# Contributions to Economics

The series *Contributions to Economics* provides an outlet for innovative research in all areas of economics. Books published in the series are primarily monographs and multiple author works that present new research results on a clearly defined topic, but contributed volumes and conference proceedings are also considered. All books are published in print and ebook and disseminated and promoted globally. The series and the volumes published in it are indexed by Scopus and ISI (selected volumes).

Samir Alamad

# Beyond Profit

## The Humanisation of Economics Through the Theory of Equitable Optimality

Springer

Samir Alamad
Coventry University
Coventry, UK

ISSN 1431-1933 ISSN 2197-7178 (electronic)
Contributions to Economics
ISBN 978-3-031-49747-6 ISBN 978-3-031-49748-3 (eBook)
https://doi.org/10.1007/978-3-031-49748-3



This Springer imprint is published by the registered company Springer Nature Switzerland AG
The registered company address is: Gewerbestrasse 11, 6330 Cham, Switzerland

Paper in this product is recyclable.

**Abstract** This book unveils a compelling call for a transformative shift in economics, ignited by the stark reality of dwindling resources amidst escalating demands. Amid this pursuit, a universal imperative remains safeguarding the well-being of all. This mandates the astute and equitable management of finite resources. Societies craft strategies rooted in their worldviews to achieve holistic well-being. These worldviews fall into two streams: secular, materialistic, and spiritual, humanitarian. The ground-breaking Equitable Optimality economic model, which we construct in this book, champions the two streams, transcending traditional economics focused solely on materialism.

This book pioneers an economic theory anchored in moral economy, values, and ethics. By weaving equity, social justice, and ethics into economics, it introduces the Equitable Optimality theory. This theory contends that economics can serve the welfare of all, offering a unique lens for economic theory and policy. Resource scarcity challenges the pursuit of universal well-being. To address this, societies devise strategies shaped by their prevailing worldviews. The prevailing worldviews are often categorised into two overarching constructs: the secular and materialistic, and the spiritual and humanitarian. The former, synonymous with conventional economics, predominantly fixates on material wealth and individual self-interest. In contrast, the latter, aligning with our proposed approach, accentuates the spiritual and humanitarian facets of human well-being and seeks to integrate ethical considerations into economic decision-making by harmonising these two constructs.

The proposed interest-balanced/free system offers an alternative to the prevailing interest-based financial economy. In this system, money creation is uncoupled from debt-based lending with interest, instead aligning with profit-sharing arrangements and societal objectives that tether it to the tangible economy. Thus, the interest-balanced/free financial economy presents a viable alternative to the interest-based paradigm, resonating with the principles of the Equitable Optimality economic model. By prioritising profit-sharing, societal objectives, justice, and equitable resource allocation, this system strives to create a more inclusive and equitable society. Nevertheless, comprehensive research and practical implementation are imperative to fully comprehend its potential impact and address any challenges that may arise during the transition.

Hence, the Equitable Optimality economic theory offers a valuable perspective within the realm of economics. Its emphasis on ethical foundations, recognition of non-monetary values, humanisation of economic agents, and a broader policy perspective enrich our understanding of economic behaviour and the pursuit of societal welfare. While not seeking to supplant conventional economic theories, it presents an alternative framework that can inspire novel approaches to economics and policymaking, all with the ultimate objective of fostering a more prosperous, resilient and stable economic model and harmonious society for all.

**Keywords** Equitable Optimality theory · Economic vision · Economic roadmap · Equitable outcomes · Rethinking economics · Ethical socio-economic

*I dedicate this work to my late father, my mother, my wife Lara and our daughters Faith and May, who always supported and encouraged me.*

# Foreword

Samir Alamad's work represents a thoughtful contribution to the growing field of Islamic economics. It is an important attempt to break new ground by positioning Islamic economics within the broader category of economics as a discipline. The approach is certainly explicitly idealistic yet attainable in an economy guided by the teachings of the Almighty. Far from one person's loss being another's gain the aspiration is for all economic participants to prosper together. It presents a more attractive model of human behaviour which all too often sees economic interaction as basically selfish, pitting individuals against each other through endless conflict. Samir Alamad introduces the concept of equitable optimality to form the basis of a new economic paradigm based on inclusion. The faith-based social contract gives fresh hope to the victims of discriminatory economic policies who no longer suffer the indignities of exclusion.

In recent years more attention has been given to Islamic finance than any other area of Islamic economics. Here again Samir Alamad provides an insightful context with the title suggesting that economic interaction moves beyond profit. This is not to imply that profit is immoral or unethical, but rather it should be part of the picture rather than the whole story. Indeed profit-sharing principles govern Islamic banking transactions. In other words if entrepreneurs and business leaders are blessed with particular talents these should be used to aid society in the service of their Maker rather than promoting material objectives and pleasure seeking. For the most talented the question they should ask themselves is how best they can contribute to social welfare and sustainable economic advance, but not merely how best to increase their personal financial balances.

Emeritus Professor
Durham University, Durham, UK

Rodney Wilson

# Preface

In the world of economics, where theories shape policies, and policies mould societies, I embark on a journey to explore the intricate tapestry of human behaviour, resource allocation, and the pursuit of prosperity. Welcome to a realm where numbers tell stories, incentives drive decisions, and the relentless pursuit of understanding guides our path. In the intricate tapestry of economics, where threads of theory and practice, wealth and poverty, growth and recession, and lending and borrowing intricately interweave, one strand often overlooked yet profoundly influential is an equitable economic model.

## Economics: Beyond the Numbers

Economics is more than just numbers, formulas, and charts; it is a discipline that unravels the intricacies of human choices and societal dynamics. It explores how individuals, businesses, and governments navigate the complex web of trade-offs to satisfy their desires and needs. Economics is about understanding the profound impacts of seemingly mundane decisions, from the choice to buy a cup of coffee to the crafting of national budgets. However, the pivotal point is how we can ensure such desires are kept in check and under control to achieve societal good, where our economic practices and policies are shaped within a just and equitable framework.

## The Art and Science of Decision-Making

At its core, economics is both an art and a science. It combines the rigour of empirical analysis with the subtlety of behavioural insights. It is a discipline that thrives on debate, for it grapples with fundamental questions that touch the essence of human existence. How do we allocate scarce resources? What drives innovation and economic growth? How do we address inequality and poverty? How can we develop an equitable economic theory to address current challenges? These questions are not just theoretical; they resonate with the realities of our world today.

## The Power and Responsibility of Economics

With great power comes great responsibility, and economics is no exception. The policies shaped by economic insights have far-reaching consequences. They impact the quality of life for millions, determine the allocation of resources, and influence the course of nations. It is therefore imperative that those who wield economic knowledge do so with wisdom and foresight, keeping in mind the broader welfare of society.

## Beyond the Classroom: A Practical Guide

This book is not just a theoretical treatise but a practical guide. While it delves into the fundamental theories and concepts that underpin economics, it also explores their real-world applications. Whether you are a student striving to grasp the intricacies of economic theory, an economist or a policy maker seeking insights to shape a better future, this book aims to bridge the gap between theory and practice.

## A Holistic Perspective

Economics is a multifaceted discipline. It encompasses microeconomics, which scrutinises individual choices and market interactions, and macroeconomics, which zooms out to study the aggregate behaviour of economies. It delves into the intricacies of behavioural economics, exploring the quirks of human decision-making, and stretches to the frontiers of environmental economics, assessing our impact on the planet.

## Empowering Critical Thinking

Throughout this journey, I encourage you to think critically, question assumptions, and challenge conventional wisdom. Economics is not a static field; it evolves with the changing dynamics of our world. By equipping yourself with the tools of economic analysis, you gain the ability to dissect complex problems, evaluate policy options, and contribute to informed decision-making. My objective of this book is to make a humble contribution towards humanising economics. I attempt to achieve this by re-evaluating and adjusting economic hypotheses and norms. My Equitable Optimality economic theory aims to contribute to a more compassionate and sustainable economic system that aligns with broader societal goals and values. This humanisation of economics is crucial for addressing pressing global challenges and ensuring a more inclusive, equitable and just economic future.

## A Global Perspective

In an era of globalisation, economics transcends borders encompassing various economic theories, ideologies, thoughts, and faith-based economic models. The forces of international trade, finance, and technology connect us in unprecedented ways. This book embraces a global perspective, acknowledging that economic challenges and opportunities are intertwined on a global scale. We explore the impact of international economic models on prosperity, the challenges of financial globalisation, and the imperative of sustainable development.

## The Road Ahead

As you embark on this journey through the fascinating world of economics, remember that knowledge is not a destination but a path. Each chapter of this book represents a stepping stone on your journey to understanding. Whether you are an aspiring economist, a policymaker, a concerned citizen, or simply curious about the forces that shape our world, this book offers a roadmap to navigate the complexities of economics.

## Acknowledgements

This book would not have been possible without the contributions of many. I extend my gratitude to the scholars, teachers, and students who have shaped the field of economics. Most importantly, I dedicate this book to those who strive for a better world through the application of economic insights.

## Join Me on This Journey

Together, let us embark on a journey into the heart of economics, where theory meets practice, numbers come alive, and the decisions of today shape the possibilities of tomorrow. Economics is more than a subject; it is a lens through which we view the world, a toolkit for solving problems, and a compass for navigating the complexities of our interconnected planet.

Birmingham, UK
30 September 2023

Samir Alamad

# Contents


| | | |
|---|---|---|
| 1 | **Setting the Stage** | 1 |
| | 1.1 Synopsis of the Issue | 1 |
| | 1.2 An Overview of the Economic Landscape Over the Years | 3 |
| | 1.3 Influence of Economics on Social Interactions | 7 |
| | 1.4 The Philosophical Aspect | 8 |
| | 1.5 How to Read This Book | 13 |
| 2 | **Basis of Conventional Economics** | 17 |
| | 2.1 Introduction | 17 |
| | 2.2 Basis of Conventional Economics | 20 |
| | 2.3 Capitalism | 25 |
| | 2.4 Capitalism Creative Destruction Approach | 28 |
| | 2.5 Conclusion | 38 |
| 3 | **Production and the Public Goods Problem in Capitalism** | 41 |
| | 3.1 Introduction | 41 |
| | 3.2 Public Goods and Private Goods | 42 |
| | 3.3 Allocation of Security Resources By the State | 48 |
| | 3.4 Conclusion | 53 |
| 4 | **Intersection of Capitalism and Anti-essentialism: The Contradictions Arising From This Encounter** | 55 |
| | 4.1 Introduction | 55 |
| | 4.2 Capitalist Regulation | 57 |
| | 4.3 Capitalism Post-development Theory | 59 |
| | 4.4 The Concept of Class and Its Relation to Identity | 62 |
| | 4.5 Challenges of Social and Individual Identity in Class Narratives | 64 |
| | 4.6 Competing Ideas of Social and Individual Identity and Their Impact on Class Politics | 66 |
| | 4.7 Conclusion | 67 |

**5 The Overselling of Globalisation** .......... 69
5.1 Introduction .......... 69
5.2 Globalisation: A Topic of Interest .......... 71
5.3 What Is Globalisation? .......... 72
5.4 Risks of Over-Globalisation .......... 76
5.5 Learning From History: A Look Back in Time .......... 79
5.6 Globalisation and Geopolitics .......... 87
5.7 Developmental Disparities in Today's World Order .......... 90
5.8 Regional Development Policies .......... 92
5.9 Conclusion .......... 93

**6 The Rise of Religious Economics Model: Critiques of the Islamic Economics Doctrine** .......... 97
6.1 Introduction .......... 97
6.2 The Case for Cultural Separatism .......... 98
6.3 Western Influence and the Economic-Political Disunity .......... 100
6.4 Rationalising the Separation Notion .......... 102
6.5 Causes of Divisions .......... 105
6.6 The Concept of One Nation .......... 106
6.7 A Question of Conflicts of Civilisations .......... 109
6.8 Identity and Understanding Sense of Self .......... 112
6.9 Critics of Islamic Economics .......... 113
6.10 Conclusion .......... 119

**7 Islamic Economics Model: The Counter Argument to Its Critiques** .......... 123
7.1 Introduction .......... 123
7.2 The Concept of One Nation (Ummah) .......... 124
7.3 Work and Productivity .......... 125
7.4 Advocating Distributional Equity .......... 127
7.5 Establishing an Economic Policy .......... 129
7.6 Conclusion .......... 134

**8 The Clash of Ideals** .......... 137
8.1 Introduction .......... 137
8.2 Normative Ideals in Contrast to Ground Realities .......... 138
8.3 Employing Material Means for Affecting Change .......... 139
8.4 The Lack of Practicality to the Normative Economics Theory .......... 140
8.5 Balancing Challenges and Opportunities .......... 141
8.6 The Material and Spiritual Aspects .......... 142
8.7 The Enlightenment Movement and Traditional Economics .......... 143
8.8 Islamic and Conventional Economics Worldviews .......... 145
8.9 Conclusion .......... 150

9 The Essence of Faith-Based Economics: The Islamic Economic Thought ... 155
9.1 Introduction ... 155
9.2 The Principle of Moderation ... 156
9.3 Ethical Competition ... 158
9.4 Overarching Principles for an Islamic Economic Policy ... 159
9.5 The Material and Spiritual in Economics ... 161
9.6 Dual Oversight and Its Scope ... 163
9.7 Elevating the Purpose of Economic Activity ... 163
9.8 The Ultimate Goal of Economic Activity ... 164
9.9 The Equilibrium Between Private and Public Interests in Islamic Economics ... 166
9.10 In the Realm of Economic Freedom and State Involvement ... 168
9.11 Conflict of Public and Individual Interests ... 169
9.12 Inflation in the Context of Islamic Economics ... 171
9.13 The State and Its Economic Role ... 173
9.14 Ethical Foundations of Islamic Economics ... 175
9.15 Achieving Economic Security ... 176
9.16 Conclusion ... 178

10 Economics and the Knowledge Crisis ... 183
10.1 Introduction ... 183
10.2 Islamisation of Economics ... 184
10.3 Framing the Economic Knowledge Crisis ... 185
10.4 Critical Flaws in Current Economics Theories ... 186
10.5 The Faith-Based Economic Theory ... 193
10.6 Advocating Spirituality ... 196
10.7 Moral Conduct and Leadership ... 196
10.8 Fighting Greed ... 199
10.9 Promoting Cooperation vs. Competition ... 200
10.10 Conclusion ... 202

11 Learning and Convergence ... 205
11.1 Introduction ... 205
11.2 The Concept of the “Great Gap” Theory ... 206
11.3 Interconnected Approach to Economic Development ... 207
11.4 Division of Labour and Specialisation for Economic Development ... 209
11.5 The Concept of Demand and Supply ... 211
11.6 Public Finances ... 212
11.7 Economic Mismanagement ... 214
11.8 Development Stages ... 215
11.9 Intellectual Decline ... 215
11.10 Gaps in Economics Research ... 217
11.11 Diversion and Deviation of Views ... 220

11.12 The Concern Regarding Financialisation of Islamic Economics . . 222
11.13 It Is Not All Doom and Gloom . . . 225
11.14 Conclusion . . . 226

**12 Rethinking Economics, Constructing the Equitable Optimality Theory Part One: Philosophical Underpinning** . . . 229
12.1 Introduction . . . 229
12.2 Interest-Bearing Money . . . 230
12.3 The Meaning of Equitable Optimality as a Theory . . . 231
12.4 Understanding Text and Context . . . 236
12.5 Meanings and Understandings Are Not a Mere Informational Text . . . 236
12.6 Contextual Understanding Is a Guiding Principle for Human Economic Behaviour . . . 238
12.7 The Equitable Optimality Worldview Advocates a Particular Economic Behaviour . . . 239
12.8 Standard of Acceptable Economic Behaviour . . . 239
12.9 A Divine-Based Economic System Is Superior . . . 240
12.10 A Comprehensive Economic Theory: Characteristics of the Equitable Optimality Theory . . . 242
12.11 Economic Law of Justice Is a Just Law . . . 244
12.12 An Effective Worldview Based on a System of Accountability . . . 245
12.13 Foundational Structure . . . 246
12.14 Utility as the Value of Something That Satisfies Human's Needs . . . 250
12.15 Key Aspects of the Proposed Theory . . . 253
12.16 Differentiating Between Economics and Economic System . . . 255
12.17 Four Economic Factors . . . 256
12.18 Conclusion . . . 262

**13 Rethinking Economics, Constructing the Equitable Optimality Theory Part Two: Macroeconomics** . . . 265
13.1 Introduction . . . 265
13.2 The Context . . . 267
13.3 Aspects of Macroeconomics . . . 268
13.4 The Demand Side of Money . . . 271
13.5 The Supply Side of Money . . . 272
13.6 Proposing a Roadmap for the Sound Transition to an Interest-Free Financial Economy . . . 274
13.7 Debt and Its Negative Impact on the Economy . . . 276
13.8 Unravelling the Interplay of Finance, Consumption, and Economic Stability . . . 280
13.9 The Real Economy . . . 282

13.10 Making the Case for an Interest-Balanced/Free Financial Economy ........ 285
13.11 Consumption ........ 290
13.12 Savings ........ 291
13.13 Investment ........ 292
13.14 Income ........ 293
13.15 Average Rate of Profit ........ 294
13.16 Labour Market ........ 295
13.17 Fiscal Policy and the Role of Government in the Equitable Optimality Theory ........ 296
13.18 Inflation, Economic Stabilisation and Growth in the Current Economic System ........ 300
13.19 Inflation, Economic Stabilisation and Growth in the Equitable Optimality System ........ 304
13.20 Moving From Interest-Based Economy to an Equitable Optimality Economy ........ 308
13.21 Conclusion ........ 309

**14 Rethinking Economics, Constructing the Equitable Optimality Theory Part Three: Microeconomics** ........ 313
14.1 Introduction ........ 313
14.2 Addressing Microeconomic Needs ........ 315
14.3 Relative Scarcity of Material Resources ........ 317
14.4 Rationality of Economic Behaviour ........ 317
14.5 The Role of Institutional Structure ........ 319
14.6 Goals of Equitable Optimality Economics ........ 320
14.7 Implications Beyond the Market ........ 321
14.8 Behavioural Motive ........ 322
14.9 Scope and Limitations of the Market ........ 323
14.10 Equilibrium Prices: Demand and Supply ........ 324
14.11 Distribution ........ 326
14.12 Labour and Wages ........ 327
14.13 Profit and Its Implication ........ 330
14.14 Income From Property ........ 332
14.15 Grants ........ 333
14.16 Production and Producers Motive ........ 333
14.17 Cost of Production and Reduced Return ........ 335
14.18 Financing and Cost of Capital ........ 336
14.19 Firm and Industry Equilibrium ........ 339
14.20 Consumer Consumption Behaviour and Hierarchy in Human Needs ........ 340
14.21 Utility and Consumer Behaviour ........ 342
14.22 Conclusion ........ 343

**15 A Vision for the Future** . . . . . . . . . . 347
15.1 Introduction . . . . . . . . . . 347
15.2 Proposing a Genuine Economic Theory . . . . . . . . . . 348
15.3 Internal Influences . . . . . . . . . . 350
15.4 The Detrimental Impact of Human Economic Actions on the Economic Ecosystem . . . . . . . . . . 354
15.5 The Call for a Responsible and Equitable Economic Model: It Is Time for Reflection and Action . . . . . . . . . . 356
15.6 What Is Proposed? The Equitable Optimality Economic Theory . . . . . . . . . . 356
15.7 The Financial Economy Proposal . . . . . . . . . . 357
15.8 Macroeconomics and Microeconomics . . . . . . . . . . 358
15.9 A Practical Roadmap to Transition to an Equitable Optimality Economy . . . . . . . . . . 359
15.10 Concluding This Journey . . . . . . . . . . 361

**References** . . . . . . . . . . 363

# Chapter 1
# Setting the Stage

## 1.1 Synopsis of the Issue

This book posits the necessity for a fresh paradigm in economics, driven by the stark realisation of limited resources juxtaposed with an ever-increasing demand for them. Yet, in this pursuit, an overarching universal imperative remains: the well-being of all humanity must be safeguarded, necessitating the efficient and equitable stewardship of these finite resources.

Societies, in their diversity, formulate strategies rooted in their worldviews to attain the holistic well-being of their constituents. These worldviews can broadly be categorised into two streams: the secular, materialistic, and the spiritual, humanitarian. The ground-breaking Equitable Optimality economic model presented herein firmly aligns with the latter, championing not only material prosperity but also spiritual and humanitarian values. This critical distinction elevates this economic theory beyond traditional frameworks, which predominantly fixate on materialistic and secular dimensions.

This book advances a novel economic theory firmly anchored in the principles of moral economy, values, and ethics, fostering a comprehensive and balanced approach to economic conundrums. By harmonising spirituality, social justice, and ethical considerations within economics, this work makes a significant contribution to the field by conceptualising the Equitable Optimality economic theory. This theory posits that economics can meaningfully contribute to the welfare of all members of society, offering an unconventional lens through which to view economic theory and policy. In scrutinising prevalent economic theories and advocating for a re-evaluation of economics, this book further distinguishes itself by positing the Equitable Optimality theory as a pioneering alternative.

This theory contends that, in the face of resource scarcity, achieving the well-being of all becomes an arduous endeavour. It necessitates the judicious and just allocation of these finite resources to meet the needs and aspirations of individuals



S. Alamad, *Beyond Profit*, Contributions to Economics,
https://doi.org/10.1007/978-3-031-49748-3_1

and communities. Every society, in this quest, devises strategies influenced by its prevailing worldview, a worldview that shapes the values, beliefs, and principles guiding resource allocation and decision-making.

Worldviews categorise into secular and materialistic, and spiritual and humanitarian constructs. The choice of worldview profoundly impacts individual and societal well-being, necessitating a re-evaluation of established economic theories. The Equitable Optimality economic theory aims for a more ethical approach, rooted in socio-economic principles.

The choice of worldview and the corresponding economic strategies wield profound implications for individual and societal well-being. Striking a balance between resource scarcity and the welfare of all mandates a conscientious examination of underlying worldviews and a reconsideration of established economic theories and their implications.

The Equitable Optimality economic theory aspires to construct a more authentic and ethical economic approach, deeply rooted in socio-economic principles and values. Achieving this vision necessitates economists to re-evaluate their methodological approaches, challenge underlying assumptions, and embrace ethical foundations that guide resource allocation and decision-making. The inclusion of third-sector institutions and a pivot from mere economic growth to comprehensive human development emerge as essential steps to nurture social well-being, equity and justice.

The proposed interest-balanced/free system offers an alternative to the prevailing interest-based financial economy. In this system, money creation is uncoupled from debt-based lending with interest, instead aligning with profit-sharing arrangements and societal objectives that tether it to the tangible economy.

Thus, the interest-balanced/free financial economy presents a viable alternative to the interest-based paradigm, resonating with the principles of the Equitable Optimality economic model. By prioritising profit-sharing, societal objectives, and equitable resource allocation, this system strives to create a more inclusive and equitable society. Nevertheless, comprehensive research and practical implementation are imperative to fully comprehend its potential impact and address any challenges that may arise during the transition.

Hence, the Equitable Optimality economic theory offers a valuable perspective within the realm of economics. Its emphasis on ethical foundations, recognition of non-monetary values, humanisation of economic agents, and a broader policy perspective enrich our understanding of economic behaviour and the pursuit of societal welfare. While not seeking to supplant conventional economic theories, it presents an alternative framework that can inspire novel approaches to economic analysis and policymaking, all with the ultimate objective of fostering a more prosperous and harmonious society for all.

## 1.2 An Overview of the Economic Landscape Over the Years

The emergence of global corporate governance and the influential role of organisations like the Council on Foreign Relations (CFR) and the World Bank in shaping global economic policies. In the 1920s, US capitalism expanded its reach to foreign markets and resources, leading to the formulation of the idea of global corporate governance. The CFR, jointly created by the Rockefeller and Carnegie foundations in 1924, became a powerful foreign policy pressure group. Over time, it developed close ties with the newly established CIA, and its membership included numerous influential figures in US politics, including secretaries of state.

The CFR's influence extended to international organisations like the United Nations (UN) and the World Bank. In the planning of the UN, CFR members played a significant role, and a substantial grant from the Rockefeller Foundation contributed to the establishment of the UN's headquarters in New York. Additionally, the CFR's members have consistently held leadership positions in the World Bank, promoting policies that further global capital penetration and standardise business practices in an open marketplace.

During the Bretton Woods Conference, the World Bank, and the International Monetary Fund (IMF) decided to make the US dollar the world's reserve currency. This decision aimed to enhance global capital penetration. To achieve this, these organisations have invested substantial resources in promoting concepts like "Good Governance" and the "Rule of Law," while also implementing anti-corruption programs in developing countries. However, critics argue that these efforts may lack transparency and accountability, as they are influenced by the same organisations that hold significant power and control over the global economic system.

The significant influence and power wielded by corporate-endowed foundations, particularly the World Bank, in shaping economic policies in the Third World. These foundations are portrayed as visionary in their strategies and methods of exerting control over global finance and markets.

Corporate-endowed foundations are depicted as administrators and channelisers of power, employing elite clubs and think-tanks to further their agendas. This network of influential organisations, including the Council on Foreign Relations (CFR) and the Trilateral Commission, works in cooperation with each other, with members overlapping and moving in and out through revolving doors. The Ford Foundation, which is seen as a liberal counterpart to the Rockefeller Foundation, is highlighted as having a well-defined ideology and working closely with the US state department to promote "good governance" and deepen democracy.

These foundations played a role in the Cold War era, working to counter the influence of communism by funding institutions like RAND, a military think-tank, and the Centre for the Study of Democratic Institutions. The Ford Foundation's activities are viewed through the lens of promoting capitalist interests, aligning with the Bretton Woods scheme of standardising business practices, and promoting efficiency in the free market.

A critical perspective on the influence and activities of corporate-endowed foundations and their role in shaping global economic policies. It portrays these foundations as instrumental in promoting capitalist interests and advancing their agendas through various networks and institutions.

The Ford Foundation's interventions and initiatives, particularly in relation to grassroots political movements and their influence in various countries, including the United States and Indonesia.

In the US, the Ford Foundation provided significant financial support to the Credit Union Movement, which aimed to provide workers with affordable access to credit. However, the foundation's focus on the first half of the movement's vision, which was to create a mass consumption society, led to workers becoming perpetually indebted, struggling to keep up with their lifestyles.

Internationally, the Rockefeller and Ford foundations began funding various non-governmental organisations (NGOs) and educational institutions, acting as quasi-extensions of the US government during the period when democratically elected governments in Latin America, Iran, and Indonesia were being toppled. In Indonesia, for instance, the Ford Foundation established a US-style economics course at the university and trained elite Indonesian students in counter-insurgency tactics with the help of US army officers. These trained students played a crucial role in the CIA-backed coup in Indonesia in 1965, which brought General Suharto to power. In return, Suharto brutally suppressed Communist rebels, resulting in the deaths of hundreds of thousands of people.

Critics suggest that the Ford Foundation's interventions and funding played a role in shaping political and economic developments in different countries, sometimes aligning with the interests of the US government. It highlights how these initiatives had significant consequences for the societies they influenced, both domestically and internationally.

Eight years later, a group of young Chilean students, later known as the Chicago Boys, were sent to the United States to receive training in neo-liberal economics by Milton Friedman at the University of Chicago, which was supported by J.D. Rockefeller. This training was part of the preparation for the 1973 CIA-backed coup that led to the death of Salvador Allende, a democratically elected socialist leader in Chile, and brought General Pinochet to power. Pinochet's regime was marked by a reign of terror, including death squads and disappearances, that lasted for seventeen years. Allende's "crime" was nationalising Chile's mines.

In 1957, the Rockefeller Foundation established the Ramon Magsaysay Prize for community leaders in Asia, named after Ramon Magsaysay, the President of the Philippines, who was a key ally in the US anti-Communist campaign in Southeast Asia. Later, in 2000, the Ford Foundation established the Ramon Magsaysay Emergent Leadership Award. The Magsaysay Award is highly regarded among artists, activists, and community workers in India, with recipients including M.S. Subbulakshmi, Satyajit Ray, Jayaprakash Narayan, and P. Sainath. However, the award's impact on the recipients has been limited, and it has been criticised for influencing what forms of activism are deemed "acceptable."

The philanthropoids, with imperialistic tendencies, aimed to create and train an international cadre that would believe in the self-interest of Capitalism and the hegemony of capital. This cadre would then assist in administering the Global Corporate Government, akin to how native elites had served colonialism. This marked the beginning of the foundations' involvement in education and the arts, becoming their third sphere of influence, alongside foreign and domestic economic policy. They invested and continue to invest substantial amounts of money in academic institutions and pedagogy.

In her insightful book Foundations and Public Policy: The Mask of Pluralism, Joan Roelofs highlights how foundations played a significant role in reshaping the teaching of political science and establishing disciplines like "international" and "area" studies. This development provided US intelligence and security services with a pool of experts proficient in foreign languages and cultures for recruitment. The ongoing collaboration between the CIA, US state department, and students/professors in American universities raises ethical questions regarding scholarship.

Corporate-endowed foundations emerge as the primary funders of the social sciences and arts, endowing courses, and student scholarships in fields such as "development studies," "community studies," "cultural studies," "behavioural sciences," and "human rights." With US universities admitting international students, a substantial number of children from the elite of Third World countries enrolled, with scholarships offered to those unable to afford tuition fees. Today, it is common for upper-middle-class families in countries like India and Pakistan to have at least one child who has studied in the US or UK. From this group, not only have emerged talented scholars and academics, but also prime ministers, finance ministers, economists, corporate lawyers, bankers, and bureaucrats who played key roles in opening up their countries' economies to global corporations.

The Foundation-friendly version of economics and political science rewarded scholars with various privileges such as fellowships, research funds, grants, endowments, and job opportunities. On the other hand, those holding Foundation-unfriendly views faced the consequences of being unfunded, marginalised, and isolated, often seeing their courses discontinued. Over time, a specific worldview emerged, presenting a veneer of tolerance and multiculturalism, but it easily transformed into racism, extreme nationalism, ethnic chauvinism, or Islamophobia when needed, all under the guise of a singular and all-encompassing economic ideology. This ideology became so pervasive that it no longer seemed like an ideology but rather the default position, the unquestioned norm. It infiltrated ordinary thinking, colonised common perspectives, and opposing it appeared as absurd or esoteric as challenging reality itself. Gradually, the notion of "There is No Alternative" took hold, implying that no other alternatives or perspectives were valid or conceivable.

Recently, thanks to the Occupy Movement, a new language has emerged on the streets and campuses of the US. Banners with slogans like 'Class War' or 'We don't mind you being rich, but we mind you buying our government' indicate a growing awareness and challenge to the prevailing economic and political system. For example, the banner that said 'Let's Bank the Muslim Way' showed that Islamic finance and banking are being seen as credible alternatives to the dominant capitalist ideology of 'There is No Alternative.' However, we must critically examine whether Islamic economics and finance are truly living up to the promise they hold.

The slogan 'There is No Alternative' is also employed in politics by Western governments to maintain support for dictators in the Middle East and other parts of the world, even in the face of widespread resentment and grassroots uprisings against these oppressive regimes. This double standard has caused frustration and disappointment among the people of these countries, who see Western governments claiming to promote democracy, justice, and fair societies, but supporting dictators who suppress their own populations and commit human rights abuses.

As a result, Western governments have lost credibility in the eyes of many people in regions where dictators are backed by these governments under the pretext of 'there is no alternative' to their rule. As long as these dictators serve the interests of Western powers, their oppressive actions are often ignored, leading to further disillusionment and scepticism among the affected populations. The discrepancy between Western rhetoric and actions has led to a loss of trust in these governments globally, particularly in countries where dictatorship is entrenched and supported by Western powers.

A century after its inception, corporate philanthropy has become deeply ingrained in our society, just like ubiquitous brands such as Coca Cola. The non-profit sector now includes millions of organisations, many of which are intricately connected to larger foundations through complex financial arrangements. Collectively, this "independent" sector possesses assets worth nearly 450 billion dollars. Some of the largest foundations include the Bill Gates Foundation ($21 billion), the Lilly Endowment ($16 billion), and the Ford Foundation ($15 billion).

As the IMF enforced Structural Adjustment policies and pressured governments to cut back on public spending for essential services like health, education, and childcare, NGOs swooped in to fill the gaps. The era of privatisation also led to the "NGO-isation" of many aspects of society. As traditional jobs and livelihoods disappeared, NGOs became significant sources of employment, even for those who may not fully support their mission. However, it is essential to acknowledge that not all NGOs are the same, and some do outstanding and transformative work.

On the other hand, there are corporate or foundation-endowed NGOs that function as mechanisms for global finance to infiltrate resistance movements. They act as shareholders in companies, seeking to control these movements from within. These organisations operate like nodes on the central nervous system of global finance, channelling its flow of influence. They serve as transmitters, receivers, and shock absorbers, constantly monitoring and adapting to every impulse without provoking host governments. Some of these NGOs, like the Ford Foundation, demand that the organisations they fund pledge not to challenge or annoy the governments of their host countries.

Inadvertently or intentionally, these NGOs also function as listening posts, gathering data from troubled areas, and contributing to an increasingly aggressive surveillance system in increasingly authoritarian states. It is no coincidence that the presence of NGOs tends to be higher in regions facing significant challenges. In a mischievous manner, when the government or certain sections of the corporate media want to discredit genuine people's movements, they often accuse them of being NGOs receiving "foreign funding." However, they are well aware that most NGOs, especially well-funded ones, actually support the project of corporate globalisation rather than opposing it.

Armed with their substantial financial resources, these NGOs have entered the global arena, enticing potential revolutionaries to become salaried activists. They provide funding to artists, intellectuals, and filmmakers, subtly steering them away from radical confrontation and directing them towards issues like multiculturalism, gender, and community development, often framed in the language of identity politics and human rights.

This transformation of the concept of justice into the industry of human rights has been orchestrated through a conceptual coup, with NGOs and foundations playing a critical role. The narrow focus on human rights allows for an atrocity-based analysis, where the broader context can be conveniently ignored. Both parties in a conflict, regardless of their underlying motivations or historical context, can be labelled as human rights violators. For example, both the Maoists and the Indian government, the Russian and Ukrainian war, the civil war in Sudan, conflicts between regimes and opposition rebels globally in different countries, or the Israeli Army and Hamas may be criticised as human rights violators, while the underlying issues of land-grabbing by mining corporations and economic colonialism by global corporations are marginalised in the discourse. This is not to undermine the importance of human rights, but rather to emphasise that they are not sufficient to fully comprehend and address the profound injustices prevailing in our world.

## 1.3 Influence of Economics on Social Interactions

There is no denying the significant impact economics has on our lives, human values, and social interactions. The influence of economics extends beyond just our economic thinking; it also shapes our ideological beliefs and values, which, in turn, play a crucial role in bringing together social groups with shared values to form their own establishments throughout history and across civilisations. Additionally, these economic and ideological values have a profound impact on how social and political groups administer their affairs and interact with other groups.

The roots of economic thought as a faith-based driver can be traced back to the advent of Islam in Mecca. The emergence of Islam sparked a religious conflict between its followers and the idol-worshipping Quraishi tribe, who viewed Islam as a threat to their materialistic way of life and their economic interests. Despite facing opposition, Islam prevailed, attracting more followers who were drawn to its principles of justice, truth, and equality. As Islam spread to other nations and societies, the need for a structured economic system became apparent.

To address the new economic challenges posed by its expansion, the management of the state economy based on religious principles gradually took shape. The establishment of the state treasury, known as the *bait al-maal*, marked the beginning of Islamic institutions responsible for managing and organising the state's economic affairs and finances. This included setting macroeconomic and fiscal policies, handling income and expenditure, managing taxes, and overseeing compulsory alms giving (zakat), among other responsibilities. As the state continued to grow, the remit of the state treasury expanded accordingly.

The economic explosion during the rise and expansion of Islam served as a strong motivation for Islamic scholars and intellectuals to deeply study and document its various aspects. Their aim was to comprehensively capture all the functions, features, principles, elements, product factors, and pricing of this faith-based economic revolution. Through their scholarly work and writings, they sought to develop a comprehensive economic theory based on human and social behaviour, shaped by Islamic values and principles.

Islamic rulers, such as Haroon Al-Rasheed, actively encouraged and supported these scholarly endeavours. For example, during his reign, numerous books were written on the topic of taxes on land (*al-kharaj*) alone, with the total number reaching up to 30 books. Similarly, other economic factors and topics, including land, pricing, labour, production, money, trade, monopoly, the economic role of government and rulers, manufacturing, agriculture, state treasury, audit, accounting, and accountability, were extensively studied and documented during this period.

These concerted efforts laid the foundation for a distinct and clear identity of Islamic economics and its underlying principles. The scholarship of these early Islamic economists not only captured the economic realities of their time but also established a lasting legacy that continues to influence Islamic economic thought and practice to this day.

## 1.4 The Philosophical Aspect

Economics and its various factors are deeply influenced by philosophical thought, which shapes its objectives, meanings, and understanding. It is essential to study this thought process, also referred to as intellect, realisation of facts, and mind, as these terms essentially convey similar meanings. Intellect denotes the thought process that an individual undergoes to arrive at conclusions about different matters. It encompasses the deductive knowledge and conclusions derived from this thought process.

The process of intellect involves four key elements: firstly, the realisation and comprehension of the current reality; secondly, human emotions and feelings; thirdly, the mind, which can be seen as the human processor; and finally, the stored knowledge and facts in the human brain. Each of these elements is crucial, and the absence of any one of them would lead to an incomplete thought process. For instance, if one lacks an understanding of existing realities or access to stored knowledge in their mind, any deducted conclusion would be mere baseless imagination.

Thus, economic thought involves the transmission of current reality, not just an image of reality, through human senses, which is then processed in the brain in the context of already stored facts and beliefs. It is then interpreted based on these realities. The importance lies in the true feeling of reality transmitted to our brain during this thought process, as it reflects a closer intellectual outcome to the actual reality. On the other hand, if the perception of reality is taken from a preconceived image or subjective understanding stored in the brain, it could distort the thought process and disconnect it from the reality perceived through our senses. Consequently, the deductive conclusions drawn from such a distorted thought process would be far from reality and would fail to objectively address the real economic matters at hand.

Indeed, the philosophical aspect of economics is crucial in understanding how economists interpret current economic realities and produce knowledge about the subject. On one hand, there are intellectual economists or thinkers who engage in a deep and reflective thought process to comprehend and analyse economic realities. They strive to derive insights and conclusions that accurately reflect the complexities of economic phenomena.

On the other hand, some individuals may act as mere transmitters of these thoughts or conclusions without engaging in the rigorous intellectual process themselves. For instance, academic lecturers at universities may convey economic knowledge and conclusions to their students without necessarily deeply reflecting on or critically examining the underlying economic realities.

However, when the thought process is driven by subjective desires and perceptions about the desired end goal, it becomes susceptible to biases and self-interest. This deviation from objective analysis can lead the thought process to prioritise achieving the desired outcome, even if it is not an accurate reflection of existing realities and facts.

As a consequence, the economic outcome and knowledge produced may be skewed to serve the interests of a small group in society, neglecting the larger group(s). Moreover, individuals might twist previously produced economic thoughts and use them as prepopulated images to justify their own desired end objectives and conclusions, even if these are not in line with actual realities.

In this context, it is crucial for economists and thinkers to remain vigilant and strive for objectivity, rigor, and accuracy in their thought process and economic analyses. A commitment to critically examining economic realities without allowing personal biases to interfere is essential in producing knowledge that serves the broader interests of society.

The philosophical assessment of economic knowledge production is indeed vital in understanding how economic ideologies and thoughts have shaped societies throughout history and continue to do so in the present day. This perspective allows us to examine how economic thought is transmitted to individuals and how they perceive and internalise this knowledge.

When economic knowledge is transmitted to individuals, it can affect them in two distinct ways. Firstly, if the new economic thought aligns with an individual's sense of reality and resonates with their life experiences, they are likely to embrace and accept this new knowledge. Even if the thought does not directly relate to their experiences, individuals might still choose to believe in it if it aligns with their desires, goals, beliefs, or ideologies. In both cases, the transmitted economic knowledge becomes a part of their existing reality and thought process, even though it originated from someone else and may not have any objective basis in reality.

Conversely, if the individual does not find a connection or mental relevance to the new economic thought, it remains mere information to them. While they may understand the context of this new knowledge, it does not resonate with their own facts, experiences, or reality. As a result, it remains detached from their senses, beliefs, and inner thinking, and they do not actively engage with it or incorporate it into their worldview.

This analysis emphasises the importance of how economic ideas are communicated and received. The transmission of economic knowledge requires a nuanced understanding of individual perceptions and experiences. To have a lasting impact, economic thought must not only be well-founded and coherent but also capable of resonating with the diverse realities and perspectives of individuals within society.

Here I would like to emphasise a significant point about the influence of meanings over mere information in shaping people's thought processes and beliefs. Indeed, meanings hold greater significance as they find resonance in individuals' thought processes, senses, and personal experiences. This allows people to connect with and relate to meanings, making them more impactful in shaping their perspectives on various matters, whether economic, social, religious, environmental, or political.

A concrete example of this phenomenon can be observed in the way people support different political parties based on their economic policies and objectives. Voters tend to choose a political party whose economic policies align with their own realities and experiences. For instance, well-off voters in the UK may support the Conservative Party because its economic policies, such as tax cuts, reduced borrowing, privatisation, and limited social security for the poor, align with their own economic interests and realities. Conversely, the working class in the UK might support the Labour Party because its economic policies, which may include increased taxes for the wealthy, higher national borrowing, nationalisation of key services, and more extensive social security benefits, resonate with their own experiences and economic needs.

This example highlights how economic policies become meaningful to individuals based on how well they relate to their personal realities and experiences. People's support for a particular political party is often driven by how closely the party's economic objectives align with their own perceptions and existing realities. This connection to meaningful policies influences people's voting decisions and reflects the importance of meanings in shaping individual perspectives and beliefs.

Indeed, the economic divide often plays a central role in shaping political ideologies and policies in countries worldwide. In many democracies, the dominant economic trends revolve around either capitalism or socialism, with opposition parties adopting different angles of these economic ideologies. The polarisation between these two major economic trends leads to a clear distinction between the policies and objectives of political parties, making it a defining factor in the political landscape.

In countries where there is a centre of the political spectrum, represented by parties with more moderate policies, they often find themselves in a challenging position when it comes to gaining power. The dominance of the major parties, whether following capitalist or socialist economic principles, makes it difficult for centrist parties to bring about significant change. Even if they manage to form a coalition government with one of the major parties, their ability to implement their distinct policies may be limited, as the major party's own policies often take precedence to maintain its voter base.

A notable example of this dynamic occurred in the UK's 2010 general elections, where a hung parliament resulted in a coalition government between the Conservative Party and the Liberal Democrats, a centrist party. While this coalition partnership aimed to form a functioning government, it presented challenges for the Liberal Democrats, as their key economic policies clashed with those of the Conservative Party. Failing to deliver on some of their promises from their political manifesto, the Liberal Democrats lost support and suffered significant losses in the subsequent general election.

This example underscores the significance of economic thought and policies in politics and highlights how economic ideologies can strongly influence the trajectory of political parties and governments. The economic divide and the alignment of political parties with specific economic ideologies can have a profound impact on the political landscape and the fortunes of political actors.

The Brexit example serves as a fascinating illustration of how the human thought process and the perception of existing realities can influence people's beliefs and actions in the context of significant political decisions. The referendum on whether the UK should leave or remain in the EU created a profound division within the country, cutting across party lines and revealing deeply entrenched ideological differences.

In the lead-up to the referendum, both major political parties, the Conservatives and Labour, found themselves divided on the Brexit issue, with some members advocating for leaving the EU and others for remaining. The debate went beyond traditional party lines, and politicians who previously supported staying in the EU found themselves campaigning to leave after the referendum results were announced.

This shift in position highlights the malleability of political beliefs and the influence of the thought process in shaping attitudes towards important decisions. The outcome of the referendum, in favour of leaving the EU, led politicians who had previously championed the benefits of EU membership to abandon their previous beliefs and align themselves with the new reality dictated by the referendum results.

This example showcases the complex interplay between political ideologies, economic factors, and individual perceptions of reality. It demonstrates how political decisions can influence and even alter existing beliefs and the thought process of individuals and groups. Additionally, it underlines the role of emotions, desires, and personal experiences in shaping people's interpretations of economic and political realities.

The Brexit scenario is a vivid reminder that political decisions are not solely driven by a fixed set of beliefs, but rather, they can be subject to change depending on the prevailing circumstances and outcomes. It reinforces the idea that economic and political thought processes are not static, but rather dynamic and subject to continuous evolution based on new experiences and information.

Indeed, the Brexit example demonstrates how the thought process and perception of reality can be influenced by political interests and the desire to maintain or gain power. After the referendum results were announced, the UK Government, despite some internal divisions, ultimately chose to accept the outcome and invoke Article 50 to leave the EU. This decision was not legally binding, but the Government saw an opportunity to align itself with the new reality and use it to its advantage.

The political interest in maintaining power and winning back voters who wanted to leave the EU played a significant role in shaping the Government's perception of the new reality. By embracing the idea of leaving the EU, the Conservative Government found a way to connect with a portion of the electorate that had favoured Brexit, and they saw this as a strategic move to secure their position in power. This newfound perception of reality, driven by political interests, became a driving force in their subsequent thought process.

The decision to become the patron of delivering Brexit, even more so than any far-right party like UKIP, who had attracted some Conservative voters, showcased the importance of political calculations in shaping the thought process of the Government. The desire to maintain power and regain support from Brexit supporters became a central aspect of their thinking, overshadowing other considerations such as the potential economic, social, and political uncertainties that Brexit might entail.

This example highlights the complex interplay between political interests, power dynamics, and the thought process in influencing major decisions. It underscores how political considerations, and the pursuit of power can lead to a selective interpretation of realities and a willingness to adopt certain outcomes as one's own, even if they were not originally part of one's beliefs. Ultimately, this kind of perception and thought process can have far-reaching implications for the country's future, as it shapes the course of action taken by the government and the impact it has on the nation as a whole.

This important observation that I have made about how the thought process of average UK citizens during the Brexit referendum was influenced by political campaigns and images presented to them. Indeed, people's perceptions and conclusions can be shaped by the information they are exposed to, and this information may or may not reflect the full complexity of existing realities and facts.

The campaign to leave the EU successfully transmitted an image and narrative that resonated with a significant portion of the population. The idea that leaving the EU would result in more jobs for British citizens and alleviate pressure on public services struck a chord with many voters, even if it did not fully capture the complexities of the situation.

Similarly, those in favour of staying in the EU may have been swayed by a different set of images and messages. They might have focused on the benefits of free movement and the contributions of EU workers to the UK economy and public services, while overlooking potential downsides.

It is essential to recognise that during campaigns and debates, simplified and sometimes selective narratives are often presented, making it challenging for voters to fully grasp the nuances and complexities of the issues at hand. As you pointed out, both sides may have overlooked certain facts or aspects of the situation, leading to an incomplete understanding of the potential consequences of their choice.

Ultimately, it can be difficult to ascertain which option best serves the national interest when competing narratives are presented, and expert opinions might vary. As events unfold and the consequences of Brexit become clearer over time, a more comprehensive assessment of its impact will likely emerge. However, your analysis underscores the significance of how information is presented and its influence on shaping people's perceptions and thought processes during critical decision-making moments like the Brexit referendum.

## 1.5 How to Read This Book

Below I provide an overview of all the chapters that this book consists of. I outline a brief synopsis about what is included in each chapter to help you map out its content and prepare you for the journey ahead in reading this book.

*Chapter 1*: In the opening chapter of this book, we embark on an exploration of the contemporary economic landscape. We delve into its intricacies and address pertinent critiques that have emerged. This chapter offers a valuable overview of the existing assumptions and perceptions surrounding capitalism and the global economy. By dissecting these foundational concepts, we lay the groundwork for the extensive journey that lies ahead in the subsequent 14 chapters.

*Chapter 2*: Our journey commences with a critical analysis of economic theories within the realms of capitalism and socialism. We delve into the reconstruction of the ethical underpinnings of private property, leading to a re-evaluation of the roles of socialism and the state. These entities, reliant on taxation and compelled membership, take on new dimensions as we unveil them as socio-psychological constructs. This realisation propels us to return to economics, advocating for a pure capitalist societal framework as an ethically guided alternative to socialism.

*Chapter 3*: Building upon our preceding chapter, we navigate the complexities surrounding public goods within capitalist production. The unique characteristics of public goods, defined by their non-excludable and non-rivalrous nature, pose challenges within the traditional framework of market exchange rooted in private property. By delving into these intricacies, we gain a deeper understanding of the unique challenges these goods present within the capitalist system.

*Chapter 4*: In this chapter, we embark on a journey into contemporary social theory, which has embraced anti-essentialism, particularly concerning identity. We explore this shift and examine how it challenges the traditional view of economic determinism within Marxian political economy. By dissecting the criticisms and limitations of economic determinism, we gain insights into the theoretical and political challenges it has faced. This chapter opens the door to a broader exploration of essentialism in contemporary social theory.

*Chapter 5*: Our exploration takes a critical turn as we assess the phenomenon of globalisation. We scrutinise how globalisation has been touted, often with undue optimism, by politicians and economists. We unravel the exaggerated claims of its benefits, including job creation, GDP growth, and positive impacts on society. By providing a balanced view, this chapter serves as a reality check, challenging prevalent perceptions of globalisation.

*Chapter 6*: In this, we embark on a fascinating exploration of faith-based economic thought, which challenges the universal economic identity promoted by globalisation. We delve into the rise of "Islamic economics," deeply rooted in Islamic scripture and traditions, within the context of "political Islam" in the twentieth century. Despite being embraced by a minority of economists known as "Islamic economists," this doctrine's social impact cannot be underestimated. This chapter offers unique insights into this faith-based perspective, providing a richer understanding of its significance.

*Chapter 7*: This immerses us in the philosophical foundations of Islamic economics. This chapter aims to offer readers a non-technical introduction to Islamic economics, exploring its core principles and foundational aspects. By shedding light on these principles, we gain a comprehensive understanding of the distinctive approach of Islamic economics. The chapter also delves into key economic instruments that put these principles into action. While not a deep economic analysis, this chapter serves as a foundational starting point for those seeking insight into this dynamic field.

*Chapter 8*: This chapter navigates the intriguing realm of comparative analysis between Islamic economics, rooted in normative ideals, and conventional economic theory, which describes the practical realities of the world. It highlights the fundamental differences in their aims: Islamic economics seeks to inspire individuals to embody higher moral and ethical values and work toward societal well-being, while conventional economics focuses on analysing economic behaviour based on idealised market conditions. By delving into these disparities, this chapter elucidates the diverging paths of these two economic paradigms.

*Chapter 9*: This delves deep into the knowledge crisis within Islamic economics. It highlights the challenge arising from the uncritical acceptance of conventional economic ideas by many Muslim economists. This uncritical approach has created a fundamental conflict between conventional economic principles and Islamic economics, a conflict that has not been adequately recognised. Attempting to reconcile these contradictory bodies of knowledge has proven unsuccessful and has hindered the development of a genuine Islamic economic theory. By critically addressing this crisis, this chapter paves the way for potential solutions and a more coherent future for Islamic economics.

*Chapter 10*: This chapter offers a path forward for resolving the crisis in Islamic economics. It advocates for rejecting the uncritical acceptance of conventional economic ideas and, instead, developing a genuine Islamic economic theory firmly grounded in Islamic principles and values. By embracing this approach, Islamic economics can provide a distinct and valuable contribution to the field of economics, offering practical solutions that align with the aspirations of Muslim societies. This chapter serves as a beacon of hope for the future of Islamic economics.

*Chapter 11*: This explores the mutual learning and convergence between Islamic economics and conventional economics. It showcases how Islamic economics has been open to drawing insights from various schools of economic thought and other social sciences, including neoclassical, Keynesian, social, humanistic, and institutional economics. This openness to learning and incorporating useful tools and perspectives has enriched the field of Islamic economics and is likely to continue to do so in the future. As both disciplines evolve, there is the potential for further convergence and mutual learning between Islamic economics and conventional economics, contributing to a more comprehensive and robust economic understanding.

*Chapter 12*: This lays the philosophical and fundamental foundations of the proposed economic theory, Equitable Optimality. It outlines a step-by-step approach to constructing a genuine economic theory grounded in ethics. This process involves re-evaluating methodological approaches to align them with an ethical socio-economic framework, critically examining foundational assumptions within economic models to ensure their coherence with ethical principles, integrating ethical values into economic analyses, acknowledging and incorporating institutional factors into economic models, shifting the focus from mere economic growth to encompass the broader concept of holistic human development, and encouraging interdisciplinary research to enhance comprehension. Moreover, this chapter emphasises the importance of contextual comprehension within the realm of economic thought and interpretation, underscoring the significance of understanding the context of economic ideas and their implications in real-life scenarios.

*Chapter 13*: Building upon the philosophical groundwork laid in the previous chapter, this chapter explores the practical implementation of the Equitable Optimality economic theory. It addresses macroeconomic aspects within this framework, providing insights into its ethical and economic foundations. The chapter critically analyses the integration of ethics into macroeconomic considerations, showcasing how the philosophy of this proposed theory is embedded in its economic operating structure as a viable alternative.

*Chapter 14*: In this chapter, we delve into microeconomics within the Equitable Optimality theory. We explore key aspects such as demand and supply analysis, market structures, consumer choice theory, and government intervention. This chapter highlights the importance of understanding distribution, income sources, wage determination, profit, and property in designing an economic system aligned with societal goals and achieving equitable outcomes. It encourages considering cooperative frameworks and social considerations in economic decision-making, emphasising the need for a broader perspective in analysing microeconomic factors and their impact on income and wealth distribution.

*Chapter 15*: The concluding chapter serves as a thoughtful and comprehensive closure to this book, summarising key arguments and contributions while inspiring readers to explore the potential of the Equitable Optimality economic theory in shaping a more equitable and just economic future. Furthermore, the chapter reflects on the journey of constructing the Equitable Optimality economic theory, highlighting the analytical tools and methodologies used to challenge conventional economic assumptions and incorporate ethical considerations. It sets forth clear policy implications and outlines steps for the implementation of this transformative economic framework. This chapter encapsulates the essence of the Equitable Optimality theory, serving as a catalyst for its practical application and integration into the broader economic discourse.

# Chapter 2
# Basis of Conventional Economics

## 2.1 Introduction

In the previous Chapter, I provided an overview of the current economic landscape and some of its criticism. We start our first step on this journey now by analysing economics and its thoughts in capitalism and socialism. The reconstruction of the ethical basis for private property precipitates, a re-evaluation of socialism and the role of the state. These entities rely on taxation and compelled membership, mirroring socialist principles. Lacking robust economic or moral justifications, they are, in essence, socio-psychological constructs.

This prompts a return to economics, focusing on a pure capitalist societal framework as the ethical alternative to socialism, according to its supporters. The ensuing sections explore how such a system addresses issues like monopoly and the production of "public goods," particularly security services. Even in a world with only one type of scarce resource, diverse norms governing exclusive ownership are conceivable. However, not all would be equally likely to be proposed and accepted. Hence, it is prudent to commence the analysis with property norms most likely to gain societal consensus.

At this stage, the discussion is not about ethics or moral justification. While the book later asserts that the "natural position" is the only morally defensible one, it currently denotes a socio-psychological category, signifying a position likely to garner public support.

So, what is this "natural position" concerning property? It entails that every individual exclusively owns their recognised asset and can employ it in ways that align with their interests, provided it does not infringe on another's rights. This ownership permits one to permit others to use their asset in various ways, forming contractual exchanges. These exchanges are characterised by mutual respect, recognising each party's domain of control over their asset. Such exchanges, while not guaranteed to be retrospectively beneficial, are inherently mutually advantageous ex ante, or they would not occur.


S. Alamad, *Beyond Profit*, Contributions to Economics,
https://doi.org/10.1007/978-3-031-49748-3_2

Conversely, uninvited actions that intrude upon or alter another person's physical integrity, using their asset in ways they disapprove of, constitute aggression. This encompasses acts like invading someone's asset without consent. Aggressive acts inherently boost one person's satisfaction at the expense of another's, by definition.

Academic assessments of socialism and capitalism vary widely and are often influenced by the perspective and values of the researcher or school of thought. Both systems have their proponents and critics, and there is ongoing debate about their merits and drawbacks. Here is a general overview of some common academic assessments of these principles:

## *Capitalism*

(a) *Efficiency and Innovation*: One of the main strengths attributed to capitalism is its ability to generate economic growth, efficiency, and innovation. The competitive nature of capitalism can incentivise individuals and businesses to produce goods and services more efficiently and to create new technologies.
(b) *Individual Freedom*: Capitalism is often praised for its emphasis on individual freedom and property rights. Proponents argue that it allows individuals to make choices about their economic activities, including what to produce, consume, and invest in.
(c) *Wealth Generation*: Capitalist systems have historically generated significant wealth, leading to higher standards of living for many people. Advocates argue that this wealth can be redistributed to address social inequalities through philanthropy and social programs.
(d) *Consumer Choice*: Capitalist economies typically offer a wide range of consumer choices, as businesses compete to meet the demands of consumers.
(e) *Incentives for Hard Work*: Capitalism is believed to provide incentives for hard work, entrepreneurship, and risk-taking because individuals can potentially reap the rewards of their efforts.

## *Critiques of Capitalism*

(a) *Inequality*: One of the most prominent criticisms of capitalism is its tendency to produce economic and social inequalities. Critics argue that it often benefits the wealthy more than the poor, leading to income and wealth disparities.
(b) *Exploitation*: Some critics argue that capitalism can lead to the exploitation of workers, particularly in low-wage industries. They claim that the pursuit of profit can prioritise the interests of business owners over the well-being of employees.
(c) *Environmental Concerns*: Capitalism's focus on economic growth and profit can sometimes disregard environmental sustainability. Critics argue that

unchecked capitalism can lead to overexploitation of natural resources and environmental degradation.

### *Socialism*

(a) *Equity*: Socialism is often lauded for its emphasis on economic and social equity. It seeks to reduce income and wealth disparities by redistributing resources and ensuring access to essential services like healthcare and education.
(b) *Social Safety Nets*: Socialist systems typically include robust social safety nets, providing citizens with healthcare, education, and other essential services regardless of their income. Proponents argue that this leads to greater social stability.
(c) *Worker Rights*: Socialism often prioritises workers' rights, including fair wages and safe working conditions. Labour unions and collective bargaining are common features in socialist systems.
(d) *Public Ownership*: In some forms of socialism, key industries and services are publicly owned or controlled, reducing the influence of private corporations.

### *Critiques of Socialism*

(a) *Economic Efficiency*: Critics argue that socialist economies can be less efficient and innovative than capitalist ones due to reduced competition and incentives for entrepreneurial risk-taking.
(b) *Bureaucracy*: Socialist systems can be criticised for their potential to lead to bureaucratic inefficiencies and slow decision-making processes.
(c) *Individual Freedom*: Some critics argue that socialism can limit individual freedom and stifle innovation and creativity by imposing too many regulations and restrictions.
(d) *Incentives*: There are concerns that socialism may reduce incentives for hard work and entrepreneurship since individuals may not reap the full rewards of their efforts.

Therefore, the assessment of socialism and capitalism often involves a nuanced examination of these systems' historical and contemporary implementations, as well as their impact on various aspects of society, including economic growth, income distribution, social welfare, and individual freedom. It is essential to recognise that there is a wide spectrum of economic systems, and real-world examples often incorporate elements of both socialism and capitalism to varying degrees. Academic debates on these principles continue to evolve as scholars explore their strengths and weaknesses in different contexts, which this study aims to achieve by suggesting an alternative to both of them.

## 2.2 Basis of Conventional Economics

The Marxian Doctrine categorises individuals as landlords or workers based on whether they own land or sell their labour. However, social classes are not subjective classifications imposed by observers; they are living entities that exist independently. Viewing society as a collection of individuals or families overlooks the consequences that arise from the existence of social classes. While the significance of social classes in purely economic theory research is debatable, their importance in practical applications and broader aspects of the social process is undeniable.

In essence, social classes were introduced in the famous statement of the Communist Manifesto, which asserts that the history of society is shaped by class struggles. Although this claim can be toned down to suggest that historical events can often be understood through the lens of class interests and attitudes, and that existing class structures play a crucial role in historical interpretation, it still provides a valuable framework akin to the economic interpretation of history itself.

The success of the class struggle principle, according to Friedman (1984, pp. 35–51), depends on the validity of the theory of classes we adopt. Our understanding of history, cultural patterns, and social change interpretations will vary depending on whether we subscribe to racial theories of classes, reducing human history to racial conflicts, or theories of classes based on the division of labour, where class antagonisms are seen as conflicts between vocational groups. Moreover, differences in analysis extend beyond the nature of classes. Disparate definitions of class interests and varying perspectives on how class action manifests also contribute to different interpretations. The subject of social classes remains rife with biases and is not yet in its scientific stage.

Interestingly, Marx never systematically developed what seems to be a pivotal aspect of his thought. It's possible that he postponed the task, assuming that his thinking heavily relied on class concepts and he didn't feel the need for a definitive statement. Alternatively, certain aspects of class theory may have remained unresolved in his own mind, hindered by difficulties arising from his insistence on an oversimplified economic conception of the phenomenon.

Marx himself and his followers offered limited applications of this underdeveloped theory, particularly evident in his History of the Class Struggles in France. However, no substantial progress has been made beyond that. Engels, Marx's chief associate, proposed a division of labour theory of classes that deviated from Marxism in its implications. Apart from scattered insights and observations found throughout Marx's writings, notably in Das Kapital and the Communist Manifesto, attempts to assemble these fragments into a cohesive theory are delicate and beyond the scope of this discussion (Rothbard 1977, p. 176).

The fundamental idea revolves around the stratifying principle based on ownership or exclusion from ownership of the means of production, including factories, machinery, raw materials, and consumer goods. Consequently, two primary classes emerge: the owners, known as capitalists, and the laborers who are compelled to sell their labour, referred to as the proletariat. Intermediate groups such as farmers, artisans, clerks, and professionals, who may employ labour but also engage in manual work, are acknowledged but considered anomalies that tend to diminish within the capitalist process.

The two fundamental classes, inherently antagonistic due to their positions, are defined not by individual volition but by the logic of their circumstances. While internal divisions and conflicts between subgroups within each class may occur and hold historical significance, they are ultimately incidental. The primary and non-incidental antagonism lies in the private control of the means of production, creating a class war between the capitalist class and the proletariat (Rothbard, 1977, p. 176).

As we will explore later, Marx attempts to illustrate how capitalists destroy each other and, eventually, the capitalist system itself through this class war. He also explores how capital ownership leads to further accumulation. However, this mode of argumentation, along with defining a social class based on ownership, raises the importance of the concept of "primitive accumulation" (Kolko, 1967).

The Marxian Doctrine, in relation to the question of how capitalists came into existence and acquired the necessary resources to exploit others, lacks explicit clarity. Marx dismisses the bourgeois notion that individuals become capitalists through superior intelligence and hard work, which he rightly ridicules. However, while this narrative may not fully capture the truth, it does hold some validity. In examining historical and contemporary facts without bias, one can observe that exceptional intelligence and effort often lead to industrial success and the establishment of positions of power. Particularly in the early stages of capitalism and individual industrial careers, saving played a significant role, although not exactly as described in classical economics (Kolko, 1967).

While it is uncommon to become a capitalist solely through saving from a wage or salary to fund a factory, saving does contribute to the process, albeit in a different manner than traditionally explained. The majority of accumulation stems from profits, presupposing their existence, which justifies differentiating between saving and accumulating. Typically, the means necessary to initiate entrepreneurship are obtained through borrowing other people's savings or utilising bank deposits created for aspiring entrepreneurs. Nevertheless, entrepreneurs usually engage in saving. Their savings serve to free them from the daily drudgery of earning a living, granting them breathing space to explore opportunities, develop plans, and secure cooperation.

From an economic theory perspective, Marx had a valid argument, although he exaggerated it, in challenging the classical authors' attribution of a significant role to saving. However, his conclusion does not follow, and the ridicule he directed at the classical theory is equally unjustified. Nevertheless, the guffaw served its purpose, aiding the acceptance of Marx's alternative theory of primitive accumulation. However, this alternative theory is not explicitly elaborated in the mentioned text.

The explanation provided by the Marxian Doctrine regarding how certain individuals acquired the power to subjugate and exploit others is not as conclusive as desired. The theory acknowledges that force, robbery, and the subjugation of the masses facilitated the exploitation and pillaging, which, in turn, reinforced the subjugation. This aligns with prevailing intellectual ideas, especially in modern times.

However, it does not fully solve the problem of explaining how certain individuals gained the power to subjugate and exploit in the first place. Popular literature often overlooks this question, and addressing it would not be suitable in the context of authors like John Reed. However, we are examining Marx's ideas (Mises, 1966, p. 359).

Marx's major theories possess a historical aspect that provides some semblance of a solution. According to Marx, capitalism emerged from a feudal society, and it is crucial to the logic of capitalism, not just a matter of historical fact. While the same question about the causes and mechanisms of social stratification arises in the feudal context, Marx largely accepted the bourgeois view that feudalism was a system of force in which subjugation and exploitation of the masses were already established. The class theory initially developed for capitalist society was extended to its feudal predecessor, along with much of the conceptual framework of economic theory. This allowed some of the most complex problems to be shifted to the feudal realm and re-emerge as data in the analysis of the capitalist system.

In this framework, the feudal exploiter simply transformed into the capitalist exploiter. Instances where feudal lords became industrialists provide some evidence supporting this view, as they would solve what remains of the problem. Historical evidence suggests that many feudal lords, especially in Germany, established and operated factories, often using their feudal rents for financial means and employing the agricultural population (sometimes their serfs) as labour. However, in other cases, the available evidence to fill the gaps is significantly limited. Frankly speaking, from a Marxian perspective, there is no satisfactory explanation for this issue without resorting to non-Marxian elements that may lead to non-Marxian conclusions (Mises, 1966, p. 359).

This highlights several criticisms of Marx's theory of social classes and its role within his overall analytical framework. One criticism is that Marx's theory of primitive accumulation, which explains the origins of capitalism, continues throughout the capitalist era, and undermines the distinction between past and present processes. Additionally, the theory does not adequately address the constant rise and fall of individual families within the upper strata of society, challenging the notion of a rigid division between capitalists and proletarians.

The argument that Marx's theory of social classes is not an independent doctrine but serves to implement and restrict the modus operandi of the economic interpretation of history. Marx's focus on economic phenomena and the narrow definition of classes as purely economic in nature limit a deeper understanding of social classes. The connection between the definition of capitalism and the definition of class division is seen as a bold analytic strategy that links the fate of social classes with the fate of capitalism, making socialism the only possible classless society. However, this tautological construction neglects other plausible principles of division and exaggerates the importance of the antagonism between capitalists and workers.

Despite its shortcomings, the theory of social classes plays an organic function within Marx's system by linking the economic interpretation of history with the concepts of the profit economy. It serves as an analytic tool that marshals all social facts and makes phenomena confocal. This overarching function is considered more important than the theory's immediate problem-solving success.

While some enthusiasts may admire Marx's theory of social classes, it is more understandable that individuals appreciate the force and grandeur of Marx's overall synthesis and are willing to overlook shortcomings in its component parts.

Now let us move to Marx's theory of exploitation and its relation to capitalist accumulation and economic progress. It argues that in a perfectly competitive economy, exploitation gains would lead capitalists to expand production and accumulate capital, as it would result in increased profits for each individual capitalist. However, this process would also lead to contradictions inherent in capitalism, such as rising wage rates and falling product prices, which would ultimately be detrimental to the capitalist class as a whole (Mises, 1974, p. 116).

Capitalist economy is not stationary but constantly undergoing revolution and change from within. New commodities, methods of production, and commercial opportunities constantly disrupt existing structures and conditions of doing business. Economic progress in capitalism is characterised by turmoil, and competition in this context works differently from a stationary process.

Marx had a clear understanding of this process of industrial change, even though his analysis and explanation of its mechanism were flawed. Marx failed to adequately distinguish the entrepreneur from the capitalist and had a faulty theoretical technique, resulting in non sequiturs and mistakes. However, the vision of the process itself served many of Marx's purposes.

Despite the shortcomings in Marx's theory of surplus value and his failure to establish a compelling explanation for the compulsion to accumulate, the passage suggests that these deficiencies can be overcome by supplying more satisfactory explanations. It argues that the driving force for accumulation can be found in the constant threat of competition from new commodities and production methods, which can turn individual profits into losses. In this way, the passage proposes an alternative explanation for the compulsion to accumulate without relying on the questionable aspects of Marx's argument. While we acknowledge the weaknesses in Marx's analysis we also highlight the significance of his insights into the process of industrial change and the driving forces behind accumulation in capitalist economies (Mises, 1974, p. 116).

Marx's prediction that real wage rates and the standard of living for the working class would fall as a result of the logic of the capitalist process. However, the passage points out that this prediction has been proven incorrect by empirical evidence, and Marxists have struggled to reconcile this discrepancy. Some attempts have been made to interpret Marx's prediction as referring to the relative share of labour incomes in total national income rather than real wage rates, but this interpretation contradicts the meaning of most passages in Marx's work (Rothbard, 1970a, p. 607).

This suggests that modern Marxists often attribute the failure of this prediction to exceptional conditions, such as colonial expansion or the opening up of new countries during the nineteenth century, which supposedly provided a temporary respite from exploitation. However, the passage notes that Marx's theoretical framework in this area is unreliable, particularly concerning the theory of the "industrial reserve army" and the unemployment resulting from mechanisation. This theory heavily relies on the work of Ricardo, but Marx's additions to it are not considered essential (Rothbard, 1970a, p. 607).

Ricardo initially believed that the introduction of machines into production would benefit the masses, but later revised his position to acknowledge the possibility of adverse effects. However, Ricardo's numerical example was meant to illustrate a possibility rather than a general rule, and he acknowledged that mechanisation could ultimately result in a net benefit to labour through its effects on total output and prices. This points out the shortcomings in Marx's prediction of falling real wages and the standard of living for the working class and highlights the unreliable nature of his theoretical framework in this area. It suggests that attempts to salvage the prediction by attributing it to exceptional conditions or interpreting it differently have not been successful (Rothbard, 1977).

Marx's contributions to the field of business cycles and notes that evaluating his work in this area is challenging. The valuable aspects of Marx's analysis consist of scattered observations and comments found throughout his writings, including letters. However, reconstructing a comprehensive theory of business cycles from these fragmented pieces is subject to interpretation and can yield different results depending on the perspective of the interpreter.

Some Marxists have attempted to find a clear-cut cycle theory within Marx's overall logic of the capitalist process. Given Marx's emphasis on the power of capitalism to develop productive capacity alongside the growing misery of the masses, it is natural to infer that crises or depressions could be attributed to under-consumption or over-production. However, Marx himself explicitly rejected the under-consumption theory and did not provide a simple theory of business cycles (Rothbard, 1977).

It is argued that Marx's "laws" of the capitalist process do not logically lead to a factor that would generate cyclical fluctuations and account for alternating periods of prosperity and depression (Friedman, 1984). While accidents, incidents, miscalculations, and external factors can be invoked to explain fluctuations, Marx's process of accumulation, described as proceeding at an even rate, does not inherently generate cycles. This lack of a fundamental explanation freed Marx to consider various elements and factors that could influence business cycles, such as the intervention of money in commodity transactions, easy money markets, population growth, expansions and contractions of credit, and other incidents and accidents (Friedman, 1984).

Despite not offering a comprehensive theory, Marx's analysis of business cycles demonstrated common sense and sound reasoning. He recognised the existence of cyclical movements before many other economists and understood aspects of their mechanism. Marx's work on business cycles, along with the French economist Clément Juglar, laid the groundwork for future cycle research, even though his explanations were not fully adequate. His preoccupation with the problem of business cycles, distinct from isolated crises, solidifies his position among the pioneers of modern cycle research.

Thus, Marx's contributions to the study of business cycles consist of scattered observations and comments rather than a comprehensive theory. While his work reveals an understanding of the cyclical nature of economic phenomena, he did not provide a satisfactory explanation for the causes of business cycles. Nonetheless, his insights and recognition of cyclical movements positioned him as an important figure in early cycle research.

Marx's theory of the inevitable catastrophe, based on the growth of misery and oppression leading to a mass revolt, is invalidated by a non-sequitur in his argument. Additionally, orthodox Marxists have questioned the proposition that concentration of industrial control is incompatible with the capitalist system. Some even argue that capitalism might gain stability through concentration. However, the passage suggests that while Marx's facts and reasoning are flawed, his prediction that capitalist evolution will undermine the foundations of capitalist society may still be true (Kolko, 1967).

Gustav Schmoller also recognised this truth without providing further explanation. The understanding that capitalist evolution will eventually destroy capitalist society has become commonplace, but Marx's vision of this truth in 1847 is considered profound. While Marx's economic analysis cannot be deemed a complete success, his contributions to individual problems, such as his treatment of the business cycle and the structure of physical capital, should be acknowledged (Friedman, 1984).

Despite Marx's theoretical shortcomings, there is a fundamental idea that runs through his analysis. Marx visualised the actual sequence of economic patterns and processes in historic time, with each state determining the next. This idea of economic theory in relation to historical analysis distinguishes Marx's work. He was the first economist of high standing to systematically integrate economic theory with historical analysis, demonstrating how the two can inform and complement each other. While Marx did not address the same integration with statistics, it is implied in his approach. The flaws and non-sequiturs in Marx's economic analysis, but it also recognises his profound vision of the inevitable destruction of capitalist society through capitalist evolution. It credits Marx with integrating economic theory and historical analysis, thereby establishing a methodological approach that would influence the future of economic theory (Mises, 1966: 357).

## 2.3 Capitalism

When we discuss the nature of the capitalist system and its impact on the behaviour and performance of individuals within the bourgeois class. It highlights the allure of business success and the fear of failure, which serve as strong motivators for individuals to engage in business activities. The rewards and punishments associated with success and failure are designed to drive the majority of businessmen to strive for success, even if their chances of achieving it are overrated. The passage likens the capitalist system to a game of poker, where spectacular prizes are awarded to a small minority of winners, further fuelling the aspirations of the majority (Fujita et al., 1999).

We note that the capitalist arrangement not only chains the bourgeois stratum to their tasks but also serves as a mechanism for selecting individuals and families to rise or fall within the class. This combination of conditioning and selection ensures that those who succeed within the capitalist system are often capable businessmen. Thus, it is argued that this selection process is not guaranteed in other forms of social organiation, and the ability of the capitalist system to select and reward individuals based on their performance is a significant achievement.

However, this raises a question about the ultimate purpose of the performance driven by the capitalist system. It suggests that the pursuit of profit, rather than social service or welfare, is the primary aim of business activities. This has been a popular opinion outside the bourgeois class, and economists have both opposed and supported this view. The classical economists, despite their biases and limited perspective, believed that the self-interest of manufacturers and traders within the institutional framework of capitalism led to maximum performance for the benefit of all (Fan and Scott, 2003; Kim, 2002). They attributed the observed increase in total output to unfettered enterprise and the profit motive.

As such, there are limitations and biases of the classical economists' views, however I should caution against dismissing their teachings solely based on these grounds. Even biased individuals can speak the truth, and propositions developed from specific cases can still have general validity. Moreover, the critics and successors of the classical economists have their own biases and preconceptions, and their perspectives are based on different but equally specific cases.

From an economic analyst's perspective, the main merit of the classical economists lies in their ability to dispel certain misconceptions about capitalist society. One of these misconceptions is the naive idea that economic activity driven by the profit motive necessarily goes against the interests of consumers or diverts production from its social goal. The classics refuted these notions and highlighted that profit-making and productive performance can coexist. They argued against the belief that private profits are always a net loss to society and advocated for a responsible long-term view.

However, there is a significant gap between recognising the compatibility of profit-seeking and productive performance and proving that the pursuit of profit will always lead to the latter. The classics were unable to bridge this gap, and their arguments, although containing some truth, were seen as a fragile construction upon closer scrutiny. Subsequent analysis of their theories, spanning into the late twentieth century and post-war developments in scientific economics, revealed the limitations of their perspective.

Therefore, delving into this later analysis may not be easily accessible to nonprofessional readers. The field of economics, like other areas of knowledge, has become more specialised and technical over time. I fully acknowledge the challenge of presenting complex economic concepts in a way that is understandable to a broader audience, but pledges to make an effort to do so.

In the first stride of economic analysis, the names of Alfred Marshall and Knut Wicksell are highlighted for their influential works. Marshall's "Principles" and Wicksell's "Lectures" were significant in shaping the minds of many and approached economic theory from a practical standpoint. While their theoretical structures differed from those of the classical economists, they retained the proposition that under perfect competition, the profit interest of producers tends to maximise production. However, as the proposition was refined and proven more accurately, it lost much of its original content and significance (Friedman, 1984).

Within the framework of the Marshall-Wicksell analysis, it can be demonstrated that firms operating under conditions where they have no control over product prices or the prices of factors of production will expand their output until the marginal cost of production equals the price they can obtain for an additional unit. In other words, they will produce as much as they can without incurring losses. This level of production is considered socially desirable. This case is referred to as perfect competition, where prices are considered parameters rather than variables from the perspective of individual firms. In this scenario, an equilibrium state can be achieved, where outputs are maximised, and all factors of production are fully employed (Friedman, 1984).

Considering the selective process that affects all firms and managers, one might hold an optimistic view of the results that can be expected from a highly selected group of individuals who are motivated by profit to maximise output and minimise costs within the framework of perfect competition. It may appear that a system conforming to this pattern would significantly reduce major sources of social waste. However, upon reflection, this optimistic view is essentially a restatement of the preceding sentence and requires further examination (Schumpeter, 1954).

Moving to the second stride of analysis, it is acknowledged that the Marshall-Wicksell analysis, like the classics, recognised the existence of cases that do not conform to the model of perfect competition. The classics also acknowledged cases of "monopoly," and Adam Smith himself observed the prevalence of practices aimed at restricting competition. However, both the classics and Marshall, despite acknowledging these exceptions, regarded them as temporary and expected them to diminish over time (Schumpeter, 1954).

This is proven to be incorrect as we have witnessed today in the twenty-first Century technological revolution boom. This is manifested by the monopoly of market access and competition by large firms in various sectors such as, oil (Shell and British Petroleum and others), Banking (HSBC, Goldman Sachs and others), technology (Google, Microsoft and others), mobile phones (Apple and Samsung), e-commerce (Amazon and Alibaba, etc.). You can list many more in various sectors such media, assets management, investment funds, pharmaceutical, food production, manufacturing and so one. The global market and economy is controlled by few big players.

Marshall, while developing the Cournot theory of monopoly and recognising the presence of firms with their own special markets where they set prices, still based his general conclusions on the pattern of perfect competition, much like the classics did. Neither Marshall, Wicksell, nor the classics fully grasped the fact that perfect competition is the exception rather than the rule. Even if perfect competition were the norm, there would be less cause for celebration than initially presumed (Kolko, 1967).

Taking a closer look at the conditions required for perfect competition, it becomes evident that outside of agricultural mass production, there are few instances where perfect competition exists. In agricultural mass production, such as the supply of cotton or wheat, farmers adapt their output based on the ruling prices, which are considered data from their standpoint.

Since all farmers act in a similar manner, prices and quantities adjust to meet the requirements of perfect competition. However, this is not the case for many agricultural products, finished products, and services in industry and trade. In these cases, individual sellers, such as grocers, filling stations, or manufacturers, have their own small and precarious markets, which they try to establish and maintain through price strategies, quality differentiation, and advertising. This pattern aligns more with monopolistic competition, where firms differentiate their products and engage in competitive strategies (Friedman, 1984, pp. 35–51; Kolko, 1967, pp. 4–5; Mises, 1966, p. 359).

Monopolistic competition, along with oligopoly (where a few large-scale firms dominate the market), becomes more prevalent in the market. These conditions make many propositions taught by the Marshall-Wicksell generation of economists and perhaps later generations of economists either inapplicable or more difficult to prove. The concept of equilibrium, which refers to a determinate state of the economic system, becomes challenging to achieve in cases of oligopoly, as there may be an endless sequence of moves and countermoves, creating an indefinite state of competition between firms (Friedman, 1984).

Even in cases where equilibrium theoretically exists, it is harder to attain and preserve than in perfect competition. Furthermore, the beneficial competition observed in perfect competition gives way to predatory or cutthroat competition, as well as struggles for control in the financial sphere. These factors contribute to social waste, including advertising costs, the suppression of new production methods, and more.

Most importantly, under conditions of monopolistic competition or oligopoly, equilibrium no longer guarantees full employment or maximum output, as defined in the theory of perfect competition. Equilibrium may exist without full employment, and the level of output is likely to be below the maximum mark. Profit-conserving strategies, which are not viable in perfect competition, become possible and prevalent in these scenarios.

Considering these observations, one might argue that this confirms what the general public, especially those not involved in business, has always believed about private enterprise. Has not modern analysis refuted the classical doctrine and justified the popular view? Is not it true that there is little alignment between producing for profit and producing for the consumer? Does private enterprise merely serve as a means to restrict production in order to extract profits described as tolls and ransoms?

## 2.4 Capitalism Creative Destruction Approach

The concept of "creative destruction" is essential to understanding capitalism as an evolutionary process. Capitalism is not a static system; it is characterised by constant economic change and innovation. This notion, initially emphasised by Karl Marx, is often overlooked in the analysis of modern capitalism.

The evolutionary nature of capitalism arises from two factors. Firstly, economic activity takes place within a social and natural environment that is subject to change. These external changes, such as wars, revolutions, and shifts in societal values, can influence and shape economic action. However, they are not the primary drivers of industrial change.

Secondly, capitalism undergoes inherent internal changes driven by its own dynamics. These changes are not solely a result of automatic increases in population or capital accumulation or fluctuations in monetary systems, although these factors can play a role. Instead, the evolutionary character of capitalism stems from the system's innate drive for innovation, competition, and the pursuit of profit (Schumpeter, 1954).

The term "creative destruction" captures this process of continuous innovation and change. As new ideas, technologies, and business models emerge, they often render existing products, industries, or firms obsolete. This process involves the destruction of outdated structures and the creation of new ones, leading to economic progress and growth (Rothbard, 1970a).

However, it is crucial to recognise that capitalism's evolutionary nature does not guarantee uniformly positive outcomes or the absence of challenges. While capitalism has shown remarkable capacity for generating wealth and improving living standards, it is also accompanied by inherent contradictions and disparities.

Therefore, understanding capitalism as an evolutionary process allows us to appreciate the dynamic nature of economic change and innovation. This perspective emphasises the importance of adaptation, competition, and the constant pursuit of new opportunities and efficiencies. Creative destruction refers to the continuous process of innovation and change within the capitalist system. It is driven by the introduction of new consumer goods, new production methods, new markets, and new forms of industrial organisation created by capitalist enterprises (Kim, 2002; Fujita et al., 1999).

The development of capitalism is characterised by qualitative changes and revolutions. For example, the evolution of farming techniques, advancements in the iron and steel industry, improvements in power production, energy, technology, communication, e-commerce, and the progress of transportation. These changes constantly revolutionise and transform the economic structure from within, destroying the old and creating the new. The concept of creative destruction is considered essential to capitalism. It is what capitalism consists of and what every capitalist concern must adapt to. It is also a process that unfolds over time, spanning decades or even centuries (Fan and Scott, 2003; Kim, 2002; Fujita et al., 1999).

Therefore, evaluating the performance of capitalism requires assessing its long-term performance rather than focusing on a specific point in time. A system that fully utilises its possibilities at any given point in time may be inferior to a system that allows for temporary setbacks or failures because those setbacks can contribute to the system's long-term performance and adaptability.

Understanding capitalism and its economic impact requires analysing it as an organic process rather than focusing solely on individual firms or industries.

Business strategies and behaviours gain significance within the context of the perpetual process of creative destruction. Merely examining the behaviour of firms at a particular moment without considering the past and future dynamics overlooks the ever-changing nature of capitalism.

Furthermore, the author challenges the traditional view of competition in economics, which predominantly focuses on price competition. It suggests that competition within rigid conditions and existing structures is less relevant than competition stemming from new commodities, technologies, sources of supply, or forms of organisation. This type of competition, which brings about significant cost or quality advantages, can profoundly impact existing firms and industries, shaking the very foundations of their operations (Kim, 2002). Thus, capitalism is an ever-evolving system driven by innovation, competition, and the continuous creation and destruction of economic structures. Recognising the significance of creative destruction and understanding its implications can lead to a different perspective on capitalist practice and its social outcomes. Which the I aim to achieve in this book.

In that context, competition, even in its potential or perceived form, has a disciplining effect on businesses. Even if a business operates in a market where there is no immediate or visible competition, the presence of potential competitors or the threat of new entrants can still shape the behaviour of the business owner. The fear of future competition prompts businesses to stay vigilant and strive to improve their relative position, even if they currently hold a dominant position in the market.

Contrary to this view, some theorists (see e.g., Schumpeter, 1954; Rothbard, 1977; Friedman, 1984) argue that in certain scenarios, businesses may settle into a quasi-equilibrium where they focus on improving aspects such as service and atmosphere rather than engaging in price competition. However, such cases of stagnation and routine are not characteristic of capitalist activity. While these situations may arise temporarily, they are not sustainable and do not benefit customers. In fact, they can lead to a negative spiral where businesses, facing reduced sales due to narrowing economic space, attempt to raise prices in agreement with each other, resulting in further sales decline.

Although these cases do exist, they are considered fringe-end cases and are not representative of the broader dynamics of capitalism. They are typically found in sectors that are far removed from the core characteristics of capitalist activity. Additionally, the transient nature of these situations is highlighted. In the retail trade example provided, the real competition that matters comes not from additional shops of the same type but from alternative forms of retail, such as department stores, chain stores, mail-order houses, and supermarkets (Fan and Scott, 2003).

These new forms of competition are likely to disrupt and eventually dismantle the stagnant structures, leading to a more dynamic and competitive market environment. Whether real or potential, competition plays a crucial role in shaping business behaviour and driving innovation and progress in capitalism. The threat of competition prompts businesses to constantly improve and adapt, and even situations of apparent stagnation are transient and eventually disrupted by new competitive forces.

For the moment, let us set aside the issues related to monopolistic and public goods production. We will now explore why many economics writings and research advocate that capitalism is economically superior compared to alternative systems. This argument is based on three fundamental reasons. Firstly, only capitalism can allocate means of production in a rational manner, considering consumer evaluations. Secondly, only capitalism can ensure that the quality of output produced reaches its optimal level, again judged by consumer evaluations, given the quality of the people and the allocation of resources. Thirdly, assuming a given allocation of production factors and quality of output, only a market system can guarantee the efficient conservation of the value of production factors over time.

When a business operates in a market, it utilises its resources to produce goods that promise a return from sales greater than the costs involved. This rational behaviour is influenced by the anticipation of market demand and the need to surpass costs. Businesses constantly evaluate whether their current allocation of resources should be maintained or reallocated due to changes in demand. The profitability of their past allocation decisions can be objectively assessed through bookkeeping, which informs whether the allocation of factors of production was economically rational for the business or its subunits. Market prices of production factors serve as a benchmark for evaluating the profitability of resource allocation (Rothbard, 1970a).

While the profit-loss criterion is an ex-post evaluation and cannot guide future ex ante allocations, it plays a crucial role in constantly testing the rationality of resource allocation from the consumers' perspective. Businesses that fail to meet the profit-loss criterion are likely to shrink or exit the market, while those that consistently succeed can prosper. Although the institutionalisation of this criterion does not guarantee that every individual business decision will be rational in terms of consumer evaluations, it ensures that the overall structural changes in the production system move towards a more rational use of resources. It facilitates the continuous redirection of factors of production from less value-productive lines to more highly valued ones by consumers (Rothbard, 1970a).

However, when the state enters the picture, the situation changes. Unlike ordinary businesses, the state can acquire income through noncontractual means such as taxes and regulations. It is not compelled to avoid losses to stay in business like other producers. This allows the state to unilaterally decide the extent and duration of subsidising its own operations and determine which competitors are allowed or restricted (Little, 1982). The state becomes independent of cost-profit considerations and no longer needs to continually test its resource allocations against the profit-loss criterion to survive as a producer. Consequently, the process of allocational decisions becomes arbitrary and irrational.

When the profit-loss criterion is absent, the allocation of resources in the absence of market forces and the state's autonomous decision-making becomes arbitrary. It does not imply that decisions are made without any constraints or purely based on whim. Constraints can be imposed, such as democratic decisions based on majority appeal or autocratic decisions based on the autocrat's perception of public opinion. However, these decisions remain arbitrary from the perspective of voluntary consumer choices (Little, 1982). Therefore, regardless of the specific allocation of resources and its changes over time, it represents a wasteful use of scarce resources.

The absence of profit requirements in the state's functioning inevitably leads to allocational chaos rather than rationality.

Murray Rothbard (1977) provides a concise summary of the problem associated with government decision-making and state production. He questions how the government can effectively allocate funds and determine the amount to spend on various activities such as building roads or investing in schools. Unlike the free market where money must be justified and withdrawn from other uses, the government's answer to shortages is often to demand more money. The profit-and-loss test in the market serves as a guide for directing the flow of productive services, ensuring that the most urgent wants of consumers are satisfied. However, the government lacks a rational way to decide how much money to spend, leading to an arbitrary allocation of resources and an inability to determine when to stop spending.

Furthermore, state production tends to result in a reduction in the quality of output. In a profit-oriented business, the quality of products or services is crucial as it affects sales and the ability to recover costs. Businesses are dependent on voluntary consumer purchases and must constantly strive to improve product quality to stay in operation and prosper. However, when the production of goods is undertaken by the state, which has independent future revenue regardless of consumer evaluations, there is less incentive to focus on product quality. State employees are less concerned about producing quality products and may prioritise their own preferences over consumer demand. As a result, state-produced goods tend to have lower quality compared to those produced in the private sector (Lucas, 1988).

Additionally, a market system is essential for efficient resource utilisation over time. Private ownership and the profit-oriented nature of enterprises establish an incentive structure where owners strive to maximise their income from sales while conserving the value of production factors. Every production act affects both income from sales and the value of production factors, and private ownership safeguards against overexploitation of capital (Hall, 2001). This incentive system allows values produced to exceed values destroyed during production. Private ownership also enables efficient adjustment of capital conservation or consumption in response to anticipated price changes, ensuring that resources are used optimally based on market conditions.

Rothbard (1977) argues that capitalism, with its rational allocation of resources, focus on product quality, and efficient resource utilisation, is economically superior to state production and government decision-making. When comparing a capitalist production system to a system where the state controls the means of production, significant differences arise, particularly in the context of a modern parliamentary democracy. In such a system, while managers may have the right to receive returns from product sales after deducting operational costs, they do not have the right to privately appropriate the gains or losses in the value of production factors.

This crucial distinction reduces the incentive to use capital efficiently over time. If individuals have the right to privately appropriate income returns from sales but lack the ability to appropriate gains or losses in capital value resulting from the usage of that capital, the institutionalised incentive structure becomes one of maximising income returns at the expense of capital value losses. In this scenario, the focus shifts from maximising total income or societal wealth based on consumer evaluations to maximising short-term income returns. This creates a situation where managers have little motivation to reduce the degree of exploitation of capital and opt for conservation when prices for the goods produced are expected to rise in the future.

For example, why would a government official choose to conserve a given stock of capital if the benefits of such conservation (increased capital value) cannot be privately enjoyed? By pursuing a conservationist policy, their income returns from sales would be reduced, while disregarding conservation would maintain their income returns without consequences. In essence, conservation would bring disadvantages without any advantages. Therefore, if state managers are ordinary individuals driven by self-interest, it is an inevitable consequence of state production that a given stock of capital will be over-utilised, ultimately leading to a decline in living standards compared to a capitalist system.

The lack of private appropriation of gains or losses in capital value under state production diminishes the incentive for efficient capital usage and conservation. This results in a suboptimal allocation of resources and a negative impact on consumer welfare compared to a capitalist system.

To address the argument that monopolistic production would arise and prevail under capitalism, several points can be made. First, available historical evidence contradicts the claim that there is a tendency towards increased monopoly under an unhampered market system. In fact, historical periods characterised by relatively freer laissez-faire capitalism, such as the period from 1867 to World War I in the United States, witnessed less development towards monopolisation and concentration of business. Instead, there was a constant trend towards more severe competition, accompanied by falling prices for most goods. It was only when state intervention and regulations increased that the trend towards monopolisation emerged (Rothbard, 1977).

Second, from a theoretical standpoint, there are reasons to doubt the notion that monopolistic tendencies would prevail in a free market. The competitive nature of a free market, with its low barriers to entry, acts as a deterrent to monopolistic practices. In a truly open market, new firms can enter and compete with established ones, thereby challenging their market power and preventing the consolidation of monopolies.

Third, even if a process of increasing monopolisation were to occur, it would not harm consumers as long as free entry into the market is ensured. The threat of potential competitors entering the market acts as a check on monopolistic behaviour. If a monopolistic firm were to raise prices or reduce quality, it would create profitable opportunities for new entrants, incentivising them to enter the market and offer better alternatives. This dynamic competition would protect consumer interests and prevent monopolies from exploiting their market power.

Lastly, the concept of monopoly prices, distinct from competitive prices, is illusory in a capitalist economy. In a competitive market, prices are determined by supply and demand forces, reflecting the interaction of various buyers and sellers. Monopoly prices, on the other hand, imply a deviation from this market-determined price. However, in a capitalist system, where competition is allowed to flourish, any attempt to set prices significantly above the competitive level would attract new entrants and erode the monopoly's market share.

Historical evidence contradicts the notion that monopolistic tendencies prevail in unhampered market systems. The theoretical characteristics of free markets, coupled with the potential for new entrants and competition, act as safeguards against monopolistic behaviour. Furthermore, the concept of monopoly prices is not applicable in a capitalist economy where competition ensures that prices align with market forces (Rothbard, 1977; Friedman, 1984).

Kolko (1967, pp. 4–5) suggests that during the period of growing competition in the United States, many business and financial leaders found competition to be unacceptable. The merger movement that took place was seen as an attempt by these leaders to regain control and counter the trends of competition. However, their efforts were largely unsuccessful.

According to Kolko (1967), new competitors emerged and economic power became more decentralised as the nation expanded. In this context, some influential businessmen came to the realisation that only the national government could effectively control and stabilise the economy. This perspective challenges the traditional view held by historians that government intervention in the economy was a response to the existence of monopoly. Instead, Kolko argues that it was the lack of monopoly power that led to government intervention. The absence of monopolistic control meant that business interests faced significant competition, which they sought to overcome by turning to the government for support.

It is worth noting that Kolko's (1967) interpretation represents a particular perspective within the realm of left-wing criticism of capitalism. While his viewpoint may be influential among critics from the left, it is important to consider multiple perspectives and engage in a broader analysis of historical evidence and economic theories to gain a comprehensive understanding of the complex dynamics between competition, monopoly, and government intervention. There are several theoretical considerations related to monopolisation and its implications for the owner of monopolised production factors.

Firstly, when a factor of production is monopolised, it is withdrawn from the market sphere, which means there is no trading of that factor and no market price for it. As a result, the owner of the monopolised factor cannot assess the monetary costs involved in withholding it from the market or using it in a particular way. This lack of market feedback makes it difficult for the owner to calculate profits and ensure the highest possible returns on investments.

Assuming that the owner is interested in maximising profits, this suggests that the owner would need to continually offer the monopolised factors on the market to ascertain if there are more lucrative ways to use them. Paradoxically, to maximise profits, the monopolist would have a permanent interest in discontinuing their position as the owner of a monopolised factor and instead desire its inclusion in the market sphere.

Moreover, monopolisation progresses, the problem of economic calculation becomes more acute for the owner of monopolised factors. The monopolist's limited knowledge of future consumer preferences and competing goods makes it increasingly difficult to detect the most profitable uses for the monopolised factors. Other entrepreneurs, occupying different positions in space and time, may perceive more lucrative opportunities for employing these factors and may be willing to purchase them from the monopolist, potentially increasing the monopolist's profits.

Monopolisation undermines the monopolist's ability to make accurate economic calculations and may create incentives for the monopolist to sell the monopolised factors to other producers, thereby increasing their profits. These theoretical considerations challenge the common assumption that monopolists always seek to maximise their own profits at the expense of consumer welfare.

Considering the extreme case of a single super-monopolist who provides all goods and services in the market and is the sole employer of everyone. In this hypothetical scenario, it is assumed that the super-monopolist has acquired and upholds their position without aggression. From a perspective of individual rights, it is argued that no one has any valid claims against the owner of this firm since the enterprise is legitimately owned. Additionally, there is no infringement on anyone's right to boycott any potential exchange. No one is forced to work for or buy from the monopolist, and individuals are free to use their earnings as they see fit.

Given these assumptions, the existence of a monopoly implies that the monopolist does not see any chance of improving their income by selling their means of production, and others do not see any opportunity to improve their income by bidding away factors from the monopolist or becoming capitalist producers themselves. This suggests that the super-monopolist is efficiently providing consumers with the most urgently wanted goods and services, as there is no alternative method that is perceived as more profitable.

Regarding the concept of monopoly prices, the question of whether monopoly prices imply a suboptimal supply of goods to consumers and whether they represent an exception to the generally superior functioning of capitalism. However, it argues that even in the case of a super-monopolist, consumers are not harmed, and the overall efficiency of the market economy is not compromised.

By stating that the theory of monopoly prices are categorically different from competitive prices deserves special treatment and analysis. However, it suggests that the analysis only reinforces the notion that monopoly does not pose a special problem that necessitates qualifying amendments to the general rule of a market economy being more efficient than socialist or statist systems. According to economic orthodoxy, specifically the Austrian school of economics represented by L. v. Mises (1966, p. 359), the definition of "monopoly price" is typically understood as follows:

Monopoly is a necessary condition for the emergence of monopoly prices, but it is not the sole condition. Another requirement is a specific shape of the demand curve. Merely having a monopoly does not automatically imply the existence of monopoly prices. For example, the publisher of a copyrighted book may have a monopoly over its distribution, but if the demand for the book is very low, even at low prices, it would not be considered a monopoly price (Mises, 1966).

Monopoly prices, on the other hand, refer to prices at which it is more advantageous for the monopolist to restrict the total quantity sold rather than expanding sales to the limit that would occur in a competitive market. In other words, a monopolist sets prices higher than what would prevail under competitive conditions to maximise their profits by limiting the quantity sold. This definition highlights the idea that monopoly prices are not simply determined by the existence of a monopoly but also depend on the specific market conditions and the monopolist's strategic behaviour in response to those conditions (Mises, 1966).

The argument presented suggests that neither the producer nor any neutral observer can definitively determine whether the prices obtained on the market are monopoly or competitive prices based on the criterion of "restricted versus unrestricted supply" as defined earlier. This is because the distinction between monopoly and competition depends on future market conditions and consumer evaluations.

According to this perspective, every producer, including a monopolist, faces a decision-making process regarding how much of a good to produce in order to maximise monetary income. This decision involves estimating the demand curve for the product and considering production costs. The producer will choose the quantity to be produced where the returns from sales (quantity sold times price) minus production costs are maximised.

In this scenario, it becomes unclear whether the resulting market price is a monopoly or competitive price. The analysis points out that there is no way to determine if the quantity produced was restricted to take advantage of inelastic demand and generate a monopoly price, or if the price reached was a competitive one based on expanded production. The producer's goal is to set the quantity produced above the level where demand becomes elastic and below the point where marginal cost equals the expected price per unit.

The argument concludes that both restriction and expansion of production are inherent in profit-maximising and market-price formation. They are interconnected aspects that cannot be separated to distinguish between monopolistic and competitive actions. This viewpoint challenges the ability to definitively classify market prices as either monopoly or competitive based solely on the criterion of supply restriction, highlighting the complex nature of price determination in real-world market settings.

The argument continues by presenting a scenario where the monopolist decides to reduce the output of the good produced from a previously higher level to a new lower level, and this decision leads to higher total returns. However, the analysis argues that even in this case, it would not necessarily be a clear instance of a monopoly price. The reason is that this reallocation of resources, resulting in a supply restriction, is indistinguishable from a "normal" reallocation that considers changes in demand (Mises, 1966).

The example given is that if the monopolist produces a unique kind of apples and faces an increase in the demand for apples as well as a higher increase in demand for oranges, the monopolist may choose to reduce apple production and allocate some of the previously used resources to produce oranges. This reallocation would lead to greater returns because the previous market price for apples would have become sub-competitive due to changes in demand. In this situation, the monopolist's decision to restrict apple production is driven by changes in relative prices and the desire to maximise profits (Mises, 1966).

However, the argument highlights that if the monopolist chooses not to produce oranges or engage in any other productive activity with the available resources but instead enjoys leisure, it indicates that the restriction in apple supply is due to changes in relative prices, specifically the increased demand for leisure. The decision to restrict output is driven by the increased value the monopolist places on leisure rather than other goods.

Therefore, the analysis asserts that the distinction between a monopoly price and a normal reallocation based on changes in demand becomes blurred. Both can lead to supply restrictions, and it is difficult to distinguish between them because they are ultimately different aspects of action and choice influenced by changes in relative prices and individual preferences.

The analysis argues that neither the monopolist nor any outside observer can conceptually distinguish restrictive actions from normal reallocations based on anticipated changes in demand. When the monopolist engages in restrictive activities that result in higher prices, it is implied that the released factors are being used for another purpose that the monopolist values more highly. This indicates that the monopolist is adjusting to changes in relative demand.

The distinction between a monopolistic restriction and a normal reallocation becomes difficult because both involve a restriction of production in one good accompanied by an expansion of production in other goods using the released factors. It is impossible to differentiate between the two situations. Even if the restriction leads to increased leisure for the monopolist instead of increased production of another good, it is still considered the expansion of the yield of a consumer good, namely leisure. There is no way to determine whether the restriction resulted in a monopoly or a competitive price, or to what extent the motive of increased leisure played a role (Rothbard, 1970a, p. 607).

Therefore, defining a monopoly price as a price attained by selling a smaller quantity of a product at a higher price is deemed meaningless, as the same definition applies to a competitive price compared to a sub-competitive price. The argument emphasises that the distinction between monopoly and competitive prices based on the quantity sold and the price alone is inadequate and fails to capture the underlying factors and motivations involved in production decisions (Rothbard, 1970a, p. 607).

The analysis concludes that there is no reason to modify the description of how a pure market economy normally works and its superiority over socialist or statist systems of production based on the monopoly question. The likelihood of a monopolistic process occurring is deemed highly unlikely both empirically and theoretically. Even if a monopoly were to exist, it would be harmless to consumers within the framework of a market system.

The argument asserts that a restrictive monopolistic price cannot be distinguished from a normal price increase resulting from higher demand and changes in relative prices. Additionally, every restrictive action by a monopolist is seen as expansionary in nature. Therefore, claiming that a curtailment of production in one line coupled with an increase in total revenue indicates a misallocation of production factors and exploitation of consumers is considered nonsensical.

An excerpt from Ludwig von Mises (1974, p. 116) is provided to illustrate this point further. He argues that blaming an entrepreneur for not producing more of a particular good while neglecting another good is arbitrary. This suggests that blaming entrepreneurs for the existence of scarcity and limited factors of production is akin to expecting an unrealistic utopia where resources are abundant and infinite. This concept reinforces the view that monopoly does not pose a fundamental challenge to the efficiency and functioning of a market economy, and it does not undermine its superiority over alternative economic systems.

This concept argues that the monopoly problem only arises when the state becomes involved in the market. The state, as a distinct enterprise, is the only entity whose prices and practices can be objectively distinguished and criticised as "too high" or "exploitative." This is because the state can enforce its prices and practices through the use of coercion and threats of violence, unlike voluntary transactions in the market.

Furthermore, the analysis (Fan and Scott, 2003; Kim, 2002; Fujita et al., 1999) suggests that the state has a natural tendency toward monopolisation and concentration due to its unique privileges and advantages. Unlike other enterprises that rely on voluntary exchange and the consent of consumers, the state has the power to tax individuals without their consent and impose regulations on property use without gaining consent. These advantages give the state a significant edge in competing for scarce resources.

The argument concludes that, if one assumes that representatives of the state are driven by the profit motive like individuals in the market, the state as an organisation will have a stronger tendency toward growth compared to any other organisation. Historical experience is claimed to support the thesis that statist systems are more prone to monopolistic growth compared to market systems, for which there is no evidence suggesting a similar tendency. The distinctive nature of the state as an enterprise and asserts that the monopoly problem is intrinsically tied to state intervention in the market. It suggests that the state's coercive power and advantages contribute to its tendency toward monopolisation and concentration, which is not observed to the same extent in market systems.

## 2.5 Conclusion

Marx's theory of social classes and its role within conventional economics is a complex and multifaceted subject. While the Marxian Doctrine categorises individuals into landlords and workers based on ownership of land or labour, this Chapter highlights the limitations of this classification in practical applications and broader social processes. The significance of social classes in understanding history and cultural patterns cannot be denied, but their economic relevance in purely theoretical research remains debatable.

We acknowledge that Marx's theory of social classes is not an independent doctrine, but rather serves to implement and restrict the *modus operandi* of the economic interpretation of history. It points out that Marx's focus on economic phenomena and the narrow definition of classes limit a deeper understanding of social classes. Despite its shortcomings, the theory of social classes plays an organic function within Marx's system by linking the economic interpretation of history with the concepts of the profit economy.

Marx's theory of exploitation and capitalist accumulation is also examined, highlighting the flaws in his analysis and the prediction of falling real wages and living standards for the working class. We propose alternative explanations for the compulsion to accumulate and the driving forces behind accumulation in capitalist economies. While Marx's insights into industrial change and the process of accumulation are acknowledged, We emphasise the unreliable nature of some aspects of his theoretical framework in this area.

Regarding business cycles, Marx's contributions are considered scattered observations and comments rather than a comprehensive theory. His understanding of cyclical movements positioned him as an important figure in early cycle research, despite not providing a satisfactory explanation for the causes of business cycles.

We also acknowledge the profound vision in Marx's analysis, especially regarding the inevitable destruction of capitalist society through capitalist evolution. Despite some flaws and non-sequiturs in his economic analysis, Marx's integration of economic theory with historical analysis established a methodological approach that would influence the future of economic theory.

Hence, Marx's theory of social classes and its relationship with conventional economics is a subject filled with complexities and limitations. While his contributions to economic theory and historical analysis are recognised, there are significant areas where his analysis falls short. Despite these limitations, Marx's work has left a lasting impact on economic thought and continues to be relevant in the discussions surrounding capitalism, exploitation, and societal progress. The study of Marx's ideas and their application to contemporary economic and social issues remains an ongoing and important endeavour for economists and scholars alike.

The nature of the capitalist system, on the other hand, and its impact on individuals within the bourgeois class is complex and multifaceted. The allure of business success and the fear of failure serve as strong motivators for individuals to engage in business activities within the capitalist system. The rewards and punishments associated with success and failure drive businessmen to strive for success, even if their chances of achieving it are overrated.

The capitalist system not only chains the bourgeois stratum to their tasks, but also serves as a mechanism for selecting individuals and families to rise or fall within the class. This combination of conditioning and selection ensures that those who succeed within the capitalist system are often capable businessmen. The ability of the capitalist system to select and reward individuals based on their performance is seen as a significant achievement.

However, the ultimate purpose of the performance driven by the capitalist system is questioned, as it suggests that the pursuit of profit, rather than social service or welfare, is the primary aim of business activities. Economists have both opposed and supported this view, and the classical economists believed that the profit motive could lead to maximum performance for the benefit of all. While the classical economists dispelled certain misconceptions about capitalist society, their theories had limitations and biases.

Subsequent economic analysis, such as that of Alfred Marshall and Knut Wicksell, recognised the existence of cases that do not conform to the model of perfect competition. Perfect competition is the exception rather than the rule, and under conditions of monopolistic competition or oligopoly, equilibrium no longer guarantees full employment or maximum output. Profit-conserving strategies become prevalent in these scenarios, leading to social waste and deviations from the idealised notions of perfect competition.

Understanding capitalism as an evolutionary process through the concept of "creative destruction" allows us to appreciate its dynamic nature and capacity for innovation and change. Capitalism is not a static system, and constant economic progress and growth arise from the destruction of outdated structures and the creation of new ones. However, capitalism's evolutionary nature also comes with inherent contradictions and disparities.

Overall, the study of capitalism and its impact on society requires an understanding of its complexities and limitations. The pursuit of profit and competition within the capitalist system drives economic change and innovation, but it also presents challenges and inequalities. Recognising the evolving and dynamic nature of capitalism helps us better grasp its effects on individuals, businesses, and society as a whole for the pursuit of developing a better economic theory. Next Chapter discusses production and its related challenges in relation to public goods.

# Chapter 3
# Production and the Public Goods Problem in Capitalism

## 3.1 Introduction

We started our first step on this journey in the previous Chapter by analysing economics and its thoughts in capitalism and socialism. We discussed that the reconstruction of the ethical basis for private property precipitates a re-evaluation of socialism and the role of the state. These entities rely on taxation and compelled membership, mirroring socialist principles. Lacking robust economic or moral justifications, they are, in essence, socio-psychological constructs.

In this Chapter we build on our discussion by analysing how public goods pose a challenge in capitalist production due to their unique characteristics and the inherent nature of market mechanisms. Public goods are goods or services that are non-excludable and non-rivalrous, meaning that once they are provided, they are available to all and one person's use does not diminish their availability to others. Examples of public goods include national defence, public parks, and street lighting.

The problem with public goods arises because they do not fit well within the traditional framework of market exchange based on private property and voluntary transactions. In a market system, goods and services are typically exchanged through prices determined by supply and demand. However, public goods cannot be easily allocated and priced in the same way as private goods, as it is difficult to exclude non-payers from benefiting and the consumption of one individual does not reduce the availability for others.

As a result, the provision of public goods through private markets tends to be inadequate. Since there is no direct mechanism for individuals to pay for and receive public goods in proportion to their preferences or usage, there is a potential for under-provision or even complete absence of certain public goods. This is known as the "free-rider problem," where individuals have an incentive to benefit from public goods without contributing their fair share.



S. Alamad, *Beyond Profit*, Contributions to Economics,
https://doi.org/10.1007/978-3-031-49748-3_3

To address the problem of public goods, governments often intervene and take on the role of providing and financing them. Through taxation or other means of revenue collection, the government can fund the production of public goods that benefit society as a whole. This is based on the understanding that public goods have positive externalities and contribute to overall social welfare, even if individuals would not voluntarily pay for them in the market.

However, the provision of public goods by the government is not without its challenges. It requires effective governance, careful resource allocation, and decision-making processes to ensure that public goods are provided efficiently and in line with societal preferences. There is also a need for transparency and accountability to address concerns about potential inefficiencies, waste, or misallocation of resources.

Public goods pose a unique challenge in capitalist production due to their non-excludable and non-rivalrous nature. Market mechanisms alone are insufficient for their efficient provision, leading to the need for government intervention. However, the provision of public goods by the government also requires careful management and accountability to ensure their effective allocation and utilisation (Fujita et al., 1999).

In this chapter, we will examine a commonly discussed scenario that supposedly challenges the notion of the economic superiority of capitalism: the production of public goods.

Specifically, we will focus on the production of security. If the assertions made in the previous Chapter about the functioning of a market economy are accurate, and if monopolies are harmless to consumers as long as consumers have the ability to boycott them and freely choose from competing producers, then one must conclude that, for economic and moral reasons, all goods and services should be produced by private entities. This includes the production of law and order, justice, and peace—areas traditionally considered suitable for state provision, as explained earlier. Instead, these should be provided through private competition in a free market. This conclusion was put forth by G. de Molinari, a renowned Belgian economist, as early as 1849, a time when classical liberalism held sway, and the terms "economist" and "socialist" were generally seen as opposites:

## 3.2 Public Goods and Private Goods

The well-established truth in political economy is this: In all cases, for any commodity that fulfils the tangible or intangible needs of consumers, it is in the consumer's best interest that labour and trade remain free because freedom in labour and trade leads to the maximum reduction in price (de Molinari, 1977). Furthermore, the interests of the consumer of any commodity should always take precedence over the interests of the producer. By following these principles, we arrive at a rigorous conclusion: In the interest of consumers of security, the production of security should remain subject to the law of free competition. Consequently, no government should have the authority to prevent another government from entering into competition or to mandate that consumers of security exclusively rely on one government for this commodity. de Molinari (1977) further asserts, "Either this argument is logical and true, or the principles upon which economic science is based are flawed".

The socialist economists (For various approaches of public goods theorists cf. J. Buchanan and G. Tullock, The Calculus of Consent, Ann Arbor, 1962; J. Buchanan, The Public Finances, Homewood, 1970; and The Limits of Liberty, Chicago, 1975; G. Tullock, Private Wants, Public Means, New York, 1970; M. Olson, The Logic of Collective Action, New York, 1965; W. Baumol, Welfare Economics and the Theory of the State, Cambridge, 1952) who disagree with Molinari's conclusion have attempted to find a way out by arguing that there are certain goods to which the principles of economic reasoning do not apply. These goods are known as public goods, and proponents of the public goods theory aim to prove that they pose a unique problem that cannot be addressed by market mechanisms. However, we will demonstrate that this line of reasoning is flawed and lacks scientific merit.

The distinction between public goods and private goods, which is commonly emphasised in economics textbooks, is said to be crucial. Public goods are defined as goods or services that provide benefits to individuals who have not directly financed their production, unlike private goods which exclusively benefit those who have paid for them. It is claimed that due to this characteristic, markets are unable to produce public goods in sufficient quantity or quality, necessitating state intervention. Various examples are provided to illustrate public goods, such as the fire brigade preventing a neighbour's house from catching fire, the police deterring burglars from both my property and my neighbour's property, and the lighthouse guiding ships at sea. However, the classification of goods as public or private is highly disputed among authors, casting doubt on the validity of the distinction itself. Despite the popularity of certain examples, such as the ones mentioned, it is argued by capitalist economists that the notion of public goods and the argument for state intervention based on their existence are illusory (de Molinari, 1977).

Before delving into the theory of public goods, it is important to assess the usefulness of the distinction between private and public goods in determining the appropriate production responsibilities for the private sector and the state. However, upon closer examination, it becomes evident that relying solely on this criterion can lead to significant difficulties rather than providing a practical solution. While some goods and services provided by the state may indeed qualify as public goods, it is not clear how many of the goods and services produced by states can be classified as such. Railroads, postal services, telephones, and streets, for example, appear to be goods whose usage can be restricted to those who finance them, making them private goods (Fujita et al., 1999).

This same categorisation applies to many aspects of security, with insurance coverage being a characteristic of private goods. However, this analysis alone is insufficient. Just as many state-provided goods seem to be private goods, there are also privately produced goods that could be considered public goods. For instance, my neighbours would benefit from my well-maintained rose garden without contributing to its upkeep (Kim, 2002). The same can be said for property improvements that enhance the value of neighbouring properties, street musicians whose performances are enjoyed by passers-by who do not contribute monetarily, or even the deodorant I use benefiting fellow bus passengers who did not contribute to its purchase (Kim, 2002).

Furthermore, everyone who interacts with me would benefit from my personal efforts to become a more likable person, despite not providing financial support for these endeavours. Given that these goods, such as rose gardens, property improvements, street music, deodorants, and personality improvements, possess characteristics of public goods, does this mean that they should be provided by the state or with state assistance?

The examples of privately produced public goods mentioned earlier highlight a fundamental flaw in the argument put forth by public goods theorists that such goods cannot be provided privately and require state intervention. These goods can, in fact, be supplied by markets. Moreover, historical evidence demonstrates that many goods currently provided by states were previously offered by private entrepreneurs or continue to be privately provided in certain countries.

For instance, postal services were predominantly private in the past, streets were financed privately and still are in some cases, and even lighthouses, which are widely cherished, were originally the result of private enterprise. Private police forces, detectives, arbitrators, and charitable organisations have also been involved in areas such as security, healthcare, poverty relief, and support for vulnerable populations. Experience overwhelmingly refutes the notion that such goods cannot be produced within a pure market system.

In addition to these observations, using the public-private goods distinction to determine the appropriate allocation of goods encounters further challenges. What if the production of so-called public goods had negative consequences for some individuals, or if the outcomes were positive for some but negative for others? For example, what if the neighbour whose house was saved from a fire by my private fire brigade actually wanted their house to burn down? Similarly, what if my neighbours dislike roses or find the scent of my deodorant unpleasant, despite benefiting from it during our shared bus rides?

Furthermore, technological advancements can alter the nature of a given good. Cable TV, for instance, was once considered a public good but has now become a private one. Changes in property laws can also influence the public-private character of goods. Consider the lighthouse, which is a public good only because the sea is considered publicly owned. However, if portions of the ocean were allowed to be privately owned within a purely capitalist society, it would be possible to exclude non-payers from benefiting from the lighthouse's services, as the lighthouse's illumination covers a limited territory.

Upon delving deeper into the distinction between private and public goods, it becomes evident that this classification is fundamentally illusory. There is no clear-cut dichotomy between the two, leading to disagreements on how goods should be classified. All goods possess varying degrees of privateness or publicness, which can change over time based on individuals' values, evaluations, and shifts in population composition. Goods are subjective and only considered as such by individuals perceiving them as scarce. They do not possess an inherent nature as goods; their status as goods is contingent on subjective evaluation (Fan and Scott, 2003).

Consequently, there is no fixed, objective criterion for classifying goods as private or public. Goods can never be inherently private or public; their categorisation depends on the number of people who view them as goods, and this can range from one person to an infinite number. Even seemingly private things, such as the interior of one's apartment or the colour of one's underwear, can become public goods once someone else starts caring about them.

Conversely, seemingly public goods, like the exterior of a house or the colour of overalls, can become highly private goods when others cease to care about them. Furthermore, every good can repeatedly change its characteristics, shifting from being a public or private good to a public or private bad, solely based on changing levels of care or indifference (Hall, 2001). Given these dynamics, it becomes evident that classifying goods as private or public cannot serve as a basis for decision-making. It would require inquiring about each individual's evaluation of every single good, monitoring continuous changes in these evaluations, and facing the impracticality of determining truthfulness (Lucas, 1988). Such an approach would render any definitive decision regarding production impossible, leading to the absurdity of a theory that would render us all deceased without any meaningful outcome.

Indeed, even if one were to set aside the aforementioned difficulties and assume, for the sake of argument, that the private-public good distinction is valid, it still fails to prove its intended point. The argument does not provide conclusive reasons why public goods, if they exist as a separate category, should be produced at all or why the state, rather than private enterprises, should be responsible for their production. The theory of public goods, after establishing the conceptual distinction, essentially states that the positive effects of public goods for non-contributors prove their desirability. However, it asserts that these goods would not be produced or would be insufficiently produced in a free, competitive market since not all beneficiaries would contribute financially. Consequently, the argument suggests that state intervention is necessary to facilitate their production.

It is argued by some researchers that this line of reasoning, commonly found in economics textbooks, including those authored by Nobel laureates (E.g., P. Samuelson, "The Pure Theory of Public Expenditure," in: Review of Economics and Statistics, 1954; and Economics, New York, 1976, Chap. 8; M. Friedman, Capitalism and Freedom, Chicago, 1962, Chap. 2; F. A. Hayek, Law, Legislation and Liberty, vol. 3, Chicago, 1979, Chap. 14, is fundamentally flawed on two accounts. Firstly, in order to conclude that the state should provide public goods that would not otherwise be produced, a normative judgment must be smuggled into the chain of reasoning. Without such a norm, the statement that certain goods would not be produced due to their unique characteristics would never lead to the conclusion that these goods should be produced.

By introducing a normative element, the public goods theorists venture beyond the realm of positive, value-free economics and enter the domain of morals or ethics. One would expect that, in order to legitimately engage in such reasoning and derive their conclusions, a theory of ethics as a cognitive discipline would be presented. However, it is noteworthy that the literature on public goods theory lacks anything resembling a cognitive ethical theory. In essence, the public goods theorists fail to provide a solid economic justification for their claim and instead rely on normative assumptions without offering a comprehensive ethical framework (Samuelson, 1937).

It is important to emphasise that public goods theorists, despite their stature as positive economists, are overstepping their authority when making pronouncements on matters where they lack expertise. While they may have stumbled upon a correct point by chance, without providing a comprehensive moral theory to support it, this notion is quickly refuted when one explicitly formulates the norm required to reach their aforementioned conclusion.

The norm necessary to justify the state's intervention in the provision of public goods can be stated as follows: Whenever it can be proven that the production of a particular good or service has a positive effect on someone but would not be produced or would not be produced in sufficient quantity or quality, unless others participate in its financing, then the use of aggressive violence against these individuals is permissible. This aggression can be direct or indirect, facilitated by the state, and these individuals may be compelled to share in the financial burden (Friedman, 1962).

It is evident that chaos would ensue if such a rule were implemented, as it essentially grants permission for anyone to use aggression against others whenever they see fit. Furthermore, it should be clear from the discussion on the justification of normative statements that this norm could never be justified as a fair principle. To argue in favour of such a norm and seek agreement for this argument presupposes, contrary to what the norm implies, that everyone's physical autonomy as an independent decision-maker is respected. The normative position underlying the public goods theorists' argument lacks justification and leads to impractical and ethically problematic consequences. Their attempt to derive policy recommendations from an incomplete economic analysis without providing a robust ethical framework is fundamentally flawed (Samuelson, 1954).

The breakdown of the public goods theory goes beyond its flawed moral reasoning; its utilitarian and economic reasoning is also fundamentally flawed. While the theory suggests that having public goods may be preferable to not having them, there is no a priori reason to assume that this preference is necessary. Some individuals, such as anarchists, may strongly oppose state action and prefer not to have so-called public goods provided by the state.

Furthermore, even if we concede the argument thus far, the leap from stating that public goods are desirable to concluding that they should be provided by the state is far from conclusive. This is not the only choice available. Since resources must be diverted from potential alternative uses to finance public goods, the crucial question is whether these alternative uses (the private goods that could have been acquired) are more valuable or urgent than the public goods. The answer to this question is clear. Based on consumer evaluations, the value of public goods, relative to competing private goods, is lower because consumers would have chosen to allocate their money differently if given the choice (Lucas, 1988). This unequivocally demonstrates that resources allocated to public goods are wasted, as they provide consumers with goods or services that are at best of secondary importance.

In essence, even if we assume the existence of public goods distinguishable from private goods, and even if we grant that a specific public good may be useful, public goods still compete with private goods. The only way to determine their relative urgency and the extent to which their production would come at the expense of more urgently needed private goods is by allowing freely competing private enterprises to provide them. Therefore, contrary to the conclusion reached by public goods theorists, logic compels us to accept that only a pure market system can ensure the rationality of producing a public good from the consumers' perspective. Only under a pure capitalist order could we guarantee that the decision on how much of a public good to produce, if it should be produced at all, is rational (Olson, 1965).

The semantic challenges and distortions that would be necessary to arrive at a different conclusion regarding public goods. It suggests that a semantic revolution of Orwellian dimensions would be required to manipulate the meaning of words and concepts to support the public goods theorists' viewpoint.

By interpreting "no" as meaning "yes," or "non-buying" as indicating a preference for non-buying over an alternative choice, or "force" as synonymous with "freedom," the public goods theorists could attempt to prove their point. However, such semantic manipulations would raise doubts about the sincerity and clarity of their arguments. It becomes unclear whether they genuinely mean what they say or if their statements lack any coherent meaning or content.

In this context, Murray Rothbard's criticism of the public goods ideologues' attempts to demonstrate the existence of market failures in the production or quantity of public goods is valid. Rothbard argues that their perspective fundamentally misunderstands the optimal functioning of a free market. The optimality of a free market does not stem from the personal ethical views of an economist but rather from the voluntary actions of all participants and the satisfaction of consumers' freely expressed needs. Therefore, any government interference necessarily deviates from this optimal outcome (Rothbard, 1970b).

This emphasises that the arguments presented by public goods theorists to prove market failures are fundamentally flawed. While it is acknowledged that markets are not perfect and there may be goods or services that cannot be produced without allowing aggression, this imperfection can be morally and economically defended. On the other hand, the supposed "perfections" of markets advocated by public goods theorists cannot be similarly justified (Olson, 1965; Baumol, 1952).

The resistance to privatising state functions and the hardship that may arise from such a transition are not valid arguments for the failure of markets. Analogously, if a person was previously allowed to harm others and is now prohibited from doing so, their discomfort cannot serve as a valid excuse to uphold the old rules. The substitution of a social order in which consumers have equal rights to determine production choices is preferable from the perspective of all voluntary consumers (Hayek, 1979).

Through logical reasoning, one can arrive at the conclusion that, for the sake of consumers, all goods and services should be provided by markets. Even if there were clearly distinguishable categories of goods, including public goods, there would be no special reason why these goods could not be produced by private enterprises. In fact, experience has shown that markets can produce various goods and services, such as postal services, railroads, electricity, telephone, education, money, and roads, more effectively and to the liking of consumers compared to the state (Hall, 2001).

While the efficiency of markets has been recognised in many sectors, there is often reluctance to accept the superiority of a capitalist economy specifically in the production of security. The rest of the chapter will delve into this topic, providing empirical material and analysis to further support the argument for the superior functioning of a capitalist economy in the realm of security production.

The question of how a system of non-monopolistic, competing producers of security would work is not a matter of pure logical analysis but requires a more speculative approach due to the lack of concrete examples and past experiences (Hall, 2001). It can be compared to asking how a market would solve the problem of hamburger production if it had previously been exclusively handled by the state. In such a scenario, one can only offer tentative answers and cannot determine the exact structure, number of companies, market size, variety of hamburgers, or other factors that would emerge. The evolution of the industry would be influenced by various factors such as demand, technology, prices of related goods, and other changing circumstances (Baumol, 1952).

While the specifics cannot be known in advance, it is possible to discuss different social orders of security production based on certain general conditions of demand for security services that are realistic in the present world. By examining the characteristics of monopolistic, state-run security production and comparing them with potential outcomes in a non-monopolistic system, insights can be gained (Landes, 1998).

To begin the analysis, it is helpful to examine the specifics of monopolistic, state-run security production, as there is ample evidence available to evaluate its validity. Once this is understood, it becomes possible to explore the potential outcomes and advantages of a non-monopolistic system of security production.

Indeed, when considering security as a public good, it must compete with other goods in the allocation of scarce resources. The resources allocated to security cannot be used for other goods that could potentially increase consumer satisfaction. Furthermore, security is not a homogeneous good but encompasses various components and aspects such as prevention, detection, enforcement, protection from different threats (e.g., robbers, rapists, polluters, natural disasters), and more. It can also be supplied in marginal units, meaning that the level of security can be adjusted incrementally (Hayek, 1979).

## 3.3 Allocation of Security Resources By the State

Now, let us consider the allocation of security resources by the state, which is funded through taxes rather than voluntary contributions and sales of its products. The state faces the challenge of deciding how much security to produce, in what aspects, for whom, and where. However, it lacks a rational method for making these decisions. From the perspective of consumers, the state's response to their security demands is arbitrary. Questions arise regarding the number of police officers and judges needed, their salaries, the allocation of their time and efforts, and the prioritisation of different types of cases.

Since resources are scarce, the time and money spent on one aspect of security cannot be spent on another. The state attempts to answer these questions, but it does so without being subject to the profit-and-loss criterion that guides market-based decision-making. Consequently, its actions are arbitrary and often result in wasteful misallocations from the consumer's viewpoint (Olson, 1965; Baumol, 1952).

State-employed security producers, to a large extent, act independently of consumer wants and tend to prioritise their own preferences. They may engage in activities that are less productive, such as excessive patrolling, targeting victimless crimes, or seeking positions of power (Landes, 1998). Meanwhile, they can be inefficient in addressing the most urgent consumer demands, such as the prevention and detection of hard-core crimes, effective punishment of criminals, recovery of stolen goods, and compensation for victims. Despite increasing budget allocations, state-employed security producers often struggle to efficiently address hard-core crime, indicating their inefficiency and the misallocation of resources.

There are important points about the lowered quality of output in state-run security systems. Since the income of state-employed police officers and judges is not directly tied to consumer evaluations of their services, there is less incentive for them to perform well. This can lead to issues such as police arbitrariness, brutality, and a slow judicial process (Callari and Ruccio, 1996).

It is also worth noting that the police and judicial system do not typically offer consumers service contracts that clearly define the procedures and expectations in specific situations. This lack of contractual clarity allows for arbitrary changes in rules of procedure over time. Additionally, when disputes arise between private citizens and the police or judges, the resolution is often handled by another police officer or judge affiliated with the same government that employs one of the parties involved. This lack of an independent third party can undermine the fairness and impartiality of the process (Little, 1982).

Furthermore, state-run police stations, courts, and prisons often suffer from overuse, poor maintenance, and unclean conditions. Since there is no inherent need to satisfy the consumers who provide their income, the motivation to maintain high standards is diminished. In cases where state-run institutions do manage to maintain a certain level of quality, it is often at a much higher cost compared to similar private enterprises.

These observations highlight some of the shortcomings and inefficiencies inherent in state-run security systems (Olson, 1965; Baumol, 1952), emphasising the need to consider alternative approaches that can better align incentives, improve quality, and ensure consumer satisfaction. The notion that a competitive system of security production would lead to permanent social conflict, chaos, and anarchy is not supported by historical evidence. On the contrary, there are several points to consider:

1. Competition and voluntary exchange: In a competitive market for security services, producers would rely on voluntary purchases, typically in the form of service and insurance contracts. This means that producers can only increase their income by improving the quality of their services as perceived by consumers. The incentive to attract and retain customers would drive producers to provide better and more diverse security offerings tailored to individual needs.
2. Diversification and consumer influence: With a diverse demand for security products among millions of consumers, producers would need to diversify their offerings. Rather than a uniform "security packet" provided by the state, a multitude of service packages would emerge in response to different security needs, occupations, risk profiles, and geographic considerations. Consumers would have a direct influence on the market by choosing the services that best meet their requirements.
3. Improved quality and accountability: In a competitive system, the treatment of consumers by security service providers would improve immediately. Employees would be incentivised to provide better services, as any maltreatment, impoliteness, or ineptitude could lead to the loss of customers and ultimately their jobs. The arbitrary behaviour, negligence, and tardiness often associated with state-run police and judicial systems would diminish.
4. Conflict resolution and arbitration: Instead of entrusting the settlement of disputes between clients and service providers to the judgment of the service provider, independent conflict arbitration would become the standard practice in a competitive system. This would ensure impartiality and fairness in resolving conflicts, removing the inherent bias in favour of the government's interests.
5. Transparent contracts and consumer rights: To attract and retain customers, security service providers would need to offer contracts that clearly define the services being provided and the obligations of both parties. Consumers would have the ability to raise valid complaints if the security producer fails to fulfil their contractual obligations. This transparency and accountability would enhance consumer rights and satisfaction.

It is important to recognise that a competitive system of security production does not guarantee a utopian society free from all crime or insecurity. However, it provides a framework that incentivises producers to meet consumer demands, improve quality, and ensure accountability. Contrary to the perception of chaos and anarchy, historical evidence suggests that competitive markets have generally led to greater efficiency, innovation, and societal well-being in various industries (Olson, 1965).

The historical evidence, as well as systematic reasons, suggest that the fear of social conflict and chaos under a competitive system of security production is unfounded. Let us examine the points raised in relation to this:

1. Historical examples: Systems of competing courts, such as those in ancient Ireland or during the Hanseatic League, have demonstrated successful functioning before the emergence of modern nation-states. Additionally, the private

police in the Wild West, which operated in a relatively competitive environment, had a crime rate that was not as high as portrayed in movies.
2. Contemporary international contacts: In modern times, millions of international contacts exist through trade and travel, and there is no evidence to suggest that there is more fraud, crime, or contract breaches in these interactions compared to domestic relations. This is achieved without a monopolistic security producer or lawmaker.
3. Coexistence of private and state security: Many countries currently have various private security producers alongside state entities, such as private investigators, insurance detectives, and private arbitrators. These private actors have been successful in resolving social conflicts and often outperform their public counterparts.
4. Institutionalised incentive structure: Establishing a competitive system of security producers requires an institutionalised incentive structure that promotes an order of law and law enforcement based on consensus. In such a system, conflicts between insured parties from different companies would not necessarily result in armed confrontations. The economic pressure on companies to retain clients would encourage them to seek peaceful resolutions. Companies would strive to provide peaceful conflict resolution measures and establish agreed-upon arbitration processes in advance. This would lead to the evolution of universally acceptable systems of law that govern relations between competing security producers.
5. Economic pressure and consensus: Independent arbitrators entrusted with resolving conflicts would depend on the support of the disagreeing companies. This would create pressure on arbitrators to find solutions acceptable to all parties involved, as dissatisfaction could lead companies to choose different arbitrators in the future. The economic pressure to retain customers and the need for consensus would drive the development of fair and just solutions.

The competitive system of security production, rather than generating more social unrest and conflict, would incentivise producers to seek peaceful resolutions, establish consensus-based systems of law, and provide effective conflict resolution measures.

Under a competitive system, it is possible for a security-producing firm to become an outlaw company that engages in aggression against others. However, it is fallacious to argue that this possibility indicates a severe deficiency in the philosophy and economics of a pure capitalist social order. The likelihood of outlaw companies emerging depends on the specific state of public opinion in a given society (Tullock, 1970).

Public opinion plays a crucial role in any social system, whether it is a statist-socialist order or a pure market economy. The current state of public opinion sets the boundaries of what can or cannot occur in a society. For example, the public opinion in West Germany would make it highly unlikely or even impossible for a Russian-type socialist system to be imposed. Similarly, in the United States, the prevailing public opinion, influenced by the natural theory of property and the libertarian philosophy on which the country was founded, would make it less likely for outlaw companies to emerge and gain support.

The likelihood of outlaw companies arising in a competitive system depends on the reactions of the public to this changed situation. If the state abolished its right to provide security with tax funds and a competitive system of security production were introduced, individuals would have to make decisions based on the new cost-benefit structure. Engaging in trade with a security producer that aggresses against others would be illegal and against one's principles of correct behaviour. The cost of supporting such a firm would be higher due to the change in legality, conscience, and public opinion (Buchanan and Tullock, 1962).

It can be assumed that the number of people supporting firms committed to honest business and protecting libertarian law would increase under a competitive system. Those committed to exploitation and aggression would likely decrease in number. In the United States, where the natural theory of property and libertarian philosophy are widespread, the support for security-producing firms committed to protecting and enforcing libertarian law would be particularly strong. The honest companies would attract the bulk of public support and financial assistance (Buchanan and Tullock, 1970).

While some individuals, especially those who benefited from the old order, might continue to support aggression, they are unlikely to be numerous or financially strong enough to succeed. The honest companies, supported by their voluntary customers, would develop the strength needed to check the emergence of outlaw producers and destroy them whenever they appear.

The likelihood of outlaw companies arising in a competitive system depends on the specific state of public opinion. Under a competitive system, the support for firms committed to honest business and protecting libertarian law would likely outweigh the support for aggression and exploitation. The voluntary support and financial assistance provided to honest companies would enable them to effectively address and eliminate any emerging outlaw producers (Buchanan and Tullock, 1970).

If, against all odds, the honest security producers were to lose their fight and an outlaw monopoly re-emerged, it would essentially mean a return to a state system. However, even in such a scenario, implementing a pure capitalist social system with private producers of security, where individuals have freedom of choice, would still be preferable to the current situation.

The implementation of a pure capitalist social system with private producers of security would provide individuals with greater freedom and choice. Even if this order were to collapse due to a significant number of people still committed to aggression and exploitation, it would have at least offered a glorious interlude of freedom and prosperity (Buchanan, 1975).

On the other hand, if this order were to survive, which is the more likely outcome, it would mark the beginning of a system of justice and unprecedented economic prosperity. A society built on the principles of individual liberty, voluntary exchange, and private property rights would create an environment conducive to innovation, entrepreneurship, and overall societal well-being. Even if there is a remote possibility of a collapse or the emergence of an outlaw monopoly, the implementation of a pure capitalist social system with private security producers would still be preferable to the current state of affairs. It would provide individuals with freedom of choice and the potential for a just and prosperous society.

## 3.4 Conclusion

This Chapter examined the challenges posed by public goods in capitalist production, due to their unique characteristics of being non-excludable and non-rivalrous. It explores the problem of how public goods do not fit well within the traditional market exchange framework based on private property and voluntary transactions. The "free-rider problem" arises because individuals have an incentive to benefit from public goods without contributing their fair share. To address this, governments often intervene and provide public goods through taxation or other means of revenue collection.

However, we argue that the distinction between public and private goods is flawed, and there is no fixed, objective criterion for classifying goods as one or the other. It points out that many goods classified as public can be produced by markets, and there are private goods with public characteristics. The text also criticises the public goods theorists for lacking a comprehensive ethical framework to support their arguments and for overstepping their expertise in moral and ethical matters.

We further argue that only a pure market system can ensure rational production of public goods from consumers' perspectives. It emphasises the efficiency of markets in producing various goods and services, including those traditionally provided by the state. In the context of security production, the text advocates for a capitalist economy's superior functioning, providing empirical material and analysis to support this claim.

The concept of a non-monopolistic, competitive system of security production presents a compelling alternative to the current state-run security arrangements. While acknowledging that the analysis requires a certain degree of speculation, the potential advantages of such a system are worth considering in light of the inefficiencies and shortcomings inherent in the existing state-provided security.

The current state-run security production suffers from arbitrary decision-making, misallocation of resources, and a lack of accountability to consumers. State-employed security producers often prioritise their preferences over consumer demands, leading to inefficiencies and suboptimal outcomes. The absence of a profit-and-loss criterion in the state-run system further exacerbates these issues, resulting in lower-quality services and a lack of incentive for improvement.

On the other hand, a competitive system of security production promises to address these deficiencies. Through voluntary exchanges and market-driven competition, security producers would be incentivised to cater to consumer demands, improve service quality, and diversify their offerings. Consumers would have the freedom to choose the security services that best suit their needs, leading to a more customised and efficient security provision.

Moreover, a competitive system would foster accountability and transparency. Private security producers would be subject to the profit motive, meaning that their income would be directly tied to consumer satisfaction. This would create a strong incentive for producers to treat consumers fairly and efficiently resolve conflicts. Independent arbitration would replace the state's biased decision-making, ensuring impartial resolution of disputes and enhancing consumer rights (Hall, 2001).

Contrary to the fear of chaos and anarchy, historical examples and contemporary international contacts demonstrate that competition can lead to more efficient and innovative outcomes. Moreover, the assumption that outlaw companies would emerge under a competitive system overlooks the crucial role of public opinion. A society built on the principles of individual liberty and voluntary exchange would likely foster widespread support for firms committed to honest business practices and protection of libertarian law.

While acknowledging the potential risks, the implementation of a pure capitalist social system with private security producers remains preferable to the current state of affairs. Even if the competitive order were to collapse or face an outlaw monopoly, it would have provided a glorious interlude of freedom, prosperity, and individual choice. The pursuit of a system that values individual liberty and voluntary cooperation is inherently worthwhile, as it offers the potential for justice, economic prosperity, and societal well-being.

In conclusion, exploring the possibilities of a competitive system of security production is a worthwhile endeavour, even if certain aspects require speculation. The potential advantages of improved quality, consumer choice, and accountability make it an appealing alternative to the current state-run security arrangements. Embracing a pure capitalist social system with private security producers holds the promise of a more just, prosperous, and free society, even in the face of potential challenges. The pursuit of individual liberty and voluntary cooperation remains an essential goal in creating a society that truly serves the needs and preferences of its members.

Next Chapter poses the question of how we choose to understand the complex interactions between different phenomena. It discusses the prevailing trend in contemporary social theory, which is anti-essentialism, particularly in discussions of identity. It challenges the notion of fixed, universal foundations for constructing identity, influenced by poststructuralist critiques.

# Chapter 4
# Intersection of Capitalism and Anti-essentialism: The Contradictions Arising From This Encounter

## 4.1 Introduction

In the previous Chapter we analysed how public goods pose a challenge in capitalist production due to their unique characteristics and the inherent nature of market mechanisms.

In this Chapter we examine how the prevailing economic trend in contemporary social theory is anti-essentialism, particularly in discussions of identity. This perspective challenges the notion of fixed, universal foundations for constructing identity, influenced by poststructuralist critiques. However, anti-essentialism has not been commonly associated with Marxian political economy, which traditionally emphasises the economy as the essential element in social systems and historical events. Economic determinism, a form of essentialism within political economy, has faced criticism and has led to theoretical and political challenges. While essentialism is often critiqued in contemporary social theory, the emphasis on economic determinism has had its own difficulties and setbacks, as seen in past socialist revolutionary projects.

An anti-essentialist perspective within Marxism focuses on causality, challenging the notion that certain influences are essential causes of a given outcome. Essentialism assumes that among various influences, some are essential while others are inessential to the occurrence of an event. In contrast, anti-essentialist strategies in Marxism, such as Althusser's concept of "overdetermination," offer a rethinking of identity and social determination. While Althusser's influence was significant in the 1960s and 1970s, his work faced dismissal and silence in subsequent years. However, there has been a resurgence of interest in Althusser's ideas, particularly in relation to anti-essentialist thought. His work aimed to develop anti-reductionist elements within the Marxian tradition and provided the theoretical and epistemological basis for anti-essentialist Marxist political economy (see for example Balibar and Wallerstein, 1991; Derrida, 1993; Kaplan and Sprinker, 1993).



S. Alamad, *Beyond Profit*, Contributions to Economics,
https://doi.org/10.1007/978-3-031-49748-3_4

Althusser's concept of "overdetermination" challenges the traditional Western philosophical and Enlightenment tradition by undermining the certainties and foundations of Western thought. Alongside other thinkers like Derrida, Foucault, Deleuze/Guattari, and predecessors such as Spinoza, Nietzsche, Freud, and Wittgenstein, Althusser contributes to a counter-tradition aimed at destabilising established notions of being, existence, identity, and knowledge. He breaks with the idea of identity based on sameness and self-resemblance, as well as with the belief in entities existing in analogical or representational relations.

Althusser's approach also disrupts the practice of assigning primacy to certain attributes while devaluing others within identity constructions. Moreover, he challenges the hierarchical oppositions of positivity/negation, necessity/contingency, importance/inconsequence, and reality/representation. While there is a contradiction in ascribing an essence to being and identity through the ontological interpretation of overdetermination, this reading enables a powerful form of anti-essentialism. It suggests that social analysis cannot find ultimate causes or definitively exclude the impact of any social or natural process in understanding the constitution of phenomena.

The question then becomes how we choose to understand the complex interactions between different phenomena. Althusser's approach emphasises that the relationship between two complexities, such as industrialisation and heterosexuality, should not be reduced to a simple cause-and-effect relationship or an assessment of their relative importance. Instead, it invites us to think about the intricate interplay between these complexities.

Althusser's notion of a "decentred structure" further emphasises the rejection of a central essence or core behind the totality of social phenomena. Unlike Hegelian totality, which posits an original essence underlying historical appearances, the Marxist totality is inseparable from its constituent elements. Each element conditions the existence of all others, resulting in a decentred structure without a central essence.

Althusser's concept of overdetermination challenges the conventional understanding of identity and events by reconceiving them as uncentered, in process and transition, and devoid of any essential tendency or reversion. According to Althusser, every identity and event is constituted by all the conditions existing in that moment, including the past and the future. This perspective undermines the hierarchical notions of importance that assign certain attributes or causes as necessary or essential, while relegating others as contingent or peripheral. Althusser critiques the conventional dialectic of A/not A, which posits positive being and its immanent negation, and instead emphasises multidimensional contradiction and complexity.

Overdetermination represents a longing or desire to uncover what is suppressed, make room for the absent, acknowledge the invisible, account for the unaccounted, and experience the forbidden. In the context of Marxist political economy, the non-economic aspects that have been hidden or overlooked have gained significance, especially in political expressions of the twentieth century. Althusser's anti-reductionist project aimed to liberate the diverse range of noneconomic social processes, not by negating the economic but by acknowledging a plethora of effectivities, with the economic being one among them (Balibar and Wallerstein, 1991). For example, Althusser describes the Russian revolution as a "ruptural unity" resulting from a convergence of various circumstances, currents, and contradictions, highlighting the inseparability of the economic contradiction from the total social structure and its formal conditions of existence.

The concept of overdetermination has played a crucial role in generating an anti-economistic and anti-essentialist body of Marxian political economy and social analysis since the publication of Althusser's early writings. It has influenced various traditions such as the French regulation school(s) of political economy, certain strands of socialist feminism, the post-Marxism of Laclau and Mouffe, critiques and re-conceptualisations of economic development theory, and the postmodern orientation of the journal *Rethinking Marxism*. These traditions, some of which explicitly draw on the theoretical strategy of overdetermination, have sought to challenge the economic essentialism present in key areas of Marxian theory. In the context of representing capitalism, considering the possibilities offered by these anti-essentialist projects, including the lens of overdetermination, becomes an intriguing proposition (Little, 1982).

## 4.2 Capitalist Regulation

One significant research program that has been built upon Althusser's work is regulation theory, which has given rise to concepts such as Fordism and post-Fordism that have gained popularity on the left. According to Alain Lipietz, who has outlined the regulationists' debt to and deviations from Althusser, Althusser's ideas allowed for a vision of a complexly structured social totality composed of multiple and diverse relations without a centre or origin. These relations exist as a fabric, mutually overdetermining one another and articulating relatively autonomous and specific relations (Kaplan and Sprinker, 1993).

Drawing on this Althusserian understanding of society, the regulationists were able to theorise the state, civil society institutions, and the realm of ideas and culture as more than mere "supports for capital." Instead, they sought to concretely specify how these elements might come to play a role in specific historical periods. The regulationists' objective is to represent capitalist development as an overdetermined process in which capitalism is constituted by its social context rather than solely by internal forces. They aim to depict capitalism as a multiplicity, a set of specificities (capitalisms), rather than as a unified and homogeneous entity (Kaplan and Sprinker, 1993).

To achieve this, the regulationists replace the transhistorical concept of the mode of production with Lipietz's notion of a "model of (capitalist) development." This model emerges contingently in specific times and places and centres around a regime of capital accumulation, which involves a macroeconomic balance between production and consumption. It is associated with a dominant technological paradigm and is stabilised over time by a mode of regulation. The mode of regulation encompasses social norms, practices, and institutions, and it acts as a mediating force that manages or mitigates the contradictions inherent in capital accumulation and capitalist social relations. The establishment of a mode of regulation allows for the smooth functioning of capital accumulation and gives rise to extended periods of economic stability and growth (Derrida, 1993).

Lipietz argues that models of development are the result of historical "accidents" rather than being determined by the functional requirements of capitalist reproduction. Therefore, capitalism appears to be a contingent phenomenon, overdetermined by specific norms and institutions, and constituted as a unique economic form in particular times and places. However, despite the apparent contextualisation or subversion of these logics, the presence of logics serves to isolate the economy from the broader social terrain. The logic of accumulation, although contingent upon external conditions, dominates the realm of economic and social events. It produces either instability and depression or growth and stability, which are the two states of being in the regulationist economy. While the accidental development of the mode of regulation alters the manifestation of the logic of accumulation, it does not displace it from the centre of effectivity (Little, 1982).

In the model of development within regulation theory, the field of contingency is divided into two types of relations: (1) contingent relations that do not stabilise accumulation but lack effectivity, and (2) relations that have effectivity but only as supports for accumulation. Only the latter type is considered within the scope of regulation theory, effectively subsuming contingency to necessity. As a result, the realm of accident loses its ability to contradict the logic of accumulation, and contingency is assimilated into the framework of necessity.

By integrating all social elements visible within the theoretical framework into a model of development centred on capital accumulation and coextensive with the social space, regulation theory marks them as belonging to capitalism. For instance, household appliances that transformed housework conditions during the Fordist era are primarily seen as consumption goods generated by capitalist mass production. Their alternative identity as productive technology in a non-capitalist context is suppressed and devalued within the context of a "capitalist" model of development. The norms and institutions constituting the mode of regulation acquire their identities within a relational structure where they function as supports for capitalism.

This approach eliminates any "exterior" that could subvert capitalism and define society or the economy as a non-capitalist space. The regulationist depiction of capitalism, despite its rich and open-ended nature, ultimately presents a familiar face. The logic of capital accumulation defines capitalism as a dynamic and growth-oriented economic system at the macro level, while profitability and competition promote technological dynamism and discipline individual capitals at the enterprise level. These economic logics unify all forms of capitalism as resemblances or replications, constituting the unchanging core and essence of capitalism.

In this perspective, capitalism's identity is not constructed relationally within a specific social articulation or through the contextualisation of the economic term in a particular discursive setting. Instead, it is based on an "empiricist" epistemology where the truth of the economic object is given within the object itself and accessible to the universal intelligence of the knowing subject. These invariant logics represent the "essence" of capitalism and allow it to impose its identity on the social field, giving primacy to its dynamics in the complex unfolding of historical events. Capitalism, as a concept, resists the destabilising force of overdetermination, displaying relative durability in defining the social field.

## 4.3 Capitalism Post-development Theory

During the post-World War II era, bourgeois economic development theory positioned industrial capitalism as the pinnacle of economic and social evolution, presenting the Western experience of capitalist development as the model for the rest of the world. Within this framework, many leftists critically viewed "development" as a capitalist phenomenon that resulted in "underdevelopment" or social and economic deformation in "developing" countries. Mainstream and left development discourses generally agreed that capitalist development initiated a process of extensive social transformation, differing mainly in their interpretations of this change as either the advent of a prosperous society or a destructive process (Little, 1982).

Both mainstream and counter-theoretical perspectives tended to be economistic, emphasising the economy as the principal driver of comprehensive social change, and monistic, perceiving development as the creation of an integrated capitalist economy from a heterogeneous and dispersed starting point.

In the 1970s, influenced by Althusser's collaboration with Balibar, a theoretical movement emerged on the left challenging the economic monism of traditional development theory. This movement sought to conceptualise social formations as potentially involving the "articulation of (multiple) modes of production," particularly in the Third World. According to Wolpe, such articulation does not necessarily assume capitalist dominance. The social formation is seen as a complex object of investigation with various possible structures: it could be structured by a single mode of production, a combination of modes with no dominance, or a combination with one dominant mode (Lucas, 1988).

This theoretical project aimed to develop a discourse of economic difference as an alternative to portraying the "complex conjuncture of the world economy" as an undifferentiated capitalist space. Additionally, it sought to theorise non-capitalist forms of economy as having constitutive effects on capitalism itself. These characteristics set this approach apart, although they were not entirely unprecedented, within the literature of Marxian political economy (Landes, 1998).

Interestingly, the issue of "capitalocentrism" became apparent in the context of this Althusserian project, particularly because individual theorists grappled with theorising the relationship between capitalism and non-capitalism within specific social contexts. Wolpe acknowledges that although there was no inherent functionalism in the concept of articulation of modes of production, in concrete analyses of social formations, theorists tended to represent the persistence of precapitalist modes of production as "functional for capital." (Hall, 2001).

Capitalocentrism, in this context, refers to the positioning of capitalism at the centre of development narratives, which tends to devalue or marginalise the possibilities of non-capitalist development. When independent commodity producers, who own their own means of production and engage in market exchange, are labelled as capitalist without recognising the distinctiveness of their economic practices, it hinders the representation of economic difference and the understanding of both capitalism and non-capitalist forms of production (Held et al., 1999). Non-capitalist forms of economy are often portrayed as primitive, backward, and incapable of independent growth and development, creating a perception that development necessitates the elimination or subordination of non-capitalist forms to capitalism.

The functional articulation of non-capitalist modes of production with capitalism, where non-capitalist elements serve as complements to capitalist reproduction, further reinforces the dominant identity of capitalism in "Third World," industrialised, and global economies. Grassroots producer cooperatives or local development initiatives, when seen as existing within a capitalist world economy, are treated as isolated pockets of non-capitalism surviving within a landscape governed by the "laws" of capitalist development or as localised sites of resistance (Lucas, 1988).

Recent left-leaning theorists have approached development as an economistic discourse rather than a universal social reality, highlighting how it has produced a dependent identity for the "Third World" under the management and surveillance of international development bureaucracies. Contrary to its promises, development is seen as bringing poverty and immiseration instead of abundance (Fan and Scott, 2003; Kim, 2002; Fujita, et al., 1999).

In the post-development literature, anti-economism and anti-Eurocentrism work together to challenge monolithic visions of the future and to acknowledge cultural and social differences, resistance to hegemony, local power dynamics, and subjectivity. However, post-development theory, like its predecessors, demonstrates a tendency toward capitalocentrism. It recognises that global capital relies not only on homogenisation but also on the consolidation of diverse and heterogeneous social forms. Even minor forms that are not fully coded by capital become targets of social subjection within the decentred system of the global economy. It becomes crucial to examine how local groups participate in this complex process and how they can evade the exploitative mechanisms of capitalist capture (Chamberline, 1933).

Furthermore, capitalism itself can produce heterogeneities, including points of non[capitalism, as part of its global economic and cultural production. A political economy analysis of global economic and cultural production should account for both new forms of capital accumulation and the local discourses and practices that arise within the structured system of global political economy, considering the production of cultural difference within this context, Quoting Pred and Watts (1992, p. 18; Cheshire and Gordon, 1998).

In these representations, the global capitalist economy is seen as the source or origin of locally manifested diversities, which exist within it spatially and causally.

The role of political economy is not to understand the existence of these diversities differently but to generate specific versions of an already established general understanding. It aims to explain how global capitalism, which is considered the essence, gives rise to heterogeneity and diversity as observable phenomena. This imperative leads post-development theory to centre its focus on the practice of an economic "science," despite its critiques of epistemological realism, economic essentialism, and modernist developmentalism (Andersson and Andersson, 2000).

It is important to note that this observation does not diminish the novelty and significance of Escobar's work or the broader post-development project. Instead, it highlights the presence of "development" within these projects and the existence of capitalism beyond the scope of overdetermination, where the determining influence of a singular factor is limited.

The question of why the economism associated with capitalism is so difficult to moderate or remove, as well as the economic monism or hegemonism prevalent in representations of capitalist society and development, can be partially addressed by examining the metaphysics of identity that Althusser sought to undermine.

Western conceptions of identity operate under an "imperative of unity," which entails the self-resemblance of an object and its one-to-one relation with the sign that represents it. In this essentialist understanding of identity, "capitalism" signifies an underlying commonality among the objects it refers to. Consequently, it is not surprising to encounter a notion of capitalism that remains essentially the same across different times and places, despite efforts by various structuralist and post-structuralist traditions to undermine the idea of sameness as the basis of meaning (Bairoch, 1988).

When capitalism is perceived as sameness, non-capitalism is either subordinated or rendered invisible, similar to the way woman is positioned in relation to man. Non-capitalism is seen as insufficient unless it is released from the binary metaphysics of identity, where A is a unified self-identical being that excludes what it is not. Thus, if capitalism/man is understood as multiple, specific, and heterogenous, always becoming what it is not, and incorporating difference within its decentred being, non-capitalism/woman can also be freed from its singular and subordinate status. Non-capitalism/woman should not be conceptualised as a simple negation or recessive ground against which capitalism/man is defined by a singular Form. The theorisation of capitalism/man as multiple and different becomes a prerequisite for conceptualising non-capitalism/woman as specific and distinct forms of existence (Jaffe et al., 1993).

Reading capitalist texts deconstructively, uncovering surplus and contradictory meanings associated with the term, and identifying the places where capitalism is constituted and inhabited by non-capitalism, allows for the destabilisation of its apparent self-identity. This strategy can be strategically effective in challenging capitalism's discursive "hegemony" and reimagining its role in social determination. However, overdetermination can be employed as an additional anti-essentialist theoretical strategy, complementing the deconstructive approach. By combining these strategies, the potential arises to undermine the discursive dominance of capitalism and reconceptualise its position in social determination. Representations of society and economy cannot be centred on a decentred and formless entity that is always different from itself and derives its shifting and contradictory identity from the ever-changing exteriors that overdetermine it (Fan and Scott, 2003; Kim, 2002; Fujita et al., 1999).

An over-determinist approach derives its power and strategic capacity from its opposition to dominant modes of understanding language categories and identity/being, much like postmodernism obtains its power from modernism. By challenging the conceptualisation of entities as autonomous, bounded, and discrete, and as unique referents that provide stable and singular meanings to signs, the strategy of overdetermination can destabilise theoretical discourse and reposition the concepts within it. Through an over-determinist lens, identities like capitalism can be seen as entirely constituted by their "external" conditions (Putnam, 2000). This approach allows us to strip capitalism of its universal attributes and evacuate the essential and invariant logics that enable it to hegemonise the economic and social landscape. Overdetermination enables us to understand capitalism's causality as coexisting with an infinity of other determinants, none of which can definitively be deemed more or less significant, while repositioning capitalism itself as an effect (Putnam et al., 1993).

The fact that the capitalist economy often evades reconceptualisation and continues to function as an organising principle and origin of meaning and causation in social theory is not simply a theoretical oversight. It also reflects the reassertion of hegemonic conceptions of language and determination that overdetermination is uniquely positioned to challenge. It demonstrates the power of overdetermination in enabling certain post-Althusserian theorists to envision an "economy" that is not singular, centred, ordered, or self-constituting, and therefore not exclusive to capitalism. However, it also underscores the resilience of the dominant conceptual context, or mode of thought, in which independent objects of thought exist separately from thought and from each other, allowing for the persistence of an autonomous economy in social representation (Mokyr, 1985).

One can argue that representations of the capitalist economy as an independent entity governed by its own logics and separate from its exteriors have facilitated capitalism's hegemony in both the economic and social realms. Conversely, one can also assert that overdetermination is a discursive strategy capable of emptying, fragmenting, decentring, and opening up the economy, thereby liberating discourses on economy and society from capitalism's grasp. However, this process is far from complete or well underway, it has only just begun.

## 4.4 The Concept of Class and Its Relation to Identity

In this part of the chapter, we explore how an alternative theory of class and a re-theorisation of social and personal "identity" can reveal a politics of class that is often overlooked in restructuring research. This suggests that by reconceptualising class, new insights, and dimensions to the relationship between gender and class can emerge. The goal is not to provide a comprehensive resolution to the theoretical troubles of the gender-class relationship but rather to demonstrate the political possibilities that come with rethinking class (Romer, 1986).

The concept of class and its relation to identity is a complex and contested topic within social and political theory. Class refers to the socioeconomic divisions and inequalities that arise from the ownership and control of resources, means of production, and labour. It traditionally focuses on the division between the capitalist class (owners of capital) and the working class (those who sell their labour power). However, class can also encompass other social groups and categories based on occupation, income, education, and social status (Rodrik, 1999).

The politics of identity, on the other hand, centres around the recognition and affirmation of various social identities such as race, gender, sexuality, nationality, and ethnicity. It aims to challenge discrimination, prejudice, and systemic oppression experienced by marginalised groups and to promote their equal rights and social inclusion.

The relationship between class and identity has been a subject of debate among theorists and activists. Some (e.g., North and Thomas, 1973; Piore and Sabel, 1984) argue that class should be the primary focus in understanding social inequality and that identity politics can divert attention from economic exploitation and material conditions. They assert that a unified working-class movement based on class consciousness is crucial for achieving transformative social change.

Others contend that identity-based struggles are essential in recognising and addressing intersecting forms of oppression. They argue that identity is not separate from class, but rather intersects with it, shaping the experiences and inequalities faced by individuals and groups. For example, individuals from marginalised racial or ethnic backgrounds may face specific forms of discrimination and economic disadvantage that are not solely explained by class position (Puga and Venables, 1998).

In recent years, there has been a growing recognition of the need to understand the interconnectedness of class and identity and to develop an inclusive and intersectional analysis. Intersectionality acknowledges that individuals and social groups occupy multiple positions of privilege and marginalisation simultaneously, and that these intersecting identities shape their experiences and social inequalities.

From a political perspective, the challenge lies in forging alliances and solidarities across different social identities and class positions to challenge both economic exploitation and various forms of oppression. It involves recognising the interplay between class dynamics and identities, and working towards inclusive and equitable social, economic, and political systems that address the needs and aspirations of diverse groups within society (Scott, 2001).

The negative effects of industrial restructuring on the working class and the challenges it poses to traditional class politics. It suggests that recent economic changes, such as increased mobility and internationalisation of capital, have led to a decline in the living standards, bargaining power, and militancy of workers. This has been particularly evident in industries that were once strongholds of working-class activism, which have since declined.

The rise of high technology and service industries, as argued by Thrift (1987, p. 207), along with the entry of women into the labour market and the prevalence of part-time and temporary jobs, has transformed the composition of the working class. These changes have undermined the traditional basis of working-class identity and consciousness, making it more difficult to mobilise the working class as a unified political force.

Studies (Thrift, 1987, pp. 207–221) paint a discouraging picture of contemporary class politics, emphasising the occupational differentiation and social segmentation of the labour market. The restructuring of industries and the development of flexible production complexes are seen as contributing to the demoralisation and increased social control of the labour force. Neo-conservative attitudes about work and life are also noted as becoming pervasive in certain regions.

The industrial restructuring, according to Storper (1995) has fractured the unity of the working class, allowing differences to be exploited for the benefit of capital. It highlights the feminisation of the labour market as a significant aspect of these changes. Both men and women are affected by the restructured labour market, with men increasingly subjected to the terms of feminised work arrangements, such as part-time and temporary jobs. Women, on the other hand, have become a central component of the restructured labour force.

This suggests that the interests of working-class men and women are converging as both genders are adversely affected by the changing nature of work. It points out that in this struggle over control of women's labour, both men and women are losing, while capital is the beneficiary (McDowell, 1991, p. 416).

The discourse of working-class decline and disempowerment that has emerged within the restructuring research program. This discourse often suggests a decreasing social importance and political relevance of class, accompanied by narratives of the traditional working class's misfortunes. It creates a vision of class politics as a diminishing force, while emphasising the development of economic structures beyond class (McDowell, 1991, p. 416).

These images of class powerlessness and decline have both discursive and non-discursive origins, and they aim to address the discursive aspects. They focus on examining how class is understood in contemporary political economy and present an alternative Marxian conception of class. They are particularly interested in how conceptions of class are embedded in visions of society and implicated in conceptions of the political subject.

## 4.5 Challenges of Social and Individual Identity in Class Narratives

There are various concepts of class within Marxian political economy. Class is primarily understood as a social group, with individuals belonging to a class based on structural or experiential commonalities. Three attributes commonly used to define social groups as classes are power, property ownership (especially means of production), and exploitation (whether they produce or appropriate surplus labour).

Different scholars have linked two or all three of these dimensions in composite conceptions of class. For example, the "classic triad" of extraction of surplus, ownership of means of production, and control of the labour process is often invoked. There is also a recognition that society is not simply structured by two major classes based on relations of production. Instead, social analysts emphasise the complex multiplicity of classes and class locations within specific historical contexts (Adams, 1996).

Various approaches have been developed to refine and complicate the conception of class. Some formulations consider class formation as a process involving political, cultural, ideological, and other forces, aiming to go beyond economism. Political processes, struggles, and the role of place are seen as important in constituting classes. Class is not solely defined by objective economic conditions but also considers the ways in which groups are formed and the subjective bases of group identification (Davis, 1999).

It is important to note that while class relations can be identified within economic structures, they do not necessarily imply complete empirical coherence or necessary political unity among class members. "Whole classes" are rarely actual political subjects, and the coherence and unity within a class are shaped by social relations and capacities (Massey, 1993, p. 43).

The theoretical and political problems that arise when dealing with complex conceptions of class. One challenge is understanding class transformation when one dimension of class changes. For example, in the case of nationalising a capitalist industry, workers become owners of the means of production. However, this change in ownership does not necessarily guarantee democratic control of the workplace or the end of capitalist exploitation. The analyst is faced with the choice of theorising an ambiguous situation or prioritising one aspect of the composite conception of class. This choice can have significant political implications (Davis, 1999).

The same problems arise when trying to understand individual class positions and social groups using a composite definition. If industrial workers experience only some, but not all, of the conditions that define class, such as having surplus value extracted from them but not owning means of production, are they considered "authentic" members of the working class? What about individuals who are exploited in a capitalist labour process but also own a small business?

These questions challenge the neat categorisation of individuals and groups into specific class identities. It raises issues of authenticity, boundaries, and the complexities of class positions in relation to multiple dimensions. The theoretical and political implications of how we define and conceptualise class can vary and influence our understanding of social dynamics and potential avenues for political action (Agnew, 1993).

Additional problems that arise when considering workers who are not directly involved in the production of surplus value. This includes workers in distribution, exchange, finance, and property sectors, as well as those who work in the domestic realm or voluntary sector. These complexities have become more urgent with recent episodes of industrial restructuring, which have further complicated the social and economic landscape (Arrighi, 1994).

The changing nature of work, such as the increase in individuals holding multiple jobs and the entry of more women into the paid workforce, as well as evolving work practices that incorporate worker decision-making, challenges traditional class mappings. Additionally, the growth of the "informal sector" and hidden workforce further complicates the relevance of conventional class analyses.

In response to these conceptual and political dilemmas, the passage suggests the need for an alternative Marxian conception of class that can address these complexities. By developing such a conception, it is hoped that these problems and questions associated with class analysis can be better navigated and understood.

## 4.6 Competing Ideas of Social and Individual Identity and Their Impact on Class Politics

The implications of defining class as a social process rather than as a social grouping. The Marxian conception of class as a "conscious coming together of those who are similarly situated by production relations" is associated with images of industrial society as a unified entity. In this view, society is theorised as a predominantly capitalist formation centred around an industrial economy, and class is understood as a social relation originating from this centre (Amin and Thrift, 1994).

This centred conception of capitalist society tends to incorporate various aspects of social life, including culture, politics, and non-capitalist economic realms, within the capitalist sector. It views social formations with capitalist class processes as capitalist formations, domestic labour as capitalist reproduction, and the state and other institutions as implicated in capitalist regulation.

These unitary and centred conceptions of capitalist society give rise to a notion of class as a binary or expanded structure based on the relations of capitalist production. They also emphasise the role of class struggle in effecting social change. In this perspective, class transformation is seen as a challenging task directed at systemic or hegemonic objects, such as entire capitalist societies. Class struggle is often portrayed as a military confrontation, requiring a coordinated effort by the working class to confront the hegemonic unity of capitalism (Brenner, 1998).

However, this view of class transformation as a monumental and rare occurrence implies that it is difficult to achieve. It suggests that class struggle can only succeed in specific historical moments when there is a combination of structural crisis and working-class mobilisation. The portrayal of class struggle as a military confrontation further reinforces the notion that a concerted and coordinated effort is necessary to challenge the hegemonic unity of capitalist formations.

Fraad et al. (1994) challenges the notion of a singular and homogeneously capitalist society centred on an industrial economy, as well as the privileging of working-class actors and the emphasis on systemic transformations in class politics. It argues for a more nuanced understanding of class that is divorced from structural or hegemonic conceptions of capitalist society.

Concepts such as the "mode of production" and the "model of development" tend to impose unity and stability on social formations, while also identifying class politics as the politics of the singular social structure. According to this view, everyday political activities can ameliorate and reform the existing society, but only systemic upheaval can bring about transformative change.

To liberate class politics from these restrictive scenarios, this proposes understanding society as a complex disunity where class can take multiple and diverse forms. It suggests that primitive communist, independent, slave, feudal, capitalist, and communal class processes can coexist within an industrialised social formation. In this conception, an advanced industrial society is not a coherent and stable unity centred solely on capitalist class relations but a decentred, fragmented, and complexly structured totality with unevenly developed and diverse class processes (Beck, 1999).

Class processes are not confined to the industrial or capitalist economy but can occur wherever surplus labour is produced, appropriated, or distributed. The household, for example, is identified as a major site of class processes, including domestic class processes where one partner produces surplus labour in the form of use values to be appropriated by the other. Exploitation can also occur in the state, educational institutions, self-employment, labour unions, and other production sites not traditionally associated with class (Hudson, 1997; Howitt, 1993).

Since class is understood as a dynamic process, the class structure constituted by the various class positions and sites is continually changing. Projects of class transformation are therefore always possible and do not necessarily require social upheaval and hegemonic transitions. Class struggles can occur whenever there is an attempt to change the way surplus labour is produced, appropriated, or distributed. The passage thus broadens the scope of class politics and emphasises the potential for class transformation in diverse contexts.

## 4.7 Conclusion

The notion of the "working class" as the collective subject of history emerged from Marxist and non-Marxist discourses that emphasised the defining role of industrial capitalism in structuring Western societies. These discourses portrayed society as structured by two major classes objectively defined by capitalist relations of production and subjectively shaped by the experiences of industrialisation. However, the discourse of class, which once depicted class as the central social relation in contemporary societies, is now being marginalised.

Critics of Marxism argue that class has become irrelevant, while Marxist theorists lament the demobilisation of the working class under contemporary capitalism. From that perspective, what has died or diminished is not class itself but rather the fictional construction of the working class and its mission, which was a product of a hegemonic conception of industrial capitalist development. As this conception has been criticised and as new social centres and competing forces have emerged, the working class has been pushed to the periphery and its significance diminished. The militaristic image of a unified collective of workers defined solely by their relation to industrial capital is receding as a social conception and a basis for transformative politics.

Despite the decline in theoretical and political prominence of the working class, it is argued that class itself can still be understood as present and pervasive. The traditional monolithic images of the working class associated with craft unionism and Fordist industries may no longer be recognised or mobilise resistance and social transformation. However, class as a social process remains an intelligible element of social development and political change. This suggests that class can be reconceptualised in different social and theoretical contexts, where new political opportunities may emerge.

The fundamental question posed in this Chapter is not whether class continues to be relevant, as socioeconomic differentiation and surplus labour appropriation remain integral to the constitution of social knowledge and political subjects. Instead, the focus is on how theorising class as a process of producing, appropriating, and distributing surplus labour can enrich theories of society and contribute to projects of social and economic innovation. Furthermore, it explores how understanding class in this way can contribute to the conceptualisation of decentred and multiple selves that are always inherently political subjects.

Viewing social subjects as constituted by multiple processes, including class processes, challenges the presumption of fixed "class interests" or "class capacities." It also resists the notion of predetermined "class alliances." Instead, this perspective opens up space for a politics of class that involves the recognition of partial identifications around class issues and the formation of strategic solidarities and alliances to bring about class transformation. However, it emphasises that these solidarities and identities are not solely determined by class but are also influenced by other discourses of identity and social differentiation.

Furthermore, this conception of class allows for the understanding that non-class-oriented social movements can have profound effects on class transformations. These movements may potentially foster the development of class diversity in ways that targeted "class politics" alone may not achieve. In other words, social movements focused on issues other than class can still contribute to broader social change and the transformation of class relations.

In the next Chapter, we critically discuss and question globalisation and its role in the economy. We examine how globalisation was oversold, with politicians and economists wrongly emphasising its benefits in terms of job creation, GDP growth, and overall positive impacts.

# Chapter 5
# The Overselling of Globalisation

## 5.1 Introduction

In the previous Chapter we examined how the prevailing trend in contemporary social theory is anti-essentialism, particularly in discussions of identity. This perspective challenges the notion of fixed, universal foundations for constructing identity, influenced by poststructuralist critiques. In this Chapter we build on that discussion by exploring the role of globalisation in constructing this notion of universality.

Prompted by the collapse of socialism in 1989, there is widespread belief in the inevitability of capitalist influence and the natural dominance of capitalism. This notion of penetration and domination is associated with the perception that the world is already or on the verge of being entirely capitalist, essentially belonging to capitalism without question (Jessop, 1999).

Globalisation was oversold, with politicians and economists wrongly emphasising its benefits in terms of job creation, GDP growth, and overall positive impacts. However, the gains were overestimated while the costs, including adverse distributional effects, were underestimated. This overselling of globalisation has had significant political consequences, eroding trust in the elites who advocated for it.

The failures of globalisation and the resulting backlash highlight several important lessons. First, it underscores the importance of science and learning in society, emphasising the need for evidence-based decision-making. Second, it emphasises the significance of shared acceptance of facts and the dangers of deliberately misleading the public. Third, it highlights the folly of disregarding the distributional consequences of economic forces, even if they contribute to overall economic growth.

The notion criticises the new protectionist measures promoted by the administration of Donald Trump, arguing that they will exacerbate the challenges faced by those already negatively affected by globalisation. Instead, the author suggests the



S. Alamad, *Beyond Profit*, Contributions to Economics,
https://doi.org/10.1007/978-3-031-49748-3_5

implementation of a comprehensive system of social protection as a solution. After discussing the failures of globalisation and their impact on the current political situation, the paper proposes a set of policies aimed at redirecting the economy and politics toward a more favourable path (Smith, 1993). These policies likely focus on addressing the distributional impacts of globalisation, promoting social protection measures, and finding a more balanced approach to economic integration.

Globalisation, the interconnectedness of economies, cultures, and societies across the world, has been a defining phenomenon of the late 20th and early twenty-first centuries. While proponents argue that it has brought unprecedented economic growth, technological advancement, and cultural exchange, critics contend that it has exacerbated inequality, eroded local cultures, and contributed to environmental degradation. This essay critically appraises globalisation by examining its economic, cultural, and environmental dimensions.

Globalisation has undeniably led to significant economic growth and development. The increased flow of goods, services, and capital across borders has facilitated economic integration, leading to higher GDP in many countries. Foreign direct investment (FDI) has enabled the transfer of technology and expertise, stimulating innovation and productivity. Moreover, globalisation has created opportunities for developing nations to participate in global trade networks, potentially reducing poverty and improving living standards.

However, these benefits are not evenly distributed. Globalisation has deepened income inequality both within and between countries. Multinational corporations, often the primary beneficiaries of globalisation, can exploit lax labour and environmental regulations in pursuit of profit, leading to precarious working conditions and environmental degradation in developing nations.

Furthermore, globalisation has made economies more susceptible to financial crises, as demonstrated by the Asian financial crisis of 1997 and the global financial crisis of 2008. The interconnectedness of global financial markets can transmit shocks rapidly, leaving developing nations particularly vulnerable. Globalisation has fostered cultural exchange, enabling people worldwide to access diverse art, music, cuisine, and ideas. This cultural diffusion can promote tolerance and understanding, breaking down stereotypes and prejudices. The internet, a product of globalisation, has facilitated this cultural exchange, connecting individuals across continents (Taylor, 2000; Wajcman, 2002).

However, critics (see e.g., Taylor, 2000; Wajcman, 2002; Yeung, 2000; Warf and Grimes, 1997; Walker, 1993) argue that globalisation has led to the homogenisation of culture, as Western cultural products dominate global markets. This "cultural imperialism" can marginalise indigenous cultures and languages. Moreover, globalisation has encouraged consumerism and materialism, potentially undermining traditional values, and identities.

Globalisation has the potential to address environmental challenges through the sharing of knowledge, technology, and resources. International agreements and organisations have emerged to combat climate change and protect biodiversity. Additionally, globalisation can incentivise sustainable practices, as companies face increasing pressure from consumers and investors to reduce their environmental footprint.

Nonetheless, globalisation often prioritises economic growth over environmental protection. The transportation of goods across vast distances contributes to greenhouse gas emissions and pollution. The pursuit of profit can result in resource overexploitation, deforestation, and habitat destruction. Moreover, globalised supply chains make it difficult to trace and regulate the environmental impact of products.

Thus, globalisation is a complex and multifaceted phenomenon with both positive and negative consequences. Economically, it has spurred growth and development while exacerbating inequality and financial instability. Culturally, it has enabled cultural exchange but also threatens cultural diversity. Environmentally, it has the potential to address global challenges but often prioritises profit over sustainability.

To maximise the benefits of globalisation and mitigate its negative impacts, international cooperation, regulation, and ethical considerations are essential. Policies that prioritise social welfare, labour rights, and environmental sustainability can help ensure that globalisation benefits all of humanity, rather than a privileged few. Ultimately, globalisation's legacy will depend on the choices we make in shaping its future trajectory.

## 5.2 Globalisation: A Topic of Interest

While globalisation has been a topic of interest for social theorists for a long time, there has been a significant increase in research on the subject in recent years. This surge in theories reflects the fact that globalisation holds immense importance and is a matter of great concern for a significant portion of the world's population. Globalisation is reshaping the lives of billions of people and transforming nations across the globe.

The impact of globalisation can be observed everywhere, from the proliferation of shopping malls in developed regions to the presence of numerous franchises within them, offering a wide range of goods and services. Additionally, protests against key international organisations like the World Trade Organisation, the International Monetary Fund (IMF), and the World Bank highlight the widespread perception that people are grappling with crucial issues (Swyngedouw, 1997).

Attitudes towards globalisation vary depending on whether individuals perceive themselves as beneficiaries or victims of its effects. Those in developed countries who benefit from globalisation tend to express less opposition to it compared to those in developing nations who feel disadvantaged by it. Opponents of globalisation not only believe it puts them at a disadvantage but also resist the control exerted by international agencies (such as the IMF) and other influential nations, particularly the United States. They fear that globalisation, or the dominance of American culture, will erode indigenous cultures (Swyngedouw, 1997).

Considering the intense public debate and academic focus on globalisation, the title of this essay may seem contradictory. How can the globalisation of nothing be discussed when globalisation itself is of such importance? It is crucial to clarify that the argument is not that globalisation is insignificant, but rather that there is a particular form of globalisation referred to as the globalisation of nothing, which holds tremendous significance.

Much of the attention, especially from critics of globalisation, has overlooked the fact that globalization is not a singular process with uniform outcomes. This essay aims to define and explore some of the primary processes encompassed by globalisation, popularly known as globalisation, in order to gain a deeper understanding of its reach and impact.

While the focus of this discussion is on consumption within the realm of globalisation, similar arguments can be extended to other aspects of the economy, such as production, as well as politics, religion, medicine, and more. Consumption is intricately linked to these social institutions (e.g., the consumption of medical services, the concept of voters as consumers), and it holds increasing importance in both developing and developed regions (Taylor, 1994). However, issues related to production also play a significant role in this analysis, particularly the distinction between mass-produced goods and services and more localised, artisanal production.

## 5.3 What Is Globalisation?

In order to proceed, it is necessary to establish some basic definitions. The concept of consumption can be understood as existing on a spectrum ranging from "nothing" to "something." "Nothing" refers to a social form that is primarily conceived, controlled, and lacking distinctive substantive content. On the other hand, "something" denotes a social form that is indigenously conceived, controlled, and rich in distinctive substantive content. It is important to note that nothing and something are not independent of each other but are mutually defined and contrasted. They exist as two poles on a continuum rather than as a strict dichotomy (Taylor, 2000).

For example, in the context of consumption, companies like the Mills Corporation create and control shopping malls that, in themselves, have little or no distinctive features except for minor variations in design and architecture. The specific content of a mall depends on the shops, goods, restaurants, employees, and customers present within it. While malls in different locations may have similar structures, there will be numerous differences in their specific contents. Moreover, people utilise malls in different ways, often in unforeseen ways, and their behaviour varies across different parts of the world (Wajcman, 2002).

If shopping malls represent the "nothing" end of the continuum, local farmers' markets can be considered as examples of "something." Farmers' markets are locally conceived and controlled, and each market has a distinct character. Farmers arrive at the market to sell their produce, and the composition of participating farmers and the offerings for sale vary from one market day to another. Once the market ends, the temporary structure is dismantled and recreated differently for the next market day. Farmers' markets are not merely nostalgic remnants of the past but continue to be important institutions in many regions worldwide, including highly developed countries (Warf and Grimes, 1997).

Opponents of globalisation (Yeung, 2000; Warf and Grimes, 1997; Walker, 1993), concerned about the homogenisation of cultures, mainly object to the spread of what can be described as "nothing." However, it is important to recognise that globalisation encompasses various types of processes. Globalisation can be defined as the compression of the world and the intensification of consciousness about the world as a whole. However, in contemporary usage, globalisation encompasses multiple transnational processes that, although global in reach, can be distinguished from one another. This essay focuses on two significant processes: glocalisation and grobalisation.

Glocalisation refers to the interpenetration of the global and the local, resulting in unique outcomes in different geographic areas. It captures the essence of how most contemporary theorists associated with globalisation theory perceive transnational processes. On the other hand, the concept of grobalisation, introduced here as a companion to glocalisation, emphasises the imperialistic ambitions of nations, corporations, organisations, etc., and their desire to impose themselves on various geographic areas. Grobalisation revolves around their interests in expanding power, influence, and profits throughout the world. It is important to note that these definitions do not imply a value judgment, as both glocalisation and grobalisation can have positive and negative aspects (Staeheli, 1999).

Therefore, consumption can be understood as existing along a spectrum from nothing to something. Shopping malls exemplify the nothing end, while local farmers' markets represent something. Globalisation encompasses a range of processes, including glocalisation and grobalisation, each with its own characteristics and implications (Staeheli, 1999).

The concept of grobalisation is closely associated with the proliferation of "nothing," such as shopping malls, while glocalisation is linked to "something," like farmers' markets. As part of the broader phenomenon of globalisation, these two processes coexist but are to some extent in conflict with each other. Grobalisation favours the spread of nothingness, whereas glocalisation supports the dissemination of something (Silvern, 1999).

Proponents of glocalisation see it as counteracting the globalisation of nothing and giving rise to a diverse range of new "glocal" forms of something. On the other hand, those who emphasise grobalisation view it as a significant contributor to the spread of nothingness worldwide. This divergence of perspectives reflects different visions of the world—some see it becoming more homogeneous, Americanised, codified, and restricted, while others perceive it as growing more heterogeneous, diverse, and free. It is important to note that both processes are occurring simultaneously and to varying degrees in different parts of the world.

While the focus of this discussion is on the globalisation of nothing, it can only be understood within the broader context of the relationship between grobalisation and glocalisation, and something and nothing. There are four basic possibilities that arise when crossing the continuum of grobalisation with the continuum of something to nothing. While these categories represent "ideal types," there are no rigid boundaries between them.

The relationship between grobalisation and nothing, as well as glocalisation and something, can be described as having an "elective affinity," as Max Weber put it. Neither element directly causes the other, but their development and diffusion tend to occur in conjunction. Glocalisation provides fertile ground for the development and proliferation of something, and something is easily glocalised. Similarly, grobalisation creates favourable conditions for the development and spread of nothing, and nothing is easily grobalised. This analysis focuses on the globalisation of nothing and the glocalisation of something because their relationship represents a crucial point of tension and conflict in the world today. There is significant pressure to grobalise nothing, and the glocalisation of something often acts as a barrier to achieving global dominance. This conflict and its implications will be further explored in the analysis (Morrill, 1999).

Grobalisation, by its nature, involves the widespread dissemination of numerous goods and services. As per the earlier definitions of nothing and something, a minimalist model with minimal content—nothing—facilitates mass distribution. A phenomenon with minimal substance is easier to centrally create, reproduce, and disseminate widely compared to one that is rich in content. Once the basic model is constructed, subsequent iterations are easily produced since there is little substance to the model (Silvern, 1999).

The proliferation of nullities (goods or services at or near the nothing end of the something-nothing continuum) assumes the presence of entrepreneurs in the broadest sense, such as corporate executives at McDonald's or Gucci, or government leaders, who are interested in expanding and exporting such minimalist creations to other parts of the world for corporate profit or national power. While some entrepreneurs create or develop phenomena that are rich, elaborate, distinctive, and idiosyncratic (the grobalisation of something), the complexity of such phenomena limits their numbers and global proliferation. World-class ballet companies, gymnastic teams, and rock groups, for example, are not easily mass-produced, and their profit potential is constrained (Morrill, 1999).

The glocal phenomena, being a unique blend of the global and the local, are more complex to reproduce in large quantities. They are often produced and marketed in limited geographic areas and in small batches, making it challenging to meet even the local demand, let alone cater to a global market. For example, the most famous restaurants in Provence are booked well in advance, and the Provencal food served in French restaurants worldwide may bear little resemblance to the authentic cuisine of Provence. The limited production area of such idiosyncratic products may also result in minimal demand. Not many people outside of France may be interested in, able to recognise, or afford Provencal food (Morrill, 1999).

In terms of dissemination, nullities are easier to extract from their original locality and export to different and diverse regions because they lack specific content. On the other hand, elaborate and distinctive phenomena are often closely tied to a particular locale and its specific tastes and demands. This makes it difficult for them to take root in other places or limits their adaptability to different geographic regions. For instance, Italian Parmigiano Reggiano, a distinctive cheese from a specific region of Italy, is globally available but on a limited scale. It has a narrow market potential outside of Italy. How well does such a unique cheese pair with Tex-Mex cuisine, Indian curry, or Chinese stir-fry? In contrast, Coca-Cola has proven easier to extract from its American origins and has been successfully exported worldwide. It complements virtually any cuisine (Tex-Mex, curry, stir-fry) and has been grobalised. As an advertising campaign in the 1990s stated, "If you don't know what it is, Welcome to Planet Earth." (Miller and Slater, 2000).

Similarly, nullities are also easier to detach from the time period in which they originated. Coca-Cola, for example, was initially produced in an era with different societal norms and less awareness of drug-related issues. It originally contained small amounts of cocaine. However, as times changed and the presence of drugs in a soft drink became unacceptable, the cocaine was removed. Coca-Cola with cocaine would be impossible to sell today, but with the offending substance removed, it can be sold almost anywhere (Lovink and Riemens, 2002).

Products may not start as nullities but gradually become nullities as they are modified over time, with many distinctive elements removed to make them marketable in different periods or locations. For instance, the taco has deep roots in Mexican culture, but much of its original essence, such as the traditional spiciness derived from hot chiles, has been eliminated (at least outside indigenous areas where the original taco is still made and consumed). This transformation turns it into a timeless, generic product that can be marketed by Taco Bell worldwide. It is much easier to distribute such globally palatable products than those that maintain strong connections to a specific time period and local area (Mele, 1999).

This concept argues that a significant dynamic within globalisation is the conflict between grobalisation and glocalisation, rather than between globalisation and the local. Globalisation is a broad concept that encompasses various transnational processes, and it already contains conflicting elements within itself. Therefore, it cannot represent a single position in the central conflict.

The importance of the local is diminished in the context of globalisation. Most of what is perceived as local has been influenced by global forces, resulting in a glocalisation where global and local elements intertwine. The truly local aspects that remain untouched by globalisation are pushed to the peripheries and interstices of local communities.

In many communities, the struggle lies between the more purely grobal and the glocal, as very few things or places remain unaffected by globalisation. The choice for communities seems to be between inherently globalised phenomena (grobalisation) and phenomena where global and local aspects mix (glocalisation). This implies the near-total triumph of the global in the world (Silvern, 1999; Morrill, 1999; Miller and Slater, 2000).

Ironically, those opposed to grobalisation can find hope in an alternative form of globalisation: glocalisation. The glocal retains important vestiges of the local, and the interaction between the grobal and the local gives rise to unique phenomena that cannot be reduced to either category alone. The glocal can be a significant source of uniqueness, diversity, and innovation (Miller and Slater, 2000).

While some may continue to support the local as an alternative to the global, the essay suggests that this effort is likely to fail due to the progressive disappearance of the truly local. Instead, supporting the glocal as an alternative to the grobal may be a more successful strategy. The glocal not only preserves cultural diversity but also fosters cultural innovation. Globalisation is not a monolithic and uniform force, offering hope to those who perceive a threat in the dominance of grobal phenomena (Silvern, 1999).

## 5.4 Risks of Over-Globalisation

The criticism that advocates of globalisation tended to overlook or underestimate the costs associated with it, particularly the negative impacts on the standards of living for individuals in advanced countries with limited skills.

One of the effects that was often neglected is the increased risk brought about by globalisation. Developing countries, in particular, face macroeconomic risks from external factors that are beyond their control. Individuals and firms are unable to adequately insure themselves against these risks or share them across society through market mechanisms. Consequently, consumers bear the burden of these risks, workers face greater insecurity, and firms may shift production to safer but less profitable activities. In the absence of efficient risk markets, all individuals may be worse off (Parnreiter, 2002).

Energy security is highlighted as a specific risk that globalisation can exacerbate (Parnreiter, 2002). The dependence of certain countries on energy imports, such as Germany relying heavily on Russian natural gas, exposes them to economic and political vulnerabilities. Disruptions in energy supply can have disastrous effects on a country's economy. The example of Russia cutting off or reducing gas supply to Ukraine in recent years serves as a reminder that these risks are not merely theoretical. The failure to adequately price the risk of such interruptions in the market is considered a market failure, similar to the failure to price the long-term consequences of global warming.

Also concerns raised by leaders in Mexico, which has become dependent on US gas, regarding the potential interruption of supply due to Donald Trump's, when he was a president) anti-Mexican stance. This illustrates how political factors can further complicate the risks associated with globalisation, as well as the limitations of presuming that humans always act rationally.

Thus, the argument is that the costs and risks associated with globalisation, including those related to energy security, were often underestimated, or ignored by proponents of liberalisation. This failure to account for such risks can have significant short-term and long-term consequences for economies and societies.

There are two important aspects of globalisation that were often overlooked or underestimated: imperfect competition and the dynamics of comparative advantage.

*Firstly*, the standard models of trade liberalisation assume perfect competition, where all firms are small. However, in reality, many trade transactions involve large corporations with significant market power. These corporate behemoths, such as Walmart, can use their market power to drive down producer prices and push small producers out of business when entering new markets. The welfare benefits predicted by standard trade models do not hold in the presence of imperfect competition. Despite this, policymakers often ignored these effects, fearing that addressing them would lead to protectionist demands from special interest groups.

*Secondly*, the advocates of globalisation failed to consider the long-term dynamics of comparative advantage. They focused on the current comparative advantage of economies without fully considering how it could change over time. For example, the shift of production from the US to China was driven by the perception that China had a comparative advantage in labour-intensive manufacturing due to cheap labour. However, China quickly learned and developed its own technological capacities, maintaining its comparative advantage in manufacturing even as wages started to rise. The learning process and technological advancement occurred at a rapid pace.

This rapid learning and technological catch-up have consequences for bringing production back to advanced countries like the US or Europe. Simply saying "let us bring manufacturing back" is not feasible because the advanced countries no longer have the necessary technology or skilled workforce. If production were to return, it would likely be based on new technologies, such as robotics, where advanced countries have a comparative advantage. However, such a shift would not revive the old manufacturing jobs but rather create mostly highly skilled jobs.

We should also emphasise the importance of spill overs and knowledge diffusion in the economy. Learning in one firm spill over to others, contributing to the formation of clusters or dense groupings of firms with similar expertise. Examples include Silicon Valley's high-tech firms or the manufacturing firms in Ohio and Michigan in the past. These spill overs play a crucial role in economic development and competitiveness (Stiglitz, 2015). Thus, the limitations of standard trade models that assume perfect competition and neglect the long-term dynamics of comparative advantage. It emphasises the need to consider the effects of imperfect competition and the rapid learning and technological progress that can reshape comparative advantage over time.

In this context, I would like to pose here and highlight several important points regarding the consequences of globalisation. The overall increase in the economic pie due to trade liberalisation may have been smaller than advocates claimed. Even when using standard models, analyses of trade agreements like the Trans-Pacific Partnership (TPP) showed minimal effects on GDP, and broader measures of well-being might even indicate smaller or negative benefits (Stiglitz, 2015).

While globalisation may have benefited some winners, the distributional consequences have been significant. Large portions of the population in developed countries have not fared well, as they received a smaller share of the increased economic pie. These distributional effects go beyond the predictions of the standard theory of comparative advantage, as globalisation can weaken workers' bargaining power and lead to wage declines or worse conditions. These effects are particularly pronounced in areas with increased unemployment, and if monetary and fiscal policies are constrained in their response (Stiglitz, 2017).

Ironically, some of the strongest advocates of globalisation have been staunch opponents of measures like trade assistance, which are necessary to ensure that no one is left behind. This contradiction implies that globalisation may not be a Pareto improvement, as there are individuals who are worse off or perceive themselves to be worse off due to globalisation. This opposition to globalisation is not surprising if a significant number of people experience negative consequences.

Moreover, we should acknowledge the contrasting experiences between different parts of the world. While some people in other countries may have benefited greatly from globalisation, it provides little comfort to the workers in America and Europe whose incomes have stagnated for a quarter of a century. This disparity can fuel the perception that the gains of others have come at their expense, reinforcing a zero-sum view of the world (Fan and Scott, 2003).

In addition to that, attributing the decline of the middle class solely to technological change offers little solace. The promise of technological progress was that it would benefit everyone, but now the middle class is told that it benefits those at the top more than anyone else. As such, globalisation has not served large parts of the country well, particularly the bottom 90%. This disconnect between economic growth and the well-being of a significant portion of the population has had profound political and social consequences (Stiglitz, 2016).

We should also not forget the failure of protectionism as a solution to the problems caused by globalisation. We argue that implementing protectionist policies, as advocated by figures like Trump, will not solve the issues faced by those negatively impacted by globalisation. In fact, the situation for those harmed by globalisation may worsen. While globalisation may not have led to significant economic growth, deglobalisation can result in a weaker economy. It is important to consider historical factors and the creation of new supply chains.

The central message is that globalization can be a positive-sum situation if well managed, benefiting citizens in all countries. However, achieving this outcome is not easy. Simply compensating those who lose out from globalisation may not be enough to regain trust in the system, as elites and politicians have been discredited. To make globalisation acceptable and ensure shared prosperity, social protection against its negative effects must be deeply integrated into the economic system.

There are several elements of a program for shared prosperity that could convince sceptics of globalisation. These include rewriting the rules of the market economy to curb corporate power, reforming corporate governance and the financial sector, increasing the minimum wage, strengthening labour market protections and workers' bargaining rights, and running the economy more tightly to bring marginalised people back into meaningful economic activity (Stiglitz, 2006). Additionally, reducing intergenerational transmission of advantage and disadvantage through strengthening public education and ensuring access to high-quality tertiary education is important. Substituting regressive taxation with progressive taxation, closing loopholes, and implementing a global minimum corporate income tax are crucial for improving income distribution. The government also needs to play a larger role in helping the economy adjust to the shift from manufacturing to a service sector economy through education and research programs. Social insurance, specifically protection against job loss and drastic wage cuts due to globalisation, is essential, and protectionism is not an effective solution.

As a result, we emphasise the need for comprehensive policies that address inequality, promote fairness, and provide social protection to counteract the negative consequences of globalisation. It argues against protectionism as a viable solution and calls for a holistic approach to ensure shared prosperity in a globalised world.

## 5.5 Learning From History: A Look Back in Time

There is a benefit of having a historical overview of the concept of globalisation, starting with the breakdown of the Bretton Woods System in the mid-twentieth century. The Bretton Woods System, established in 1944, aimed to promote economic growth by managing exchange rates and trade flows among nation-states. However, by the 1960s, the system faced challenges as trade imbalances and the decline of the U.S. dollar's value put pressure on the pegged currency rates. This led to the end of the Bretton Woods era in 1973 when major economies, including Japan and European states, were forced to float their currencies (Stiglitz, 2017).

During the 1970s, with the rise of neoliberalism, research began to emphasise the transnational nature of the economy, highlighting the influence of international business and capital markets. The power of the nation-state appeared diminished as private international financial activities encroached on governmental sovereignty. The idea of "international political economy" gained traction, especially as states struggled with trade imbalances, inflation, and slow growth (Summer et al., 1993).

By the end of the 1970s, the concept of "globalisation" emerged, suggesting the complete disengagement of the economy from the nation-state. The book "The New International Division of Labour" published in 1977 played a significant role in defining globalisation as a worldwide redistribution of production, enabling companies to exploit low-wage labour in poorer countries. Dependency and interdependency became central to this understanding of globalisation, with the authors arguing for a single worldwide capitalist system that transcended geographical distance. Theodore Levitt's 1983 work on corporate strategy further emphasised the homogenisation of markets and the end of domestic territoriality (Summer et al., 1993).

Although discussions on globalisation within business studies declined in the late 1980s, the concept gained prominence in broader social science discourse in the 1990s. However, there were critics who challenged the idea of a completely globalised economy. Paul Hirst and Grahame Thompson's book "Globalisation in Question" argued that nationally cantered processes and the role of the state in managing economic affairs had not been overturned by cross-border activities. They compared the contemporary world economy to the belle epoque period of the early twentieth century, highlighting that current levels of integration were similar to those of a century ago (Stiglitz, 2017).

The development of the concept of globalisation, its roots in the breakdown of the Bretton Woods System, and the evolving understanding of the global economy within business studies and social science discourse. It showcases differing perspectives on the extent and nature of globalisation, with some emphasising its transformative power and others highlighting the continued importance of the nation-state and national processes in the global economy (Stiglitz, 2017).

The Hirst and Thompson book, "Globalisation in Question," marked a turning point in the discourse on globalisation. It expanded the scope of the discussion beyond current affairs and challenged the concept of globalisation, putting it on the defensive. In response to this critique, a book titled "Global Transformations: Politics, Economics, and Culture" was published in 1999 by David Held, Anthony G. McGrew, David Goldblatt, and Jonathan Perraton. The authors positioned themselves as "transformationalists" who sought to provide a comprehensive analysis of globalisation.

"Global Transformations" acknowledged that globalisation had a historical background but argued that the contemporary configuration of globalisation displayed unprecedented qualitative differences. The erosion of the internal/external distinction of the nation-state was identified as the central concern of the book. The authors claimed that the current era of globalisation is characterised by a new geography of power and privilege that transcends political borders and regions.

The book presented a robust social scientific evaluation and also advocated for a political agenda, particularly the idea of "cosmopolitan governance." The authors asserted that the operation of states in an increasingly complex international system limits their autonomy and impinges on their sovereignty.

"Global Transformations" became one of the most cited works on globalisation and received praise from influential figures in history and social sciences. The book aimed to provide a comprehensive synthesis of various arguments on globalisation, making it a valuable resource for evaluating the claims of contemporary globalisation.

In terms of defining globalisation, the authors echoed Anthony Giddens' definition, stating that it refers to the spatio-temporal processes of change that transform the organisation of human affairs by linking human activity across regions and continents. They conducted a comparative historical analysis of different epochs of globalisation: premodern, early modern, modern, and contemporary. However, the meaning of the term "modern" is not clarified in the book, and the temporal markers are necessary to distinguish the contemporary era from the modern era, contrasting it with the arguments presented by Hirst and Thompson (Stiglitz, 2017).

Held et al. propose a two-fold thesis that is shared by many scholars in the field: we have entered a new era of history where territorial power distinctions are eroding, and the state-economy axis, particularly in advanced capitalist states, provides compelling evidence of global enmeshment. However, the evidence they present does not adequately address the objections raised by Hirst and Thompson.

In terms of economics, Held et al. discuss production, trade, and finance as key aspects of globalisation. They argue that foreign direct investment (FDI) and the export of production and distribution systems are at unprecedented levels, leading to the transnational power of global corporations. However, the reality is that global FDI is highly concentrated and unevenly distributed. Only a handful of countries are heavily involved in FDI, and the destinations for investments are predominantly European rather than truly global. Studies have shown that FDI has remained stagnant for some countries over the past two decades, and the expected increase in investments to low-wage locations has not materialised (Stiglitz, 2016). Furthermore, multinational production represents less than 10% of output even in the most integrated economies.

Moreover, national policies and trajectories continue to shape ownership structures, corporate governance, worker relations, competitor relations, financing, research and development, in-house trade, and international investment strategies. These factors vary significantly between countries such as the United States, Germany, and Japan, indicating that national contexts still play a crucial role (Stiglitz, 2017).

The analysis by Held et al. (1999) raises questions about the extent of global integration in the economic sphere and the uniqueness of contemporary globalisation compared to a century ago. Their emphasis on the state-economy axis and their selection of a narrow case study set of advanced capitalist states limit the generalisability of their arguments and fail to fully address the objections raised by critics.

Held et al.'s (1999) arguments regarding trade globalisation are also subject to scrutiny. They highlight the geographical extension and intensification of trade, as measured by trade-to-GDP ratios, to support their claim of a new era of trade globalisation. However, the majority of the world economy, approximately 80 percent, remains national, and global trade flows are highly uneven. For instance, Africa below the Sahara accounted for just 1% of world trade in the 1990s, indicating significant disparities.

While there has been a slight increase in world exports relative to world GDP since World War II, the distribution of trade suggests regionalisation rather than globalisation. Trade among European Union (EU) partners has grown substantially, but extracontinental trade for individual states and the EU as a whole has stagnated or declined. Geographical factors such as shipping costs, time lag, cultural differences, and regional agglomerations play a significant role in shaping trade patterns and contribute to the development of regional trade blocs.

In terms of international finance, the argument for contemporary economic globalisation often relies on factors such as reduced controls and taxes on capital movement, liberalisation of domestic regulations, offshore accounting, and large-scale currency trading. While it is true that capital mobility is less restricted today compared to the Bretton Woods era, patterns of international finance remain uneven, and national distinctions persist even within international flows. The concentration of financial activity in upper-income countries and the growing polarisation between rich and poor countries demonstrate the asymmetries in international finance.

Domestic institutional decisions, historical factors, policies, and cultural differences all influence financial internationalisation (Kim, 2002).

Furthermore, corporate practices and financial markets are still deeply rooted in national political and cultural structures. While international trade levels continue to increase, the focus is more on regional circuits rather than truly global integration. It raises the question of whether the current integration is truly unique or if there are precedents in history, as highlighted by Hirst and Thompson's analysis of the belle epoque.

In summary, the arguments presented by Held et al. regarding trade and international finance in support of contemporary globalisation face criticism due to the uneven distribution of trade flows, regionalisation tendencies, and the enduring influence of national structures. The claim of a new era of globalisation is challenged by historical precedents, as highlighted by other scholars.

Regarding international production, the focus of Held et al. on six wealthy states shows that only Sweden experienced a substantial increase in outward foreign direct investment (FDI) from 1914 to 1994. Other countries such as Japan, the United States, and Germany remained at similar levels, while France and the United Kingdom witnessed significant contraction. When considering world FDI relative to world GDP, the levels in the late 1990s did not surpass those of 1913. This indicates that multinational corporations were already flourishing before World War I and played a crucial role in the internationalisation of production. Various industries, including automobiles, telephones, cameras, and food products, had already achieved multinational and multiregional status during that period (Leamer and Storper, 2001).

Similarly, international trade today does not show a significant increase compared to the pre-war era. Analysing the six advanced industrial states mentioned by Held et al., only Germany experienced a notable expansion in total merchandise trade relative to GDP. France, Sweden, and the United States saw slight growth, while Japan experienced a slight reduction, and the United Kingdom underwent significant de-internationalisation. Comprehensive data compiled by Christopher Chase-Dunn also indicates a moderate increase in world trade as a percentage of world GDP from 1913 to 1995. This challenges the notion that a completely new stage of global integration has emerged in recent years (Hall, 2001).

In terms of securities markets, capital integration during the belle epoque period actually exceeded current levels by many measures. European savings banks underwent consolidation and national centralisation, channelling more domestic capital into international markets. Financial centres in France, Germany, Holland, Belgium, Switzerland, and the United States were interconnected with highly mobile international capital markets. The majority of the world's population, approximately 89 percent in 1908, lived in economies with convertible currencies under the gold and silver standards (Stiglitz, 2017).

When comparing net capital flows of the pre-World War I era to those of today for the six wealthy states highlighted by Held et al., only Germany showed an increase, while the United States remained the same and France, Japan, Sweden, and the United Kingdom indicated decline. The overall aggregate number for these economies has also declined to about two-thirds of the 1913 level. The significant capital flows and foreign investments during the late nineteenth and early twentieth centuries, particularly in countries like Britain, France, and Germany, far exceeded the levels seen today. Additionally, the financial market openness and speed of spreading panic during the gold-era were greater and more volatile compared to the present (Leamer and Storper, 2001).

In conclusion, the evidence presented challenges the notion of a completely new era of globalisation by showing that international production, trade, and capital integration had already reached significant levels before World War I. The belle epoque period demonstrated remarkable precedents for the global integration that is often described as unique to the present era (Leamer and Storper, 2001).

The critique of the globalisation literature suggests that it often overlooks the locally specific and contested nature of policy and power production. This leads to a projection of a singular and abstract logic that is presumed to cover the entire globe. This conceptual approach emerged after a decade of methodological reflection in economics that aimed to shed naturalist assumptions and embrace the complexities of multiple equilibria, imperfect competition, and historical contingencies (Hall, 2001).

However, the dominant notion of political power in globalisation studies is rooted in the Westphalian system, which defines sovereignty as the self-determining authority of a bordered territorial space. The Westphalian model, which emerged in the twentieth century, established centralised political units and territorial states as the basis of the international political system. Sovereignty, understood as freedom from external authority, reduces domestic politics to an abstract equivalence across all states, disregarding local variations. This approach treats the economy as either contained within the state or as a supra-territorial threat to state sovereignty. Consequently, it minimises the local production and interrelation of political and economic power while isolating cross-border commerce as a global abstraction (Kim, 2002).

Moreover, the Westphalian model is often presented as evidence of the epochal global change brought about by globalisation, suggesting that the clear and unambiguous boundaries of political rule are being blurred. However, international pressures on state sovereignty are not new, and historical responses have been locally dependent and highly variable. The presumption of the Westphalian model underestimates state power in the present while overestimating it in the past (Kim, 2002). It also fails to acknowledge the complex interplay between relative autonomy and complex interdependence that modern states have always possessed.

In light of this critique, subsuming the variant operations of boundaries, domestic rule, and international law under the single rubric of "sovereignty" obscures more than it reveals. The evidence shows that domestic rule has frequently been subject to external authority and intervention, as major peace treaties from Westphalia to Helsinki have compromised the Westphalian model, according to Stephen Krasner (Stiglitz, 2017).

Thus, there is a need to consider the locally specific and contested nature of policy and power production in globalisation studies, rather than relying on an abstract notion of political power derived from the Westphalian system.

Historical analysis challenges the Westphalian periodisation of territoriality, which is the linchpin of the entire model. Actual centralisation of enforceable state authority emerged only in the last third of the nineteenth century, as industrial capitalism transformed the control of land and reconfigured it through alliances of new and old elites. It was during this period that lawyers and historians projected the origins of state sovereignty back to the Westphalian Treaty, creating a mythological narrative that became the basis for twentieth-century international relations theory and today's globalisation studies (Stiglitz, 2017).

However, even in the late nineteenth century, international economic flows were already undermining the rhetoric of Westphalia. Weak states of that era, like many in recent history, surrendered fiscal autonomy to foreign governments, creditors, and international commissions in order to secure development loans. The gold standard system, which approached near-total integration of world currencies, subordinated the national monetary policies of both rich and poor states to the demands of gold parity and reserves. Even Britain, often seen as the hegemonic conductor of the system, had its options nullified on several occasions and had to rely on borrowing from other central banks to maintain sterling convertibility (Stiglitz, 2017).

Both weak and strong states were compromised by the pre-war world economic order, but the conditions and consequences were not uniform. Domestic distinctions and national decisions remained significant. Different approaches were used by major players in the gold standard system to uphold currency strength, leading to diverse local and systemic effects. Smaller economies negotiated with the international system differently, influenced by their specific local factors and geopolitical contexts. Historical factors such as domestic distributional conflicts, elite preferences, institutional settings, and developmental strategies shaped unique relations to the international economic order and its pressures (Stiglitz, 2015).

Therefore, the contemporary era does not represent a new economic regime or a new system of states. The abstraction of politics and economics, as often seen in the presentist globalisation literature, oversimplifies the complex dynamics of world power. The comparisons made with the past in this literature are inherently distorted, and when political and economic forces are understood as reciprocally constructed, the constraints on contemporary governments appear exaggerated and not fundamentally new. The territorialised state has always needed to manage the mobile flows of international wealth, and while there are inflections and variations, power is not inherently supra-territorial but rather created and negotiated at the site of decision. Domestic, national, and regional variations challenge the claim that power transcends political borders (Stiglitz, 2016).

Historical analysis reveals the limitations and distortions of the Westphalian model and challenges the simplistic dichotomy between politics and economics in the study of globalisation. It emphasises the importance of understanding the complexities and variations of power dynamics in different historical contexts (Stiglitz and Greenwald, 2014).

The process of economic integration during the nineteenth century was not solely driven by voluntary agreements or market forces. European states and the United States employed direct coercion, often through gunboat diplomacy, to secure their economic interests. This coercion involved imposing guarantees of extraterritoriality, unsupervised trade, and low customs duties on foreign lands. Naval forces were deployed to protect the interests of bondholders and investors, and asymmetrical treaties remained in force for extended periods (Stiglitz, 2017).

Furthermore, economic intervention by states took the form of direct colonial control. Colonial seizures were often accompanied by violence, and the enforcement of occupation and extraction was a daily reality. British control in particular had a significant impact on trade. While other countries protected their textile manufacturers with import prohibitions or high duties, British control eliminated Indian tariffs entirely, leading to a flood of British merchandise. Britain also invested heavily in state-backed railroad construction in India to secure cotton supplies. Colonial powers exerted control over the transportation of goods, restricted local tariffs, and legislated measures to favour the metropolis (Stiglitz and Greenwald, 2010).

The neoclassical economists, in their analysis, tend to ignore the economic relevance of colonialism and its interconnections with the broader world economy. Colonialism played a crucial role in generating surpluses, such as India's opium trade with China, which financed further colonisation and the acquisition of wealth. These coerced surpluses with Asia enabled Britain to accumulate capital and venture into the world market, while running deficits with Euro-American trading partners (Stiglitz and Greenwald, 2014).

By focusing primarily on prices, the neoclassical model overlooks the enduring significance of colonialism and its multifaceted economic impact. It treats colonialism as a singular event that initiates free trade, disregarding the ongoing role of political power in shaping and expanding markets. Political interventions, ranging from financial interventions to labour enforcement and military force, were instrumental in driving global integration during the nineteenth century. The description of the mid-century world economy as liberal or free trading is thus problematic, and an analysis that separates the state and the economy falls short in providing a comprehensive understanding of global integration.

Scholars of the early modern period have an advantage over those analysing the nineteenth century in terms of recognising the reciprocal relationship between the state and the economy. They are not burdened by the competing universalisations of state and economy that emerged in the nineteenth century. However, there is a question of whether a worldwide scale of analysis is applicable to the early modern period. Some studies of this period, including those in the next volume under discussion, may describe long-distance network linkages rather than a truly global system. Additionally, in an attempt to fit Europe into a global frame, it is sometimes portrayed as a dependency of larger global forces (Stiglitz and Greenwald, 2010).

Andre Gunder Frank's book "ReOrient: Global Economy in the Asian Age" presents a structuralist account of a single global world economy with a worldwide division of labour and multilateral trade from 1500 onward. Frank argues that class, state, and culture are all dependent on the world economic system. He sees Europe's hegemony as brief and declining, but its particularistic analytic legacy from the nineteenth century persists.

Frank considers Afro-Eurasia as a single economic system dating back 5000 years, with Song China dominating from around 1000 CE. Europe played a marginal role until its American extractions after 1500 allowed it some presence in the Asian market. Frank relies on evidence of early modern silver flows, which enriched Europe through trade and were exchanged for commodities in China. He also highlights long-term economic cycles, with a China-cantered expansive phase from around 1400 to the eighteenth century, followed by a contractive phase that affected Europe differently due to its higher wages and finite silver supply. Europe's industrialisation led to temporary global dominance, but East Asian economies began emerging ascendant by the late twentieth century.

While Frank's holistic perspective offers a vision of global unity and challenges Eurocentric presumptions, the periodisation he presents is not convincing. Examining components such as currency, trade, and economic cycles, as well as his critique of Eurocentrism, reveals discrepancies. For example, early modern Chinese prices were not significantly influenced by silver imports, as European and Chinese money circulated in separate currency systems. Additionally, China's domestic expansion in the eighteenth century led to inflation unrelated to the international flow of bullion.

Therefore, while scholars of the early modern period have a better understanding of the reciprocal relationship between the state and the economy, there are challenges in applying a worldwide scale of analysis and in periodising global integration in a convincing manner.

Frank's argument for a single global system leads him to advocate for a holistic approach and critique non-holistic perspectives as Eurocentric. However, this rigid criticism leads to logical and historical contradictions. Frank's statement that "commonalities" are more important than differences is self-cancelling, as acknowledging commonalities necessitates differentiation. Frank aims to raise social science to the level of history theory, but universalising historical knowledge is itself a product of Europe's engagement with the wider world and can be seen as a form of Eurocentrism.

A more nuanced perspective is offered by A. G. Hopkins' "Globalisation in World History" and C. A. Bayly's "The Birth of the Modern World, 1780–1914," which present Europe within a polycentric history. These works view early modern empires as drivers of globalisation and understand the reconfiguration of the empire form in the nineteenth century into a global system of states. While Hopkins draws on the description of tightening large-scale networks from Held et al., the concept of globalisation in this context lacks clarity and does not add much to the discussion.

The Qing Empire, for example, expanded in a different way from European merchant empires. It transformed adjoining lands into sedentary agricultural communities, focusing on domestic production and market patterns rather than foreign trade. Describing the Qing Empire as a form of "globalisation" raises questions about the conceptual connection between different historical networks and present-day globalisation. The authors of these works present a transactional method that emphasises the dynamic relations between interior and exterior forces in shaping social formations. Mislabelling this approach as "globalisation" undermines its analytical value.

While Frank advocates for a holistic approach and criticises Eurocentric perspectives, his rigid criticism leads to contradictions. Works by Hopkins and Bayly offer a more nuanced understanding of the polycentric nature of early modern history and the reconfiguration of the empire form in the nineteenth century. Describing historical networks as "globalisation" lacks conceptual clarity and fails to capture the dynamic relations that shape social formations.

## 5.6 Globalisation and Geopolitics

It approaches irrefusably, hesitantly, terrible as fate, the great task and question: how shall the Earth as a whole be managed? (Friedrich Nietzsche, 1885).

The question of how the Earth as a whole should be managed is indeed a monumental and complex task. It requires addressing a wide range of interconnected issues, including environmental sustainability, social equity, economic development, and political governance. Finding a comprehensive and universally accepted answer to this question is challenging due to the diverse interests, values, and priorities of different nations, societies, and individuals.

However, there are ongoing efforts at various levels to tackle global challenges and work towards more effective global governance. International organisations such as the United Nations, along with regional organisations and agreements, play a crucial role in fostering cooperation and addressing global issues. Initiatives like the Sustainable Development Goals (SDGs) provide a framework for collective action and guide global efforts towards a more sustainable and equitable future.

Managing the earth as a whole requires recognising the interconnectedness of different regions and systems and promoting cooperation and collaboration among nations. It necessitates addressing issues such as climate change, biodiversity loss, poverty, inequality, and conflicts, which transcend national boundaries and require collective solutions.

Achieving effective global management also requires inclusivity and respect for diverse perspectives and voices. It involves engaging with various stakeholders, including civil society organisations, indigenous communities, businesses, and academia, to ensure a holistic and participatory approach to decision-making.

While the task of managing the earth as a whole is daunting, it is crucial to recognise the urgency and importance of addressing global challenges collectively. By fostering international cooperation, promoting sustainable development, and embracing inclusive governance, we can strive towards a more just, prosperous, and sustainable world for future generations.

Therefore, it is important to acknowledge the historical context of the emergence of a global system and the complexities involved in analysing it. Here are some key points from our earlier discussion to help you follow this analysis:

(a) Existence of a Global System: The text argues that early modern historians have not convincingly shown the existence of a global system during their period. The global scale of power and integration did not truly emerge until the second half of the nineteenth century.
(b) Abstraction of Economy and State: The passage criticises the reliance on the abstraction of economy and state in understanding global history. It suggests that analysing transactional effects and historical contexts is more effective in historicising globalisation.
(c) Local and Global Interconnections: Geyer and Bright's work highlights how during the mid-nineteenth century, competing autonomous centres of regional rule encountered interregional connections in their reproduction of power. European interventions and technologies played a role, but indigenous and regional trajectories were also significant in shaping developments.
(d) Changing State Power: The text explains how the efforts to manage global competition led to changes in state power dynamics in different regions. European imperialism shifted from surplus extraction to social organisation and created global circuits of control.
(e) Unravelling of Imperial Order: Despite efforts to manage global affairs, the European order was challenged by increasing local resistance and self-renewal in various regions. This resistance aimed at asserting local autonomy and limited the degree of European control.

Overall, there are several factors are discussed that contributed to the unravelling of the European imperial order and the intensification of political tensions between European states:

(a) Global Crisis and Interconnectedness: The Russo-Japanese War is highlighted as the first "global crisis" that had reverberating effects on European dynamics. The war's aftermath influenced various European interactions and events, such as the Anglo-French entente cordiale, the Moroccan crisis, the Triple Entente, and the Russian revolution, among others. These events demonstrated the interdependent networks of global power and challenged attempts to organise territorial dispensation.
(b) Geopolitical Recognition: Geopolitical analysis, exemplified by H. J. Mackinder's pronouncement, acknowledged the emergence of a new globality that would sharply impact political and economic systems worldwide. This recognition intensified the demand for the consolidation of state power, signalling an "intensification of territoriality."
(c) Challenges to the Gold Standard: The survival of the gold standard, beneficial to elites at its core, relied on the credibility and cooperation of participant states. However, domestic political pressures in Western Europe, the United States, Southern Europe, and South America shifted priorities away from currency convertibility toward national concerns such as unemployment and inflation. Geopolitical tensions among imperial states also eroded their willingness to cooperate on maintaining the gold standard.

(d) Economic Internationalisation and Political Tensions: The deepening internationalisation of the economy led to increased political tensions between European states. The integration of world markets brought prosperity to some, but it also posed challenges. Rising import pressures prompted countries to raise tariffs to protect domestic industries, leading to a competitive squeeze between European states. Moreover, concerns over unrestricted migration and its perceived threat to political authority and cultural order resulted in the implementation of immigration policies and border controls that aimed to nationalise and militarise domestic populations.

These factors contributed to the complex and interconnected dynamics that shaped the late nineteenth and early twentieth centuries, leading to the erosion of European imperial order and the intensification of political struggles between states (Stiglitz and Greenwald, 2014). We should also not forget how the internationalisation of the economy contributed to an arms race among European powers in the early twentieth century:

(a) Arms Race: The aftermath of the Russo-Japanese War triggered an arms race among rival states. Russia initiated a rearmament drive, and Germany, perceiving an advantage, increased its arms expenditures and militarised its diplomacy. Britain and France responded with military expansions and joint war planning with Russia. Other countries, including Austria-Hungary, Italy, Serbia, and Romania, also increased their military budgets.
(b) Competition for Resources: As consumers, states competed for resources that were experiencing higher earnings elsewhere. Accessing easily exportable capital became costlier for Britain, France, and Germany. Mobilising labourers also became challenging, as industrial wages and returns to peasants were rising. States employed strategies such as increasing the reserve army, innovating military doctrine for shorter and less costly wars, and promoting nationalism to convince resource holders to accept reduced compensation.
(c) Strategic Assessments and Uncertainty: States faced complex and uncertain strategic assessments. They had to navigate their compromised market circumstances while making conjectures about their rivals' intentions. Perceptions of rival states' preparations for war reinforced the arms race, amplifying the stakes of resource mobilisation.
(d) Escalation and Panic: Germany, fearing increasing inferiority after the second Moroccan crisis, initiated a massive acceleration of its land strength, triggering a new phase of the arms race. With each measure and countermeasure, the constraints on resource mobilisation worsened for each state, fuelling a sense of panic about a potentially unfavourable future. Ultimately, 2 years after the Moroccan crisis, the European blocs entered into war driven by the fear of being disadvantaged in the future.

The internationalisation of the economy, combined with the arms race and competition for resources, created a volatile and uncertain environment that led to the outbreak of World War I.

## 5.7 Developmental Disparities in Today's World Order

Neoclassical theories of development emphasise that political challenges can hinder development programs that do not adequately consider the spatial integration of economic activity. We have also suggested that the intricate network of relationships between urbanisation and development operates at all levels of GDP per capita, and economic development can be achieved through a diverse range of manufacturing and service sectors. Even simple craft-based or small firm-based industries, which were previously seen as incompatible with sustainable development, have shown potential for economic growth.

It is crucial to refocus attention on the developmental possibilities of cities and regions within the context of globalisation because they generate significant positive externalities in the increasingly interconnected global economic system. In less-developed countries, agglomeration is vital for development not only because it enhances economic productivity but also because it facilitates specialisation within the global division of labour and serves as a foundation for export-oriented growth.

As globalisation progresses and economic exchanges become more liberalised, dense productive agglomerations have emerged worldwide. This development is complemented by inter-agglomeration competition and complementarity, where different agglomerations in various regions compete or cooperate with each other. Agglomerations are also often connected to less-developed peripheral areas, particularly when certain production units within commodity chains find it advantageous to locate in decentralised sites.

This phenomenon is particularly evident in branch plant operations with standardised production activities and cost-efficient procurement and distribution structures. However, it has led to increasing regional income inequalities within many developing countries. Even in developed countries, the period of intensive globalisation coupled with neoliberal policy measures has resulted in widening gaps in per capita incomes between sub-national regions. This issue is exacerbated in regions with low labour mobility, such as the UK and most of continental Europe compared to the United States.

Per capita income differences between countries have historically diverged during much of the nineteenth and twentieth centuries. However, from the 1960s to the 1980s, there were signs of convergence. Unfortunately, this trend has been reversed over the past decade, despite significant advancements in technologies of spatial interaction (Stiglitz and Greenwald, 2010).

Even as communication and transportation costs decreased rapidly in the nineteenth century, there was a significant "great divergence" in income levels. This suggests that the decline in costs alone does not guarantee convergence. To understand these dynamics, it is essential to examine the ways in which regional development contributes to lasting structural and compositional differences between economies.

One key question is why certain regions succeed in establishing high-performing economic systems while others struggle or experience decline. Traditional economic theories do not fully explain these processes. Neoclassical theories assume that successful behaviour emerges spontaneously from the broader economic and social context, while new growth theories focus on the accumulation of knowledge and its positive effects on the economy as a whole.

However, these theories overlook the concrete habits and relationships through which knowledge and expertise are created and utilised in economic activities. These relational assets, which are not easily reproduced from one place to another, play a crucial role in regional development. Understanding these relational assets and their contribution to economic action requires further exploration and analysis (Stiglitz, 2017).

In our previous discussion, we highlighted the significance of network membership and untraded interdependencies in regional development (Storper and Venables, 2002). Untraded interdependencies are strongly influenced by the local cultural context and are not easily transferable from successful to less successful regions. Agglomerations, which possess certain endogenous characteristics, also have a considerable impact on local development prospects.

Even in industries where best practices diffuse rapidly across countries, there are often uneven levels of productivity across space. This suggests that regional economic development involves a combination of exogenous constraints, the reorganisation and accumulation of local assets, and political mobilisation focused on institutions, socialisation, and social capital. The success of agglomerations in creating localised increasing returns effects, which depend on cultural and institutional foundations, is crucial to the overall development process (Akerlof and Shiller, 2015).

It is puzzling that these differences in productivity and development levels exist not only in industries with similar technologies and managerial practices but also in industries that tend to concentrate in large urban centres. This implies that there are significant endogenous determinants, both at the local and national levels, that influence the functioning of agglomerations and their contribution to economic development.

While increased trade, foreign investment, and technology diffusion have the potential to contribute to development, they do not automatically lead to productivity convergence (North and Thomas, 1973; Mokyr, 1985; Wade, 1990; Landes, 1998; Clark and Feenstra, 2003). Many of the endogenous conditions that underlie local economic development and facilitate integration into the global economy are cultural or institutional in nature. They involve the formation of routines and social structures that support economic activities.

It is important to note that joining the high-income convergence club and achieving sustained economic development in today's world requires countries to sustain successful agglomerated development processes. However, this does not diminish the significance of balanced and sustainable rural development as an essential component of overall development.

## 5.8 Regional Development Policies

The regional dimensions of development policy require careful consideration and cannot be equated with simple urbanisation or macroeconomics. Development policy should focus on cultivating the multiple benefits that arise from regionalised production systems and the complex intra- and inter-regional conditions that govern agglomeration (Akerlof and Shiller, 2015). Negative aspects of interregional competition must also be addressed to ensure smooth development.

Historically, regional development policies have often taken the form of stimulus packages aimed at specific localities to initiate growth or counter stagnation. These packages vary across countries but typically include industry subsidies, tax breaks, infrastructure provision, capital investment schemes, and labour retraining programs. However, these approaches, in isolation, neglect the critical organisational and institutional foundations necessary for regional growth and competitiveness (Stiglitz and Greenwald, 2014).

In recent decades, there has been a growing body of literature and practical experiments emphasising the importance of these foundations in regional development. Regional economies are interconnected through human and organisational interdependencies, often untraded, that generate positive externalities accessible to local firms but owned by none. These positive externalities manifest in various aspects of regional economic activity, such as information flows, learning processes, craft traditions, and business networks (Stiglitz and Greenwald, 2010).

These positive externalities form a "regional economic commons," representing elements of economic advantage that emerge from agglomeration but cannot be reduced to individual ownership and control. They contribute to overall regional success, particularly in a globalising economy. However, positive externalities are typically undersupplied in market relations, leading to suboptimal investment in critical social assets. Policy interventions are necessary to rectify this undersupply and address moral hazards that can generate negative externalities (Stiglitz and Greenwald, 2014).

Policy interventions can take various forms, including governmental agencies, civic associations, private-public partnerships, or other institutional arrangements based on local traditions and political sensibilities. While intervention is needed in regions at all levels of poverty or prosperity, it is most challenging in areas with significant deficits in physical and relational assets. This type of intervention differs from traditional urban policies focused on infrastructure, housing, transportation, and urban public finance. Instead, it emphasises the coordination of urban production systems and requires extensive social and political engagement to involve local stakeholders in public debates and collective decision-making (Stiglitz and Greenwald, 2014).

It is important to note that objections may arise regarding the level of government intervention, with some arguing that it is preferable to live with market failures than with policy interventions. Nonetheless, recognising the importance of regional economic commons and the need for coordinated development processes can lead to more effective and sustainable development policies.

Therefore, there are some challenges and risks associated with regional economic development and policy interventions. It points out that public agencies can make mistakes and encourage rent-seeking behaviour, which can hinder effective development. It emphasises the importance of sustaining a regional economic common that offers compensating returns to coordination, allowing for policy interventions that enhance the local economy (Akerlof and Shiller, 2015).

However, rising levels of local activism in regional economic development also introduce risks. These risks manifest as irrational development races, fiscal wars over subsidies and investments, talent and resource poaching between regions, and locational tournaments for large inward investments. Interregional competition for first-mover advantages, especially in emerging industries, can lead to misallocation of resources if not properly coordinated.

In pursuit of agglomeration economies, some analysts argue that development policy should focus on productivity improvements in dynamic agglomerations, even if it increases social tensions. Others suggest that limiting inequality through income redistribution can lead to more viable long-term development programs. These competing perspectives highlight the need for effective central/regional coordination and a more equitable spatial distribution of political power.

At different geographic scales, tensions over development disparities persist, including at the global scale in the context of intensified globalisation. The current regime of globalisation, influenced by the ideology of the Washington Consensus, may dilute central government policies that promote regional income equalisation. This, coupled with contractionary monetary and fiscal policies, can exacerbate interregional income divergence.

In light of these challenges, there is an argument for a consideration of the economic geography of globalisation and its regional foundations in the reorganisation of governance institutions. Achieving balanced responses to the competing claims of growth and equity remains crucial, even as spatial economic reorganisation necessitates rethinking the approaches to address them.

## 5.9 Conclusion

The opposition between decision-making and the flow of capital has been dissolved. We have also moved away from the self-centred perspective of the present that defines the "modern" as a uniquely significant era. To understand globalisation as the creation and reproduction of localised circumstances, we must emphasise historical explanations rather than a predetermined narrative. If we recognise that contemporary history has roots in the late nineteenth century, why did discussions of globalisation only gain prominence recently? After World War II, the Bretton Woods System was established to promote national economic growth.

However, the previous gold standard, which isolated economic decisions from national demands, had already become challenging to sustain due to democratic pressures before 1914. After World War II, the expectations and needs of populations made the revival of the gold standard impossible. The dismantling of Bretton Woods reduced systemic support for managing growth, but most core states maintained a post-war social contract focused on directing economic policies toward national growth and social welfare.

Even in countries like Britain and the United States, where Margaret Thatcher and Ronald Reagan advocated for the separation of politics and economics, state interventions and protections actually increased. This shift did not entail an impossible separation of public decisions from private wealth but rather aimed to free economic policies from popular pressures. The initial surge in globalisation literature emerged in this period, primarily in business and economics journals. While international capital movements, offshore production, and global trade had increased since Bretton Woods, they had not reached epochal levels that necessitated new terminology.

In this phase, the neoliberal rhetoric that abstracted economic and political spheres, giving prominence to the former's de-territorialised nature, became crucial for understanding "globalisation." The literature on globalisation experienced a temporary decline but saw a significant increase in works following the end of the Cold War. Economics was joined by extensive contributions from sociology and political science, solidifying globalisation as the dominant theme of our time.

The second phase of the globalisation discourse, which was more extensive than the first, emerged as a result of the ideological crisis following the collapse of the Soviet system. From 1914 onwards, the intense conflicts between competing social formations allowed states to articulate their economic priorities in terms of international politics. For corporate capitalism, communism, authoritarian regimes, and fascist nationalisms, the economy was seen as a means of mobilisation. It was not only viewed as a resource distribution system but also as a weapon. Even the neoliberal agenda, which strongly advocated for an autonomous economy, positioned itself in opposition to an ideology embodied by specific states, particularly the Soviet Union.

However, after the end of the Cold War, major powers could no longer justify state control over the economy in the context of large-scale conflicts. The political and economic tracks for these advanced capitalist states lost their parallel logic and signposts. Francis Fukuyama's influential book in 1992, "The End of History and the Last Man," marked not the end of ideology but rather the crisis faced by capitalism in terms of its ideological foundation within a political framework. The left fared better than neoliberals like Fukuyama, as figures such as Bill Clinton, Tony Blair, and proponents of the "third way" came to power, asserting the role of an efficient regulator for the state in capital reproduction.

While it is accurate to define "globalisation" as a neoliberal agenda, this characterisation only applies to the first phase of its discourse. The second phase has also encompassed the agendas of conservatives, third-way liberals, social democrats, Marxists, and cosmopolitans, each attempting to reclaim a political objective in response to this crisis and the opportunities it presents for ideological formation.

For the poor and the weak, wealth and borders serve as dividing lines, trapping billions in closed and inescapable worlds. On the other hand, the rich and powerful present the judicious reproduction of capital as the purpose of political community.

However, recent elections in the North Atlantic region, which have seen a shift away from third-way governments, indicate that this may not be sufficient. Additionally, the events of September 11, the subsequent "War on Terrorism," and the US-led war in Iraq have opened up the possibility of a new political objective. In October 2001, President Bush spoke from Travis Air Force Base in California, which is primarily responsible for providing rapid global mobility. He stated, "The terrorists attacked the World Trade Centre, and we will defeat them by expanding and encouraging world trade."

We should also consider the importance of considering economic geography in the context of development theory and policy, particularly in relation to agglomeration economies and regional dynamics. Conventional economic theories of development have often overlooked geographical factors. However, economists with an interest in agglomeration economies and regional dynamics are starting to rectify this neglect.

Agglomeration economies, characterised by externalities and increasing returns effects, play a significant role in the development process. They are seen as potent and immobile elements of economic organisation, akin to firms, sectors, and nations. Therefore, regions should be recognised as integral units of economic reality, and development theory should take this into account.

Thus, development theory has traditionally focused on macroeconomic variables as the primary approach to understanding development. However, it argues that this perspective alone is no longer sufficient and calls for a broader understanding that includes economic geography. The recognition of economic geography in development theory raises new questions at regional, national, and international scales. This Chapter aimed to move beyond traditional development theory and provide initial responses to the questions raised by considering the geographical aspects of the globalisation process.

We take this discussion further in the next Chapter as we discuss this matter by focusing on a faith-based economic thought that provides a different perspective to capitalism and socialism, and we also examine its critique. As you can see we are on a clear path in this journey to reach our destination in building our proposed economic theory, so stay with me on this journey and stay tuned.

[illegible] Conclusion

[illegible]

[illegible] Finally.

[illegible]

# Chapter 6
# The Rise of Religious Economics Model: Critiques of the Islamic Economics Doctrine

## 6.1 Introduction

In the previous Chapter, we critically discussed and questioned globalisation and its role in the economy. We examined how globalisation was oversold, with politicians and economists wrongly emphasising its benefits in terms of job creation, GDP growth, and overall positive impacts. While globalisation advocates a notion of universal economic identity, it overlooks other religious, cultural, and ideological systems that it may conflict with this notion. In this Chapter we discuss this matter by focusing on a faith-based economic thought that provides a different perspective to capitalism and socialism, and we examine its critique.

The rise of "Islamic economics," a doctrine rooted in Islamic scripture and traditions, has become a significant aspect of the broader movement known as "political Islam," "Islamic fundamentalism," or "Islamism" in the twentieth century. Although only a small minority of economists who follow the Muslim faith, referred to as "Islamic economists," embrace this doctrine, its social impact cannot be ignored.

Islamic economics aims to establish an economic system aligned with Islamic principles and has its foundations formed in the 1940s. By the 1970s, numerous countries had begun implementing these principles, such as the establishment of centralised Islamic redistribution systems called zakat in Pakistan, Malaysia, and elsewhere. Over 60 countries now possess Islamic banks that claim to offer interest-free alternatives to conventional banking. Some countries, including Pakistan and Iran, have even prohibited all forms of interest, mandating banks, including foreign subsidiaries, to adopt ostensibly Islamic methods of deposit taking and loan making (Chapra, 1992). Efforts are also underway to apply religious norms to price setting, bargaining, and wage determination. Furthermore, numerous other initiatives are being considered.



S. Alamad, *Beyond Profit*, Contributions to Economics,
https://doi.org/10.1007/978-3-031-49748-3_6

While these developments may suggest that Islamic economics arose as an economic agenda, its origins can be traced back to late-colonial India as a means of creating and safeguarding a distinct Muslim identity. Initially, the economic aspects of Islamic economics were secondary to its Islamic character. The objective here is to examine and substantiate this claim.

Limited research exists regarding the origins of Islamic economics, likely due to the doctrine's rhetoric. Islamic economics asserts that it reflects the unchanging and eternal teachings of Islam, which may discourage inquiries into its origins, as if probing its origins were akin to investigating the origins of Islam itself. According to this perspective, Islamic economics has existed since the dawn of Islam, with modern Islamic economists merely rediscovering forgotten teachings. However, this view is flawed. Some economic ideas and practices categorised as inherently Islamic are relatively new inventions, while others have only recently acquired religious significance. Additionally, the concept of Islamic economics itself emerged in the twentieth century. Consequently, the reasons for the doctrine's existence and its subsequent development of Islamic norms, banks, and redistribution systems are far from obvious.

Furthermore, the Islamic world's overall economic development, in comparison to Europe and North America, is relatively low, creating a perplexing situation. It is not immediately evident why Muslims, regardless of their devoutness, would turn to Islam for economic solutions. Granted, Islam's heritage offers principles, policies, and practices that can be applied to modern economic problems, and during the early centuries of the religion, lands ruled by Muslims experienced notable economic progress. However, if these undisputed facts are the justification and explanation for Islamic economics, why did the doctrine not emerge earlier? If the answer lies in the persistent underdevelopment of the Islamic world, which has prompted a search for alternative economic programs, it is worth noting that the Islamic world's economic prime occurred nearly a millennium ago. The need for economic reforms has been apparent for centuries, yet Islamic economics is a relatively recent phenomenon, spanning only a few decades.

## 6.2 The Case for Cultural Separatism

The emergence of Islamic economics in late colonial India was driven by a larger campaign to safeguard the religious identity and traditional culture of the country's substantial Muslim minority, which constituted over a fifth of the total population. During the 1930s, as demands for Indian independence grew, an increasing number of Muslims began to fear that a Hindu-dominated India would subject them to hostility and discrimination. These concerns were exacerbated by the mounting indebtedness of Muslim farmers, who were mainly indebted to Hindu moneylenders willing to seize the lands of defaulters. While the British had set up safeguards against expropriation, there was uncertainty about whether a Hindu-led government would uphold these protections. In response to these anxieties, certain Muslim leaders began advocating that Indian Muslims constituted a separate nation entitled to their own state, leading to the birth of the idea of Pakistan, which eventually became a reality within 15 years.

However, there were Muslim figures who opposed the idea of a separate state, arguing instead for cultural autonomy. They believed that Muslims needed cultural autonomy rather than political independence, and they viewed these two objectives as incompatible. One notable leader among them was Sayyid Abu'l-A'la Mawdudi (1903–1979), the founder of Jama'at-i Islami (Party of Islam), first in India and then in Pakistan. Mawdudi objected to the idea of a national homeland for Indian Muslims, asserting that they were a "brotherhood" entrusted with "a comprehensive system of life to offer the world." He argued that if Muslims practiced Islam faithfully, the question of a national homeland would become irrelevant (Brohi, 1990).

He acknowledged the threats faced by Indian Islam but believed that cultural reassertion, rather than political separation, was the preferred solution. He advocated for his community to turn inward and revive the traditions that had once brought them power, glory, and prosperity. As part of this revival, he promoted the concept of Islamic economics. It is unclear who initially introduced this concept into the discourse of Indo-Islamic society, but it gained popularity through Mawdudi's sermons, speeches, and publications. Alongside "Islamic economics," Mawdudi coined or popularised other terms that became essential components of Islamist discourse, including "Islamic ideology," "Islamic politics," "Islamic constitution," and "Islamic way of life." (Mawdudi, 1963).

In his extensive writings, Mawdudi (1963) argued that for India's Muslims to survive as a community, they needed to consider Islam not only as a system of faith and worship but as their complete way of life. He asserted that "true Muslims" merged their personalities and existences into Islam, subordinating all their roles to the one role of being Muslims. They lived as Muslims in all aspects of life, whether as fathers, sons, husbands or wives, businessmen, landlords, laborers, or employers. Mawdudi noted that while a minority of Muslims were fully immersed in Islam, allowing religion to control every aspect of their lives, the majority barely practiced their religion. He described them as believing in Allah, offering prayers, and partially abstaining from forbidden actions.

However, beyond these limited domains, their lives lacked religious influence and were driven solely by personal considerations and self-interest in their preferences, daily transactions, business activities, and social relationships. Mawdudi (1963) argued that this group of "partial Muslims" had not achieved anything significant. On the contrary, by relegating Islam to the private sphere, they had weakened the Muslim community and facilitated the rise of "infidels." He believed that their limited adherence to Islamic norms posed a greater danger to Indian Islam than the impending transfer of political power to the Hindus. Moreover, he warned that even within an Islamic polity like Pakistan, a Muslim community could lose its religious identity. Mawdudi feared that the creation of Pakistan would give its citizens a false sense of communal safety, further diminishing Islam's relevance in their daily lives.

Mawdudi and his associates were convinced by this reasoning that the Muslim nationalists' proposed solution to the problem was misguided. While the nationalists sought territorial partition for political independence, Mawdudi believed that cultural reassertion was necessary to ensure religious survival. To revitalise their culture, Muslims needed to consistently display their religiosity in public. They had to be conscious of how their behaviours differed from non-Muslims in every aspect of their activities, making it clear that they were Muslims. Economic activities, being carried out outside the home, had the potential to enhance the visibility of Islam. For instance, if Muslim traders followed Islamic contracting procedures and Muslim consumers made distinctly Islamic choices, Islam would become more prominent, creating an environment where Islam appeared highly relevant to everyday decision-making. Mawdudi emphasised the growing significance of economics as a reason for Muslims to maintain their economic behaviours in accordance with Islamic principles. He observed that economic problems had become a dominant subject of discussion and scientific research, seemingly overshadowing other aspects of human affairs (Mawdudi, 1963).

Mawdudi's focus on bringing economics under the purview of religion was crucial to his broader objective of defining a self-contained Islamic order. Regardless of one's opinion on his agenda, he accurately recognised that with technological progress, economics was becoming increasingly significant in daily life worldwide. In a technologically primitive and static society, where one's career is determined by family background, traditional agricultural practices are followed, and non-subsistence goods are scarce, economic decision-making does not require much attention (Mawdudi, 1990). However, in a technologically advanced world, where individuals make career choices, women pursue careers outside the home, investment decisions require monitoring, and markets offer abundant options, economic decision-making consumes a considerable amount of time. Consequently, if economic choices are viewed as secular activities, economic advancements will make Muslim existence appear increasingly secular. On the other hand, if economic choices are regarded as religious activities, economic development does not have to diminish the perceived role of Islam in the lives of Muslims (Mawdudi, 1978).

## 6.3 Western Influence and the Economic-Political Disunity

The Muslim nationalists failed to recognise the dangers identified by Mawdudi, according to his explanation. He attributed this to the fact that many of them had received education in colleges like Aligarh University, which were specifically established to provide Muslims with Western knowledge. These nationalists had been influenced to think like Westerners, leading them to attempt to reshape Islam in the image of irreligious Western materialism. Mawdudi argued that the ideology of "Muslim nationalism" was inherently contradictory (Mawdudi, 1950). He questioned how nationalism could be compatible with a universal religion that transcends local identities. He even went as far as to claim that the envisioned state, Pakistan, would be "pagan," and its leaders would be like "Pharaohs and Nimrods." However, once Pakistan became a reality, Mawdudi accepted the new situation and expanded his mission to include making the state itself Islamic. He distinguished between a "Muslim state," in which the majority of citizens happened to be Muslim, and an "Islamic state," which adhered to Islamic principles. He then began to fight against what he considered Western influences on Pakistan's social, economic, and political systems (Mawdudi, 1960).

Over time, Mawdudi's anti-Western rhetoric became less strident, and his positions became more nuanced. However, during the time of India's partition, his main concern was the impact of the West, referring to the civilisation comprising Western Europe, North America, and its cultural offshoots elsewhere. He observed that an increasing number of Muslims were adopting Western literature, customs, sports, and attire, considering Western culture superior to their own. They were evaluating Islam based on Western criteria instead of judging the West by Islamic criteria. This led to a sense of superiority among some Muslims, creating a division within the Muslim community between those perceived as modern and progressive and those seen as traditional and backward. Furthermore, English literacy became a prerequisite for civil service jobs, further accentuating the communal division (Nasr, 1996).

Mawdudi attributed the splitting of the Muslim community not only to his fellow Muslims who viewed Westernisation as a means of personal advancement but also to the West itself. He believed that the West, with its recent material advancements, aimed to diminish Muslim achievements, making them appear unimpressive. Some Western statesmen and intellectuals openly expressed their disdain for non-Western cultures, particularly singling out Islam as uncivilised and irrational. Duncan Black Macdonald, an Islamicist, had stated that the essential difference in the Oriental mind was an inability to construct a system concerning observable things, leading them to ignore incompatible elements. Macdonald believed that Muslims would have to abandon Islam to make peace with the twentieth century and approved of efforts to limit Islam's social role. He praised the Young Turks of the Ottoman Empire for their willingness to assimilate the civilisation of Christendom and modernise Islam, even if it meant Islam had to yield in certain areas (Naqvi, 1994).

Indeed, contemporary perspectives consider such statements as crude and simplistic. However, during the pre-partition era in India, they were prevalent. Edward Said's polemic against Orientalism (1978) highlights how such views were commonplace at that time. For Mawdudi and his followers, these statements served as evidence that Westernised Muslims had aligned themselves with a new crusade against Islam. Khurshid Ahmad, a member of Mawdudi's inner circle and a later prominent contributor to Islamic economics, refers to Lord Macaulay, a British statesman, who stated the need to create a class of individuals who would act as intermediaries between the British rulers and the Indian population. These individuals were expected to be Indian in blood and colour but English in taste, opinion, morals, and intellect. The implication was clear: Islam had to be defended against such influences (Mawdudi, 1963).

## 6.4 Rationalising the Separation Notion

Mawdudi's upbringing in a family suspicious of modern knowledge and his lack of formal Western education likely contributed to his apprehensions about the West. This led him to overlook the diversity within the West and equate Western cultural expansionism with the West as a whole. Despite his motivations and perceptions, he was correct in noting that increasing contact with the West was causing many of India's Muslims to reject their own heritage (Mawdudi, 1976a, b). During that time, the majority of India's Muslims were illiterate, with only 6.4% of those aged five or above being able to read according to the 1931 census. The educated minority often attended traditional schools that focused on religion and avoided modern science. The community was largely impoverished and had disproportionately few major entrepreneurs. Dissatisfied with these circumstances, ambitious Muslims, like many non-Muslims in India and around the world, realised that adopting new technologies and developing new mindsets were key to prosperity (Mawdudi, 1950).

Mawdudi was also correct in observing that India's Muslims lagged behind other major groups in making the necessary adaptations. In 1931, only 0.9% of Muslims aged five or above were literate in English, compared to 1.2% of the entire Indian population. Furthermore, two decades earlier, only 1.3% of Muslims were in professions requiring education beyond elementary level, compared to 1.5% of the total population. This discrepancy is particularly noteworthy as the advanced professions were primarily urban, giving Muslims, who were more urbanised than the general population, an advantage in entry. These patterns were influenced by two historical factors: Indian Islam drew its followers mostly from the lower end of the caste system, and Muslims were overrepresented among artisans whose skills became less valuable with industrialisation (Mawdudi, 1990).

Lastly, Mawdudi's belief that Westernisation weakened the influence of religion on personal worldviews and interpersonal relationships was justified. His writings foreshadowed Luckmann (1967) concept of "religious privatisation," which argues that as Western religion became confined to private domains, it exerted less control over individual religiosity and lifestyles. In Europe and North America, adherents of religious denominations had increasing discretion in practicing their religion. Attendance at religious services became more flexible, and diversity within denominations became more accepted. Consequently, religion lost some of its significance in determining marriage, residential choice, and employment. Based on the ongoing evolution of the West, Mawdudi reasonably predicted that the Westernisation of India's Muslim community would weaken the control of official Islam over the beliefs and behaviours of individual Muslims. He also anticipated that the practice of Indian Islam would become more diverse, although his rhetoric may have exaggerated the extent of these effects.

Mawdudi's proposed response to reverse Islamic privatisation and promote religiosity in public settings was rooted in a universal principle of group solidarity. Movements aimed at preserving or rebuilding group solidarity often emphasise visible markers of group identity, which limit interactions across group boundaries and foster a sense of belonging among group members. This can be seen in religious sects referred to as cults, where strict behavioural codes are imposed on members, making them distinct from non-members and strengthening their bond with each other (Nasr, 1996).

In late-colonial India, Mawdudi was not the first to advocate for Islamic norms to cultivate Muslim solidarity. Muslim nationalists had already encouraged Muslims to differentiate themselves by wearing the "Jinnah cap," in response to Hindu identification with the "Gandhi cap." Enforcing Islamic behaviours was not a departure from Islamic history either. Traditionally, Islam placed greater emphasis on orthopraxy (behavioural correctness) rather than orthodoxy (doctrinal correctness). For example, the regular recitation of sacred texts was considered more important than understanding their meaning. Even in non-Arab lands, the call to prayer and the prayers themselves were predominantly in Arabic, a language not widely understood. Notably, there is no equivalent term for "orthodox" in major Islamic languages, and the term "Sunni," which refers to the largest branch of Islam, means orthoprax. In Islam, being a good Muslim is typically determined by observable behaviours rather than adherence to a specific doctrine, as seen in Protestant Christianity. The Islamic concept of heresy is often defined as "behavioural nonconformism" rather than doctrinal deviation (Naqvi, 1994).

The uniqueness of Mawdudi's program lay not in emphasising Islamic orthopraxy, but in updating its content to address new challenges. He sought to redefine Islamic orthopraxy in response to the irreversible and universal effects of Europe's Enlightenment and Industrial Revolution. His goal was to enable certain adaptations while preserving communal identity. Recognising the centrality of economic change in modernisation, Mawdudi believed that Muslims needed to learn how to make economic adjustments in a distinctly Islamic manner to avoid a loss of identity. He saw the development of Islamic economics as a pressing challenge, as it would specify the economic components of a new Islamic orthopraxy. While Mawdudi presented this agenda as a return to Islam, it can be seen as a manifestation of Westernisation. The discipline of economics originated in Europe, and it was not previously a distinct field of knowledge within the Islamic intellectual heritage. Muslim economic thought, as a separate branch of discourse, only emerged more recently under Western influence.

The emergence of Islamic economics as a distinct concept is notable when examining the intellectual trajectory of Mohammad Iqbal, a prominent poet-philosopher in India before Mawdudi's time. In 1902, Iqbal (1964) published a book titled "Ilmul Iqtesad" (Science of Economics), which, given his later evolution towards Islamism, is strikingly secular in nature. A few years later, after embracing Islamism, Iqbal no longer considered economics as a key instrument of change. However, he did recognise the economic backwardness of the Islamic world. In 1909, he lamented the deterioration among Indian Muslims, noting the pale and faded faces of Muslim boys in schools and colleges. His proposed solution to this crisis of underdevelopment, however, did not include an economic dimension. He urged Muslims to revive their traditions that had brought glory and prosperity to their ancestors and to refrain from imitating Hindus.

From Iqbal's perspective, it may be inferred that the solution to economic matters lay in rediscovering old Islamic principles. Nevertheless, the concept of a specifically Islamic form of economics was absent from his work. Notably, major bibliographies of Islamic economics do not list any of Iqbal's writings. This lack of interest in developing an Islamic form of economics was shared by other influential figures who made significant contributions to Islamic thought in the decades preceding Mawdudi's emergence. Prominent activists such as Muhammad Abduh, Jamal ad-Din al-Afghani, and Sayyid Ahmad Khan, whose speeches and writings are well-known, show no interest in Islamising economics.

Furthermore, the development of Islamic economics was not a goal of pan-Islamism, an international movement that sought to unite Muslims worldwide under a common banner. Pan-Islamists were primarily concerned with resisting European military advances and protecting Muslim holy sites. While a few pan-Islamists expressed concerns about economic exploitation and favoured economic resistance against non-Muslim rulers, the notion of identifying or rediscovering distinctly Islamic economic practices was absent from their campaigns. The cultivation of an economic doctrine grounded in Islamic teachings was also non-existent within the pan-Islamist movement.

While the Muslim activists of the late-nineteenth and early twentieth centuries did not prioritise the development of Islamic economics, their calls for a return to Islam laid the groundwork for Mawdudi's initiatives. Their diverse interpretations of what it meant to return to Islam prepared the masses for Mawdudi's broader campaign of Islamisation. Mawdudi's argument that Islam is a comprehensive way of life was not a new concept, but what set him apart was his serious consideration of its concrete implications (Mawdudi, 1963).

During Mawdudi's time, a significant number of Muslims in India and beyond were acutely aware of the Islamic world's political powerlessness and economic backwardness compared to the West. They formulated various responses, some of which were diametrically opposed to Islamisation. One response was secularist modernism, which accepted the advantages of Western civilisation and sought to privatise Islam akin to unobtrusive Protestant Christianity, aiming to align with the West. This approach became the official policy in modern Turkey under its first two presidents, Ataturk and Inonu. The post-Ottoman regime aimed to import Western civilisation entirely and marginalised Islam, shifting Turks' primary loyalty from religion to nation (Shaban, 1971).

Another response, Muslim modernism, exemplified by the movement for Pakistan, pursued Westernisation without perceiving any conflict with the promotion of an Islamic identity. It identified Islamic precedents for reforms designed to meet secular goals. While secularist modernism essentially rejected the sanctity of Islamic scripture, Muslim modernism paid lip service to the comprehensive wisdom of Islam, pretending that it was the ultimate source of authority. The difference between them lies in stylistic and tactical choices, rather than substance. Both types of movements may adopt policies such as import restrictions, justifying them through either secular theories of economic development or a more vague religious rationale (Macdonald, 1971).

By contrast, two other responses staunchly opposed Westernisation and regarded Islam as the primary source of wisdom. The more extreme variant, conservative Islamism, rejected Western civilisation and adhered to familiar cultural forms without seeking change. By Mawdudi's time, conservative Islamism was more popular among the masses and low-level religious functionaries than among religious leaders of his stature. Mawdudi's response, referred to as reformist Islamism, aimed for a religious revival that promotes modernisation without Westernisation. He recognised the urgency to creatively address the Western challenge and insisted that reforms must have an Islamic character. He rejected pursuing reforms to appease global opinion and focused on Islam as the guiding force for change (Malik, 1996).

## 6.5 Causes of Divisions

Mawdudi claimed to speak on behalf of all Muslims, except for those he deemed "partial Muslims" who had received a Western education. However, he never had the support of a majority of India's Muslims, let alone widespread support from Muslims outside of India. As we have seen, Muslims responded to the Western challenge in diverse ways. This variation can be attributed to differences in upbringing, education, and exposure to different cultures. Those with traditional backgrounds faced disadvantages in a Westernising society, while individuals with Western education and contacts had certain privileges. Additionally, some individuals had a vested interest in preserving traditional patterns of authority, fearing a shift of power to modern professionals in a Westernised society (Lewis, 1993).

Another factor contributing to the variation in responses was individuals' capacity to navigate cultural clashes and reconcile elements from different cultures. People differ in their ability to synthesise cultural elements or compartmentalise conflicting cultural demands. For example, fasting during Ramadan may pose challenges for productivity in certain professions, leading individuals to feel torn between fulfilling religious obligations and professional duties. Such individuals may be more receptive to responses that involve choosing one culture over the other (Lewis, 1993).

Mawdudi recognised the inner conflicts experienced by many Muslims, torn between Eastern and Western influences, tradition, and adaptation. He believed that controlling the influence of the West would alleviate these tensions. His agenda aimed to provide distinctly Islamic alternatives to behaviours that Muslims perceived as Western. By infusing work with religious significance and perceiving work and worship as interconnected, Mawdudi sought to create a unified Muslim identity, free from cognitive and moral dualism. In this aspect, Mawdudi's agenda shared similarities with the secularist modernist approach, both seeking to discard certain cultural influences to prevent dualistic thinking. Furthermore, Mawdudi's approach to Islamisation through an updated Islamic orthopraxy paralleled the secularist campaign to weaken Islamic culture by promoting the adoption of Western appearances and lifestyles (Lewis, 1975).

The headgear law introduced in Turkey in 1925, which mandated the abandonment of the fez in favour of Western headgear, was part of a broader cultural reconstruction effort. While it may appear insignificant or even comical, the law held great significance at the time. Dress, particularly headgear, served as a visible symbol through which Muslims expressed their allegiance to the Islamic community and their rejection of Western influence. By adopting Western appearance, a Turk would publicly identify with the West and remove a prominent symbol of their Islamic heritage. Similar visibility-focused reforms were also carried out in Iran under Reza Shah Pahlavi during the 1920s and 1930s, aiming to showcase Iran's Westernisation (Mardin, 1993).

Mawdudi's agenda, like these Westernisation campaigns, recognised that the coexistence of Western and Islamic cultural influences created personal tensions and social instability. The difference lay in their chosen approach to resolving this tension. Both secularists and reformist Islamists were aware of past reforms that had resulted in mental dualism, such as the educational reforms of the mid-nineteenth century. During that time, rulers in Egypt and the Ottoman Empire sought to provide Muslims with the benefits of Western education while preserving the traditional educational system. This led to a split in knowledge and values among educated Muslims, with one side emphasising the centrality of Islam and traditional values, while the other side embraced European Enlightenment values such as freedom and progress.

The avoidance of mental dualism required a unified system of education within a unified culture. However, there were different approaches to achieving this unity. Turkey under Ataturk and Iran under Reza Shah pursued one strategy, while Mawdudi and other reformist Islamists sought an alternative path towards unification.

## 6.6 The Concept of One Nation

Mawdudi, similar to secular modernists like Ataturk and Reza Shah, aimed to foster a strong sense of historical and emotional attachment to a particular civilisation. However, while Ataturk and Reza Shah sought to enhance identification with the West and distance their people from the broader Islamic world, Mawdudi emphasised the notion of the universal Muslim community, the umma, as the primary source of identity and loyalty for individual Muslims. According to Mawdudi, the umma transcends tribal, national, regional, and local ties, operating based on traditional principles of Islamic solidarity (Lewis, 1993).

To strengthen awareness of the umma, Mawdudi emphasised the similarities and historical bonds among the world's Muslim peoples, downplaying their cultural, linguistic, historical, and political differences. He portrayed such distinctions as insignificant and suggested that they would lose significance or dissolve if Muslims were to restore the vitality of the umma. In his historical writings, Muslim diversity and discord were seen as exceptions, while what was similar among different regions was deemed authentic and important because it was Islamic. Harmony among Muslims was considered natural, while disharmony was viewed as a sign of deviation from Islamic principles (Mawdudi, 1963).

However, Mawdudi's concept of the umma was not based on ongoing and observable interactions among its members who personally knew each other. It was an "imagined community" in the sense that most members would have limited personal connections within the vast umma. Furthermore, the concept contradicted prevailing social realities. Economic relations among Muslim nations were minimal, as they primarily traded with Europe, and many Muslims identified strongly with smaller ethnically, linguistically, and regionally defined communities rather than the Islamic umma (Lewis, 1993). Even among those who sought to invigorate the Islamic umma, there were significant differences in interpretation, tactics, and strategy. The differences among regionally separated Muslims were often not minor, and they often upheld hereditary caste divisions similar to Hindus rather than subscribing to the principle of innate equality found among some Muslim and Christian Arabs (Jalal, 1995).

Indeed, Mawdudi's vision of strengthening the Islamic umma did not account for the technological advancements that were shrinking distances and facilitating increased contact between geographically distant Muslims. While improved transportation and communication could potentially enhance the unity and homogeneity of the umma, they also exposed Muslims to non-Muslim influences, making the desired isolation of the umma increasingly challenging to achieve. As Muslim and non-Muslim lifestyles converged, individual Muslims would find it easier to develop loyalties that crossed civilisational boundaries.

However, addressing these technological challenges would have complicated Mawdudi's message and potentially weakened its appeal. His political mission required him to present the forces of globalisation as controllable and to emphasise the importance of preserving and strengthening the communal identity of Muslims. The Jama'at-i Islami sought to define what behaviours were considered properly Islamic by updating the norms of Islamic orthopraxy, with Islamic economics being one of the outcomes of their efforts. They also advocated for increased interactions and affinities among members of the global Muslim community, while minimising relations with outsiders (Lewis, 1993).

Mawdudi (1963) vision focused on preserving and enhancing the distinct Islamic identity in the face of global influences, while downplaying the challenges posed by advancing technology and the convergence of cultures. You are correct to argue that the issue of group identity is not unique to Islam, and every society experiences individuals with confused identities and movements seeking to define and strengthen group boundaries. Cohesive groups offer familiarity, trust, easy communication, and emotional comfort, which can create a natural constituency for activists promoting identity-related agendas. In pre-partition India, both the Jama'at-i Islami and the Muslim League emerged as significant political players because they addressed concerns related to group identity in different ways.

While identity construction played a role in their appeal, individual political commitments are driven by a range of motives that go beyond identity. In the case of Mawdudi and the Jama'at-i Islami, their early works sought to establish that Islamic solidarity and uniformity would bring material benefits to Muslims, along with security of identity. However, unlike the communist movements that relied heavily on theoretical frameworks, Mawdudi and his followers did not provide an elaborate theory to support their claim that Muslims would fare better within a segregated Islamic umma compared to a multi-religious society (Haneef, 1995).

Instead, Mawdudi's persuasive strategy relied on presenting the "Golden Age" of Islam, the period of the Prophet Muhammad's leadership and the early caliphs, as evidence of the benefits of Islam. He portrayed this era as one of efficiency, justice, cooperation, and self-sacrifice, emphasising its superiority over the preceding era of ignorance (*jahiliya*). Mawdudi argued that subsequent attempts at Islamic renewal had been limited in scope and had not produced a comprehensive ideological movement that encompassed all aspects of life. He positioned his own mission as a fresh attempt at Islamic renewal, claiming that its comprehensiveness would make it more successful than previous efforts (Macdonald, 1965).

Mawdudi and the Jama'at-i Islami appealed to the evidence of Islam's Golden Age and the perceived shortcomings of subsequent periods to convince their audience of the material advantages and superiority of Islamic solidarity. While they did not provide an elaborate theoretical framework, they presented historical examples and emphasised the need for a comprehensive Islamic movement to achieve lasting success.

There is an important point regarding the framing of historical references to elicit a sense of loss and generate support for a particular agenda. Cognitive psychologists have found that losses tend to have a greater impact on individuals than equivalent gains, leading people to be more responsive to promises of improvement when framed as eliminating a loss. Reformers often use historical reference points that make changes look like degeneration to emphasise the need for change and appeal to people's emotions (Luckmann, 1967).

Mawdudi employed this tactic by focusing on the Golden Age of Islam, a period revered by Muslims, to foster a sense of loss and highlight the alleged degeneration of Islamic society under "un-Islamic" influences. While the accuracy of his interpretation of Islamic history can be questioned, his vision of the Golden Age resonated with his audience and was easily communicated because it had long been part of Islamic discourse.

It is true that the early period of Islam was characterised by harsh living conditions, and the early Islamic community faced internal conflicts and disagreements. The historical accuracy of Mawdudi's depiction of the Golden Age can be debated, but it served his purpose of attributing the problems faced by Muslims to the perceived degeneration of Islamic society. Accuracy about early Islamic history may have been less important to Mawdudi than the persuasive power of framing history in a way that supported his argument (Kuran, 1993).

Furthermore, the histories of various Muslim peoples include periods of economic growth, scientific achievements, and artistic flourishing, such as the Abbasid Caliphate, Muslim Spain, Safavid Iran, the Ottoman Empire, and Mughal India. However, these periods did not receive much attention in Mawdudi's writings because they conflicted with his thesis. Invoking the glories of these cosmopolitan states would have undermined his argument that Muslims thrive best when they retreat into their own communal shells. It would also challenge the notion of the Golden Age's alleged perfection, as these later periods represented sustained improvements (Kuran, 1989).

Mawdudi's selective use of historical references and his focus on the Golden Age of Islam served to evoke a sense of loss and reinforce his argument for the need to withdraw into a distinct Islamic identity. Accuracy in historical representation may have been sacrificed in favour of a persuasive narrative that supported his ideological goals.

## 6.7 A Question of Conflicts of Civilisations

The campaign by Jama'at-i Islami to isolate Muslims from non-Muslim influences aligns with Huntington (1996) thesis on the clash of civilisations, which posits that the primary source of global conflict is the interaction between the West and non-Western civilisations. According to Mawdudi (1978) and his companions, Islam and the West were seen as incompatible, locked in a battle for the loyalty and identity of Muslims.

However, Huntington (1996) thesis has been criticised for overlooking the homogenising effect of economic development and people's receptivity to cross-cultural influences. Urbanisation, industrialisation, and modern education have contributed to the convergence of non-Western and Western lifestyles, even as cultural resistance movements emerge in response to the disruptive nature of these transformations. The movement led by Jama'at-i Islami was rooted in the belief that Islamic civilisation would lose its distinctive features without active efforts to counteract non-Muslim influences.

Another criticism of Huntington (1996) thesis is the difficulty in defining civilisations. Boundaries between civilisations can be arbitrary, and each civilisation encompasses significant diversity within it. Yet cultural protectionists often act as if civilisations are well-defined entities. Mawdudi, for instance, disregarded the diversity of aspirations among individual Muslims. Despite the vast differences in lifestyles and circumstances of Muslims in different regions, he claimed to speak for all Muslims. Defining who is a Muslim itself presents challenges, as evidenced by debates among religious leaders regarding the criteria for being considered Muslim (Kuran, 1986).

While there are parallels between the ideas of Jama'at-i Islami and Samuel Huntington (1996) clash of civilisations thesis, criticisms of the thesis highlight the complex nature of cultural interactions, the influence of economic development, and the challenges in defining and representing civilisations and their diverse populations.

The belief in civilisational conflict and the clash between Islam and the West is not limited to a Eurocentric perspective. The Jama'at-i Islami and other Islamic movements embrace the conviction that Islam is engaged in a war of civilisations. This notion is evident in the early contributions to Islamic economics, including those by Sayyid Qutb and Muhammad Baqir al-Sadr.

Qutb (1970), influenced by Mawdudi, portrayed Islam as a self-sufficient system that does not seek to imitate or align with other systems. However, even in his writings, Western influences are discernible, with concepts such as full employment and social justice being twisted to fit within an Islamic framework. Qutb's interpretations supported the idea of Islam offering a comprehensive system in conflict with the West (Heyworth-Dunne, 1939).

Similarly, al-Sadr's (1961) work, "Iqtisaduna: Our Economics," extends Mawdudi's comparison between the Islamic economic system and its main rivals, capitalism, and socialism. Al-Sadr sought to demonstrate Islam's superiority over socialism, which was gaining popularity in the Arab world at the time (Mallat, 1993). He emphasised Islam's role in providing an alternative to the dominant economic ideologies (Rahnema and Nomani, 1990).

The Iranian Revolution of 1978–79, led by Ayatollah Khomeini (1985), was driven by the goal of restoring Islam's central role in society. While economic concerns were present, Khomeini prioritised the restoration of group identity, social cohesion, and moral guidance through Islam. He believed that both communism and the West posed threats to Islam and had already influenced many Muslims. Thus, the revolution encompassed a broader challenge beyond economic direction.[1]

These examples illustrate the prominence of the theme of civilisational conflict in Islamic movements and the use of Islamic economics as a means of resistance and asserting the distinctiveness of Islam in the face of Western ideologies.

The concept of a clash of civilisations, as perceived by many Muslims including Islamists and secularists, is not without merit. They see Islam and the West engaged in a struggle for influence and dominance over Muslims. This perception has existed for decades, and the term "clash of civilisations" confirms what they have already believed. Islamists consider it a defence of their cultural identity, while secularists view it as a clash between contrasting cultural models.

Economics has indeed become one of the battlegrounds in this civilisational struggle. Some Muslims perceive Western economic thought, policies, and

---

[1] Recent expositions include Chapra (1992) and Naqvi (1994). For critiques of the literature, see Behdad (1989, 1994), Kuran (1986, 1989, 1993) and Haneef (1995).

For critical overviews of the practice of Islamic economics, see (Rahnema and Nomani, 1990; Kuran, 1993, 1995; Richards and Waterbury, 1996, Ch. 14; Malik, 1996, Chaps. 3–4).

The fears were not baseless. Some Hindu politicians envisioned a centralised Hindu raj, and they considered the terms "Hindu" and "Indian" as synonymous. Moreover, certain Hindu-dominated local governments had treated Muslims as undesirable aliens. (See Aziz, 1967, esp. Chaps. 2–3). As tensions between Muslims and Hindus mounted, certain leaders on both sides fanned hostilities by reviving memories of old grievances.

For examples of Mawdudi's writings and addresses published in prepartition India, see Jihad in Islam ([1939], 1976), Let Us Be Muslims ([1940], 1990), Islam and Ignorance ([1941] 1976), and Islamic Way of Life ([1948], 1950). Scholarly analyses of Mawdudi's thought include: (Nasr, 1996; Aziz, 1967; Lerman, 1981; Binder, 1961, pt. 1).

institutions as a threat to their cultural identity, while others are concerned about efforts to give economics an Islamic character. The advent of Islamic banking, for example, has been seen by some as part of a larger scheme to promote Islamic fundamentalism and establish a regressive political union (Denny, 1989).

It is important to note that not all Westerners or Muslims are actively engaged in this civilisational clash. However, if a substantial number of participants define the conflict in civilisational terms, then the evidence suggests the existence of a longstanding struggle. Economics plays a role in this clash, reflecting the concerns of those who view Western economic influence as a threat and those who seek to give economics an Islamic framework (Hodgson, 1974).

While contemporary Muslims have been receptive to Western technologies and products, the clash of civilisations can also be understood as the difficulty individuals face in synthesising or selecting among the various civilisations they encounter. Muslims have embraced modern science and technology, and there is no inherent incompatibility between Islam and modernisation when examining production and consumption patterns.

The clash of civilisations is a perception held by many Muslims, and economics has become a contested battleground in this struggle for cultural identity and influence. However, it is important to recognise that not all individuals are actively involved, and Muslims have demonstrated their ability to adopt modern technologies and participate in the global economy. Hechter (1987) makes an important point about the psychological and emotional aspects of cross-civilisational diffusion in production and consumption. Even if individuals voluntarily choose certain products or lifestyles, they may still experience distress, guilt, or a sense of cultural displacement. This human response is natural when individuals perceive a clash between their own cultural values and the influences they are exposed to.

Islamist discourse often highlights this distress, emphasising the challenges and conflicts that pious Muslims face in navigating modernity. The term "Westoxification" coined by Jalal Ale Ahmad in Iran reflects the social alienation he perceived as a result of contact with the West (Behdad, 1994). Similarly, Turkish Islamists argue that Western civilisation has created a consumer culture that breeds perpetual dissatisfaction and leads to a sense of spiritual disconnection. They believe that believers struggle to uphold their Islamic values amidst the temptations of material wealth and increased consumption, causing distress when they feel they are not living a truly Islamic life (Kuran, 1997).

These concerns were also expressed by early opponents of Turkish Westernisation, such as poet Necip Fazil Kisakurek, who felt culturally displaced and rediscovered Islam as a means to find authenticity and meaning in life (Kuran, 1993).

In this context, the notion of a clash of civilisations is consistent with the rapid diffusion of new technologies and goods. The exposure to different cultures and influences can heighten the perceived clash, as individuals grapple with the conflicts between their own cultural values and the external forces shaping their lives. The diffusion of new technologies and goods can be seen as one of the underlying causes of this clash, exacerbating the distress and tensions experienced by individuals.

## 6.8 Identity and Understanding Sense of Self

Identity confusion is a common phenomenon that occurs when individuals experience uncertainty or conflict in understanding and defining their sense of self. It can arise from various factors, including cultural influences, societal expectations, personal experiences, and exposure to diverse value systems. The repercussions of identity confusion can be significant and wide-ranging, impacting individuals' psychological well-being, social interactions, and decision-making processes.

1. Psychological impact: Identity confusion can lead to feelings of anxiety, depression, and a lack of self-esteem. Individuals may struggle to understand their place in the world, resulting in a sense of internal dissonance and a loss of direction. The psychological distress arising from identity confusion can affect overall mental health and hinder personal growth.
2. Social interactions: Identity confusion can affect how individuals relate to others and form social connections. It may result in difficulties in establishing authentic relationships and a sense of belonging. Individuals may struggle to find like-minded individuals or communities that align with their evolving identity, leading to feelings of isolation and alienation.
3. Decision-making: Identity confusion can also impact individuals' decision-making processes. Uncertainty about one's values, goals, and beliefs can make it challenging to make choices that align with a coherent sense of self. Individuals may feel torn between different paths or influenced by external expectations, which can lead to indecisiveness and dissatisfaction with life choices.
4. Conflict and identity politics: Identity confusion can contribute to societal tensions and conflicts, particularly in contexts where group identities play a significant role. When individuals experience uncertainty or perceive threats to their cultural, ethnic, or religious identities, it can lead to defensive reactions, polarisation, and identity-based conflicts.

Addressing identity confusion often involves a process of self-reflection, exploration, and self-acceptance. This may include seeking support from mental health professionals, engaging in personal development activities, and connecting with communities or individuals who share similar values and experiences. It is important to foster an environment that promotes inclusivity, acceptance, and understanding, allowing individuals to navigate their identities with greater confidence and clarity.

Implicit in the foregoing argument has been that individuals derive a measure of inner satisfaction from a secure and unambiguous identity. Since our focus is on economic thought and behaviour, it is worth recognising that many influential schools of modern economics downplay, if not ignore, matters of identity. Indeed, much of economics treats the benefits of identity as nil and its social role as negligible, thus avoiding the need to address how people cope with identity-related concerns. In reality, the need for a well-defined identity competes with needs that every school of economics recognises, like food, shelter, and financial security (Richards and Waterbury, 1996). Moreover, just as a person whose house suffers damage will undertake repairs, people whose identity has lost focus or become depreciated will try to redefine themselves and establish a clearer sense of who they are. The repair task may involve, we have seen, efforts to reformulate economics itself.

That concerns over identity account for the emergence of Islamic economics does not mean, of course, that these fully account for its subsequent evolution. Once the doctrine had been outlined, various actors found it a convenient vehicle for advancing political and economic aims unrelated to identity. A milestone in the evolution of Islamic economics was reached with the Arab oil boom of the 1970s. Led by Saudi Arabia, the boom's major Arab beneficiaries felt obliged to step up their support for pan-Arab and pan-Islamic movements, and Islamic economics was among the causes that received vast assistance. Accordingly, the first Islamic commercial banks started operation in 1975, as did the Islamic Development Bank, established to transfer petrodollars to predominantly Muslim developing countries through interest-free instruments. The period of the oil boom saw also the enhancement of the institutional infrastructure of Islamic economics. New institutes of Islamic economics came into being, and departments of Islamic economics were started in various parts of the Islamic world. Also, journals of Islamic economics began publication, and well-funded international conferences of Islamic economics became a regular occurrence (Kuran, 1990, 1995).

Once Islamic economics acquired the trappings of an academic discipline, it gained new complexities. Researchers steeped in Islamic economics went looking for new problems to address, and various applications of Islamic economic principles, including Islamic redistribution and Islamic banking, stimulated new debates. To this day, however, Islamic economics has remained preoccupied with defining the modern Muslim identity. One cannot make sense, therefore, of either contemporary Islamic economic thought or the current applications of Islamic economics without paying attention to the factors that stimulated its genesis half a century ago. The major stimulus to the emergence of Islamic economics was the perception of Mawdudi and his political associates that the Indo-Muslim community was losing its identity (Ahmad, 1978).

## 6.9 Critics of Islamic Economics

The emergence and popularity of Islamic economics, according to its critics (see e.g., Nasr, 1996; Kuran, 1993; Crone, 1987; Roy, 1994), can be attributed to several factors, despite its perceived shortcomings in terms of economic performance. The following points help explain its existence and appeal:

(a) Cultural preservation: Islamic economics serves as a means of preserving and promoting Islamic cultural values and identity. It provides a framework that adheres to fundamental Islamic teachings and principles, which are seen as essential for maintaining a distinct Islamic identity in the face of globalisation and Western influences.

(b) Moral and ethical considerations: Islamic economics emphasises the importance of moral and ethical principles in economic transactions. It seeks to create an economic system that aligns with Islamic teachings, focusing on justice, fairness, and social welfare. The appeal lies in the belief that economic activities should be guided by religious values, promoting a sense of accountability and righteousness.
(c) Spiritual fulfilment: Islamic economics offers a pathway for Muslims to align their economic activities with their religious beliefs. By adhering to Islamic economic principles, individuals may seek spiritual fulfilment and a sense of piety. This connection between economic choices and religious devotion can be a motivating factor for individuals to embrace Islamic economics.
(d) Solidarity and community support: Islamic economics encourages Muslims to support religious causes and contribute to the betterment of their communities. By promoting economic practices that prioritise the welfare of society, it fosters a sense of solidarity and collective responsibility among Muslims. This can be appealing to individuals who value community support and the notion of working for the greater good.
(e) Symbolic resistance: Choosing Islamic economics can be seen as a form of symbolic resistance against perceived Western hegemony and cultural dominance. It represents a rejection of Western economic models and a desire to establish an alternative system based on Islamic principles. The popularity of Islamic economics may stem from a desire to assert cultural independence and resist assimilation into a global culture seen as Western-centric.

While the economic effectiveness of Islamic economics may be subject to debate, its significance lies in its role as a cultural and ideological force within the Muslim community. It offers a distinct economic framework that resonates with those seeking to maintain Islamic identity and values in an increasingly interconnected world.

## *The Cultural Aspect of the Critique*

The emergence and focus of Islamic economics on cultural rather than economic concerns can be seen through several key factors:

(a) Cultural autonomy and identity: The founders of Islamic economics, such as Maududi, were motivated by the desire to protect and preserve Muslim cultures in the face of increasing Western influences. They sought to establish a distinct Islamic identity and cultural autonomy, which they believed was threatened by Western secularism and the erosion of Islamic values.
(b) Resistance to Westernisation: Islamic economics became a means to resist the perceived Westernisation of Muslim societies. By promoting an economic system rooted in Islamic principles, proponents aimed to counter the cultural influence of the West and maintain a distinct Islamic identity.

(c) Self-governance according to Islamic prescriptions: In countries like Pakistan, where Islamic economics has received significant attention, the focus on Islamic economic principles aligns with the broader goal of self-governance based on Islamic prescriptions. Islamic economics is viewed as a means to establish and strengthen the Islamic identity of the state and its citizens.
(d) Differentiation from established economic doctrines: Islamic economics emphasises its distinctiveness from mainstream economic doctrines. By highlighting prohibitions on interest (*riba*) and seeking to provide alternative financial mechanisms, such as Islamic banking, it aims to differentiate itself from conventional economic systems and offer a uniquely Islamic approach to economic practices.

It is worth noting that the primary emphasis of Islamic economics has been on establishing an Islamic framework and addressing cultural concerns rather than solving pressing economic problems. While economic performance and practicality may not be the primary focus, the appeal of Islamic economics lies in its ability to provide a sense of cultural identity, resistance to Westernisation, and adherence to Islamic values within economic activities.

Islamic economics often focuses on issues and topics that may seem irrelevant or outdated to modern readers. This emphasis on classical Islamic sources and traditional practices reflects the cultural and historical roots of Islamic economics. It seeks to draw from and adhere to Islamic teachings as they were understood during earlier periods.

However, this focus on classical Islamic sources and traditional practices has resulted in limited substantive contributions to economic discourse in terms of addressing contemporary economic issues. Islamic economics has been criticised for its incoherence, impracticality, and lack of relevance to modern economic challenges. Its emphasis on topics like barter rules, slave rights, and other antiquated practices may detract from engaging with more pressing economic issues of the present era.

While Islamic economics has gained attention and influence in certain countries, such as Pakistan and Iran, its practical impact on addressing contemporary economic challenges has been limited. The focus on cultural identity and adherence to Islamic principles has often overshadowed the development of comprehensive and practical economic theories and frameworks that can effectively address modern economic problems (Khomeini, 1985; Agwani, 1967; Ahmad, 1991).

It is important to note that this observation does not dismiss the significance of cultural identity and the role it plays in shaping economic perspectives and practices. The cultural function of Islamic economics should be understood in relation to its emphasis on preserving Islamic values and fostering a distinct Islamic identity, rather than its ability to provide comprehensive economic solutions.

## *Islam vs. the West Critique: Confrontational Aspect*

Indeed, proposals to restrict interest-based finance and promote profit-and-loss sharing can be evaluated within secular economic discourse, stripped of their Islamic vocabulary. The merits of such proposals can be assessed using the same standards by which secular economists evaluate other financial practices. There is nothing inherently anti-Western about considering alternative economic systems or questioning certain practices in finance.

However, it is worth noting that Islamic economists often frame their arguments against interest and other financial practices within a broader moral and cultural context. They draw on Islamic authorities, such as the Quran, to support their positions and emphasise the compatibility of these practices with Islamic values. This moral discourse of Islamic economics can create a perception that the behavioural standards of Islam are in conflict with those of the West.

Islamic fundamentalists, including proponents of Islamic economics, do view international politics through the lens of a clash of civilisations, as described by Samuel Huntington (1996). They seek to strengthen social and economic bonds among Muslim communities, with the goal of establishing an Islamic common market and, in some cases, a pan-Islamic state. They may also aim to reduce commercial and industrial ties with the West to protect Muslims from what they perceive as un-Islamic cultural influences.

It is important to recognise that these perspectives represent specific ideological viewpoints and do not necessarily reflect the correct view and wisdom of Islam, nor views of all Muslims or Islamic economists. The relationship between Islamic economics, cultural identity, and Western influences is complex and multifaceted, and it varies among different individuals and contexts.

The contradiction between the objective of a self-segregating pan-Islamic union and the morality advocated by Islamic economics is indeed a significant challenge. Islamic economics promotes a collectivist morality rooted in medieval Islamic civilisation, which emphasises restrictions and limited economic linkages. This approach encourages Muslims to primarily interact within their own ethno-religious subgroups, hindering economic cooperation and integration across subgroup boundaries (Said, 1978).

In contrast, medieval Western Europe promoted an individualist morality that facilitated interactions and economic cooperation beyond subgroup identities. This individualist morality contributed to Europe's economic dominance over the Islamic world. By seeking to revive the collectivist economic morality, Islamic economics may inadvertently impede the goal of improving living standards for Muslim communities and hinder the formation of an Islamic common market.

It is important to recognise that the civilisational clash associated with Islamic economics is not simply a collision of old and new values. While Islamic economics draws on living traditions, its objective of ending political and economic fragmentation in the Muslim world represents an effort to break free from historical divisions (Rodinson, 1973). However, historical precedent shows that even the earliest Islamic state was unable to eliminate the social significance of tribal and other divisions among Muslims.

The fundamentalist strategy of strengthening the Islamic identity of Muslim communities as a means of breaking nonreligious solidarity patterns may be self-defeating. However, it is important to acknowledge the revolutionary element of this strategy, as Islamic fundamentalists attempt to achieve a task that even early Muslims were unable to accomplish (Mottahadeh, 1995).

## *The* Homo Economicus *vs.* Homo Islamicus *Argument*

The clash between Homo Economicus and Homo Islamicus arises from the tension between individual Muslims' aspirations for economic advancement and their desire to maintain an Islamic lifestyle. Islamic economics portrays certain economic practices as immoral, which creates a conflict for Muslims who recognise the need for economic adaptation and prosperity. This clash within individual Muslims leads to discomfort and a sense of internal conflict.

When individuals experience discomfort or guilt, they typically strive to reduce it. Social psychology experiments have shown that individuals who believe they have harmed others tend to engage in acts of rehabilitation to alleviate their guilt. However, these acts often focus on general moral commendation rather than directly addressing the specific harm caused. For example, individuals who thought they broke a camera in an experiment became more willing to help someone in need in general, but they did not offer to pay for a new camera specifically.

In the context of Islamic economics, this suggests that Muslims may seek to alleviate their guilt or reconcile the clash between economic aspirations and an Islamic identity by engaging in acts of religious piety, supporting religious causes, or contributing to charitable endeavours. These actions may provide a sense of atonement and moral righteousness without directly addressing the economic conflicts they face.

The clash between Homo Economicus and Homo Islamicus highlights the challenges faced by individual Muslims in navigating their economic pursuits and maintaining an Islamic identity. Islamic economics plays a role in heightening this clash and shaping individuals' responses to the tensions they experience.

Muslims who engage in economic practices portrayed as immoral may seek to exonerate themselves through acts of altruism or by participating in religious activities that carry Islamic significance. They may donate to charitable causes, assist the handicapped, join public prayers, make donations to mosques, participate in Islamic political rallies, or display symbols of Islamic piety through their clothing.

The revival of medieval economic injunctions, which may be viewed as nuisances in contemporary settings, does not necessarily lead to changes in economic behaviour. Instead, it tends to promote various forms of religious participation. Islamic economists often highlight the presence of greed, corruption, dishonesty, deceit, and exploitation in contemporary Muslim communities (Kuran, 1995).

While these problems are indeed prevalent, simply praising Islamic virtue is not enough to address them effectively.

In order to address these issues, institutional reforms are necessary. Improvements in the legal system, industrial standardisation, and the removal of anti-competitive regulations can help make socially undesirable behaviours more costly. Merely emphasising the problems without implementing institutional changes will only serve to make Muslims more conscious of their moral failings (Iannaccone, 1992). This may lead them to seek compensation for their perceived deficiencies through outward displays of piety.

The revival of medieval economic injunctions and the emphasis on Islamic virtue in response to economic practices portrayed as immoral can lead to a focus on religious participation rather than substantial changes in economic behaviour. Addressing the social and economic challenges faced by Muslim communities requires comprehensive institutional reforms (Gibb, 1947).

The existence of Islamic banks, which claim to shun interest but often employ similar practices disguised through alternative terminology, is an exception to the resistance to institutional redesign in Islamic economics. While the operations of these banks may not fully conform to the ban on interest, they still serve as a means of guilt reduction for depositors and borrowers who perceive Islamic banking as morally superior to conventional banking (Kuran, 1990).

Islamic banks cultivate an image of moral superiority through their contributions to Islamic causes and by incorporating signs of Islamic devotion within their branch offices, such as prayer areas, Quran verses on the walls, veiled female tellers, and religious literature available to customers.

Another source of guilt in Islamic economics arises from its internal inconsistencies. Islamic economists themselves hold divergent views on many substantive matters, and their programs are marked by internal contradictions. These conflicts and tensions stem from the fact that the fundamental sources of Islam themselves contain inconsistencies. For instance, while some accounts of Prophet Muhammad's sayings suggest that Islam rejects interference with market freedoms, other classical Islamic texts and historical precedents indicate a tradition of tight economic regulation.

As a result, a devout Muslim striving to adhere to all Islamic injunctions may find it impossible to lead a life that is beyond doubt entirely consistent with Islamic law. Regardless of their economic choices, they may constantly question whether some of their actions conflict with the spirit, if not the letter, of Islamic teachings. Consequently, a sense of guilt may persist, and the pursuit of a wholly "properly Islamic" life may prove elusive.

### *The Islamic Economic Morality Argument*

Religion, despite being viewed by influential thinkers such as Karl Marx, Auguste Comte, and Sigmund Freud as a manifestation of ignorance or weakness, continues to exert significant influence on intelligent and educated individuals. Recent research in evolutionary psychology suggests that religion taps into our innate moral sense, which plays a role in defining right and wrong. Therefore, even if the morality of Islamic economics is ill-suited to modern economic conditions, it can continue to exert influence due to its role in nourishing the moral sense and promoting a stronger Islamic identity.

However, under current global circumstances, adhering strictly to the morality of Islamic economics would limit individual and collective wealth accumulation while reinforcing Islamic identity. The vast majority of Muslims are willing to adopt financial and commercial mechanisms developed in the West, just as contemporary Italians use Arabic numerals. Nonetheless, many Muslims perceive their identity as being threatened, particularly because Islamic fundamentalism views any adaptation as a form of cultural surrender.

As a result, even Muslims who can justify their own economic adaptations may question whether their behaviours contribute to the erosion of their society's Islamic identity. In their desire to preserve that identity, they experience an internal clash of civilisations. They seek peace by compensating for their perceived transgressions through acts that symbolise Islamic defiance and separatism. Paradoxically, in their quest to live up to the ideal of Homo Islamicus, they inadvertently serve the anti-assimilationist goals of Islamic fundamentalism. This paradox arises from the impossibility of fully embodying the ideal of Homo Islamicus in a complex and interconnected world.

## 6.10 Conclusion

This Chapter discusses the rise of "Islamic economics" as a significant aspect of the broader "political Islam" movement in the twentieth century. Islamic economics aims to establish an economic system aligned with Islamic principles and has its roots in late-colonial India as a means to safeguard a distinct Muslim identity according to its critics. The Chapter argues that while economic aspects were secondary to its Islamic character, the concept gained momentum through the efforts of figures like Sayyid Abu'l-A'la Mawdudi.

Mawdudi, the founder of Jama'at-i Islami, promoted the idea of Islamic economics as part of a larger campaign to preserve cultural autonomy for Indian Muslims. He believed that by emphasising visible markers of group identity, Muslims could strengthen their communal bond and promote their religiosity in public settings. Mawdudi's program sought to redefine Islamic orthopraxy, especially in economic matters, to address the challenges of modernisation while preserving a distinct Muslim identity.

We also explore Mawdudi's concerns about Western influences on Indian Muslims and their adoption of Western cultural practices. He believed that Westernisation weakened the influence of religion on personal worldviews and interpersonal relationships, leading to a division within the Muslim community. Mawdudi's response was rooted in the principle of group solidarity, and he saw the development of Islamic economics as a pressing challenge to specify the economic components of a new Islamic orthopraxy.

Moreover, the Chapter highlights the emergence of Islamic economics as a distinct concept during Mawdudi's time, with its origins not being a goal of previous pan-Islamist movements or influential figures like Mohammad Iqbal. While many Muslim activists called for a return to Islam, Mawdudi's serious consideration of its concrete implications set him apart. His initiatives prepared the masses for his broader campaign of Islamisation and paved the way for the development of Islamic economics.

Furthermore, the Chapter discuss critics of Islamic economics who raise several points concerning its cultural aspects, confrontational stance towards the West, clash between Homo Economicus and Homo Islamicus, and its emphasis on Islamic economic morality. We examined these critiques in-depth and here is a summary of them:

(a) Cultural Aspect: Islamic economics is often seen as a means of preserving and promoting Islamic cultural values and identity. Critics argue that its founders, such as Maududi, were motivated by a desire to protect Muslim cultures from Western influences and establish a distinct Islamic identity. By resisting Westernisation and promoting self-governance based on Islamic prescriptions, Islamic economics may prioritise cultural concerns over practical economic problem-solving.
(b) Confrontational Stance Towards the West: Some proponents of Islamic economics view international politics through a "clash of civilisations" lens, seeking to establish an Islamic common market and reduce ties with the West to protect Muslims from perceived un-Islamic cultural influences. This confrontational aspect can create a perception of conflict between Islamic and Western values, further emphasising cultural identity and resistance to Westernisation.
(c) Clash between Homo Economicus and Homo Islamicus: The clash between individual economic aspirations and the desire to maintain an Islamic lifestyle can lead to discomfort and internal conflict for Muslims. Islamic economics portrays certain economic practices as immoral, creating a tension for individuals seeking economic adaptation and prosperity while adhering to Islamic values. In response, some Muslims may engage in religious acts or symbols of piety to alleviate guilt without directly addressing economic conflicts.
(d) Emphasis on Islamic Economic Morality: The morality of Islamic economics, rooted in medieval Islamic civilisation, may limit individual and collective wealth accumulation in modern economic conditions. While many Muslims are willing to adopt Western financial and commercial mechanisms, strict adherence to Islamic economic morality may be perceived as necessary for preserving Islamic identity. This emphasis on moral righteousness can inadvertently serve the goals of Islamic fundamentalism by promoting Islamic defiance and separatism.
(e) Limited Substantive Contributions: Critics argue that Islamic economics' focus on classical Islamic sources and traditional practices may detract from engag-

ing with pressing contemporary economic issues. This limited substantive contribution to economic discourse and its emphasis on antiquated practices may hinder its practical impact on addressing modern economic challenges.

Therefore, critics highlight various concerns regarding Islamic economics, including its cultural emphasis, confrontational stance towards the West, and the clash between economic aspirations and Islamic values. While Islamic economics plays a role in fostering a distinct cultural identity and providing a moral framework for economic transactions, it may face challenges in addressing contemporary economic problems effectively.

In the next Chapter we examine the counter argument for the critics of Islamic economics and its founding objective to balance the discussion objectively.

# Chapter 7
# Islamic Economics Model: The Counter Argument to Its Critiques

## 7.1 Introduction

The previous Chapter discussed the rise of "Islamic economics" as a significant aspect of the broader "political Islam" movement in the twentieth century, and as a response to globalisation and the notion of universal identity. We analysed how Islamic economics aims to establish an economic system aligned with Islamic principles and has its roots in late-colonial India as a means to safeguard a distinct Muslim identity according to its critics.

The objective of economic analysis has evolved over time, with three major focuses of development. In the first half of the nineteenth century, economic analysis primarily dealt with the problem of distribution. After 1870, the focus shifted to the optimal allocation of resources among competing ends. In more recent times, particularly with the resurgence of macroeconomic theory by Keynes, economic science has been concerned with economic policy issues related to employment, aggregate demand generation, and price stabilisation (Schumpeter, 1968).

Modern economics has been predominantly focused on the idea of satisfying the economic man, often referred to as Marshall's "homo-economicus." This concept is based on the assumptions of total, free, and perfect competition. However, alongside this mainstream approach, a new economic order has been emerging, known as Islamic Economics (Choudhury, 1981).

Islamic Economics revolves around the efficient allocation of resources guided by a transcendental consideration, the promotion of the laws of God on Earth, to establish a righteous community. The principles of Islamic economics form the philosophical basis of this economic system. This Chapter aims to outline these principles in non-technical language, providing an introductory understanding of Islamic economics. It also discusses some key economic instruments that put these principles into action. While the paper does not engage in elaborate economic analysis, it serves as a starting point for readers seeking insight into this field.



S. Alamad, *Beyond Profit*, Contributions to Economics,
https://doi.org/10.1007/978-3-031-49748-3_7

During the early nineteenth century, the social and economic conditions in the Muslim world were predominantly agrarian and traditional, resembling pre-modern societies. The modes of production and social values were similar to those of medieval times, with minor urban exceptions. The majority of the population lived in rural areas under semi-feudal conditions, facing exploitation by landlords and occasional tax collectors. Communication systems were also underdeveloped during this time (Sulayman, 1968).

However, rapid changes occurred throughout the century, transforming the socio-economic landscape. The establishment of Muhammad Ali's rule in Egypt brought law, order, peace, and security, which were crucial prerequisites for economic development. Previously, the nomadic unrest and Bedouin uprisings had posed challenges for both the people and the government, but Muhammad Ali's policies addressed these issues. The settlement of land ownership led to the breakdown of tribal links and the emergence of socioeconomic differentiation (Hussaini, 1971).

As individual ownership of land and taxation responsibilities increased, the traditional village community began to disintegrate. Guilds, which had organised industrial production in the past, were also affected by Muhammad Ali's reforms and the influx of European goods. The commercial system underwent changes, and guilds shifted their functions to supplying labour and services rather than organising production (Hussaini, 1971).

Overall, the early nineteenth century witnessed significant transformations in the social, economic, and political spheres of the Muslim world, with Muhammad Ali's rule in Egypt playing a significant role in bringing stability and initiating reforms.

## 7.2 The Concept of One Nation (Ummah)

Islamic economics goes beyond the conventional viewpoint of economic analysis by incorporating the principle of *Tawheed* and Brotherhood as its foundational principle. *Tawheed*, meaning unity or oneness, summarises the essence of Islamic economics by guiding human interactions and relationships in light of their relationship with God. It emphasises that beyond the mechanisms of market exchange, resource allocation, and maximising utility and profits, there lies a more fundamental truth, which is social justice (Naqvi, 1978).

In Islam, the understanding and implementation of social justice stem from the knowledge and practice of the principles of the Quran (Quran, Surah 55, verse 9.).. The principle of *Tawheed* and Brotherhood establishes a connection between our responsibilities towards fellow human beings and our duties towards God (Quran, Surah 2, verse 30–31). Practically, this principle manifests through equality and cooperation among individuals. The Quran emphasises the unity of humanity, stating that all humans are created from a single soul and that men and women are interdependent, (Quran, Surah 4, verse: 1).

A direct consequence of the principle of *Tawheed* and Brotherhood is the recognition that everything in the heavens and the earth belongs to God. Islamic economics acknowledges that God has created the good things of the world for the service of humanity. Human beings, as the vicegerents of God on Earth, are entrusted with the just use and distribution of these resources. This principle underscores the importance of responsible stewardship and equitable distribution of wealth and resources in Islamic economics (Choudhury, 1981).

In Islamic economics, the elimination of *riba,* which refers to interest or usury, is considered imperative in order to establish the principle of *Tawheed* and Brotherhood. *Riba* is seen as a form of exploitation and oppression, as it allows for the accumulation of wealth in the hands of a few at the expense of lowering wages and causing unemployment.

In the neo-classical economic theory, the distribution of the total annual gross product of a nation is divided into three components: capital inputs for further production, wages, and the capitalist's surplus value in the form of profits, interest, and rents. With the presence of interest, capital accumulates and the rate of profit either falls or becomes constant, while the rate of interest rises and investment decreases. This can lead to lower wages or unemployment as capitalists strive to maintain their profits (Schumpeter, 1968).

In Islam, *riba* is not limited to interest on loan capital but encompasses any unjust increase in individual or state claims of ownership beyond what is considered lawful. The abolition of interest is seen as a means to check the exercise of excessive private ownership and to put an end to the oppression and exploitation of the labour force. It is important to note that Islamic economics does not advocate for a socialist economic doctrine, but rather aims to establish a cooperative system based on free enterprise while ensuring social justice and equitable distribution of wealth.

## 7.3 Work and Productivity

The second principle of Islamic economics is based on the concept of work and fair compensation. It states that an individual's wages should be proportionate to the amount and type of labour performed. The measurement of labour could be in man-hours, and different professions may have specific categories of labour with corresponding wages. These wages would be constrained by the minimum rent determined for the specific category of labour in demand.

If an individual acquires income greater than what is due to them based on their labour and resources, it is considered a form of excess known as "*rububiyyah*," which implies sole proprietorship of the means of production. According to Islamic economic principles, all means of production fundamentally belong to God, so exceeding this limit is seen as an act of excess (Choudhury, 1978).

Under the category of excess, rent on plain land and sharecropping are prohibited, but rent on money capital is allowed. Prophet Muhammad's saying is mentioned to support the prohibition of rent on plain land, emphasising the importance of cultivating the land rather than renting it out. However, when land has been cultivated and developed through labour and capital inputs by the owner, it would be unjust for them to forgo the exchange value created without receiving anything in return. In such cases, it is suggested that rent should be paid in monetary terms rather than in crops (Ibn-al Qayyim, n.d.).

It is important to note that while rent was prohibited on plain land, it was allowed on cultivated and utilised land. Sharecropping, on the other hand, was prohibited in Islamic economics.

In the Islamic exchange system, the conditions for Pareto optimality, which are the first-order conditions of efficiency in a perfectly competitive market, differ from those in a conventional exchange system. In a pure exchange economy, the marginal conditions for Pareto optimality are typically based on the ratio of marginal utilities of products and wages.

However, in the Islamic exchange system, where the principle of equality and cooperation is emphasised, the marginal utility of an owner is not solely determined by the returns from rents but also by the equitable wages given to the labourer. Similarly, the marginal utility of the labourer depends not only on the amount of wages received but also on the just amount of rents given to the employer.

This introduces a distortion in the economic system compared to the conventional framework. Consequently, the Islamic solution to the exchange problem results in what is known as a Second-Best Solution, deviating from the ordinary concept of Pareto optimality.

This Islamic exchange system considers additional variables such as product and wage variables in the utility functions of individuals, leading to a different perspective on efficiency and Pareto optimality compared to the conventional economic framework. In an Islamic economy, the concept of a Second-Best Solution is realised through the essence of cooperation between labour and employers in a productive work environment. This cooperation acts as a corrective force in resource allocation and promotes a more realistic state of the market economy. It aligns with the principles of equity and social justice emphasised in Islamic economics.

Once the allocation principle concerning land rent and profit-sharing is established, Islam allows for profits to be earned from the produce of the land. Consequently, the value of the product sold in the market is determined by wages, rents, and profits. This concept aligns with Adam Smith's notion of the "natural price" of a commodity, which encompasses factors such as labour, rent, and profit in determining its value (Bailey, 1971).

The idea of a Second-Best Solution in an Islamic economy emphasises the importance of cooperation, equity, and social justice in achieving a more realistic and efficient allocation of resources. In an Islamic economy, the principle of cooperation extends beyond the labour-employer relationship and encompasses the broader economic system. It replaces the idea of competition that is prevalent in modern market economies. Instead of firms competing against each other, Islamic economics encourages partnerships and cooperation among firms. When firms find themselves struggling to compete, they are encouraged to form partnerships with more successful enterprises. These partnerships involve mutually agreed-upon profit-sharing rates (Choudhury, 1974).

This system of profit-sharing, known as *mudarabah*, is a prominent feature of both the private and public sectors in an Islamic economy. It pervades various economic activities and promotes cooperation among stakeholders (Choudhury, 1974).

In a modern market economy, such partnerships and cooperative arrangements may be seen as a departure from the ideal of perfect competition. They may be viewed as reducing the efficiency of resource allocation, particularly in cases of mergers and oligopolistic competition. The principles of perfect competition may not fully exist in the context of an Islamic economy.

The fundamental difference between the principles of cooperation in Islamic economics and competition in modern market economies leads to variations in the functioning of institutions and challenges the conventional notion of economic efficiency. It highlights the distinctiveness of the Islamic economic system and its approach to resource allocation and economic organisation.

## 7.4 Advocating Distributional Equity

The third major principle of Islamic economics is the right of society to redistribute private property. This principle is supported by several Quranic verses (Quran, Surah 59, verse 7–9; and Surah 8, verse 41.). In an Islamic economy, the chief sources of national income and transfer payments used for redistributive purposes include *zakah* (tax on wealth exceeding a certain exemption level called *nisab*), *sadaqah* (voluntary charity), *ghanimah* (war booty), *fai* (property acquired in war without fighting), *fidth* (a part of fai distributed similar to *zakah*), *kharaj* (tax on lands conquered during war), and *'ushr* (*zakah* on crops).

The Quran does not specify that these funds must be spent exactly as they were during the early period of Islam. The specific distribution patterns of funds during that time were shaped by the exigencies of the era. For example, the distribution of four-fifths of *ghanimah* among Muslim soldiers in the early period of Islam was due to the absence of a standing army and state treasury to finance it. However, in a modern Islamic state, the army can be regularly paid, and war acquisitions would be added to the state treasury.

Similarly, the remaining one-fifth of *ghanimah* can be directed towards the state treasury to support organised social assistance programs. The portion that was allocated to the Prophet and his near kin during the early period of Islam can now be returned to the government for public works.

In the case of *zakah* expenditure, it can be channelled into organized social assistance programs managed by the state. The categories of expenditure for *zakah* funds can be expanded to include employment creation programs, family welfare initiatives, rehabilitation of the elderly, unemployment insurance, income support during economic losses, and other relevant programs. Even though the rate of *zakah* can be varied marginally, the original fixed rate of 2.5 percent on assessed wealth exceeding the *nisab* level should be maintained.

Indeed, at a micro-level, the Islamic law of inheritance plays a significant role in redistributing private property. The Quran emphasises the importance of inheritance and its purpose is to prevent the concentration of wealth in the hands of a few individuals (Quran, Surah 4, verse 17). Equitable redistribution of income and wealth is a responsibility of both the Islamic state and individuals. It is based on the principles of *Tawheed* (unity of God) and Brotherhood. The objective of this redistribution is to utilise national income and wealth productively for the benefit of society, promoting employment and welfare for all citizens.

A historical example that reflects this principle is the treatment of early Muslim refugees who found refuge in the city of Medina. They were integrated into society as equal members and provided opportunities to utilise their skills and abilities. Those who were able to cultivate land were given land, traders were allowed to engage in business, and those who needed assistance received support from their fellow believers. Islamic economics aims to create a just and equitable society by promoting the redistribution of wealth and providing opportunities for individuals to thrive and contribute to the welfare of the community.

The concept of zakah in Islamic economics plays a significant role in economic activity. *Zakah* is associated with an income multiplier effect, whereby the imposition of *zakah* on idle assets encourages their productive use and leads to increased investment. This increased investment, in turn, generates higher income through the multiplier effect. Therefore, a higher *zakah* rate can result in increased income, investment, and labour force participation.

The principle of distributional equity in Islam implies that the state has a responsibility to efficiently distribute national output among individuals and institutions. This recognition allows for a certain degree of government intervention in the Islamic economy. Unregulated freedom of enterprise and excessive profits can be seen as socially undesirable, as it may lead to inequitable wealth accumulation. To address this, Islamic economics advocates for the control and distribution of wealth through mechanisms such as the Bait al-Mal (public treasury) in an Islamic state (Alamad, 2019a).

In addition to the obligatory tax of *zakah,* individuals are also encouraged to spend in the path of God for the propagation of truth. Furthermore, Islam prescribes rules for inheritance, ensuring that private property is not concentrated in the hands of a single individual after one's death. Lawful heirs, including children, near relatives, and distant relatives, are entitled to fixed shares of the deceased's property, as stated in the Quran. Islam also encourages individuals to allocate a portion of their property for welfare projects through making a will, with the recommended limit not exceeding one-third of their property (Alamad, 2019a).

These principles of wealth distribution and social responsibility reflect the values and objectives of Islamic economics, aiming to create a more equitable society and ensure the well-being of individuals and the broader community.

## 7.5 Establishing an Economic Policy

To establish the viability and workability of the three major principles of Islamic economics, they need to undergo testing on two grounds.

The first ground is rational economic analysis. While Islamic economics may not align with modern economics in all aspects, it should be capable of consistent economic analysis based on assumptions and behaviours, whether normative or positive, at both micro and macro levels. This means that the principles should be able to withstand economic scrutiny and provide a coherent framework for understanding economic phenomena within an Islamic context.

The second ground is practical application. The principles should be capable of being translated into practical policies and implemented through suitable Islamic policy instruments. This requires developing mechanisms, institutions, and instruments that align with the principles of Islamic economics to facilitate their implementation in real-world economic systems. These policy instruments should be designed to effectively achieve the objectives of an Islamic economic system, such as equitable distribution, social justice, and the promotion of individual and collective well-being.

By subjecting the principles of Islamic economics to these two grounds of testing, it becomes possible to assess their feasibility, effectiveness, and compatibility with economic analysis and practical application. This evaluation is essential for determining the viability and workability of an Islamic economic system in theory and practice.

In the practical application of the three fundamental principles of Islamic economics, there are four key policy instruments that play a crucial role. These instruments help in implementing the principles and shaping the economic system in line with Islamic values.

a) **Eradication of *Riba* (Interest):** One of the central tenets of Islamic economics is the prohibition of interest on capital, known as *riba*. This principle calls for the elimination of interest-based transactions and the development of alternative financial systems that adhere to Islamic principles, such as profit-sharing and equity-based financing. Islamic financial institutions, such as Islamic banks, have been established to provide interest-free financial services and promote economic activities without relying on interest-based transactions.

In Islamic economics, the concept of riba extends beyond loan interest and encompasses any form of unjust and exploitative excess in economic transactions. It includes both monetary and non-monetary transactions where one party unfairly gains at the expense of the other.

In a monetary exchange, riba refers to the excessive increase demanded or received over the principal amount in a loan or debt. This concept originated from the practices of pre-Islamic Arabs who would charge additional amounts on loans that were not based on productive activities but rather on the passage of time (Haneef, 1995).

When goods are exchanged by weight or measure, Islamic principles emphasise the need for strict equality in weight and measure and immediate delivery of both goods. This ensures fairness and eliminates any form of exploitation or unjust gain. However, if the goods being exchanged are of different species, strict equality is not insisted upon, but immediate delivery is still required.

In modern exchange economies, interest is often seen as necessary to cover the cost of capital and promote economic efficiency. However, in Islamic economics, the concept of interest as an exogenous variable set by lenders is viewed as speculative and divorced from the actual proceeds of production. The Islamic economic system aims to establish a more just and equitable framework that discourages unjust enrichment and promotes productive activities based on mutual cooperation and fairness (Alamad, 2019b).

By adhering to the principles of *riba*-free transactions and ensuring fairness and equity in economic exchanges, Islamic economics seeks to create an economic system that aligns with the values and principles of Islam. In Islamic economics, the concept of profit-loss sharing (PLS) is emphasised as an alternative to interest-based transactions. Mudarabah is one such mechanism within the framework of PLS.

Under the *mudarabah* arrangement, one party (the investor or financier) provides the capital, while the other party (the entrepreneur or manager) contributes labour, skills, and expertise. The profit generated from the business venture is then shared between the parties based on an agreed-upon ratio, while any losses incurred are borne by the investor (Choudhury, 1974).

The principle of *mudarabah* ensures that the rewards and risks of the business are shared between the capital provider and the entrepreneur. It aligns with the Islamic economic principle of cooperation and fairness, as both parties have a stake in the success of the venture (Alamad, 2017b).

By adopting profit-loss sharing mechanisms like *mudarabah*, Islamic economics aims to promote investment in productive activities and discourage speculative behaviour. It encourages a more equitable distribution of wealth and fosters a sense of shared responsibility in economic transactions.

It's important to note that while *mudarabah* is a prominent example of profit-loss sharing, there are other Islamic financial contracts and mechanisms such as *musharakah* (partnership), *wakalah* (agency), and *murabahah* (cost-plus financing) that also contribute to the principles of equity and fairness in Islamic finance and economics (Alamad, 2017a).

b) **Institution of Mudarabah (Profit-Loss Sharing):** Mudarabah is a system of profit-loss sharing in economic ventures. It encourages cooperation and partnership between capital providers and entrepreneurs. In this system, one party provides the capital, while the other party manages the business operations. Profits are shared based on pre-agreed ratios, and losses are shared according to the capital contribution. Mudarabah promotes risk-sharing and aligns the interests of capital owners and entrepreneurs, fostering a more equitable distribution of wealth and promoting entrepreneurial activities (Alamad, 2017b).

The absence of interest in Islamic banking brings about significant differences compared to conventional banking. Islamic banks operate based on the principles of Shariah, which prohibit the charging or paying of interest (*riba*) on loans or investments. Instead, Islamic banks engage in profit-sharing and asset-backed transactions that align with Islamic principles.

Regarding the creation of liquidity, Islamic banks cannot create money through the interest-based fractional reserve system used by conventional banks. In an interest-based system, banks can expand their balance sheets by creating money through lending, which increases the money supply and liquidity in the economy. However, in Islamic banking, the creation of money through interest is not permissible (Alamad, 2017a, 2019b).

Islamic banks, therefore, rely on alternative mechanisms to provide financing and liquidity. They participate in partnerships and profit-sharing arrangements with clients, providing funding for investment projects based on shared risks and returns. Islamic banks also engage in asset-backed transactions, such as trade financing or leasing, where the underlying assets serve as collateral.

The absence of interest in Islamic banking is intended to promote fairness, ethical conduct, and discourage speculative behaviour. It aims to ensure that financial activities are linked to real economic transactions and productive investments. While the absence of interest may impose certain limitations on the operations of Islamic banks, it also encourages more equitable and sustainable economic practices.

It's worth noting that Islamic finance has developed various financial instruments and mechanisms to meet the needs of individuals and businesses while adhering to Islamic principles. These include profit-sharing contracts, lease-based contracts, and Islamic bonds (sukuk), among others. The objective is to provide financing and investment opportunities that align with Islamic ethics and promote economic growth and stability.

In an Islamic economy, the absence of interest-based monetary policies necessitates alternative approaches to managing economic fluctuations. Instead of manipulating interest rates, Islamic economics emphasises real economic activities and the principles of profit-sharing and risk-sharing.

The institution of mudarabah, which you mentioned, is one such mechanism in Islamic finance. Mudarabah refers to a partnership where one party provides the capital (*rab-al-maal*) and the other party provides the expertise and labour (*mudarib*). Profits generated from the joint venture are shared based on a pre-agreed ratio, while losses are borne by the capital provider. This profit-sharing arrangement ensures a direct link between investment and returns, as well as a fair distribution of profits (Alamad, 2020).

In an Islamic economy, the focus is on promoting productive investment and entrepreneurship rather than relying solely on monetary policy to manage economic fluctuations. By encouraging profit-sharing and risk-sharing, Islamic finance aims to align the incentives of investors and entrepreneurs with the overall growth and stability of the economy.

The absence of interest-based monetary policies does present challenges in terms of liquidity management and monetary control. However, Islamic financial institutions have developed alternative tools and instruments to address these challenges. For example, Islamic banks engage in various financing modes such as *murabaha* (cost-plus financing), *ijara* (leasing), and sukuk (Islamic bonds) to provide liquidity and investment opportunities (Alamad, 2016).

It's important to note that the objective of Islamic economics is not merely to replicate the functions of conventional monetary policies but to establish an economic system based on ethical principles and equitable distribution. By promoting genuine economic activities, risk-sharing, and fair profit-sharing, Islamic economics aims to create a more stable and just financial system.

Indeed, the institution of *mudarabah* in public-private sector joint ventures can contribute to risk diversification and encourage real investment in the economy. Public enterprises, with their ability to distribute risk capital across multiple investment projects, exhibit a greater tolerance for risk compared to individual private investors (Alamad, 2019b).

By adopting a risk-neutral approach, the public authority can allocate capital to various investment projects, promoting economic growth and development. This encourages the flow of money capital into productive investments, which in turn leads to the creation of real assets and infrastructure.

In an Islamic economy, there is a focus on maintaining an optimal allocation of capital between consumption and investment. Excessive consumption is discouraged, as it can lead to the misallocation of resources and hinder long-term economic growth. The institution of *mudarabah*, with its emphasis on profit-sharing and risk-sharing, serves as a mechanism to encourage investment in real capital while ensuring a balanced allocation of financial resources.

By promoting real investment and discouraging excessive consumption, Islamic economics aims to foster sustainable economic development and equitable wealth distribution. This approach aligns with the principles of fairness, social justice, and long-term economic stability advocated in Islamic teachings.

c) **Elimination of *Israf* (Wasteful Consumption):** Islamic economics emphasises responsible and moderate consumption, discouraging wastefulness and extravagant spending. The principle of *israf* calls for individuals and societies to avoid excessive consumption and utilise resources wisely. This principle encourages sustainable practices and responsible consumption patterns that consider the well-being of individuals, society, and the environment (Alamad, 2017a).

In an Islamic economy, the concept of *israf*, or excessive and wasteful consumption, is strongly discouraged. The principles of Islamic economics prioritise the production and consumption of necessaries and comforts of life, while discouraging the production and consumption of luxuries. This helps to prevent the wastage of resources and promotes responsible use of factors of production and goods (Naqvi, 1978).

Islamic economic principles also encourage savings and real investment, as they are seen as avenues for increasing productive capacities and improving the overall welfare of society. The emphasis is on allocating income into productive investments that generate long-term benefits and contribute to economic growth.

In the context of intertemporal allocative efficiency, the study of Islamic economics shifts the focus from the modern consumer theory's analysis of consumption patterns to the welfare analysis of income allocation, particularly into real investment. This necessitates the development of a choice-theoretic approach to individual and social ordering that aligns with the principles of the Islamic integrated value system. Islamic welfare economics becomes a priority area of study to understand how resources should be allocated between investment and consumption to maximise societal welfare and promote economic well-being within the Islamic framework (Choudhury, 1980).

d) **Institution of *Zakah* (Social Assistance):** *Zakah* is an organised form of social assistance and wealth redistribution in Islamic society. It is a mandatory tax imposed on eligible individuals and businesses whose wealth exceeds a certain minimum threshold (*nisab*). *Zakah* funds are collected and distributed to specific categories of recipients, such as the poor, the needy, debtors, and others mentioned in Islamic teachings. The institution of zakah aims to reduce inequality, alleviate poverty, and provide social support to those in need.

*Zakah*, as a pillar of Islamic faith, holds significant economic significance in the Islamic framework. It serves as a means of purifying accumulated wealth and addressing the issue of wealth inequality by providing for the basic needs of all members of society. Islam recognizes the potential for wealth accumulation and does not object to individuals earning large sums. However, it places a responsibility on the wealthy to ensure that others are not deprived of their basic necessities (Alamad, 2019a).

One key aspect of *zakah* is its opposition to hoarding. According to Islamic principles, a portion of a person's wealth should be spent on living necessities, comfort, productive investment, charity, and for the benefit of Muslims in general and in the way of God. Any remaining wealth that remains idle for a year becomes liable for *zakah* taxation (Alamad, 2019a).

The revenue generated from *zakah* consists of a levy on idle wealth, a percentage of agricultural produce, a portion of mineral wealth, and a tax on the earnings from capital. The funds collected through *zakah* are then distributed to various categories, including the poor, the needy, the propagation of Islam, those in bondage, those in debt, wayfarers, the functionaries who collect and distribute *zakah*, and other noble causes that require financial support. It should be noted that while the principle of *zakah* remains immutable in Islam, the specific methods of collecting and distributing it can vary in accordance with the broader aspects of the mentioned categories of expenditure (Choudhury, 1980).

Overall, *zakah* serves as an important mechanism for promoting social welfare, reducing wealth inequality, and fulfilling the principle of providing for the basic needs of all members of society within the Islamic economic framework.

These four policy instruments help translate the principles of Islamic economics into practical application by providing a framework for financial transactions, encouraging equitable partnerships, promoting responsible consumption, and establishing a system of social assistance and wealth redistribution. By implementing these instruments, an Islamic economic system seeks to foster an inclusive and just economy that aligns with Islamic values and promotes the well-being of individuals and society as a whole (Alamad et al., 2021).

Thus, the principles of Islamic economics provide a fundamental philosophy that can shape the development programs of Muslim nations. By embracing these principles as a new value system of economics, Muslim societies can integrate their social values with their economic strategies, leading to sustained and meaningful growth. The establishment of a New International Economic Order, as proposed by scholars like Reddy, would further align development objectives with social and ethical values (Alamad et al., 2021; Kuran, 1990).

In Muslim societies, Islamic values naturally form the foundation of such a development order. Considering the potentials of Islamic economics becomes crucial in any form of economic development, as it provides a framework that upholds the principles of justice, social welfare, and equitable distribution of wealth. By embracing Islamic economics, Muslim nations can contribute to a new era of joint national science and technology policies while promoting a harmonious blend of economic development and social values (Alamad, 2017b).

It is recommended that Muslim nations clearly identify their national priorities in social values and establish strong linkages with their economic development strategies. This fusion of values and economic goals can pave the way for sustained growth and contribute to the shaping of a New International Economic Order based on the principles of Islamic economics.

## 7.6 Conclusion

Economic analysis has undergone significant evolution over time, with shifting focuses on distribution, resource allocation, and macroeconomic policy. In recent times, alongside the mainstream economic approach of satisfying the "economic man," Islamic Economics has emerged as an alternative economic order. Rooted in Islamic principles, this system seeks to achieve efficient resource allocation while upholding social justice and adhering to the laws of God. This summary outlines the key principles of Islamic economics and discusses their practical implementation in economic activities.

A) The Concept of One Nation (*Ummah*): At the core of Islamic economics lies the principle of *Tawheed,* emphasising unity and social justice. The belief in one God directs human interactions and relationships, promoting equality and cooperation among individuals. Islamic economics recognises that all resources belong to God and are to be used responsibly for the benefit of humanity. To establish this, the elimination of *riba* (interest) is crucial as it prevents the accumulation of wealth at the expense of others.
B) Work and Productivity: Islamic economics advocates for fair compensation based on labour performed, discouraging excess profits and rent-seeking

behaviour. The principle of *mudarabah* (profit-loss sharing) e.g., promotes cooperation between capital providers and entrepreneurs, encouraging productive investment and equitable distribution of profits. By focusing on real economic activities, Islamic economics challenges conventional monetary policies and aims to foster sustainable economic growth.

C) Advocating Distributional Equity: In Islamic economics, society has the right to redistribute private property to ensure equitable wealth distribution. This principle aligns with the Islamic law of inheritance, preventing the concentration of wealth in the hands of a few individuals. Zakah, a mandatory tax on wealth exceeding a certain exemption level, plays a crucial role in economic activity, encouraging the productive use of idle assets and stimulating investment.

D) Elimination of *Israf* (Wasteful Consumption): Responsible and moderate consumption, known as *israf*, is emphasised in Islamic economics. This principle discourages wastefulness and extravagant spending, promoting sustainable practices and resource conservation. By addressing issues such as overconsumption and environmental degradation, Islamic economics underscores the importance of preserving resources for future generations.

To establish the viability and workability of Islamic economics, it must undergo rational economic analysis and practical application. Alternative financial instruments, such as profit-sharing contracts, Islamic bonds (*sukuk*), and equity-based financing, replace interest-based transactions. Islamic banks play a central role in this system, providing interest-free financial services and adhering to Shariah principles.

Institution of *mudarabah* promotes risk diversification and encourages real investment, while the elimination of *israf* encourages businesses and individuals to adopt sustainable practices. The concept of distributional equity is translated into practical policies through various sources of national income and transfer payments, ensuring the welfare of society.

Therefore, Islamic economics offers an alternative economic order rooted in principles of social justice, cooperation, and ethical behaviour. By eliminating interest, promoting profit-sharing, and encouraging responsible consumption, it aims to achieve equitable wealth distribution and sustainable economic growth. While presenting challenges in practical implementation, Islamic economics provides an inspiring model that emphasises the ethical dimensions of economic activities and their impact on individuals, society, and the environment.

The principle of *israf* in Islamic economics advocates for responsible and moderate consumption, discouraging wastefulness and extravagant spending. This concept is rooted in the idea that resources are a trust from God and should be utilised wisely and in a manner that benefits individuals, society, and the environment.

Wasteful consumption, or *israf*, is considered contrary to the principles of justice and social responsibility in Islamic economics. It goes against the idea of equitable distribution and the concept of *Tawheed*, which emphasises unity and responsibility towards fellow human beings.

The prohibition of *israf* is not only applicable to individuals, but also extends to businesses and the state. In an Islamic economic system, businesses are encouraged to avoid excessive consumption of resources, and the state is responsible for ensuring the efficient and sustainable use of national resources.

By promoting responsible consumption, Islamic economics aims to address issues such as overconsumption, environmental degradation, and the depletion of natural resources. It emphasises the importance of preserving resources for future generations and ensuring the well-being of all members of society.

Furthermore, the principle of *israf* aligns with the idea of social justice and equitable distribution. When resources are used responsibly, there is a greater opportunity to meet the needs of all individuals and reduce disparities in society. To implement the principle of *israf*, Islamic economics advocates for practices such as conservation, recycling, and sustainable production methods. It encourages businesses to adopt environmentally friendly practices and consumers to be mindful of their consumption habits.

Overall, the concept of *israf* in Islamic economics serves as a reminder of the ethical dimension of economic activities and highlights the interconnectedness between economic decisions and their impact on society and the environment. By adhering to this principle, individuals and societies can contribute to a more sustainable and just economic system.

The next Chapter shed a light on the objections raised about comparing Islamic Economics, which involves normative ideals, with conventional economic theory, which describes ground realities. I also discuss that Islamic economics is not meant to merely describe the world but to bring about positive changes in it.

# Chapter 8
# The Clash of Ideals

## 8.1 Introduction

As discussed in the previous Chapter, some researchers criticised Islamic economics and its practicality as an economics system. We also assessed how economic analysis has undergone significant evolution over time, with shifting focuses on distribution, resource allocation, and macroeconomic policy. In recent times, alongside the mainstream economic approach of satisfying the "economic man," Islamic Economics has emerged as an alternative economic order. Rooted in Islamic principles, this system seeks to achieve efficient resource allocation while upholding social justice and adhering to the laws of God. The objections raised about comparing Islamic Economics, which involves normative ideals, with conventional economic theory, which describes ground realities, are addressed in this Chapter.

In this Chapter, I discuss that Islamic economics is not meant to merely describe the world but to bring about positive changes in it. The Message of the Prophet Muhammad focused on highlighting and rectifying elements that required transformation to align with Islamic principles. Thus, Islamic Economics seeks to set high ideals to guide the path of improvement, even though achieving those ideals entirely may be challenging. It serves as a guiding star, setting the direction for the journey of societal progress, even if it cannot be fully realised.

It is essential to recognise that conventional economic theory itself is not entirely positive or descriptive of real-world conditions. Instead, it also presents an idealised vision of an ideal market society with perfect competition, price-taking firms and consumers, no collusion or monopolies, and no information or transactional failures. While economists acknowledge that these idealised conditions are rarely found in reality, they are still proposed as goals to strive for due to their theoretical properties (Kenny, 1999).

In this context, the difference between the two approaches lies in the nature of their respective ideals. Conventional economic theory envisions a market society



S. Alamad, *Beyond Profit*, Contributions to Economics,
https://doi.org/10.1007/978-3-031-49748-3_8

based on cutthroat competition and survival of the fittest, which might be in conflict with Islamic economics ideals of cooperation, generosity, and social welfare. On the other hand, Islamic Economics presents ideals that are consistent with compassion, cooperation, and service to society.

This Chapter argues that Islamic Economics aims to create a transformative vision based on Islamic ideals, while conventional economic theory also presents its own set of idealised conditions to strive for. The methodological difference lies in the nature of their respective ideals, with Islamic Economics focusing on creating a more just and compassionate society in line with Islamic teachings.

## 8.2 Normative Ideals in Contrast to Ground Realities

The objection that normative ideals of Islamic Economics cannot be compared with positive theories of conventional economics is valid to some extent, but it can be addressed by considering the purpose and methodology of each approach.

Islamic Economics, as rooted in the teachings of the Quran and the practices of Prophet Muhammad, is primarily concerned with guiding human behaviour, and creating positive change in society. It sets forth visionary ideals to inspire individuals and societies to work towards achieving excellence and fostering generosity, cooperation, and compassion. The focus is on guiding human conduct towards moral and ethical behaviour, which is considered more important than merely describing the ground realities of human existence.

While some critics (Issawi, 1950; Ghazanfar, 2003; Watt, 1972) may argue that actual Muslim behaviour in Islamic countries does not fully conform to the Quranic ideals, it does not invalidate the significance of these ideals as guiding principles. The Quran and the teachings of the Prophet acknowledge that human beings have weaknesses and imperfections but encourage them to strive for improvement and righteousness.

On the other hand, conventional economic theory, while often considered a positive theory, also presents an idealised vision of a perfectly competitive market society. This idealised model assumes certain conditions that rarely exist in the real world, such as perfect competition, complete information, and absence of externalities and transaction costs. Despite its deviation from real-world complexities, economists use this ideal model to analyse economic phenomena and suggest policies to approximate these ideal conditions (Siddiqi, 1992a, 1992b; Alamad et al., 2021).

The key difference lies in the objectives of these visions. While Islamic Economics aims to inspire individuals to embody higher moral and ethical values and work towards societal well-being, conventional economic theory aims to analyse and predict economic behaviour based on idealised market conditions.

Therefore, Islamic Economics, while rooted in normative ideals, serves a distinct purpose from conventional economics. It sets a moral compass and offers a transformative vision, encouraging individuals and societies to strive for higher values, compassion, and cooperation while recognising human imperfections. In contrast, conventional economics offers analytical tools for understanding market behaviour based on idealised conditions, despite their divergence from reality (Essid, 1995). Both approaches can coexist, addressing different aspects of human society and economic behaviour, while each serves its unique purpose and offers valuable insights for shaping the world we live in.

## 8.3 Employing Material Means for Affecting Change

The objection that Islamic economics ideals may not have any real effect due to the gap between lofty ideals and ground realities can be addressed in the following manner:

Firstly, it is essential to challenge the assumption that materialistic theories are the only means of bringing about change in society. While conventional scientific methods prioritise the study of material means and causal laws, Islamic thought posits that ideals and visions can indeed influence the material world. The rise of Islamic economics is a historical example that counters the claim that material causes are the sole determinants of societal change. Prophet Muhammad inspired the Bedouin Arabs with a vision and Islamic ideals, leading them to transform their society and have a profound impact on the world (Spengler, 1964).

Secondly, Islamic economics emphasise the significance of inner transformation and spirituality, which can drive external actions. When individuals are motivated by a genuine desire to follow Islamic principles and embody ideals such as compassion, cooperation, and generosity, their actions can bring about positive changes in the material world. This inner transformation guides individuals to engage in activities that benefit society and promote social justice (Sarakhsi, 1978).

Lastly, the objection assumes that Islamic economics ideals and material means are mutually exclusive. However, in reality, they can complement each other. The pursuit of Islamic economics ideals can lead to the development of real-world institutions and economic policies that align with principles of justice, fairness, and societal welfare. Islamic economics provides a framework that incorporates both moral and material dimensions, enabling policymakers to create systems that serve the well-being of individuals and society as a whole (Misri, 1981; Alamad et al., 2021).

Therefore, Islamic economics ideals are not disconnected from material reality; they can serve as guiding principles that inspire meaningful actions and contribute to the betterment of society. By recognising the value of spiritual transformation and aligning it with material means, Islamic Economics offers a holistic approach to addressing the challenges faced by societies.

We present evidence to demonstrate how abstract and intangible ideals and visions can impact the course of history without relying solely on material means. A notable example is Karl Marx's vision of a classless society based on justice, equality, and brotherhood, which inspired and influenced millions, despite his own deterministic analysis of economic trajectories proving to be incorrect (Solo, 1981).

Furthermore, Karen Pfeifer's research on wage-profit shares in Egyptian firms revealed that Islamic firms offer higher wages but lower profits compared to non-Islamic firms, indicating the influence of Islamic values on their economic behaviour (Pfeifer, 2001).

Additionally, Najam's study on philanthropy among immigrant Pakistanis in the USA showed that they contribute significantly more to charity than other communities with similar income, owing to their adherence to Islamic injunctions (Najam, 2007).

## 8.4 The Lack of Practicality to the Normative Economics Theory

The objection raised is that the ideals presented in Islamic economics are not realistic and practical, considering the imperfect nature of human beings and their tendencies towards greed and selfishness. The argument is that a more concrete and grounded theory is needed, which reflects the realities of the world as observed in existing Islamic societies.

To address this objection, we can turn to the concept of *Jahilliya*, which means the age of ignorance prevalent before the advent of Islam, which bears similarities to modern society. Both eras are characterised by widespread oppression, injustice, and exploitation of the weak by the powerful. The Quran explicitly discourages the concentration of wealth in the hands of a few, a problem that persists in modern times. Stiglitz (2011) points out that in the USA, the top 1% of the population owns 40% of the country's assets. Carter (2011) criticises the top 1% for leading the country into war and economic devastation while leaving the less fortunate to bear the burdens. The recent financial crisis in 2008 resulted in bankers evicting millions from their homes for non-payment of interest.

Moreover, contemporary societies still struggle with various social evils reminiscent of *Jahilliya*. Loose sexual morals, alcohol, drugs, and the abandonment and trafficking of children are issues that exist even today. To prevent thousands of abandoned babies, "safe haven" laws have been introduced in many states in the USA, allowing mothers to leave their children at designated hospitals without facing any questions (Carter, 2011).

By pointing out these parallels, it becomes evident that certain issues witnessed in the age of ignorance persist in modern societies, highlighting the relevance and practicality of Islamic economics ideals for addressing contemporary challenges. Islamic economics is historically renowned for bringing enlightenment and revolutionising the world. Despite its humble beginnings with ignorant, illiterate, and semi-barbaric Arabs, it led to the creation of a civilisation that dominated the world for a millennium. However, it was prophesied that Islam would become a stranger in the future, and today, Muslims are criticised for deviating from the teachings of Islam and indulging in various prohibited actions (Mahdi, 1964).

To address this objection, one must have faith in Islamic economics' transformative power. Just as it revolutionised the world centuries ago, it has the potential to bring about positive change today. The message of God, embodied in Islam, is a precious gift to humanity, as stated in the Quran (Surah Al-Ma'idah, 5:3): "This day have I perfected your religion for you, completed My favour upon you, and have chosen for you Islam as your religion."

Embracing the true Islamic economics and aligning one's actions with its principles can lead to positive changes in individuals and society as a whole. Rather than dismissing the ideals of Islamic economics as impractical, one must have faith in its ability to guide people towards righteousness and a better way of life. By adhering to the true spirit of Islamic economics, Muslims can once again find the path of enlightenment and bring about meaningful transformation in the world.

Today, not only has Islamic economics become unfamiliar to many Muslims, but they have also lost faith in its ability to provide comprehensive and perfect guidance for contemporary challenges. Instead, the prevailing belief is that the solutions to current problems lie in adopting conventional economics and science, technology, and social and political institutions. However, just as Islamic economics provided a complete and effective solution fourteen centuries ago, its core teachings on spirituality, piety, reliance on God, and emulating the exemplary conduct of the Prophet Muhammad remain sufficient to address our present-day issues (Siddiqi, 1992a, 1992b).

The problems faced by the Islamic world cannot be adequately resolved through foreign investments, international financial institutions like the IMF, democratic reforms, or institutional changes alone. Instead, Islamic economics offers a profound lesson on spirituality and individual conduct that can form the foundation for solving modern challenges. By striving to realise the potential within themselves and fostering a sense of unity within the Ummah (the Muslim community) as a cohesive entity, Muslims can replicate the efforts of Prophet Muhammad (S.A.W.) and achieve similar success (Siddiqi, 1992a, 1992b).

In essence, the comprehensive Islamic economics framework, when genuinely practiced and implemented, can provide the answers to the problems faced by Muslims today, transcending the dependence on external sources for solutions. By returning to the spiritual essence of Islamic economics and embracing the principles of unity and righteousness, the Islamic world can find the path to progress and prosperity.

## 8.5 Balancing Challenges and Opportunities

The global financial crisis of 2008 exposed a significant failure in economic theory, which has been acknowledged even by prominent figures like Larry Summers, the former United States Treasury Secretary. Many economists, including Nobel laureates, have criticised the prevailing economic theories for their inability to comprehend and predict the crisis accurately. Despite these critiques, the economics profession has been slow to respond with substantial changes to the conventional syllabus and hiring practices (Stiglitz, 2011; Alamad, 2016).

The field of economics produces a considerable number of Ph.D. graduates each year, and the existing mechanisms for evaluations, tenure, and publications in academia have considerable inertia, making it challenging to shift directions quickly. This situation can be likened to the US Steel Industry's inability to adopt fourth-generation steel furnaces when they were invented by the Japanese because of their significant investments in obsolete technology (Carter, 2011).

Similarly, in economics, the established practices and infrastructure make it difficult for the field to embrace alternative theories and approaches that might better explain and address real-world economic challenges. The lack of a swift response to the crisis and the failure to adapt to changing circumstances highlight the need for critical evaluation and reform within the economics profession to better serve society's needs and address complex economic issues (Stiglitz, 2011).

The failures in conventional economic theories, as highlighted by the 2008 global financial crisis, present a significant opportunity for the Islamic world to develop and build an Islamic economics on new and solid foundations. Unlike conventional economists who are bound by heavy investments in obsolete knowledge and the limitations of neoclassical economics, Muslim economists have the advantage of being able to explore alternative and transformative approaches (Stiglitz, 2011).

The Quran provides deep wisdom and guidance on managing the economic affairs of a society, offering a coherent worldview that is radically different from the failed methodologies of materialism and logical positivism. While many new schools of thought have emerged after the 2008 crisis, most of them offer only partial remedies because they lack an alternative foundation that can truly revolutionise economic thinking (Carter, 2011).

Islamic teachings in the economic realm provide an opportunity for the Islamic world to lead the way out of the current global challenges. Just as it did fourteen hundred years ago, the Quran offers complete and perfect guidance that can guide Islamic economics towards a more just, compassionate, and sustainable path. By embracing these teachings and developing a distinct Islamic economic approach, the Islamic world has the potential to make a positive impact and provide solutions to the world's economic problems.

## 8.6 The Material and Spiritual Aspects

Secular and materialist worldviews prioritise the material aspect of human well-being while often overlooking the spiritual dimension. They argue that allowing individuals to pursue their self-interest and maximise their wants according to their preferences will lead to the highest material well-being. Such worldviews may not recognise the role of Divine guidance in human life and rely solely on human reasoning to develop strategies. Values and government intervention are usually seen as unnecessary in the efficient and equitable allocation and distribution of resources.

The belief is that market forces, driven by competition, will naturally ensure that individual self-interest serves the social interest (Kenny, 1999).

On the other hand, religious worldviews consider both the material and spiritual aspects of human well-being. They do not necessarily reject the importance of reason in human development but recognise its limitations and seek to complement it with divine revelation. They also acknowledge the value of individual freedom and the pursuit of self-interest in human development. However, they emphasise the need for moral values and good governance to temper these freedoms and pursuits. The goal is to ensure that the well-being of all is realised, and social harmony and family integrity are preserved, even as individuals pursue their self-interest. In religious worldviews, the notion of moral values and ethical conduct plays a significant role in guiding individual behaviour and decision-making for the greater good of society (Maqrizi, 1956).

Among the prevailing worldviews, there are varying degrees of emphasis on material and spiritual goals, as well as differences in the role of moral values and government intervention in shaping human affairs. Material goals primarily focus on physical comfort and well-being through the acquisition of goods and services, while spiritual goals encompass elements like closeness to God, inner peace, happiness, honesty, justice, care, cooperation, family and social harmony, and the prevention of crime and disorder. Although spiritual goals may not be easily quantifiable, they play a crucial role in achieving overall human well-being (Allouche, 1994).

Given the limitation of resources, an excessive emphasis on material aspects may lead to the neglect of spiritual elements. The varying emphasis on material and spiritual aspects of well-being can significantly impact the economic disciplines of different societies. In certain cases, the pursuit of material gain might overshadow other essential dimensions of human existence.

Paul Feyerabend (1993, p. 3), in the introduction to the Chinese edition of his book "Against Method," openly acknowledged that first-world science is just one form of science among many. When it tries to claim a monopoly or superior status, it risks transforming into a political pressure group rather than a genuine instrument of research. This statement highlights the need for openness to diverse worldviews and their contributions to understanding and addressing human problems and challenges.

## 8.7 The Enlightenment Movement and Traditional Economics

The continuity and similarity in the value systems of major religions, including Judaism, Christianity, and Islam, stem from Islam's belief in the preservation of the core messages of previous Revealed religions. The Quran asserts that the teachings delivered to Prophet Muhammad were also given to the Messengers before him (Al-Quran, 41:43). Had conventional economics continued to evolve in alignment with the Judeo-Christian worldview as it did prior to the Enlightenment Movement of the seventeenth and eighteenth centuries, the distinction between conventional and Islamic economics might not have been significant.

However, the Enlightenment Movement had a profound impact on intellectual disciplines in Europe, instilling a secular, value-neutral, materialistic, and social-Darwinist worldview, although this influence was not all-encompassing. Despite the theoretical adoption of a secular and value-neutral stance, not all economists embraced materialism or social-Darwinism in their personal lives, and many continued to be guided by their religious worldviews. Koopmans (1969) aptly noted that beneath the surface of an economist, one could often find a moralist. Consequently, while conventional economics theoretically adopted the Enlightenment worldview's secular orientation and neglected the role of value judgments and good governance in resource allocation and distribution, in practice, the pre-Enlightenment tradition persisted to some extent (see Baeck, 1994, p. 11).

Indeed, the market system, with its secular and materialist worldview, brought about a prolonged period of prosperity in the Western market-oriented economies. However, this remarkable prosperity did not result in the eradication of poverty or the fulfilment of all individuals' needs in alignment with the values of Judeo-Christian traditions, even in the wealthiest nations. Persistent income and wealth inequalities have endured, and economic instability and unemployment have also contributed to the hardships faced by the less fortunate. Despite rapid economic development and a phenomenal increase in wealth, achieving both efficiency and equity has proven to be challenging and elusive (Koopmans, 1969).

The field of economics has faced persistent criticism from various well-meaning scholars throughout history. For instance, in England, Thomas Carlyle (in his work "Past and Present" (1843), John Ruskin (in "Unto this Last" (1862), and Charles Dickens (in "Hard Times", 1854–55) ridiculed the dominant doctrine of *laissez-faire*, which emphasised self-interest. Carlyle famously referred to economics as a "dismal science" and rejected the notion that uncontrolled private interests would naturally lead to the public welfare (see Jay & Jay, 1986). Similarly, in America, Henry George (1879), in his book "Progress and Poverty", criticised the stark contrast between wealth and poverty resulting from the prevailing economic system. He pointed out that if all the benefits of progress only serve to create vast fortunes, increase luxury, and deepen the divide between the rich and the poor, then true progress is not achieved, and the situation cannot be sustainable in the long run (George, 1955, p. 10). These critiques questioned the prevailing economic ideologies and called for a more equitable and compassionate approach to economic affairs.

Modern economic development, despite its progress, has been accompanied by various negative consequences. It has failed to meet the basic needs of a significant portion of the population and has exacerbated income and wealth inequalities (Easterlin, 1974, 1995, 2001; Oswald, 1997; Blanchflower & Oswald, 2000; Diener & Oshi, 2000; Kenny, 1999). Moreover, it has been associated with the breakdown of family structures and has not been able to provide inner peace and happiness to individuals (Easterlin, 1995, 2001; Oswald, 1997; Blanchflower & Oswald, 2000; Diener & Oshi, 2000; Kenny, 1999).

In response to these problems and the aftermath of the Great Depression in the 1930s, the laissez-faire approach lost its prominence. The Keynesian revolution and the rise of socialist ideas brought about a call for more government intervention in the economy. However, it became evident that government intervention alone could not completely solve all socio-economic issues. There is a recognition that motivating individuals to act ethically and responsibly is essential. This is where the moral foundation of society becomes crucial, as it can inspire people to do what is right and refrain from harmful actions. Neglecting ethics in economics has limited the effectiveness of welfare economics and descriptive economic analysis (Easterlin, 1995, 2001; Oswald, 1997; Blanchflower & Oswald, 2000).

Nobel laureate Amartya Sen has advocated for a greater integration of ethical considerations into economics to enhance its productivity (1987, pp. 78–79). Scholars Hausman and McPherson also assert that an economy that actively engages with the moral dimensions of its subject matter can be more insightful and beneficial (1993, p. 723). Thus, there is a growing acknowledgment of the importance of ethics in shaping economic behaviour and policy-making.

## 8.8 Islamic and Conventional Economics Worldviews

Islamic economics stands apart from conventional economics in its fundamental worldview. While conventional economics is gradually returning to its pre-Enlightenment roots, Islamic economics has always remained rooted in a religious worldview that rejects secularism and value neutrality. Its primary focus is on ensuring the genuine well-being of all individuals, regardless of their gender, age, race, religion, or wealth (Siddiqi, 1992a, 1992b).

In contrast to communism, which seeks to abolish private property, and laissez-faire economics, which solely relies on self-interest and competition, Islamic economics takes a balanced approach. It does not aim to eliminate private property or prevent individuals from pursuing their self-interest. Instead, it acknowledges the role of the market in efficiently allocating resources. However, Islamic economics goes beyond the market mechanism alone and recognises that competition may not be enough to safeguard the overall social interest (Sen, 1987).

Islamic economics places a strong emphasis on human brotherhood, socio-economic justice, and the well-being of all members of society. It achieves these goals through an integrated approach that combines moral values, the market mechanism, families, society, and effective governance. In this context, the concept of human brotherhood and socio-economic justice is deeply ingrained, guiding the principles and practices of economic affairs.

By prioritising the values of compassion, equity, and social welfare, Islamic economics strives to create an economic system that fosters an inclusive and just society. It emphasises the importance of moral values, cooperation, and good governance to ensure that the benefits of economic activities are fairly distributed and contribute to the overall well-being of society.

(a) **The Role of the Market, Families, Society, and Government**

The functioning of human society involves multiple institutions, such as the market, families, society, and government. These institutions are interconnected, and the interactions within each of them have significant implications for the overall well-being of society.

While the market plays a crucial role in efficiently allocating resources based on individual self-interest, an overemphasis on self-interest without moral restraints can lead to detrimental effects in other institutions. In particular, the family, which is the source of human input into society, may suffer if mutual sacrifice and care are lacking. Strong families are essential for providing loving care and proper upbringing for children, who represent the most important input not only in the market but also in society and government (Easterlin, 2001; Oswald, 1997).

If families disintegrate due to a focus solely on self-interest, the overall quality of the human input into all institutions may decline. For instance, children raised in unstable or uncaring environments may struggle to become productive members of society and contribute to economic growth. Moreover, a decline in family values and the willingness to make sacrifices can negatively impact social cohesion and trust within the broader society (Kenny, 1999).

Additionally, if fertility rates fall below the replacement level due to a lack of family cohesion and mutual sacrifice, it can pose challenges for society's sustainability and social security systems. A declining population may strain economic growth and lead to difficulties in maintaining support for an aging population (Blanchflower & Oswald, 2000; Diener & Oshi, 2000).

Therefore, Islamic economics recognises the importance of nurturing strong families and promoting mutual sacrifice, compassion, and care within society. It emphasises the need for moral values and good governance to complement the market mechanism and ensure the well-being of individuals and the broader community. By upholding the principles of human brotherhood, socio-economic justice, and the holistic development of individuals, Islamic economics aims to create a balanced and thriving society that benefits everyone.

(b) **The Role of Moral and Ethical Values**

Islamic economics differs from conventional economics in its emphasis on moral values and individual and social reform. While conventional economics often assumes individuals' behaviour and preferences as given, Islamic economics focuses on moral uplift and aims to change human behaviour, tastes, and preferences for the better. This moral uplift is viewed as essential for promoting general well-being and complementing the price mechanism in the market (Easterlin, 2001).

In Islamic economics, individuals are expected to pass their claims through a moral filter before entering the market. This helps filter out conspicuous consumption and wasteful claims on resources, leading to a more efficient use of resources and a reduction in inequities. The market mechanism then takes over to further allocate resources, but the moral filter ensures that the distribution is just and equitable.

The discipline of Islamic economics recognises that material well-being is essential but argues that the market alone may not fulfil all human needs, especially the spiritual ones. Excessive focus on self-interest can lead to the concentration of wealth in a few hands, leaving others deprived. In contrast, Islamic economics emphasises the importance of sacrifice and fulfilling obligations towards others, which leads to greater social harmony and a sense of responsibility towards the less fortunate (Siddiqi, 1992a, 1992b).

The question arises: Why would rational individuals sacrifice their self-interest for the sake of others? In Islamic economics, the concept of God-consciousness (*Taqwa*) plays a significant role. Individuals are motivated to act ethically and make sacrifices because of their belief in divine accountability and their desire to seek spiritual growth and inner peace.

Islamic economics and conventional economics both deal with resource allocation and distribution, but Islamic economics adds a strong emphasis on moral values and individual responsibility. By complementing the market mechanism with morally-based value judgments, Islamic economics aims to create a more equitable and just society that fulfils not only material needs but also spiritual well-being.

(c) **The Concept of the Hereafter**

In contrast to conventional economics, Islamic economics places a strong emphasis on the concepts of the innate goodness of human beings and the Hereafter. These concepts provide a deeper understanding of human motivation and behaviour, which conventional economics often overlooks.

According to Islamic beliefs, human beings possess an innate goodness that goes beyond merely pursuing self-interest. They are capable of altruism and making sacrifices for the well-being of others. This innate goodness plays a significant role in shaping individual behaviour and societal interactions (Fischel, 1992).

Additionally, the concept of the Hereafter in Islam extends the perspective of self-interest beyond the temporal world. It emphasises that actions in this life have consequences in the afterlife. Thus, self-interest is not confined to short-term gains but also includes considerations of moral and ethical conduct that affect one's standing in the Hereafter (Fischel, 1992).

In Islamic economics, the interplay between the innate goodness of human beings and the long-run perspective of self-interest creates a motivating mechanism for individuals to be not only efficient but also equitable and caring. The pursuit of self-interest is aligned with fulfilling obligations towards family, society, and the environment, as these actions have implications beyond this world.

Due to these fundamental differences in perspective, the three core concepts of conventional economics—rational economic man, positivism, and laissez-faire—do not receive the same intellectual approval in Islamic economics. Islamic scholars reject the narrow and materialistic view of human behaviour and advocate for a more holistic approach that considers spiritual, moral, and social dimensions in economic decision-making.

Islamic economics integrates the concepts of innate goodness and the Hereafter to provide a broader and more compassionate view of human behaviour. By recognising the long-run perspective of self-interest and the importance of moral values, Islamic economics seeks to promote not only efficiency but also equity and social welfare, ultimately aiming to create a just and caring society.

(d) **Rational Economic Human**

The concept of rationality in human behaviour is widely acknowledged, but there are differing viewpoints on its definition (Sen, 1987, pp. 11–14). In the conventional economics perspective, rationality is often equated with pursuing self-interest, maximising wealth, and satisfying personal wants, akin to the "moral equivalent of the force of gravity in nature" (Myers, 1983, p. 4). In this framework, society is seen as a collection of individuals solely driven by self-interest.

However, in Islamic economics, rationality goes beyond the pursuit of self-interest in this worldly life. It extends to the Hereafter through the adherence to moral values, which helps restrain self-interest and fosters social interest. Scholars[1] like Al-Mawardi (d. 1058) and Ibn Khaldun (d. 1406) emphasised the importance of moral values in guiding individual tastes and preferences, fostering social harmony, and promoting righteousness (Al-Mawardi, 1955, pp. 118–120; Ibn Khaldun, n.d., p. 158). Islamic economics rejects the notion of a "rational economic man" focused solely on self-interest, and instead, emphasises the integration of moral values for the well-being of both individuals and society as a whole.

(e) **Conceptual Positivism**

In contrast to conventional economics, positivism, which advocates complete neutrality towards ends and normative judgments (Robbins, 1935, p. 240; Friedman, 1953), does not align with Islamic intellectual thinking. In Islamic economics, all resources are perceived as a trust from God, and human beings are held accountable for their use. Thus, the utilisation of resources must adhere to the terms of this trust, which are defined by religious beliefs and moral values. Justice is central to Islamic economics, and the concept of human brotherhood within Islamic economics is inseparable from fair and equitable allocation and distribution of resources. The positivist notion of value-neutrality is incompatible with the Islamic economics worldview, as the ethical and moral dimensions play a fundamental role in the allocation and distribution of resources in a just and equitable manner.

(f) **The Concept of Pareto Optimality**

In Islamic economics, the emphasis on justice is integral to achieving balanced development, a concept that has been highlighted by Muslim scholars[2] throughout

[1] Some of these scholars include Abu Yusuf (d. 798), al-Mawardi (d. 1058), Abu Ya'la (d. 1065), Nazam al-Mulk (d. 1092), al-Ghazali (d. 1111), Ibn Taymiyyah (d. 1328), Ibn Khaldun (d. 1406), Shah Walliyullah (d. 1762), Jamaluddin al-Afghani (d. 1897), Muhammad 'Abduh (d. 1905), Muhammad Iqbal (d. 1938), Hasan al-Banna (d. 1949), Sayyid Mawdudi (d. 1979), and Baqir al-Sadr (d. 1980).

[2] Some of these authors include al-Katib (d. 749), Ibn al-Muqaffa (d. 756) al-Nu'man (d. 974), al-Mawardi (d. 1058), Kai Ka'us (d. 1082), Nizam al-Mulk (d. 1092), al-Ghazali (d. 1111), al-

history. This aligns with the recent focus of Development Economics on the importance of justice (Abu Yusuf, 1933/34, p. 111; Al-Mawardi, 1955, p. 27; Ibn Taymiyyah, 1961–63, Vol. 18, p. 166). According to their teachings, rendering justice and eradicating injustice not only brings spiritual blessings and rewards in the Hereafter but also accelerates the development of the country, increases wealth, and ensures security and well-being for the society.

However, the concept of pareto optimality does not align with the principles of Islamic economics. Pareto optimality asserts that a situation is optimal if no individual can be made better off without making someone else worse off. This view conflicts with moral values that prioritise the well-being of all over absolute efficiency. Islamic economics recognises the importance of sacrifice by the well-to-do to uplift the well-being of the less fortunate. This is exemplified by the religious obligation of Muslims to pay Zakat, which is a form of charity equivalent to 2.5 percent of their net worth, for the benefit of the poor and needy. The concept of Pareto optimality is, therefore, not relevant in the paradigm of Islamic economics, which places a strong emphasis on social justice and equitable distribution of resources.

(g) **Role of the State**

In Islamic economics, moral values need to be not only promoted but also enforced for their effectiveness in society. The responsibility for ensuring compliance with moral norms and restraining socially harmful behaviour lies with the state. This includes preventing injustice, fraud, and transgressions against others' rights and property. While the Qur'an provides moral guidelines, the state plays a crucial role in implementing and upholding these norms through proper upbringing, incentives, deterrents, regulations, and an impartial judiciary. Prophet Muhammad himself emphasised the restraining role of the state, stating that God restrains through the sovereign more effectively than through the Qur'an (al-Mawardi, 1955, p. 121).

Throughout history, leading Muslim scholars have emphasised the importance of an effective government in preventing injustice and ensuring social welfare (al-Mawardi, 1960, p. 5). However, this role of the state does not imply regimentation or extensive ownership and operation of the economy by the government. Classical Islamic scholars, such as al-Dimashqi and Ibn Khaldun, expressed disapproval of the state becoming directly involved in the economy. Instead, they emphasised that the state should adopt a welfare-oriented approach, moderate its spending, respect property rights, and avoid excessive taxation. This approach to governance aligns with the concept of 'good governance,' which has become widely recognised as an essential aspect of effective state management. The state's role in Islamic economics is not to dominate the economy but to ensure justice, protect property rights, and promote the general welfare of society through ethical governance.

Turtushi (d. 1127). (For details, see Essid, 1995, pp. 19–41.)

## 8.9 Conclusion

In this chapter, we delved deeper into the objections raised about comparing Islamic Economics, rooted in normative ideals, with conventional economic theory, which describes ground realities. We argued that Islamic economics is not meant to be mere descriptions of the world but rather tools to bring about positive changes in it. The teachings of Prophet Muhammad (SAW) focused on highlighting and rectifying elements that required transformation to align with Islamic principles. As a result, Islamic Economics sets high ideals to guide the path of improvement, even though achieving those ideals entirely may be challenging. It serves as a guiding star, setting the direction for the journey of societal progress, even if it cannot be fully realised.

Moreover, it is crucial to acknowledge that conventional economic theory itself is not entirely positive or merely descriptive of real-world conditions. Instead, it also presents an idealised vision of an ideal market society, assuming perfect competition, price-taking firms and consumers, no collusion or monopolies, and no information or transactional failures. While economists recognise that these idealised conditions are rarely found in reality, they are still proposed as goals to strive for due to their theoretical properties.

The crucial difference between the two approaches lies in the nature of their respective ideals. Conventional economic theory envisions a market society based on cutthroat competition and survival of the fittest, which might be in conflict with Islamic ideals of cooperation, generosity, and social welfare. On the other hand, Islamic Economics presents ideals that are consistent with compassion, cooperation, and service to society.

This chapter argues that Islamic Economics aims to create a transformative vision based on Islamic ideals, while conventional economic theory also presents its own set of idealised conditions to strive for. The methodological difference lies in the nature of their respective ideals, with Islamic Economics focusing on creating a more just and compassionate society in line with Islamic teachings.

By recognising this distinction and understanding the purpose and methodology of each approach, we can appreciate the unique contributions and insights they offer to address the challenges faced by societies. Islamic Economics provides a moral compass to guide human behaviour and inspire positive change, while conventional economics offers analytical tools to understand economic phenomena and suggest policies for improving market conditions.

As a result, both Islamic Economics and conventional economic theory have their place in shaping our understanding of human behaviour and economic systems. While the former sets visionary ideals to inspire positive change in society, the latter proposes idealised market conditions to strive for. Each approach serves a distinct purpose and offers valuable insights for societal progress and well-being. By recognising the complementarity of these approaches, we can foster a more comprehensive understanding of economic behaviour and work towards creating a more just and compassionate world.

The objection that normative ideals of Islamic Economics cannot be compared with positive theories of conventional economics is valid to some extent, but it can be addressed by considering the purpose and methodology of each approach.

Islamic Economics, as rooted in the teachings of the Quran and the practices of Prophet Muhammad (SAW), is primarily concerned with guiding human behaviour, and creating positive change in society. It sets forth visionary ideals to inspire individuals and societies to work towards achieving excellence and fostering generosity, cooperation, and compassion. The focus is on guiding human conduct towards moral and ethical behaviour, which is considered more important than merely describing the ground realities of human existence.

While some critics may argue that actual Muslim behaviour in Islamic countries does not fully conform to the Quranic ideals, it does not invalidate the significance of these ideals as guiding principles. The Quran and the teachings of the Prophet (SAW) acknowledge that human beings have weaknesses and imperfections but encourage them to strive for improvement and righteousness.

On the other hand, conventional economic theory, while often considered a positive theory, also presents an idealised vision of a perfectly competitive market society. This idealised model assumes certain conditions that rarely exist in the real world, such as perfect competition, complete information, and absence of externalities and transaction costs. Despite its deviation from real-world complexities, economists use this ideal model to analyse economic phenomena and suggest policies to approximate these ideal conditions.

The key difference lies in the objectives of these visions. While Islamic Economics aims to inspire individuals to embody higher moral and ethical values and work towards societal well-being, conventional economic theory aims to analyse and predict economic behaviour based on idealised market conditions.

Therefore, Islamic Economics, while rooted in normative ideals, serves a distinct purpose from conventional economics. It sets a moral compass and offers a transformative vision, encouraging individuals and societies to strive for higher values, compassion, and cooperation while recognising human imperfections. In contrast, conventional economics offers analytical tools for understanding market behaviour based on idealised conditions, despite their divergence from reality. Both approaches can coexist, addressing different aspects of human society and economic behaviour, while each serves its unique purpose and offers valuable insights for shaping the world we live in.

Employing Material Means for Affecting Change: The objection that Islamic economics ideals may not have any real effect due to the gap between lofty ideals and ground realities can be addressed in the following manner:

Firstly, it is essential to challenge the assumption that materialistic theories are the only means of bringing about change in society. While conventional scientific methods prioritise the study of material means and causal laws, Islamic thought posits that ideals and visions can indeed influence the material world. The rise of Islamic economics is a historical example that counters the claim that material causes are the sole determinants of societal change.

Secondly, Islamic economics emphasise the significance of inner transformation and spirituality, which can drive external actions. When individuals are motivated by a genuine desire to follow Islamic economics principles and embody ideals such as compassion, cooperation, and generosity, their actions can bring about positive changes in the material world. This inner transformation guides individuals to engage in activities that benefit society and promote social justice.

Lastly, the objection assumes that Islamic economics ideals and material means are mutually exclusive. However, in reality, they can complement each other. The pursuit of Islamic economics ideals can lead to the development of real-world institutions and economic policies that align with principles of justice, fairness, and societal welfare. Islamic economics provides a framework that incorporates both moral and material dimensions, enabling policymakers to create systems that serve the well-being of individuals and society as a whole.

Therefore, Islamic economics ideals are not disconnected from material reality; they can serve as guiding principles that inspire meaningful actions and contribute to the betterment of society. By recognising the value of spiritual transformation and aligning it with material means, Islamic Economics offers a holistic approach to addressing the challenges faced by societies.

The Material and Spiritual Aspects: Secular and materialist worldviews prioritise the material aspect of human well-being while often overlooking the spiritual dimension. They argue that allowing individuals to pursue their self-interest and maximise their wants according to their preferences will lead to the highest material well-being. Such worldviews may not recognise the role of Divine guidance in human life and rely solely on human reasoning to develop strategies. Values and government intervention are usually seen as unnecessary in the efficient and equitable allocation and distribution of resources. The belief is that market forces, driven by competition, will naturally ensure that individual self-interest serves the social interest.

On the other hand, religious worldviews consider both the material and spiritual aspects of human well-being. They do not necessarily reject the importance of reason in human development but recognise its limitations and seek to complement it with divine revelation. They also acknowledge the value of individual freedom and the pursuit of self-interest in human development. However, they emphasise the need for moral values and good governance to temper these freedoms and pursuits. The goal is to ensure that the well-being of all is realised, and social harmony and family integrity are preserved, even as individuals pursue their self-interest. In religious worldviews, the notion of moral values and ethical conduct plays a significant role in guiding individual behaviour and decision-making for the greater good of society.

Among the prevailing worldviews, there are varying degrees of emphasis on material and spiritual goals, as well as differences in the role of moral values and government intervention in shaping human affairs. Material goals primarily focus on physical comfort and well-being through the acquisition of goods and services, while spiritual goals encompass elements like closeness to God, inner peace, happiness, honesty, justice, care, cooperation, family and social harmony, and the prevention of crime and disorder. Although spiritual goals may not be easily quantifiable, they play a crucial role in achieving overall human well-being.

Given the limitation of resources, an excessive emphasis on material aspects may lead to the neglect of spiritual elements. The varying emphasis on material and spiritual aspects of well-being can significantly impact the economic disciplines of different societies. In certain cases, the pursuit of material gain might overshadow other essential dimensions of human existence.

# Chapter 9
# The Essence of Faith-Based Economics: The Islamic Economic Thought

## 9.1 Introduction

The previous Chapter provided insights on the objections raised about comparing Islamic Economics, which involves normative ideals, with conventional economic theory, which describes ground realities. It also discussed that Islamic economics is not meant to merely describe the world but to bring about positive changes in it.

The aim of this Chapter is to discuss economics in religions and its faith-based economic approach. However, it was proven difficult to find any comprehensive faith-based economic framework, except for Islamic economics. While the original intention was to discuss religious-based economic thoughts of different faiths, due to this challenge, this Chapter focuses on one faith-based economic thought, the Islamic economics framework.

Given the stability of usury in the modern economy in non-Islamic countries and Islamic countries alike, we address the harmonisation between the Islamic and non-Islamic financial systems concerning the crucial issue of usury and the contemporary economic necessity.

The Islamic economic thought is based on clearly defined principles in its religious texts, on which the analysis and discussion in this Chapter is based upon. For example, Prophet Muhammad said: Whoever cheats is not a true believer. The Prophet said, "A buyer and a seller have the option of cancelling or confirming the bargain unless they separate, and if they spoke the truth and made clear the defects of the goods, then they would be blessed in their bargain, and if they told lies and hid some facts, their bargain would be deprived of God's blessings." [Sahih Bukhari, Hadith 1937; Sahih Muslim, Hadith 2286; Sunan al-Kubra al-Nasa'i, Hadith 9520].

For a Muslim, both selling and buying are permissible, provided they do not involve deceit in the commodity or the price. If a defect is present, it must be explicitly stated; otherwise, it is a form of deception and any profit from it is forbidden, as is said in another narration. [Sahih Muslim, Hadith 2287].



S. Alamad, *Beyond Profit*, Contributions to Economics,
https://doi.org/10.1007/978-3-031-49748-3_9

Hoarding is prohibited: The Prophet said, “It is unlawful for a Muslim to hoard for more than forty days, except for a house or an animal or a well.” [Sunan al-Kubra al-Nasa’i, Hadith 9596]. Regarding hoarding, it is forbidden for a Muslim to hoard goods for more than forty days, unless it is for a house, an animal, or a well. Some scholars have restricted the prohibition of hoarding only to necessities, while the prevailing view is more comprehensive.

It is evident that these teachings from the Quran and Hadith emphasise the principles of justice, honesty, and ethical behaviour in economic transactions. The prohibition of usury, deceit, hoarding, and unfair practices aims to ensure a fair and just economic environment that benefits society as a whole.

Another economic principle within the framework of moral teachings is the duty of managing wealth and utilising it for the betterment of society. This entails avoiding extravagance and abstaining from excessive accumulation of wealth, as both sides should be aligned with the betterment of society. This is because every participant in an economic exchange should contribute to the welfare of the community.

Prophet Muhammad’s teachings accentuate the importance of balanced trade, where both parties benefit, and society prospers. He said as mentioned earlier, “The buyer and the seller have the option of cancelling or confirming the bargain unless they separate, and if they spoke the truth and made clear the defects of the goods, then they would be blessed in their bargain, and if they told lies and hid some facts, their bargain would be deprived of God’s blessings.” [Sunan Abu Dawood, Hadith 1997; Musnad Ahmad, Hadith 1; Sunan al-Darimi, Hadith 8428]. This is a framework that regulates financial dealings and advocates for transparency.

The essence of Islamic economics encompasses not only individual well-being but also the collective welfare of society. This balance is maintained through principles like moderation, restraint, and adherence to ethical conduct. The practice of moderation and the avoidance of excess contribute to the overall vitality of the economy and its participants, ensuring a thriving economic environment.

## 9.2 The Principle of Moderation

It is noteworthy that while individuals are entitled to enjoy the worldly pleasures within ethical boundaries, excess, extravagance, and indulgence are discouraged. Islam economics encourages wealth distribution and spending on family and personal needs, advocating for a balanced and equitable approach to wealth management.

The Quran and the Prophet’s teachings underline the significance of moderation and the avoidance of extremes in economic matters. Extravagance, waste, and excessive accumulation are discouraged, as they can lead to societal discord and economic instability. This reflects Islam’s holistic approach to economic principles that prioritise individual and communal well-being.

Thus, Islam charts a moderate path in its economic behaviour, avoiding extremes. This balance is highlighted in the Quran, where it says, “And do not waste [resources]. Indeed, He does not like the wasteful." [Quran, Surah Al-Isra, 17:26]. Islamic teachings and traditions strongly discourage extravagance and even prohibit it in many instances. Extravagance is seen as a source of harm to both the individual and the community. It can lead to committing sins, erode moral values, and weaken a person's resolve. The Quran also emphasises the concept of moderation and balanced spending, advocating for a lifestyle that ensures individual and communal well-being.

Islamic economics promotes a harmonious and just society, where wealth is not concentrated in the hands of a few while others suffer. Islam economics encourages the responsible management of wealth, allowing individuals to enjoy the blessings of life while fulfilling their social obligations.

The Quran also warns against the negative consequences of excess and indulgence, both on an individual level and in a societal context. It cautions that indulgence can lead to moral degradation and societal decay. This concept extends to the entire community, as indulgence and excess can disrupt the balance of society and lead to its destruction.

Islamic economics further emphasise the interdependence of actions and consequences, stressing that the negative outcomes of indulgence and extravagance are inevitable. This highlights the importance of following a middle path, where economic activities are carried out with moderation and ethical considerations. In essence, Islamic economics advocates for responsible wealth management that benefits both individuals and the community. It encourages the avoidance of excess and indulgence, aiming to establish a just and balanced economic system that fosters societal well-being and prosperity.

In terms of ethical teachings regarding wealth pertains to the owner of wealth refraining from exploiting their financial position to gain political influence in directing state affairs and pursuing their material interests. This involves harnessing the tools of governance to satisfy their sinful desires, at the expense of other segments of society.

Islam economics encourages refraining from exploiting wealth and influence to achieve illegitimate personal goals. The Qur'an says, "Do not invalidate your charities with reminders or injury as does he who spends his wealth [only] to be seen by the people and does not believe in God and the Last Day" [Al-Baqarah: 264].

Islam economics advocates respecting values and ethics in the proper use of wealth and influence to prevent corruption and injustice. Using influence to further personal interests at the expense of community interests contradicts Islamic values and ethical principles.

The Quran and the Prophetic traditions advise against pursuing power and influence for personal gains. They emphasise that authority and power should be used for the public good and the welfare of society, through managing public affairs with sincerity and fairness. Islam considers the economy and governance as tools to serve humanity, promoting a balance between individual and communal interests. It urges avoiding the misuse of wealth and influence for purposes that harm society and promote corruption.

By consistently following these ethical principles and restrictions, Muslims can build a just and balanced society, economically and socially, where everyone enjoys fair opportunities and strives for the common good.

## 9.3 Ethical Competition

Regarding competition, Islamic economics encourages healthy competition for goodness and promotes striving for excellence in performing good deeds and productive activities while fostering cooperation. This is a fundamental principle of the Islamic economy.

The Quranic injunctions repeatedly emphasise pursuing beneficial competition and striving for excellence. Beneficial competition is a concept that encompasses direct and indirect competition, encompassing various economic activities. Healthy competition can lead to cost reduction in production, making goods and services more affordable to consumers. This is a virtuous cycle created through the market's competitive dynamics.

However, competition is not solely about economic gains; it also involves compassion and ethical behaviour. Muslims are advised to advise their fellow Muslims in economic endeavours, offering help and guidance rather than seeking to harm or undermine them. This approach strengthens the sense of brotherhood and cooperation within the community.

In contrast, capitalist economic practices often prioritise economic gains above ethical considerations. The non-faith-based economic philosophy often asserts that economic incentives and gains are the primary justifications for human activities, regardless of any ethical or social considerations. This approach has contributed to the prevalence of a materialistic and self-centred mindset in many societies.

Critics of Western capitalist economic practices argue that this perspective has led to a deterioration of human values and the loss of a higher purpose in life. The pursuit of economic gain has become an end in itself, overshadowing more meaningful and virtuous goals. This approach has transformed businesses from being means to achieve a good life into ends in themselves, with the acquisition of wealth becoming the ultimate objective.

Therefore, Islamic economics advocates a balanced approach to competition that encompasses both economic growth and ethical values. Competition is encouraged in Islamic economics, but it should be pursued with compassion, ethical behaviour, and the well-being of society in mind. This stands in contrast to some Western economic ideologies that prioritise economic gain above all else, potentially leading to a decline in ethical values and a skewed sense of purpose in life.

Similarly, the Western economy moved towards forming monopolistic conglomerates, successfully launching from the window of capitalism towards monopoly. Its actual monopoly was restrained by controlled abundance, orchestrated prices, and its control over domestic and international markets. The automatic mechanism of supply and demand was corrupted, freedom of exchange was abolished, and this aided in the accumulation of a few. Its influence expanded to grasp various economic activities both domestically and globally, until it managed to compete in diverse economic activities.

Furthermore, these are aspects of Islamic ethical teachings, as they relieve from indirect costs burdened by society, the primary source of private ownership. We observed their mention, along with a comparison to the Western economy, to elucidate Islamic economics' stance on wealth ownership.

It remains for us to complete the Islamic economics view of wealth and ownership, and the positive and negative implications it carries. We need to consider: How does Islamic economics - considering these costs - direct an individual who possesses wealth towards a certain direction in investing that wealth?

## 9.4 Overarching Principles for an Islamic Economic Policy

In the economic field, Islamic economics has principles and specific foundations that encompass a distinct economic policy. The application of these principles and policies was seen with precision during the time of the Prophet Muhammad and the rightly guided caliphs, and it is associated with the opinions of various scholars over different eras, and we are not here to pass judgment on them.

Islamic economics is a collection of general economic principles derived from the Quran and the Sunnah, coupled with an economic system that is built upon these principles, adaptable to various environments and eras. Thus, it possesses the following overarching aspects:

a) **Steadfast Principles:** These are a set of economic principles derived from Quranic and Sunnah texts, adhered to by Muslims in different times and places. Examples include the prohibition of usury and exploitation, as well as guidelines for trade and transactions.
b) **Applicability and Flexibility:** This refers to the methods, plans, and economic solutions adopted by the ruling authority in an Islamic society to apply the economic principles of Islam to the prevailing material conditions of the society. This allows for adaptation to changing circumstances while remaining rooted in Islamic economic principles.
c) **Diversity of Interpretation:** The application of these principles can differ based on individual juristic opinions. They may vary due to the changing context of time and place, but they are all rooted in the divine sources of Islamic economics.

These principles were applicable in various ways throughout Islamic history. Islamic scholars and jurists developed economic frameworks for the Islamic state, and their views varied depending on the time and place. The actual implementation is subject to the scholars' interpretations of the religious texts.

The practical implementation of these principles remains a subject of ongoing scholarly debate, reflecting the dynamic nature of Islamic economics' applicability to different societies and contexts. Scholars and researchers are striving to find ways to bridge the gap between Islamic teachings and the contemporary economic realities, recognising that the true challenge for Islamic society lies in linking its teachings with the material world it inhabits.

It is possible to express these applications in the form of economic systems or models that adhere to principles of Islamic economics and cater to the needs of modern society. These economic systems are not fixed in stone but rather flexible to address the unique economic challenges faced by each society and era.

- **One Unified Economic Doctrine**: In Islamic economics, there is only one unified economic doctrine, which is based on the principles and economic guidelines derived from the Quran and Sunnah (teachings of Prophet Muhammad). This doctrine encompasses a distinct economic policy and is governed by specific principles. Within the boundaries of these principles and guidelines, and within the framework of this economic policy, there can be variations in the application and the forms of Islamic economic systems based on the changing circumstances of time and place. These variations do not contradict the essence of the doctrine. Rather, they reflect the flexibility and adaptability of Islamic economics to different social, temporal, and spatial contexts. This understanding is supported by the fact that the essential principles of Islam remain constant, while their application may vary.
- **Different Economic Applications or Systems**: The way the principles and guidelines of Islamic economics are put into practice can vary among researchers and scholars, depending on the changing circumstances of their societies. This does not negate the overall Islamic economic doctrine, but rather accounts for the diverse contexts in which it is applied. This can be observed in various Islamic countries that adopt different economic policies, all within the framework of Islamic principles. This is not to omit the fact that most of those countries follow and adapt conventional economic policies.
- Some countries might emphasise public ownership or a strong role for the state in economic activities, while others might opt for a more market-oriented approach. These variations in approach are based on different interpretations of the same Islamic economic principles, all aiming to create economic systems that adhere to the tenets of Islam.
- **Difficulty of Research in Islamic Economics**: Researching Islamic economics presents challenges due to two main factors:

   i. Closure of the Gate of Ijtihad: Since about a thousand years ago, there has been a general lack of consensus among Islamic scholars regarding new interpretations and legal opinions (ijtihad). This has led to a lack of development in Islamic economic thought, hindering the adaptation of traditional principles to contemporary economic conditions.
   ii. Complex Economic Realities: The intricacies of modern economic life are such that merely understanding the vast Islamic jurisprudence and theology is not enough. Researchers in Islamic economics are also required to possess a deep understanding of technical economic theories and contemporary

economic systems to formulate practical solutions that align with Islamic economics principles.

Hence, the concept of Islamic economics is based on unchanging principles derived from the Quran and Sunnah. However, the application of these principles can vary within different contexts and economic systems. The difficulty in researching Islamic economics lies in the limitations imposed by historical factors and the need for scholars to bridge the gap between traditional Islamic teachings and modern economic complexities.

## 9.5 The Material and Spiritual in Economics

The material and spiritual aspects in the Islamic economy is an important part of its structure. In various economic systems, whether individualistic or collective, economic activity is generally focused on achieving material gains. This could mean maximising profits in capitalist economies or satisfying public needs and achieving material welfare in socialist economies. However, in Islamic economics, economic activity, while being material in nature, is imbued with a religious or spiritual dimension.

This spiritual dimension is rooted in a strong sense of awareness and reverence for God. In Islamic economics, individuals feel that they are not only dealing with others but also with God. This sense of spiritual connection leads to a different approach to economic activities.

There are several implications of this spiritual dimension in Islamic economics:

a) **Faith-Based Nature:** Islamic economic activity is driven by the faith and spiritual devotion of individuals. The pursuit of material gain is not the sole objective; seeking God's pleasure and fearing His judgment are equally important.
b) **Dual Oversight and Inclusiveness:** Islamic economic practices are subject to both material and spiritual oversight. The economic transactions are not only evaluated based on their material outcomes but also on their ethical and spiritual dimensions.
c) **Higher Purpose of Economic Activity:** The primary goal of economic activity in Islamic economics goes beyond mere material gain. Economic activities are carried out with the intention of pleasing God and seeking His reward.

This spiritual foundation has a significant impact on various aspects of economic behaviour and transactions within the Islamic economic framework. It shapes the motivations, intentions, and ethical considerations that guide economic decisions. Additionally, the emphasis on spirituality helps maintain a balance between material pursuits and spiritual growth, preventing excessive focus on material accumulation.

As a result, Islamic economics introduces a unique approach where economic activity is not detached from spiritual values. The integration of material and spiritual dimensions leads to a more balanced and purposeful economic behaviour, promoting both material welfare and spiritual growth.

The connection between the material and the spiritual in Islamic economics forms a significant characteristic of the Islamic economy and its orientation, which imbues economic activities with a sense of faith and spiritual contentment.

Here, a crucial point arises, which has been a subject of contemplation for many, including experts. In Islamic economics, the demarcation between the material and the spiritual, as well as between worldly and otherworldly matters, is not distinct. Many material or worldly pursuits undertaken by individuals can possess a spiritual or otherworldly dimension within the framework of Islam, provided they are executed with the intention of seeking God's pleasure and are directed towards Him.

For example, a companion of the Prophet once observed a robust young man diligently working. Some companions suggested that if he was working to support his young children, he was indeed in the path of God. If his labour was to aid elderly parents, he was still in the path of God. Even if he was striving for his own benefit, he remained in the path of God. The Prophet confirmed that all these actions, when accompanied by noble intentions, are considered to be in alignment with God's way.

This underscores that in Islamic economics, there is no inherent conflict between religion and worldly matters, and there exists no metaphysical divide between material and spiritual realms. Instead, Islamic economics recognises that various activities can be infused with spiritual significance, contingent upon intention and the pursuit of God's satisfaction.

Furthermore, faith in Islamic economics transcends mere belief; it entails a revived faith linked to productivity, equitable distribution, kindness, and support for others. It is faith that ultimately benefits the community. Consequently, Prophet Muhammad emphasised that monasticism has no place in Islam, asserting that true devotion lies in serving God and being industrious within the community.

In essence, Islamic economics integrates the material and the spiritual, channelling different actions towards the intention of seeking God's approval. This integration ensures that both material and spiritual endeavours are oriented toward a productive and virtuous existence, rather than being compartmentalised or conflicting components. Spirituality in Islamic economics is the pursuit of righteousness, seeking the pleasure of God. It is about aligning one's actions with the divine will and seeking God's contentment. The Quran explains that: God is pleased with those who engage in righteous deeds, and it is through these deeds that individuals will be rewarded on the Day of Resurrection.

In this context, the concept of "annihilation in God" ascribed to Jamal al-Din al-Afghani refers to a deep state of spiritual surrender to God. However, the broader message suggests that true spirituality lies in conforming to the teachings and ethics ordained by God, leading to the betterment of individuals and their ultimate happiness.

The essence of Islamic economics spirituality is rooted in virtuous actions, sincere intentions, and a continuous connection with God's guidance and teachings. It is a holistic approach that emphasises the integration of faith, good deeds, and ethical behaviour as the path to achieving both spiritual enlightenment and worldly contentment.

## 9.6 Dual Oversight and Its Scope

- Oversight in Contemporary Economic Systems:

Within contemporary economic systems, oversight in conducting economic activities primarily relies on external regulations defined by the law. This oversight is limited and constrained. Prophet Muhammad once said, "There is no obedience in sin. Obedience is only in what is good." [Sahih Muslim, Hadith 2277]. This indicates the importance of adherence to ethical standards and legal regulations.

- Oversight in Islamic Economics:

In the realm of Islamic economics, there is both oversight from legal or religious authorities and a parallel internal oversight. This internal oversight is grounded in the believer's faith in God and the accountability in the Hereafter. Undoubtedly, this serves as a strong deterrent for ethical behaviour and the legitimacy of economic activities. It reinforces the sense of responsibility that Muslims have towards their actions, as they are not only answerable to human authorities but also to God.

The economic principles in Islamic economics are nurtured by this religious awareness and are deepened. Muslims find themselves naturally adhering to Islamic economic teachings, driven by their belief and faith. This commitment becomes intrinsic, voluntary, and a conscious choice not influenced by external authorities.

This contrasts with prevailing practices in contemporary economic systems, where religious ethical considerations in economic activities are often overlooked. This is evident in the attempts of many individuals within these systems to evade responsibilities or engage in deviations from economic norms, especially when they perceive a lack of state supervision or regulatory control.

## 9.7 Elevating the Purpose of Economic Activity

- In all contemporary economic systems, material interests are an End in themselves:

In all contemporary economic systems, material interests are pursued for their own sake, whether in the form of maximising profit or achieving material sufficiency and prosperity. This pursuit has led to the intense materialistic struggle inherent in capitalist societies, as well as the drive for economic control and dominance that characterises socialist economies. Despite the accomplishments attained by both capitalist and socialist economies, whether in terms of monetary gain or material prosperity, these gains and prosperity are themselves threatened due to the ongoing fierce competition between these economic systems. This competition persists as long as material wealth remains the ultimate goal.

- In Islamic economics, material interests are pursued but Not for their Own Sake:

In Islamic economics, material interests are pursued, yet not as ends in themselves. Instead, they serve as means to achieve higher goals and human welfare. According to the Islamic economics perspective, this world is cultivated for the Hereafter, and humans are stewards of it. Wealth in Islamic economics is not an ultimate end; rather, it is a tool. Muslims are tasked with seeking and utilising wealth, but not for its own sake. Instead, wealth is viewed as a means to effectively fulfil one's needs and responsibilities. The accumulation of wealth is guided by ethical considerations and a sense of accountability before God.

Thus, in Islamic economics, wealth is not sought simply for its own sake. Instead, Muslims use it as a means to remember and speak of God's blessings. It's a means to support oneself and others, and a source of gratitude. The emphasis is on using wealth as a way to fulfil responsibilities and express gratitude to God.

Islamic economics encourages the responsible and ethical utilisation of wealth. The Prophet Muhammad (peace be upon him) said: 'If a person equips himself with what is sufficient for his needs, Allah will bless his self-sufficiency and independence.' [Sahih Muslim, Hadith 1263]. This approach prevents both the pursuit of wealth for its own sake and its wasteful use. Islamic economics envisions wealth as a tool to support the welfare of individuals and society while maintaining a balanced and ethical perspective on its acquisition and distribution. This vision stands in contrast to the materialistic pursuits that often dominate contemporary economic systems.

## 9.8 The Ultimate Goal of Economic Activity

One of the most distinctive features of Islamic economics is that the ultimate goal of economic activity is to develop and enhance the world, to bestow its blessings upon all, rather than to pursue economic control, dominance, or the exclusive benefit of a specific group or nation. This stands in contrast to the focus of capitalist and socialist economic systems.

In Islamic economics perspective, humanity is considered the vicegerent of God on Earth, and it is a continuous obligation to elevate the concept of vicegerency by building and revitalising the world, harnessing its resources for the betterment of individuals and future generations. The Quran says: "It is He who made you successors upon the Earth…" (Quran, 35:39).

Accordingly, the Prophet Muhammad (peace be upon him) advised: "If the Day of Judgment comes while you have a palm-cutting in your hands and it is possible to plant it before the Hour comes, you should plant it." [Sahih Muslim, Hadith 1143]. This illustrates the proactive attitude of an individual in contributing positively to the development of the world.

The essence of Islamic economics lies in its holistic approach, combining material and spiritual aspects. Its policies are grounded in the sense of accountability before God. This aspect differentiates it from other economic systems. It ensures that economic activities are carried out in a responsible and ethical manner, aligned with the teachings of Islam. The oversight in Islamic economics is not solely based on legal regulations, but also on the moral compass derived from faith in God and a sense of responsibility for the well-being of humanity.

Islamic economics is characterised by its humanistic and spiritual dimension, rooted in seeking the pleasure of God in all economic endeavours. This is why it emphasises the cultivation of resources for the greater good, as opposed to the exploitation or concentration of wealth. It aims to eliminate exploitation, control, conflict, and war from economic relations, ultimately striving to establish a world characterised by cooperation, love, and peace. Therefore, Islamic economics offers a profound alternative to prevailing economic systems by intertwining material and spiritual values, emphasising stewardship and social responsibility, and envisioning economic activities as a means to fulfil the higher purpose of human life.

The highest goal of economic activity is to rebuild and revive the world, and to ensure that its blessings are enjoyed by all, rather than economic control or dominance by specific groups or nations, as seen in capitalist or socialist economic systems. In Islamic economics, humans are considered stewards of God on Earth and are constantly tasked with elevating the level of stewardship by developing and harnessing the world's resources for their service and the benefit of future generations.

Moreover, Islamic economics emphasises that economic activity should be directed towards achieving both material and spiritual well-being. This approach is rooted in the belief in God and accountability in the Hereafter. The Prophet Muhammad is reported to have said, 'None of you truly believes until he loves for his fellow Muslim what he loves for himself.' [Sahih Muslim, Hadith 123]. This perspective guides economic goals and elevates them to a higher purpose of collective prosperity and individual contentment.

Islamic economics stands out with its human-centred and spiritual dimension, sourced from the pursuit of God's pleasure in conducting economic activities directly. This distinctiveness is further reinforced by the guarantee and strength of implementing its economic teachings. The regulatory framework of Islamic economics is not only based on legal principles but is also anchored in faith in God and accountability. This leads to a balanced approach where economic activities serve the purpose of enhancing individual and collective well-being, while upholding ethical and moral values.

In Islamic economic theory, the concept of public interest (*maslaha*) is crucial. Any social or economic arrangement aims to achieve *maslaha* by promoting benefit and preventing harm. The nature of *maslaha* may be specific or general and may vary depending on the policy of the socio-economic system. Islamic economic systems differ based on their approach to these two forms of public interest. Some capitalist systems prioritise individual interest, while socialist systems focus on collective interest.

Islamic economics is characterised as a middle path, as derived from the Quranic verse: 'Thus We have made you a middle nation.' (Al-Baqra, 2:143). This moderation is not an absolute mathematical equation, but rather a relative social moderation. It embodies the principle that all matters should be balanced in accordance with the circumstances of time and place. However, in exceptional circumstances such as wars, famines, or epidemics, where reconciling individual and public interests becomes challenging, the public interest takes precedence over individual interest.

In conclusion, the core principle of Islamic economics is the pursuit of public interest. It emphasises striking a balance between individual and societal welfare. The flexibility of the system is evident in its recognition of varying circumstances and the need to adapt to exceptional situations. Islamic economics seeks to achieve equilibrium and justice between individual and public interests, guided by Islamic values and ethics, for the sustainable well-being of society as a whole.

## 9.9 The Equilibrium Between Private and Public Interests in Islamic Economics

The aim of organising social or economic systems is to achieve benefit and prevent harm. However, this benefit can be private or public, specific, or general. Here, different social and economic systems diverge based on their policy towards these two interests. Capitalist countries tend to prioritise individual interests, while socialist countries prioritise the collective interest.

Islamic economics stands out from the start with a distinct economic policy that is not solely based on the individual (as in individualism) or solely on society (as in socialism). Instead, its foundation is in balancing and harmonising the interests of individuals and society. This concept is expressed in the Quranic verse: 'Thus We have made you a middle nation.' (Al-Baqra, 2:143).

However, it is important to note that this moderation is not an absolute mathematical equation but rather a relative social balance. This principle is applied to various aspects of life and is adaptable according to different circumstances of time and place. This is illustrated by the Prophet's saying: 'If there is harm, there is no obligation.' It means that in exceptional circumstances, such as wars, famines, or epidemics, public interest takes precedence over individual interest.

To summarise this point:

i. The essence of Islamic economics is public interest.
ii. Islamic economics is characterised by its flexibility and adaptability to different situations.
iii. The concept of benefit (*maslaha*) is the basis of Islamic economic theory.

a. **Differences in interests vary with circumstances**

Achieving interests differs based on circumstances; what is considered beneficial in certain conditions may not be so in other conditions. In this sense, Imam Ash-Shatibi says in his book "Al-Muwafaqat": 'Benefits and harms can change based on situations. They can be beneficial or harmful in one situation but not in another.' This idea has been used by some scholars of Islamic jurisprudence to refute the accusation of usury regarding interest provided by savings accounts or similar benefits, such as those offered by government bonds and investment certificates.

Prioritising interests according to their importance is also important. Similarly, the interests pursued by society are arranged according to their significance. There are absolute necessities, such as preserving life, which, if lost, would endanger one's existence, like safeguarding religion, self, progeny, wealth, or intellect. On the other hand, there are improving necessities, which refer to those things required for a decent life, and if lost, would cause distress and difficulty.

However, these necessities are not on the same level. One necessity might be neglected if it conflicts with a more important necessity. Therefore, consuming alcohol, which is generally forbidden, becomes permissible in cases of extreme thirst, as preserving life takes precedence over preserving modesty. Similarly, exposing the *'awrah* (private parts) becomes permissible if it's required for a medical treatment, as medical treatment is a necessity.

These principles have led to opposition to a life of luxury in Islamic economics, especially when essential needs are not fulfilled for some members of society. This principle was strictly followed by Caliph Umar ibn al-Khattab, who used to repeat the verse from the Quran: 'And take provisions, but indeed, the best provision is Taqwa' (Quran, Surah Al-Baqarah, 2:197).

b. **Reconciling individual interests with communal interests in times of conflict**

In capitalist economics, an individual's goal is to prioritise their interests first and contribute to society secondarily. This leads to full freedom in economic activities and ownership. Capitalism justifies this by asserting that when individuals pursue their interests, they indirectly contribute to society's welfare. However, this economic policy has advantages, such as encouraging personal initiative and entrepreneurship, as well as rapid economic growth. It also has disadvantages, like the disparity between the wealthy and the poor and the emergence of class divisions.

On the other hand, socialist economics prioritises communal interests over individual interests. In this system, the state intervenes in all economic activities and abolishes private ownership of the means of production. Socialism justifies this by claiming that when society's interests are prioritised, individual interests are achieved indirectly. Since an individual's value is determined by their community, their progress and material well-being are dependent on the community's growth and development. While socialism has benefits like satisfying public needs and avoiding unemployment and economic crises, it also has drawbacks, including stifling personal incentives and creating bureaucratic complexities.

As for Islamic economics, it has existed for over fourteen centuries and has had a distinct economic policy from the very beginning. This policy does not primarily rely on individualism like capitalist systems, nor solely on collectivism like socialist systems. Instead, it aims to safeguard and balance both individual and communal interests, seeking harmony between them.

One of the key principles in Islamic economics is that both individual and communal interests are intertwined and protecting one is essential for the protection of the other. This is reflected in the Quranic verses such as: "There is no harm in [accepting] the benefits that people offer you willingly, and you may eat of the bounty of God if you believe in it." (Quran, Surah Al-Ma'idah, 87). Moreover, the Prophet Muhammad provides a simple yet profound example of this harmony, as narrated by Ibn Majah: "If three people embark on a journey, they should appoint one of them as their leader. If they each take turns in this role, they will never agree. So, choose a leader." (Ibn Majah, Hadith No. 511).

This principle is further supported by the narration where the Prophet likened the unity of individual and communal interests to passengers on a ship. If one of them is given a portion closer to the source of water, all will be saved; otherwise, they would perish. However, some disputed this and suggested that each person gets their portion. Consequently, the ship was destroyed, and they all perished. (Reported by Ibn Majah, Hadith No. 819).

In application, Islamic economic solutions stand out from capitalist or socialist alternatives due to their ability to achieve a balance between individual and communal interests. This is evident in three main areas: economic freedom, state intervention in economic activities, ownership rights, and wealth distribution.

## 9.10 In the Realm of Economic Freedom and State Involvement

In the Islamic economy, economic freedom for individuals is coupled with state involvement in economic activities, but this involvement is not exclusive. The two coexist in balance. Both aspects are simultaneously addressed by Islamic economics, not as exceptions but as essential elements.

a) When Islamic economics endorses individual economic freedom, it places numerous restrictions on economic activities. For example, it prohibits producing alcohol, engaging in usury, monopolising markets, hoarding wealth without production, spending wealth in ways that do not benefit society, infringing upon others' rights, and excessive price setting. Additionally, Islamic economics ensures that economic freedom aligns with religious beliefs and societal well-being, establishing a monitoring system resembling state oversight to ensure economic activity's legitimacy.
b) When individuals are collectively incapable of fulfilling necessary economic activities, Islamic economics requires state involvement. This might encompass

infrastructural development, establishment of heavy industries like steel, or production of goods with no individual profitability but societal importance, such as weapons of defence. In both cases, Islamic economics seeks to maintain the balance between individual and communal interests, as emphasised in the Quranic verse: "And do not squander [your wealth] wastefully. Indeed, He does not like the wasteful." (Quran, Surah Al-Isra, 26).

**In the realm of ownership:**

In capitalist economies, private ownership is dominant, and public ownership is limited to cases where state intervention is necessary.

In socialist economies, public ownership prevails, with limited private ownership recognised based on societal needs.

In Islamic economics, both private and public ownership coexist. Islamic economics' view of ownership is not absolute; it is restricted in terms of acquisition, scope, limits, and usage. Ownership serves a societal function, as the true owner is considered to be God, and humans are stewards. Therefore, ownership must be exercised responsibly, considering societal welfare and religious obligations. If individual ownership poses a threat to society, the state can intervene.

**In the realm of wealth distribution:**

In capitalist economies, wealth distribution depends on individual ownership and leads to significant disparities.

In socialist economies, wealth distribution is generally based on work, but disparities may still arise due to varying capacities and talents.

In Islamic economics, wealth distribution is based on a combination of personal responsibility and communal support, with priority given to basic needs followed by societal well-being. This is in line with the Quranic principle: "And in their wealth there is acknowledged right for the needy and the destitute." (Quran, Surah Al-Dhariyat, 19).

In all these areas, economic principles of Islamic economics aim to establish a balanced and just system that considers both individual and communal interests while upholding ethical and religious values.

## 9.11 Conflict of Public and Individual Interests

Prioritising the public interest over individual interest, except when reconciliation is impossible. In the case of conflict between Islamic political and economic policies, it should aim for balance or moderation between private and public interests. However, if extraordinary circumstances like wars, famine, or epidemics arise, public interest takes precedence unanimously, considering it as a right from God that surpasses other rights. This is what the proponents of Islamic jurisprudence express: mitigating private harm to prevent greater public harm, or choosing the lesser harm over the greater, or when two harms conflict, prioritising the greater good.

When extremist interpretations of Islamic economics are endorsed: Certainly, during exceptional circumstances such as wars, famines, and epidemics, the application of Islamic economics might lean more towards extremist interpretations. It is observed that in societies characterised by deprivation and poverty, a Muslim is not allowed to possess more than what suffices them, and the state is obliged to redistribute excess wealth to provide citizens with at least the basic necessities.

This is in line with the Quranic verse: "Seek the life to come by means of what God granted you, but do not neglect your rightful share in this world." (28:77). In these circumstances, some interpretations might go beyond conventional Islamic economic principles. They are tailored to the context of severe deprivation and aim to establish a just distribution of resources.

The view of Abu Dhar Al-Ghifari: Towards the end of Caliph Uthman's rule, the companion Abu Dhar Al-Ghifari expressed the idea that Muslims should not possess more than what satisfies their basic needs. This perspective can be considered an Islamic economic alternative in non-ordinary situations. Specifically, when a privileged few accumulate wealth while many suffer from poverty, this principle becomes relevant. The idea is that affluence should only be allowed after eradicating poverty and ensuring no one is left deprived.

This perspective does not criticise prosperity itself, but the excessive accumulation of wealth. It acknowledges that in certain circumstances, Islamic economics can temporarily lean towards such a view as a solution. In light of the above, it is vital to avoid misinterpreting Islamic economics' principles. Abu Dhar Al-Ghifari's view should be seen as a context-specific remedy, not a universal rule. It shows the flexibility of Islamic economics thought when addressing unprecedented challenges, with the ultimate goal of achieving justice and eliminating poverty.

**Three main conclusions**

From our previous study, we can draw three main conclusions:

a) The primary outcome is that the core of Islamic economics is the pursuit of the public interest. The realisation of these interests varies based on time and place. Prioritising interests should be based on their importance, which means that it is not permissible in a society for those in authority to allocate resources lavishly on personal luxuries while neglecting public needs and essential facilities.
b) The second outcome is that Islamic economic policy hinges on balance, moderation, and harmonising individual and collective interests. The economic approach in Islam is distinct from both capitalism and socialism, incorporating different concepts. When addressing economic issues, an Islamic economic solution is aligned with the balance and moderation between individual and collective interests.
c) The third outcome is that under circumstances where distribution fails and there is not enough to meet basic needs, private ownership is not upheld, and individual interests are sacrificed for the common good, ensuring equitable distribution. This sacrifice serves the goal of securing the well-being of all individuals, as providing for everyone is considered the right of God that supersedes other rights.

Thus, while Islamic economics may share common ground with certain economic systems, it retains its unique perspective. The fundamental principle is to prioritise the common good and secure the well-being of all members of society. This demonstrates the flexibility of Islamic economics thought in responding to specific circumstances while upholding the principles of justice and equity.

## 9.12 Inflation in the Context of Islamic Economics

Defining or pinpointing inflation is a challenging task, mainly because it is a complex and unstable phenomenon. It exhibits various types and is caused by diverse factors. However, the common thread among the different forms of inflation is its disruptive nature, posing a threat to economic stability and jeopardising developmental efforts. Inflation is characterised by a disturbance in the flow of monetary and goods/services transactions, leading to a sustained increase in prices that is not easily controlled.

Economists have recognised that inflation results from an imbalance between actual supply and demand in the economy. This refers to an increase in real or monetary demand compared to the total aggregate supply, implying an excess of demand over available goods and services. This scenario eventually leads to a continuous rise in prices that is hard to curtail.

The foundation of modern economics indirectly exacerbates and sustains inflation over time. If this foundation were replaced with alternative principles, it could potentially provide a more effective remedy for numerous economic challenges. Islamic economic foundations, in particular, diverge significantly from the contemporary structure, with one of the key distinctions being the prohibition of usury (*riba*). Economic policy in Islamic economics is built on the prohibition of interest, extending to both interest on loans and deposits. This eliminates the typical practice of seeking interest to support investments and finance projects, which often exacerbates inflation due to the increase in the cost of goods.

A company that resorts to interest to increase its investments adds the interest amount to its production costs. Consequently, it raises the prices of its goods to maintain a certain level of profit. This, in turn, causes inflation since the excess liquidity in the economy is not being absorbed by production.

By highlighting an economy built on the foundation of interest prohibition, we can predict that interest will either become limited or completely confined. This would lead to a situation where borrowing becomes restricted, potentially causing essential sectors of the economy to rely on investments without borrowing. This shift could replace financial risks with entrepreneurial risks, contributing to stable, long-term growth.

In essence, the economic system will likely shift towards achieving equilibrium by limiting or removing the practice of interest, which could lead to a transition from financial debt-based solutions to a more asset-based model of economic development.

Zakat is considered a fundamental cornerstone and important pillar on which the economic structure of Islamic economics is built. With its various capabilities, Zakat can contribute significantly to mitigating inflation in several ways. It has the potential to absorb excess demand, promote wise spending, encourage savings and investment, and play a crucial role in addressing certain negative effects of inflation, particularly in the distribution of wealth.

Zakat serves as an effective mechanism to control inflation by curbing excessive government expenditure. Islamic economics emphasise that Zakat should not be responsible for financing government spending. Instead, Zakat is directed towards the impoverished and can be used to alleviate the cost of living and reduce the suffering of the less fortunate, thus contributing to reducing inflationary pressures.

It is widely recognised that a major factor contributing to inflation is an increase in government expenditure. This can be addressed by directing Zakat funds to specific areas, such as debt repayment for those in need. This not only supports individuals in paying off their debts but also reinforces credit and borrowing, as the creditor will be more assured of the borrower's ability to repay. This, in turn, promotes economic activity and growth.

Similarly, directing Zakat towards debt repayment encourages lending and borrowing, providing a supportive environment for credit activity. This is because borrowers will have a greater sense of assurance that they can repay their debts, thereby encouraging them to engage in productive economic endeavours.

Zakat should not be seen as a temporary solution for combating inflation. Its effects are continuous throughout the year, with its impact on reducing overall demand and increasing the availability of goods and services remaining consistent. Thus, Zakat has the potential to aid in maintaining a balance between monetary and goods supply, which helps control inflation.

Inflation poses numerous difficulties for certain segments of society, such as individuals on fixed incomes or those whose occupations are not sufficiently remunerative to cope with rising prices. Zakat can be instrumental in providing relief to these individuals and mitigating the impact of inflation on their lives.

Therefore, Zakat, with its multifaceted impact, can play a pivotal role in addressing inflation. By supporting productive economic activities, encouraging savings and investment, and aiding those in financial need, Zakat contributes to stabilising the economy and mitigating the effects of inflation on vulnerable segments of society.

In reality, scholars have indicated the role of Zakat in alleviating the negative effects of inflation. See: "Al-Amwal" by Abu Ubaid, p. 709, 199.

Islamic economy is… What is its essence? What is its goal? What does it seek? What are its foundations? In light of these questions, if this is the affected category, then when this affected category is constrained within the limits of the poor and the destitute, or is allocated to small professions, or is directed to the indebted class, the Zakat can be spent in a single category among the eight categories, or it is permissible to focus on a single category. It is permissible to allocate Zakat to one category or more than one category, depending on the situation. (See: "Al-Mughni" by Ibn Qudamah)

Some of the scholars, like Abu Ubaid in "Kitab al-Amwal," supported this view. The reality is that this approach has the potential to improve the existing relationship between the total demand and supply forces, when supporting small professions, small-scale investments, and aiding the indebted class. This has the potential to increase the actual supply of goods and services, contributing to control inflation. By effectively distributing Zakat, it can be used to mitigate the impacts of inflation. However, certain small-scale industries can be influenced by inflation. Once Zakat is distributed, it can revive many dormant sectors that were hampered by inflation. See: "Al-Mughni" by Ibn Qudamah, p. 882.

This approach has the potential to enhance the relationship between the total demand and supply forces in the economy. Supporting small professions, small-scale investments, and aiding the indebted class could increase the actual supply of goods and services. This contributes to controlling inflation through the proper distribution of Zakat. Inflation can affect small industries, but the distribution of Zakat can reactivate these industries. See: "Bidayat al-Mujtahid wa Nihayat al-Muqatdid" by Ibn Rushd, p. 818.

Moreover, if the revenue from Zakat is insufficient to meet the needs of the deserving class, some scholars suggest that there is no harm in delaying the distribution of the Zakat over a longer period, such as three years, as a way to mitigate its impact. (See: "Al-Amwal" by Abu Ubaid). It is possible that Zakat could be delayed if the community is in dire need, especially for the deserving class, and undoubtedly, this helps maintain economic stability for the country.

## 9.13 The State and Its Economic Role

The role of state economy in the balance of Islamic economics: The Quran primarily emphasises the concept of governance in relation to the righteous ruler. This is evident in various aspects, including:

a) Numerous verses discuss the creation of entities and beings that serve humanity, such as in the verse: "And He created cattle, in which there is warmth for you and benefits, and from them you eat." (Surah An-Nahl, 16:5).
b) The Quran also mentions celestial bodies, focusing on their organisation and governance.
c) Several verses emphasise the concept of divine appointment, highlighting the attributes of those who strive for good and righteousness, as seen in: "Then We made Our chosen servants successors." (Surah Al-Qasas, 28:5).
d) Additionally, there are verses that discuss Allah's power to create and develop, as in: "Did you then think that We had created you in jest (without any purpose), and that you would not be returned to Us?" (Surah Al-Muminun, 23:115).

The Quranic approach emphasises that people are not to become heedless in seeking material benefits from the world. Rather, they are expected to engage in economic and developmental activities, which elevate them towards realising goodness and benefiting humanity. This is evident in the verse: "Say, 'Who is there to forbid the beauty and provision which Allah has produced for His servants?'" (Surah Al-A'raf, 7:32)

States should not just focus on their own prosperity, as God reminds us in Surah Hud (11:63): "He said, 'O my people, is my family more significant to you than Allah? And you take Him as a mere cast behind your backs!'"

Human development is an imperative element of civilisation. However, it must be guided by principles that uphold faith, the Hereafter, and the welfare of society. Although we might observe temporary dominance by those who cause corruption, it is certain that such dominion is fleeting. The Quran has stated, "And We did not grant everlasting life to any human being before you. So if you die, will they live forever?" (Surah Al-Anbiya, 21:34)

A righteous state is one that governs according to divine principles, unifying all people equally. Such a state fosters solidarity, ensuring equitable distribution among the rich, the poor, the beneficiaries, and the needy. To fulfil this role, the state must execute economic policies that directly correlate with improving the economic circumstances of individuals. This involves preventing societal harm and securing general welfare. For example, the state should establish social security measures and maintain economic balance through methods that Islamic economics permits. It should enforce justice, eliminate corruption, and promote beneficial endeavours.

The scope of state intervention in economic activities should be determined by the extent of benefit it provides to society. If the harm outweighs the benefit, the state should intervene, and grant freedoms as deemed necessary. As Abu al-Ala al-Mawdudi (1980) expressed, "Islamic governance does not essentially mean that the government engages in business, trade, or landownership. The primary function of the state is to establish the nation, guide it towards goodness, uphold justice, eradicate corruption, enjoin good, and serve the collective welfare of society.

Therefore, the economic role of the state would include:

i. Organisation of the economic market: The definition of the market, its etiquettes, prohibitions, and the role of the state in regulating it.
ii. The Issue of Pricing: The state's jurisdiction regarding pricing, ruling on pricing, its methodology, and different perspectives on the matter, as well as the state's role in this domain.
iii. Dealing with monopoly: The state's stance on the issue of monopoly.
iv. Monetary regulation: The functions and significance of money, its development, the role of the state in regulating it, and its connection to economic stability.
v. Food security and economic development: Providing food security and striving for economic development.
vi. Outlining the prerequisites for economic development, its pillars, funding sources, and the assurance of its continuity.

## 9.14 Ethical Foundations of Islamic Economics

Economics is the driving force of nations and peoples, especially in this era where some nations are held captive by materialism. Materialism is considered the fine line between progress and backwardness, and all matters of virtue or corruption are intertwined with it. The path to advancement, resilience, and safeguarding an entity from vulnerabilities lies only through understanding and implementing ethical guidelines.

Hence, economic studies must be at the forefront, deeply interwoven with politics, finance, and religious knowledge. In the realm of economic transactions, Islamic economics places great emphasis on ethical principles that guide the causes of integrity and righteousness. These principles are not limited to any specific sector; however, it is important to note that studying these texts allows us to comprehend Islamic economics' approach to economic dealings. It is characterised by good intentions, elevated aspirations, and noble objectives, aiming for prosperity and virtue.

In elucidating Islamic teachings on economics, it is crucial to recognise that Islamic economics has never been isolated; it has perpetually linked its teachings with moral and doctrinal beliefs. This linkage forms a solid foundation for people, guiding their actions with unwavering faith and genuine intention.

In organising economic affairs, the aim of the Islamic economics community is to prepare society, strengthen the pillars of peace, security, and solidarity, all within the framework of established traditions and without deviating from the essential principles. Islamic economics' foundation lies in principles, grounded in wisdom and benefits. "Ibn al-Qayyim" said, "The objectives of Islamic law aim at the welfare of the people in both this life and the Hereafter. It encompasses justice in its entirety, mercy in its entirety, benefits in their entirety, and wisdom in its entirety." These objectives ensure that rights are respected, mischief is prevented, and the path of virtue is upheld.

Islamic economics allows individual rights such as ownership and inheritance, but it encircles these rights with ethical and moral boundaries, rooted in faith and its dictates, binding on every individual. What is rightfully owned cannot be enjoyed at the expense of others' harm. When the exercise of a right leads to harm, it must be relinquished, adhering to the principle: "No harm should be inflicted or reciprocated." This curbs the abuse of rights.

Islamic economics does not prohibit enjoying the good in life, but it forbids excess and wastefulness, urging communal sharing. While the wealthy have the right to enjoy their possessions, they are prohibited from extravagant and heedless living. The rich are obligated to assist the less fortunate, ending unemployment, and aiding the destitute when they are capable.

Islamic economic transactions are built on a general principle: permissibility unless explicitly prohibited. This principle opens the door to gain, making all lawful earnings from buying, selling, renting, and various other dealings permissible, except for specific prohibited actions, such as contracts involving injustice, deception, and exploitation.

Hence, Islamic economic principles are inherently moral and considerate of others' well-being. They aim at balanced and just transactions, discouraging exploitation and fostering cooperation and societal welfare. The primary objective of the state is to achieve legitimate interests, whether they are necessities or improvements. If these objectives are contradicted by the actions of someone in their financial transactions, then their actions become invalid. Examples include:

a) **Distorting inheritance and will**: Inheritance and wills as prescribed by God are intended to spread goodwill and cooperation, distributing wealth among heirs and beneficiaries. This prevents hoarding and ensures equitable wealth distribution.
b) **Harming others with wealth**: Using wealth to harm others, whether as an individual or an institution, goes against the purpose of community development and welfare.
c) **Hoarding wealth**: Not investing wealth for productive purposes leads to poverty in the society and contradicts the principles of Islamic economics.
d) **Wasting wealth**: Wastefulness or miserliness are both extreme actions that are discouraged in Islamic economics.

Islamic economics encourages earning, investing, and saving, while discouraging unemployment and begging without justification. Prophet Muhammad said, "It is better for you to take your rope, go to the mountains, cut some firewood, carry it on your back, and sell it, and thereby save your face than to beg from people, whether they give you or refuse." [Sahih Muslim, Hadith, 253].

However, this earning should be pursued with a conscientious approach, considering the welfare of fellow human beings. This aligns with the values and ethics taught by Islamic economics. Islamic economics is not merely about generating wealth, but about fostering a balanced and just society, where economic activities are integrated with moral principles and ethical behaviour.

Therefore, Islamic economics is not a separate domain from social awareness and moral obligations. It encompasses belief, morality, and ethics in a holistic manner, emphasising community welfare, justice, and the responsible use of resources.

## 9.15 Achieving Economic Security

The world in which we live is sharply divided economically, with a stark divide between the wealthy and the impoverished, or between developed and developing nations. This economic division holds deep significance, as the wealthy nations constitute less than a quarter of the global population yet possess over three-quarters of the world's total wealth.

Conversely, the remaining three-quarters of the global population lives on a fraction of the world's total wealth. Among these nations, there are severely impoverished countries that reside at the edge of survival, encompassing vast areas in Africa and parts of Asia. The majority of Muslim-majority countries are considered part of the developing world, and many of them are among the most poverty-stricken. An examination of the world map shows that almost all Muslim-majority countries are situated in Asia and Africa, both regions classified as the third world, where around 17% of the Muslim population lives in poverty.

Interestingly, a significant number of Muslim-majority countries possess more natural resources than some affluent nations. Therefore, it is important to note that these countries lack certain elements crucial for development, primarily capital and technology. Consequently, they require the assistance of the international community to acquire these elements.

The core issue we are discussing here has been extensively deliberated among prominent thinkers within the Islamic world. The primary challenge lies in how to lift Muslim-majority nations from the grip of economic subordination and underdevelopment. This prompts us to consider how to ensure economic security for people.

The economic underdevelopment experienced by most Muslim-majority countries can be attributed to their need to break free from cycles of dependency and economic backwardness. It is the responsibility of the international community to assist developing nations in adopting measures for economic development. These nations lack the vital components required for growth, particularly financial resources, and advanced technology. Their limited resources hinder their progress and necessitate support from the global society.

Removing legal barriers: The international law for development focuses on two key aspects:

i. Eliminating legal barriers that hinder development. These barriers were imposed by colonial powers during the colonial era to serve their interests.
ii. Establishing positive rules in international law that promote cooperation and foster closer relations among nations, while affirming the responsibility of the strong to aid the weak.

Consequently, it is necessary for Muslim-majority countries, especially those within the third world, to seek legal frameworks that enable economic assistance. Regrettably, this often occurs within the confines of financial organisations, lacking a comprehensive understanding of the collective nation. If people fully embraced Islamic economics and its principles, economic challenges would have been minimised."

This approach focuses on the economic disparities in the world, especially among Muslim-majority countries, and the need for economic security and assistance within this context. It emphasises the importance of international cooperation and legal frameworks to address economic challenges and disparities among Muslim-majority nations.

## 9.16 Conclusion

If we look at the trajectory of global civilisation, we can see that Muslims once held a prominent position in technology and leadership. Muslim countries are rich in resources that are essential for advancing scientific and technological progress, as well as achieving economic prosperity. It is evident that Muslim countries faced numerous challenges and divisions, leading to a fragmented entity that hindered the potential of Islamic fertility in various fields. This Chapter discussed in-depth what is meant by Islamic economics, its principles, fundamentals and founding aspects.

The role Islamic economics aspires to regain demands that every Muslim, in their place and homeland, contributes to enhancing their country's economy. They must consistently work towards reinforcing cooperation between nations in technological and economic domains, grounded in the teachings and principles of Islamic economics.

Cooperation, solidarity, and unity among Muslims are divinely ordained concepts, emphasised in the Quranic verses and the teachings of Prophet Muhammad. These principles should not remain mere slogans; the real challenge lies in imbuing them with sincerity, good intentions, and positive actions in application. For example, to address economic challenges, the idea of establishing a shared Islamic economics market was proposed, aimed at expanding the scope of trade exchange among Muslims. However, for this to succeed, a unified effort is necessary.

Nonetheless, the practical reality within the Islamic economics includes the establishment of Islamic economic institutions, such as the Islamic Development Bank, an affiliate of the Organisation of Islamic Cooperation. This bank significantly contributes to advancing development in many Islamic countries. Despite this, the potential for an Islamic economics market has yet to fully materialise.

Realistically, there are existing Islamic economic establishments, like the Islamic Development Bank, which plays a crucial role in promoting development in numerous Muslim nations. Yet, there is a lack a comprehensive Islamic economic system. The desired achievement of economic security for people necessitates intensifying economic and technical cooperation and highlighting the facets of Islamic economics solidarity across various dimensions. This way, economic independence for the Islamic economics can be realised.

Undoubtedly, development in Muslim nations requires substantial funds that can be invested to increase production. This results in elevated individual income, which can be saved after optimising consumption within reasonable limits. The surplus income or savings are then cycled back into investment and various developmental projects, thus boosting production and individual empowerment. This chain reaction expands the circles of production, investment, and developmental initiatives.

Development is rightfully considered a human right, and it necessitates utilising the elements of production effectively, such as natural resources and financial assets. Islamic economics encourages investment in these productive resources while emphasising moderation in consumption, abstaining from extravagance, and avoiding the hoarding of wealth.

Recognising that development cannot occur without knowledge, the Islamic economics should pursue an economically suitable development strategy tailored to its social and economic conditions. Acquiring technology from other countries is permissible as long as it aligns with Islamic society's circumstances and does not harm Muslims or compromise their sovereignty.

Cooperation and technological advancement within the Islamic world can enhance the nation's technological capacity. This includes creating technology innovations suitable for the economic and social context of Muslim societies. Such efforts protect Muslim countries from dependency on industrialised markets. Economic development cannot be isolated from social and cultural growth. Economic progress is essential for safeguarding human rights across all domains.

**Economic Crises**

The eight categories of Zakat channels hold shares that are intended to secure the vulnerable in society against economic disasters. Zakat comes to the rescue of Muslims and shields them from the danger of economic downturns and hardships. The economic effects of Zakat extend their influence over numerous individuals and the entire society. For example, consider the *Ibn al-Sebeel* (the wayfarer) bank in the present era, which supports students studying abroad, specialising in beneficial fields. Similarly, those compelled to leave their homeland and part with their assets to seek refuge from wars and killing, Zakat ensures that Muslims are not left defenceless against economic catastrophes. Thus, Zakat is a unique system ensuring Muslims' protection from economic crises and their diverse consequences.

In this contemporary era, Islamic economics faces the challenge of an incomplete economic identity, which diminishes the place of religion and its impact on people's lives. Economic experts within the Islamic knowledge must enhance Muslims' treatment and offer them avenues for ethical investments. The ummah should extend its reach to establish a unique Islamic development bank that accumulates funds. Moreover, Islamic scholars should work to apply Zakat more broadly to counter potential deficiencies within Islamic resources.

Economics focuses on material and economic values, often neglecting spiritual and religious values. This imbalance weakened the role of religion and diminished its influence on societies. The Islamic world is facing a challenge from these influences that must be met with determination and strength. This is because Islam guards the purity of faith, the excellence of worship, and the power of influence. The unity within the Islamic economic sphere should be achieved by reinforcing Islamic economics principles. By fostering Islamic cooperation and strengthening economic ties, Muslims can achieve balance between human relations and economic activities, thus harmonising their ethical and behavioural actions according to Islamic economics.

Islamic economics thought preceded in establishing the standards, and although these standards have evolved over time in accumulating knowledge and gaining experience, they have been widely embraced by many economists worldwide. Through studying Islamic economics and Islamic jurisprudence, we observe that this methodology in decision-making is deeply rooted in our culture. Scholars and jurists within the Islamic community have employed this approach and techniques for centuries, which continue to be fascinating. Despite their various names, what Ibn Qayyim says in his book "Al-Fawā'id" (See: Al-Fawā'id by Ibn Qayyim, p. 48) about the fundamental principle is noteworthy.

The core principle is to prioritise good and ward off harm. Thought is the origin of will, seeking love, and renouncing hatred. The most beneficial thought is the one related to the benefits of the afterlife, the paths leading to them, and warding off their harms. These are the four essential thoughts, followed by another four: thoughts concerning the benefits of the worldly life and the ways to attain them, thoughts concerning the harms of the worldly life and how to avoid them.

Islamic economics, what is it, what constitutes it, what is its aim, and what are its foundations? Here, the Islamic economics viewpoint establishes the foundation for decision-making and planning for the distant future (the Hereafter) and the near future (the worldly life). Islamic economics is seen as one aspect among many of its diverse aspects. Ibn Qayyim repeats the methodology of balancing between benefits and harms, which can also be termed as gains and losses or economic perspective, in various areas. He states that the balance between benefits and harms can be viewed from a religious perspective or an economic perspective.

This is illustrated through various examples and scenarios, as well as the balance between pleasures and pains, and the choice between two difficult options. The process of making decisions becomes simpler when guided by understanding the causes, their implications, and the concept of forsaking what is lesser in favour of what is greater. Ibn Qayyim underscores that understanding the causes and context makes the decision easier. One should be well-acquainted with the situation in order to strike a balance between different aspects.

He (See: Al-Fawā'id by Ibn Qayyim, p. 80) emphasises that the wise should not be deceived by the illusion of pleasure, and if painful things are forsaken, it should be in favour of avoiding a greater harm. Here, the distinction between intelligent and foolish individuals becomes apparent. The wise recognises the difference between temporary pleasure and enduring pain, while the foolish might fail to differentiate between the two. Therefore, forsaking lesser pleasure for greater benefit and accepting pain for avoiding greater harm is an art that requires understanding and judgment.

In conclusion, Ibn Qayyim's work provides insightful guidance on decision-making based on the principle of balancing benefits and harms. This principle, deeply rooted in Islamic thought, serves as a valuable framework for making informed choices and managing various aspects of life effectively.

Therefore, we find that this guidance in economic thought and Islamic thought revolves around two fundamental principles:

a. Maximising benefits,
b. Minimising harm.

Islamic economics aims to maximise benefits and minimise harm. This concept has contributed to Islamic jurisprudence in deriving many principles used in deducing legal rulings for various issues that can be applied in different domains. Some of these principles include:

- What cannot be fully achieved should not be abandoned.
- Repelling harm takes precedence over bringing benefits.
- There should be no harm inflicted or reciprocated.
- Minimise harm by choosing the lesser of two evils.

These principles are intertwined with economic considerations. Some scholars believe in the just principle of compensating those harmed, such as compensating for damage to property or the seisure of investments. This should include evaluating the value of damage or confiscation and what was gained from it, like the profit gained from the property.

In essence, compensation accounts for the value of the missed opportunity or the loss that the affected person bears. Additionally, if one cannot achieve full benefits, they should not engage in activities that will lead to irreversible losses.

As narrated, Ibn Taymiyyah was passing by a group drinking alcohol, and he was told that alcohol was prohibited as it distracted from prayer and remembrance of Allah, and it prevented others from their Islamic duties. He let them be. Ibn Taymiyyah argued that commanding good and forbidding evil becomes obligatory when the greater evil is removed, applying the principle of weighing benefits against harms in economic theory.

This could bridge the gap between theoretical and applied knowledge, fostering innovation in contemporary issues. So, why the delay in tapping into this intellectual heritage? The concept of pleasure (لذة) according to Ibn Qayyim is equivalent to benefits in economic terms, and the concept of pain (ألم) is equivalent to losses in economic thinking. However, the key distinction lies in the fact that in conventional economics, pleasure is considered a benefit regardless of how an individual perceives it, while pain is seen as a loss. This is applicable even if the actions involve consuming alcohol, cigarettes, engaging in prostitution, or taking drugs in countries where these activities are not prohibited.

In contrast, in an Islamic economics framework, pleasure is divided into two categories, just as Ibn Qayyim distinguished between permissible benefits and illicit ones. In permissible benefits, a balanced approach is adopted, considering the principle of maximising benefits within the permissible boundaries. However, in the case of forbidden benefits, a more cautious approach is followed, aiming to minimise harm. This involves avoiding greater harm (leaving what is prohibited) and seeking lesser harm (engaging in permissible actions).

For example, alcohol, cigarettes, prostitution, and drugs might be considered beneficial by some individuals or groups within society, but they come with broader societal harms. Policymakers in Islamic economics need to discern between general harm and individual or specific group benefits. This distinction is a hallmark of the decision-making methodology in the Islamic economic thought.

I hope you have been able to see the value I was trying to demark here in this Chapter when I referred to benefiting from a divine economic system and ignoring the label if it would be a barrier for some. In the next Chapter I discuss the knowledge crisis in Islamic economics, and critically evaluate the root causes of this knowledge crisis.

# Chapter 10
# Economics and the Knowledge Crisis

## 10.1 Introduction

The previous Chapter discussed in-depth what is meant by Islamic economics, its principles, fundamentals and founding aspects. The discussion was purely based on the perspective of Islamic economics and analysis from religious texts. In this Chapter, I discuss critically the knowledge crisis in Islamic economics, and its factors. The current crisis in the discipline of Islamic economics stems from the uncritical acceptance of conventional economic ideas by most Muslim economists. This has led to a fundamental conflict between conventional economic principles and Islamic economics views, which has not been properly recognised. Attempting to combine these contradictory bodies of knowledge has proven unsuccessful and has hindered the development of a genuine Islamic economic theory.

This Chapter discusses how the crisis in Islamic economics can be resolved by rejecting uncritical acceptance of Western economic ideas and developing a genuine Islamic economic theory based on Islamic principles and values. By doing so, Islamic economics can offer a distinct and valuable contribution to the field of economics and provide practical solutions that align with the aspirations of Muslim societies.

To address this crisis, alternative foundations need to be established for constructing a truly Islamic economic theory. This would involve re-evaluating the methodological framework and underlying assumptions used in the discipline. Islamic economics should be based on the principles and values derived from Islamic teachings, rather than attempting to fit conventional economic models into an Islamic context.

By going back to the core principles of Islam and incorporating them into economic analysis, a more coherent and meaningful approach to Islamic economics can be developed. This would require careful consideration of Islamic views on wealth


S. Alamad, *Beyond Profit*, Contributions to Economics,
https://doi.org/10.1007/978-3-031-49748-3_10

distribution, social justice, ethical behaviour, and the role of the individual and community in economic activities.

Moreover, Islamic economic theory should be developed with a critical and independent approach, acknowledging its distinctiveness from conventional economic theories. Embracing Islamic values and principles in economic analysis will lead to more relevant and effective policy prescriptions that address the unique needs and challenges faced by Muslim societies.

## 10.2 Islamisation of Economics

The project of "Islamisation of Knowledge" remains crucial for the Muslim Ummah (community). The education received by the younger generation plays a vital role in shaping the future of any community. However, many Muslim children today receive a secular Western education that often includes assumptions and values conflicting with basic Islamic teachings. One such example is the idea of the separation of state and religion, which goes against the Islamic understanding of religion as a comprehensive way of life that should also guide public affairs.

To address these conflicts, many Muslim intellectuals argue for the assimilation of Western knowledge into an Islamic framework. This involves integrating the traditional corpus of Islamic knowledge with modern Western knowledge, seeking a harmonious synthesis that respects Islamic principles while benefiting from advancements in various fields.

In support of this vision, the Organisation of Islamic Conference (OIC) established two universities—the International Islamic Universities of Islamabad and Malaysia—explicitly dedicated to the integration of Islamic and Western knowledge. Additionally, numerous initiatives across the Islamic world are striving to achieve this goal.

The Islamisation of Knowledge project aims to create an education system that upholds Islamic values while embracing modern scientific and intellectual achievements. By doing so, it seeks to equip Muslims with the ability to navigate contemporary challenges while remaining grounded in their faith and traditions. The Islamisation of Knowledge is a crucial endeavour for the Muslim community, as it seeks to bridge the gap between traditional Islamic teachings and the modern world, enabling Muslims to contribute positively to society while maintaining their identity and values.

Due to its immense significance, considerable individual and collective efforts have been invested by Muslims to achieve the goal of Islamisation of Knowledge. Despite some limited successes in specific areas, the overall outcome can be regarded as a failure. Scholars who dedicated their lifetimes to this endeavour have acknowledged this failure, as will be demonstrated shortly. Various explanations have been put forth to account for this failure. Our objective is to present a new diagnosis of the underlying reason.

We contend that the failure to achieve the Islamisation of Knowledge can be attributed to significant conflicts between Islamic perspectives on the nature and purpose of human existence and conventional viewpoints. Regrettably, many involved in the Islamisation project have not fully recognised the extent of these conflicts. Consequently, their attempts have involved trying to reconcile two incompatible bodies of knowledge, which, as we will argue, is an impossible task. This inherent incompatibility is the primary reason for the failure of these endeavours.

To maintain focus, this Chapter will specifically address the area of 'Islamic Economics' or the project of Islamising the Western discipline of economics. The broader principles underpinning social sciences in the West and their discord with Islamic teachings have been discussed in Zaman's work titled "Origins of Western Social Sciences" (2009).

## 10.3 Framing the Economic Knowledge Crisis

There are various indications of the failure of the project to develop an Islamic alternative to Capitalist Economics. Esteemed scholars in the field of Islamic Economics have expressed their discontent with the current state of affairs. Umer Chapra (2000, p. 375) states that "... Islamic economics has been unable to come to grips with ... the problems faced by Muslim countries."

Nejatullah Siddiqi (2008) suggests that "All is not well with Islamic economic(s) ... The grand idea of providing an alternative to capitalism and socialism ... has yielded to a desire to join the flock." Monzer Kahf (2004) in "Islamic Economics: What Went Wrong" points out:

Moreover, Islamic economists failed to propose a specific agenda for political economics that is based on their branch of knowledge, despite the necessity for such an agenda. It seems to me that the present generation of Islamic economists is exhausted and already consumed in the activities of Islamic banking and finance, leaving the task of deeper theoretical analysis, and filling the gaps to the next generation.

These pioneers of the field have dedicated their lives to its development. However, critics have been even more critical. For instance, Sohrab Behdad (1994), discussing the implementation of Islamic Economics in Iran under Ayatullah Khomeini, remarks that "It has become apparent that Islamic Economics is not capable of presenting a viable social alternative."

Similarly, Timur Kuran (1997) contends that "Islamic economics did not emerge from a drive to correct economic imbalances, injustices, or inequalities ... (but to) restore Islamic community's self-respect. Because Islamic economics was developed to serve cultural and political ends, it did not have to meet scientific standards of coherence, precision, or realism." In simpler words, Kuran suggests that Islamic Economics lacks substance or content and is merely a part of an effort to create a distinct Islamic identity.

Despite numerous efforts to create one, there is no standardised textbook of Islamic Economics. The diversity of opinions among Muslim economists is vast, and there is no consensus on the definition of "Islamic Economics," nor a clear model of what an ideal Islamic economic system would look like in concrete and practical terms.

Acknowledging these challenges, leading scholars argue that Islamic Economics is still in its infancy. They suggest that, like Western economics, it will take time for Islamic economics to evolve and mature. However, such advice for patience also admits the current state of failure. In the following discussion, we will argue that the problem is more fundamental, and the current approaches to the development of Islamic Economics are destined to fail. I will propose alternative and more promising directions for its advancement later on.

## 10.4 Critical Flaws in Current Economics Theories

The current economic theories, as presented in textbooks used in Economics departments in the USA and Europe, are based on four fundamental assumptions. However, all of these assumptions are incorrect, and their acceptance leads to contradictions that cannot be resolved in light of Islamic economics. To address this issue, it is essential to reject conventional economic theories and methodologies and instead adopt the background assumptions provided by Islamic economics. In this section, we will define, discuss, and refute these four background assumptions of modern Western economic theories. By doing so, we aim to pave the way for a new approach that aligns with the principles of Islamic economics and realities of human existence.

(a) **Universal laws**

Economic theories in conventional economics are often treated as universal laws of economic behaviour, assumed to be invariant across time and space. Economists approach their discipline by studying aspects of the economic environment and behaviour that are considered independent of historical context. Consequently, historical explanations of economic events are not typically included in economic theory, as they are not seen as generalisable across different periods and regions.

For example, the inter-war economy of Germany provides an illustrative example. After World War I, Germany faced heavy reparations payments as a punishment for its defeat. Keynes predicted that this injustice might lead Germany to revolt and potentially cause another war within two decades. However, a modern economist analysing this historical period may focus solely on creating a macroeconomic model to study the impact of foreign taxes on Germany's GDP (Ariely, 2008a, 2008b).

The limitation of this approach is that it overlooks the most critical aspect of the German economy during that time, the resentment and anger of the population due to the unjust economic burden imposed on them. This social and historical context played a crucial role in shaping the events that followed, leading to the rise of Hitler, the outbreak of World War II, and significant changes in the global economic landscape (Ariely, 2008a, 2008b).

In Islamic economics, historical and social contexts are considered essential in understanding economic phenomena. The rejection of the assumption of universal economic laws allows for a more nuanced and comprehensive analysis of economic events and their underlying causes. Emphasising the role of historical context in economic analysis enables a more holistic understanding of economic systems and contributes to more accurate policy recommendations.

The neglect of historical factors in mainstream economic theories has been acknowledged by prominent economists like Douglass North, a Nobel Prize laureate. North highlights the limitations of standard economic theories in understanding the complex and ever-changing real world. He argues that to comprehend economic, political, and social changes, a fundamental shift in the way we think and approach economic analysis is necessary (Stiglitz, 2011).

Unfortunately, Islamic economists, by adopting the framework assumptions of modern economic theories, have inadvertently limited their ability to incorporate historical explanations for economic events. They have accepted the notion that historical explanations cannot be universal laws and, therefore, may not hold the same weight as general economic principles. This has restrained them from fully utilising historical context in their analyses.

However, the Quran itself employs both particular historical explanations and universal laws to illustrate economic, social, and political concepts. Islamic economists need not shy away from incorporating historical explanations as a methodological principle, as the Quran itself uses this approach. By embracing the full spectrum of economic analysis, including historical context, Islamic economists can develop more comprehensive and nuanced understandings of economic phenomena and better address the challenges of an ever-changing world.

(b) **Theories are best expressed in a mathematical form**

European history, influenced by the conflict between science and Christianity, led to the emergence of science as a rival to religious knowledge. This resulted in an exaggerated emphasis on science as the sole valid source of understanding the world. Physics, in particular, became the ideal model for scientific thought, given its focus on measurement and quantification. Lord Kelvin famously stated that without measurement, true knowledge is lacking, while with measurement, knowledge is gained (Kung, 2006).

The concept of the "quantitative imperative," which emphasises the centrality of measurement, gained prominence. This idea was deeply rooted in the development of physics and permeated other scientific disciplines as well, including economics. Economic theories started to be formulated in mathematical form, often imitating models borrowed directly from physics. Economic thinkers, especially neoclassicals, adopted these mathematical models, sometimes verbatim, without considering their practical relevance (McCloskey, 1983).

This imitation of physics and the pursuit of mathematical elegance in economic theories has led to admiration for complex mathematical models even when their practical applicability is questionable. As a result, the practical relevance of economic theories has often been overshadowed by their mathematical sophistication. This inclination towards mathematical elegance over practicality has hindered the development of economic theories that are more attuned to the complex and ever-changing real world.

Renowned economist Paul Krugman has criticised the field of economics, stating that it went astray because it mistook the beauty of mathematics for truth. In a discussion on the state of economics organised by the American Economic Association (AEA), it was concluded that "Economics as taught in graduate schools has become increasingly preoccupied with formal technique to the exclusion of studying real-world problems and issues" (AEA, 2008).

Blaug (1985), in his work "Disturbing Currents in Modern Economics," also highlighted concerns about "formalism" in modern economics, which refers to the overuse of mathematical models with more attention to rigor than content. An illustrative example of this dominance of mathematical reasoning over economic reasoning can be seen in the Arrow-Debreu model of General Equilibrium. While the model is extremely well developed mathematically, its economic assumptions of complete markets, zero costs of transactions and information, and price-taking behaviour by all agents are highly unrealistic.

Despite its deficiencies on the economic front, Arrow and Debreu went on to receive Nobel Prizes for the mathematical precision of the model. An intellectual grandchild of the Arrow-Debreu model is the DSGE (Dynamic Stochastic General Equilibrium) model, which has been blamed for the global financial crisis of 2008. The failure of mathematically sophisticated economic theories has become so glaringly obvious that a Congressional Committee was set up to investigate the role of deficient economic theories in the global financial crisis of 2008 (Congressional Committee, 2009).

In testimony before this committee, Solow (1956) commented on the extreme lack of realism in the DSGE model, stating, "A thoughtful person, faced with the thought that economic policy was being pursued on this basis (i.e., DSGE models), might reasonably wonder what planet he or she is on." The flaws in these mathematically driven economic theories have become evident, raising doubts about their applicability to the real world.

Indeed, Umar Ibn al-Khattab., the second Caliph of Islam, demonstrated the use of censuses to ensure just and equitable distribution of revenues generated from Muslim conquests. Moreover, Muslims have made significant contributions to mathematical knowledge throughout history.

While there are no objections to the appropriate use of mathematics and statistics in economics when they are relevant and useful, McCloskey (1983) argues that some applications of mathematics in economics are merely for show and lack practical value. Samuelson's skill at mathematics may be impressive, but the actual mathematical models used in certain cases may be irrelevant or distract from the essential economic issues at hand.

Milton Friedman (1990) pointed out that economics has increasingly become an arcane branch of mathematics rather than a discipline focused on addressing real economic problems. Therefore, it is essential to use mathematics judiciously in economic analysis, ensuring that it enhances understanding and insights into real-world economic issues, rather than merely serving as a display of technical prowess.

(c) **Materialism of economic theories**

The materialistic nature of both Karl Marx's doctrine of material determinism and the foundations of modern Western economic theory poses two significant conflicts with Islamic economics ideas.

Firstly, material determinism, as believed by Marx and implicitly embedded in Western economic theory, denies the role of God in shaping human affairs. In contrast, the Quran emphasises God's active intervention in historical events and sets conditions for receiving divine help in the present. The clockmaker model prevalent in the West, where God is seen as the initial creator who no longer interferes with the universe, contradicts the Islamic perspective of an involved and responsive God.

Secondly, material determinism reduces human agency, vision, and ideologies to mere outcomes of material conditions. Marx even asserted that economic circumstances determined the development of human philosophies. However, the irony lies in the fact that Marx's vision of a classless society inspired millions of people in Russia and China, leading to significant social and political changes despite the absence of substantial material means. This contradicts his theory, which posits that societies should progress from agrarian to capitalist before eventually transitioning to communism.

The materialistic nature of certain economic theories conflicts with the core Islamic economics belief in an active and intervening God and the significant impact of human agency, vision, and ideology on shaping societies. As such, a proper integration of Islamic teachings and principles into economic theories would require a more nuanced and comprehensive approach that respects both the spiritual and material dimensions of human existence.

Modern economic theory, with its focus on utility maximisation and treating human beings as mere inputs in production functions, often overlooks the profound impact that inspired leaders can have on the destiny and fortunes of a nation. Islamic economics emphasises the power of affection and unity that can be fostered among people through divine intervention.

In contrast to the reductionist view of individuals as selfish utility maximisers, the Quran acknowledges the role of God in creating affection and love between people's hearts. It highlights that no amount of material wealth or resources can replicate or replace the affection divinely established among individuals. This recognition of the intangible and spiritually significant aspects of human relations sets Islamic economics apart from some aspects of modern economic theory, which tend to focus predominantly on material factors and self-interested behaviour. Quran says: "And (moreover) He hath put affection between their hearts: not if thou hadst spent all that is in the Earth, couldst thou have produced that affection, but Allah hath done it: for He is Exalted in might ..." (Quran, 8:63).

Prophet Muhammad (peace be upon him) is an exemplar of an inspired leader who transformed the fate of his community through his character, teachings, and guidance. His role in bringing people together, establishing justice, and fostering unity serves as a reminder that human potential and leadership can go beyond the narrow scope of utility-maximising individuals in economic models.

By acknowledging the importance of spiritual and emotional dimensions in human interactions and recognising the potential of inspired leadership to influence societies positively, Islamic economics offer a broader perspective on the complexities of human behaviour and the dynamics of social change. This holistic approach can complement economic analyses and lead to a more comprehensive understanding of human actions and their impact on society.

Islamic economics recognises that the most valuable treasures, such as the unity and cohesion of the Ummah (Muslim community) established through the efforts of Prophet Muhammad, cannot be acquired solely through material means. This perspective contradicts the methodological foundations of conventional economic theories, which often emphasise material factors and utility maximisation as the primary drivers of human behaviour and progress.

In recent times, there have been major failures in economic theories that have prompted some economists to explore invisible and immaterial factors as potential drivers of material progress. Scholars like Zak and Knack have conducted seminal studies on trust and economic growth, acknowledging the role of intangible factors such as the quality of institutions, property rights, and social norms in shaping economic outcomes (Zak & Knack, 2001).

These efforts to consider invisible causes of economic progress represent a departure from conventional economic thinking. Nobel Laureate Ronald Coase has critiqued existing economics for its limited relation to real-world phenomena, highlighting the need to consider factors beyond purely materialistic ones. Nonetheless, such critiques have not gained widespread acceptance among mainstream economists.

Islamic economics, on the other hand, provide valuable insights that go beyond the narrow materialistic scope of traditional economic theories. Islamic economic principles emphasise the importance of justice, fairness, trust, and ethical conduct in economic interactions, and they acknowledge the significance of social institutions and norms in shaping economic outcomes. These teachings offer a more holistic and advanced understanding of human behaviour and social progress.

Hence, Islamic economic principles encompass a broader view of human interactions and progress, incorporating both material and immaterial factors. By considering the teachings of Islam, economists can gain valuable insights into social justice, ethics, and the interplay of visible and invisible factors that influence economic development and the well-being of societies.

(d) **Economics theories are not normative**

Economic theories are often categorised into two types: positive and normative. Positive theories are considered to be factual and objective, dealing with describing and explaining economic phenomena as they are observed in the real world. In contrast, normative theories involve value judgments and cannot be empirically tested or verified. The claim made by some is that conventional economic theories are primarily positive, focused on describing economic facts and behaviour.

For example, Samuelson and Nordhaus (2010) assert in their book "Economics" that positive economics describes the actual facts of an economy, while normative economics involves value judgments. Similar claims can be found in various conventional economics textbooks. However, upon closer examination, it becomes evident that this claim is not entirely accurate, as predictions made by economic theories often contradict actual observed behaviour of firms and consumers.

One particular area that highlights the discrepancy between economic theory and real-world behaviour is consumer behaviour. The field of behavioural economics has emerged precisely because of the recognition that actual consumer behaviour does not always align with the predictions of traditional economic theories, which are based on the assumption of utility maximisation.

Numerous examples of systematic discrepancies between economic theories and observed consumer behaviour have been documented. Authors such as Daniel Ariely (2008) in "Predictably Irrational" and Richard Thaler (1994) in "Quasi-Rational Economics" have provided extensive evidence that challenges the notion of utility maximisation as the sole driver of consumer decision-making.

Thus, the claim that conventional economic theories are purely positive and accurately describe real-world economic behaviour is not entirely true. The emergence of behavioural economics and the numerous examples of observed deviations from standard economic predictions highlight the need for a more comprehensive understanding of human decision-making and behaviour in economic contexts. One line of investigation reveals the importance of considering human drives for understanding, achievement, and feelings of reciprocity, trust, etc., to understand behaviour in different economic environments (Mehmood, 2011). Another area of research emphasises the role of social norms in shaping human conduct (Biccieri, 2006).

Nobel Prize Laureate Herbert Simon's work introduced the concepts of "satisficing" and "bounded rationality," which provide better descriptions of observed human behaviour than the traditional economic assumption of "maximisation." Ariely's work, titled "The Fallacy of Supply and Demand," illustrates the phenomenon of "anchoring," where initial decisions about the value of new products are arbitrary and not revised based on new information. This leads to arbitrary decisions about price and value that can be exploited by marketeers.

Consumer choices at cafeterias are systematically influenced by factors like the sequence in which choices are listed, contrary to the predictions of economic theory. This behavioural tendency can be utilised to "nudge" consumers toward healthier choices (Koehler & Harvey, 2004).

Empirical studies of Vickrey 2nd price auctions show that people frequently bid over their private values, contrary to the optimising strategy predicted by economic theory. This behaviour is due to cognitive errors and has been demonstrated in experimental studies (Kagel & Roth, 1995).

Regarding firm behaviour: Efficiency wage theories demonstrate that firms often pay laborers higher wages than their marginal product, which contradicts simple-minded profit maximisation assumptions (Mehmood, 2011).

Theories of internal organisation of firms reveal that they cannot be treated as homogenous entities pursuing a single goal. There are conflicts of interest between owners, managers, and employees, as highlighted in the Principal/Agent literature. Greenwald and Stiglitz (1990) have developed a theory of firms that considers informational asymmetry and aligns better with observed firm behaviour than neoclassical theory. Findings from the theory of Industrial Organisation show that firms often behave differently from the assumptions of competitive markets presented in economics textbooks (Kagel & Roth, 1995).

Bergmann (2007) criticises the unrealistic theories in economics, noting that much of the material about business behaviour found in economics textbooks and the theoretical developments in leading academic journals were not based on empirical accuracy or validation. She points out that many economic theories were simply constructed by economists without substantial empirical evidence.

The assumption that prices are determined by the equilibrium of supply and demand, a fundamental concept in traditional economics, has faced challenges in real-world situations. The Great Depression highlighted the fact that labour markets can remain out of equilibrium for prolonged periods, which contradicts the standard demand and supply model. Keynes provided an explanation for this phenomenon, suggesting that wages are rigid downwards.

However, this still raises the question of why such rigidity exists. The failure of labour markets to clear at the supply and demand equilibrium has led to the need for government intervention to restore equilibrium. Instances of persistent unemployment in various countries further support the notion that labour markets do not always clear as predicted by traditional economic theories. Multiple explanations have been proposed to account for this market failure, and Mehmood (2011) provides a survey of these various explanations.

The research conducted by Card and Krueger (1997) challenged the predictions of the traditional supply and demand model in the context of minimum wage policies. Their study indicated that raising minimum wages might not lead to the expected decrease in employment, as the standard model suggests, but could potentially increase employment. This finding sparked controversy and received strong opposition from some economists.

In an interview about their research, Card acknowledged that the simple supply and demand model might not fully describe how employers operate in the labour market. He indicated that alternative theories might offer better explanations for certain observed phenomena that do not align with the basic demand and supply framework.

The controversy surrounding their research was so intense that Card decided to step away from further research on the minimum wage topic. He mentioned losing friends and facing criticism from some colleagues who felt that their work was betraying the principles of economics as a whole.

Additionally, Zaman and Saglam (2010) demonstrated that the Marshallian theory of supply and demand, which explains price formation in a single market, conflicts with general equilibrium theory (GET). General equilibrium theory extends the principles derived from single-market theory to multiple markets. This indicates that the principles leading to price formation in a single market can yield contradictory outcomes when applied to multiple markets.

These examples illustrate how traditional economic theories can encounter challenges and contradictions when confronted with real-world situations and empirical evidence. Indeed, the foundations of economic theory, both in microeconomics and macroeconomics, are largely built upon the concepts of supply and demand and the notion of equilibrium. However, as previously discussed, when we examine actual consumer behaviour, firm behaviour, and price determination in the real world, we find significant discrepancies between these observed behaviours and the theoretical predictions derived from economic models.

Consumer behaviour often deviates from the standard utility maximisation hypothesis, leading to the emergence of behavioural economics as a distinct field that studies the discrepancies between theoretical predictions and observed behaviour. Similarly, firm behaviour is often more complex and diverse than the simplistic profit-maximisation assumption frequently assumed in economic models.

Moreover, the concept of equilibrium, which assumes that markets naturally tend towards a state of balance between supply and demand, is not always supported by empirical evidence. For example, the persistence of unemployment during the Great Depression and the possibility of minimum wage increases leading to increased employment, as shown by Card and Krueger's (1997) research, contradict the standard equilibrium predictions.

Due to these inconsistencies between economic theory and real-world observations, it can be argued that economic theory is not a positive theory in the sense of being grounded in empirical evidence and conformity to observations. Instead, it relies heavily on a priori assumptions, axioms, and mathematical formulations that might not align well with actual human behaviour and economic phenomena.

The acknowledgment of the disparities between economic models and empirical evidence has led some economists, like Joseph Stiglitz, to criticise the ideological nature of some economic theories and their departure from the principles of scientific inquiry.

Therefore, the existence of substantial disparities between observed behaviour and economic theories highlights the need for a more realistic and empirically grounded approach to economic analysis, which can better explain and predict real-world economic phenomena.

## 10.5 The Faith-Based Economic Theory

In an Islamic alternative to economic theory, three fundamental issues serve as the foundation of this approach:

a) Transforming human beings: The primary goal of a Muslim's actions, including the study of economics, is to be directed towards God's will. The teachings of Prophet Mohammad aimed to bring about a spiritual transformation within his companions, helping them understand the purpose and meaning of their existence as defined by the Quran (95: 4–5). This transformation recognises the potential within human beings to attain the highest spiritual state or descend to the lowest moral level. Islamic teachings, including those in the economic domain, aim to help individuals realise their potential and strive towards a higher moral and spiritual state. Quran says: (13:11) "Verily, God does not change men's condition unless they change their inner selves".

b) Shaping economic institutions: Islamic economics emphasises the importance of shaping economic institutions and practices in accordance with Islamic principles. This involves adopting a system of economic governance that aligns with the teachings of the Quran and Hadith (sayings and actions of Prophet Muhammad). Economic institutions should promote justice, fairness, and ethical conduct, avoiding exploitation and oppression. Issues such as wealth distribution, trade practices, and financial transactions must be designed to ensure social welfare and equitable distribution of resources.
c) Emphasis on moral and ethical values: Islamic economics places a strong emphasis on moral and ethical values in economic decision-making. Profit-making is not the sole motive; rather, economic activities are expected to be guided by ethical considerations and social responsibility. This approach aligns with Islamic economics on economic justice, charity, and caring for the less fortunate in society.

It should be noted that developing a comprehensive Islamic economic theory requires a deeper exploration of the Quranic principles and Hadith, as well as a critical evaluation of conventional economic theories in light of Islamic economics. Quran says: (13:11) "Verily, God does not change men's condition unless they change their inner selves". While this brief outline highlights key foundational aspects, a more detailed and rigorous study is essential to establish a comprehensive and coherent Islamic economic framework. This endeavour may lead to a more profound understanding of economics in the context of Islamic economics principles and values, ultimately contributing to the well-being and flourishing of individuals and communities in the Islamic world.

The Islamic economics approach to economics is indeed different from materialistic teachings. While conventional economic theories often prioritise material conditions and wealth accumulation as the primary means to achieve human welfare and development, Islamic teachings emphasise a more holistic approach that places human well-being and spiritual growth at its core.

In the Islamic economics perspective, material prosperity is considered a means to an end rather than an end in itself. The ultimate goal is to fulfil the spiritual and material needs of individuals and communities, promoting social justice, and ensuring the well-being of all members of society. This human-cantered approach recognises that true development and progress cannot be achieved solely through economic growth or material wealth. Instead, it requires empowering individuals and communities with capabilities, freedom, and opportunities to pursue a life of dignity, virtue, and self-realisation.

Scholars like Amartya Sen and Martha Nussbaum (2011) have echoed similar sentiments, advocating for a human capabilities approach to development. They emphasise that the focus should be on enhancing people's capabilities and freedoms, allowing them to lead fulfilling lives and participate in shaping their own destiny.

In essence, the Islamic economic alternative to economics seeks to strike a balance between material well-being and spiritual growth, prioritising the well-being of human beings over material possessions. This approach emphasises social justice, compassion, and ethical conduct, ultimately aiming to create a just and harmonious society where all individuals can thrive and prosper.

Indeed, Islamic economics provides a unique and comprehensive approach to human development that goes beyond what is typically available in conventional secular thought. The profound teachings of Prophet Muhammad and the Quran have inspired Muslims to strive for excellence in all aspects of life, including personal development, moral conduct, and social justice.

a) Concept of Human Excellence: In the Islamic tradition, the ultimate goal of human development is to attain excellence in character and conduct. Muslims are encouraged to follow the example of Prophet Muhammad as a role model for personal growth and ethical behaviour. The emphasis on developing virtues such as compassion, honesty, generosity, and humility leads to a well-rounded and morally upright individual.
b) Balance between Material and Spiritual Well-being: Islamic teachings promote a balanced approach to life, emphasising both material and spiritual well-being. While material prosperity is not discouraged, it is always viewed as a means to fulfil one's responsibilities and serve the greater good. The pursuit of wealth is tempered by the recognition of the transient nature of worldly possessions, and the need to prioritise spiritual growth and the development of one's relationship with God.
c) Social Justice and Welfare: Islamic economics places a strong emphasis on social justice and the welfare of all members of society. The concept of Zakat (charitable giving) and other forms of wealth redistribution are fundamental aspects of Islamic economic principles. Muslims are encouraged to help those in need and support the less fortunate through various charitable acts.

Moreover, Islamic economics also promotes ethical business practices, fair trade, and responsible stewardship of resources, ensuring that economic activities are conducted with moral principles in mind.

Overall, the Islamic approach to human development transcends mere material progress and economic growth. It seeks to nurture individuals who are not only economically prosperous but also spiritually enlightened, socially just, and morally upright, contributing to the well-being of their communities and society as a whole. This holistic approach to human development is one of the unique contributions of Islamic teachings to the world.

## 10.6 Advocating Spirituality

The strong spiritual focus of Islamic economics, as exemplified by the life of Prophet Muhammad (peace be upon him), sets Islamic Economics apart from conventional materialistic approaches. The ultimate purpose of all human endeavours, including economic activities, is to seek the pleasure of God. As the Quran states: (73:7–8) Lo! [the struggle to establish the Deen] keeps you very busy in the daytime. So remember the name of thy Lord and devote thyself with a complete devotion. That is, even being busy with the struggle to establish the Faith during the daytime should not distract you from the remembrance of God, and some significant portion of the nights should be fully devoted to God. This spiritual orientation gives Islamic Economics a unique ethical foundation and a higher purpose beyond mere material gains.

In Islamic Economics, the pursuit of wealth and economic prosperity is not an end in itself but rather a means to fulfil one's responsibilities as a trustee (*khalifah*) of God's resources. People are encouraged to be conscious of their actions and intentions, ensuring that their economic activities are conducted with ethical integrity, social responsibility, and the welfare of all members of society in mind.

The emphasis on corporate social responsibility (CSR) in conventional economics often stems from a utilitarian perspective, where companies may engage in socially responsible actions to enhance their public image and increase profits. In contrast, Islamic Economics promotes genuine concern for social problems and the well-being of society as a moral and religious duty.

The concept of accountability and transparency in Islamic Economics is also grounded in spirituality. The idea that individuals will be held accountable by God for their actions, including their economic dealings, encourages ethical behaviour and discourages corrupt practices. Moreover, the spiritual focus of Islamic Economics also extends to the treatment of employees and workers. Islamic teachings emphasise fair wages, just treatment, and ethical conduct in business dealings, promoting a harmonious and morally upright work environment.

The spiritual focus of Islamic economics instils a higher sense of purpose and responsibility in economic activities. It encourages individuals and businesses to align their actions with ethical principles and social justice, thereby contributing to the betterment of society and earning the pleasure of God. The integration of spirituality and ethics into economic practices is a unique and valuable aspect of Islamic Economics that distinguishes it from purely materialistic approaches.

## 10.7 Moral Conduct and Leadership

The emphasis on moral leadership and training in Islamic Economics is deeply rooted in the teachings of Prophet Muhammad (peace be upon him) (Quran 21:107). As a mercy to all of creation, his mission was not only to convey the message of

Islam but also to exemplify its principles through his actions and character (Quran 33:21). Islamic economists are called upon to follow his example and actively engage in moral training, both for themselves and their students.

In Islamic economics, moral training is not limited to mere outward actions; it includes the inner dimensions of intentions and feelings with which actions are performed. This holistic approach to morality is essential in developing genuine compassion, empathy, and mercy towards others (Quran 8:63). Islamic economists must not only advocate for feeding the poor but also inspire and educate others to participate in acts of charity and social welfare (Quran 76:8–9).

The moral mission of education in Islamic Economics contrasts with the conventional economics trend of abandoning moral values in the pursuit of knowledge. In many conventional institutions, the focus shifted away from character-building, leading to a disconnection between academic knowledge and ethical conduct. The consequences of this detachment are evident in the lack of trust in business and economic institutions, as expressed by Harvard Professor Zubof (2009).

Islamic Economics, on the other hand, integrates moral principles into the very fabric of economic activities (Kahf, 2004). The principles of Islamic economics emphasise honesty, integrity, fair treatment, and social responsibility in economic transactions and business dealings. Islamic economists are called to be ethical role models and to instil these values in their students to create a generation of morally conscious and socially responsible individuals.

Prophet Muhammad (peace be upon him) served as a transformative leader, guiding people not only through words but also through his exemplary character (Quran 33:21). Islamic economists must strive to follow this path, seeking to be sources of positive change in society by embodying and imparting moral values in their work, research, and teaching (Kahf, 2004). By infusing moral leadership into the study and practice of economics, Islamic economists can contribute to building a more just, compassionate, and sustainable economic system that aligns with the broader objectives of Islam.

The concept of engagement and struggle as a means to knowledge is deeply ingrained in Islamic economics, particularly through the example of Prophet Muhammad (peace be upon him) and his Companions. Islamic economists are called upon not to remain detached and neutral observers but to actively participate in the world, striving to bring about positive change and economic justice (Quran 29: 69).

The process of struggle in the path of God is seen as a means of guidance and knowledge. By engaging in the struggle for justice and societal improvement, Islamic economists can gain insights and understanding that go beyond theoretical constructs or abstract analysis. The practical experience of addressing real-world economic issues allows them to better comprehend the complexities of the economic system and its impact on people's lives.

In contrast to the dichotomy between positive and normative economics, Islamic Economics is seen as transformative. It emphasises taking action to bring about concrete changes aligned with Islamic economics principles, rather than merely studying the world as it is or describing an ideal state of affairs. Islamic economists are encouraged to implement the teachings of Islam in their personal lives and guide their students to do the same.

The transformative approach in Islamic Economics is exemplified in the teachings of Prophet Muhammad (peace be upon him), who led his companions in striving for social justice, compassion, and fairness. Following this path, Islamic economists are called to engage with economic challenges and work towards solutions that align with the values and principles of Islamic economics.

By adopting a transformative approach, Islamic Economics aims to have a meaningful impact on the well-being of individuals and society, rather than being limited to theoretical discussions. The focus on moral training, compassion, and social responsibility is central to this approach, ensuring that economic decisions and actions are driven by ethical considerations and a sincere desire to serve humanity.

Hence, Islamic Economics is rooted in the principles of engagement, struggle, and transformation. Islamic economists are called upon to actively participate in changing the world for the better, guided by Islamic values and teachings. Through this process of struggle and moral leadership, they seek not only to understand economic phenomena but also to bring about positive and lasting change in society, in the spirit of Prophet Muhammad's mission and the teachings of Islam.

Indeed, the approach of Islamic Economics sharply contrasts with the detached observer stance advocated in conventional economic methodology. Conventional economists often seek to discover universal laws and formulate positive theories that describe observed economic phenomena without making normative judgments or engaging in policy matters. This detachment is seen as essential for maintaining scientific objectivity and avoiding value judgments.

On the other hand, Islamic Economics places a strong emphasis on the transformative role of economists as activists and reformers working to bring about positive change in society. The teachings of Prophet Muhammad (peace be upon him) and Islamic principles encourage engagement with the world to address social and economic injustices actively.

The contrast between Western economic theory and Islamic economic systems can be summarised by the difference between "selfishness and competition" versus "generosity and cooperation." Conventional economics often assumes that individuals act out of self-interest and compete to maximise their utility, whereas Islamic economics emphasises the values of generosity, cooperation, and social welfare.

In conventional economics, self-interested behaviour is often viewed as the driving force behind economic decision-making, leading to the idea of the "rational economic man." This perspective can sometimes neglect the role of compassion, moral values, and social responsibility in shaping economic behaviour.

Islamic economic systems, on the other hand, place an emphasis on the importance of moral and ethical considerations in economic activities. Islamic economics encourage individuals and societies to act generously, consider the welfare of others, and cooperate for the common good. Economic decisions and policies are expected to align with these values, promoting economic justice and social welfare.

The foundations of Islamic economics are deeply rooted in the spiritual and moral teachings of Islam, which promote compassion, mercy, and social responsibility. This approach provides a distinct perspective on economic affairs, shifting the focus from mere material accumulation to the well-being of individuals and society as a whole.

Thus, the contrast between conventional economic theory and Islamic economic systems lies in their underlying philosophical foundations. Conventional economics often emphasises self-interest and competition, while Islamic economics is rooted in generosity, cooperation, and compassion. The transformative and socially responsible approach of Islamic economics encourages economists to actively engage with economic issues and work towards creating a just and equitable society.

## 10.8 Fighting Greed

The contrast between conventional economic methodology, which often explains economic behaviour as a consequence of selfishness and greed, and Islamic economics on generosity is evident in the Quranic verses and the actions of Prophet Muhammad (peace be upon him).

In Islamic economics, generosity is highly valued and is considered a virtuous act that brings one closer to God. The Quran repeatedly emphasises the importance of spending for the sake of God and helping those in need. Muslims are encouraged to give charity both in public and private, without seeking any worldly rewards but only seeking the pleasure and reward from God (Quran 2:274).

The Quranic verse (2:219) explicitly indicates that Muslims are commanded to spend beyond their needs for the sake of God, signifying the significance of generosity and charity in Islam.

The generosity of Prophet Muhammad (peace be upon him) serves as an exemplary model for all Muslims. He was known for his kindness, compassion, and willingness to help others in need, regardless of their background. His actions reflect the essence of Islamic economics on generosity, as he never turned away anyone seeking his assistance and was as generous as the rain, as mentioned by Sufyan bin Umayyah.

Contrary to the conventional economic perspective that attempts to explain charity and generosity solely as manifestations of long-run selfishness, Islamic economics views acts of charity as motivated by love for God and seeking His pleasure alone. Muslims believe that their acts of charity are a means of spiritual purification and an expression of gratitude for the blessings bestowed upon them by God.

The concept of generosity in Islamic economics stands in sharp contrast to the notion of selfishness and greed often associated with Western economic theories. Islamic economics places great importance on acts of charity and encourage Muslims to be generous and compassionate towards others, motivated by love for God and the desire to seek His pleasure. This emphasis on generosity as a means of spiritual development and social welfare is a distinctive aspect of Islamic economic thought (Kahf, 2004).

Indeed, in genuine Islamic economics, the emphasis on generosity and spending on others is a fundamental aspect of economic behaviour. Islamic economists must not only preach but also actively practice these principles, serving as role models for their students. By engaging in projects that aim to help the poor and disadvantaged, they can instil in their students the importance of compassion and social responsibility, in addition to the theoretical knowledge of economics.

This practical experience of actively contributing to the well-being of others must be an integral part of the Islamic economics curriculum of studies, enabling students to internalise the values of generosity and selflessness. By doing so, Islamic economists can contribute to fostering a society that prioritises the welfare of others over individual gain.

This approach contrasts sharply with conventional economic teachings that often promote self-interest and individualistic behaviour. Studies have shown that economists, as a group, tend to exhibit more selfish tendencies compared to individuals in other professions (Kirchgässner, 2005). This highlights the need for an alternative economic approach that emphasises moral values and societal welfare, which are essential components of Islamic economics.

By incorporating a strong moral and social dimension into economic teachings, Islamic economists can promote a more compassionate and just economic system. By actively practicing and teaching generosity, they can inspire students to become agents of positive change, working towards a society that prioritises the well-being of all its members. This transformative approach is fundamental to Islamic economics, which seeks to bring about meaningful and sustainable changes in the world through the application of Islamic economic principles and values.

## 10.9 Promoting Cooperation vs. Competition

Islamic economic principles emphasise the importance of promoting community feeling and cooperation among all members of society. The Quran repeatedly encourages unity and cooperation, emphasising that Muslims should support and help one another in righteousness and piety (Quran, 2:5). The concept of brotherhood and love among believers is highly valued and is seen as a unifying force that transcends divisions and fosters a sense of shared responsibility (Quran, 8:62,63).

In contrast to the competitive nature often promoted in conventional economic systems, Islamic economics emphasises collaboration and mutual support. This cooperative attitude has significant implications for various aspects of economic behaviour and transactions. For example, in the market for insurance, a cooperative approach can address problems such as moral hazard and adverse selection, which are often challenging to manage in competitive settings.

By nurturing a spirit of cooperation and solidarity, Islamic economics seeks to create a society that values the welfare of all its members. This approach encourages individuals to look after the needs of others as they would their own, fostering a sense of shared purpose and collective well-being. As a result, Islamic economic systems strive to promote social harmony, reduce inequality, and ensure the equitable distribution of resources and opportunities.

The emphasis on cooperation over competition aligns with the broader principles of Islamic economics, which advocate for unity, compassion, and the promotion of communal welfare. Through these values, Islamic economics aims to create a just and compassionate society where individuals work together to uplift one another and contribute to the greater good.

The contrast between the norm of selfish profit maximisation in conventional economic systems and the emphasis on cooperation in Islamic economics has significant implications for firm behaviour and societal outcomes.

In conventional economic theory, the pursuit of profit maximisation often leads to firms engaging in collusive behaviour to gain advantages over consumers. Collusion can result in higher prices, reduced competition, and decreased consumer welfare. Therefore, laws and regulations are put in place to prevent such collusive activities and promote fair competition in markets.

On the other hand, Islamic economic ideals of service and societal welfare discourage firms from engaging in collusive behaviour. In an Islamic economic system, firms are encouraged to cooperate and work together to provide the best possible service to society, prioritising the well-being of consumers over selfish profit motives. This cooperative orientation is driven by the spiritual values and rewards of the (hereafter) and is exemplified in historical Islamic societies through the institutions of *Awqaf* (charitable endowments).[1]

Islamic societies historically demonstrated the potential of spiritually oriented behaviour in fostering cooperation and service to society. The Prophet Muhammad's teachings and the practices of his companions set high standards of excellence, where individuals would serve others even when faced with personal hardships. The concept of feeding others while being hungry and acting to earn the pleasure of God exemplified the selflessness and cooperation present in these societies.

Modern economic theory, influenced by the theories of evolution, often assumes that competition among individuals and firms leads to the survival of the fittest and ultimately benefits the economy as a whole. However, this notion does not apply in societies where human beings are spiritually developed and prioritise the welfare of others over selfish gains, as exemplified in Islamic teachings and practices.

By emphasising cooperation and selflessness, Islamic economics offers an alternative vision that aims to create a more compassionate and equitable society. The ideals of service and cooperation, deeply rooted in Islamic teachings, can guide economic behaviour and lead to positive outcomes for individuals and the entire community.

---

[1] The concepts of Awqaf and historical Islamic practices are well documented in various Islamic literature, including religious texts and historical accounts. However, specific citations for this section are not provided in the original response.

## 10.10 Conclusion

Over the last few decades, there has been a revival of interest in Islamic economics. However, it is still in its early stages of development when compared to the well-established and sophisticated discipline of conventional economics, which has undergone a long and rigorous process of development over more than a century. This raises the question of whether a new discipline in economics is needed, and if so, what Islamic economics is, how it differs from conventional economics, and what contributions it has made over the centuries. This Chapter aimed to briefly address these questions.

It is widely acknowledged that resources are limited compared to the demands placed on them. Nevertheless, virtually all civilisations recognise the importance of ensuring the well-being of all human beings. Achieving this well-being may remain an unattainable dream if scarce resources are not utilised efficiently and equitably. To achieve this, every society must develop an effective strategy, influenced consciously or unconsciously by its worldview. If the underlying worldview is flawed, the strategy may fail to promote the well-being of all. Worldviews can broadly be categorised into two theoretical constructs: secular and materialist, and spiritual and humanitarian.

Conventional economics, which dominates the global discourse, is primarily rooted in secular and materialist worldviews. It focuses on self-interest, rational behaviour, and market forces as the driving factors of economic behaviour. However, this approach has faced significant criticism, particularly in light of recurring economic crises and rising social inequalities.

In contrast, Islamic economics is based on a spiritual and humanitarian worldview. It centres on the ethical and moral dimensions of economic behaviour, emphasising justice, fairness, and the well-being of all individuals. Islamic economics operates within the framework of Islamic teachings, including the Quran and the Hadith (sayings and actions of Prophet Muhammad S.A.W.), which provide guidelines on economic activities.

One of the key differences between Islamic economics and conventional economics is the concept of *riba*, which prohibits interest-based transactions in Islamic finance. Instead, Islamic finance adheres to principles of profit-sharing, risk-sharing, and asset-backing, fostering more equitable economic arrangements. Islamic economics also emphasises the importance of social welfare and the eradication of poverty. The concept of zakat, a mandatory charitable contribution, is a central pillar of Islamic economics, serving as a mechanism to redistribute wealth and address social inequalities.

Over the centuries, Islamic economics has made notable contributions to various fields. During the Islamic Golden Age, Islamic scholars made significant advancements in areas such as monetary theory, trade, and Islamic finance. Today, Islamic economics continues to gain recognition, with Islamic finance institutions operating worldwide and research in Islamic economics expanding.

While conventional economics has a well-established history, the emergence of Islamic economics signifies an important opportunity to develop a discipline rooted in ethical and humanitarian principles. By embracing a spiritual and humanitarian worldview, Islamic economics seeks to address the shortcomings of conventional economics and promote economic well-being for all members of society.

Furthermore, the inclusion of ethical and normative considerations in economics is essential, especially when dealing with issues of social justice, wealth distribution, and the well-being of society. Islamic economics explicitly incorporates normative values derived from Islamic teachings into economic analysis, acknowledging that ethical considerations play a crucial role in shaping economic behaviour and outcomes.

Islamic economics, as a normative discipline, emphasises the pursuit of a just and equitable economic system that adheres to the principles of Islam. The concept of *Maqasid* al-Shariah (the objectives of law) guides economic policies and ensures that they align with the broader goals of Islamic economics, such as promoting human welfare, social justice, and the well-being of the community. By embracing the normative dimension of economic analysis, Islamic economics offers a more comprehensive and holistic approach that considers both material and moral aspects of human existence.

There is a need to demark the road to a genuine Islamic economic theory to address the crisis in the discipline of Islamic economics. It is crucial to reject the uncritical acceptance of conventional economic ideas and embark on a path of establishing a genuine Islamic economic theory. This involves re-evaluating the methodological framework and underlying assumptions used in the discipline.

The first step is to acknowledge and recognise the fundamental conflict between conventional economic principles and the views of Islamic economics. Attempting to merge these contradictory bodies of knowledge has proven unsuccessful and has hindered the development of a coherent Islamic economic theory. Instead, Islamic economics should be rooted in the principles and values derived from Islamic teachings, allowing it to stand on its own merits and offer a unique contribution to the field of economics.

Secondly, Islamic economists must embrace alternative foundations for economic analysis that align with Islamic principles. This entails rejecting the uncritical adoption of universal laws, excessive reliance on mathematical formalism, and materialistic assumptions prevalent in conventional economic theories. By doing so, Islamic economics can move beyond the limitations of conventional economic models and develop a more meaningful and relevant approach to economic analysis.

Thirdly, Islamic economists need to approach economic analysis with a critical and independent mindset. While recognising the contributions of conventional economic thought, they must not shy away from developing distinctly Islamic economics perspectives and theories. By incorporating Islamic economics values and principles into economic analysis, Islamic economists can offer practical solutions that address the unique needs and challenges faced by Muslim societies.

Moreover, Islamic economics must prioritise the welfare of society and the promotion of social justice over mere profit maximisation. By integrating ethical considerations into economic analysis, Islamic economics can emphasise responsible and sustainable economic practices that prioritise the well-being of individuals and communities.

By going back to the core principles of Islam and incorporating them into economic analysis, Islamic economics can offer a coherent and meaningful approach that aligns with the aspirations of Muslim societies. Rejecting uncritical acceptance of conventional economic ideas and developing a genuine Islamic economic theory will enable Islamic economics to contribute effectively to the field of economics and provide practical solutions that promote social justice, ethical behaviour, and the well-being of individuals and communities.

In the next Chapter we explore insights and contributions provided to us by the knowledge structure of Islamic economics. Islamic economists have also been open to drawing insights from various schools of economic thought and other social sciences, including neoclassical, Keynesian, social, humanistic, and institutional economics.

# Chapter 11
# Learning and Convergence

## 11.1 Introduction

The previous Chapter discussed how the crisis in Islamic economics can be resolved by rejecting uncritical acceptance of conventional economic ideas and developing a genuine Islamic economic theory based on Islamic principles and values. By doing so, Islamic economics can offer a distinct and valuable contribution to the field of economics and provide practical solutions that align with the aspirations of Muslim societies.

Nonetheless our discussion in the previous chapters, while Islamic economics and conventional economics may have different emphases and approaches, they also share commonalities. Both disciplines deal with the allocation and distribution of scarce resources, and both involve making value judgments, whether explicit or implicit, in their analyses. It is important to note that conventional economists have never been entirely value-neutral, and they too have made value judgments based on their beliefs and perspectives.

Over time, the paradigm of conventional economics has evolved, recognising the significance of good governance, and incorporating a moral dimension into economic analysis. Prominent economists have emphasised the importance of ethical considerations in understanding economic behaviour and outcomes. This evolution in conventional economics aligns with some aspects of Islamic economics, which has always placed great emphasis on moral values and the broader well-being of society.

In this Chapter we explore insights and contributions provided to us by the knowledge structure of Islamic economics. Islamic economists have also been open to drawing insights from various schools of economic thought and other social sciences, including neoclassical, Keynesian, social, humanistic, and institutional economics. This openness to learning and incorporating useful tools and perspectives has enriched the field of Islamic economics and will likely continue to do so in the



S. Alamad, *Beyond Profit*, Contributions to Economics,
https://doi.org/10.1007/978-3-031-49748-3_11

future. As both disciplines continue to evolve, there is potential for further convergence and mutual learning between Islamic economics and conventional economics.

The concept of a generation is a useful way to distinguish and compare different stages of development or changes that occur over time. In the context of studying the evolution of thinking and ideas in the discipline of Islamic economics, the Chapter divides the scholars into two generations based on a time span of approximately forty years. However, determining the exact duration of a generation can vary, and there are different opinions on this matter (Ibn Khaldun, 1967).

For example, Ibn Khaldun considered a generation to be forty years, referring to the time it takes for a particular generation of human beings to vanish. He used the example of the Children of Israel, who spent forty years wandering in the desert after leaving Egypt to build a new generation capable of facing life's challenges and fulfilling the prophetic mission (Ibn Khaldun, 1967).

However, the duration of a generation is not always fixed at forty years and can differ in various contexts. Prophet Muhammad (peace be upon him) mentioned that the best generation is his generation, followed by the generations that come after them. Their time spans were not equal, as the Prophet's prophetic life was twenty-three years, while his companions and their followers lived longer.

Furthermore, the concept of generation can vary depending on the context and the object being referred to. For example, in the field of technology, the term "generation" is used to refer to specific stages of development or improvement, such as first-generation, second-generation, and so on.

Therefore, the concept of a generation is a useful tool for studying changes over time, but its duration may differ depending on the context and the subject of study. In the context of Islamic economics, the Chapter divides scholars into two generations based on a time span of around forty years for the purpose of analysis and comparison.

## 11.2 The Concept of the "Great Gap" Theory

The concept of the "Great Gap" theory, which suggests that there was a period of over 500 years of intellectual stagnation between the Greeks and the Scholastics in the history of economic thought, is a fallacy. Islamic economics, during this period, made significant contributions to various economic concepts that were later developed in conventional economics. These contributions cover a wide range of areas, demonstrating an interdisciplinary approach and understanding of economic principles (Islahi, 1996).

Some of the economic concepts that were developed by Muslim scholars long before they appeared in conventional economics include:

1. Interdisciplinary approach: Islamic economics integrated principles from various fields, including philosophy, ethics, law, and theology, into its economic thought (Ghazanfar, 2003, p. xi).

2. Property rights: Muslim scholars discussed the importance of property rights and the need for secure ownership, which is crucial for economic development (Ibn Khaldun, n.d., p. 141).
3. Division of labour and specialisation: Islamic economists recognised the benefits of division of labour and specialisation in enhancing productivity (Al-Mawardi, 1960, p. 5).
4. Saving and investment: The role of saving and investment in promoting economic development was emphasised by Muslim scholars (Abu Yusuf, 1933/34, p. 111).
5. Price determination: Both demand and supply were recognised as factors influencing prices, and the interplay of these forces was studied (Ibn Khaldun, n.d., p. 306).
6. Money and exchange: Islamic economics delved into the characteristics of money, counterfeiting, currency debasement, and Gresham's law (Ibn Khaldun, n.d., p. 296).
7. Banking and finance: Muslim scholars developed concepts related to banking, including checks, letters of credit, and principles of banking (Ibn Khaldun, n.d., p. 188).
8. Labour supply and population: Issues related to labour supply and population were discussed by Muslim economists (Ibn Khaldun, n.d., p. 158).
9. Role of the state: The importance of the state in promoting justice, peace, and stability for economic development was recognised (Al-Mawardi, 1960, p. 5).
10. Principles of taxation: Muslim scholars discussed principles of taxation and the role of the state in collecting revenue (Ibn Khaldun, n.d., p. 306).

It is essential to acknowledge these significant contributions made by Muslim scholars in the field of economics during the so-called "Great Gap" period. Their works not only enriched intellectual activity during that time but also influenced later European scholars, including the Scholastics. The acknowledgment of these contributions can help remove the misconception of a significant gap in economic thought during that period (Islahi, 1996). The recognition of the intellectual and sophisticated writings from the Islamic civilisation is crucial for a comprehensive understanding of the historical development of economic thought.

## 11.3 Interconnected Approach to Economic Development

The Muqaddimah by Ibn Khaldun is a prime example of the multidisciplinary approach adopted by Islamic economics. Unlike the conventional economics of his time, Ibn Khaldun did not limit his focus to economic variables alone. Instead, he recognised that human well-being is the result of complex interactions between various economic, moral, social, political, demographic, and historical factors. These factors are interconnected, and none of them can contribute optimally without the support of others (Ibn Khaldun, n.d.).

Central to this multidisciplinary framework was the concept of justice, which held a pivotal place in the Islamic worldview. Muslim scholars understood that justice is essential for development and that the absence of justice can lead to decline and disintegration in society.

Ibn Khaldun's work in the Muqaddimah represents the culmination of the contributions made by various scholars over the centuries. He sought to draw lessons from history to understand the rise and fall of civilisations, ruling dynasties, and states. Instead of merely documenting historical events, he aimed to establish cause-and-effect relationships in the study of historical phenomena. Ibn Khaldun's approach was driven by a quest for understanding the "how" and "why" of historical developments, rather than a simple account of what happened (Ibn Khaldun, 1967).

Through this multidisciplinary and dynamic approach, Islamic economics demonstrated a deeper understanding of the complexities of human societies and their development. It recognised that economic factors alone cannot lead to sustained development and progress. Instead, a comprehensive understanding of the interplay between economic, moral, social, and political aspects is crucial for achieving genuine and lasting development. This holistic approach remains a valuable contribution of Islamic economics to the field of economics and social sciences.

Ibn Khaldun's analysis stands in stark contrast to the neoclassical economist's simplification of confining the study primarily to short-term static analysis of markets, assuming that all other factors remain constant (North, 1994, p. 549). Instead, Ibn Khaldun's approach revolves around the human being as the central focus of analysis. He recognised that the rise and fall of dynasties or civilisations are closely dependent on the well-being or misery of the people. However, well-being cannot be solely attributed to economic variables, as conventional economics has often emphasised.

Instead, Ibn Khaldun acknowledged the interconnected and interrelated role of moral, psychological, social, economic, political, demographic, and historical factors in shaping the well-being of societies (Ibn Khaldun, n.d., p. 141). He viewed these factors as dynamically interacting with one another over an extended period. In this framework, one factor may act as a trigger mechanism, influencing the others either in the same direction or differently.

If the other factors do not react in the same direction, the decay in one sector may not spread to the others, leading to the possibility of reform or a slower decline. However, when multiple factors react in the same direction, the decay gains momentum through a chain reaction, making it challenging to isolate individual causes from the effects. This holistic and multidisciplinary dynamic approach allows Ibn Khaldun to have a clear vision of how different factors work together over time to influence the development or decline of a society.

In contrast, neoclassical economics, with its ceteris paribus assumption, often oversimplifies the complexity of real-world interactions. This limited approach may be suitable for short-term static analysis, but it falls short in comprehending the intricate dynamics of socio-economic systems and their long-term development (North, 1994, p. 549). As Nobel-laureate Douglass North points out, a lack of understanding of how economies develop makes neoclassical economics an inappropriate tool to prescribe effective policies for inducing development.

By contrast, Ibn Khaldun's multidisciplinary dynamics offer valuable insights for formulating socio-economic policies that can improve overall societal performance. His approach embraces the complexity of human societies and acknowledges the ever-changing nature of interactions between various factors, making it more suitable for understanding and influencing real-world development processes (Ibn Khaldun, n.d., p. 141).

Indeed, Islamic economics has made significant contributions to economic theory through the works of numerous Muslim scholars. These scholars, including Abu Yusuf (d. 798), al-Mawardi (d. 1058), Ibn Hazm (d. 1064), al-Sarakhsi (d. 1090), al-Tusi (d. 1093), al-Ghazali (d. 1111), al-Dimashqi (d. after 1175), Ibn Rushd (d. 1187), Ibn Taymiyyah (d. 1328), Ibn al-Ukhuwwah (d. 1329), Ibn al-Qayyim (d. 1350), al-Shatibi (d. 1388), Ibn Khaldun (d. 1406), al-Maqrizi (d. 1442), al-Dawwani (d. 1501), and Shah Waliyullah (d. 1762), have offered valuable insights into various economic concepts.

Their understanding and analysis of economic principles were so profound that some of their theories can be considered as forerunners to more sophisticated modern formulations of these theories. These contributions span a wide range of economic ideas, encompassing subjects such as taxation, property rights, division of labour, labour supply, the role of money and exchange, principles of taxation, and the importance of saving and investment for development (Ghazanfar, 2003). Their intellectual endeavours have left a lasting impact on the development of economic thought, and their works have played a crucial role in shaping the foundations of Islamic economics as a distinct field of study.

## 11.4 Division of Labour and Specialisation for Economic Development

Muslim scholars have emphasised the importance of division of labour and specialisation for economic development long before these concepts were fully developed in conventional economics. They recognised that self-sufficiency is neither feasible nor desirable and that individuals need to cooperate and specialise to meet their diverse economic needs.

For example, al-Sarakhsi (d. 1090) highlighted the interdependence of different economic activities, stating that farmers rely on weavers for clothing, while weavers rely on farmers for food and raw materials like cotton for their cloth (1978, Vol. 30, p. 264). Al-Dimashqi, writing about a century later, expanded on this idea, explaining that individuals cannot master all industries due to the limited span of their lives. Thus, they are necessitated to live in cities and collaborate with others to fulfil their mutual needs (1977, pp. 20–21).

Ibn Khaldun further developed this concept and emphasised the advantages of cooperation and specialisation. He observed that through mutual cooperation, individuals can satisfy their economic needs far more effectively than trying to do everything themselves (p. 360). This idea is reminiscent of the theory of comparative advantage, which is commonly attributed to David Ricardo in conventional economics, formulated in 1817.

These early insights from Muslim scholars illustrate their understanding of the benefits of division of labour, specialisation, and cooperation in promoting economic development. Their contributions to economic thought were well ahead of their time and have significantly shaped the foundations of economic theory.

The discussion on division of labour and specialisation in Islamic economics naturally led to an emphasis on trade and exchange, as well as the importance of well-regulated and properly functioning markets. A stable and reliable monetary system was also recognised as essential, with money serving as a measure, medium of exchange, and store of value. However, the prevalent bimetallism during that time, with both gold and silver coins circulating together, and varying supply and demand conditions for these metals, led to fluctuations in the exchange rate between the two types of coins.

Another complication arose from the debasement of currencies by governments, particularly in later centuries, as a means to address fiscal challenges. This practice was condemned by Islamic scholars like Ibn Taymiyyah (d. 1328), al-Maqrizi (d. 1442), and al-Asadi (d. 1450), as it violated the principles of honesty and integrity in measures of value. This phenomenon of bad coins driving good coins out of circulation was later recognised in the West in the sixteenth century and became known as Gresham's Law.

The need to finance expanding domestic and international trade in the Muslim world led to the development of a sophisticated financial system. Financiers, known as *sarrafs*, performed functions similar to modern banks. By the time of Abbasid Caliph al-Muqtadir (908-32), they were already fulfilling the basic functions of modern banks and had their own markets, similar to Wall Street in New York and Lombard Street in London, to cater to the banking needs of commerce, agriculture, and industry. This financial system facilitated the use of checks (*sakk*) and letters of credit (hawala), with the English word "check" derived from the Arabic term "*sakk*." The Muslim world's financial institutions were able to mobilise significant monetary resources to finance various economic activities, such as agriculture, crafts, manufacturing, and long-distance trade (Ghazanfar, 2003).

Overall, the contributions of Islamic economics to the understanding of trade, exchange, money, and banking were remarkable, and they played a crucial role in shaping the economic practices of the time. The knowledge and advancements made by Muslim scholars in these areas were well ahead of their time and have left a lasting impact on the development of economic thought and financial systems worldwide.

## 11.5 The Concept of Demand and Supply

Muslim scholars in the past demonstrated a clear understanding of the role of both demand and supply in determining prices. For instance, Ibn Taymiyyah (d. 1328) recognised that price fluctuations might result not only from unfair practices but also from changes in output or the import of goods that are in demand. If demand for a commodity increases while its supply declines, the price rises (Ibn Taymiyyah, 1961-3, Vol. 8, p. 523).

Even earlier, al-Jahiz (d. 869) made similar observations, stating that the availability or scarcity of a commodity in the market affects its price. Anything readily available is considered cheap due to its abundance (supply), while its scarcity (demand) leads to higher prices (al-Jahiz, 1983, p. 13).

Ibn Khaldun expanded on this understanding by noting that both an increase in demand or a decrease in supply would cause prices to rise, while a decline in demand or an increase in supply would result in lower prices. He advocated for moderate prices between excessively low and excessively high levels, as this would benefit both traders and consumers. Stable prices with a relatively low cost of living were preferred for both economic growth and equity, as bouts of inflation or deflation could harm equity and reduce efficiency and incentives. However, he also emphasised that low prices for necessities should not be achieved through state price fixing, as it would undermine production incentives (Ibn Khaldun: 398).

Thus, Muslim scholars of the past recognised the dynamic interplay between demand and supply in determining prices and sought a balance that would promote prosperity, equity, and overall economic well-being (Ibn Taymiyyah, 1961-3, Vol. 8, p. 523; al-Jahiz, 1983, p. 13; Ibn Khaldun: 398). Their insights remain relevant and contribute to the understanding of demand and supply dynamics in modern economics.

Ibn Khaldun's insights into the determinants of demand and supply were remarkably comprehensive. He identified several factors that influenced demand, including income, price levels, population size, government spending, societal habits, customs, and overall development and prosperity (Ibn Khaldun, 1967, pp. 398–404). On the other hand, he recognised that supply was determined by demand itself, order, stability, the relative rate of profit, human effort, the size and skill of the labour force, peace and security, and the technical development of society (pp. 306–308, 395–396, 363, 399–403).

It is noteworthy that Ibn Khaldun's understanding of the role of both demand and supply in determining value was ahead of his time, particularly when compared to early Western economists. Pre-classical English economists mainly emphasised the role of labour and cost of production in value determination. The notions of both demand and supply did not fully appear in English writings until the late eighteenth and early nineteenth centuries (Thweatt, 1983). Even then, it took until the early nineteenth century for the appreciation of both demand and supply in determining market prices to become more widespread (Groenewegen, 1973).

While Ibn Khaldun (1967) was ahead of conventional economists in recognising the significance of demand and supply, it is essential to acknowledge that he did not have access to some modern economic concepts like demand and supply schedules, elasticities of demand and supply, and equilibrium prices, which are central to contemporary economic discussions. Nonetheless, his pioneering work laid the foundation for later developments in economic thought regarding the determinants of value.

## 11.6 Public Finances

### (a) **Taxation**

The principles of taxation and public finance were well understood and emphasised by both pre-Islamic and Muslim scholars long before the ideas were articulated by Adam Smith. Caliphs Umar, Ali, and Umar ibn Abd al-Aziz emphasised the importance of collecting taxes with justice and leniency, ensuring that taxes were not oppressive and did not burden the people beyond their ability to pay. Tax collectors were also instructed not to deprive the people of their basic necessities of life (Abu Yusuf, 1933/34, pp. 14, 16, and 86).

Abu Yusuf, who served as an advisor to Caliph Harun al-Rashid, argued for a just tax system that not only increased revenues but also contributed to the overall development of the country (Abu Yusuf, 1933/34, p. 111). Similarly, al-Mawardi emphasised that the tax system should be fair to both the taxpayer and the treasury, striking a balance that did not burden the people excessively while ensuring adequate funding for public expenses (al-Mawardi, 1960, p. 209).

In the Muqaddimah, Ibn Khaldun forcefully stressed the principles of taxation. He quoted a letter from Tahir ibn al-Husayn, advising his son Abdullah ibn Tahir, Governor of al-Raqqah, to distribute taxes among all people fairly and without exemption based on nobility, wealth, or official positions. The emphasis was on equity and neutrality in taxation, ensuring that taxes were distributed based on capacity to pay (Ibn Khaldun, p. 308). Elsewhere, Ibn Khaldun also emphasised the principles of convenience and productivity in taxation.

These principles, laid down by early Islamic scholars, reveal their advanced understanding of public finance and the importance of a just and effective tax system. Their ideas on taxation and public finance predate Adam Smith's canons and provide valuable insights into economic governance and development.

Ibn Khaldun's (1967) understanding of the effect of taxation on incentives and productivity was remarkably advanced, and he seems to have anticipated the concept of optimum taxation, which was later formalised by Arthur Laffer. In the Muqaddimah, Ibn Khaldun dedicated two full chapters to this subject, emphasising the importance of reducing the burden of taxation on businessmen to encourage enterprise and stimulate economic activity (p. 280).

He argued that when taxes are light, people are incentivised to be more active, and business expands, leading to greater satisfaction and increased tax revenues overall (p. 279). However, he cautioned that as the needs of the state increase over time, tax rates may rise gradually, which can have an adverse impact on incentives. Higher tax rates can discourage business activity, leading to a decline in both economic productivity and tax revenues (pp. 280–281). In other words, he observed that there is an optimal point where lower tax rates can generate higher tax revenues due to increased economic activity, but beyond that point, higher tax rates can lead to decreased economic activity and lower tax revenues (p. 279).

Ibn Khaldun (1967) attributed this relationship between taxation, incentives, and economic activity to the psychological effect of unjust treatment on people's willingness to work and acquire wealth. He emphasised that unjust taxation can reduce the will of individuals to earn and acquire wealth, leading to decreased economic activity and stagnation in the markets (pp. 286–287). Consequently, tax revenues would also decline (p. 362).

Therefore, Ibn Khaldun advocated for justice in taxation, emphasising that fair and moderate tax policies would be more beneficial in generating economic prosperity and higher tax revenues than oppressive and excessive taxation (p. 308). His insights into the relationship between taxation, incentives, and economic activity demonstrate his deep understanding of economic principles, which were well ahead of his time.

(b) **Public Spending**

Ibn Khaldun recognised the significant role of the state as a factor of production and its impact on the economy through public expenditure and taxation. He believed that government spending plays a crucial role in promoting production and economic activity. The state, being the largest market for goods and services, contributes to the overall development of the economy (pp. 286 and 403). When the government decreases its spending, it not only leads to a decline in business activity and profits but also results in reduced tax revenue (p. 286).

According to Ibn Khaldun (1967), higher government spending is beneficial for the economy as it allows the state to support the population, maintain law and order, and ensure political stability (pp. 306 and 308). He drew an analogy of government spending being like water that makes the surroundings green and fertile, while a lack of government spending leaves everything dry and barren (p. 369).

Interestingly, Ibn Khaldun also analysed the multiplier effect of government spending on the economy, anticipating some aspects of Keynesian economics. He argued that when the ruler spends tax revenues, it circulates among the population, benefiting various segments of society. This circulation of wealth among the people, as well as their spending, contributes to economic activity and prosperity. However, if the ruler withholds tax revenues from spending, it deprives the population of the benefits, leading to a decline in business activity, profits, and tax revenues (p. 286).

Overall, Ibn Khaldun recognised the importance of government spending in supporting economic development, fostering business activity, and ensuring prosperity for the society. His insights on the role of the state in the economy demonstrate his far-sighted understanding of economic dynamics, making him a notable forerunner to modern economic theories on public expenditure and its impact on economic growth.

## 11.7 Economic Mismanagement

Ibn Khaldun's analysis on the causal link between bad government and high grain prices sheds light on the impact of economic mismanagement during his time. He pointed out that when a dynasty's public administration becomes corrupt, inefficient, and oppressive in its taxation practices, it negatively affects the incentive for farmers to cultivate the land. As a result, grain production and reserves fail to keep up with the rising population, leading to supply shortages during times of famine, which in turn causes prices to escalate (pp. 301–302).

Al-Maqrizi (1956), who had first-hand knowledge of economic conditions during his time as a market supervisor, applied Ibn Khaldun's analysis to understand the economic crisis in Egypt during the 1403–06 period. He identified that weak and corrupt political administration, along with bribery-based appointments of public officials, led to oppressive taxation to recover bribes. This situation dampened the incentive to work and produce, resulting in a decline in output. The crisis was further aggravated by the excessive issuance of copper *fulus* (coins), or fiat money, to cover state budget deficits, leading to currency debasement and inflation. All these factors, combined with the famine, exacerbated the economic situation, causing hardship for the poor and impoverishment of the country.

Al-Maqrizi's (1956) analysis demonstrates his understanding of the socio-political determinants of the prevailing 'system crisis,' taking into account corruption, bad government policies, and weak administration. He recognised that these factors played a role in exacerbating the impact of the famine, which otherwise could have been better managed without significant adverse consequences for the population. This notion of socio-political factors exacerbating the impact of natural disasters is reminiscent of Amartya Sen's entitlement theory, which also attributes the misery of the poor during famines and natural disasters to economic mismanagement by illegitimate governments (Sen, 1981).

In this regard, al-Maqrizi's writings (1956) about the Circassian Mamluks and the later Ottoman period show that his insights into economic mismanagement and its consequences were well ahead of his time, making him a forerunner of later economic and political theories on the effects of government policies on socio-economic outcomes.

## 11.8 Development Stages

Ibn Khaldun's analysis of the stages of development in society, as outlined in his work Muqaddimah, illustrates the progression from a primitive Bedouin stage to the emergence of villages, towns, and urban centres with an effective government. Throughout this development, agriculture, industry, and sciences also evolve, and the influence of values and the environment on this progression is recognised (Muqaddimah by Ibn Khaldun, 1967, pp. 35, 41–44, 87–95, 120–148, 172–176).

Waliyullah (1992), who lived later in the eighteenth century, further expanded on the concept of stages of development. He identified four distinct stages that societies go through, starting from a primitive existence and culminating in a well-developed community with a *khilafah*, which he envisioned as a morally-based welfare state. Walliyullah, like Ibn Khaldun, emphasised the importance of political authority for the well-being of society. For this authority to serve the people's well-being, it must possess the characteristics of a *khilafah*. In various writings, Walliyullah applied this analysis to the conditions of his time.

In his analysis, Walliyullah observed that the luxurious lifestyle of rulers, along with their costly military campaigns and increasing corruption in the civil service, led to oppressive taxation on productive sections of society such as farmers, traders, and craftsmen. Consequently, these productive segments lost interest in their occupations, and output declined. This, in turn, led to a decline in state financial resources and an overall impoverishment of the country (Waliyullah, 1992, Vol. I, pp. 119–152).

Both Ibn Khaldun and Walliyullah adopted a multidimensional approach, considering moral, political, social, and economic factors to explain the economic phenomena and the rise and fall of their respective societies. This comprehensive perspective on development and societal progression made them notable forerunners in understanding the complex interactions that shape the course of civilisations over time.

## 11.9 Intellectual Decline

The lack of further development in Islamic economics after Ibn Khaldun's time can be attributed to several factors. One crucial reason is that Ibn Khaldun lived during a period of political and socio-economic decline in the Muslim world. He was a shining intellectual figure in a time when the overall progress of the Muslim society was waning. As Ibn Khaldun himself emphasised, sciences and intellectual pursuits tend to flourish when a society is advancing and progressing (Ibn Khaldun, 1967, p. 434). This principle is evident in the history of the Muslim world, where sciences experienced rapid advancement during the "Golden Age" from the eighth to the twelfth century, followed by a gradual deceleration of progress over the centuries that followed (Sarton, 1927).

During this period of decline, the focus shifted away from scientific and intellectual endeavours, including economics. Political illegitimacy and corruption crept into governance, leading to the misallocation of state resources for personal gain rather than investing in education and nation-building functions. As a result, the decline in political authority triggered a chain reaction, affecting all other sectors of society and the economy.

Furthermore, the intellectual tradition in the Muslim world faced challenges from external forces, including invasions, colonisation, and political disruptions. These factors, along with internal struggles and conflicts, contributed to a decline in the flourishing intellectual climate that was once prevalent.

Despite a few isolated scholars making valuable contributions in specific areas, such as al-Maqrizi (1956), al-Dawwani, and Waliyullah (1992), the sustained intellectual momentum needed for the further development of Islamic economics did not materialise. Consequently, Islamic economics remained integrated within the broader framework of social and moral philosophy within Islam, rather than evolving as a distinct and separate intellectual discipline in line with the theoretical foundations laid down by Ibn Khaldun and his predecessors.

The rapidly rising Western civilisation took over the torch of knowledge from the declining Muslim world and has kept it burning with even greater brightness. All sciences, including the social sciences, have made phenomenal progress. Conventional economics became a separate academic discipline after the publication of Alfred Marshall's great treatise, Principles of Economics, in 1890 (Schumpeter, 1954, p. 21). With such a great achievement to its credit, there is no psychological need to allow the 'Great Gap' thesis to persist.

It would help promote better understanding of Islamic civilisation in the West if textbooks started giving credit to Muslim scholars. They were "the torchbearers of ancient learning during the medieval period" and "it was from them that the Renaissance was sparked and the Enlightenment kindled" (Todd Lowry in his 'Foreword' in Ghazanfar, 2003). Watt (1972) has been frank enough to admit that, "the influence of Islam on Western Christendom is greater than is usually realised" and that, "an important task for Western Europeans, as we move into the era of the one world, is … to acknowledge fully our debt to the Arab and Islamic world" (Watt, 1972, p. 84).

Conventional economics, however, took a wrong turn after the Enlightenment Movement by stripping itself of the moral basis of society emphasised by Aristotelian and Judeo-Christian philosophies. This deprived it of the role that moral values and good governance can play in helping society raise both efficiency and equity in the allocation and distribution of scarce resources needed for promoting the well-being of all. However, this has been changing.

The role of good governance has already been recognised and that of moral values is gradually penetrating the economics orthodoxy. Islamic economics is also reviving now after the independence of Muslim countries from foreign domination. It is likely that the two disciplines will converge and become one after a period of time. This will be in keeping with the teachings of the Qur'an, which clearly states that mankind was created as one but became divided as a result of their differences and transgression against each other (10:19, 2:213 and 3: 19). This reunification [globalisation, as it is new called], if reinforced by justice and mutual care, should help promote peaceful coexistence and enable mankind to realise the well-being of all, a goal the realisation of which we are all anxiously looking forward to.

## 11.10 Gaps in Economics Research

Currently there are several research gaps in the field of Islamic economics:

a) Lack of Empirical Studies: There is a scarcity of empirical research in Islamic economics. While the first generation of scholars focused on theoretical work and the establishment of Islamic banks and financial institutions, the second generation has not significantly shifted towards empirical studies (Siddiqi, 2008). The absence of empirical research limits our ability to assess the effectiveness of Islamic economic institutions, evaluate achievements, and plan for the future.
b) Discrepancy between Muslim Ideals and Conduct: There is a dearth of research on the gap between the ideals prescribed by Islamic economics and the actual economic behaviour of Muslims. Understanding contemporary Muslim economic behaviour is crucial for improving the alignment of economic practices with Islamic principles (Siddiqi, 2008).
c) Poverty Removal, Inequality, and Development: Islamic economic literature lacks sufficient coverage on poverty removal, inequality reduction, and economic development. These crucial areas have not received enough attention, despite the emphasis on poverty elimination and inequality reduction in early Islamic economic literature (Kahf, 2004; Siddiqi, 2004).
d) Inadequate Focus on Poor-Friendly Institutions: While Islam advocates for propoor institutions such as zakat (obligatory almsgiving), *sadaqat* (voluntary charity), and *awqaf* (endowments), Islamic economics has not given enough attention to these topics. Even Islamic banking and finance, often considered the jewel of Islamic economics, have been criticised for being largely irrelevant for the poor (IERC, 2008).

Addressing these research gaps could lead to a more comprehensive and practical understanding of Islamic economics and its potential impact on poverty reduction, inequality, and sustainable economic development in Muslim societies. Conducting more empirical studies and incorporating a focus on the poor-friendly institutions advocated by Islam would be essential steps towards achieving this goal.

Zaman (2008, p. 17) proposes that effective *da'wah* (preaching and invitation) to Muslims to pay *zakah* (obligatory almsgiving) and adopt the simple lifestyles recommended by Islam could potentially eliminate poverty in Islamic societies. However, he rightly emphasises that this claim needs to be supported and validated through empirical studies. Throughout history, there have been instances of denial or evasion of *zakah*, indicating that relying solely on *da'wah* might not be sufficient to address poverty. Enforcing authority and efficient management are also essential in ensuring that *zakah* is collected and distributed effectively to those in need.

Moreover, while *zakah* and equitable distribution are crucial for poverty alleviation, they alone may not be enough to completely eliminate poverty. Economic growth and development are equally important factors in addressing poverty in Muslim countries. Many Muslim nations possess abundant natural resources and fertile lands, making sustainable development a vital challenge for the international community. Achieving growth with sustainability should be a key focus, but unfortunately, little attention has been given to this topic.

Khurshid Ahmad (1980) and Chapra (1994) have explored the concept of "*tanmiyah* with *tazkiyah*," which entails material growth alongside human development and improvement. Despite their contributions, progress in this direction has been limited in subsequent years. Additionally, works on the environment and sustainable development within an Islamic economic framework are not yet substantial.

To address poverty comprehensively, there is a need for a holistic approach that combines effective *da'wah*, fair distribution of wealth through *zakah*, and sustainable economic development. Empirical studies and further research in these areas would be instrumental in formulating practical and effective strategies to combat poverty in Islamic societies.

In the field of economics, public finance was one of the earliest areas to attract the attention of Muslim scholars, with exclusive writings dating back to the second century Hijrah (eighth century CE). This development was natural, considering the expanding territory of the Islamic state, new sources of income, emerging heads of expenditure, and other socio-economic challenges. However, at present, there are very few works on taxation, fiscal policy, social welfare, and development financing in Islamic economics. These works tend to follow the same pattern as their predecessors, often lacking in-depth analysis of the current reality faced in modern living (Siddiqi, 2008, p. 10).

While the first generation of scholars may have had an excuse, as they needed to explore and understand their heritage in these areas, it was expected that the second generation would advance the study by incorporating the current situation and reality into their research.

Despite the commitment of many Muslim states to Islamise their economies, public finance and fiscal policy have not received much attention from writers and researchers. There is a need for fresh thinking in this aspect of Islamic economics, especially since some traditional sources of government revenue, such as fay', *ghanimah, jizyah*, and tributes, are no longer relevant in the modern context. *Kharaj*, which was a significant source of government financing in earlier centuries, has also lost its importance in the modern period (Zarka, 2008, p. 27).

As a result, there is a pressing need to thoroughly discuss and analyse what the sources of public revenue would be for a modern Islamic state and what its expenditure policy should be. With the changing economic landscape and new challenges, the exploration of contemporary solutions and approaches is essential for effective public finance management within the framework of Islamic economics.

An important gap in the field of Islamic economics is the absence of a unified and well-defined Shari'ah (Islamic law) methodology. Many scholars have noted that Islamic economists have not properly discussed methodology in their works. When attempts were made to discuss methodology, it was often limited to *usul al-fiqh*, which is understood as the methodology of Islamic law or jurisprudence. This lack of a comprehensive and specific methodology has been a significant concern in the field (Haneef, 2012, p. 146). The Institute of Islamic Economics (IEI) recently addressed this issue by making it one of the main themes of discussion in a workshop.

Another area of concern is the research on the history of Islamic economic thought and the economic history of Muslim peoples. While such research started before the 1950s, it is still considered a thinly researched area (Siddiqi, 2008, p. 4). The focus on practical aspects of Islamic economics and the drive towards financialisation has left very few scholars paying attention to the study of the history of Islamic economic thought.

Research in this area has been specific to certain languages, regions, and periods, often focusing on Arabic, the Middle East, and up to the ninth/fifteenth century. Other regions and languages, such as Andalus, West Africa, Turkey, Persia, Southeast Asia, and Far East Asia, have not received sufficient attention in these studies. Moreover, the research has often been cantered on the economic thought of a few personalities, neglecting the ideas of others. To bridge this gap, there is a need for more intensive and extensive research that includes various personalities, ideas, periods, languages, and regions to create a comprehensive and systematic history of the subject (Islahi, 2008, p. 347).

Zaman (2012a) raises a valid concern that despite numerous efforts, there is still no comprehensive textbook of Islamic economics. Mannan (1970) produced one of the earliest textbooks on the subject, attempting to provide an Islamic perspective on each topic. However, as modern Islamic economics has evolved and the literature on the topic has grown exponentially, there is a need for a more systematic and up-to-date textbook on Islamic economics.

This sentiment is shared by many scholars, and there are ongoing efforts at both individual and institutional levels to produce an authentic and standard textbook on Islamic economics. The Islamic Economics Research Centre (IERC) also acknowledges various research gaps and challenges faced in the field of Islamic economics, as outlined in their document "A Proposed Strategic Vision for Future Research in Islamic Economics" (IERC, 2008, p. 40).

Some of these challenges include addressing issues related to globalisation, environmental concerns, access to basic necessities like housing, drinking water, and clean air, managing rapid technological changes, fostering flexible labour markets, dealing with the flow of hot money and foreign capital, coping with rising anxiety levels that outpace rising living standards, tackling gender relations and family problems, and addressing challenges arising from an aging population. Unfortunately, these issues have not received adequate attention in the works of the second generation of Islamic economists.

## 11.11 Diversion and Deviation of Views

The existence of diversity of opinions and differences on various issues is not uncommon among intellectuals, including those in the field of Islamic economics (Zaman, 2012a). These differences often arise due to varying interpretations and understandings of complex economic concepts and principles. Over time, some of these differences may be narrowed down, lose their significance, or even disappear altogether, as scholars gain more experience and insights.

However, there are two significant departures in the field of Islamic economics presented by eminent scholars Masudul Alam Choudhury and Asad Zaman. Both scholars have received education from prestigious Western institutions and have expertise in mathematics and econometrics, respectively. They share a common criticism of Western economics and advocate for eliminating neoclassical economics influences from Islamic economics (Choudhury, 2010; Zaman, 2012b). Nevertheless, their approaches to the subject diverge greatly.

Choudhury's writings are characterised by philosophical and mathematical jargon that may be difficult for most readers to comprehend, while Zaman presents his ideas in a more straightforward and understandable language. They criticise each other's approaches, with Choudhury referring to Zaman's thinking as "utopian," and Zaman suggesting that Choudhury's focus on mathematics overlooks the practical challenges in applying complex mathematical theories to economics (Choudhury, 2010, p. 181; Zaman, 2012b).

Choudhury emphasises "*tawhidi* economics," which incorporates Islamic principles into economic analysis, while Zaman advocates for "spiritual economics," which integrates spiritual and ethical dimensions into economic analysis (Zaman, 2012b). Their differences extend beyond methodology and theoretical approaches, leading to a critical examination of each other's ideas.

Therefore, the existence of diverse opinions and debates in the field of Islamic economics is a natural aspect of intellectual discourse (Zaman, 2012a). However, the distinct approaches and criticisms presented by scholars like Choudhury and Zaman demonstrate the complexities and challenges involved in developing a unified and well-defined methodology for Islamic economics.

Choudhury's exploration into the *Tawhidi* epistemology of the Islamic world system began in the 1990s and has continued persistently in his subsequent works (Zaman, 2012b). His ideas have been significantly influenced by Ibn Arabi's concept of "*Wahdat al-Wujud*" or the Oneness of Being, which forms the basis for his *Tawhidi* arguments as presented in his book "Science and Epistemology in the Qur'an" (Choudhury, 2006b).

Choudhury's approach goes beyond the realm of religious dissemination of thought. According to him, Tawhid, understood as the law of divine oneness expressed through the epistemic law of unity of knowledge, is a highly methodological worldview that applies uniformly to all sciences, without being confined to being labelled as "Islamic" in any specific manner (Zaman, 2012b). In this sense,

Choudhury's *Tawhidi* approach can be considered a universal and comprehensive framework for knowledge and understanding.

Choudhury asserts that the *Tawhidi* methodological worldview is derived through analytical investigation and discourse based on the Quran, the Sunnah (traditions of the Prophet Muhammad), and critical examination of historical works from comparative perspectives (Choudhury, 2006a). He believes that the current state of confusion and disarray in Islamic economics can be remedied by returning to the *Tawhidi* methodological worldview and establishing a unique and universal epistemology for the entire socio-scientific order, derived from the teachings of the Quran and the Sunnah, and through scholarly discussions and applications (Zaman, 2012b).

In Choudhury's view, much of Islamic economics has faced challenges and limitations and has not been able to fulfil its potential (Zaman, 2012b). He believes that a rejuvenation of the discipline can be achieved by embracing the *Tawhidi* approach as a foundation for knowledge and understanding, thereby establishing a solid and coherent basis for the development of Islamic economics.

The concept of "Tawhidi economics" has been viewed by some scholars as an abstract idea with limited practical relevance, similar to the concept of "general equilibrium" in economics, which is beautiful in theory but challenging to achieve in practice (Zaman, 2012a). *Tawhidi* economics, as advocated by Masudul Alam Choudhury, is based on the idea of divine oneness and unity of knowledge, but its application in real-world economic scenarios may face challenges and complexities.

On the other hand, Asad Zaman emphasises what he calls "Spiritual Economics," which centres on the strong spiritual focus of Islam and contrasts it with conventional materialistic approaches to economics (Zaman, 2012a). According to Zaman, the pursuit of knowledge and efforts to change the world in Islamic economics are driven by the sole purpose of pleasing Allah. This spiritual focus is seen as a defining characteristic of Islamic economics, differentiating it from other existing economic approaches.

Mainstream Islamic economists recognise the significance of the spiritual aspect of Islamic economics, as highlighted by Zaman. However, they contend that "Spiritual Economics" presents only a partial view of the entire system of Islamic economics (Zaman, 2012a). They argue that while the spiritual focus is essential, it should be complemented by an understanding of the other economic principles and concepts that form the complete framework of Islamic economics.

Thus, the debates between scholars on the concepts of "Tawhidi economics" and "Spiritual Economics" revolve around striking a balance between the spiritual aspect and the practical economic principles within the overall framework of Islamic economics. Both perspectives are essential, and a comprehensive understanding of Islamic economics requires integrating both the spiritual and material dimensions to achieve a holistic approach.

The field of Islamic economics currently exhibits multiple streams of thinking, each advocating different approaches, and principles. These streams are still evolving, and their definitive shapes have not yet been fully established. The main streams of thought in Islamic economics include:

a) **Mainstream Islamic Economics:** This stream represents the majority of scholars in the field of Islamic economics. It is based on the application of Islamic principles, ethics, and values to economic issues. Mainstream Islamic economics aims to develop economic theories and policies that align with Islamic teachings and promote social justice, equity, and ethical conduct.
b) **Tawhidi Economics:** This stream is inspired by the concept of Tawhid, the oneness of God and unity of knowledge. Scholars in this stream advocate for a methodological worldview based on Tawhid, seeking to apply it across various sciences, including economics. The idea is to derive economic principles and policies from the Quran, the Sunnah, and critical analysis.
c) **Spiritual Economics:** This stream emphasises the strong spiritual focus of Islam in economic discourses. It centres on the notion that all economic endeavours and knowledge acquisition should be directed towards pleasing God. Scholars in this stream highlight the contrast between the spiritual focus of Islamic economics and conventional materialistic approaches.
d) **Conventional Assumptions with Modifications:** Some scholars propose adopting certain conventional economic assumptions, such as self-interest, maximisation, and rationality, but with modifications to align them with Islamic principles and values. This approach seeks to integrate elements of conventional economics into Islamic economic frameworks.
e) **Islamic Socialism (Historical):** Before the fall of communist systems, there was a stream of thought known as "Islamic socialism." This approach attempted to blend socialist economic principles with Islamic teachings to create an economic system based on social justice and equitable distribution of resources.

While these streams of thought exist in the field of Islamic economics, their prominence and influence may vary. In the future, these streams may further develop into distinct schools of thought, or the principles of survival of the fittest and academic discourse may lead to the consolidation or integration of some ideas. The ongoing evolution of Islamic economics will continue to be shaped by intellectual debates, research, and practical application of economic principles in the context of Islamic teachings and societal needs.

## 11.12 The Concern Regarding Financialisation of Islamic Economics

The issue of 'financialisation' in Islamic economics and banking has become a matter of concern for leading scholars of the first and second generations (El-Gamal, 2006). Financialisation refers to the increasing influence of financial markets, institutions, and practices on various aspects of the economy, including Islamic finance. The frustration stems from the perceived widening gap between theoretical principles and their practical implementation, especially in the area of banking and finance.

The proponents of Islamic banking and finance have emphasised the value-based nature of the industry, intending to operate under the principles of the Islamic spirit (El-Gamal, 2006). They envisioned Islamic finance as an industry that would prioritise faith and ethics, aiming to earn reasonable profits while investing in merit goods and services that are beneficial to society.

However, in practice, various providers of financial products and services in the Islamic finance sector have primarily resorted to "negative screens" (El-Gamal, 2006). Negative screens refer to the exclusion of certain sectors or industries that are considered non-compliant with Islamic principles, such as alcohol, gambling, or conventional banking. While this exclusion is important, it is seen as a narrow interpretation of Islamic finance's potential and social impact.

The dissatisfaction arises from the fact that many Islamic financial institutions and products often mimic conventional financial products with slight modifications to avoid explicit violations of Islamic principles (El-Gamal, 2006). Critics argue that the original spirit of Islamic finance, which aimed to promote economic justice, social welfare, and ethical conduct, is getting overshadowed by the focus on profit maximisation and financial innovation.

Some scholars and practitioners in the field of Islamic economics and finance are concerned that the profit motive and increasing financial complexity have taken precedence over the original goals of promoting social welfare and economic justice in Islamic finance (El-Gamal, 2006). This perceived shift towards financialisation raises questions about whether the industry is staying true to its foundational principles and whether there is a need for more ethical and socially responsible practices within Islamic finance.

The practical implementation of Islamic banking and finance has faced challenges in staying true to its theoretical foundations. While it was originally claimed that partnership and risk-sharing were at the core of Islamic banking and finance, in practice, debt-based finance has gained dominance, including sukuk based on ijarah, *salam,* and *istisna'* (Siddiqi, 2006). There was once controversy surrounding the legitimacy of *murabahah*, a cost-plus financing arrangement, but it has now become widely accepted (Siddiqi, 2006).

Additionally, new financial instruments like *tawarruq* and *'inah* have been introduced in Islamic finance as a way of obtaining cash against future payment (Siddiqi, 2006). Despite being presented as sale and purchase transactions, experts argue that these practices bear little difference from interest-based lending and borrowing (Siddiqi, 2006). From a macroeconomic perspective, Islamic banks practicing *tawarruq* face the same challenges as conventional banks providing interest-based loans to their clients (Siddiqi, 2006). This has raised concerns about the lack of integration between the real sector of goods and services and the financial sector in Islamic finance.

The prevalence of debt-based financing and the introduction of financial instruments that resemble conventional practices have sparked debates among scholars and practitioners in Islamic economics and finance (Siddiqi, 2006). Some argue that the increasing use of debt-based instruments diminishes the original spirit of Islamic finance, which was founded on principles of partnership, risk-sharing, and ethical conduct.

The disconnect between the theoretical emphasis on partnership and risk-sharing and the prevalence of debt-based financing raises questions about the direction of Islamic finance and its adherence to the ethical and social objectives of Islamic economics (Siddiqi, 2006). There is a need for continued dialogue and critical evaluation to ensure that the practical implementation aligns with the principles and values espoused in Islamic economics.

The development of financial engineering in Islamic banking and finance has sometimes deviated from the original objectives and spirit of Islamic economics and finance (Zaman, 2012a). Over time, there has been a decline in consulting and seeking guidance from original and classical Islamic sources, while the reliance on legal stratagem has increased. This has led to concerns about the role of Shariah Supervisory Boards, as some Shariah advisers may have a strong background in Islamic law (*fiqh*) but lack expertise in economics (Zaman, 2012a).

As a result, their focus might be primarily on fulfilling legal requirements rather than considering economic criteria or rationale (Zaman, 2012a). To compete with conventional financial institutions, Islamic banks and financial institutions have engaged in financial engineering to develop products that comply with Islamic legal rules (*fiqh*) but may not align with the higher objectives (*maqasid*) of Shariah (Zaman, 2012a).

Financial engineering in this context often prioritises financial goals and monetary gains over social goals (Zaman, 2012a). As a consequence, certain financial products and practices may satisfy the legal requirements but fall short in meeting the broader social objectives set by Islamic economics (Zaman, 2012a).

The tension between financialisation and the fulfilment of *maqasid* (Shariah objectives) highlights the need for a more balanced and principled approach in Islamic finance (Zaman, 2012a). While the development of financial products and services is essential for competitiveness, it should also be guided by a deeper understanding of the *maqasid* and the ethical principles of Islamic economics (Zaman, 2012a). This requires a collaborative effort from scholars, practitioners, and regulators to ensure that the financial industry adheres to both the legal requirements and the broader ethical and social objectives of Islamic economics and finance (Zaman, 2012a).

The phenomenon of 'financialisation' within Islamic economics has led to a significant focus on the banking and finance sector, making it the most rapidly growing segment. Consequently, other sectors such as *zakah* and waqf have been overshadowed, creating a perception that Islamic economics revolves around Islamic banking and finance. Initially, the proponents of Islamic banking and finance emphasised the differences between Islamic and conventional financial products. However, the current trend is geared towards developing products that closely resemble their conventional counterparts, reducing the gap between Islamic and conventional financial practices.

This shift in approach has made it easier for multinational Western banks to enter the Islamic finance market, posing growing competition to indigenous financial institutions in the Islamic world. As a result, there is a risk of Islamic institutions losing their distinct identity if they do not reform and adhere to genuine Islamic principles and practices. This concern is shared by a majority of scholars, and efforts are being made at various levels to address this issue and ensure a return to authentic Islamic conduct in the field of Islamic banking and finance (Zaman, 2012a).

## 11.13 It Is Not All Doom and Gloom

Islahi (2015) holds a more positive view regarding the performance of the second generation of Islamic economists. While there may be some dissatisfaction with the current state of affairs, it is believed that the discipline of Islamic economics is still progressing despite its ups and downs. It is acknowledged that there has been an excessive focus on Islamic banking and finance, with form sometimes taking precedence over substance, and the discipline being termed as "Islamic Economics Light" in some cases (Nienhaus, 2012).

However, it is important to recognise that not all scholars from the second generation have accepted the current situation, and there are many who are actively working to correct the course and establish future directions for the field. Furthermore, the second generation has made significant contributions in various areas, such as risk analysis, hedging, risk sharing, and microfinance.

New scholarly work by economists and scholars like Alamad (2017a, b, 2019a, b, 2023; Alamad et al 2021), Van Greuning and Iqbal (2008), al-Suwailem (2006), Askari et al. (2012), Obaidullah (2008), and Obaidullah and Abdul-Latif (2011) have addressed topics that were previously lacking in research (Zaman, 2012a). Therefore, the writer believes that there is hope for improvement and a positive trajectory for Islamic economics, despite some shortcomings and challenges faced by the second generation of Islamic economists.

The research on the history of Islamic economic thought has made significant progress, despite certain limitations. Works by scholars like Siddiqi (1964, 1982), Mirakhor (1987), Hosseini (2003), Ghazanfar (2003), and Islahi (2015) have challenged the Schumpeterian great gap thesis (1954) and highlighted the profound contributions made by Muslim scholars in the history of economics. These studies have shed light on the intellectual heritage of Islamic economic thought and have influenced some mainstream economists to reconsider and integrate it into the broader economic discourse. Additionally, research efforts have been made to explore post-Khaldunian era Muslim economic thinking and other regions and languages, providing insights into previously unexplored areas (Islahi, 2009, 2010, 2011).

The first-generation Islamic economists, who are still actively contributing, continue to enrich the discipline with their valuable works. They serve as a source of guidance and inspiration for the current and future generations of Islamic economists. Presently, there are several research institutes dedicated to Islamic economics, banking, and finance, along with specialised journals and an increasing number of courses and teaching departments on the subject. It is essential to note that not all of these endeavours are confined to the trends of banking and finance, and there are dissenting voices that offer rays of hope and innovation for the field's future. Despite a flood of literature on Islamic economics over the past 40–50 years, including some that may be transient, valuable contributions that benefit humanity remain and continue to shape the discipline (The Qur'an 13:17) (Zaman, 2012a).

## 11.14 Conclusion

This Chapter examined economic insights and contributions of scholars within the discipline of Islamic economics. The recent financial crises that have occurred in the global economy have had significant impacts on economists worldwide. These crises have compelled economists to re-examine the fundamentals of their theories and practices, leading to a reawakening of interest in the concept of "financialisation." The financial crises were, in essence, a crisis of the system itself, with excessive debt driven by interest-based and risky financial instruments being the root cause behind them. These events have reinforced the conviction and self-confidence of the first-generation Islamic economists, who have long advocated for an alternative economic system based on Islamic principles.

Moreover, the financial crises have also served as a wake-up call for many second-generation Islamic economists, who were previously attempting to emulate conventional banking and finance practices in an Islamic context. It has prompted them to reconsider their approach and return to the fundamental principles of Islamic economics. The crises have also had a profound impact on the new generation of economists, creating a strong desire among them to study and implement the core values and principles of Islamic economics.

In response to the financial crises, several seminars and symposia have been held, providing platforms for discussions on the root causes and potential remedies. Islamic economists have emphasised that excessive lending, risk-shifting, interest (*riba*), excessive risk (*gharar*), gambling (*maysir*), and speculation (*mujazafah*) were the main factors behind the financial crisis in conventional finance. They have also highlighted the inherent tendency of the capitalist system to experience frequent crises.

In contrast, the Islamic economic system, based on ethical values and principles, such as risk-sharing and equitable distribution of wealth, has been presented as an alternative that can help avoid similar financial crises. By adhering to the principles of Islamic economics and incorporating risk-sharing mechanisms, the Islamic economic system offers a different approach to financial stability and sustainability (Oran, 2012). The financial crises have thus spurred a critical evaluation of the present state of Islamic economics and have motivated economists to develop robust solutions to prevent similar occurrences in the future.

Islamic economics, since its revival in the modern era, has sought to present a balanced economic system that offers an alternative to the extremes of socialism and capitalism. During the early days of its resurgence, the first-generation Islamic economists focused on establishing the supremacy of Islamic economics over the dominant economic systems of capitalism and communism. They presented a convincing case for the viability of an Islamic economic system, which was based on the principles of social justice, equity, and ethical conduct (Mawdudi, Siddiqi, Rai'uddin, Hamidullah, Ahmad, Abdul-Hakim, Alamad, and al-Sibai).

As time progressed, the second-generation Islamic economists faced the challenges posed by the widespread prevalence of interest-based banking and finance. They responded by advocating for interest-free and participatory financial institutions as an alternative to the conventional banking system. This led to the establishment of Islamic banks and financial institutions that adhered to Islamic principles and avoided interest-based transactions.

Now, the current generation of Islamic economists faces the new challenges brought about by globalisation. The world has become a global village, and the problems and concerns of humanity are interconnected. In this context, Islamic economics needs to address issues such as environmental sustainability, equitable development, poverty eradication, and shared prosperity. These challenges are not specific to a particular region or community but are shared concerns of all humanity.

The next generation of Islamic economists must adopt a global approach and spread the message of Islamic economics to all corners of the world. They need to demonstrate how Islamic economics can offer practical solutions to the problems faced by humanity at large. The Islamic Economics Research Centre (IERC) emphasises the need for Islamic economics to embrace the causes of humanity and address their problems as its own (IERC, p. 41).

By doing so, Islamic economics can play a vital role in contributing to the well-being of humanity and promoting a more just and equitable global economic system. It can provide a holistic and ethical approach to economic issues, balancing economic growth with social welfare and environmental sustainability. Embracing this approach and addressing the challenges of globalisation can pave the way for the continued relevance and impact of Islamic economics in the modern world.

# Chapter 12
# Rethinking Economics, Constructing the Equitable Optimality Theory Part One: Philosophical Underpinning

## 12.1 Introduction

The current crisis in the discipline of economics, as was discussed in the previous Chapter, whether conventional or faith-based can be attributed to the uncritical acceptance of modern capitalist economic ideas. This has led to a methodological framework and underlying assumptions that conflict with the faith-based views and principles. The attempt to merge these contradictory bodies of knowledge has proven unsuccessful, resulting in a lack of coherence and clarity in such attempts.

We also explored insights and contributions provided to us by the knowledge structure of Islamic economics. Which has drawn insights from various schools of economic thought and other social sciences, including neoclassical, Keynesian, social, humanistic, and institutional economics.

To address this crisis and build a genuine economic theory, alternative foundations need to be established. These foundations should be rooted in socio-economic principles, values, justice, and beliefs. The following steps can help in constructing a more authentic economic theory, which I coin as the Equitable Optimality economic theory, drawing on lessons learned from existing capitalist theories and value-based approaches from faith-based economic thought and other theories. We achieve this objective by:

a) Revisiting Methodological Framework: We re-evaluate the current methodological approaches and ensure they are aligned with the Equitable Optimality economic theory. This economic theory should not be viewed as a mere extension of mainstream economics, but it has its own distinct approach.
b) Re-examining Assumptions: Questioning the underlying assumptions made in economic models and theories that were formulated decades ago to assess its relevance today, and to ensure they are consistent with the Equitable Optimality economic principles. For example, assumptions related to human behaviour,



S. Alamad, *Beyond Profit*, Contributions to Economics,
https://doi.org/10.1007/978-3-031-49748-3_12

utility maximisation, and profit-seeking may need to be re-evaluated in light of the Equitable Optimality economic theory ethics.

c) Embracing Ethical Foundations: Integrating the Equitable Optimality economic theory ethical values, such as justice, compassion, and fairness, into economic policymaking and analyses. These values should guide decision-making and resource allocation to foster social welfare and equitable distribution of economic resources.
d) Incorporating Third-Sector Institutions: Recognising and incorporating third-sector institutions, such as endowments, charities, *zakah*, into economic models. These institutions play a crucial role in promoting social justice and poverty alleviation.
e) Emphasising Human Development: Shifting the focus from mere economic growth to holistic human development. Economics should prioritise the well-being of individuals and communities, aiming to enhance their spiritual, social, and economic welfare.
f) Engaging with Scholars: Encouraging collaboration between economists and scholars from other disciplines to ensure that economic theories are in line with the Equitable Optimality economic theory and its philosophy.
g) Promoting Interdisciplinary Research: Fostering interdisciplinary research that bridges social studies, ethics, and economics. This approach will enrich the understanding of Equitable Optimality economics as we formulate it herein and its implications for society.

By adopting these alternative foundations, we can pave the way for a genuine and robust economic theory. It would not only provide a coherent framework for economic analysis but also align with the principles and values of the Equitable Optimality economic theory, leading to a more meaningful and effective approach to economic development and social welfare in global societies.

## 12.2 Interest-Bearing Money

The issuance of interest-bearing money by governments is a rare occurrence in monetary history. Typically, such actions are taken during times of crises to stimulate demand for money, as interest-paying currency becomes more appealing to hold. For example, during the Civil War era in the USA, around 20% of the money supply in the Southern Confederacy paid interest, allowing for an opportunity to study the implications of interest and non-interest-bearing money (Burdekin & Weidenmier, 2002).

According to the legal restrictions theory, interest-bearing money should drive out non-interest bearing money from circulation, unless there are laws or legal restrictions preventing this outcome. In the case of the Southern Confederacy, Burdekin and Weidenmier (2002) explore why non-interest-bearing money remained the predominant medium of exchange despite the presence of a considerable amount of interest-bearing money. They find that the state and Confederate governments enforced de facto legal restrictions, compelling banks to accept both types of money. To ensure compliance, these governments threatened to resume specie convertibility if banks did not accept both Gray-back interest and non-interest-bearing liabilities at par. Fearing a loss of their gold stocks with specie resumption, banks complied with this policy, leading them to hold a significant proportion of their reserves in interest-bearing money.

Interestingly, non-interest-bearing money continued to circulate more widely in the Confederate economy. This can be attributed to banks' rational choice to hold money that paid interest (Makinen & Woodward, 1999). The practical considerations of preserving gold reserves and avoiding the consequences of specie resumption motivated banks to maintain both types of money in circulation.

Legal restrictions played a crucial role in maintaining the coexistence of interest and non-interest-bearing money during the Civil War era in the Southern Confederacy. The threat of specie resumption compelled banks to accept both types of money, ensuring the continued circulation of non-interest-bearing money alongside its interest-bearing counterpart.

You may be wondering at this point, what is the relation between this and the new economic theory I am outlining here? This is a sensible question, which I will explain further as we progress in constructing this economic theory in this Chapter and the also in Chaps. 13 and 14. For now, it is important to bear in mind the crucial negative role that interest-based money plays in the economy, and how restrictions existed in the past around it have been completed abolished in current economic theories and policies.

## 12.3 The Meaning of Equitable Optimality as a Theory

I start this Chapter by clearly articulating the foundations and framework of the Equitable Optimality economic theory, and what I mean by this coined name for this economic theory. This Chapter is the first building block in constructing this economic theory and will be followed by further two chapters to complete the construction of this theory. This theory refutes the economic concept of 'Pareto Optimum', by providing a new perspective.

The concept of pareto optimality does not align with the principles I outline here for the Equitable Optimality economic theory. Pareto optimality asserts that a situation is optimal if no individual can be made better off without making someone else worse off. This view conflicts with moral values that prioritise the well-being of all over absolute efficiency. Our economic theory recognises the importance of sacrifice by the well-to-do to uplift the well-being of the less fortunate.

Vilfredo Pareto, an Italian economist and sociologist, made the observation that approximately 80 percent of the wealth was concentrated in about 20 percent of the population. He first noticed this distribution while studying income and wealth patterns in his native Italy in the late nineteenth century. This observation later became known as the Pareto Principle, the 80/20 Principle, or the Law of the Vital Few (Sanders, 1987).

The Pareto Principle has since been applied to various fields beyond economics, including business, management, and productivity. It suggests that in many situations, a small percentage of inputs or efforts (the 20 percent) yield a disproportionately large percentage of outputs or results (the 80 percent). This principle is widely recognised and has practical applications in optimising resource allocation, identifying key contributors, and improving overall efficiency in various contexts (Sanders, 1987).

In economics, the Pareto Principle underscores the concentration of wealth, where a minority of individuals or entities possess the majority of resources. This distribution can have significant implications for economic policies and societal well-being, as it can lead to income inequality and social disparities. Business leaders like Jack Welch recognised the value of the 80/20 Principle in streamlining their organisations and identifying the most impactful contributors. By focusing on the "vital few" who have a substantial impact on performance, businesses can increase efficiency and productivity. Welch's approach of categorising employees into the top-performing, potential-rising, and underperforming groups enabled him to create a high-performing team (Sanders, 1987).

Applying the 80/20 Principle in business involves identifying the most critical points that drive success and focusing on those aspects. By prioritising the vital few actions that have the most significant impact, businesses can streamline their operations and improve overall performance.

While the Pareto Principle is a valuable tool that offers insights into the distribution of outcomes and the identification of key contributors in various fields, it is not a suitable principle for just allocation of economic resources. By understanding and applying this principle, I make the case for the alternative concept I am suggesting here. This new proposed concept can help policymakers make strategic decisions that lead to greater economic efficiency, fairness, productivity, and success.

In that context, the opposite concept to Pareto optimality in economics is known as "Pareto suboptimality/inefficiency" or simply "inefficiency". While Pareto optimality refers to a state where no one can be made better off without making someone else worse off, Pareto inefficiency implies that it is possible to make at least one individual better off without making anyone else worse off.

In other words, a situation is considered Pareto inefficient if there are potential changes or reallocations of resources that could improve the well-being of at least one person in society without reducing the well-being of anyone else. Pareto inefficiency suggests that resources are not allocated optimally, and there is room for improving overall societal welfare without harming anyone. Pareto efficiency and Pareto inefficiency are fundamental concepts in welfare economics and the analysis of economic efficiency and equity. They are often used to evaluate the desirability of economic policies and allocations of resources.

On the other hand, in economics, "equitability" typically relates to concepts of fairness and justice in the distribution of resources or benefits. "Suboptimality" generally means that a situation is not at its most efficient or optimal state. Therefore, after an extensive research and analysis, I settled on "Equitable Optimality" as a name for this economic theory because "Equitable Optimality" suggests a theory that focuses on situations where fairness, justice or equity considerations result in outcomes that are not ONLY economically efficient or optimal, but also equitable. 'Equitable' is an adjective that describes the type of optimality being referred to, emphasising fairness and equity. In this context, "optimality" refers to the state of being optimal or the best possible outcome. Thus, "Equitable Optimality" conveys the idea of striving for the best possible outcome with a focus on fairness and equity. It's a compound term that combines these concepts effectively.

As a result, the concept of Pareto optimality is, therefore, not relevant in the paradigm of this proposed economic theory, which places a strong emphasis on social justice and equitable distribution of resources. In this economics system of exchange, the pursuit of Equitable Optimality, which is a first-order condition of efficiency in a perfectly competitive market, takes a different approach compared to conventional economic exchange systems. In a pure exchange economy, optimality is typically based on the ratio of marginal utilities of products and wages.

However, in this proposed economic exchange system, the focus is on the principle of equity and cooperation between individuals. This means that the marginal utility of an owner is not solely determined by the returns from rents, but also by the equitable wages given to the labourer. Similarly, the marginal utility of the labourer depends not only on the amount of wages received, but also on the just amount of rents given to the employer.

This incorporation of additional variables, such as product and wage variables in the utility functions of individuals introduces a deviation from the conventional framework, resulting in what is known as a Second-Best Solution. This means that the solution, I am proposing here for constructing this economic theory, to the exchange problem does not strictly adhere to the traditional concept of pareto optimality.

Therefore, the focus I am placing here in this proposed theory is on cooperation and equitable relationships between labour and employers that plays a vital role in resource allocation. I also extend this focus to other economic aspects and variables in constructing this theory. It promotes a more realistic state of the market economy, aligning with the principles of equity and social justice emphasised in this economic theory. If we analyse economic downturns, economic crises and cycles we find that overall root causes are attributed to aspects contrary to the underlying principles of the Equitable Optimality economic theory that I am introducing in this book.

The emphasis on fairness, justice and cooperation in this theory aims to achieve an outcome that benefits the broader society rather than just maximising individual utility. This approach recognises the interdependence of various stakeholders in the economic system and aims to create a more inclusive and just society, which will extend and influence the global economy. To illustrate this concept further I use the following image that is widely used online in relation to achieving justice, you may consider it a cliché, however it is a good visual illustration of our economic reality and what needs to be done to remove the barrier and achieve economic and social justice for all stakeholders.

As illustrated in Fig. 12.1 above and discussed in this Chapter thus far, while equality might seem to be the right approach it would not achieve the equitable outcome. Moreover, while I seek equitable economics in this proposed theory by using various tools, which will be discussed further herein and the next chapters, to ensure equity, the desired outcome by the Equitable Optimality economic theory is to achieve justice and look beyond profit. This justice is achieved by moving from equity to economic justice by removing any barriers that hinder this objective. It is believed that all current applied economic theories and global economic policies are located in the first two boxes of the image, i.e., Reality and Equality to varying extents.

Economic policies are formulated with the objective of addressing and dealing with humans' affairs. This proposed economic policy aims to achieve highest level

**Fig. 12.1** Illustration of an equitable approach [Image credit: we were not able to identify the original originator of this image which is freely available and widely used online with various variations, nonetheless, we acknowledge and credit the original designer of this image whoever they are, available at: https://twitter.com/VocesUnidasOrg/status/1547279953229746183/photo/1]

of prosperity for mankind, with the view of the overall society rather than an individual or small group of individuals. Thus, it could be summed up as an economics theory to achieve and satisfy the needs of humans, not the individual and it is for society not for a group of individuals without consideration to what connect them and link them together.

As a result, this worldview does not permit the production and consumption of harmful items or economic activities. This approach eliminates such harmful activities from being an economic factor of consideration or of benefit in its economic policy, whether such policy is directed to people of faiths, Muslims, Christians, Jews, Hindu etc. or no faith at all living together in the same community/society. You may think and possibly argue that I am an ambitious idealist, and this is not realistic. I would ask that you bear with me and follow my argument throughout, and the steps I lay down in articulating this proposed theory and how it works in practice in this Chapter and the next two chapters. Then you can make your own judgement on its viability, bearing in mind I am not claiming it has the solution for everything.

Indeed, this economic worldview, which I articulate here, emphasises the intertwining of economic policies and human prosperity, with the ultimate goal of achieving social contentment and human happiness. In this approach to economics, the pursuit of wealth and economic prosperity is not seen as separate from spiritual pursuits and the attainment of goodness in this world and the afterlife world for those who believe in it.

In this context I would like to quote a Quranic verse that highlights the balanced approach to economic well-being and spiritual fulfilment. It encourages seeking the home of the hereafter, which emphasises the importance of spiritual growth and righteousness. At the same time, it also emphasises not forgetting one's portion of lawful enjoyment in this world, recognising that economic prosperity and enjoying the blessings provided by God are not to be neglected and not being contradictive (Quran, al Qasas 28: 77). I find this verse fascinating, as it guides people to enjoy this life to the fullest within acceptable boundaries, at the same time remember that humans are also accountable for their actions. A very simple but powerful economic concept.

In the same context the Bible states: "Give, and it will be given to you. A good measure, pressed down, shaken together and running over, will be poured into your lap. For with the measure you use, it will be measured to you." (Luke 6:38 NIV).

However, this pursuit of prosperity should be within the boundaries of justice, fairness, and ethical behaviour. The Quran advises against seeking mischief on Earth, which includes committing great crimes, oppression, tyranny, and corruption (Quran, al Qasas 28: 77). Our approach to economics, as proposed here, seeks to ensure that economic activities and policies are conducted in a manner that does not harm others and does not lead to injustice or exploitation. This theory advocates for a balanced and ethical approach to economic prosperity, considering both material well-being and spiritual growth. It emphasises the pursuit of goodness, justice, and fairness in economic activities, aiming to create a society where all individuals can thrive and find contentment in this world.

## 12.4 Understanding Text and Context

My philosophical exploration, which underpins the economic theory I am constructing here, regarding understanding text and context is profound and important in the realm of economic thought and interpretation. Indeed, the meaning of a text extends beyond its literal words; it is also about grasping the contextual nuances and implications it conveys. A mere literal interpretation might not capture the full depth and richness of the intended message.

The understanding of economic thought goes beyond the surface-level information provided by texts. Instead, it involves comprehending the underlying meanings and connecting them to the realities experienced in everyday life. This process of contextual understanding helps to bring economic ideas to life and makes them more relevant and applicable to individuals and societies.

By understanding the context of economic thought, people can internalise its meanings and relate it to their own experiences and existing realities. In doing so, economic thought becomes more than just an abstract idea or theory; it becomes a tangible and applicable concept with real-life implications. As individuals see how these ideas align with their daily experiences, the economic thought gains credibility and becomes a guiding force in their decision-making and actions.

The distinction I draw between mere informational text and meaningful contextual understandings is essential. It highlights the need to look beyond surface-level information and delve deeper into the meaning and relevance of economic ideas. By doing so, economic thought becomes a more powerful tool for shaping societies and individuals' lives, as it is grounded in reality and connected to their own experiences.

This philosophical perspective reminds us of the importance of engaging with economic thought in a holistic and nuanced manner. It encourages us to seek not only the literal meaning of economic texts but also to explore their implications and connections to our everyday realities. In doing so, we can develop a more comprehensive and meaningful understanding of economic concepts and their impact on our lives.

## 12.5 Meanings and Understandings Are Not a Mere Informational Text

Economics provides meanings and understandings that are directly linked to our existence, and our mind can relate to it when it is able to do so. If the mind is not able to relate to it and understand its meanings directly, it can understand its meaning with a high level of certainty. Thus, it can relate such understandings to reality that it senses without any doubt.

It has been debated in the classical books of the principles of jurisprudence, see e.g. (Al-Ghazali, 1997; Al-Haithami, 2010) that all thoughts have understandings and meanings. This means it has a reality and existence in one's mind, which can be realised, or if not in few cases, it can be accepted with high level of certainty because the mind can relate to it and it can be actually realised. This is what I hope to achieve here. If the Equitable Optimality economic theory at this point cannot be realised as a reality and existence in the reader's mind, it ca be accepted, at least, with high level of certainty. Until it is realised by the end of this book, or if not, perhaps later on when it spreads further and get implemented.

Therefore, it has been said that a belief is a way of life because it has an existing reality in this life, and I do believe in this proposed economic theory. Every meaning and thought within it has a fact in an individual's mind that is realised by his/her senses and resonates in their mind. Thus, a sound mind forms the basis of all obligations on us as individuals, which our beliefs are built on, and such obligations are always addressed to the sound mind.

For example, the Quran says: "And He has subjected to you (humans) the night and the day, the sun and the moon; and the stars are subjected by His Command. Surely, in this are proofs for people who understand.", (Quran, Al Nahil 16: 12). Also, " And in the Earth are neighbouring tracts, and gardens of vines, and green crops (fields), and date-palms, growing into two or three from a single stem root, or otherwise (one stem root for every palm ), watered with the same water, yet some of them We make more excellent than others to eat. Verily, in these things, there are Ayat (proofs, evidences, lessons, signs) for the people who understand". (Quran, Al Ra'ed 13: 4). "And among His Signs is that He shows you the lightning, for fear and for the hope, and He sends down water (rain) from the sky, and therewith revives the earth after its death. Verily, in that are indeed signs for a people who understand". (Quran, Roum 30:24).

Therefore, the belief in the existence and oneness of God, happens as the mind realise through its senses that God exists, and this is a must; given that all the signs we have seen and accepted in our thoughts which lead to this conclusion as the earlier verses of the Quran state, acknowledging the views of those of no faiths. Those signs realised through one's senses and realisation of existing reality and have been imprinted in the brain. Such subsequent realisation is the outcome of the first, which is the belief in God and what that entails of realities that resonate with many who believe in it, and which we connect with through our senses and understanding.

As a result, it has become a reality and an understanding in one's mind, based on the already established understanding of realisation through our senses of the Quran and facts it represents in one's mind. While one may accept the above, so what about the belief in predestination whether good or bad, I would say the same rationale applies. Predestination is realised through one's senses which connect to various events happen to us throughout our life. This results in a direct realisation in one's mind of predestination through actual life experiences. Therefore, the belief for its believers is based on existing understandings with absolute certainty and meanings that resonate in people's mind, which they act and react towards it.

The other part of the equation is guiding economic principles and rules, which interact with people's daily life and is subject to understanding life circumstances and the dynamic interpretation of such rules and principles to address changing and developing world. This interpretation should be established on a correct understanding of the context in the texts and its wisdom and objectives. If this goal is achieved, then this is an indicator that the interpretation of the rules and principles meet its intended wisdom and injunctions. Otherwise, another more correct interpretation should be pursued for better understanding ad conclusion that connects with reality and resonates in people's mind.

Hence, the philosophical principles that we outline here for this proposed economic theory become an understanding that has an existing reality that connects with people's mind through their senses. Thus, these economic philosophical principles and rules are not just information or ideas acknowledged in people's minds. Rather, they are an understanding and meanings that require actions and set a guiding framework for people's behaviour.

## 12.6 Contextual Understanding Is a Guiding Principle for Human Economic Behaviour

As the text has a context and actual meanings in life it acts as a guiding framework for a man's behaviour in this life, including economic behaviour. The economic philosophical principles and rules as prescribed in the text, which the text literally refers to, and its context which refers to the meaning and understanding of the text are all confined to the belief in it. Therefore, these economic philosophical principles provide a way of life that should be followed and observed at all times according to its context and meanings. This sets out a practical behavioural framework to be implemented and followed in our economic behaviour on Earth. As a result, we must accept that this economic philosophy provides two key things:

Firstly, it provides meanings that regulate man's behaviour in this life and how to be successful as an economic agent. Thus, an individual should follow this context and understanding as a guiding principle in all aspects of his/her life, which reflects the knowledge and understanding, not the informative element. If a person just follows the informative side only, it becomes empty of its original contextual meanings as a guiding framework for regulating man's economic behaviour and a way of life that addresses and resolves all life's aspects.

Secondly, it becomes an information like any other, such as geography, history or literature that relates to theory rather than a dynamic meanings and guiding principles for economic prosperity. Hence, viewing this economic philosophy from that lens will render it a type of information that individuals of faiths or no faith relate to it equally void of any contextual meanings and understandings that influence people's life and economic behaviour. This is the case nowadays where we see economic policies, but we do not see this economic philosophy in its contextual meanings and wisdom being implemented and practiced as it should be by those who brand themselves as policymakers! Therefore, one does not go without the other, they both go hand in hand.

## 12.7 The Equitable Optimality Worldview Advocates a Particular Economic Behaviour

As we have learned, this economic philosophy depicts a particular path in life for economic behaviour. It provides a way of life that includes meanings and regulations of how individuals must live their life within this economic worldview. This worldview governs all aspects of an individual's economic life, such as economic, financial, social, resource consumption, political economy, etc... It provides broad guidelines that help individuals navigate through life, its challenges, requirements, and problems. Accordingly, it has set out meanings and understandings for people, but did not limit their mind and intellectual horizons. It also regulates people's behaviour, but it does not restrict their effort and endeavour.

This then formulates a worldview about economics and people's way of life that ensures they live prosperous, dignified, responsible, wholesome, equitable life within this guiding framework. This worldview also explains while an individual should enjoy this life and available economic resources, however, should always remember that this life is not by itself the ultimate goal. Hence, an individual's life on this Earth has a purpose and it is not meaningless. It must be lived and enacted according to this economic philosophy's worldview, and all acts, deeds and behaviours in this worldview are measured and accounted for accordingly.

## 12.8 Standard of Acceptable Economic Behaviour

This economic philosophy worldview, as discussed earlier, acts as a standard for an individual's behaviour that should be complied with at all times to achieve its objectives. Some have indirectly deviated from this worldview and lost their compass because they moved away from its economic philosophy and no longer have a standard that they can measure their deeds and behaviours against. Consequently, this deviation has affected their economic practices and judgements. They started to get involved in interest-based capitalist or socialist financial practices, which do not fit with this worldview, and started accepting it as a normative economic and financial practices. Others lost their ethical compass and have become passive in their behaviour and indifferent about doing the right thing, promoting the good and fighting evil as and when it takes place.

As a result, the first type of people, i.e., those who completely deviated from this worldview and embraced other views, have went astray and indulged in self-interest. Thus, adopting another system to be the regulating framework for man's deeds and behaviours, whether that system is capitalism or socialism over doing the right thing is a deviation from this worldview. This is not by anyway advocating a specific religious view, but we have seen what man-made rules have done to our world, therefore, we should consider divine wisdom and guidance and incorporate it in our economic worldview.

The other type of people who diverted from this worldview are those who ditched any element of faith and religion even if it addresses serious economic or social problems. They do not represent this worldview in their deeds and behaviour, ordain the good and forbid the bad, acting as an example to others or make things right when it needs to be put right. The economic philosophy that Equitable Optimality does not accept is passive behaviour, such as people not taking active part in the affair of their society under the excuse of 'I do not like politics, or I do not want to be involved in politics'. Prophet Muhammad e.g., said: Whoever of you does not care for the affairs of Muslims, he is not one of them. The affairs of Muslims are anything of concern to them and their well-being, such as politics, economics and financial policies, social and environmental policies. A policy in that sense means looking after and taking care of all Muslims' affairs, and this is a religious requirement. This goes to people of all faiths or no faith, not only Muslims.

Those two types of people failed because they do not have a criterion that they could apply to their deeds and behaviour, which would be the judge of such deeds. So, their philosophical and ethical compass is broken, and they cannot differentiate between what is permitted, which is encouraged, what is obligatory or a principle that must be fulfilled, what is disliked and better to be left and what is forbidden and must be avoided. This criterion acts as a compass for all of us anywhere and at any time to guide our deeds, behaviours, sayings, and interaction with others in relation to what is permitted, obligatory or prohibited. God's wisdom and mercy necessitate that this criterion that governs and regulates people's deeds and behaviour is not subject to and dictated by mind. However, God has made this criterion comprehensible by the mind, and this criterion is an important feature of a sound legislative system.

Hence, if deeds and behaviours were subject to the mind as a criterion, it will lack objectivity and consistency. What is bad in the mind today could change to be good tomorrow because our brain and behaviour are driven by our human desires, interests and wants. This will also differ from a person to others, from a community to others and from a country to others. Therefore, a divine judging criterion or standard that regulates humans' deeds, behaviours and acts on Earth is superior for a system of accountability to work.

## 12.9 A Divine-Based Economic System Is Superior

A legislation and law put in place by God is superior to any other manmade rules, as the faith-based worldview advocates. This is derived from the monotheism concept like in Islam, which is the belief in the oneness of God. As the creator and planner are two of God's attributes, so the legislator. The Quran says: "... and made the word of those who disbelieved the lowermost, while the word of God that became the uppermost, and God is All-Mighty, All-Wise.", (Quran, al Tawbah 9:40). The word of God means here God's law (Shariah) as it is His word sent down to people to follow it and abide by it. The Quran, as well as the Bible, also makes it clear that God's rulings, legislations, and system is superior to any other and must be followed, "O you who believe! Make not (a decision) in advance before God and His Messenger, and fear God. Verily! God is All-Hearing, All-Knowing.", (Quran, al Hujuraat 49:1). As God's legislations are superior to any other, it fulfils the objective of the legislator in achieving people's benefit and what is in their interest on Earth.

The faith-based worldview explains the role of religious principles, which is put in place by the Legislator for social good and people's interest. People's benefit is achieved by either bringing a benefit to them or protecting them from a harm coming to them. The Quran articulates this point in the following verse: "O mankind! There has come to you a good advice from your Lord (i.e. the Qur'an, enjoining all that is good and forbidding all that is evil), and a healing for that (disease of ignorance, doubt, hypocrisy and differences,) Which is in your breasts, a guidance and a mercy (explaining lawful and unlawful things) for the believers.", (Quran, Yunus 10:57).

Guidance and mercy in this verse means bringing good to you or protecting you from harm for your own interest. However, determining what is of interest to us as humans or not is according to this faith-based framework only as an objective legislation enacted to achieve that goal for humans. The Quran illustrates this point in the following verse, "… And We have sent down to you the Book (the Quran) as an exposition of everything, a guidance, a mercy, and glad tidings for those who have submitted themselves (to Allah as Muslims)." (Quran, al Nahel 16:89).

Therefore, as a guiding exposition of everything, any new matter, in the Islamic worldview, would be referred first to the Quran for ruling and guidance. Then to the Sunnah of prophet Muhammad that illustrated the Quranic rulings, explained them, and expanded on them. Both legislative sources provide objectives and wisdom that explain the Legislator objective of permitting something or forbidding other. Those objectives act as pointers for jurists to enact them as a base for extracting rulings and laws at any time to address new matters. These new laws and rulings are a legal extension derived from the original sources i.e., the Quran and the Sunnah (prophetic traditions), and are supported by them as it was not reached to in isolation of the religious framework. Consequently, there is nothing in the world that could happen or exist which does not have a guiding principle or a pointer on how to deal with it in the Islamic law, as the verse above clearly states 'an exposition of everything'. This is also confirmed in the following verse, "… We have neglected nothing in the Book, then unto their Lord they (all) shall be gathered." (Quran, al Ana'am 6:38). Thus, this is important to achieve justice in Islamic law when holding humans accountable for their actions and behaviour.

This interest that we discussed above is aimed to be achieved for mankind collectively not for an individual. Achieving an individual's interest does not fit with a divine legislation meant for the benefit of mankind. As humans our mind is limited by what we know and rationalise through our senses and intellectual realisation. Therefore, our decisions are based on what we perceive as benefit or interest to us based on our limited awareness and knowledge. This is in addition to the fact that such decisions will be influenced by our own individual interests and goals (e.g., the agency theory), rather than a more collective view of the benefit of wider society. Therefore, many things that may appear at present to be of interest and benefit for people, would become in a short while bad and harmful to the same group of people. An obvious example is the subprime mortgage crisis of 2008, where those receiving such mortgage loans that banks dished out to them left and right to maximise their profits appeared to be good for them and achieving their interest in buying their own home.

However, this was not the case, and the negative consequences of those financial practices became evident in 2008 during the financial meltdown. The subprime mortgage loans, which lacked proper backing by real assets, were given to people who believed they could afford them at the time. This belief was influenced by false positive realisations, driven by banks' eagerness to provide loans at, and in many cases exceeding, 100%, leading individuals to convince themselves that it was in their best interest. Their limited knowledge played a role in this misjudgement.

Unfortunately, this perception was completely shattered when a financial crisis, caused primarily by those very banks that were supposed to act in their customers' best interest, emerged. The impact on those who received these mortgage loans was severe, leaving them in a much worse financial situation than before taking on the loans. This highlights the uncertainty inherent in determining what is truly beneficial or harmful for us as human beings. Only a divine legislation, guiding our actions and behaviour throughout life, can provide absolute clarity in this matter.

While some, like atheists, may disagree with this philosophy and raise objections, I respectfully doubt that they can present a strong argument to refute it. Thus, a human's true interest and benefit can only be absolute when it originates from a superior framework, in this case, God. A human brain can then recognise, rationalise, and be guided by these divine principles to achieve the standard set by God, which we should strive to follow in our actions and decisions.

## 12.10 A Comprehensive Economic Theory: Characteristics of the Equitable Optimality Theory

The proposed Equitable Optimality economic theory is distinguished from any other theory, regulations, and rules by being comprehensive, inclusive, and all encompassing. Thus, any event that may happen has a ruling and a guiding answer about how to deal with it within this framework that addresses anything matters to people, their actions, and behaviours. This is demonstrated by the fact that this theory is a dynamic approach, and this would still be the case for the future. Its comprehensive nature, applicability, inclusivity, and dynamic character makes it relevant and applicable everywhere and makes it timeless.

One of the most important characteristics of Equitable Optimality's worldview is justice and being just. This justice is emphasised in different ways within its structure to ensure all people are treated equally, and for the self-accountability and the system of reward and punishment to work justly and effectively. This key characteristic is also supported and emphasised in religious and conventional texts.

In this context, the Quran says, "Verily, God enjoins Al-Adl (i.e. justice) and worshipping none but God Alone - Islamic Monotheism) and Al-Ihsan [i.e. to be patient in performing your duties to God, totally for God's sake and in accordance with the Sunnah (legal ways) of the Prophet in a perfect manner], and giving (help) to kith and kin (i.e. all that God has ordered you to give them e.g., wealth, visiting, looking after them, or any other kind of help): and forbids Al-Fahsha' (i.e all evil deeds, e.g. illegal sexual acts, disobedience of parents, polytheism, to tell lies, to give false witness, to kill a life without right), and Al-Munkar (i.e all that is prohibited by Islamic law: polytheism of every kind, disbelief and every kind of evil deeds), and Al-Baghy (i.e. all kinds of oppression), He admonishes you, that you may take heed." (Quran, al Nahel 16:90).

If we carefully analyse this verse in the Quran, we find that it sets a framework for a just society that is supported by equitable and just economic system. The excerpt from the Quran, (Surah An-Nahl, 16:90), conveys a profound message about the fundamental principles that guide human economic behaviour, emphasising the concepts of justice, excellence, kindness, and the prohibition of various forms of evil. This verse encapsulates the core values and ethical framework of a healthy society, providing individuals with a comprehensive guideline for leading a righteous and virtuous life.

a) **Justice (*Al-Adl*):** The verse begins by emphasising the paramount importance of justice. The term "*Al-Adl*" refers to a state of equilibrium, where individuals are treated fairly and impartially. This concept extends beyond mere legal justice to encompass economic, moral and social justice as well. The injunction to uphold justice underscores the principle of treating all individuals with equity and fairness, irrespective of their social, economic, or religious backgrounds.
b) **Excellence (*Al-Ihsan*):** The concept of "*Al-Ihsan*" calls for individuals to go beyond fulfilling their obligations and to perform their duties with sincerity, dedication, and excellence. It involves carrying out one's responsibilities in a manner that reflects devotion to God and adherence to the best forms of behaviours and conduct. This commitment to excellence is a reminder that individuals should strive to excel in all aspects of their lives, from personal conduct to interactions with others.
c) **Kindness (Giving to Kith and Kin):** The verse also emphasises the importance of maintaining close ties with family members and stakeholders and providing them with support and assistance. This encompasses financial help, emotional care, and maintaining familial bonds. The Quranic directive to care for kith and kin underscores the significance of fostering strong family and social relationships and supporting one another in times of need.
d) **Prohibition of Evil Deeds (*Al-Fahsha', Al-Munkar, Al-Baghy*):** The verse goes on to enumerate the acts that are explicitly prohibited as being socially harmful. "*Al-Fahsha'*" refers to indecent and immoral actions, including illegal sexual acts and lying. "*Al-Munkar*" encompasses all actions that are deemed

forbidden by Islamic law, such as disbelief, polytheism, and any form of evil conduct. "*Al-Baghy*" denotes oppression and transgression against others' rights and dignity. By forbidding these actions, this text underscores the importance of maintaining a moral and ethical standard that safeguards individuals' well-being and societal harmony.

e) **Admonition for Reflection:** The verse concludes by stating that these commandments and prohibitions are provided as admonitions for individuals to reflect upon. It encourages introspection and self-awareness, urging individuals to consider their actions in light of these principles. This reflective approach allows individuals, also as economic agents, to align their behaviour with this framework, and to strive for continuous self-improvement.

Hence, this text encapsulates a comprehensive ethical framework that underpins this proposed economic theory. It highlights the interconnectedness of justice, excellence, compassion for family and fellow humans, and the avoidance of evil deeds as essential components of an individual's life. By adhering to these principles, individuals are called to lead lives characterised by integrity, kindness, and a commitment to higher moral standards. It also emphasises on reflection which serves as a reminder that adherence to these principles is a continuous journey towards spiritual and economic growth and moral development.

## 12.11 Economic Law of Justice Is a Just Law

Justice in the Equitable Optimality's worldview from the above discussion and perspective is placed on an equal footing to monotheism, and oppression is against monotheism. So, oppression strips any legal economic system or a policymaker from any legitimacy even if this individual is a practicing individual, and claiming to be a good individual. Thus, the founding principle of this economic theory and its worldview is justice, which is enshrined in every aspect of the Equitable Optimality economic theory, and that is an attribute of a divine law and would not be achieved in any other worldly laws or legislations.

Therefore, it is believed that economic justice can be only achieved by implementing normative law and rules that ensure everyone is treated with justices. As such, one of the key higher objectives of the Equitable Optimality theory is economic and social justice and fair distribution of economic resources among all stakeholders. That is why this higher objective and economic aspiration can only be achieved by fully implementing the Equitable Optimality economic theory and its principles.

Economic justice is embedded in the Equitable Optimality economic theory when it is put in place for people to follow, and it should be manifested when people implement it in all their activities and behaviours. Thus, it is not acceptable that we ask for economic justice on Earth if we block this justice by not following a just law, the latter is required for the former to be fulfilled.

Achieving a balanced and just economic system requires a deep analysis of the laws and rules that this system is derived from. Therefore, when studying the Equitable Optimality economic theory a researcher should analyse its worldview, its objectives, and principles within its contextual context. Current economic theories and ideologies, such as capitalism and socialism are perceived by many researchers (Kahf, 2004; Siddiqi, 2004, 2006; Zaman, 2008, 2012b; Zarka, 2008; Ahmad, 1980; Chapra, 1994; Alamad, 2017a, b, 2019a, b, 2023; Alamad et al., 2021; Van Greuning & Iqbal, 2008; Nienhaus, 2012) to be not balanced and do not achieve the benefit of all stakeholders in society. It rather focuses on the interest of a small group that obtains most benefits and accumulate wealth on expense of the larger group in society, or completely diminish the rights of people to earn and own wealth legitimately on the other side of the economic spectrum, in the case of the socialist economic philosophy.

This balance is an important aspect in the Equitable Optimality economic worldview, which covers all aspects of people's life. This however is not achievable in any manmade laws as evident in our life. It is normal for existing laws to be limited, out of date or require to be amended on ongoing basis to stay relevant. Nonetheless, sometimes it appears to be contradictory, subjective, and subject to many interpretations. Therefore, the Equitable Optimality framework is comprehensive, just and balanced which ensures that the law is merciful as well at the same time.

For example, in many countries that implement a civil law influenced by the French laws (such as, Jordan, Syria and Lebanon), the law says if someone's car was parked by his/her house and someone fell down from a building (any floor) and landed on that person's car, whether was just injured or died as a result, the owner of that parked car is responsible as a consequence. How such law can be merciful or deliver justice, I will leave this with you to think about it as there are many other similar examples in our current laws that are manmade laws. The Quran says "And strive hard in God's cause as you ought to strive (with sincerity and with all your efforts that His Name should be superior). He has chosen you (to convey His Message of Monotheism to mankind by inviting them to His religion, of Islam), and has not laid upon you in religion any hardship, it is the religion of your father Ibrahim (Abraham) (Islamic Monotheism)...", (Quran, al Hajj 22: 78).

## 12.12 An Effective Worldview Based on a System of Accountability

For an economic system to be effective it should be based on justice. Justice requires that those who follow this system in every aspect of their actions and behaviours are rewarded. This reward is not necessarily a monetary reward in terms of money and other items of value, as they are expected to follow the law for their own benefit and interest regardless. But, as this life is a passage and a test for the Next Life, where everyone would be held accountable for their deeds, and if passed the test they will be rewarded with paradise for eternity. However, on the other hand those who ignore the law and disobey its guidance and rules should be held to account. This accountability could be partially served in this life, even though some wrongdoers may do all sort of things and oppress many people and escape this life without punishment. However, they will not escape the accountability and the punishment that follows in the Hereafter, or being exposed publicly before or after their death, as reported in the media in many cases.

As the Equitable Optimality economic system is just also merciful, the door for repentance and forgiveness is always open if wrongdoers repent and put things right, by giving back people their right and what is taken unjustly from them. However, when the law is not implemented bad people may escape justice in this life, but will not escape the divine justice. To ensure its effectiveness, the Equitable Optimality theory is based on a system that incentivises goodness and punishes evil deeds. It places more emphasis on doing good, by giving multiple rewards for such good deeds, and one sin for each bad deed to ensure a balanced approach is in place. Punishment in the Equitable Optimality system is not a goal; it is only a deterring measure to achieve justice and encourage good deeds.

Hence, the Equitable Optimality economy is also derived from this divine law ensures justice is implemented, achieves inclusivity, and punishes for breaching its rules. A system that would be still applicable even if the two parties to an economic dealing agreed to not observe it, e.g., agreed to undertake an interest-based lending transaction. While this transaction might serve their immediate personal interest, it breaches the law and its balance as it compromises its meanings, objectives, and social justice. Therefore, the Equitable Optimality economic system is a comprehensive approach that does not stop at the individual's benefit. It ensures that its objective is humanistic and considers the social good.

## 12.13 Foundational Structure

In this worldview of economics, I advocate that economic policies are closely linked to the Equitable Optimality philosophy and principles of what is permissible and prohibited for humans. This linkage ensures that economic activities and policies are guided by its objectives, aiming to achieve the well-being and benefit of individuals and society as a whole.

Figure 12.2 outlines the structure of the proposed Equitable Optimality economic theory, mapping out its key aspects and components, which are explained in details in this chapter and Chaps. 13 and 14.

One of the key principles of this theory is the protection of property rights, both for public ownership and private ownership. It forbids any infringement of such ownership rights, and this applies equally to individuals and the state. The fulfilment of financial obligations to others is treated with the same importance as the duty of paying the obligatory public dues or taxes. This underscores the significance of upholding economic justice and respecting the rights of individuals and society.

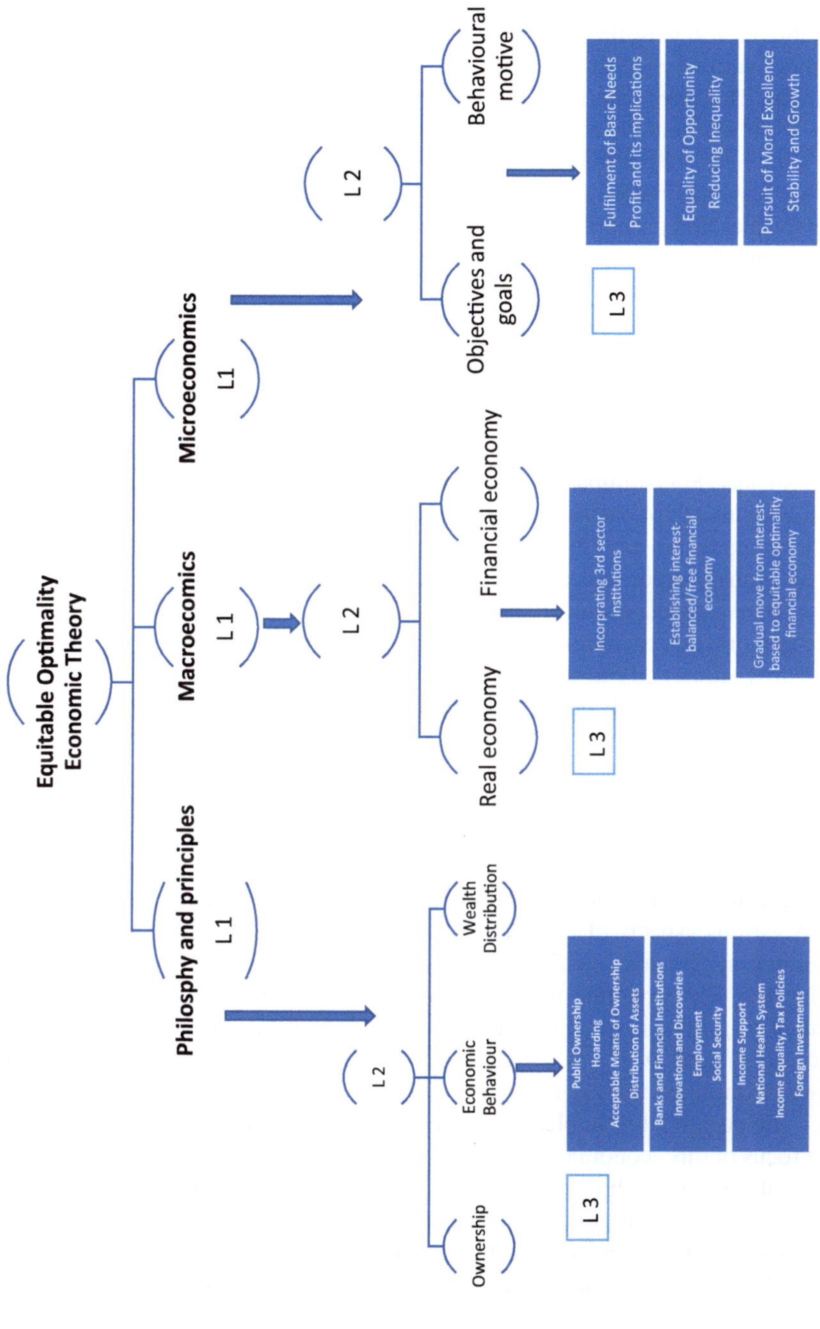


**Fig. 12.2** Mapping out the Equitable Optimality economic system

Economic legislation in this worldview considers the interests of both individuals and society. When macro-economic policies and rules are formulated, they are designed to benefit the wider society while considering the interests of individuals. For example, allowing the state to collect taxes/funds from individuals but only from their surplus wealth beyond their standard needs, and at a specific rate per annum. This approach aims to achieve the objective of economic welfare for society while maintaining economic balance and justice, and also ensuring the individual's interests are not ignored.

In this way, this theory seeks to create an economic system that is in harmony with the values and principles of Equitable Optimality, promoting fairness, justice, and social welfare for all members of society. It emphasises the responsibility of individuals and the state to uphold economic ethics and principles while striving for the well-being and prosperity of the entire community.

Moreover, in this economic worldview, individual ownership and the accumulation of wealth are indeed recognised and encouraged, but with the principle of not infringing on the rights and interests of others. This principle ensures that economic activities are conducted in a manner that respects the rights and well-being of the broader society. For example, while an individual is entitled to build their property or farm, they must not obstruct public roads or passages in the process, as it would negatively impact others. This same principle applies to economic activities undertaken by global corporations, such as Microsoft, Shell, Google, Apple, Amazon, Alibaba, Banks, assets management firms etc.

Furthermore, this economic worldview emphasises the importance of hard work, seeking provisions, and earning a living to achieve prosperity both for the individual and society as a whole. It promotes simplicity in earning money and defines clear guidelines for ownership, rights, and obligations, as well as various contracts involved in economic activities.

The structured approach to ownership and the movement of assets aims to enable people to earn and make profits in a principled manner without causing harm to the economy or triggering economic crises. This economic worldview views economic reasoning and financial contracts as broad guidelines, while offering detailed guidance on various aspects of economic activities, including labour, sales contracts, ownership transfers, and agency fees.

Moreover, this economic theory and its worldview treats giving something as equivalent to gifting it when transferring ownership from one party to another. It also considers agency fees as similar to rental fees in lease contracts. These guidelines are meant to be followed by everyone adhering to this worldview to maintain balance and ensure a fair implementation of economic policies.

The focus of this economic worldview extends beyond achieving economic prosperity; it also regulates how prosperity is attained. By addressing both the "What" and "How" in economic policies, it strives for a just and balanced social and economic prosperity that provides stability and happiness for both individuals and society as a whole. This approach aligns with the principles of equity and social justice emphasised in this approach to economics, creating an economic system that fosters the well-being of all members of society.

The economic worldview I present in this theory indeed distinguishes between the means of generating economic benefit (capital and labour) and the ownership and utilisation of such benefit. It prohibits benefiting from certain sources of capital, such as usury, gambling, and activities that harm societies and individuals. It also restricts engaging in labour that falls under prohibited activities. This aspect of the worldview emphasises ethical considerations and aims to ensure that economic activities are in line with the principles and values of this theory.

However, when it comes to ownership and accumulating wealth, this theory provides various legislations and contracts, such as sale contracts, leasing, inheritance, gifting, reviving non-utilised land, and wills. These mechanisms enable individuals to rightfully own and accumulate wealth within the boundaries set by law, promoting a fair and just distribution of resources.

Regarding economic resources in general, this worldview recognises that they are part of God's creation and are meant to benefit humanity. Divine scriptures acknowledge that God has created everything on Earth for the benefit of humans and that there are signs in these resources for those who contemplate deeply. This time I quote the Bible which says: "One who oppresses the poor to increase his wealth and one who gives gifts to the rich—both come to poverty" (22:16 NIV- New International Version).

While this economic worldview provides guidelines for the utilisation and ownership of resources, it does not prescribe specific methods or techniques for extracting and benefiting from these resources in the process of economic production. This aspect is left to human creativity, experience, and societal needs as they evolve over time. The principles I outlined here for this theory offer a framework for conducting economic activities within the bounds of ethics and morality, leaving room for human innovation and development.

Thus, this economic worldview is concerned with the ethical and just utilisation of economic resources and the fair accumulation of wealth while recognising that the means of generating economic benefit may vary and evolve over time. It aims to guide individuals, corporates, governments, and societies toward economic activities that align with the principles of equity, justice, and social welfare. Indeed, this economic worldview recognises that minerals, oil, and other economic resources are part of God's creation and have been provided for the benefit of humanity. God has entrusted humans with the responsibility of extracting and utilising these resources, but within the framework of ethical guidelines to ensure their responsible and beneficial use.

As humans have advanced in science and technology, they have developed ways to utilise these resources for various purposes, such as powering machinery, vehicles, and factories. This utilisation is a result of economic and industrial revolutions that have shaped the modern world. However, this economic worldview emphasises that such utilisation must be in accordance with the broader guidelines that prioritise the interest of society and protect the well-being of individuals and future generations.

If the utilisation of economic resources, such as oil, becomes harmful to people, the environment, and other living beings on earth, it goes against the principles of this economic worldview. In such cases, this utilisation would be considered unlawful as it goes against the original purpose of these resources being provided for the benefit of mankind.

It guides the relationship between private and public interest in utilising economic resources. It also recognises the importance of public values in shaping private value and prioritises the interest of society over individual interests when conflicts arise. Solidarity, fairness, responsibility, and compassion are essential values emphasised in this worldview, alongside economic dynamism, and efficiency. Therefore, it encourages responsible and ethical utilisation of economic resources, ensuring that the interest of society and the well-being of individuals are prioritised. It emphasises the values of solidarity, fairness, and compassion to create a more just and equitable economic system that benefits all members of society.

## 12.14 Utility as the Value of Something That Satisfies Human's Needs

Here I provide a comprehensive description of utility and how it is comprised of two aspects:

a) human desires to acquire certain values or things of importance, and
b) the key characteristics of these desired values in addressing societal needs. The utility, in this context, can indeed be the outcome of both labour and capital.

Capital plays a significant role in satisfying human needs, and possessing wealth is a common human instinct. It is through the possession of capital and wealth that individuals can acquire various assets and resources to meet their needs and desires. Labour, on the other hand, serves as a means for individuals to earn money, whether it be in the form of fiat currency or other assets (Chapra, 1994).

The process of acquiring wealth and assets can happen through various means, such as transferring assets from one individual or group to another. This possession of wealth can take different forms, including acquiring assets for consumption or usage, benefiting from labour, or engaging in exchanges with countervalues, such as sales and leases. Additionally, wealth can be transferred without exchanging a countervalue through actions like gifting, inheriting, donating, and lending assets.

The interplay between capital and labour serves as the key principles in satisfying human needs, with wealth and assets being pivotal in the pursuit of utility. The possession and exchange of wealth take various forms, each contributing to individuals' ability to acquire and utilise resources that address their desires and societal needs.

A clear understanding of the key economic problem as seen from this economic worldview, specifically within value centred approach would yield better and more effective economic policies. The problem is not merely about possessing capital or finding wealth and economic resources, but rather revolves around how capital and wealth are acquired, accumulated, and utilised, as well as how wealth is distributed within society.

Within the context of this economic worldview, I emphasise three key rules to address this economic problem:

a) **Ownership:** This rule pertains to how humans can utilise and benefit from economic resources, goods, and services. It involves recognising and respecting ownership rights while ensuring that economic resources are used in a manner that aligns with ethical and social values.
b) **Economic Behaviour**: This rule focuses on the utilisation and usage of economic resources, wealth, goods, and services. It emphasises responsible economic behaviour, encouraging individuals to act in ways that promote social well-being, sustainability, and fairness.
c) **Wealth Distribution**: This rule deals with how capital and economic resources are distributed within society, taking into consideration the values of economic dynamism, efficiency, solidarity, fairness, and responsibility. The aim is to establish a system that ensures a just distribution of wealth and resources, reducing inequality and promoting social cohesion.

By adhering to these three key rules, this proposed economic worldview seeks to create a balanced and ethical economic system that serves the greater good of society. It emphasises the importance of considering not only individual economic interests but also the well-being and prosperity of the community as a whole.

Ownership of economic resources and wealth belongs all to God who created it for humans and gifted it to them to use it fairly and responsibly. I again quote a religious text in relation to this point. The Quran says "…And give them something (yourselves) out of the wealth of God which He has bestowed upon you…", (Quran, al-Noor 24: 33). Thus, God explains clearly that the true owner of economic resources and wealth is Him only when He said: "give them out of the wealth of God". When this ownership is transferred to people God affected that by the pronoun (their) instead of His as shown in the following verse "…if then you find sound judgement in them, release their property to them…", (Quran al-Nisa 4: 6), also "Take sadaqah (alms) from their wealth in order to purify them and sanctify them with it…," (Quran al-Tawba 9:103).

This transfer of ownership from God to humans was affected on the basis of trusteeship or vigerency "Believe in God and His Messenger (Muhammad), and spend of that whereof He has made you trustees. And such of you as believe and spend (in God's Way), theirs will be a great reward", (Quran, al-Hadid 57: 7). So, humans are given the right to utilise and benefit from the economic resources and wealth that God entrusted them with, but not forgetting that the true owner of all of this wealth is God, and that everything belongs to Him.

This type of human engagement is regulated through both general and specific economic policies. Fundamentally, this encourages economic policies and business transactions to secure the basic needs for all human beings, and these should be within the general ambit of permissible transactions. The concept of vigerency is essentially the concept of representation of God's ruling on Earth, conferred on mankind. The Quran says, "And (remember) when your Lord said to the angels: Verily, I am going to place vigerent (mankind) generations after generations on earth. They said: Will You place therein those who will make mischief therein and shed blood, while we glorify You with praises and thanks and sanctify You. He (God) said: I know that which you do not know." (Quran, al-Baqara 2: 30). In another religious text, this time from the Bible: Then he said to them, "Watch out! Be on your guard against all kinds of greed; life does not consist in an abundance of possessions." (Luke, 12:15, NIV-New International Version).

The point I am making here in relation to this economic worldview is that ownership and wealth distribution are regulated by the concept of permission from the original true owner. This permission serves as the basis for determining individual ownership rights and how wealth can be lawfully possessed and transferred through legitimate means. The rules and principles set out in this worldview guide how ownership is managed and the rightful transfer of wealth from one party to another.

Wealth distribution is influenced by various factors, including the size of wealth owned by individuals and the satisfaction of human needs. The concern arises when wealth distribution becomes unequal and concentrated in the hands of a small group, leading to social injustice and marginalisation of a larger segment of society. To address this issue, the Equitable Optimality economic worldview discourages economic monopoly, hoarding, and usury, as these practices lead to restricted circulation of wealth and inequality.

Instead, the Equitable Optimality economic worldview encourages a more just and wider distribution of wealth by promoting investment and economic ventures that involve both capital and labour. This ensures that the benefits of economic activities are shared between parties and contribute to the well-being of society as a whole. The concept of Zakat in the Islamic system, the religious tax, further ensures the redistribution of wealth to assist the less advantaged and needy in society, helping to eliminate poverty and create a more prosperous community. This concept if applied correctly in any economic system (religious or otherwise) would provide an important economic lever.

The distinction between means of acquiring wealth, such as labour, and growing wealth through economic activities like buying, selling, and leasing, highlights the interdependence of these factors. Our economic worldview encourages a balanced approach where economic activities are conducted with consideration for the welfare of society and the principles of justice and fairness. By adhering to these principles, this proposed economic theory which aims to create an economic environment that promotes social justice, equity, equality, and the well-being of all individuals in society.

## 12.15 Key Aspects of the Proposed Theory

Following the detailed discussion earlier about the proposed Equitable Optimality economic theory, I outline here the key aspects of this theory to ensure you are following with me its key structure. This economic theory encompasses a comprehensive set of principles and guidelines that aim to create a just and equitable society. Some key aspects include:

a. **Ownership:** Economic resources are considered the trusteeship of all humans, as they are God's creation. Private individual ownership is allowed, but subject to specific rules and guidelines.
b. **Public Ownership:** Resources deemed essential for public interest are protected as public ownership, ensuring their accessibility and availability to all members of society.
c. **Hoarding:** Accumulation of wealth without productive use is discouraged, and the state is responsible for implementing economic policies that promote development and prevent wealth concentration.
d. **Acceptable Means of Ownership:** Legitimate means of acquiring ownership include labour, reviving unutilised land, inheritance, gifts, donations, zakat, marriage dowry, compensation for damages, and finding assets without known owners.
e. **Banks and Financial Institutions:** Financial activities are allowed, but under the supervision of a state regulatory authority to ensure adherence to principles of this theory and meet public needs.
f. **Innovations and Discoveries:** Scientific and medical advancements, e.g., are considered public ownership and cannot be monopolised by individuals or groups.
g. **Employment:** The state is responsible for ensuring employment opportunities for all individuals, regardless of their class, background, religious beliefs, or other characteristics.
h. **Social Security:** This economic system guarantees social security and provides dignified livelihood for those in need, including the elderly and people with special needs.
i. **Income Support:** Low-income individuals with dependents are provided with financial support by the state to ensure their well-being.
j. **National Health System:** A free national health system is provided by the state to ensure equal access to healthcare for all citizens.
k. **Income Equality:** Measures are taken to address income inequality and achieve social-economic balance in society.
l. **Distribution of Assets:** Assets of public ownership are distributed to economically disadvantaged individuals to enable economic growth and development.
m. **Tax Policies:** The state can implement tax policies on the wealthy to support social welfare programs.
n. **Foreign Investments:** Foreign investments are allowed only if they serve the economic needs and benefit of the country.

Indeed, distinguishing between the three aspects of economic thought is crucial in understanding the different perspectives and objectives within economics:

1. **Economic Theory and Analysis:** This aspect focuses on the exploration and study of economic laws, causalities, and various phenomena. Economists in this domain seek to understand and identify patterns, relationships, and mechanisms that govern economic activities without necessarily making value judgments. The aim is to develop models and theories that explain how the economy functions and how it responds to various stimuli. For example, studying the determinants of supply and demand, the impact of changes in interest rates on investment, or the effects of trade policies on international commerce fall under economic theory and analysis.
2. **Economic Policy:** This aspect delves into the identification and formulation of suitable economic methods and strategies that a government or policymaker can adopt to achieve specific economic objectives. Economists in this field analyse the consequences of different policy measures and propose recommendations to address economic challenges and goals. Their aim is to guide policymakers in making informed decisions to stabilise economies, promote growth, manage inflation, or address unemployment. Economic policy researchers often weigh the advantages and disadvantages of different policy options and consider their potential impacts on various economic indicators.
3. **Economic System or Economic School of Thought:** In this aspect of economic thought, economists develop and defend a comprehensive set of economic principles, beliefs, and ideologies that form an economic system or school of thought. These economic systems represent broader perspectives on how economies should be structured and managed. Different economic systems might advocate for varying degrees of government intervention, market regulation, or resource allocation. For example, capitalism, socialism, and Islamic economics represent distinct economic systems or schools of thought, each with its own set of principles and values that guide their understanding of economic activities and their desired outcomes.

Therefore, economic thought encompasses these three interconnected aspects: theory and analysis for understanding economic laws, economic policy for guiding government actions, and economic systems or schools of thought that represent broader ideologies shaping economic beliefs and practices. These aspects contribute to a comprehensive understanding of the economic landscape and the range of perspectives within the field of economics.

## 12.16 Differentiating Between Economics and Economic System

Economics is defined as the science of studying economic life, its cycle, and economic phenomena, by linking those economic phenomena with causes and influencing factors that control it in society, (Al-Ghazali, 1997).

Economic system, on the other hand, is the set of laws and rules that are designed to regulate our economic life (Al-Ghazali, 1997) directly and practically. This means, as I discussed earlier when articulating the structure of my proposed economic theory, it is the economic principles and policies that govern the relationship between humans and capital, in terms of obtaining money, ownership rights, utilisation of money, expenditure, economic development and investment, and ensuring an economic equilibrium in society is achieved.

In that context I would like to draw again on the religious economic worldview. The faith-based economic thought is incapsulated in four economic rules, which are:

a. All economic resources and wealth belong to God, the Quran says "…And give them something (yourselves) out of the wealth of God which He has bestowed upon you…", (Quran, al-Noor 24: 33). Due to the importance of money in the faith-based economic thought, it was mentioned 76 times in the Quran in various forms, such singular, plural, definite and indefinite forms. This shows the importance of money, its role and influence in humans' life in the faith-based economic thought.
b. People are God's vigerences and trustees, "…, and spend of that whereof He has made you trustees. And such of you as believe and spend (in God's Way), theirs will be a great reward", (Quran, al-Hadid 57: 7). So, humans are given the right to utilise and benefit from the economic resources and wealth that God entrusted them with, and they are required to observe this trust in how they utilise it, earn it and spend it "The parable of those who spend their wealth in the way of God is that of a grain of corn: it groweth seven ears, and each ear hath a hundred grains. God giveth manifold increase to whom He pleaseth; and God careth for all and He knoweth all things." (Quran, al-Baqara 2: 261).
c. Hoarding money (e.g., gold, silver, wealth, precious commodities) is prohibited. This is because of the negative economic impact resulting from hoarding wealth without being invested in the real economy to achieve economic development, "And those who hoard up gold and silver, and spend them not in the way of God, announce unto them a painful torment." (Quran, al-Tawba 9: 34).
d. Circulation of wealth is an obligation; this is to address inequality of wealth distribution and ensure social justice of economic resources. The faith-based economic worldview is against the restricted circulation of wealth in the hand of a small group of people because of the negative economic impact on society from this practice, "…in order that money may not become a fortune used by the rich among you", (Quran, al-Hasher 59: 7).

## 12.17 Four Economic Factors

There are four identified basic types of economic factors in the world that have been the subject of extensive research by economists, which are land, labour, capital, and entrepreneurship. Land comprises all natural resources and supply which humans require as a fundamental factor for the production of all goods. Labour is a measure of work done by humans. It includes a variety of techniques and types of work. The level and quantity of labour force, as a factor of economic resources, always seems to be increased to achieve desired economic growth. Capital is an economic driver for durable goods that are used in production of goods or services. An entrepreneur is an individual or group that marshals resources in the production of final goods, which generate more capital and resources to make an impact on the global economy.

These four economic factors, as shown in Fig. 12.3, are combined in the production process to produce outputs that meet human needs. Humans have to make trade-offs and choices due to the scarcity of the available economic resources. The allocation of these four economic resources will directly affect the economic problem. Therefore, through the advancement of human society to present day, two major economic systems were formed to make the allocation of these resources to be efficient and productive. These are planned economy and mixed economy.

Economic system is an organised way to allocate its economic resources and apportions commodities and services in society among the population. It involves

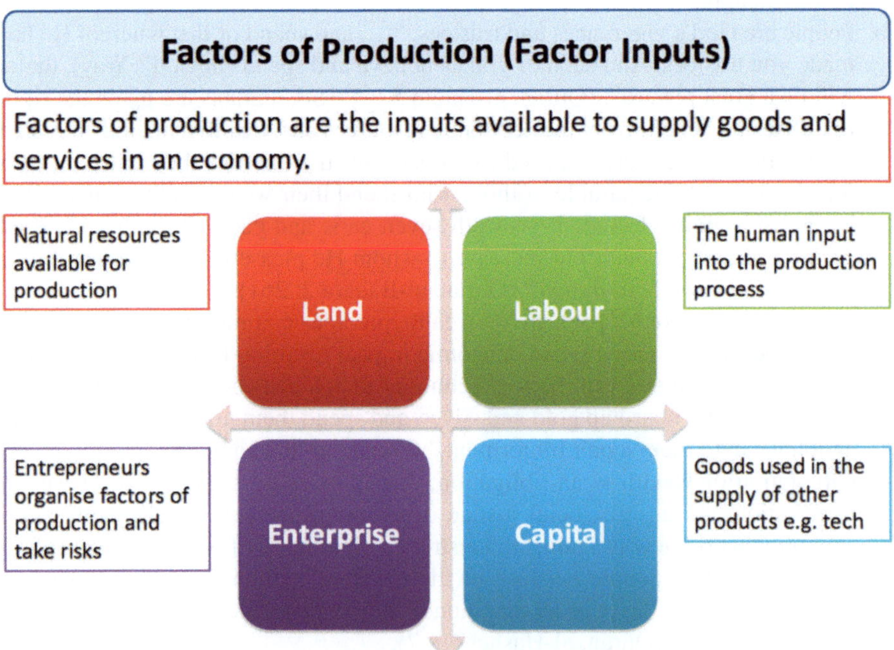


**Fig. 12.3** Economic factors of production

production, allocation of production inputs, distribution of outputs, land availability, financial institutions and government policies, household earnings and expenditure. This earning of allocated economic resources and capital takes the form of wages, rent, profit and interest (in the conventional sense).

Thus, the strength of an economic system is determined by the status of the development of social productive power and their social relations. The economic system of a society, called the basic system or the basic economic system, provides the overall directions of the social economic activities. Therefore, once the economic system in a society was established, they would have their social development remain unchanged to bring the nation to achieve the goal of prosperity. Thus, if the fundamental changes occur in allocation of resources and goods, the economic system of this society will be changed to respond to various changing circumstances. This helps minimise the impact of economic downturns, which I aim to achieve in this proposed new economic theory.

The economic resources theory is one of the key economic theories that is debated and discussed in most of the economic systems. The same economic challenge is faced by all societies, which is addressing the problem of how to fully utilise the scarce resources in the economy. This economic question always exists and is debated by economists throughout many generations. This is because the demands of people are infinite, and the supply that is available to satisfy market demand is limited due to the limited available economic resources.

In that respect, there are two dominant contradictory economic systems or views in relation to the economic resources, capitalism, and socialism. Capitalism's view advocates capital (wealth) maximisation as the main principle of its economic system, leaving the method and level of achieving that open without any rules. On the other spectrum, socialism, and communism as part of it is against private capital and wealth ownership whether entirely or partially, and advocates labour as the main principle of its economic system. Their moto is 'if you do not work, you do not eat'.

The economic theory I am proposing here, on the other hand, in relation to economic resources is based on human needs and human endeavours. Its economic system is based on capital private ownership and labour to increase and maximise wealth, this concept is support in the religious texts. For example, the Quran says: "He it is, Who has made the earth subservient to you (i.e. to live and utilise its resources e.g. to do agriculture on it), so walk in the path thereof and eat of His provision…." (Quran, al-Mulk 67:15). Also, "…you may disperse through the land, and seek the bounty of God (by working, making wealth etc.)", (Quran, al-Jumua' 62: 10).

It was also reported that prophet Muhammad said: there is never a better food for son of Adam (humans) than a food they eat as a result of their own labour i.e., their own work. So, the instruction to work and earn wealth in the above religious texts is to denote permissibility. This means that labour and ownership of capital permissible, but not free which supports our economic approach in this proposed theory. Therefore, while labour and ownership of capital are permissible, this permissibility is subject to rules that regulate it, and is not free of any rules or governing framework, as the case may be with other economic systems, such as capitalism. In this context, I expand the discussion more below on the four factors of production.

a. **Land**

Land is an agriculture economic resource, the form of its production is decided by the method of its ownership, how it is used and not through labour, entrepreneurship, or equipment. This is because this aspect is part of economics as a science, rather than being a feature of an economic system. Thus, our theory conceptualises this economic resource from the view of land ownership and possession. This ownership is affected by a purchase of a land, inheritance, reviving a dead land or other legitimate method. A dead land means a land that is not owned by anyone or exploited in any way of land usage. Reviving a dead land is by making use of it by way of farming it, planting trees, building on it or other means of utilisation that makes use of the land. It is reported that prophet Muhammad said: (whoever builds a land that is not owned by anyone, he/she would have a claim over it).

The same applies when a government allocate an exploited land to anyone who can farm it, build it, invest it, or make good use of it. Land allocation and distribution was practiced by prophet Muhammad and those who ruled after him, on a condition that the land should be invested and made good use of it. It was reported that prophet Muhamad gave a man called Bilal ibn al-Harith al-Muzani a land called al-'Aaqiq, when Omar ibn al-Khattab became a Caliph said to him: you were given that land by the prophet to make good use of it by farming it, building it etc. and not to build a fence around it and leave it or deny other people from making use of it. Then Omar ordered him to take from the land what he is able to utilise of it and work in it and return the rest to the state ownership, so it can be allocated to other people.

This view of land and how land ownership is obtained and is utilised ensures fair usage of it. Those who keep a land without making a good use of it by cultivating it, building it, investing it and so on for a long period. Then, the land will be taken from them and given to other people who would make good use of it for the benefit of society, to fulfil the objective of this economic resource. Imam al-Shafi'i (the founder of the Shafi'i school of thought) narrated that prophet Muhammad said: (old land, with no known owner for a long time, belongs to God and His messenger and this land ownership is passed to you if you revive it and make use of it. Anyone who builds a fence around a land with no owner and leaves it for three years without making use of it, has no ownership rights to it after that period).

b. **Capital**

Capital takes the form of various things. Manufacturing e.g., is judged according to what it produces in accordance to the Islamic legal maxim 'manufacturing is assessed based on what is produced'. For example, manufacturing drinks and juices to grow and maximise capital is permissible. However, brewing or manufacturing alcoholic drinks is prohibited, and consequently any capital growth and income as a result from it due to social harm it may cause by or to those who consume it. Anas ibn Malik narrated that: prophet Muhammad cursed 10 things in relation to alcoholic drinks, those who drink it, those who offer it, sell it, buy it, manufacture it, brew it etc… While this faith-based view acknowledges that there is a commercial benefit in producing and selling alcohol, it also considers the harm caused by it which outweigh the benefits. The Quran says "They ask you (O Muhammad) concerning alcoholic drink and gambling. Say: In them is a great sin (harm), and (some) benefit, for men, but the sin of them is greater than their benefit." (Quran, al-Baqara 2: 219).

This worldview also advocates that certain type of capital cannot be owned by an individual or a group in society, and it should be only owned by the state due to its strategic economic importance for all people, such as natural oil and electricity. Therefore, as manufacturing is based and powered by raw materials and economic natural resources, capital as an economic resource in that context should be researched from that perspective. These could be divided into three types. Firstly, minerals, metals in the ground (such as gold, silver, copper, led, iron etc.) and oil. The ownership of any of these items or similar items or the land that they are found in it should belong to the state and not individuals or a group of people. This is because of the national and social importance of these resources, and it should not be manipulated by small group in society. Secondly, the ownership of coasts, seas, rivers, places of worship and public and national parks. Thirdly, ownership of what is mutually shared by people, such as water and energy resources should not be an individual ownership.

The prophetic saying, "people are partners in three: water, sustenance, and fire," provides a guiding principle for an alternative economic view that emphasises the collective ownership and management of certain essential resources. This view is in line with the economic worldview we present here, where the ownership of economic resources is seen as belonging to all human beings collectively, and these resources are considered as part of God's trust to mankind.

Applying this principle to capital and ownership, our economic view distinguishes between private and public ownership based on the underlying purpose and the produced outcome of the economic resources. If an economic resource, such as electricity, is primarily intended for public use and serves essential needs of the society, then it is considered as public ownership. On the other hand, if it is primarily used for private purposes, it can be considered as privately owned. The decision is guided by how the resource traditionally benefits people and affects their daily lives.

In the case of public ownership, the state acts as a trustee and manages these resources on behalf of the people, ensuring fair and equal distribution of their benefits. The income generated from such resources can be used for the social and economic development of the society, which ultimately contributes to the economic prosperity and well-being of the entire population.

This alternative economic view emphasises the collective interest and well-being of the society over individual ownership and profit. By treating certain essential resources as public goods, it seeks to prevent the concentration of wealth and ensure that the benefits of these resources are shared by all. It aligns with the values of equity, justice, and social welfare, which are central principles in the faith-based economic worldview.

This perspective encourages a more egalitarian distribution of economic resources and emphasises the role of the state as a trustee in managing these resources for the benefit of society as a whole. It highlights the importance of economic policies and systems that promote fairness, balance, and social welfare in achieving economic prosperity for everyone.

c. **Labour**

Labour is the other three factors of production i.e., land, capital and entrepreneurship do not result in economic outputs without labour. Human effort is the key driver of economic factors of production, an individual farms a land, manages a factory, manufactures goods and trades. Thus, labour is an important source of wealth, as it is required for farming, manufacturing, and trading, which means it is an independent factor of production. Labour refers to human effort whether in the form of physical or mental activities. Therefore, the person performing this labour is called labourer, while it is more accurate description of the person who works for others to be called 'hired' as argued by some researchers.

This is due to the meaning of each and what each of labourer and hired refers to, as the former refers to the labour whether physical or mental activities being performed by the person requires such labour. While the latter refers to hiring someone who is a skilled worker to do such activities. In return performing the required work, this person is paid a fee, which is paid in monetary value or in kind according to this view. Economists define a contract of hire as a contract for a benefit in return for a compensation. They make the objective of making this contract to achieve a benefit, and fee or compensation paid in return to the hired person on the basis of achieving this benefit.

This means they placed the achieved benefit as the basis to determine the fee or financial compensation paid. In that context the hiring person receives the sought benefit for the hired worker, which becomes his own, in return he/she transfer their ownership of the agreed fee or money to the hired worker. This interpretation is what Jurists understood from the following verse in the Quran in relation to feeding babies by mothers after divorce where fathers are required to compensate them financially for breast feeding their babies, "… Then if they breast feed the babies for you, give them their due payment …", (Quran, Al-Talaq 65: 6).

Therefore, the subject matter of a hire contract either the benefit achieved, such as the clothes done by a tailor or furniture made by a carpenter, or the subject matter of the contract is the benefit obtained from the hired person themselves, such as a gardener or a nurse. It is reported that prophet Muhammad said: Whoever believes in God and the Day of Judgement, shall not hire a person until he agrees the hire fee with him/her. By analysing the meaning of economics as a science, economic system, and economic policy we conclude based on the understanding of those three meanings that economics is concerned with production and its increase, which is a universal meaning. While economic system is concerned with how wealth is generated and distributed, which is different among nations, whereas capitalism and communism are different to the theory we propose. As for economic policy, it is the economic roadmap for achieving national prosperity within the boundaries of the proposed economic worldview.

Hence, it becomes clear that the current global gap between different economic classes today is not the outcome of economic policy, is actually the outcome of the economic system that is concerned with wealth creation and distribution. Thus, the economic system I advocate here aims to guarantee for individuals their economic needs and necessities. Not only that, it also guarantees the space for healthy competition in providing labour to achieve complementary economic prosperity and for individuals to strive for a better economic life.

However, a question can be posed here about what determines what economic needs and necessities mean today? The answer is that it is important that basic economic needs are defined clearly and controlled. Which means that an individual is guaranteed a dignified life where basic economic needs are made available for individuals to live a healthy life where those basic economic needs are guaranteed. Such needs are determined based on time i.e., the era we live in, customs and place. For example, basic economic needs at a time of a global or national disaster, famine, or war (e.g., the second World War and the ration system introduced in the UK during the war to meet basic economic needs and preserve life) will be different to basic economic needs at a time of peace, stability, and economic prosperity.

Therefore, it is safe to say that basic economic needs across history in terms of goods are food, housing, clothing, and transport. As for basic services, this includes education and healthcare which should be freely available and accessible to all individuals in a society without discrimination on any basis. This is how the proposed economic view addresses this factor of production.

d. **Entrepreneurship**

This fourth factor of production is discussed by economists across the board, and also referred to in the classical writings of Islamic economics as trade (*tijarah*). Trade is the means by which produced goods and products from land and manufacturing is sold in the market, which makes trade equally important as the other three factors of production in an economy. Trade is considered as the fourth factor of production, alongside land, labour, and capital. Trade plays a crucial role in the economy as it involves the exchange and distribution of goods and products that are produced from land and manufacturing.

One of the key principles in cross-border trade in our proposed view is that the trader, not the goods, is the central focus. This means that the rules that apply to the goods being traded are determined by the rules that apply to the trader engaging in the trade. The reason for this is that cross-border trade falls under specific rules that govern trade among nations, including those in a state of war.

Regarding taxes on cross-border trade, the level of such taxes and types varies from capitalism, socialism, and Islamic economics. An alternative economic system e.g., prescribes specific rates for Zakat (compulsory religious tax on wealth) to be paid for imported goods. Traders pay ¼ of a tenth, and foreign traders living in Muslim countries or having treaties with those countries pay ½ of a tenth of the trade capital. Traders who have obtained sponsorship to import goods into countries pay one-tenth (1/10) as a custom tax.

It is important to note that while these rules were supported by the practice of the second caliph, Omar Ibn Al-Khattab, and the consensus of the companions of Prophet Muhammad at that time, they are not currently implemented or imposed by any Muslim country. Instead, contemporary man-made tax laws are typically used in modern trade transactions. The historical rules mentioned in classical Islamic economics writings serve as a reference point to understand the perspective of Islamic economics on cross-border trade and taxation.

## 12.18 Conclusion

This Chapter aimed to clearly outline the philosophy and founding foundations of the proposed Equitable Optimality economic theory. In doing so, it discusses and refers to various economic systems and thoughts where relevant. The steps to construct a more authentic economic theory include re-evaluating methodological approaches to align with ethical socio-economic framework, questioning underlying assumptions in economic models to ensure consistency with ethics, integrating ethical values into economic analyses, recognising, and incorporating institutions into economic models, shifting focus from mere economic growth to holistic human development, and promoting interdisciplinary research to enrich understanding.

Additionally, this Chapter emphasises the significance of contextual understanding in economic thought and interpretation. Economics texts provide meanings and understandings that connect with human existence and guide economic behaviour. The context of economic thought is essential for grasping the underlying meanings and implications of economic ideas and relating them to real-life experiences.

The proposed economic theory in this Chapter seeks to align with principles and values, providing a guiding framework and economic behaviour. It emphasises justice, fairness, and ethical conduct in economic activities and aims to create a more inclusive and just society, fostering social welfare and equitable distribution of resources.

To address current economic thoughts and practices and build a genuine economic theory, alternative foundations need to be established. These foundations should be rooted in socio-economic principles, values, and beliefs. The following steps where implemented in constructing a more authentic economic theory, as proposed here in this Chapter, drawing on lessons learned from existing capitalist theories and value-based approach from Islamic economic thought:

a) Revisiting Methodological Framework: Economists should re-evaluate their methodological approaches and ensure they are aligned and appropriate. This new proposed economics theory should not be viewed as a mere extension of mainstream economics but should have its own distinct approach.

b) Re-examining Assumptions: Question the underlying assumptions made in economic models and theories to ensure they are consistent with moral values and principles. For example, assumptions related to human behaviour, utility maximisation, and profit-seeking may need to be re-evaluated in light of the framework we developed here.
c) Embracing Ethical Foundations: Integrate ethical values, such as justice, compassion, and fairness, into economic analyses. These values should guide decision-making and resource allocation to foster social welfare and equitable distribution.
d) Incorporating Third-Sector Institutions: Recognise and incorporate social impact institutions into economic models. These institutions play a crucial role in promoting social justice and poverty alleviation.
e) Emphasising Human Development: Shift the focus from mere economic growth to holistic human development. Economics should prioritise the well-being of individuals and communities, aiming to enhance their spiritual, social, and economic welfare.
f) Promoting Interdisciplinary Research: Foster interdisciplinary research that bridges studies of moral economy, ethics, and economics. This approach will enrich the understanding of economics and its implications for society.

By adopting these alternative foundations that we aim to do in the economic theory we introduce, economists can pave the way for a genuine and robust alternative economic theory. It would not only provide a coherent framework for economic analysis but also align with the principles and values of a moral economy, leading to a more meaningful and effective approach to economic development and social welfare in societies globally.

The Chapter also delves into the concept of "Interest-Bearing Money" and explores its historical implications in the context of the Civil War era in the Southern Confederacy in the US. It explains how legal restrictions played a vital role in maintaining the coexistence of interest and non-interest-bearing money during that time, providing a nuanced perspective on monetary history and policy.

Furthermore, we highlighted the importance of understanding text and context in the study of economics and its broader application in economic thought. Contextual understanding helps individuals internalise the meanings and implications of economic ideas, making economic thought more relevant and applicable to real-life experiences.

Ultimately, the proposed economic theory seeks to align with conventional principles and values where possible, providing a guiding framework for new economic way of life and economic behaviour that address current and future economic challenges. It emphasises justice, fairness, and ethical conduct in economic activities and aims to create a more inclusive and just society, fostering social welfare and equitable distribution of resources.

This economic worldview governs all aspects of life, providing broad guidelines to navigate through life's challenges and requirements. While the pursuit of prosperity is encouraged, it should be within the boundaries of justice and ethical behaviour, recognising the interdependence of various stakeholders in the economic system. By adhering to this proposed economic worldview, we can achieve both material well-being and spiritual growth, living a purposeful and meaningful life that reflects our beliefs and values.

This Chapter is the first building block in constructing the Equitable Optimality economic theory, which sets out its foundations and philosophy. The construction of this economic theory continues in the next Chapter as we start shaping its practical application in the macroeconomic context. Therefore, it is important to comprehend this Chapter before moving on to the next one.

# Chapter 13
# Rethinking Economics, Constructing the Equitable Optimality Theory Part Two: Macroeconomics

## 13.1 Introduction

In the previous Chapter, I discussed the first building block in the construction of the Equitable Optimality economic theory, setting out its foundations and philosophy. The Chapter's primary objective was to provide a clear exposition of the philosophy and fundamental principles that underpin the proposed economic theory, the Equitable Optimality. In achieving this aim, it delved into various economic systems and ideologies where relevant. It discussed that the process of constructing a more genuine economic theory encompasses several critical steps. These steps encompass re-evaluating methodological approaches to align with an ethical socio-economic framework, critically examining foundational assumptions within economic models to ensure their coherence with ethical principles, integrating ethical values into economic analyses, acknowledging and incorporating institutional factors into economic models, shifting the focus from mere economic growth to encompass the broader concept of holistic human development, and encouraging interdisciplinary research to enhance comprehension.

Furthermore, this chapter underscores the importance of contextual comprehension within the realm of economic thought and interpretation. Economic texts provide meanings and interpretations that resonate with human existence and shape economic behaviours. Understanding the context of economic thought proves essential for grasping the inherent meanings and implications of economic concepts and linking them to real-life experiences.

This Chapter discusses part two of developing the Equitable Optimality economic theory, after we discussed its theoretical and philosophical underpinnings in the previous Chapter. Now, it is time to start calibrating the philosophical aspects into practical implementation, discussing how the philosophy of this proposed theory is embedded in its economic operating structure as a viable alternative. In this Chap. I address the issues of macroeconomics.



S. Alamad, *Beyond Profit*, Contributions to Economics,
https://doi.org/10.1007/978-3-031-49748-3_13

Macroeconomics is a branch of economics that deals with the study of the economy as a whole, rather than focusing on individual economic agents like households or firms. It examines the aggregate behaviour of economic variables such as total output (Gross Domestic Product, or GDP), unemployment, inflation, and national income. Macroeconomists analyse the factors that influence the overall performance of an economy and seek to understand how different policies and events can impact its growth, stability, and development.

The key objectives of macroeconomics include understanding the determinants of economic growth, employment levels, price stability, and the balance of trade. Macroeconomists study how changes in government policies, international trade, monetary systems, and fiscal measures can affect these key macroeconomic variables.

Some of the central topics within macroeconomics include:

*Economic Growth*: Macroeconomists study the factors that contribute to long-term economic growth and prosperity in a country. They examine how factors like investment, technological progress, and education impact an economy's ability to produce more goods and services over time.

*Unemployment*: Macroeconomics addresses the causes and consequences of unemployment. It analyses the various types of unemployment (frictional, structural, and cyclical) and assesses the effectiveness of policies to reduce unemployment rates.

*Inflation*: Refers to the sustained increase in the general price level of goods and services in an economy. Macroeconomists investigate the causes of inflation, its effects on purchasing power, and the tools available to control inflation, such as monetary policy.

*Fiscal and Monetary Policy*: These are two key tools that governments and central banks use to influence the overall economy. Fiscal policy involves government spending and taxation, while monetary policy involves the control of the money supply and interest rates by central banks. Macroeconomists analyse the impact of these policies on aggregate demand, output, and inflation.

*Trade and Exchange Rates*: Macroeconomics examines the role of international trade and exchange rates in determining a country's economic performance. It explores how trade balances, tariffs, and exchange rate fluctuations affect a country's growth and competitiveness in the global economy.

*Business Cycles*: Macroeconomists study fluctuations in economic activity over time, known as business cycles. They investigate the causes of booms and recessions and explore ways to stabilise the economy during these fluctuations.

To analyse these topics, macroeconomists use various models and methodologies, such as the aggregate demand-aggregate supply model, the Phillips curve, and the IS-LM model. They also use statistical data and econometric techniques to understand the relationships between different macroeconomic variables.

Macroeconomics plays a crucial role in informing policy decisions by governments, central banks, and international organisations. Policymakers rely on macroeconomic analysis to design strategies that aim to achieve sustainable economic growth, price stability, and full employment.

## 13.2 The Context

Macroeconomics encompasses various aspects of society's income distribution, including wages, profits, and rents. This division was particularly relevant during the classical economics era when these incomes corresponded to the three social classes: workers, capitalists, and landlords. However, in modern economies, especially in advanced countries, this division is challenged as many workers now earn profits through stock ownership, and certain professionals can also earn 'rent.'

Government actions often impact aggregate quantities like money supply, credit levels, taxes, subsidies, and grants, making them important subjects of study in the context of macroeconomics. This includes both monetary and fiscal policies.

Despite its distinct focus, macroeconomics is not entirely separate from microeconomics. Many tools and concepts developed in microeconomic analysis remain relevant in macroeconomics. Concepts like supply and demand, equilibrium, and the maximisation hypothesis continue to play a significant role in macroeconomic analysis. However, macroeconomics introduces unique concepts such as full employment, economic growth, and tools like the multiplier and the Phillips curve.

Methodological points discussed in the previous chapter are equally relevant to this chapter, particularly when addressing policy issues involving the role of the state in the economy. The substantial reduction of interest-based economies is a fundamental distinction in the Equitable Optimality economic theory, significantly impacting attitudes toward money and credit and their roles in the system. Consequently, the demand and supply of money and credit in an interest-free system become crucial subjects in this economic theory. However, being realistic and as the intent is to develop a practical economic theory that can be implemented, I am not proposing to completely eliminate interest-based money supply systems, as this would an impossible and unrealistic objective. However, I call in this theory for a balancing measure with elements from the real economy that would off-set negative impact of the existing interest-based system on the economy.

Interest plays a crucial role in savings and investment decisions, acting as a link between financial and real markets. Understanding how these two markets are linked in the absence of interest, as well as the determinants of savings and investment decisions in an interest-free profit-sharing system, becomes vital in an economics framework with this perspective. The practice of profit-sharing system and other trade-based finance modes in an interest-free system introduces the rate of mark-up as an additional variable to be studied.

Furthermore, studying the interrelationship between the rate of profit, rate of interest, and rate of mark-up in real-world economies where Equitable Optimality economic theory operates in an otherwise interest-based system is also important. These considerations shape the economic dynamics and decision-making processes in an Equitable Optimality economy and require careful examination and analysis within the framework of macroeconomics within this context.

According to Stiglitz and Greenwald (2003) credit differs from money in several significant ways. Firstly, money is uniform and identical, while credit varies in quality depending on the borrower. Each borrower's creditworthiness may differ, leading to variations in the terms and conditions of credit arrangements.

Secondly, regulating the supply of money is comparatively easier for the Social Authority than influencing the supply of credit. The central bank or government can control the money supply through various monetary policy tools, such as open market operations, reserve requirements, and interest rates. However, managing the supply of credit requires dealing with multiple financial institutions and borrowers, making it more complex to control.

Thirdly, the supply of credit involves information processing. Lenders need to gather and assess information about borrowers' creditworthiness, repayment capacity, and risk profile. Additionally, credit supply also entails risk-bearing by the lender, as there is a chance of default by the borrower.

Considering these distinctions, three alternatives for credit supply are commonly compared: interest-bearing loans (IBL), mark-up trade arrangements (MTA), and supplying funds on a profit-sharing basis (PS). Each of these approaches differs in terms of information costs, risk levels, and regulatory feasibility.

## 13.3 Aspects of Macroeconomics

In macroeconomics, it is essential for us to grasp the fundamental variables that frequently appear in subsequent discussions. Below is a list of these aspects, along with brief definitions, as commonly presented in standard textbooks on macroeconomics. Additionally, we should explain how to compute their values. Some qualitative variables, crucial for the behaviour of economic agents but challenging to quantify, are also provided, and their significance will become clearer as we proceed. Notably, the rate of mark-up, which has been previously defined, is included in the list.

1. Y: National Income, or real output of a country during a year. It is essential to distinguish between real income and money income, gross income and net income, total income, and disposable income.
2. C: Consumption, referring to total annual consumption unless otherwise specified.
3. I: Investment, distinguishing between gross and net investment.
4. S: Savings, referring to total annual savings unless otherwise specified.
5. E: A new variable not typically considered in conventional analysis. It represents total annual expenditure in the cause of Allah or social expenditure.
6. N: Employment, standing for the total labour employed.
7. P: Price level.
8. MS: Total money supply.

9. MD: Total money demand.
10. RP: Average rate of profit.
11. W: Average rate of wages.
12. CI: Minimum level of consumption for an individual.
13. PS: Ratio of profit sharing.
14. U: Rate of mark-up.
15. R: Rate of interest.
16. M: Moderation principle.
17. GI: Social goals of investment.
18. OE: Social objectives of employers.
19. L: Social considerations before labourers.

These variables are crucial in macroeconomic analysis and provide the foundation for understanding economic phenomena, policy formulation, and decision-making. As we delve deeper into the subject, the significance and interrelationships of these variables will become more apparent in the context of the Equitable Optimality economic theory.

In the context of our proposed theory, commencing a discussion in macroeconomics with an emphasis on money and banking is preferred for two significant reasons. First, money and credit, along with their demand and supply, play a critical role in determining other macroeconomic variables. Understanding their functions and management is crucial to understand how they influence key economic indicators. Second, this subject serves as a fundamental departure point for analysis in an interest-free or interest-balanced economy, where the management of money and credit can significantly alter economic outcomes. Therefore, it is essential to highlight the distinctive institutional arrangements in an Equitable Optimality system and explore their implications before delving into the theory of income determination.

Money serves as a medium of exchange, allowing for general acceptability in transactions. To fulfil this role, it must also act as a store of value between exchanges and as a unit of account or measure of value. Moreover, since money serves as both a store and measure of value, it facilitates deferred payments, with debts being made and repaid in monetary terms. These functions are upheld through social conventions supported by legal sanctions. It is worth mentioning how money emerged from society's experience with barter and the inefficiencies of such a system.

It is also essential to provide a brief description of various modern forms of money, such as coins, currency notes, demand deposits, and more recently cryptocurrencies and digital currencies. Deposits subject to checking and withdrawal on demand are considered money as they fulfil the functions mentioned earlier. Additionally, there are "near" monies that can perform similar functions to varying degrees. Government bonds, particularly those issued by countries like the United Kingdom and United States, are often considered the closest substitutes to money.

Mutual funds and other financial institutions holding a significant amount of high-quality bonds can also effectively supply credit to businesses and may offer withdrawal facilities to their clients-depositors. However, credit, while performing many money-like functions, is not easily regulated through simple quantitative measures like reserve requirements. The complexity of modern financial markets makes them less amenable to straightforward quantitative control and analysis.

This complexity arises due to credit's multifaceted role and its interplay with various financial instruments, making traditional regulatory measures insufficient for effective control and analysis. As we progress in formulating our theory, understanding these intricacies will be essential in appreciating the dynamics of the Equitable Optimality economic system and its unique approach to monetary management and banking.

The efficiency of money in fulfilling its functions is contingent upon the stability of its value, specifically its purchasing power. This stability, in turn, is determined by the balance between the demand for money and its supply.

When the demand for money matches its supply, the value of money remains relatively stable, and it can effectively serve as a medium of exchange, a store of value, and a unit of account. In such a scenario, individuals and businesses can confidently engage in transactions, plan for the future, and use money as a reliable measure of value.

However, if the demand for money exceeds its supply, a situation known as excessive demand, the value of money increases, resulting in deflation. In this case, the purchasing power of money rises, leading to a higher value of goods and services that can be purchased with the same amount of money. While this may initially appear advantageous, deflation can discourage spending and investment, as individuals and businesses anticipate even lower prices in the future, resulting in economic stagnation.

On the other hand, if the supply of money surpasses its demand, a condition referred to as excessive supply or inflation occurs. Inflation causes the value of money to decline, meaning that more money is required to purchase the same goods and services. As a consequence, inflation erodes the purchasing power of money, leading to rising prices and a reduction in the real value of savings. This can result in economic instability, as consumers may experience a decrease in their standard of living and businesses face uncertainty in planning and decision-making.

Therefore, our proposed theory is based on the efficient functioning of money, which depends on maintaining a balance between its demand and supply. When the demand for money aligns with its supply, the stability of its value is preserved, allowing money to effectively perform its roles as a medium of exchange, store of value, and unit of account. However, imbalances between demand and supply, such as deflation and inflation, can disrupt the efficient functioning of money and impact overall economic stability. Therefore, policymakers and central banks must carefully manage the money supply to achieve an optimal balance that supports sustainable economic growth and price stability. In the context of the Equitable Optimality economic system, the management of money and credit should align with ethical principles and values, fostering equitable distribution of wealth and promoting social welfare.

## 13.4 The Demand Side of Money

Money serves as a medium of exchange, facilitating transactions for both consumers and businesses. Similarly, credit plays a crucial role, especially for businesses, by enabling them to make necessary payments, such as wages and raw material purchases. Individuals and businesses also hold cash for precautionary reasons, as uncertainties in the future may require immediate access to cash.

Holding cash comes with an opportunity cost, as it means forgoing potential income that could be earned by investing in other assets. In an interest-free or interest-balanced economy as I advocate here in the proposed theory, alternative income-yielding assets range from shares and investment accounts with banks that meet the philosophical underpinnings of this theory to physical assets like real estate or equipment, which could generate rents or rentals. The cost of holding cash is thus the expected return on these alternative assets. Despite this cost, individuals and businesses prefer holding cash due to the convenience and security it offers for transactions and precautionary needs.

The demand for money to hold is inversely related to the expected rate of return on income-yielding assets. As the expected return on these assets increases, individuals and businesses may reduce their demand for money, choosing instead to invest in those assets. Conversely, a decline in the expected rate of return on alternative assets may lead to an increase in the demand for money to hold.

Keynes initially recognised speculative demand for money, which was directly related to bond prices in a simple world where bonds were the primary alternative to holding cash. However, in a more realistic setting, where wealth owners have multiple income-yielding asset options with varying degrees of liquidity, a separate speculative motive is not necessary. Instead, changes in the expected rates of return from different assets can lead wealth owners to adjust their asset allocation, potentially involving temporary holdings of cash when transitioning between assets. These temporary holdings should not be mistaken for changes in the overall demand for money, as they are merely a part of the wealth owners' portfolio reallocations. For the sake of simplicity, these temporary holdings can be assumed away in economic analysis.

The responsiveness of the demand for money to changes in the expected rate of return on income-yielding assets in an interest-free/balanced economy is a subject that requires empirical research. However, at the theoretical level, it can be argued that the demand for money curve will have a negative slope. This means that as the expected rate of return on alternative income-yielding assets increases, the amount of cash held for transactions and precautionary purposes will decrease, and vice versa.

The position of the demand for money curve relative to the Y axis (quantity of money demanded) will also depend on the level of income. At higher levels of income, more cash will be held at every expected rate of return, and vice versa. Nevertheless, the curve will never touch the Y axis, as long as there is a positive level of income, and there will always be some assets with a positive expected rate of return. Similarly, it will never touch the X axis, assuming that there will always be some convenience afforded by holding cash for transactions.

The speculative demand for money, which Keynes related to the rate of interest, does not apply to an interest-free economy, or would apply with minimum effect to an interest-balanced economy. This is because the expectations regarding the rate of return on shares, investment accounts, and other assets in an interest-free/balanced economy are not 'self-justifying' as they are in the case of bond prices and the rate of interest. In an interest-free/balanced economy, expectations about the rate of return on investments are likely to reflect real productivity and economic conditions rather than being solely driven by changes in subjective feelings.

For example, if economic conditions improve, generating expectations of a higher rate of profit, according to the model, the demand for money to hold may decline as people reduce their cash holdings for transactions and precautionary purposes. However, the actual increase in the rate of profit does not necessarily generate expectations of a decline in the rate of profit. Expectations in an interest-free/balanced economy are based on real factors and changes in these expectations will likely be tied to changes in real economic conditions rather than mere shifts in subjective sentiments of wealth owners.

Certainly, the issue of the demand for money and its relationship with income-yielding assets, as well as the concept of liquidity preference and risk, has been extensively studied by economists. As mentioned, two seminal works on this topic are Baumol (1952) and Tobin (1958), both provided valuable insights into the demand for money and its connection to various factors like interest rates and risk preferences. Their work laid the foundation for understanding the motives behind holding money.

However, in the context of an interest-free/balanced economy, there is a need to update the analysis to accommodate the unique features and characteristics of such a system. The insights offered by economists Stiglitz and Greenwald (2003) in their work 'Towards a New Paradigm in Monetary Economics' are particularly relevant for understanding the dynamics of an interest-free monetary system.

Incorporating Stiglitz and Greenwald's (2003) insights would enable a more comprehensive understanding of how income-yielding assets in an interest-free/balanced economy, as I propose here, may carry different expected rates of return, varying degrees of ease in convertibility to cash, and different levels of risk. This updated analysis could shed light on the implications for the demand for money in such an economic context.

Therefore, in a study focused on macroeconomics in the Equitable Optimality perspective, it would be essential to refer to and integrate the works of Baumol, Tobin, Stiglitz, and Greenwald to provide a comprehensive and contemporary understanding of the demand for money and its relevance in an interest-free/balanced economy.

## 13.5 The Supply Side of Money

In the context of our proposed Equitable Optimality theory, the fundamental principles and mechanisms of banking operations differ from conventional banking. The key distinction lies in how money is created and its relationship with real economic activities.

## *Conventional Banking System*

In the conventional banking system, money is primarily created through the process of lending and borrowing. When a bank provides a loan to a borrower, it credits the borrower's account with the loan amount. This new money comes into existence as a debt, and the borrower is obligated to pay it back with interest over time. This interest on loans becomes the main source of income for conventional banks. However, this process of creating money through debt does not necessarily have a direct link with the real production of goods and services in the economy.

## *Interest-Free/Balanced Banking in the Equitable Optimality System*

In this system, banking operates based on the philosophical principles I outlined in the previous Chapter, which advocate for moving away from the charging or paying of interest, towards an interest-free banking system. However, acknowledging the substantial challenges in doing so as the global economy currently is an interest-based system, I proposed an Interest-Balanced system. This system if founded on a planned large shift from an interest-based system to an interest-balanced economic system. Then, moving gradually in the global economy in planned and steady steps to a global economy that is more balanced, and possibly with greater weighting towards an interest-balanced economic system. This proposed interest-balanced economic system would start with 50/50 split, and then move in clearly defined steps to increase the weighting of an interest-balanced economic system gradually by 7–10% (7–10%) every five (5) years.

Instead, the focus is on profit-sharing and investment activities. In this banking system, money is created through investment and partnership arrangements, where the bank and the customer share the risk and rewards of the investment.

One prominent example for this is where the bank acts as an investor, and the customer provides the entrepreneurial expertise. Profits generated from the investment are shared between the bank and the customer based on a pre-agreed ratio, while losses are borne by the investor (the bank) unless they result from the customer's negligence or gross misconduct.

Another mode is encouraging partnership models of financing arrangements, which involves a joint partnership between the bank and the customer in a specific business venture. Both parties contribute capital and share profits and losses according to their respective equity participation.

The linkage between money creation and the real economy in Equitable Optimality banking system is more direct. Money is created when investments are made in real economic activities, leading to the creation of goods and services, job opportunities, and overall economic growth. As a result, the money supply in an interest-free/balanced economy is inherently tied to the expansion of productive economic activities, fostering a more stable and sustainable economic system.

Therefore, the contrast between interest-free/balanced banking and conventional Western banking lies in how money is created and the linkage between money creation and real economic activities. Equitable Optimality banking system emphasises investment and profit-sharing, ensuring a stronger connection between money supply and the growth of the real economy, while conventional banking relies on debt-based lending, which may not always be directly tied to real production and economic growth.

## 13.6 Proposing a Roadmap for the Sound Transition to an Interest-Free Financial Economy

Moving from an interest-based financial economy to an interest-free financial economy is a complex and multifaceted challenge that requires careful consideration of economic, legal, and social factors. Such a transition would represent a significant departure from the existing global financial system, which is deeply entrenched in interest-based banking and lending practices. In this section, we will explore several practical approaches and strategies that could facilitate this transition, emphasising the importance of a gradual and well-planned shift as discussed in the previous section.

### *Alternative Finance As a Model*

One practical approach to transitioning towards an interest-free financial economy is to draw inspiration from alternative finance models. This model promotes profit and loss-sharing arrangements and asset-backed financing. In this model financial institutions operate under these principles, and their success suggests that interest-free finance is not only feasible but also commercially viable.

Governments and central banks could encourage the growth of this finance model by creating a regulatory framework that accommodates its financial institutions. This framework would need to address issues related to taxation, accounting standards, and legal structures to ensure that alternative financial products can compete on a level playing field with conventional interest-based products to achieve this transition over time.

### *Promotion of Ethical and Socially Responsible Finance*

Another practical approach to move towards an interest-free financial economy is to promote ethical and socially responsible finance. This approach encourages financial institutions to consider the social and environmental impact of their investments and lending practices. It aligns with the principles of ethical finance, which prioritise investments that contribute to the well-being of society and the environment.

Governments can incentivise ethical finance by offering tax benefits or subsidies to financial institutions that prioritise ethical investments. They can also require financial institutions to disclose the environmental and social impact of their investments, allowing consumers to make more informed choices about where they deposit their money and how institutional and consumer economic behaviour is pushing towards ethical interest-free economy.

### *Development of Alternative Financial Instruments*

To transition towards an interest-free financial economy, it is essential to develop alternative financial instruments that provide attractive returns to investors without relying on interest payments. This can be achieved by creating innovative financial products based on profit-sharing, equity investments, and risk-sharing.

One example is the development of equity-based crowdfunding platforms, where investors buy shares in start-ups and small businesses in exchange for a share of future profits. This model provides an alternative to traditional debt financing.

### *Support for Financial Inclusion*

A critical aspect of transitioning to an interest-free financial economy is ensuring that all segments of society have access to financial services. Financial inclusion initiatives can help bring unbanked and underbanked populations into the formal financial system, providing them with opportunities for saving and investment.

Governments and international organisations can support financial inclusion by promoting digital financial services, creating financial literacy programs, and offering microfinance options that do not rely on interest-based lending.

### *Gradual Phasing Out of Interest-Based Instruments*

To transition from an interest-based financial economy, policymakers may consider a gradual phasing out of interest-based instruments. This could involve setting a timeline for the discontinuation of certain interest-bearing products and gradually reducing the availability of interest-based loans. This transition timeline could be similar to the one that governments in the UK, Europe and the US put in place for transitioning to electric vehicles and phasing out diesel and petrol vehicles due to their negative environmental impacts.

During this transition period, governments and central banks can encourage the adoption of interest-free alternatives and provide financial institutions with the necessary support and incentives to make this shift. This gradual approach can minimise disruptions to the financial system and allow businesses and consumers to adapt gradually.

### *International Collaboration and Standards*

Transitioning to an interest-free financial economy may require international collaboration and the development of global standards for ethical and interest-free finance. Countries that are committed to this transition can work together to create a supportive international environment. International organisations such as the United Nations, the World Bank and the International Monetary Fund can play a role in facilitating this transition by promoting ethical finance principles and providing technical assistance to countries seeking to adopt interest-free financial systems.

Moving from an interest-based financial economy to an interest-free financial economy is a complex endeavour that requires careful planning, collaboration, and innovation. While it represents a significant departure from the existing financial system, practical approaches such as the ones outlined above as a roadmap, promoting ethical finance, developing alternative financial instruments, supporting financial inclusion, phasing out interest-based instruments gradually, and fostering international collaboration can facilitate this transition.

It is essential to recognise that such a transition will not happen overnight, and it will require the commitment of governments, financial institutions, regulators, and civil society. Moreover, the success of this transition will depend on the ability to create financial products and systems that provide attractive returns to investors while adhering to interest-free principles. Moreover, educating the market, investors, and consumers about the benefit of this approach to all stakeholders and the global economy. Ultimately, the goal is to create a financial system that is not only economically sound but also ethically and socially responsible, contributing to the well-being of individuals and society as a whole.

## 13.7 Debt and Its Negative Impact on the Economy

Household debt constitutes funds borrowed by individuals, often from financial institutions or banks, encompassing obligations such as mortgages, personal loans, student loans, and outstanding credit card balances. Conversely, commercial debt pertains to financial obligations incurred by corporate and commercial entities. This distinction is essential for understanding financial dynamics.

Within the context of the United Kingdom, the ratio of debt to household income experienced a notable shift. It increased from 85% in 1996 to its zenith at 156% in

2008. Subsequently, during the 2008/09 recession, financial institutions displayed hesitancy in extending loans, while consumers exhibited reduced inclination towards credit. This convergence of factors led to a decline in the household debt-to-income ratio to 128% by late 2015. The following years witnessed an acceleration in household debt growth, culminating in the debt-to-income ratio escalating from 132% in Q4 2015 to 136% in Q4 2017, before subsiding to 132% by late 2019.[1]

The emergence of the Covid-19 global pandemic further influenced household debt dynamics. Although total household debt and the debt-to-income ratio experienced a gradual increase, propelled by mounting mortgage debt, this growth was offset by consumer repayments of unsecured debt. Commencing from Q1 2022, the debt-to-income ratio embarked on a downward trajectory, reaching 129% in Q1 2023, partially attributed to elevated interest rates.[2]

Figure 13.1 shows the level of household debt as a percentage of UK disposal income to illustrate the level of interest-based lending.

The rise in living costs has driven individuals to rely on both savings and debt to meet essential needs. This phenomenon has been accentuated by the escalating cost of living. Consequently, debt advice organisations like StepChange and Citizens Advice reported an upsurge in clients seeking debt assistance. The UK's Office for National Statistics (ONS) survey revealed that among adults witnessing a cost-of-living increase in July–August 2023 compared to the previous month, 19% resorted to higher credit utilisation in response.[3]

The interest rate framework established by the Bank of England significantly influences borrowing costs. However, the decision to set interest rates for consumers ultimately rests with individual banks and financial entities. Against the backdrop of soaring inflation, the Bank of England commenced a series of interest rate

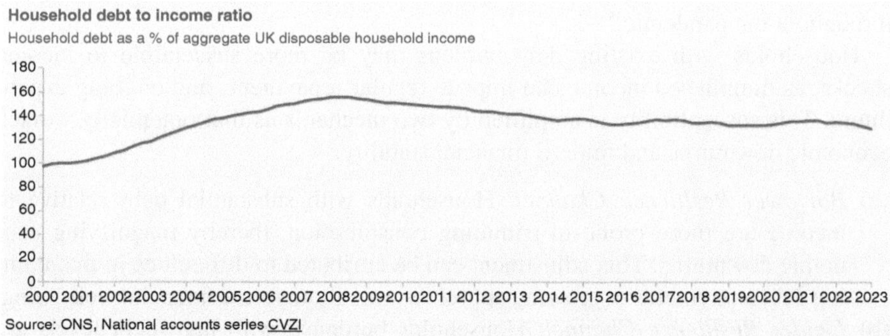


**Fig. 13.1** Household debt to income ratio

[1] Financial Lives January 2023: Consumer experience of the rising cost of living Financial Conduct Authority, 26 July 2023.

[2] https://www.bankofengland.co.uk/monetary-policy-report/2023/august-2023.

[3] Economic and fiscal outlook – March 2023 Office for Budget Responsibility, 15 March 2023.

hikes in December 2021. This trend culminated in the interest rate reaching 5.25% by August 2023.[4]

It is worth noting that while debt can have short-term benefits by boosting economic growth through heightened consumer spending, the presence of elevated debt levels within an economy can exacerbate the severity and duration of a recession in the medium term. This was corroborated by the Global Financial Stability Report (GFSR) in October 2017, which underscored the importance of managing financial stability to ensure sustained economic growth. The report also highlighted the interconnectedness of financial conditions and the distribution of future GDP growth.

Notably, households burdened with substantial debt have historically displayed a greater tendency to curtail spending during and post-recession, thereby heightening the likelihood of loan defaults and subsequently impacting lenders. The COVID-19 crisis has introduced unique challenges, affected households' financial situations and influencing their capacity to service debts. The pandemic's impact on income and employment opportunities has been a prominent characteristic of the crisis.

Historical patterns have shown that households with elevated debt levels tend to amplify economic shocks. Such households, grappling with mounting debt repayments and financial concerns, may drastically reduce spending, thereby increasing the risk of default or resorting to savings. This phenomenon can lead to negative feedback loops and exacerbate economic downturns while also posing threats to financial stability.

Research aimed at evaluating the impact of household debt on economic performance during the COVID-19 pandemic showed the negative impact of debt. The study examines the shock's impact on different household segments, their responses, and the subsequent implications for their debt burdens. Leveraging data provided by the Bank of England, this study utilises a combination of aggregate statistics and household surveys to gain comprehensive insights into household debt dynamics throughout the pandemic.[5]

Households with existing debt burdens may be more susceptible to income shocks, as diminished income can impede regular repayments and ongoing expenditure. This susceptibility is amplified by two mechanisms that potentially worsen economic downturns and imperil financial stability:

(a) *Borrower Resilience Channel*: Households with substantial debt relative to income are more prone to trimming consumption, thereby magnifying economic downturns. This adjustment can be attributed to difficulties in maintaining debt repayments or growing apprehensions about future financial well-being.
(b) *Lender Resilience Channel*: Households burdened with high debt levels are more liable to default on their obligations, causing losses for lenders. This dynamic can impede lenders' capacity to provide credit to the broader economy, thus exacerbating economic contractions.

[4] Monetary Policy Report - August 2023 Bank of England, 3 August 2023.

[5] Monetary Policy Report - August 2023 Bank of England, 3 August 2023.

Empirical evidence[6] underscores the linkage between household debt and the magnitude of consumer spending reductions during economic downturns. For instance, research indicates that countries characterised by elevated household debt relative to income observed more substantial declines in aggregate consumption during the global financial crisis. This trend is echoed in individual household behaviour, with those carrying higher pre-crisis mortgage debt relative to income being more inclined to adjust their spending.

It is worth noting that households entered the COVID-19 pandemic in a more resilient financial position compared to the aftermath of the global financial crisis. Factors such as lower interest rates, post-financial crisis reforms, and a better-capitalised banking system have contributed to this enhanced resilience. Additionally, the policy response to the pandemic, including measures such as the Coronavirus Job Retention Scheme (CJRS) and the Coronavirus Self-Employment Income Support Scheme (SEISS), has curtailed the impact on household incomes to a significant extent.

This research recognises that renters have been more adversely affected by the pandemic's financial repercussions compared to homeowners. Renters have faced challenges such as job losses or furloughs more frequently, which could have broader economic implications due to potential credit defaults and the possible sale of properties by buy-to-let landlords.

In conclusion, the relationship between debt and economic performance during an economic shock is vital. We examined various channels through which debt dynamics interact with economic shocks and potentially magnify their impact. We leveraged comprehensive household surveys and data to shed light on the complex interplay between household debt, economic downturns, and financial stability.

Debt and indebtedness hold the potential to provide a transient impetus to economic expansion in the short term, primarily due to the augmented expenditure of borrowing households. Nevertheless, in the medium term, an elevated prevalence of debt within an economy can contribute to exacerbating the severity and protraction of economic recessions. This effect is underscored by the behaviour of households encumbered with substantial debt levels, particularly evident during and following recessions.

Specifically, households burdened by high debt levels tend to exhibit more pronounced reductions in spending compared to their counterparts with lower indebtedness. This phenomenon is especially noticeable in the aftermath of economic downturns. Furthermore, this subset of households demonstrates a heightened propensity to default on their outstanding debt obligations, thereby causing financial losses for lending institutions.

The combination of reduced spending and heightened default rates among heavily indebted households can compound the depth and duration of a recession. This interconnectedness is a key factor in understanding the nuanced relationship between debt, economic performance, and financial stability. Therefore, our

[6] Monetary Policy Report - August 2023 Bank of England, 3 August 2023, available at: https://www.bankofengland.co.uk/monetary-policy-report/2023/august-2023.

proposed theory argues for a balanced approach of interest-balanced/free financial economy, with more weighting of the real economy to minimise the negative impact of the debt-based economy. This will be discussed further in the coming sections.

## 13.8 Unravelling the Interplay of Finance, Consumption, and Economic Stability

In the intricate tapestry of economics, where threads of theory and practice, wealth and poverty, growth and recession, and lending and borrowing intricately interweave, one strand often overlooked yet profoundly influential is household debt. Seemingly commonplace, yet intricately connected to the vibrancy of modern economies, the role of household debt is both a boon and a bane. It can catalyse economic growth but also precipitate financial crises. It can elevate living standards but also deepen inequality. It can foster consumption but also sow the seeds of recession.

In this section and the sections that follow, I will take you on a journey through the complex landscape of household debt, shedding light on its multifaceted nature and far-reaching consequences. As economists, policymakers, and concerned citizens, we must grasp the intricacies of this financial force that shapes the well-being of individuals and the stability of nations.

### *The Paradox of Household Debt*

Household debt, characterised as the accumulated financial obligations of individuals and families, is a multifaceted phenomenon. At first glance, it may seem a means to an end, a tool for purchasing homes, financing education, or smoothing consumption. However, beneath this seemingly benign exterior lies a paradox.

In the short term, household debt acts as an economic accelerant, fuelling spending and stimulating demand. Borrowing families can furnish their homes, send their children to college, and indulge in the occasional splurge, all thanks to loans and credit. This debt-driven consumption injects vigour into economies, fostering growth, creating jobs, and increasing prosperity.

Yet, as we delve deeper into this intricate web of financial commitments, a different picture emerges. The seductive allure of easy credit can lead households down a perilous path. As debts accumulate, financial pressures mount. The obligation to meet interest payments and repay principal can strain budgets, curbing discretionary spending and reducing the capacity to save. When the inevitable economic downturn arrives, these debt-laden households find themselves ill-prepared to weather the storm.

### *The Tug of War: Short-Term Gain vs. Long-Term Pain*

This tug of war between the short-term benefits and long-term consequences of household debt lies at the heart of our exploration. We dissect the economic dynamics at play, examining how borrowing can both boost and hinder economic growth.

In the immediate aftermath of borrowing, consumption rises, businesses thrive, and the economy flourishes. However, this economic buoyancy is often built on shaky ground. The increased financial fragility of heavily indebted households renders them vulnerable when adversity strikes.

When economic headwinds blow, whether due to a global financial crisis or a localised shock, indebted households are more likely to retrench. Their reduced spending reverberates throughout the economy, triggering a cascade of consequences. Businesses face diminished demand, leading to layoffs and reduced investments. Unemployment rises, and economic growth falters. In essence, the debt-driven boost becomes a debt-induced drag.

### *Navigating the Challenges*

As we embark on this exploration of household debt, we confront a fundamental question: How can societies harness the benefits of borrowing while mitigating the risks? This question is not only of academic interest but of paramount importance to policymakers and individuals alike.

Throughout this journey, we confront numerous facets of this challenge. We investigate the impact of interest rates, government policies, and financial regulations on household debt. We assess the resilience of households in the face of economic shocks and explore how they adapt to changing financial circumstances. We consider the broader implications for economic stability and financial resilience, pondering whether there are viable strategies to navigate these treacherous waters.

Our exploration does not confine itself to the realm of economics alone. Indeed, understanding household debt necessitates a multidisciplinary approach. We draw upon insights from psychology, sociology, and behavioural economics to comprehend the decisions individuals make when borrowing and repaying debts. We delve into the ethical dimensions, questioning the responsibilities of both borrowers and lenders in this intricate financial dance.

While this exploration is intended to deepen our understanding of household debt, it also serves a broader purpose—the imperative of financial literacy. As individuals and communities, we must equip ourselves with the knowledge and tools to navigate the complex financial landscapes we inhabit. Whether you are a student contemplating your first student loan, a homeowner managing a mortgage, or a policymaker shaping economic regulations, this journey into the world of household debt holds relevance.

## 13.9 The Real Economy

As our proposed economic theory is rooted in the real economy, I should discuss this aspect briefly before moving on in our discussion.

The term "real economy" refers to the tangible production and consumption of goods and services in an economy. It encompasses all the physical and productive activities that create value and contribute to the overall economic output. The real economy is contrasted with the financial economy, which deals with financial transactions, investments, and the trading of financial assets (see e.g., Palley, 2012; Gordon, 2014; Stiglitz, et al., 2009; Stockhammer, 2017). The real economy is crucial for economic growth, job creation, and the overall welfare of individuals and societies. It is the foundation upon which financial activities and transactions are built, and its performance is closely monitored by policymakers and economists to guide economic policies and ensure sustainable development.[7]

The real economy plays a crucial role in driving economic growth and job creation, and this importance is supported by various academic discussions and theories. I list some of those below to illustrate this discussion.

*Production and Output*: The real economy represents the actual production of goods and services, which is the basis for economic growth. According to classical economic theories, such as the neoclassical growth model, the increase in production and output leads to economic expansion and higher GDP levels (Solow, 1956). This growth, in turn, creates opportunities for investment, innovation, and employment.

*Labour Market Dynamics*: The real economy is directly linked to the labour market. As production increases, firms require more labour to meet the rising demand for goods and services. This leads to job creation and reduces unemployment rates. Empirical evidence supports the positive relationship between economic growth and job creation (Calmfors, 1995).

*Income Generation*: In the real economy, individuals and households earn income from their labour and entrepreneurial activities. This income is a critical determinant of consumer spending, which is a key driver of economic growth. As people have more disposable income, they can spend on goods and services, further boosting demand and production (Keynes, 1936).

[7] Palley (2012), pp. 391–410. doi:10.1080/09538259.2012.674390 This article discusses the post-Keynesian approach to understanding the real economy and its relevance in modern economic analysis. Gordon (2014). Retrieved from https://www.nber.org/papers/w19895 This working paper explores the slowdown in U.S. economic growth and its implications for the real economy. Minsky (1982). M. E. Sharpe. In this book, economist Hyman Minsky discusses financial instability and its impact on the real economy. Stiglitz et al. (2009). Report by the Commission on the Measurement of Economic Performance and Social Progress. Retrieved from https://www.insee.fr/en/statistiques/fichier/2019951/GDPBeyond2008.pdf This report presents a comprehensive analysis of economic measurement and the need to go beyond GDP to better capture the well-being and performance of the real economy. Stockhammer (2017), pp. 1253–1274. doi:10.1093/cje/bew053 This article examines the impact of wage-led versus profit-led demand on the real economy, drawing insights from the works of Kalecki and Minsky.

*Investment and Capital Accumulation*: Economic growth in the real economy encourages firms to invest in new technologies, machinery, and infrastructure to meet the expanding demand. Investment contributes to capital accumulation, which, according to the neoclassical growth theory, leads to sustained economic growth in the long run (Solow, 1956).

*Human Capital Development*: A growing real economy provides opportunities for skill development and human capital accumulation. As firms expand and require a skilled workforce, individuals invest in education and training to enhance their employability. Human capital development contributes to increased labour productivity and economic growth (Becker, 1964).

However, it is essential to acknowledge that the relationship between the real economy, economic growth, and job creation is not without challenges:

(a) Economic Cycles and Fluctuations: The real economy is subject to business cycles, characterised by periods of economic expansion and contraction. Economic downturns can lead to job losses and lower economic growth. Theories like Keynesian economics emphasise the role of government intervention in managing these cycles through fiscal and monetary policies (Keynes, 1936).
(b) Structural Changes: Technological advancements and changes in consumer preferences, as it is clearly witnessed nowadays, can lead to structural shifts in the real economy. While innovation can boost productivity and create new industries, it may also render some jobs obsolete, leading to unemployment and skill mismatches (Autor et al., 2003).
(c) Inequality and Distribution: The benefits of real economic growth may not be evenly distributed among all segments of society. Some individuals and groups may experience rising incomes and improved job opportunities, while others face stagnation or job insecurity (Piketty, 2014). Income inequality can hamper the inclusive growth and well-being of a society.

Thus, the real economy's significance for economic growth and job creation is firmly established in economic theory and empirical research. However, policymakers must address the challenges and inequalities that may arise from economic fluctuations and structural changes to ensure sustainable and inclusive growth in the real economy. Our proposed Equitable Optimality theory which advocates real economy provides some solutions that are rooted in its economic and philosophical approach for the real economy's challenges that we discussed above. It ensures equality of distribution, managed structural change via e.g., the PS system, and minimise the impact of economic cycle, in a much better way than the financial economy. Therefore, if we analyse and contrast the real economy with the financial economy, we can conclude the following.

The real economy and the financial economy are two interconnected components of an overall economic system, but they operate differently and serve distinct purposes:

1. Definitions:

- Real Economy: The real economy refers to the production, distribution, and consumption of goods and services. It involves physical transactions, such as manu-

facturing products, providing services, and engaging in trade. The real economy encompasses industries, businesses, and households engaged in tangible economic activities.
- Financial Economy: The financial economy, also known as the financial sector, deals with the management and exchange of financial assets, such as stocks, bonds, currencies, and derivatives. It includes banks, financial institutions, investment firms, and financial markets where financial instruments are traded.

2. Nature of Transactions:

- Real Economy: Transactions in the real economy involve the exchange of physical goods and services for money. For example, when a company sells a product to a customer or when a person pays for a service, it is a real economy transaction.
- Financial Economy: Transactions in the financial economy involve the exchange of financial assets or instruments. These transactions are often intangible and involve contracts or agreements. For instance, buying shares of a company's stock or investing in a mutual fund involves financial economy transactions.

3. Focus and Purpose:

- Real Economy: The real economy focuses on the production and consumption of goods and services to meet the needs and wants of individuals and businesses. Its purpose is to create value, generate income, and foster economic growth and development.
- Financial Economy: The financial economy focuses on the mobilisation and allocation of capital and resources. Its purpose is to facilitate investment, savings, and risk management. It plays a crucial role in channelling funds from savers to borrowers and in providing financial services.

4. Risks and Returns:

- Real Economy: In the real economy, risks and returns are directly related to the production and sale of goods and services. Companies and individuals face operational risks and uncertainties, and their returns are based on the success of their business activities.
- Financial Economy: In the financial economy, risks and returns are associated with financial assets and investments. Financial markets can be subject to volatility and speculation, leading to potentially higher returns but also higher risks, such as market risk and credit risk.

5. Impact on the Overall Economy:

- Real Economy: The real economy has a tangible impact on the overall economic growth and employment levels. When production and consumption increase, it leads to higher GDP growth and more job opportunities.
- Financial Economy: The financial economy influences the allocation of capital and resources, affecting the efficiency of the real economy. It can contribute to

economic growth by facilitating investment and capital formation, but it can also create risks, as seen during financial crises.

Hence, our proposed economic theory advocates more balance towards the real economy. The key changes that our proposed theory argues for are directed to the financial economy as discussed above, and in the previous Chapter. Ensuring that the financial economy is an interest-balanced system shifting towards an interest-free system gradually. This is achieved by amending the nature and purpose of the activities of the financial economy to be aligned with the Equitable Optimality economy. I aimed to draw this contrast between the real economy and financial economy, so you (the reader) can appreciate the impact of each on the economy in light of the theory I am proposing as an alternative. I hope I was successful in making that clearer.

I would further draw your attention to the Focus, Risk and Return aspects of the discussion above and how this leads to the last point of Overall Economic Impact. This is why I am calling for Rethinking Economics in light of the proposed theory and how it deals with these aspects of the real and financial economies. Real economy deals with the tangible production and exchange of goods and services, driving economic growth and job creation.

On the other hand, the financial economy deals with intangible financial assets and transactions, playing a crucial role in mobilising capital and managing risks, which can be done in a more tangible way aligned to the real economy as we argued. Both the real and financial economies are essential components of an overall economic system, and their interactions can significantly impact the overall economic performance and stability. However, they can be based on different more normative approaches, particularly in the case of the financial economy.

## 13.10 Making the Case for an Interest-Balanced/Free Financial Economy

In the interest-balanced/free financial economy, banking companies operate based on the principles of partnership, mark-up trades and profit-sharing. These banks accept deposits from the public through two types of accounts: current accounts payable on demand and investment accounts on the basis of profit-sharing. Many economists and policymakers may argue that might be unrealistic. I fully acknowledge the fact that the financial economy is dependent on interest as an interest-based model. However, let us take many steps back, after we have seen various economic and financial crises caused by the current financial economy model, we find that interest (usury) was banned across all religions and also philosophy of previous civilisations. Thus, surely this is a clear indicator why we should move gradually from this financial economy model as I outline in this proposed theory. In the section I present supporting discussion of this fact, and I would urge you to bear this mind throughout the book, then you would appreciate why I include religious supporting thoughts and statements within my book while I am discussing an economic theory.

During the fourth century BC, Aristotle espoused the view that money, while serving as a medium of exchange, lacked intrinsic value because it was a human social construct devoid of inherent utility. Additionally, Aristotle argued against charging interest, deeming it fundamentally wrong because, apart from its lack of intrinsic worth, money lacked self-replicating properties (Aristotle, 1948). This perspective was shared by other influential thinkers like St. Thomas Aquinas, who contended that money could not reproduce itself, and St. Bonaventure, who unequivocally stated that money did not yield fruit by itself (Aquinas, 1948).

Aristotle identified two primary purposes for money. Firstly, it was meant to provide for the household, a necessity imbued with honour. Secondly, it was intended for retail trade, a mode of exchange in which individuals gained from one another but was considered unnatural. He further argued that although money was designed for exchange, it should not be used to generate interest as it was intended for consumption. Aristotle explicitly defined usury as "the birth of money from money," a concept he rejected as the most unnatural way of accumulating wealth since the offspring (interest) was identical to the parent (the principal) (Aristotle, 1948).

Throughout history, the charging of interest has been a contentious subject, extensively debated by philosophers. While it was common practice to levy a fee for lending money or goods, various civilisations introduced regulations to either completely ban interest or, at the very least, restrict the amount that could be charged. Simultaneously, investments in trade and partnerships, where investors assumed some level of risk, were generally permitted, and even encouraged. In the early centuries AD, debates on usury and its permissibility were chiefly led by religious scholars such as St. Thomas Aquinas, Ibn Rushd, and John Calvin. In subsequent centuries, as Church and State separated in Europe, the debate shifted to parliaments and prominent economists of the era, including Adam Smith (Goff, 1990).

In Judaism, both the Torah and the Talmud unequivocally prohibit the charging of interest on loans, making no distinction between charitable personal loans and commercial ones. Two Hebrew terms are employed to describe interest: "Neshekh," which literally means "a bite" and conveys the painfulness of such charges to the debtor, and "Ribbit," which translates to "increase" and denotes the gain on the creditor's side (Jewish Encyclopedia, 1906).

The essence of these Jewish laws prohibiting interest is deeply rooted in religion (Levine, 2010). The Torah explicitly identifies the prohibition on interest in various verses, including Deuteronomy 23:20–21, Exodus 22:24, and Leviticus 25:36–37 (The Holy Bible, n.d.). While there are many similarities between the Torah and the Old Testament, the interpretations between both religions differ slightly. In the Torah, for instance, Deuteronomy 23:21 specifies, "You may [however] give interest to a gentile, but to your brother, you shall not give interest, in order that the Lord, your God, shall bless you in every one of your endeavours on the land to which you are coming to possess" (The Holy Bible, n.d.).

Within the context of Christianity, early definitions of usury drew upon various teachings, including those of St. Ambrose and St. Jerome. These theologians asserted that usury encompassed anything received in return for a loan that exceeded the principal amount lent. Usury was not limited to money loans but applied to loans involving any asset. Prohibitions against usury were also embedded in historical documents such as the Capitulary of Nijmegen (806 AD), which declared, "There is usury wherever one demands more than one gives," and Gratian's Decretum, which stated, "Everything that is demanded beyond the capital is usury" (Levine, 2010).

Biblical references, including Deuteronomy 23:19–20, Exodus 22:25, and Leviticus 25:35–37, consistently condemned the idea of profiting from money itself. Both the Old and New Testaments regarded earning money through usury as a sin, as was the mere expectation of gaining more than the principal amount lent. Charging a higher price for a sale on credit was also considered implicit usury. The legal code additionally mandated that all gains obtained through usury be fully reimbursed to the rightful owner (Levine, 2010).

In his Summa Theologica, penned between 1225 and 1274, St. Thomas Aquinas delved into the sin of usury in question LXXVIII, posing four sub-questions for contemplation. He questioned whether it was sinful to receive usury for a loan, whether any other consideration for a loan was lawful, whether one was obliged to return gains acquired through usurious practices, and whether it was permissible to borrow money at usury. Aquinas argued that receiving usury for a loan was unjust for multiple reasons. It involved the sale of something that did not exist, perpetuated inequality among individuals, which contradicted justice, and essentially traded in fictitious commodities (Aquinas, 1948).

During Aquinas's era, theologians did not dismiss the notion that capital could be employed productively, with those providing capital deserving compensation for making it available. Their primary objection lay with lending at interest when no economic purpose was served or when the lender assumed no risk (Aquinas, 1948).

Adam Smith, in his seminal work "The Wealth of Nations," echoed similar sentiments. He contended that "something ought everywhere to be paid for the use of money" since money could be employed profitably in various endeavours. Smith advocated that the lowest rate of interest charged should slightly exceed the level required to compensate for occasional losses to which lending was exposed, acknowledging the inherent credit risk faced by lenders. While Smith opposed anti-usury laws, he believed in establishing a maximum interest rate slightly above the market rate on a secure investment, thus preventing excessive speculation (Smith, 1776).

In contrast to Christianity, where religious doctrine takes precedence, Islam places greater emphasis on ethics and collective morality rather than religion itself (Goff, 1990). While the core of Islamic Law consists of the Quran and the Sunnah, it has not always provided explicit answers to the application of its principles in daily life. Much like in Judaism and Christianity, religious philosophers in Islam utilised various techniques to provide further clarity on a range of matters. These methods included Ijma'a (consensus of independent jurists from the Ummah of the Prophet), Qiyas (analogy or case law), and ijtihad (interpretation).

Similar to Christianity and Judaism, Sharia contains references to the prohibition of usury, primarily found in chapters such as Al-Baqarah (2), Al-Imran (3), and Ar-Rum (30). The ban on interest in Islamic tradition is typically interpreted as absolute and without qualification.

The Arabic term "*riba*" is commonly translated as "increase" or "excess." In the strictest sense, it refers to an amount or rate due in excess of the principal of a loan. However, the most accurate interpretation has been a subject of historical controversy, given room for interpretation in the associated verses. Omar Ibn al-Khattab, for example, expressed uncertainty about whether riba referred to usury (excess) or had a broader meaning of increase. In the latter case, any inequality in a trade, such as the exchange of unequal quantities or qualities of assets, would be considered usury. While some scholars restrict *riba* to money and money-like assets, Omar advised caution by adding "give up usury or anything resembling it" (Al-Suwaidi, 1993).

During the fourteenth century AD, in the time of Ibn Khaldun, economic activity was constrained by the Quran and the Sunnah. Many commercial transactions were forbidden, and *riba* was viewed as an illicit gain applicable not only to loans but also to brokers and traders (Armstrong, 2000). Ibn Khaldun made references to usury in his writings, acknowledging that money changing occurred but specifying that "the money-changer must not grant credit and receive increment." He also noted the risks associated with money changing and declared "any loan bringing benefit [to the lender] is unlawful."

However, the prohibition of *riba* did not imply that profit-making was forbidden. On the contrary, wealth generation was highly valued, benefiting both individuals and society. The interplay between supply, demand, and price was recognised, allowing merchants to sell goods at prices influenced by market forces. They were permitted to sell at a profit, provided that demand warranted it. Additionally, storing goods until prices improved was allowed. A clear distinction was drawn between profit, defined as income derived from effort and strength, and capital accumulation, represented by profits exceeding the merchant's needs (Al-Suwaidi, 1993).

Therefore, it is not academically and scholarly appropriate to ignore all the above religious condemnation of interest (usuary) on the basis that economics has no religion. As researchers and scholars, we should consider all facts and concepts, and acknowledge them even when they disagree with our thinking or ideological stance. While I fully consider the criticism of religion by some researchers and its exclusion of our economic life according to their views, we should draw clear distinction between religion itself and its divine teachings on one hand, and those who miss-practice it and misrepresent it on the other hand. Our views about religious concepts should not be based on wrong practices by those who represent any religion, it should be based on understanding the text and context of the true divine text and make our judgement accordingly. Moreover, while it is claimed that religions are divisive and a source of division and conflict, I have to say that we should clearly acknowledge the religious unity among all major religions globally, as discussed above, regarding banning any involvement with interest-based transactions, which is considered a sinful act. This religious unity about this economic notion surely must count for something and for us to contemplate and consider in our economic debates the wisdom behind it and take note of that.

Now, let us continue with the discussion on how we can move from interest-based financial economy towards interest-balanced and eventually to an interest-free financial economy according to this proposed economic theory. In this context, interest will be replaced with profit sharing alternatives, as explained below in relations to banking products and deposits.

*Current Accounts*: Depositors who open current accounts are essentially providing loans to the banks, and their deposits are repayable on demand. However, since these deposits act as guaranteed repayments to depositors, they are not entitled to any dividend or interest. Thus, they are interest-free accounts.

*Investment Accounts*: Banks also invite deposits into investment accounts, where depositors become partners with the bank in a profit-sharing arrangement. In this setup, the depositors agree to share in the profits generated by the bank's investments using these deposits. However, they also bear the risk of any losses that may occur as a result of those investments.

The main business of these banks in this approach revolves around providing funds to businesses on the basis of profit-sharing, which is rooted in the real economy. Instead of traditional interest-based lending, the banks enter into partnerships with entrepreneurs and participate in business management. They may also engage in activities such as buying and leasing physical assets, earning rents and rentals.

Another practice in this alternative banking system is a credit-sale financing arrangement, where the bank purchases goods on behalf of a client and sells them to the client at a markup, with the price to be paid later on an instalment basis. This enables the bank to earn a profit without resorting to interest-based transactions.

Furthermore, banks also offer various customary banking services, such as safe deposits, money transfers, acting as agents, and providing other services for fees, as long as interest is not involved. This approach can be easily visualised with recent emergence of alternative digital banking and FinTech financial services.

To oversee the monetary system and regulate the supply of money, there exists a central bank in the economy. The central bank has the authority to create money and control its supply. It can add to the money supply by providing investible funds to the government for public sector enterprises or to commercial banks, which, in turn, supply these funds to businesses. This could take different forms, including purchasing shares in public sector enterprises or creating central deposits and opening investment accounts with commercial banks, allowing them to invest in the real sector.

Economists have different perspectives on the monetary system, particularly regarding the role of commercial banks in money creation. Some economists advocate for a fractional reserve system in banking, where commercial banks are allowed to create new money through the lending process. Others argue in favour of a 100% reserve system, wherein only the central bank has the authority to create new money in line with the growth of real output (production).

Under a fractional reserve system, commercial banks create new money by lending out a portion of the deposits they receive. This money creation process is based on the expectation that the funds will be used for productive projects, generating profits that can cover the banks' liabilities. However, if the projects financed by the loans turn out to be unproductive and result in losses, the money returned to the bank will be reduced by the amount of the loss incurred.

In contrast, a 100% reserve system, as we argue in our theory, advocates that money creation should only occur through the central bank, and this process should be linked to the expansion of real output (the growth of the economy). In this system, commercial banks supply funds for productive projects through profit-sharing investment, ensuring that the supply of money is directly connected to the supply of goods and services in the economy. Consequently, money creation is tightly tied to actual economic output.

The introduction of a trade-based model of finance, into the current financial model does not fundamentally alter the correspondence between money supply and real output in the interest-balanced/free Equitable Optimality system. Financing production through money created in the process of lending, as seen in conventional interest-based systems, fails to maintain this correspondence because loan repayment and interest returns are not directly linked to actual output.

In the interest-balanced/free banking system, interest-free loans would have a minor role, and the vast amounts of outstanding debts commonly seen in conventional systems, as well as their ease of monetisation, would not be possible. Debts arising from mark-up sale financing and other trade-based financial instruments in this system do not exhibit the characteristics of interest-bearing debts.

To further elaborate on these points, I should provide detailed explanations of both conventional banking and Equitable Optimality banking. This should be followed by a brief discussion of other financial intermediaries in contemporary interest-based systems, as well as how these intermediaries would function in the interest-balanced/free system as envisioned by this theory. This will help the understanding of the key differences and principles that underpin the two systems.

## 13.11 Consumption

In an interest-free economy, assuming that the monetary authority will expand the supply of money (MS) in correspondence with the growth of real output, the supply of money would be a function of the level of income (Y) and the price level (P). On the other hand, the demand for money (MD) would be a function of the level of income and the expected average rate of profit in the economy (?).

The spending behaviour of income recipients in the society is characterised by allocating a major part of their current income to consumption. Additionally, income recipients are assumed to allocate part of their income to support others in the form of gifts, grants, and contributions to social institutions, including the state. The remaining income after consumption expenditure (C) is then divided between expenditure on others (E) and saving (S), such that:

$$Y = C + S + E$$

The consumption function is influenced by various factors, but in the short run, the single most influential factor is income. For individuals within this proposed economic theory, consumption is subject to certain constraints, and other restricted items under the moral and ethical principles. Furthermore, there are strong injunctions against indulgence in luxury, waste, and extravagance in consumption. Pareto-optimum-oriented consumers are encouraged to exercise moderation in their expenditure on consumption.

This notion of moderation is denoted by the symbol 'm' and acts as an argument in the consumption function. Consumers who tend to spend more than the average level of consumption in the community would feel uneasy about doing so, leading them to reduce their consumption in the next period. With this in mind, the consumption function can be formulated as:

$$C = ?+ f(y,m)$$

This formulation represents the aggregation of individual consumption functions, considering the factors of income and the degree of moderation in consumption for pareto-optimum-oriented individuals.

## 13.12 Savings

In an interest-balanced/free economy, income plays a central role in determining the amount saved by an individual. Other factors influencing this decision are generally long-term and relate to stable factors such as personal habits, the desire to provide for the future, and leaving an inheritance for children. These additional motives for saving should be explained. Another significant motive for saving is the desire to earn income through investment of the savings. Therefore, the expected rate of profit (denoted as?) should be considered as a determinant along with the level of income (Y), leading to the formulation:

$$S = f(Y,?)$$

To better understand the close link between the decision to save and the decision to invest in an interest-balance/free economy, it is essential to consider what a saver is likely to do with their savings. In this context, the saver has three main options:

(a) Investing in Physical Assets: The saver becomes an investor by purchasing physical assets capable of yielding a rent or rental income. This option may be preferred due to psychological satisfaction from ownership, higher return expectations, or potential capital gains. However, these benefits need to be balanced against associated risks and management costs.
(b) Investing in Financial Assets: The saver can buy shares, other financial assets, or deposit money into "investment accounts". By doing so, the saver is effectively financing investments, leaving the real decisions on how much to invest

and where to be taken by corporations issuing shares or financial assets or firms obtaining profit-sharing funds from banks. This option may be chosen for its convenience, lower risk, easier convertibility into cash, or differences in returns compared to the first alternative.

(c) Keeping Savings in Cash: The saver may opt to keep their savings in cash, either in hand or in demand deposits. This choice may result from risk aversion or a strong precautionary motive.

In practice, wealth owners often diversify their savings by creating a portfolio that includes all three forms of keeping savings: physical assets, financial assets, and cash. The allocation of total savings among these components may be influenced by the factors mentioned above.

## 13.13 Investment

In the context of an interest-balanced/free economy, the concept of investment retains its conventional meaning, as taught in standard textbooks. Investment refers to the process of allocating financial resources to various projects, ventures, or assets with the expectation of earning returns in the future.

In the case of the Equitable Optimality economics, decisions regarding how much to invest, where to invest, and in which line of production are typically made by entrepreneurs who organise and manage production. Initially, these decisions may be taken independently of the capital supplier. However, in a profit-sharing and interest-balanced/free system, where production is not solely financed by loans, these decisions are subject to review by the financier. This is particularly important in markup financing, where the financier must consider the likelihood of the financed firm facing bankruptcy. The final investment decisions must have the concurrence of both the financier and the firm.

One of the most critical factors influencing investment decisions is the expected rate of profit. All else being equal, both entrepreneurs and financiers are more likely to invest more at higher expected rates of profit and vice versa.

It is important to note that assuming financiers and producers to be solely profit-maximisers would not align with the principles of Equitable Optimality economics. As discussed in the previous chapter, Equitable Optimality economic behaviour is characterised by considering the interests of consumers, labour, other producers, and society as a whole. Investment decisions in an Equitable Optimality economy are guided not only by financial considerations but also by social priorities set by the state or expressed through public opinion.

Additionally, individual or collective views on what is in the best interest of society, especially concerning employment, essential goods and services, defence, etc., play a significant role in investment decisions. We represent these considerations with the symbol?, making it an argument in the investment function. Lastly, investment is also influenced by the level of income in the economy. The investment function in an interest-balanced/free economy can now be formulated as:

$$I = f(Y, ?, ?).$$

## 13.14 Income

In the context of income determination in an interest-balanced/free economy, two key equilibrium conditions need to be satisfied: equilibrium in the product market and equilibrium in the money market.

(a) Equilibrium in the Product Market: Equilibrium in the product market is achieved when total savings (S) equal total investment (I). Savings (S) represent the portion of income that households do not consume but instead save for future use or investment purposes. Investment (I) refers to the expenditure made by businesses and entrepreneurs to create additional productive capacity.

$$S = I$$

The equality of savings and investment ensures that all produced goods and services find buyers in the market. It is essential to maintain this equilibrium to prevent imbalances in the economy and avoid issues like unsold inventories or insufficient demand for goods and services.

(b) Equilibrium in the Money Market: Equilibrium in the money market requires that the demand for money (MD) equals the supply of money (MS). The demand for money depends on the level of income (Y) and the expected average rate of profit ($\gamma$). On the other hand, the money supply (MS) is determined by the central bank, which expands the money supply in correspondence with the growth of real output (Y).

$$MD = MS$$

The money market equilibrium ensures that the amount of money available is sufficient to facilitate transactions and meet the demand for money in the economy.

To analyse income determination, we conduct the analysis in real terms, assuming a constant price level (P). However, if we wish to take changes in the price level into consideration, we can divide the money supply (MS) by the price level (P):

$$MS\,MD = -----P$$

Along with discussing income determination, I also introduce the concepts of average and marginal propensities to consume (APC and MPC, respectively) and the average and marginal propensities to save (APS and MPS, respectively). These concepts help us understand how changes in income affect consumption and saving behaviour.

Additionally, the concept of the multiplier and its role in the theory of income determination should be explained along conventional lines. The multiplier effect shows how an initial change in autonomous spending (such as investment or government expenditure) leads to a multiplied impact on the total income in the economy. This multiplier effect is crucial in understanding how changes in spending can lead to changes in income and economic activity.

## 13.15 Average Rate of Profit

In an interest-balanced/free economy, the average rate of profit (?), which has been denoted as $\gamma$ in the discussion, plays a crucial role. However, to avoid confusion, it is essential to clarify that there are multiple profit rates involved in the economy. Let's simplify matters by assuming that all investment takes place through intermediaries (banks) on a profit-sharing basis.

The three important profit rates are as follows:

(a) Rate of profit accruing to savers who deposit money in banks' 'investment accounts.'
(b) Rate of profit accruing to banks (before the depositors' share is distributed).
(c) Rate of profit accruing to the ultimate investor, i.e., the producer who uses these funds.

Let us denote the profit rate accruing to the business enterprise as "p." The banks' rate of profit (before sharing with depositors) is "f * p," where "f" is the profit-sharing ratio (assumed to be less than 1). The depositors' rate of profit is "f^2 * p."

The average rate of profit in the economy as a whole, denoted as "?," represents the rate f^2 * p. It is important to note that "?," in this context, refers to the expected value and not the realised value. The realised value comes into play in equilibrium when "?," and the level of income (Y) are determined by simultaneous equilibrium in the money market and the product market.

Thus, the determination of "?," and Y is explained through the simultaneous equilibrium between the money market and the product market in an interest- balanced/free economy. Additionally, we introduce the IS-LM curves analysis in the context of an interest-based system, leading to the determination of equilibrium levels of Y and the rate of interest (r). The points of similarity as well as the differences between the two approaches should be highlighted.

At this stage of the analysis, the rate of mark-up in financed investments comes into play. The determination of this rate would take place in the same market where the cash prices are determined, i.e., the real market. The forces of supply and demand for real assets that determine their spot prices would also be relevant in determining their deferred prices (rate of mark-up).

However, it is noted that empirical data to support this hypothesis are currently unavailable. Therefore, further research and data collection would be required to explore this aspect in detail.

## 13.16 Labour Market

In analysing income determination, it is essential to consider the labour market and the role of employment (N) in determining real output (Y). To simplify the analysis, the production function is taken as given, and there is a given stock of capital (K). The production function is represented as:

$$Y = f(N,K)$$

where Y is the real output, N is the level of employment, and K is the stock of capital.

In the labour market, the level of employment (N) is determined by the equilibrium between the demand and supply of labour. Marginal productivity of labour plays a key role in the demand for labour function. However, economic agents in an Equitable Optimality economy also consider social goals and not just economic advantages. To account for these social goals, two additional arguments are introduced:

(a) ? in the demand for labour function, which represents everything other than money that the demander cares for.
(b) ?' in the supply of labour function, which represents everything other than money that the supplier of labour cares for.

The demand for labour function is represented as: w = f(N,?).where "w" stands for the real wage rate (wages adjusted for the price level).

Similarly, the supply of labour function is represented as: w = g(N,? ').

To achieve equilibrium in the labour market, the real wage rate (w) determined by the demand and supply of labour must be such that: f(N,?) = g(N,? ').

This equation gives us the equilibrium values of the real wage rate (w) and employment (N) given the values of? and? '. Additionally, it determines the equilibrium value of the money wage rate (W) given the price level (P).

The aggregate demand and supply curves for labour are derived by summing the respective curves at the firm level and then at the industry level. This process helps understand the overall equilibrium in the labour market, where the demand for labour equals the supply of labour, leading to the determination of real wages and employment levels.

Constructing the aggregate supply curve involves analysing how equilibrium employment (N) and output (Y) vary with changes in the price level (P). By adjusting the price level, we can observe how equilibrium employment responds, and then, using the production function, we can determine the corresponding variation in equilibrium output supplied. This information helps us plot the economy's aggregate supply curve.

Once the aggregate supply curve is determined, it can be compared to the aggregate demand curve, representing the total spending in the economy. The interaction between the aggregate supply and aggregate demand curves allows us to simultaneously determine the equilibrium output and price level in the economy.

To construct the aggregate demand curve, we can consider successive changes in investment, which affect the equilibrium level of output (Y) on the demand side of the economy involving both the money market and the product market.

Alternatively, we can bring together consumption (C), social expenditure (E), and investment (I) to calculate the total spending (C + E + I), which equals the total output (Y) in the economy, as it consists of consumption, social expenditure, and investment:

$$C + E + I = Y.$$

This equation shows that the aggregate demand (C + E + I) equals the total output (Y). By plotting different levels of aggregate demand against the corresponding levels of aggregate supply, we can determine the equilibrium output and price level.

By comparing the aggregate demand and aggregate supply curves, we can find the point where they intersect, representing the equilibrium level of output (Y) and the corresponding price level (P) in the economy. This intersection indicates the simultaneous determination of output and the price level in the interest-balanced/free economy in our theory.

## 13.17 Fiscal Policy and the Role of Government in the Equitable Optimality Theory

Fiscal policy in the Equitable Optimality economy is designed to align with the principles of the philosophical objective of this theory, which we discussed in the previous Chapter. Nonetheless, let us summarise the key points:

(a) Objectives of Fiscal Policy: In the Equitable Optimality economy, fiscal policy aims to achieve four major objectives. These objectives emphasise social justice, equitable distribution, and the well-being of society as a whole:

- need fulfilment,
- economic development,
- reducing income and wealth inequality, and
- ensuring economic stability.

(b) Addressing Need Fulfilment: Fiscal policy can directly address the needs of the less privileged by implementing transfer payments, providing free essential goods and services, and offering subsidies to producers of crucial goods and services.

(c) Reducing Inequality: The government can reduce income and wealth inequality by redistributing wealth and income from the rich to the poor. This can be achieved through various means, such as progressive taxation, social welfare programs, education, and providing tools for the poor to improve their earning capacity.

(d) Promoting Economic Development: Fiscal policy can promote economic development by investing in infrastructure, strategic projects, and sectors crucial for economic growth. Providing incentives to private enterprises and involving the public sector directly can also stimulate economic development.

(e) Ensuring Economic Stability: Fiscal policy plays a role in maintaining economic stability by timing public spending appropriately and using taxation and borrowing to inject or withdraw purchasing power from the economy as needed.

(f) Trade-offs and Incidence of Taxes: The trade-offs involved in fiscal policy, such as balancing spending and taxation to achieve policy objectives. The incidence of direct and indirect taxes, as well as the impact of government expenditure, should also be analysed.

(g) Fiscal Policy Equilibrium: In an equilibrium situation, government expenditure (G) plus private consumption (C), investment (I), and net exports (E) equals total output (Y) which is also equal to private consumption (C), private savings (S), and taxes (T). This equilibrium is represented as: $C + E + I + G = Y = C + S + T$, and in equilibrium, $I = S + (T - G)$.

(h) Multiplier Effect and Fiscal Impact: The multiplier effect of government expenditure and how deficit financing ($G > T$) and surplus budget ($G < T$) can have different impacts on the economy.

(i) Limitations of Macroeconomic Policies: The limitations of fiscal policy in developing countries with capital shortages, where fiscal constraints may restrict the scope of policy measures should also be considered in this proposed economic framework.

Understanding the role of fiscal policy in the Equitable Optimality economy, shows how economic decisions and policy measures are aligned with the principles of social justice and well-being in such a system. Achieving a reduction in the inequality of wealth and income distribution can be accomplished through various means. One approach is to transfer a portion of the wealth and income of the wealthy to the less privileged. Additionally, diverting a part of the current income to the poor, along with enhancing the earning capacity of the impoverished through education, training, and providing tools of trade and equipment, can contribute to this objective.

To foster economic development, several strategies can be employed. Building essential infrastructure through public sector investment and implementing projects for the production of goods and services crucial for economic growth are crucial steps. Better utilisation of natural resources and manpower resources can be achieved by incentivising private enterprises and encouraging direct involvement of the public sector.

In order to minimise economic fluctuations and ensure stability, careful timing of public spending is essential. Utilising taxation, borrowing, and loan repayment as instruments for injecting purchasing power into the system or withdrawing it when necessary can help maintain economic stability.

Conventional fiscal economics extensively explores how government expenditure, debt policy, and taxation can be harnessed to achieve some of the aforementioned objectives. However, policymakers must consider trade-offs in their decision-making process. Additionally, analysing the incidence of direct and indirect taxes and evaluating the impact of government expenditure in this context is essential.

Previously, we noted that the equilibrium level of income (Y) is determined by the equality of total consumption (C), expenditure on other goods and services (E), and investment (I) with total income (Y) allocated to consumption (C), expenditure on others (E), and saving (S). Now, with the inclusion of government expenditure (G) and taxes (T), the equilibrium condition becomes:

$$C + E + I + G = Y = C + E + S + T$$

Where G represents government expenditure on consumption and investment, and T denotes taxes. In equilibrium, investment (I) is equal to saving (S) plus the difference between taxes and government expenditure (T - G), signifying that any excess of taxes over government expenditure contributes to savings.

It is essential to explain the multiplier effect of government expenditure and its impacts on the economy under deficit financing ($G > T$) and surplus budget ($G < T$). Moreover, the limitations of macroeconomic policies in developing countries, particularly those facing capital shortages, should be emphasised.

In the Equitable Optimality economy, debt policy is not likely to play a prominent role since interest cannot be paid on loans. Instead, the government may be able to raise significant amounts of interest-free loans in emergency situations like war or famine.

Fiscal analysis in the Equitable Optimality perspective necessitates special attention to the collection and utilisation of profit-sharing funds, which play a pivotal role in the economy. The government can acquire investible funds from the public by selling shares of public enterprises or issuing investment certificates to create a general pool for investing in public sector projects. The profit-sharing ratio, the percentage of profit given to the fund provider, can be manipulated by the government to attract more funds. In this manner, mobilisation of investible funds becomes a fiscal policy tool, largely replacing debt policy.

For example, in Islamic majority countries globally, Zakat is a unique levy in this economic system and holds significant importance in fiscal policy. It is an obligatory form of charity that individuals are required to pay annually, 2.5% of their wealth. The term “zakat” literally means “purification” and “growth,” signifying the purification of one's wealth by giving a portion of it to those in need and the growth of the community through social welfare.

Zakat is considered a religious duty for Muslims, and its collection and utilisation are overseen by relevant authorities or institutions. It is seen as a way of promoting social justice, eradicating poverty, and ensuring the well-being of the less fortunate members of society. We argue that Zakat falls under our Equitable Optimality economic theory as it aligns with its fiscal policy objectives. It forms part of the fiscal policy for Muslims majority countries, which governments can leverage. Non-Muslim countries can also devise something similar that is not based on religious duty, something that suits more the nature of their conventional economic system.

Zakat is typically levied on specific assets or forms of wealth, which include money, gold, silver, agricultural produce, livestock, and trade goods. The rate of zakat is usually a fixed percentage of the value of these assets. Different categories of wealth may have different zakat rates. For example, the rate for cash assets might be lower than that for gold or agricultural produce.

The collected zakat funds are allocated to specific heads of expenditure as prescribed. These include providing support to the poor, helping the needy, assisting those in debt, contributing to eradication of human trafficking and modern slavery, aiding stranded travellers, and various other charitable purposes that promote the welfare of society.

Zakat also aligns with several of the fiscal policy objectives in the Equitable Optimality economy. It directly addresses the reduction of inequality by transferring wealth from the affluent to the less fortunate members of society. It serves the goal of need fulfilment by supporting those in need and the destitute. Furthermore, zakat plays a vital role in promoting economic development as it channels funds to productive activities that benefit the less privileged and contribute to the growth of the economy.

By integrating zakat, or its alternatives in the context of conventional economies, into fiscal policy, the government can enhance its ability to achieve social and economic objectives. The efficient collection and proper utilisation of zakat funds can significantly contribute to poverty alleviation, the provision of basic necessities, and the overall well-being of the society, thereby fostering a just and balanced economic system.

Noting that the zakat base includes various capital assets, part of the current income, and savings, it is expected that zakat revenue will constitute a significant percentage of the Gross National Product (G.N.P) in such economy. However, at present, there is a lack of reliable empirical studies relating to zakat revenue in Muslim majority countries.

In analysing the impact of zakat on the economy, it is assumed that all zakat is actually paid out of current income, even though it is assessed on capital assets. The government, being responsible for zakat collection, treats all zakat revenue as part of its government expenditure (G). Similarly, all zakat revenue, whether from current income or past wealth, is considered as taxes (T), regardless of its origin.

To estimate the amount of income transferred from zakat payers to zakat recipients, certain assumptions are made. Let K represent the total stock of capital in society, with some of it owned by zakat recipients (kr) and the rest by non-recipients (kn), such that $K = kn + kr$. Zakat is levied on some forms of capital, denoted by zk at an average percentage rate, but no zakat is assessed on kr.

Additionally, savings are annually subject to zakat at a particular rate (zs), and only some parts of the current income, such as agricultural and mineral resources, are subject to zakat at a rate zy. To calculate the total zakat due and collected, a weighted average of zk, zs, and zy, represented by z, is used.

The total zakat collected (Z) is given by the equation: $Z = z(k.kn + sn.k.Kn + Kn)$.

Where: sn represents the propensity to save of non-recipients, Yn is the total income of non-recipients (excluding zakat recipients), k is the overall output capital ratio (y/k), Kn is the capital owned by non-recipients, and Z represents the total amount of zakat collected from non-recipients, assessed on their annual savings, part of their income, and some of their capital assets.

A number of economists have attempted to develop a macroeconomic theory of income distribution in a capitalist economy. One approach is to analyse the impact of an annual transfer due to zakat, which can be expressed as a fraction of current income ($Z = z.kn\ (k(1 + sn) + 1)$).

Substituting k.K for Y (national income) on the right-hand side of the equation, we can observe that in the short run, when z, k, and sn are fixed, the percentage share of national income transferred to zakat recipients depends on the share of non-recipients in the total social capital stock (Kn). In the limiting case when all social capital is owned by non-recipients, so $Kn = k$, the zakat share of national income would be at its highest.

Furthermore, both of these relationships indicate that in the long run, the percentage share of zakat in national income is positively related to the capital output ratio (1/k) and the propensity to save of non-recipients. This suggests that higher capital output ratios and higher savings by non-recipients will lead to a larger share of national income being transferred through zakat.

## 13.18 Inflation, Economic Stabilisation and Growth in the Current Economic System

Inflation, as a general rise in the price level, can be categorised into two main types: demand-pull inflation and cost-push inflation. Demand-pull inflation is a result of an increase in aggregate demand in the economy, leading to upward pressure on prices. On the other hand, cost-push inflation is caused by an upward shift in the aggregate supply curve due to increased production costs, such as higher wages or increased input prices. At the time of writing this Chapter in 2023 the global economy has been in severe economic cycle and inflation of the two types, the cost-push and demand-pull, at the same time, particularly in the UK.

The aggregate demand curve for output shows a negative relationship with the price level P, as a rise in prices reduces the real money balances and savings of consumers, leading to a decrease in demand to maintain desired levels of real balances and savings. This negative slope gives us the downward-sloping aggregate demand curve. On the other hand, the aggregate supply curve for output has a positive slope with respect to P, meaning that as prices rise, firms are willing to produce and supply more output.

We should highlight here the distinction between economies operating at full employment of resources and those with unemployed labour and unused capacity. In the context of the Keynesian analysis, the concept of deflationary and inflationary gaps should be discussed. Similarly, in the classical model, the focus should be on the role of the money supply as the only source of inflation.

It is essential to differentiate between cases of temporary shortages or disturbances leading to short-term inflation and more persistent cases of chronic inflation. Additionally, the asymmetry in the impact of price changes on the supply of credit due to information asymmetry should be noted. This means that the impact of price changes on credit availability and borrowing behaviour may not be predictable, and it can vary based on the information available to lenders and borrowers. A thorough understanding of the nature and causes of inflation is crucial for analysing its impact on an economy and formulating effective policy responses.

Inflation is a significant macroeconomic concern that central banks worldwide aim to control. Traditionally, the relationship between money supply and inflation has been a fundamental concept in monetary theory. According to the Quantity Theory of Money (QTM), an increase in the money supply leads to proportional inflationary pressures (Bernanke et al., 2004). However, the conventional wisdom linking money supply and inflation has been challenged, particularly in the context of central banks' unconventional monetary policies like quantitative easing (QE). This critical analysis examines the limitations of the money supply as the sole driver of inflation in light of QE and its associated problems (Mishkin, 2007; Woodford, 2012; Svensson, 2011).

## *The Quantity Theory of Money and Its Limitations*

The Quantity Theory of Money suggests that changes in the money supply directly impact the price level in an economy, assuming constant velocity of money. In its simplest form, the equation can be represented as $M * V = P * Y$, where M is the money supply, V is the velocity of money, P is the price level, and Y is real output. This theory implies that an increase in the money supply will result in a proportional increase in the price level (inflation) if the velocity and output remain constant (Mishkin, 2007).

However, empirical evidence has shown that the link between money supply and inflation is not always straightforward. Numerous factors, including expectations, market psychology, and supply-side shocks, can influence inflation. For instance, during periods of economic downturn, as witnessed during the 2008 financial crisis, central banks implemented QE to inject money into the economy. Yet, inflation remained subdued despite a significant expansion of the money supply. This raises questions about the validity of the Quantity Theory of Money in explaining inflation dynamics in the modern economy (Woodford, 2012; Svensson, 2011).

## *The Role of Central Banks' Quantitative Easing*

Quantitative easing is an unconventional monetary policy that involves central banks purchasing financial assets, such as government bonds and mortgage-backed securities, from the open market to increase the money supply and stimulate economic growth. The primary goal of QE is to lower long-term interest rates and encourage borrowing and spending to revive economic activity.

In the aftermath of the 2008 financial crisis, major central banks, including the Federal Reserve, the European Central Bank, Bank of England, and the Bank of Japan, adopted QE on an unprecedented scale. However, the effectiveness of QE in boosting inflation has been subject to debate.

For example, the Bank of England (BoE) began its quantitative easing (QE) program in March 2009, in response to the global financial crisis that began in 2008. The program involved the central bank purchasing financial assets, primarily government bonds, to inject liquidity into the financial system and stimulate economic activity during a period of economic turmoil. The Bank of England has implemented multiple rounds of QE since then, both during and after the financial crisis, to support the UK economy and manage monetary policy.

Quantitative easing (QE) has had various effects on the UK and the global economy and its currency, including potential negative consequences. Talking specifically about the UK economy as an example, here are some ways in which QE might have negative affected the UK economy and the value of its currency (GBP):

(i) *Inflation Concerns:* One of the primary concerns associated with QE is inflation. When BoE engaged in QE, it injected a significant amount of money into the financial system. If this money is not absorbed by increased economic activity, which it was not, it can lead to rising prices. While some inflation is generally desirable, excessive inflation can erode the purchasing power of a currency, negatively impacting consumers and savers.

(ii) *Currency Depreciation:* QE puts downward pressure on the country's currency. When BoE creates new money to purchase assets, it increases the supply of the GBP currency. An increase in the supply of a currency, especially when other factors remain constant, leads to a depreciation of its value relative to other currencies. In the case of GBP, this could lead to a weaker exchange rate, which what exactly happened.

(iii) *Income Inequality:* QE can contribute to income inequality. The benefits of QE often flow to those who hold assets such as stocks and bonds, as these asset prices tend to rise when central banks purchase them. Those who do not own these assets may not experience the same level of wealth appreciation, potentially exacerbating income disparities.
(iv) *Asset Bubbles:* The injection of liquidity through QE also leads to speculative behaviour and the formation of asset bubbles. Investors may chase higher returns in riskier assets, leading to overvaluation in certain markets. If these bubbles burst, it can lead to financial instability and economic downturns.
(v) *Low Interest Rates:* QE typically involves lowering interest rates through the central bank's asset purchases. While low-interest rates can stimulate borrowing and spending, they can also reduce the income earned by savers and pension funds, potentially impacting their financial well-being.
(vi) *External Pressures:* A depreciating currency creates external pressures, particularly if a country relies heavily on imports. A weaker GBP leads to higher import costs, potentially contributing to imported inflation.

It is important to note that the impact of QE can vary depending on the specific circumstances of the economy and how the policy is implemented. Central banks often use QE as a tool to support economic growth and stabilise financial markets during periods of crisis. While it can have negative consequences, it is also intended to provide much-needed liquidity and stimulate economic activity, but is that the best way of providing liquidity!

The actual effects of QE on an economy and its currency can be influenced by a complex interplay of factors, including the overall economic environment, global economic conditions, and the specific design of the QE program. The central bank typically carefully monitors these effects and may adjust its policies accordingly to achieve its objectives.

## *The Problem of Money Supply and Inflation Disconnect*

The global experience with QE has revealed several challenges in linking money supply and inflation:

- Liquidity Traps: In certain situations, increased money supply may not lead to higher inflation if the economy is trapped in a liquidity trap. A liquidity trap occurs when nominal interest rates are at or near zero, limiting the effectiveness of monetary policy. During such times, consumers and businesses may hoard money instead of spending or investing it, undermining the transmission mechanism of QE.
- Asset Price Inflation: Central bank asset purchases under QE can inflate asset prices, such as stocks and real estate, without a corresponding increase in consumer price inflation. This phenomenon, known as asset price inflation, widens income inequality and can create financial instability.

- Expectations and Anchored Inflation: Inflation expectations play a crucial role in shaping actual inflation. If people believe that inflation will remain low or stable, it can become a self-fulfilling prophecy. Central banks' commitment to maintaining price stability through inflation targeting frameworks has contributed to anchoring inflation expectations, even in the face of increased money supply.

The idea that money supply is the sole source of inflation has been challenged, especially in the context of central banks' unconventional policies like QE. While the Quantity Theory of Money remains a foundational concept in monetary economics, its limitations have become evident in the modern economy. Central banks' experience with QE has shown that factors beyond money supply, such as liquidity traps, asset price inflation, and inflation expectations, significantly influence inflation dynamics (Woodford, 2012; Svensson, 2011). More recently inflation rate in the UK exceeded 10%. As a response the Bank of England increased interest rate from historic low of 0.25% to a staggering rate of 5.5% to control inflation. While retail goods inflation was around 18%.

I argue in the Equitable Optimality theory that this classical approach to respond to inflation by central banks needs to be revisited and rethought. I call for rethinking our economics in relation to such events in the context of new economic order, economic drivers and global economic changes and challenges, including new advancement in technology and geo-political challenges.

For example, the approach taken by the Bank of England in our example above, increased interest rate on loans, put consumers and businesses in a financial difficulty with typical average residential loan increased on an average by £350 a month. This is on top of rises in the prices of everything. All businesses and services providers put their prices up due to inflation, higher wages, and rising costs of everything including borrowing. While I would argue a balanced financial economy as I explained earlier with less concentration on interest-based system, would show a completely different economic outcome that is more favourable. This is a theory which of course needs testing.

## 13.19 Inflation, Economic Stabilisation and Growth in the Equitable Optimality System

Defining or precisely identifying inflation is a complex undertaking due to its multifaceted and dynamic nature. Inflation manifests in various forms and arises from diverse factors. However, a common thread across these different manifestations is its disruptive impact, posing a threat to economic stability and undermining developmental efforts. Inflation can be characterised by a disturbance in the flow of monetary and goods/services transactions, leading to a sustained increase in prices that is challenging to manage.

Economists have recognised that inflation is a consequence of an imbalance between the actual supply and demand within an economy. This imbalance arises when real or monetary demand outpaces the total aggregate supply, indicating an excess of demand relative to the available goods and services. Such a situation results in a continuous upward spiral of prices that is difficult to rein in.

As central banks continue to navigate economic challenges and design effective monetary policies, understanding the complexities of inflation and its drivers becomes imperative. Further research is needed to explore the interplay between money supply, financial markets, and real economic activity to develop more nuanced and robust models of inflation in the contemporary macroeconomic landscape.

In the short run, both monetary and fiscal policies can play significant roles in dealing with disturbances in the economy, even in the Equitable Optimality model based on profit-sharing. Despite the absence of an interest rate, the monetary authority can still regulate the supply of money to maintain real balances at the desired level. This can be achieved through various means, such as open market operations or adjusting reserve requirements for banks.

Fiscal policy, on the other hand, can be utilised to increase or decrease aggregate demand as per the prevailing economic conditions. Government expenditure can be adjusted to stimulate demand during periods of low economic activity, while taxation can be used to reduce demand during periods of high inflation.

In the long run, the self-correcting nature of the Equitable Optimality model based on profit-sharing should be explained. As the expected rate of profit, denoted by?, increases, both investment demand and the supply of savings increase. However, the actual realised profits may not match the expectations, leading entrepreneurs to revise their expectations. If realised profits are lower than the expected rate of profit, investment demand will decrease, which counteracts the tendency of the price level to rise.

An exogenous rise in the expected rate of profit,?, may temporarily raise the price level by increasing investment demand more than the decrease in consumption demand. However, the sustainability of this rise in prices will depend on the extent to which expectations regarding the rate of profit are realised in practice. If expectations are based on realistic production possibilities rather than mere speculative factors, the economy is likely to experience more stable and sustainable growth.

Overall, while the Equitable Optimality model based on profit-sharing provides unique characteristics, it can still benefit from the use of conventional monetary and fiscal policies to manage short-term disturbances and maintain economic stability. The focus on realistic expectations and prudent investment decisions will be crucial in ensuring long-term economic growth and stability in the Equitable Optimality economy.

The profit-sharing system in the Equitable Optimality economy provides an additional stabilising mechanism that can counteract inflationary rises in prices. As the expected rate of profit, denoted by?, increases due to a rise in the price level, brp (the ratio of entrepreneurial profits claimed by financial intermediaries as suppliers of investible funds) may also rise. This increase in brp has a dampening effect on investment demand by entrepreneurs, thereby mitigating the inflationary pressures arising from higher?.

Moreover, when the expected rate of profit,?, is supported by an increase in actually realised profits, it is likely to sustain itself over time. This sustainability occurs because expectations regarding profits are often based on past performance. As? continues to rise and entrepreneurs invest more, output and employment expand.

However, when the economy reaches its full employment limits, realised profits start falling short of expectations. As a result, the expected rate of profit,?, stabilises around a certain value, which puts a stop to the further rise in the price level, P. This stabilisation helps prevent excessive inflation and contributes to the overall stability of the Equitable Optimality economy.

The profit-sharing system, with its focus on realistic profit expectations and the distribution of profits among various economic agents, plays a vital role in maintaining price stability and promoting long-term economic growth in the Equitable Optimality economic framework.

In the context of inflation and growth in the Equitable Optimality economic framework, the real sources of output growth are attributed to labour, natural resources, and technological progress. The growth of labour supply is linked to population growth, while labour productivity is influenced by motivation, education, training, and the overall state of knowledge in society. A higher level of knowledge is essential for discovering and utilising natural resources more effectively. Technological progress, which is a significant driver of growth, is directly connected to the state of knowledge and motivation in the economy.

In this system, the expected rate of profit, denoted by?, plays a critical role as a signal for growth potentialities. When? rises, it stimulates both investment and savings. Increased investment leads to expanded output and production capacity, which allows the economy to accommodate larger savings without causing any adverse effects on aggregate demand. As a result, the system becomes capable of absorbing a larger aggregate supply, and the process of sustainable economic growth is facilitated as long as the growth potential exists.

In essence, proper motivation and the expansion of knowledge are crucial for fostering long-term economic growth in the Equitable Optimality economic model. By encouraging investments and promoting technological progress, the Equitable Optimality economic system aims to achieve stable and sustained growth while mitigating the impact of inflationary pressures through its unique profit-sharing mechanism.

The foundation of modern economics inadvertently exacerbates and perpetuates inflation over time. However, alternative economic principles, like the ones I am proposing here, could potentially offer more effective solutions to a range of economic challenges. The Equitable Optimality economic foundations, in particular, diverge significantly from contemporary structures, with one of the key distinctions being the diversion from interest. In this economic policy, interest, both on loans and deposits, is not a factor of the proposed model. This departure from the conventional practice of seeking interest to support investments and finance projects can contribute to inflation by increasing the cost of goods.

When a company resorts to interest to finance its investments, it effectively adds the interest amount to its production costs. Consequently, the company raises the prices of its goods to maintain a certain level of profit. This, in turn, contributes to inflation since the excess liquidity in the economy is not absorbed by increased production.

By envisioning an economy founded on the absence of interest, we can anticipate a scenario where interest becomes limited or entirely eliminated. This would result in restrictions on borrowing, potentially leading crucial sectors of the economy to rely on investments without borrowing. This shift could replace financial risks with entrepreneurial risks, fostering stable and long-term economic growth.

In essence, the economic system might transition toward equilibrium by curbing or eliminating interest practices, thereby shifting from debt-based solutions to a more asset-based model of economic development.

Zakat (a form of Islamic almsgiving) like economic instruments possess several capabilities that can significantly mitigate inflation. Zakat has the potential to absorb excess demand, promote responsible spending, encourage savings and investment, and play a crucial role in addressing certain negative effects of inflation, particularly wealth distribution.

Zakat serves as an effective mechanism for controlling inflation by curbing excessive government expenditure. It should not be used to finance government spending. Instead, Zakat is directed toward the impoverished and can be employed to alleviate the cost of living for the less fortunate, thus helping reduce inflationary pressures. Initiatives that exist currently in our conventional economy in the form of food banks, charities providing shelters and so on, which are not fully supported and organised as to be an economic instrument to address inflation.

A recognised contributor to inflation is increased government expenditure. This can be addressed by channelling charitable funds to specific areas, such as debt repayment for those in need. This not only supports individuals in paying off their debts but also bolsters credit and borrowing, as creditors gain more confidence in the borrower's ability to repay. This, in turn, promotes economic activity and growth.

Similarly, directing charitable funds toward debt repayment encourages lending and borrowing, fostering a supportive environment for credit activity. Borrowers are more likely to engage in productive economic activities when they have greater confidence in their ability to repay their debts, thereby stimulating economic growth.

Charitable funds should not be viewed as a temporary solution to combat inflation. Its effects are continuous throughout the year, with its impact on reducing overall demand and increasing the availability of goods and services remaining consistent. Thus, charitable funds has the potential to help maintain a balance between monetary and goods supply, aiding in inflation control.

Inflation poses numerous challenges for specific segments of society, including individuals on fixed incomes or those in occupations with inadequate compensation to cope with rising prices. Charitable funds can play a vital role in providing relief to these individuals and mitigating the impact of inflation on their lives.

Therefore, charitable funds, with its multifaceted impact, can play a pivotal role in addressing inflation. By supporting productive economic activities, encouraging savings and investment, and aiding those in financial need, charitable funds contribute to stabilising the economy and mitigating the effects of inflation on vulnerable segments of society.

## 13.20 Moving From Interest-Based Economy to an Equitable Optimality Economy

Moving from a capitalist economy to the Equitable Optimality economy involves several crucial changes that can be analysed in comparative static terms. The transition centres around three key factors. Firstly, interest is replaced by profit-sharing, thereby restoring the vital role of profits in resource allocation. Secondly, social objectives are introduced, influencing individual economic agents through variables such as E, z,?,?, and? ', while addressing the fulfilment of basic needs for the poor and promoting moderation in consumption for the wealthy through variables? and m in the consumption function.

Under the influence of the E and Z functions, part of the national income is transferred from the rich to the poor, assuming there are economically disadvantaged individuals in society. Additionally, the introduction of? and m in the consumption function is expected to reduce the consumption of the rich and increase the consumption of the poor. However, the overall effect on total consumption cannot be predicted in advance.

Social objectives, symbolised by?, introduced in the investment function, may direct investment towards socially prioritised areas. This may lead to increased investment, depending on the existing production possibilities. While the change in investor behaviour indicated by? could alter the composition of aggregate supply in line with social priorities, the actual volume of investment will depend on prevailing conditions.

Considering social objectives in workers and employers (?' &?) may positively impact labour productivity (motivation) and wages (employers sharing profits with workers). This could also affect employment levels and working hours, potentially leading to increased production.

Encouraging moderation in consumption by the wealthy would reduce conspicuous consumption and decrease the consumption demand from the rich, while ensuring a minimum level of consumption for all, thereby increasing the consumption demand from the poor. Fiscal and monetary policies would play a crucial role in reinforcing and ensuring these behavioural trends. The overall transition aims to align economic activities with social priorities and promote a more equitable and balanced economic system.

The replacement of interest with profit sharing stands out as the most powerful instrument of change in our model. Through our analysis, it becomes evident that the Equitable Optimality model exhibits greater self-correcting abilities and higher stability compared to the capitalist model. Unlike the capitalist system, the Equitable Optimality model does not exhibit a tendency for an inflationary trend to perpetuate itself.

Two fundamental characteristics of the Equitable Optimality model contribute to this enhanced stability. Firstly, the creation of money is directly tied to production possibilities, ensuring a more balanced monetary system. Secondly, profit expectations in the Equitable Optimality model are not self-justifying; they are subject to correction based on actual production possibilities and realised profits. The absence of interest, the reinstatement of the rate of profit's role in resource allocation, and the incorporation of expected profits instead of interest in cost functions will lead to increased investment, employment, and overall output.

Therefore, the changes introduced in the Equitable Optimality economic theory are expected to elevate the economy to a higher level of employment and output. They will also bring about a shift in aggregate demand and aggregate supply towards essential needs and socially desirable consumption and investment. Furthermore, these changes will foster a more equitable distribution of income and wealth, while also promoting greater stability, industrial harmony, and social cohesion within the economy.

## 13.21 Conclusion

In this Chapter, we have kept most of the analytical tools developed by modern economics, while introducing some critical departures in behavioural assumptions and institutions. The prominent change is the elimination of interest, providing new approach to addressing inflation, and the introduction of profit sharing as the primary mechanism for resource allocation. Additionally, social objectives are incorporated alongside self-interest for economic agents such as consumers, producers, and labour.

In this proposed economic model, the government plays an active role in the economy, aiming to maintain stability, promote growth, and achieve a redistribution of income and wealth to ensure universal need fulfilment, social solidarity, and cohesion. While these policy objectives are widely recognised, conventional economic theory often lacks strong analytical support for them. However, the presented theory addresses this issue by integrating a redistributive measure unique to its proposed model. Moreover, the theory includes the principles of moderation in consumption and the guarantee of a minimum standard of living for all individuals.

Despite these advancements, there is still a need to develop new analytical tools, particularly for studying income distribution within the Equitable Optimality economic context. Current macro-distribution models may not adequately capture the nuances of the Equitable Optimality economic model, thus presenting a challenge that requires further exploration and refinement.

This Chapter discusses the role of fiscal policy in the Equitable Optimality economy, a theoretical economic model based on profit-sharing and social objectives. The main objectives of fiscal policy in this model are to address need fulfilment, promote economic development, reduce income and wealth inequality, and ensure economic stability. Fiscal policy achieves these goals through various means, such as transfer payments, subsidies, progressive taxation, and investment in infrastructure and strategic projects.

The Chapter also highlights the limitations of conventional macroeconomic policies, such as the Quantity Theory of Money, in explaining inflation dynamics in the modern economy, particularly in the context of central banks' quantitative easing (QE) measures. QE, an unconventional monetary policy, involves the central bank purchasing financial assets to increase the money supply and stimulate economic growth. However, the effectiveness of QE in boosting inflation has been subject to debate, as other factors, like liquidity traps, asset price inflation, and inflation expectations, can influence inflation dynamics.

Moreover, the Chapter emphasises the importance of considering social objective]es in the Equitable Optimality model to achieve a more equitable and balanced economic system. These social objectives influence individual economic agents' behaviour and resource allocation decisions, aiming to address the needs of the poor and promote moderation in consumption for the wealthy. The article also discusses the transition from a capitalist economy to the Equitable Optimality economy, highlighting the crucial changes in interest-based systems to profit-sharing and the introduction of social objectives.

Overall, the Equitable Optimality model with its focus on profit-sharing, social objectives, and more nuanced approaches to inflation challenges offers a unique and potentially more stable economic framework compared to conventional capitalist economic models. However, further research and empirical testing are needed to explore the effectiveness and feasibility of this economic system in real-world applications.

It is clear that our proposed theory focuses on advocating an interest-balanced/free banking system as an alternative to the interest-based system. We explored the key features of both systems to better understand their differences and how the interest-balanced/free system aligns with the principles of the Equitable Optimality economic model.

In the conventional banking system, money is primarily created through the process of lending. When a bank provides a loan to a borrower, it creates new money in the form of a deposit in the borrower's account. This money is essentially created as a debt, and the borrower is required to pay back the loan with interest.

The main source of income for banks comes from charging interest on loans. When borrowers repay the loans, they not only repay the principal amount but also pay interest on the loan. The interest charged by banks is the primary mechanism through which they earn profits. Most conventional banks operate on a fractional reserve system, where they are required to hold only a fraction of their deposits as reserves and can lend out the rest. This means that a significant portion of the money in the economy is created through the lending process by commercial banks.

Critics of the conventional system argue that money creation through lending can lead to a disconnect between the financial economy and the real economy. The expansion of money supply may not always be directly tied to real economic activities and may lead to speculative bubbles and financial instability.

While in the interest-balanced/free banking system, money creation is based on profit-sharing and investment activities rather than interest-bearing debt. Banks create money through investment and partnership arrangements with customers, sharing both the risk and rewards of the investment. Instead of charging interest on loans, banks in this system earn income through profit-sharing with their depositors. Depositors who open investment accounts become partners with the bank, and their returns are tied to the profitability of the investments made by the bank.

The primary business of banks in this system revolves around providing funds for businesses on the basis of profit-sharing. Banks enter into partnerships with entrepreneurs and participate in business management, encouraging a stronger link between money supply and real economic activities.

As proposed in our theory, an ideal implementation of the interest-balanced/free system would advocate for a 100 percent reserve system, where only the central bank has the authority to create new money. Commercial banks would act as intermediaries, providing funds for productive projects through profit-sharing investment.

By focusing on investment in the real economy and profit-sharing, the interest-balanced/free banking system aims to establish a direct link between money supply and the expansion of productive economic activities. This alignment with the real economy seeks to foster a more stable and sustainable economic system. The interest-balanced/free system is guided by ethical principles that discourage the charging and paying of interest. It seeks to promote equitable distribution of wealth and social welfare, aligning with the broader objectives of the Equitable Optimality economic model.

To further develop this proposed theory and its implications for macroeconomics, it would be crucial to provide more specific details on the mechanics of the interest-balanced/free banking system. Exploring how such a system could be implemented, the regulatory framework it would require, and the potential challenges and benefits it may present would contribute to a comprehensive analysis of the theory's feasibility and impact.

Additionally, integrating the insights of economists such as Stiglitz and Greenwald (2003) on the demand for money and its relationship with income-yielding assets in the context of an interest-free/balanced economy could enhance the understanding of the monetary dynamics in your proposed model. This would further strengthen the foundation for studying the implications of the Equitable Optimality economic system and its unique approach to monetary management and banking.

Overall, the proposed theory presents an interesting, comprehensive, and innovative perspective on macroeconomics, emphasising a real economy-focused approach and advocating for an interest-balanced/free banking system to achieve equitable and sustainable economic outcomes. In the next chapter we will build on this discussion within the context of Microeconomics. I will further delve into how the Equitable Optimality economic theory can be implemented on the Microeconomic level.

# Chapter 14
# Rethinking Economics, Constructing the Equitable Optimality Theory Part Three: Microeconomics

## 14.1 Introduction

I have discussed in-depth in the previous Chapter the macroeconomic side of the proposed Equitable Optimality economic theory and all its relevant aspects. As the objective is to establish a comprehensive worldview of the Equitable Optimality theory, in this Chapter I discuss the microeconomic side of this theory and its related aspects to complete the cycle.

Microeconomics is a branch of economics that focuses on the study of individual economic agents, such as consumers, firms, and markets. It analyses the behaviour of these agents and the interactions that take place in specific markets, aiming to understand how individual decision-making shapes the allocation of resources and prices. In an academic discussion, several critical aspects of microeconomics play a crucial role in understanding economic phenomena and formulating policy recommendations (Stiglitz and Greenwald, 2003). This Chapter discusses key aspects of microeconomics in the context of the Equitable Optimality theory, including demand and supply analysis, market structures, consumer choice theory, and the role of government intervention.

One of the fundamental aspects of microeconomics is demand and supply analysis. This analysis examines the factors that influence the quantity of goods and services consumers are willing and able to buy at various price levels (demand) and the quantity of goods and services producers are willing and able to sell at different price levels (supply). The interaction between demand and supply determines the market equilibrium price and quantity. Understanding demand and supply is essential for assessing market dynamics, price changes, and consumer behaviour.

The observation I make here is that traditional economics, as it has developed over time, has largely been based on the behaviour and experiences of people in the British Isles, Western Europe, and North America since the seventeenth century. While economics claims universality, it is acknowledged that its foundations have not fully


S. Alamad, *Beyond Profit*, Contributions to Economics,
https://doi.org/10.1007/978-3-031-49748-3_14

considered the behaviours and values of peoples of other regions, underdeveloped, and developing societies, or faith-based societies, such as Muslim, Christian, Sigh and Hindu societies where religion plays an important part in directing economic behaviours.

To address this deficiency, microeconomic analysis in the Equitable Optimality theory aims to imagine how people would behave under the influence of its philosophical approach encompassing their values wherever they are in the globe. This approach will be supplemented by historical evidence of faith-based behaviour and contemporary data on some societies.

The Equitable Optimality perspective encompasses unique norms of behaviour and societal goals, providing ample room for positive and normative studies in economics. It delves into the examination of policies that can help achieve the Equitable Optimality society's objectives. With the Equitable Optimality theory perspective's distinct values and principles, it can shed light on various aspects of positive and normative economics, offering a fresh outlook on policies tailored for economically marginalised societies today.

Consumer choice theory is another critical aspect of microeconomics. It delves into how consumers make decisions about what to buy given their limited budget and preferences. Through utility analysis and indifference curve theory, economists study how individuals allocate their income to maximise their satisfaction or well-being. This analysis provides insights into how changes in prices, income, or preferences affect consumer behaviour and, consequently, market demand (Stiglitz and Greenwald, 2003).

Market structures also play a vital role in microeconomic analysis. Different market structures, such as perfect competition, monopoly, oligopoly, and monopolistic competition, have distinct characteristics that influence the behaviour of firms and market outcomes. For example, in a perfectly competitive market, firms are price takers, while in a monopoly, a single firm holds significant market power. Understanding market structures helps economists assess the level of competition, pricing behaviour, and efficiency in different industries.

The role of government intervention in markets is another critical aspect of microeconomics. Governments can influence market outcomes through various policies, including taxation, subsidies, price controls, and regulations. The analysis of market failures, such as externalities and public goods, provides a basis for understanding when government intervention is necessary to achieve socially optimal outcomes.

Moreover, microeconomics explores the concept of producer and consumer surplus, which measures the benefits received by producers and consumers in a market. Consumer surplus represents the difference between the maximum price consumers are willing to pay for a good or service and the actual price they pay. On the other hand, producer surplus is the difference between the minimum price producers are willing to accept for a good or service and the actual price they receive. These surpluses help measure the overall welfare or economic efficiency in a market (Stiglitz and Greenwald, 2003).

Additionally, microeconomics investigates factors that influence production and costs for firms. The theory of production and cost analyses how firms combine inputs (e.g., labour and capital) to produce goods and services and how costs vary with changes in output levels. Understanding production and cost functions is crucial for firms in making production decisions and optimising their operations.

Microeconomics also studies market failure and the potential inefficiencies in resource allocation. Externalities, public goods, information asymmetry, and imperfect competition are some of the reasons why markets may fail to allocate resources efficiently. The analysis of these market failures guides policymakers in designing interventions to correct these inefficiencies and achieve a more optimal allocation of resources.

Furthermore, game theory is an essential aspect of microeconomics, especially in the analysis of strategic interactions between different agents. Game theory studies decision-making in situations where the outcome of one's choice depends on the actions of others (Stiglitz and Greenwald, 2003). It is particularly relevant in understanding competition and cooperation among firms, bargaining between buyers and sellers, and decision-making in various economic situations.

Therefore, microeconomics covers a wide range of critical aspects that are fundamental to understanding individual economic agents' behaviour and market interactions. Demand and supply analysis, consumer choice theory, market structures, government intervention, producer and consumer surplus, production and cost functions, market failures, and game theory are all central elements of microeconomic analysis. Together, they provide valuable insights into how individuals and firms make economic decisions and how markets allocate resources and determine prices. In this Chapter, I aim to examine those aspects from the perspective of the Equitable Optimality theory. This understanding is essential for formulating effective economic policies and achieving efficient and equitable outcomes in various economic settings.

## 14.2 Addressing Microeconomic Needs

Economics from the Equitable Optimality theory perspective begins by understanding the holistic nature of human beings and their chief concern in life. Survival with dignity is of utmost importance, but it must align with the ultimate goal according to a specific ideological value, whether this ideological value is rooted in a religious belief or driven by worldly desire. In the case of the former, it seeks the pleasure of God through submission to His will and the pursuit of values and objectives that are pleasing to Him. This transcends personal interests, as it emphasises the ordering of human life on earth in accordance with divine guidance. While in the latter it will be the opposite.

The Equitable Optimality theory's concern with economic life goes beyond mere need fulfilment; it encompasses the concept of value-oriented development. The objective is to increase resources and utilise them for the betterment of humanity, promoting a vigorous and efficient life. Economics from the Equitable Optimality theory's perspective goes beyond basic needs and extends to a broad range of economic activities aimed at achieving the overall well-being of individuals and society. It includes considerations of environmental balance, distributive justice, and progress in aesthetic and spiritual dimensions.

Central to this approach is the notion of freedom within the framework of submission to natural laws. It means that human beings are free to pursue values and objectives while adhering to objectives values and principles. This freedom is intrinsic to being human and is integral to the economic perspective in Equitable Optimality theory. By encompassing these fundamental principles, microeconomics in the context of Equitable Optimality theory embraces a comprehensive vision of human prosperity and societal development.

In the study of economics, a distinction can be made between needs that can be satisfied through measurable and marketable goods and services and those that cannot, such as love, affection, and a sense of belonging. While traditional economics primarily deals with the first type of needs, it is essential to recognise the significance of the second type as well.

Understanding needs and their fulfilment is crucial because individual economic activities and social policies are driven by the necessity to meet these needs. Moreover, the Equitable Optimality theory places great importance on universal need fulfilment, making it a subject worthy of significant attention. Scholars, especially Shatibi,[1] have discussed needs extensively from a faith-based perspective, and contemporary works in humanistic economics, social economics, and ethics in economics can also provide valuable insights[2] (see e.g., Restakis, 2010; Bowles, 2016; Nelson, 2006; Little, 2002).

---

[1]Abu Ishaq al Shatibi (d. 790 H./1388 CE) famous for his study on the goals of Shari'ah. See: Masud (1977).

[2]Humanistic Economics:

1. "Humanising the Economy: Co-operatives in the Age of Capital" by John Restakis (2010)—This book explores the potential of co-operatives as an alternative economic model that prioritises human well-being and democratic decision-making over profit maximisation.
2. "The Moral Economy: Why Good Incentives Are No Substitute for Good Citizens" by Samuel Bowles (2016)—This book delves into the role of ethics and intrinsic motivations in economic behaviour and argues that the success of economic systems relies on the cultivation of good citizens rather than solely relying on external incentives.

Social Economics:

1. "Economics for Humans" by Julie A. Nelson (2006)—This book provides a social economics perspective that emphasises the importance of social interactions, care work, and human values in shaping economic outcomes and policies.
2. "Social Economics: Current and Emerging Avenues" edited by Jonathan B. Wight and John F. Tomer (2019)—This edited volume offers diverse perspectives on social economics, covering topics such as sustainable development, inequality, social justice, and human flourishing.

Ethics in Economics:

1. "Ethics, Economics and Politics: Principles of Public Policy" by Little, I. M. D. (2002)—This book explores the intersection of economics and ethics, examining how ethical considerations influence economic decision-making and policy.
2. "The Economics of Ethics and the Ethics of Economics: Values, Markets, and the State" by Geoffrey Brennan and Hartmut Kliemt (2010)—This book delves into the ethical dimensions of economic institutions and systems, questioning the role of markets and the state in promoting human welfare and justice.
3. "Economics and the Virtues: Building a New Moral Foundation" edited by Jennifer A. Baker and Mark D. White (2016)—This edited volume explores the virtues and moral character in economic decision-making and policy, offering insights into the relationship between economics and ethics.

Although economic theory often focuses on analysing 'wants' backed by purchasing power within the functioning of the market, economics is not solely confined to the study of markets. As a social science, it must also consider the broader goals of society, with universal need fulfilment being among the primary objectives. By incorporating such considerations, economics can address the holistic well-being of individuals and the greater community.

## 14.3 Relative Scarcity of Material Resources

Moving from the discussion of needs and their fulfilment, we now focus on the concept of relative scarcity of material resources and the pursuit of higher values and missions. In our observation of reality, resources may be flexible and expandable, but scarcity remains a constant factor, necessitating labour and enterprise to obtain the means required for fulfilling needs and pursuing goals. This scarcity compels individuals to make choices and engage in economic decision-making, a subject of significant importance.

To comprehend how choices are made, certain assumptions must be made about the decision-maker and the external world. These assumptions pertain to the availability of information, the motives of the decision-maker, their level of awareness, and the consistency of their decisions. Additionally, societal factors and institutions come into play, such as the extent of individual freedom in decision-making and any constraints that might limit this freedom. Understanding the critical role these assumptions play in shaping the outcomes of our economic analysis.

Furthermore, in economics, it is necessary to abstract certain aspects of reality to facilitate analysis, generalisation, and the derivation of universal or broadly applicable conclusions, even though these conclusions may have known limitations. The complexity of reality often requires simplification to focus on the essential aspects and patterns that relate different economic facts. By omitting details and considering only key factors, economists can gain a deeper understanding of economic phenomena.

## 14.4 Rationality of Economic Behaviour

In the context of economic behaviour, the concept of 'rationality' is often discussed in conventional economics textbooks. However, a brief critique of this concept reveals that the traditional portrayal of the "economic man" as an entirely

---

These references cover a range of topics and perspectives in humanistic economics, social economics, and ethics in economics. They provide valuable insights into how economics can be informed by human values, social interactions, and ethical considerations, moving beyond traditional neoclassical economic approaches.

self-interested, profit-maximising individual is not always reflective of real human behaviour.

It is possible to reject the idea of the economic man while still acknowledging a different form of rationality in decision-making. What is crucial is that individuals make choices after careful consideration, based on relevant information, and with the intention of achieving their known objectives.

In this perspective, rationality is not confined to maximising monetary gains or personal benefits. Instead, it encompasses a broader range of factors, such as personal values, ethics, and societal goals. Individuals may prioritise social well-being, ethical considerations, or other non-monetary aspects in their decision-making process. Such a notion of rationality recognises that human behaviour is shaped by diverse motivations and objectives, and it considers a more comprehensive understanding of human nature and decision-making.

In traditional economics, the concept of rationality is often linked to the idea of the "economic man," who is depicted as entirely self-interested, rational, and profit-maximising. According to this view, individuals are assumed to make decisions based solely on their own narrow financial gains, seeking to optimise their utility or wealth.

However, critics argue that this portrayal of the economic man is overly simplistic and does not capture the full complexity of human behaviour. In our proposed Equitable Optimality theory, we argue that in reality, people's decisions are influenced by a wide array of factors, including personal values, beliefs (religious or otherwise), social norms, ethics, and concerns for others' well-being. As a result, individuals may prioritise goals beyond material wealth and pursue objectives that align with their personal beliefs and societal values.

In recent years, economists have recognised the limitations of the traditional economic rationality concept and have explored alternative approaches to understanding decision-making. Some of these alternative perspectives include:

1. Behavioural Economics: This branch of economics acknowledges that human behaviour is influenced by cognitive biases, emotions, and social influences. Behavioural economists study how these factors impact decision-making, leading to choices that may not always align with traditional economic rationality.
2. Pro-Social Behaviour: People often engage in pro-social behaviour, where they act in ways that benefit others, even at a personal cost. This behaviour reflects a form of rationality that considers the well-being of others and contributes to social welfare.
3. Ethical Considerations: Decision-making can be guided by ethical principles, such as fairness, justice, and environmental sustainability. Individuals may prioritise actions that are consistent with their moral beliefs, even if they entail financial sacrifices.
4. Psychological Well-Being: Rationality can encompass considerations of psychological well-being, which involves seeking experiences and activities that contribute to personal fulfilment and happiness, rather than solely focusing on monetary gains.

Therefore, in our proposed economic theory, we argue that rationality is guided by the principles of philosophical underpinnings that we established in Part One of the development of the Equitable Optimality theory, which promote social justice, equitable distribution, and ethical conduct. Economic choices are made in accordance with these philosophical underpinnings, aiming to achieve both personal well-being and societal welfare.

Thus, the concept of rationality in economic behaviour is evolving beyond the traditional economic man. It recognises that individuals' decisions are shaped by a complex interplay of economic, social, ethical, and psychological factors. This broader understanding of rationality allows for a more comprehensive analysis of human behaviour and decision-making in economic contexts.

## 14.5 The Role of Institutional Structure

The institutional framework plays a defining role in shaping the economic decisions and activities within a society. In the Equitable Optimality theory and its context of society, the following institutional arrangements are key:

i) Ownership rights are recognised both for individuals and society, acting as trustees in managing and utilising this ownership. Private property is considered a trust, involving responsibilities towards others and subject to limitations in its acquisition, use, and disposal. Similarly, public property is also regarded as a trust, with those in charge being accountable to both people and the public good.
ii) Freedom of enterprise and contract is allowed but within constraints that safeguard the interests of others. Competition is permitted, with a careful consideration to avoid harm to others.
iii) In joint enterprises, profits are shared among all participants who bear the associated risks and uncertainties. Lenders, who are guaranteed repayment of the principal, are not entitled to any additional returns.
iv) Political organisation should be based on mutual consultation.
v) People are encouraged to support and care for one another, and voluntary organisations have a role in this regard. The state holds the responsibility and authority to ensure the realisation of the goals of this proposed economic theory through collective action. Individual rights are inviolable, and the people have the power to appoint state functionaries.

Therefore, the Equitable Optimality institutional framework emphasises a balance between individual rights and societal welfare, with principles of trust, accountability, mutual support, and collective action forming the basis of economic and political activities.

In this context, it is important to highlight the key differences between the institutional pattern assumed in the Equitable Optimality economics and that in conventional economics. Four specific points stand out:

1. Constraints on Freedom: In the Equitable Optimality economics, while freedom of enterprise and contract is granted, it is subject to constraints aimed at protecting the interests of others. Private property is considered a trust, and there are limitations on its acquisition, use, and disposal to ensure social welfare. In contrast, conventional economics often assumes unrestricted individual freedom in economic decision-making.
2. Obligations Attending Upon Rights: the Equitable Optimality economics recognises that ownership rights come with obligations towards others. Private property holders are required to fulfil their responsibilities towards society and are accountable for their actions. In conventional economics, property rights are often viewed as absolute, without explicit reference to social obligations.
3. Emphasis on Mutual Consultation, Cooperation, and Helping Behaviour: In the Equitable Optimality economics, the concept of mutual consultation (collective decision-making) is integral to political organisation, emphasising collective decision-making and cooperation. There is an emphasis on helping those in need and caring for one another. These social values are not always explicitly incorporated in conventional economic models.
4. Role of the State in Realising the Equitable Optimality Goals: The state in the Equitable Optimality economics is seen as an active participant in the economic process, responsible for ensuring the realisation of the Equitable Optimality goals, such as social justice, equitable distribution of wealth, and universal need fulfilment. In conventional economics, the role of the state may be limited to correcting market failures and providing public goods.

Despite these significant departures, conventional economic analysis remains useful in the context of the Equitable Optimality economics. Both systems share the assumptions of private property, free enterprise, and competition. The Equitable Optimality economics complements these assumptions with additional principles to promote a more balanced and socially responsible economic system, minimising negative consequences and guiding economic activities towards positive outcomes.

## 14.6 Goals of Equitable Optimality Economics

The fundamental goal of the Equitable Optimality economy is to achieve economic well-being, which is deeply rooted in its philosophy. Economic well-being is not pursued in isolation but in harmony with higher moral, ethical and social values. It involves men and women producing, distributing, and consuming wealth in a way that allows them to lead well-provisioned lives, and cooperate and treat each other with fairness and equality.

In this context, the following specific goals are emphasised:

1. Fulfilment of Basic Needs: Ensuring that all humans have access to essential needs such as food, clothing, shelter, medical care, and education.
2. Equality of Opportunity: Providing equal opportunities to all individuals, regardless of their background or social status, to achieve their full potential.
3. Reducing Inequality: Preventing the concentration of wealth and income, and striving to reduce economic inequality to avoid the misuse of wealth for dominating others.
4. Pursuit of Moral Excellence: Allowing individuals the freedom to pursue moral and ethical virtues in their economic activities.
5. Stability and Growth: Ensuring a stable and growing economy that is capable of achieving the above-mentioned goals.

These goals form the foundation of the Equitable Optimality economy, reflecting its ethical and social dimensions in addition to its economic considerations.

## 14.7 Implications Beyond the Market

Recognition of certain societal goals and the acknowledgment of an institutional framework that restricts unfettered market forces and involves an active role for the state move economics beyond the scope of a purely free market economy. While economic analysis will still examine market mechanisms, such as the interaction of demand and supply to determine prices, it will also go further. This is because relying solely on market mechanisms cannot guarantee the fulfilment of basic needs for all individuals or the realisation of other societal objectives mentioned earlier.

In situations where certain individuals lack the means to fulfil their needs due to factors like age, disability, or lack of opportunities, interventions beyond the market are necessary. One potential solution is to transfer income or wealth to these individuals, enabling them to participate in the market like others. However, implementing such transfers raises questions about who should contribute, how much should be transferred, and what mechanisms should be used for the transfers.

Moreover, economic analysis should explore whether the social authority (the state or governing body) should confine itself to short-term income transfers or consider long-term solutions, such as redistributing property to address underlying inequalities. Additionally, addressing unemployment and enhancing earning capacity through education and training should also be part of the economic study.

In essence, economics must consider a broader array of interventions and policy measures that extend beyond the market, as they play a crucial role in achieving societal goals and addressing the needs of vulnerable individuals.

## 14.8 Behavioural Motive

The recognition of societal goals and the acceptance of constraints and obligations on property rights and freedom of enterprise have significant implications for the motives of economic agents like consumers and producers. In contrast to the conventional notion of the "economic man" solely driven by self-interest, such a perspective acknowledges that a goal-oriented economy with social considerations cannot rely solely on single-minded self-interest.

In the Equitable Optimality economy, self-interest is not rejected, but it is recognised that other motives coexist with it, shaping and constraining individual decision-making. These additional motives include caring for the well-being of others, reflecting the principles which emphasise man's concern for fellow human beings.

This recognition of dual concern implies that individuals not only care about their own interests but also consider the interests of others in their decision-making. The relative strength of these two concerns and the scope of "others" for whom one cares may vary from person to person, depending on different circumstances and contexts. However, the acknowledgment of dual concern highlights that unadulterated self-interest is not the sole determinant of behaviour in the Equitable Optimality economy, and social considerations and caring for others play a significant role.

In the context of producers, we move away from the strict assumption of profit maximisation and acknowledge the presence of various other motives beyond profit. This more flexible and realistic assumption recognises that producers may be influenced by considerations related to labour, consumers, other producers, or society as a whole. This approach is not only relevant to Equitable Optimality economics societies, but also holds true for societies worldwide.

By allowing for a mix of profit-motivated behaviour, personal motives, and motives related to others, we create a more accurate representation of how economic agents make decisions. This concept of optimisation, rather than strict maximisation, better captures the complexity of decision-making processes, especially when considering Equitable Optimality economic value orientations that may influence producers' actions.

The same principle applies to all economic agents, including consumers, labourers, and others. In each case, the interests of others are likely to play a role in decision-making. By incorporating these various motives and considerations into economic analysis, we enhance the realism and utility of our approach, leading to a more comprehensive understanding of economic behaviour.

Indeed, economics as a social science has a formative role, not just a descriptive one. The way economic theories are constructed and the assumptions they rely on can shape human behaviour and influence economic outcomes. For instance, the prevalent emphasis on profit maximisation or utility maximisation as the primary motive for economic agents can lead to cutthroat competition, unethical practices, and inequitable distributions of wealth.

The consequences of these assumptions can be seen in various real-world scenarios, such as corporate scandals, environmental degradation due to profit-driven decisions, and widening income inequality. These outcomes are often rationalised and justified using economic theories that prioritise self-interest and financial gain.

To humanise economics, it is essential to question and modify these assumptions. This what out constructed Equitable Optimality theory aim to achieve by acknowledging and incorporating a broader range of motives and values in economic analysis. As a result, we create a more holistic and ethical understanding of economic behaviour. This could involve recognising the significance of social responsibility, environmental sustainability, and equitable distribution of resources in shaping economic decisions and policies.

By re-evaluating and adjusting economic hypotheses and norms, our theory aims to contribute to a more compassionate and sustainable economic system that aligns with broader societal goals and values. This humanisation of economics is crucial for addressing pressing global challenges and ensuring a more inclusive and just economic future.

## 14.9 Scope and Limitations of the Market

The market plays a vital role in an economy with private property and freedom of contract. It is the primary mechanism through which goods, services, and productive resources are exchanged, allowing individuals and firms to meet their needs and achieve their economic goals.

In the market, individuals and firms act as both demanders and suppliers. People demand consumer goods and services for their personal consumption, while also supplying labour and other services to earn income. Owners of land, buildings, and machinery, for example, can sell or rent out these assets to generate income.

Firms, on the other hand, demand factors of production, such as labour and capital, to produce various goods and services that they supply to consumers. The interaction of demanders and suppliers in the market leads to the determination of prices, which serve as the basis for exchange. It is important to note that the market is not limited to households and firms. The government and other social institutions also participate as demanders and suppliers in the market, influencing economic activity through their spending and production decisions.

The concept of the "circular flow of economic life" helps illustrate the interdependence and flow of economic activities. This model demonstrates how income earned from supplying goods and services is used to purchase other goods and services in the market, creating a continuous cycle of economic transactions.

Understanding the functioning of the market is essential for comprehending how economic decisions are made, how resources are allocated, and how prices are determined. However, it is equally crucial to recognise that the market has its limitations and may not be the sole means of achieving all societal goals, especially in the Equitable Optimality economy that prioritises social justice, equitable distribution, and moral values.

Indeed, the efficient functioning of the market relies on economic agents behaving honestly and fairly, which fosters trust among participants. When there is a free flow of relevant information to all market participants, it enhances market efficiency further. However, the market's effectiveness can be undermined by the exercise of economic power for private advantage, leading to market failures and moral hazards.

In a market environment, information deficiencies, fraud, and deception can distort the equilibrium between demand and supply, leading to suboptimal outcomes. Such issues can create asymmetries in information, where some parties have access to more information than others, resulting in unfair advantages and unfair distribution of resources.

The Equitable Optimality theory addresses these problems by advocating for a moral reorientation of economic agents. The principles of honesty, fairness, and transparency are emphasised to create an ethical market environment. Additionally, the social authority, which can be the government or relevant institutions, plays a crucial role in ensuring market stability and fairness. It intervenes to correct market failures, enforce regulations, and protect the interests of society.

Despite the emphasis on moral orientation and the role of the social authority, it is essential to acknowledge that no economic system can entirely eliminate all problems. Imperfections may persist, and some challenges may remain unresolved, requiring continuous efforts to improve and adapt economic policies and regulations. While the Equitable Optimality theory seeks to address market failures and moral hazards through moral reorientation and social intervention, it is essential to recognise that no economic system is without limitations, and continuous efforts are needed to achieve the desired economic outcomes.

## 14.10 Equilibrium Prices: Demand and Supply

Certainly, the concept of equilibrium prices being determined by the interaction of demand and supply is fundamental in economics. To understand this concept, we can use demand and supply schedules and curves.

The market demand curve illustrates the relationship between the price of a commodity and the quantity demanded by consumers. Generally, the demand curve slopes downward from left to right, indicating that as the price of a commodity decreases, the quantity demanded increases, and vice versa. This negative relationship is based on the law of demand, which states that *ceteris paribus* (all other factors remaining constant), the quantity demanded of a good or service decreases as its price increases.

It is important to note that there can be exceptions to this general pattern. For example, certain luxury goods might have an upward-sloping demand curve, indicating that as their price increases, their perceived status and desirability also increase, leading to higher demand. Similarly, some goods might have perfectly elastic demand, where consumers are willing to purchase any quantity at a specific price and none at a higher price, resulting in a horizontal demand curve.

The precise shape of the market demand curve can be influenced by various factors, such as consumer preferences, income levels, and the availability of substitute goods. However, a detailed discussion of the logical justification for the downward-sloping demand curve is beyond the scope of this explanation.

In equilibrium, the market price and quantity will be determined at the point where the demand curve intersects the supply curve. At this price, the quantity demanded equals the quantity supplied, ensuring that there is no shortage or surplus in the market. The market reaches a stable state, known as equilibrium, where both buyers and sellers are satisfied with the prevailing conditions.

Certainly, the supply schedule and the supply curve are crucial components in understanding how the market mechanism works. The supply schedule represents the quantities of a commodity that producers are willing to supply at various prices of the commodity. When these individual supply schedules are combined, we get the market supply curve, which indicates the total quantity of the commodity supplied in the market at different prices.

The typical market supply curve slopes upward from left to right, reflecting the relationship between price and quantity supplied. This positive slope is primarily due to increasing costs of production in the short run. As the market price rises, producers find it more profitable to supply larger quantities of the commodity. Conversely, when prices fall, some producers may find it unprofitable to continue producing at higher costs, leading to a decrease in supply.

It is essential to recognise that the shape of the supply curve may vary depending on the time period considered. Instantaneous market supply may exhibit different characteristics compared to short-run and long-run supply curves. Short-run supply allows for adjustments in variable factors, such as labour and raw materials, while long-run supply incorporates technological changes as well. This may result in supply curves with varying slopes, including curves that slope downward from left to right or even vertical curves.

However, when discussing supply and demand in introductory economics, the focus is generally on short-run supply curves for manufactured consumer goods. While using these curves for explanatory purposes, it is crucial to remember that the supply of specific commodities can be influenced by various factors unique to that particular market.

It is also essential to differentiate between movements along the supply curve and shifts of the supply curve. A movement along the curve occurs when there is a change in the quantity supplied caused by a change in the price of the commodity. On the other hand, a shift of the supply curve occurs when the entire curve moves due to changes in production costs, technology, or other relevant factors.

The equilibrium price of a commodity is a crucial concept in understanding how markets function. It is the price at which the quantity willingly supplied by producers is equal to the quantity willingly demanded by consumers. This point of equilibrium is indicated by the intersection of the supply curve and the demand curve. At this price, the market clears, meaning that there is no excess supply or excess demand for the commodity.

It is essential to emphasise the significance of this equilibrium point in explaining our proposed theory. The equilibrium price is the prevailing market price, and no other price can persist in the market as long as all other factors remain constant. This concept is fundamental in understanding price determination in a specific market.

However, it is important to note that the concept of equilibrium assumes "other things to be constant," which includes factors such as the prices of related commodities and the overall state of other markets. This assumption allows for a simplified analysis of price determination in a particular market and is referred to as "partial equilibrium." In reality, many factors affecting markets are constantly changing, leading to a state of disequilibrium.

While partial equilibrium analysis is a useful tool to understand how individual markets function, it is essential to recognise that in the real world, markets are interconnected, and changes in one market can influence other markets. Thus, actual markets are more complex and dynamic than the partial equilibrium analysis suggests.

Stability in prices over time can also be attributed to factors beyond purely economic considerations. Customary practices and social conventions can influence price determination, as consumers and producers may choose to maintain certain behaviours and not react immediately to changes in external factors like income, prices of substitutes, or production costs. In-depth exploration of these "non-economic" factors is essential for a more comprehensive understanding of market dynamics, but it may be more appropriate for advanced economic study.

## 14.11 Distribution

The process of distribution, specifically the initial distribution of income and wealth, is a crucial aspect of understanding economic life. Access to the market and the ability to participate in economic activities is determined by individuals' purchasing power, which is derived from their incomes and accumulated wealth. Without sufficient purchasing power, there is no effective demand for goods and services in the market, and without demand, there is no incentive for producers to supply goods.

While traditional economics often discuss distribution after covering consumption and production, we have reversed the order to highlight the significant importance of the initial distribution of income and wealth in shaping economic outcomes. By doing so, we emphasise that the pattern of production and consumption is heavily influenced by the initial distribution of resources.

This emphasis is especially relevant in the context of our focus on universal need fulfilment and other societal goals. Correcting the imbalance in the initial distribution of income and wealth becomes essential in achieving these objectives, as it directly impacts the ability of individuals to participate in the market and fulfil their needs.

Rather than trying to modify the final outcomes of the economic process, which may be inefficient and ineffective, addressing the root cause of inequality and imbalances at the source is more conducive to creating a just and equitable economic system. By paying attention to the distribution of income and wealth from the outset, we can ensure that all individuals have the means to participate in the market and lead fulfilling lives, aligning with the broader objectives of our proposed economic model.

Incomes can be acquired through several sources, each with its unique characteristics. One significant source is property, which can be acquired through ownership or inheritance. Some assets, like houses and cars, provide direct satisfaction to their owners, while others, such as land, buildings, machinery, and financial assets like cash, shares, and stocks, generate income streams for their owners over time.

Work is another primary source of income, encompassing various forms of labour, professional services, managerial roles, and entrepreneurship. The quality of work is influenced by an individual's education, training, health, and nutrition, which directly impact their ability to earn wages or salaries. Entrepreneurial profits, on the other hand, are distinct from contractual income as they are uncertain and non-contractual, arising from decision-making in the face of risk and uncertainty.

Grants represent another source of income, where individuals, institutions, or governments provide financial assistance to alleviate suffering or recognise merit. These grants may be given based on need or merit, often considering past or future services rendered. Grants play a significant role in economic life, especially when considering both welfare programs provided by modern states and the support given within families.

In the following discussion, we will delve into a more detailed analysis of the various categories of income, exploring their characteristics and implications for economic life.

## 14.12 Labour and Wages

The determination of wages in the labour market involves the application of the demand and supply framework, similar to the analysis of other prices. Demand for labour, like any factor of production, is a derived demand, meaning that it is derived from the demand for the final goods and services that labour helps produce. To understand this concept, it is crucial to discuss the notions of physical productivity, the value of the product, and revenue productivity.

However, calculating the marginal revenue productivity of labour, which forms the basis for the demand curve for labour, can be challenging due to several factors. The marginal productivity theory faces limitations, primarily stemming from market imperfections, such as lack of divisibility, labour mobility, and complete information. Assumptions like constant returns to scale can also contribute to its limitations. These issues have been extensively discussed in the economic literature.

Another important consideration when analysing wages is the impact of institutional and historical factors, which can lead to rigidity in wage structures and perpetuate wage differentials over time. Despite these limitations, the notion of marginal productivity as the basis for labour demand is retained due to the lack of alternative theories. Nevertheless, economists must be aware of these limitations and consider them when applying the theory to real-world scenarios.

Indeed, the supply of labour is a complex concept that involves various factors. The typical individual supply curve for labour assumes that as the number of hours worked increases, the pain or disutility associated with work also increases. However, this assumption does not always hold true. Sometimes, the absence of work itself can be painful, regardless of the loss of income involved. In other words, useful work is often considered a basic human need.

Using indifference curves between leisure and hours of work to bypass this issue also does not fully address the problem, as leisure is not always a substitute for the kind of work that is seen as essential for human well-being. Moreover, human behaviour in terms of supplying labour is significantly influenced by institutional arrangements within a society. Factors such as the availability of grants based on need, the opportunity to choose between different types of work, and the chance to participate in management can all impact an individual's decision to supply labour.

At the macroeconomic level, the shape of the labour supply curve involves the entire population, its composition, and its rate of growth. In between the individual labour supply curve and the economy-wide labour supply curve, we have the supply of labour curve for a particular industry, as well as the supply curve for a particular firm within that industry. For explanatory purposes, an upward sloping curve may be used for the former case, and a horizontal curve (representing unlimited supply at the prevailing wage rate) for the latter case. However, specific considerations related to other factors should be considered when dealing with specific situations.

The determination of wages for a particular kind of labour can be shown by bringing together the supply of labour curve for a specific industry and the demand for labour curve by that industry. The upward-sloping supply curve can be justified on the basis that as higher wages are offered in a particular industry, labourers are attracted away from other industries to work in this specific one, assuming other factors remain constant. On the other hand, the downward-sloping demand for labour curve at the industry level is obtained through the horizontal summation of the demand curves of firms within that industry, which are based on the marginal revenue productivity of labour in these firms.

However, we can introduce a modification to the usual hypothesis that every economic agent seeks to maximise its own profits and labour seeks maximum wages. In this modified scenario, both labourers and their employers, the producers, may care for each other and for others in society, including other labourers, producers, and consumers.

In such a context, several situations may arise:

1. There may be increasing returns to scale, where the total revenue product is more than the sum of the marginal products, enabling the producer to pay wages higher than the revenue productivity of labour, if the situation calls for such a measure.
2. Labour may be paid a wage higher than the marginal revenue productivity at the expense of returns to capital and enterprise, i.e., out of profits, if the situation calls for such a measure.
3. Consumers may agree to a higher price for a product, resulting in an increase in the marginal revenue productivity of labour, which then allows for higher wages to be paid to labour, should the situation require it. This can be thought of as a tax per unit of the product on consumers, with the proceeds being added to wages.
4. Labour may agree to a wage lower than its marginal revenue productivity, allowing increased profits to be reinvested in the industry to create more jobs or to enable producers to lower the price of the commodity in the interest of consumers. The lower price will eventually lower the marginal revenue productivity, making it equal to the lower wage rate.

These scenarios illustrate the complexity of wage determination when factors such as concern for others, social considerations, and the interplay of multiple agents come into play. It shows that the market for labour is not solely governed by profit maximisation and self-interest but can be influenced by various social and ethical factors as well.

In a cooperative framework where economic decisions are made through mutual consultation and economic agents consider the interests of others along with their own, the possibilities of various outcomes related to wage determination cannot be easily dismissed. Such a scenario might occur during a period of collective effort to lift people out of poverty or in response to an emergency situation like war or a natural disaster. In this context, the traditional marginal productivity theory and the usual supply curve can still be used for studying wages in the context of long-run competitive equilibrium. However, the additional factors arising from the motivations of economic agents and the assumed institutional arrangements need to be considered when drawing conclusions for specific situations.

The concept of collective bargaining and the role of the government in wage settlements should also be analysed within the same framework. Advantages and disadvantages of minimum wage legislation can also be discussed in this light. The key point to consider is that when labour and employers are driven solely by self-interest without concern for each other or the broader society, it often leads to confrontation and conflicts that government intervention may struggle to resolve in the long run. On the other hand, when both parties are mindful of each other's interests and those of the society as a whole, and decisions are made through mutual consultation, achieving industrial peace becomes easier. These are just some of the possibilities within this cooperative context that the Equitable Optimality theory conceptualise in its model. The role of information and the influence of public opinion can also be brought into focus to better understand the dynamics of wage determination in such a setting.

Indeed, the issue of power in economics is significant, especially when it comes to labour facing organised employers. Understanding who holds power, when it is exercised, and its effects are crucial aspects of economic analysis. However, given the scope of this topic and the focus on economics of - perspective, we may have to analyse this topic for a more specialised discussion on labour and industrial relations.

It is important to note that the exercise of economic power within a framework of profit maximisation often leads to conflicts that the market alone may not be capable of resolving. The Equitable Optimality theory addresses this issue on multiple levels: by promoting more equitable distribution of economic power, constraining the pursuit of mere profit maximisation, and, if necessary, allowing intervention in the market by relevant authorities.

## 14.13 Profit and Its Implication

In the Equitable Optimality economy, the concept of profit and profit-sharing plays a crucial role due to the proposed financial economy model of interest-balanced/free concept. Individuals have the freedom to engage in entrepreneurial activities, taking on risk and uncertainty in the hope of earning a reward, which is known as profit. Profit can arise from various economic ventures, and individuals can enter into partnerships to share the net income based on agreed-upon proportions.

Entrepreneurs, regardless of their skill level, can participate in partnerships with others to undertake various tasks and share the resulting profits. This allows for a more flexible and dynamic approach to income generation compared to fixed wages. Professionals like lawyers, engineers, doctors, and others can also form consultancy services and share the net revenues among themselves.

In contrast to interest, which is either positive or zero, profits can be positive, zero, or negative. Instead, both the reward for entrepreneurship and the return on money capital are treated as profits. The income of the entrepreneur is referred to as profits, while the return to the owner of the capital is called profit-share. Both profit and profit-share are derived from the gross profits of joint enterprises.

It is important to note that the division of joint profits between the entrepreneur and the capital owner is contractual. If the enterprise generates no profits or losses, the profit-share is zero, and the capital is returned to the capital supplier. In case of losses, the capital supplier bears the losses, which are deducted from the capital before its return, resulting in a negative profit-share.

This distinction between profit and profit-share facilitates economic analysis and ensures alignment with the philosophical principles of the Equitable Optimality economic theory which proposes an alternative model to interest, while encouraging entrepreneurial endeavours and shared risk-taking among economic agents.

The determination of profits and profit-shares involves analysing the joint return to both capital and enterprise. This joint return, known as gross profits, is the difference between the total revenue and the total cost of a firm. The forces of supply and demand, which determine the price of the firm's product and the prices of the productive services and raw materials it uses, also play a significant role in determining the return to capital and enterprise at the microeconomic level.

However, it's important to note that the average level of profit in the economy cannot be fully explained through microeconomic analysis alone. Macroeconomic factors come into play, including the overall level of income in the economy and, in the long run, factors such as technological advancements and the supply of entrepreneurship.

For a comprehensive understanding of profit determination at the macroeconomic level, further analysis is needed, considering the interplay of various economic factors that influence the overall level of profits in the economy. This includes factors like aggregate demand, overall economic performance, government policies, and the long-term trajectory of economic growth and development.

While microeconomic forces of supply and demand play a role in determining profits and profit-shares at the firm level, a more extensive macroeconomic analysis is required to comprehend the average level of profit in the entire economy. This broader perspective involves examining multiple economic variables and their interactions to full appreciate the overall dynamics of profit determination at the macro level.

In an interest-balanced/free economy based on profit-sharing, the division of the joint return to capital and enterprise into profits of the entrepreneur and profit-share of the supplier of capital is also influenced by the forces of supply and demand. The ratios of profit-sharing between the depositor and the bank (or any other financial intermediary) and between the bank and the entrepreneur play a crucial role in determining this division. Additionally, to provide a comprehensive view, an analysis of the shares market should be done, explaining how the rate of return on equity capital outside the banks is determined.

It is important to note that the conventional analysis of return to capital typically includes the concept of the productivity of capital, which is used to explain the rate of interest. However, in an interest-free/balanced system, the concept of interest changes significantly. Interest becomes an institutional phenomenon specific to the capitalist economy, attributing positive value productivity to money capital invested in productive enterprise.

In an interest-free/balanced system, the return to capital is combined with the reward of enterprise, and the two are separated based on prior agreement between the parties involved. The resulting return to money capital, referred to as profit-share, can be positive, zero, or negative, depending on the actual outcomes of the productive enterprise. If the enterprise incurs a loss, profit-share will be negative, and the capital-owner will bear the loss.

Regarding capital goods (tangible assets), as distinct from money capital, their expected value productivity is typically reflected in their rentals or lease charges. This ensures that the expected productivity of capital goods is accounted for in the economic system, even in an interest-free/balanced context.

## 14.14 Income From Property

Indeed, property is a major source of income in various forms. Money capital, when exposed to risk and uncertainty in productive enterprise, can earn profit-share for its owner. This profit-share is the return on capital resulting from joint enterprise with an entrepreneur. Landed property, on the other hand, can earn rent. Rent is the price paid for the benefits derived from using land for different purposes, such as building and cultivation. The rate of rent per acre is determined by the forces of supply and demand in the market.

Similarly, buildings of all kinds can also earn rent for their owners based on the benefits they provide to tenants or users. The rent for buildings is also determined by supply and demand factors.

Durable goods like machines, equipment, and vehicles can be rented out, and the income earned from such rentals is called 'rentals.' The rental income is the price charged for using these durable goods, and like other rents, it is also determined by supply and demand.

Another way to earn income through property is by entering into profit-sharing arrangements in productive enterprise. For instance, the owner of cultivable land can collaborate with a farmer. The landowner provides the land and seeds, while the farmer contributes labour for cultivation. Both parties then share the resulting crop based on a prior agreement.

In an interest-free/balanced economy with profit-sharing arrangements, property can be a versatile and dynamic source of income, with various types of property generating different forms of revenue, such as profit-share, rent, and rentals. These incomes are subject to market forces and agreements between parties, reflecting the dynamic nature of economic interactions in such an economy. There are various forms of income that can be derived from property in an interest-balanced/free economy. Profit-sharing arrangements, as mentioned earlier, can extend beyond just money capital and land to other durable goods like vehicles, buildings, and machinery.

For example, the owner of an aircraft can enter into an agreement with an aircraft operator, where both parties divide the daily fare based on an agreed percentage. The cost of maintaining and repairing the aircraft would typically be borne by the owner. Similarly, other durable goods like buildings and machinery can also be supplied by their owners to entrepreneurs, manufacturers, or shopkeepers who participate in the productive process. The returns from such arrangements would be in the form of profit-share rather than rent or rentals.

It is important to note that money capital, although a form of property, cannot be rented out directly as it needs to be converted into goods and services to enter the production process. Rent and rentals are specifically associated with durable goods, which generate income based on the benefits they provide or services they render.

Economists have made distinctions in the realm of land rent, particularly between scarcity rent and differential rent. Scarcity rent arises due to the overall scarcity of land, while differential rent arises from differences in land fertility or location. These distinctions help in understanding the nature and application of economic rent.

## 14.15 Grants

Grants indeed play a significant role in achieving the goals of an economy that aims to ensure the fulfilment of basic needs for all individuals. In the Equitable Optimality economic framework, grants are provided through various means, including obligatory intra-family and interfamily grants, obligatory almsgiving from the well-to-do to the needy, philanthropical grants, and additional measures taken by the state to collect more from those who can afford it and ensure need fulfilment for those in need.

By redirecting sufficient income towards those who do not have enough through wages, rents, profits, or profit-shares, the economy can broaden access to the market and provide greater freedom to all economic agents. The guarantee of a minimum level of living through grants ensures that individuals have their basic needs met, reducing the need for destructive competition and inhumane struggle for survival.

However, it is essential to be cautious of potential risks, such as beneficiaries developing dependency on grants or abusing the system. Appropriate measures should be implemented to minimise such risks, drawing from the experiences of welfare states in post-World War II Europe. Overall, grants can play a crucial role in achieving a more equitable and socially just economic system, where the well-being of all individuals is considered, and basic needs are fulfilled for everyone.

## 14.16 Production and Producers Motive

The conventional assumption of profit-maximisation as the sole motive of producers is not always realistic. In reality, producers are influenced by a multitude of objectives and considerations beyond just making profits. In both capitalist and Equitable Optimality societies, producers may be motivated by various factors, including:

1. Social Concerns: Producers may be driven by a desire to contribute positively to society by producing goods and services that meet people's needs or improve their lives in material, moral, or aesthetic ways.
2. Social Responsibility: In Equitable Optimality societies, individuals are assumed to take the interests of others into consideration. Producers may see it as their duty to produce essential goods and services that benefit the community or goods necessary for defence and security.

3. Employment Generation: In times of high unemployment, producers may be motivated to create job opportunities for the community.
4. Reputation and Image: Producers may be concerned about their reputation and the image of their businesses. Building a good reputation can attract more customers and enhance their standing in society.
5. Power and Prestige: For some individuals, owning a large firm can bring power and prestige, which may act as a motivation for production.
6. Custom and Tradition: Cultural and traditional values may influence producers' decisions and choices in the types of goods and services they produce.

In economic analysis, it is crucial to acknowledge and consider these various motives and objectives that producers may have. The real-world behaviour of producers is shaped by a mix of these factors, and the pursuit of profit is just one aspect of a more complex set of motivations. This broader perspective can help in understanding the dynamics of production and the role of producers in an economy.

In the Equitable Optimality economy, the motive for production for producers is driven by a combination of ethical principles, social responsibility, and the pursuit of common welfare rather than solely by profit maximisation. A just economy seeks to address issues of fairness, equality, and the well-being of all stakeholders, including workers, consumers, and the broader community. As such, the motive for production goes beyond narrow self-interest and focuses on creating sustainable, equitable, and socially beneficial outcomes.

Here are some key aspects of the motive for production in a Equitable Optimality economy. Producers are motivated to create goods and services that contribute to the well-being and happiness of individuals and society as a whole. The goal is to enhance human flourishing and foster a sense of community and interconnectedness, rather than simply pursuing profits at the expense of social welfare.

Moreover, producers are guided by ethical principles in their business practices. This means adhering to fair labour practices, ensuring workplace safety, respecting human rights, and promoting environmental sustainability. Ethical conduct is considered essential, and producers prioritise the impact of their actions on various stakeholders. Ensuring Long-Term Sustainability, focusing on long-term sustainability rather than short-term gains. Producers recognise the importance of preserving resources, protecting the environment, and maintaining ecological balance for future generations.

Furthermore, stakeholder engagement is an important aspect. Producers engage with various stakeholders, including employees, consumers, communities, and suppliers, to ensure that their needs and interests are considered. Transparent communication and inclusive decision-making processes are valued. Also, producers are motivated to address economic inequality by creating opportunities for upward mobility, fair wages, and equitable distribution of resources. The aim is to narrow the wealth gap and foster a more inclusive economic system.

Social and environmental impact measurement is another crucial aspect. Producers should consider not only financial metrics but also social and environmental impact as important indicators of success. Social accounting and reporting mechanisms are used to assess the positive contributions and potential negative externalities of production processes. Focusing on human-centred innovation. Producers are motivated to innovate and create products and services that address real human needs and improve the quality of life. Innovation is driven by a human-centred approach, rather than merely by market demands.

In addition to supporting local and sustainable economies. Producers prioritise local economies and support small-scale producers and businesses. They seek to minimise dependency on exploitative global supply chains and promote sustainable production and consumption.

Therefore, the motive for production aligns with the principles of distributive justice, social equity, and environmental stewardship. It emphasises the importance of economic activities that promote the well-being of individuals and society while considering the broader social and ecological impacts. In such an economy, producers play a crucial role in contributing to the common good and fostering a more equitable and sustainable global economy.

The motivations of the owner of money capital are also influenced by a mix of objectives. While seeking a return on their capital is a primary concern, they may also have other considerations in mind. The supplier of money capital might be willing to support projects that align with their social and ethical values, such as environmentally friendly initiatives or businesses that serve the community's needs.

The rate of return that satisfies the supplier of money capital or the producer would depend on their specific mix of objectives. For some, achieving social goals alongside a reasonable rate of return might be more important, while others may prioritise higher profits and be less concerned about other social objectives.

The expected rate of return on capital plays a crucial role in the decision-making process for both the supplier of money capital and the producer. If the expected return is not sufficient to satisfy their objectives, they may not be motivated to invest in a particular project or production endeavour. On the other hand, if the expected rate of return aligns with their objectives, they will proceed with the investment and organise production accordingly to achieve their financial and non-financial goals.

Overall, the complexity of human motivations and objectives highlights the need to consider a diverse set of factors when analysing economic decisions, including investment and production choices. Economic actors are driven by a combination of profit motives and social considerations, and understanding this interplay is essential for a comprehensive understanding of economic behaviour.

## 14.17 Cost of Production and Reduced Return

The Law of Diminishing Returns is a fundamental concept in economics that explains how the addition of more units of a variable input (e.g., labour) to a fixed set of inputs (e.g., land and machinery) eventually leads to diminishing marginal returns. Initially, as more units of the variable input are added to the production process, total output increases. However, beyond a certain point, the additional output gained from each additional unit of the variable input starts to decrease, resulting in diminishing marginal returns (Graafland, 2009).

Let us consider an example of agricultural production. Suppose a farmer has a fixed amount of land and machinery (fixed inputs) and hires additional labour (variable input) to cultivate the land. Initially, each additional worker improves productivity and total output rises. However, as more workers are added, the land becomes crowded, and the output gained from each additional worker starts to decline. This happens because the fixed land and machinery cannot accommodate an unlimited number of workers efficiently. The same example applies to factories, corporations, and any other productive sector.

The Law of Diminishing Returns highlights the importance of balancing inputs in the production process. It suggests that there is an optimal combination of inputs that maximises total output. Beyond that point, adding more of the variable input becomes less efficient and may result in higher costs without proportional increases in output.

The Law of Diminishing Returns as Samuelson and Nordhaus (1985, p. 36) argue is closely related to the concept of returns to scale. Returns to scale refer to the change in output that occurs when all inputs are increased proportionally. If output increases proportionally more than the increase in inputs, it is called increasing returns to scale. If output increases proportionally less than the increase in inputs, it is called decreasing returns to scale. If output increases proportionally to the increase in inputs, it is called constant returns to scale.

Regarding the upward sloping variable and average cost curves, the diminishing returns to the variable input lead to these curves' shape. As the variable input becomes relatively scarce compared to the fixed inputs, the cost of producing each additional unit of output increases, causing the upward slope of the curves.

It is essential to note that technological advancements and improvements can counteract the diminishing returns and lead to higher overall productivity. The idea of the "new economy" defying the law of diminishing returns may refer to technological innovations that have significantly increased productivity in certain sectors, allowing for sustained or increasing returns to scale.

Therefore, the Law of Diminishing Returns is an essential concept in economics that helps understand how changes in inputs affect total output and costs. It highlights the need for efficient resource allocation and the role of technology in overcoming limitations posed by the law.

## 14.18 Financing and Cost of Capital

In the Equitable Optimality economy, the concept of interest is marginalised, and therefore, loans with an interest rate are not the main driver. Instead, financing is based on profit-sharing arrangements or equity participation.

1. Equity Participation: The producer can invest his/her own capital into the business, which means they become the sole owner of the firm. In this case, all the profits and losses belong to them. However, this limits the scale of the firm to the extent of the owner's personal wealth.
2. Issuing Shares: To raise more capital, the producer can invite equity participation from other investors by issuing shares of the firm. Shareholders, by buying these shares, become part-owners of the company and have ownership rights. Their return on investment is tied to the firm's performance, and they earn profits (or dividends) based on the company's profitability. Shareholders do not have direct involvement in the day-to-day management of the firm but may have voting rights in major decisions depending on the type of shares they hold.
3. Financing through Profit-Sharing: Financial institutions and financiers can provide money capital to a firm on the basis of profit-sharing. In this arrangement, the bank acts as a financial intermediary and provides funds to the producer without charging interest. Instead, the bank and the producer agree to share the profits generated by the business in an agreed-upon ratio.

For example, if a producer needs money capital to start a business, the financing party may provide the required funds in exchange for a share of the future profits. If the business performs well and generates profits, the bank receives a portion of those profits as agreed. However, if the business incurs losses, the bank shares in those losses as well.

It is important to note that this finance model emphasises ethical and socially responsible investment, and the use of funds should not support activities that are considered unethical or harmful to society. Thus, in the Equitable Optimality economy, the focus is on achieving a just and equitable distribution of wealth and promoting economic activities that benefit society as a whole. Financing methods such as profit-sharing and equity participation align with these principles by promoting risk-sharing, discouraging exploitative practices, and encouraging productive economic activities that create value for society.

In that context, the cost of capital and its distinction from other fixed costs is insightful. In an interest-free/balanced economy, the return on money capital is based on profit-sharing, and it becomes an important consideration for the entrepreneur when undertaking a business venture.

The expected rate of profit, rather than a fixed return on capital, would be a more relevant element to consider in cost accounting. The entrepreneur, through profit-sharing arrangements, aims to achieve a rate of profit on capital that satisfies the supplier of money capital. The agreed-upon ratio of profit-sharing serves as a guide for the entrepreneur to strive for a target rate of profit that meets the expectations of the capital suppliers.

The flexibility in profit-sharing ratios allows the entrepreneur to adjust the expected rate of profit to align with the market conditions, business strategies, and the satisfaction of the capital providers. By varying the profit-sharing ratios, the entrepreneur can ensure that both parties are content with the financial arrangement and that the return on money capital is commensurate with the level of risk and reward.

In this interest-free/balanced system, the risk and reward are shared between the entrepreneur and the capital providers, fostering a cooperative and equitable approach to business. This aligns with the Equitable Optimality principles of justice, social responsibility, and ethical conduct in economic activities. The profit-sharing mechanism not only incentivises entrepreneurial efforts but also ensures a fair and just distribution of wealth among stakeholders.

There is an important distinction between an interest-based borrowing system and a profit-sharing system for working capital. In the conventional interest-based system, interest is treated as a fixed cost and becomes a part of the variable cost of the firm. The entrepreneur must cover the cost of interest, and the equilibrium and shutdown points are determined accordingly in a competitive market.

However, in an interest-free/balanced economy operating with working capital obtained on the basis of profit-sharing, the situation changes. The return to capital, which is obtained through profit-sharing, is not a predetermined cost for the firm. It is directly linked to the profits earned by the firm. As a result, the variable cost curve can be separated into two components: one that includes the expected rate of profits and one that does not.

This separation provides the firm with manoeuvrability in the short run, allowing it to adjust its profits and costs by varying the ratio of profit-sharing and thereby influencing the return to capital. This flexibility is not available in an interest-based system, where the interest cost is fixed and determined by external market rates.

However, it is crucial to note that in the long run, the difference between the two systems diminishes. In the long run, the suppliers of capital on profit-sharing basis would expect to receive their promised returns, aligning the actual profits with the expected rate of return. Consequently, the manoeuvrability enjoyed by the firm in the short run converges to the expected rate of return in the long run to fulfil the expectations of capital providers.

Indeed, the difference in the notion of the cost of capital between interest-based and profit-sharing systems has significant implications for analysing the employment of capital and labour in the production process. In the interest-based system, the market rate of interest is used as the price of fixed capital, and it is equated to the rentals of physical capital in the equal product curve analysis. This is because in a competitive market, the market rate of interest and the rentals of physical capital tend to be equal.

However, in a profit-sharing system, where the return to capital is based on a profit-sharing arrangement, there is no fixed rate of interest. Instead, there is an expected rate of return on the money capital supplied on a profit-sharing basis. The rate of rentals of physical capital may move closely with the expected rate of return on money capital in the market, but they are not contractually fixed and cannot be directly equated.

In the short run, this distinction allows the individual firm in a profit-sharing system to have some manoeuvrability in adjusting costs and profits, enabling it to deviate from the least-cost combination of labour and capital indicated by the price line and equal product curves. This manoeuvrability is not available to firms in the conventional competitive market, as they must adhere to the least-cost combination to survive.

The profit-sharing system also opens up the possibility for individual firms to create more jobs for labour, even at the expense of higher costs per unit of output. This can be done on a limited scale in the short run. However, for such a policy to be sustainable in the long run and on a larger scale, it would require the general adoption of such practices by all firms in the industry. Additionally, creating more jobs can also be achieved through mutual consultations between producers and labour, where labour may accept a lower wage rate, resulting in a change in the slope of the price line and increased employment of labour.

Hence, the flexibility and adaptability of a profit-sharing system can offer alternative possibilities for decision-making and resource allocation, fostering a more cooperative and equitable economic environment.

## 14.19 Firm and Industry Equilibrium

The equilibrium of the firm and the industry plays a crucial role in understanding how markets function and how resources are allocated.

For an individual firm, equilibrium is reached when it produces the quantity of output where marginal revenue (MR) equals marginal cost (MC). At this point, the firm maximises its profits because producing more or less would result in lower profits. The equilibrium output level can be found by identifying the quantity where MR = MC on the firm's marginal revenue and marginal cost curves. The corresponding price is determined by the intersection of the firm's demand and supply curves.

In a perfectly competitive industry, where all firms are price takers and there is free entry and exit, the industry's supply curve is obtained by horizontally summing the individual firms' supply curves at each price level. The industry's equilibrium is reached at the price where the industry's supply curve intersects the demand curve. At this equilibrium price, each firm in the industry produces the quantity where MR = MC, and all firms earn zero economic profit in the long run. This ensures that resources are efficiently allocated.

In the long run, the industry can adjust the number of firms to achieve equilibrium. If firms are making profits, new firms will enter the industry, increasing supply and driving down prices until profits are reduced to zero. Conversely, if firms are incurring losses, some firms will exit the industry, reducing supply and causing prices to rise until losses are eliminated. This process continues until the market reaches a long-run equilibrium with firms earning only a normal rate of return on their capital investment.

It is important to note that in the real world, markets are rarely in perfect equilibrium due to constant changes in demand, technology, and other factors. Thus, firms and industries are often in a state of disequilibrium, constantly adjusting to changing conditions to find new equilibria. Economic agents must be adaptive and responsive to these changes to remain competitive and successful.

The analysis presented is a useful framework for understanding the consequences of various policy decisions by firms in a competitive market setting. By quantifying policies and tracing their effects on revenue and cost curves, it becomes possible to determine how changes in supply, output, and prices may occur. This approach can shed light on the impact of decisions made by individual firms or groups of firms on the overall industry and market equilibrium.

However, it's important to recognise that in real-world markets, the assumptions of perfect competition, homogeneous products, and large numbers of buyers and sellers may not always hold true. In cases of monopoly, oligopoly, or monopolistic competition, the behaviour of firms may differ significantly from that in a perfectly competitive market. For example, in a monopoly, a single firm has market power and can set prices above marginal cost to maximise its own profits. Oligopolies, which consist of a small number of large firms, may engage in strategic behaviour, such as price-fixing or collusion, to maximise joint profits. Monopolistic competition involves firms producing differentiated products and using advertising and branding to establish product differentiation.

When firms have multiple objectives beyond just profit maximisation, such as social or ethical considerations, their behaviour may diverge further from the predictions of traditional economic models. In such cases, the distinction between cost curves that include expected profits and those that do not becomes even more relevant, as firms may be willing to accept lower profits in pursuit of other objectives.

Hence, while the analysis presented provides a valuable starting point for understanding market behaviour, it is essential to acknowledge the complexities of real-world markets and the varied motivations of economic agents. Economic models should be flexible enough to accommodate different objectives and behaviours while still offering insights into market dynamics and resource allocation.

## 14.20 Consumer Consumption Behaviour and Hierarchy in Human Needs

Consumer behaviour is indeed influenced by a hierarchy of needs, as proposed by Abraham Maslow (1943) in his theory of human motivation[3]. According to Maslow's hierarchy of needs, individuals are motivated to fulfil certain basic physiological

[3] In this seminal paper published in Psychological Review in 1943, Maslow introduced his theory of human motivation, commonly known as Maslow's hierarchy of needs. The theory proposes that human motivation is structured in a hierarchical manner, with basic physiological needs at the foundation and higher-level needs related to self-actualisation and personal growth at the pinnacle.

needs first before moving on to higher-level needs. The hierarchy is typically depicted as a pyramid with five levels:

1. Physiological needs: These are the most fundamental needs for survival, such as food, water, shelter, and clothing. Consumers will prioritise meeting these needs before anything else.
2. Safety needs: Once physiological needs are reasonably satisfied, individuals seek security, safety, and stability in their lives. This may include seeking protection from physical harm, having a stable living environment, and financial security.
3. Love and belongingness needs: After securing safety, people seek social connections, love, and a sense of belonging. This involves forming relationships, friendships, and finding a sense of community and acceptance.
4. Esteem needs: Once social needs are met, individuals desire recognition, respect, and a sense of accomplishment. This may involve seeking success, achieving goals, and gaining recognition from others.
5. Self-actualisation needs: At the top of the hierarchy, individuals pursue personal growth, self-discovery, and realising their full potential. This may involve pursuing creative endeavours, engaging in meaningful activities, and seeking personal fulfilment.

As consumers move up the hierarchy, their spending patterns may change. Basic needs like food and shelter are essential and often have relatively inelastic demand, meaning that changes in price have a limited effect on consumption. However, as individuals' needs for social belongingness and self-esteem come into play, their spending may become more discretionary and responsive to price changes.

The concept of consumer behaviour is complex and influenced by various factors, including income, preferences, cultural influences, and external stimuli (such as marketing and advertising). Therefore, while the hierarchy of needs provides a useful framework for understanding consumer motivations, individual behaviour can still vary significantly based on personal circumstances and experiences. As consumers satisfy their physiological and safety needs, their purchasing decisions become influenced by social and psychological factors, which can make predicting their behaviour more complex.

*Status and Symbolism*: Products like luxury cars, designer clothing, and high-end gadgets often serve as status symbols. Their desirability goes beyond their functional benefits, as they convey social status, success, and prestige. A rise in the price of such products may increase their exclusivity and appeal as symbols of affluence, making them even more desirable to certain consumer segments.

*Aspirational Consumption*: Consumers may aspire to own products associated with a particular lifestyle or image, even if they are beyond their immediate needs or financial means. Brands that are perceived as aspirational and iconic can

This paper has had a profound impact on the field of psychology and has influenced various disciplines, including humanistic psychology, organisational behaviour, and education.

command higher prices, and consumers may be willing to pay more to align themselves with the image portrayed by these brands.

*Perceived Quality and Value*: Consumers may associate higher prices with superior quality and performance, leading them to believe that more expensive products offer better value. In some cases, people may be willing to pay premium prices for items they believe will last longer or provide a better experience.

*Brand Loyalty and Identity*: Consumers often develop strong attachments to certain brands based on emotional connections and positive experiences. Brand loyalty can override price sensitivity, and consumers may continue to purchase products from their preferred brands despite price increases.

*Experiential Purchases*: Consumers may prioritise experiences over material possessions, leading them to spend on travel, entertainment, or unique experiences that fulfil their social and emotional needs rather than material goods.

*Conspicuous Consumption*: Some consumers may engage in conspicuous consumption, where they buy luxury items to display their wealth and social standing. In such cases, the higher price of a product may increase its appeal as a conspicuous status symbol.

*Personal Expression*: As consumers seek products that align with their identity and personal values, factors like aesthetics, design, and uniqueness become more important. Personal expression through possessions can be a key driver of purchasing decisions.

Due to the multifaceted nature of consumer behaviour in this context, price changes may not always lead to straightforward outcomes. Higher prices may increase desirability for certain products as status symbols, while at the same time, consumers may seek alternatives that fulfil their functional needs at a lower cost. Companies must carefully consider these psychological and social factors while formulating their marketing strategies to meet the evolving needs and preferences of their target audience.

## 14.21 Utility and Consumer Behaviour

The conventional approach of analysing changes at the margin and considering substitution effects is valuable for goods that satisfy basic needs. However, applying utility analysis, including indifference curves, to consumer behaviour in a broader sense is problematic. This approach overlooks the hierarchical nature of human needs and fails to account for various factors influencing choices beyond just price changes. Nonetheless, concepts like price elasticity of demand and income elasticity of demand remain useful in conducting analyses.

When explaining the indifference curves technique to students, it should be clarified that its application should be restricted to studying consumer choices between goods and services that satisfy similar needs, such as different food options or housing alternatives. However, it cannot be effectively used to analyse choices involving goods and services fulfilling different needs, such as comparing food and shelter to social prestige and efficiency, due to the absence of a valid marginal rate of substitution in such cases. Each specific scenario requires consideration of unique factors, making generalisations impractical.

The assumption that consumers seek to maximise utility or satisfaction implies that all goods and services possess a common denominator called utility, which can be measured or compared. However, this notion is not entirely convincing considering the hierarchy of human needs and the multifunctional nature of certain commodities, which may serve multiple needs. This complexity makes it difficult to generalise consumer equilibrium analysis.

Therefore, while utility analysis and indifference curves offer insights into consumer behaviour for goods satisfying similar needs, their application to diverse needs and preferences is limited. For a comprehensive understanding of consumer choices, other factors such as social status, personal values, and experiential preferences should also be considered alongside price and income effects.

In the context of the Equitable Optimality economic theory, it is essential to acknowledge that consumers not only prioritise meeting their personal needs but also hold a genuine concern for others within the society. They are especially attentive to the well-being of those who are struggling to have their basic necessities fulfilled. Additionally, consumers care about the overall interests of the society, encompassing aspects such as environmental preservation, prudent use of scarce resources, employment opportunities, trade balances, and capital accumulation. Their decisions are influenced by these considerations, provided they have access to relevant information.

These social concerns can significantly impact consumers' choices of goods and services, as well as the quantities they opt to purchase. Moreover, their responses to changes in prices may also be influenced by these broader societal considerations. In certain cases, factors beyond price may play a dominant role in consumer choices. For example, the consumption of essential goods that are in short supply, imported items when the society calls for import reduction, and goods and services that are encouraged or discouraged due to environmental implications, all demonstrate how social considerations can guide individual demand.

It is essential, therefore, that a comprehensive study of consumer demand incorporates these social factors. By recognising the impact of altruistic and societal concerns on consumer behaviour, a more accurate understanding of market dynamics can be achieved, enabling policymakers and businesses to make more informed decisions and promote ethical, socially responsible practices.

## 14.22 Conclusion

In this Chapter, we have made a conscious effort to be realistic and take into consideration factors that are often neglected in conventional economic theories. We recognise that economic agents, including consumers, producers, labourers, and others, do not solely pursue their self-interest but also care for others and take the interests of society into account. In the Equitable Optimality economic theory which we propose, this is the norm, where individuals are expected to be mindful of the broader goals of the economy and respect the institutional arrangements. This approach also reflects the reality in many countries, where economic agents often demonstrate a greater sense of social responsibility compared to the single-minded pursuit of self-interest depicted in conventional economic theory.

By incorporating these factors, our analysis aims to provide a more helpful and relevant understanding of economic life as it exists in practice and in alignment with the Equitable Optimality economic philosophy. While it may not be as elegant as conventional analysis, it compensates for the loss with its increased realism and applicability to real-world situations. Additionally, this approach acknowledges the potential for cooperation among market participants and the importance of mutual consultation. Such cooperation and consultation can be instrumental in achieving social and economic goals of the Equitable Optimality economic theory.

Although we have not explicitly brought the state into the model, it is essential to recognise that there may be instances where state intervention and participation are necessary. As we delve into macroeconomics, there will be opportunities to explore the role of the state as an active participant in shaping and guiding economic policies in accordance with our proposed theory.

It is evident that the Equitable Optimality theory perspective brings a unique and holistic approach to the study of economics. By incorporating societal goals, ethical considerations, and a broader range of motives in economic analysis, this perspective offers a fresh outlook on economic policies and decision-making. Some of the key implications and contributions of the Equitable Optimality theory perspective are:

1. Ethical Foundation: The Equitable Optimality theory establishes a strong ethical foundation for economic analysis, emphasising the importance of social justice, equitable distribution of resources, and caring for others' well-being. This ethical framework guides economic decision-making and policy formulation towards achieving societal welfare.
2. Recognition of Non-Monetary Values: Unlike traditional economic theory, which often focuses solely on monetary gains and individual self-interest, the Equitable Optimality theory recognises the significance of non-monetary values and motives in shaping economic behaviour. This includes considerations of social welfare, environmental sustainability, and ethical conduct in economic activities.
3. Humanising Economic Agents: By acknowledging a mix of motives and values in economic decision-making, the Equitable Optimality theory humanises economic agents, portraying them as complex individuals who care about others and pursue broader societal goals. This perspective provides a more accurate representation of human behaviour in economic contexts.
4. Broader Policy Considerations: The Equitable Optimality theory perspective calls for a broader range of interventions and policy measures beyond the market to address societal goals and meet the needs of vulnerable individuals. This

includes income transfers, redistributive measures, and investment in education and training to enhance earning capacity.
5. Emphasis on Social Responsibility: The Equitable Optimality theory places a strong emphasis on social responsibility, both for individuals and institutions. It recognises the obligations that come with property rights and freedom of enterprise and encourages individuals to consider the well-being of others in their economic decisions.
6. Redefining Economic Goals: The Equitable Optimality theory redefines the goals of the economy, placing importance on basic needs fulfilment, reducing inequality, and pursuing moral excellence. These goals go beyond mere economic growth and profit maximisation, reflecting a more comprehensive vision of economic well-being.
7. Combating Market Failures: The Equitable Optimality theory perspective acknowledges the role of government intervention in addressing market failures and promoting socially optimal outcomes. This includes correcting externalities, providing public goods, and ensuring a fair and competitive market environment.
8. Holistic Understanding of Human Prosperity: By encompassing a broad range of economic activities and societal dimensions, the Equitable Optimality theory provides a holistic understanding of human prosperity and well-being. It considers not only material needs but also the progress in aesthetic, spiritual, and social dimensions.

The Equitable Optimality theory offers a fresh and comprehensive outlook on economics, integrating ethical considerations, societal goals, and a broader range of motives into economic analysis. This approach aims to create a more compassionate, sustainable, and just economic system that aligns with the values and well-being of individuals and society as a whole. By addressing microeconomic needs from this perspective, economists can formulate more effective economic policies and achieve efficient and equitable outcomes in various economic settings.

The discussion in this Chapter highlights the critical importance of distribution in understanding economic life, particularly the initial distribution of income and wealth. The initial distribution determines individuals' purchasing power, which is essential for effective demand in the market. Emphasising the significance of distribution in achieving societal goals, the discussion suggests correcting imbalances in income and wealth distribution to create a just and equitable economic system.

The sources of income are explored, including property, work, and grants. Property, acquired through ownership or inheritance, generates income streams or direct satisfaction. Work, including labour, professional services, and entrepreneurship, influences income based on education, training, and health. Grants, given based on need or merit, play a significant role in welfare programs and family support.

The determination of wages in the labour market involves demand and supply analysis. Institutional and historical factors can lead to wage rigidity and perpetuate wage differentials over time. The concept of labour supply involves factors like pain associated with work, individual decisions influenced by societal arrangements, and macroeconomic factors. In a cooperative framework where economic decisions are made through mutual consultation and concern for others, the determination of wages is influenced by various social and ethical factors.

Profit and profit-sharing play a crucial role in an interest-balanced/free economy. Entrepreneurs take on risk and uncertainty to earn profit, which can be positive, zero, or negative. The division of joint return to capital and enterprise into profit and profit-share is contractual and depends on ratios influenced by supply and demand.

Property is a major source of income, including profit-share, rent, and rentals. Profit-sharing arrangements extend beyond money capital and land to include durable goods like buildings and machinery. Various forms of income can be derived from property, reflecting the dynamic nature of economic interactions in an interest-balanced/free economy.

Overall, the Chapter highlights the importance of understanding distribution, income sources, wage determination, profit, and property in designing an economic system aligned with societal goals and achieving equitable outcomes. It encourages considering cooperative frameworks and social considerations in economic decision-making, emphasising the need for a broader perspective in analysing macroeconomic factors and their impact on income and wealth distribution. Next Chapter is the conclusion where I share my final and concluding thoughts about what we have discussed in this book and the steps I followed in constructing the Equitable Optimality economic theory.

# Chapter 15
# A Vision for the Future

## 15.1 Introduction

The current crisis in economics knowledge can be attributed to the uncritical adoption of capitalist economic ideas by many economists globally. This has resulted in a methodological framework and underlying assumptions that clash with Equitable Optimality principles, making it challenging to integrate the two bodies of knowledge successfully. Consequently, the development of a genuine Equitable Optimality economic theory has been hindered.

While there has been a revival of interest in alternative economics in recent years, it is still in its early stages compared to the well-established conventional economics, which has evolved over centuries. The driving force behind the need for a new economic discipline arises from the recognition of limited resources compared to the numerous demands placed upon them. However, it is universally acknowledged that the well-being of all individuals should be ensured, necessitating efficient and equitable utilisation of these scarce resources.

Various societies devise strategies based on their worldviews to achieve the well-being of their members. These worldviews can be broadly categorised into secular and materialist, and spiritual and humanitarian perspectives. Equitable Optimality economics falls into the latter category, emphasising not only material well-being but also spiritual and humanitarian values. This distinction sets Equitable Optimality economics apart from conventional economics, which tends to prioritise materialistic and secular aspects.

To address this crisis of knowledge in economics and establish an authentic economic theory, this book argues for a critical rethinking and reassessment of the underlying assumptions and methodological framework of conventional economics. By proposing a new economic theory grounded in moral economy, values, and ethics, this book provides a holistic and balanced approach to economic issues. Integrating spirituality, social justice, and ethical considerations into economic


S. Alamad, *Beyond Profit*, Contributions to Economics,
https://doi.org/10.1007/978-3-031-49748-3_15

analysis, the Equitable Optimality economic theory offers a unique perspective on economic theory and policy that can contribute to the well-being of all members of society.

This proposed theory recognises that the scarcity of resources makes achieving the well-being of all a challenging task. It requires efficient and equitable utilisation of these scarce resources to meet the needs and aspirations of individuals and communities. Each society must develop strategies influenced by its worldview, shaping the values, beliefs, and principles guiding resource allocation.

A flawed worldview can hinder a society's ability to achieve the well-being of all. Misguided or skewed assumptions and values can lead to policies and strategies that do not result in optimal outcomes for the entire community.

Worldviews are often divided into two main constructs: the secular and materialist, and the spiritual and humanitarian. Economics tends to align with the former, emphasising material wealth and individual self-interest. The proposed approach in this book aligns with the latter, emphasising the moral, ethical, and humanitarian dimensions of human well-being and incorporating ethical considerations into economic decision-making.

In the end, the choice of worldview and corresponding economic strategies can significantly impact the well-being of individuals and society as a whole. Striking a balance between addressing resource scarcity and ensuring the well-being of all requires a conscious and thoughtful consideration of the underlying worldview and a rethinking of current economic theories and their implications.

## 15.2 Proposing a Genuine Economic Theory

This book posits the necessity for a fresh paradigm in economics, driven by the stark realisation of limited resources juxtaposed with an ever-increasing demand for them. Yet, in this pursuit, an overarching universal imperative remains: the well-being of all humanity must be safeguarded, necessitating the efficient and equitable stewardship of these finite resources.

Societies, in their diversity, formulate strategies rooted in their worldviews to attain the holistic well-being of their constituents. These worldviews can broadly be categorised into two streams: the secular, materialistic, and the spiritual, humanitarian. The ground-breaking Equitable Optimality economic model presented herein firmly aligns with the latter, championing not only material prosperity but also spiritual and humanitarian values. This critical distinction elevates this economic theory beyond traditional frameworks, which predominantly fixate on materialistic and secular dimensions.

This book advances a novel economic theory firmly anchored in the principles of moral economy, values, and ethics, fostering a comprehensive and balanced approach to economic conundrums. By harmonising spirituality, social justice, and ethical considerations within economic analyses, this work makes a significant contribution to the field by conceptualising the Equitable Optimality economic theory.

This theory posits that economics can meaningfully contribute to the welfare of all members of society, offering an unconventional lens through which to view economic theory and policy. In scrutinising prevalent economic theories and advocating for a re-evaluation of economics, this book further distinguishes itself by positing the Equitable Optimality theory as a pioneering alternative.

This theory contends that, in the face of resource scarcity, achieving the well-being of all becomes an arduous endeavour. It necessitates the judicious and just allocation of these finite resources to meet the needs and aspirations of individuals and communities. Every society, in this quest, devises strategies influenced by its prevailing worldview, a worldview that shapes the values, beliefs, and principles guiding resource allocation and decision-making.

Worldviews categorise into secular and materialistic, and spiritual and humanitarian constructs. The choice of worldview profoundly impacts individual and societal well-being, necessitating a re-evaluation of established economic theories. The Equitable Optimality economic theory aims for a more ethical approach, rooted in socio-economic principles.

The choice of worldview and the corresponding economic strategies wield profound implications for individual and societal well-being. Striking a balance between resource scarcity and the welfare of all mandates a conscientious examination of underlying worldviews and a reconsideration of established economic theories and their implications.

The Equitable Optimality economic theory aspires to construct a more authentic and ethical economic approach, deeply rooted in socio-economic principles and values. Achieving this vision necessitates economists to re-evaluate their methodological approaches, challenge underlying assumptions, and embrace ethical foundations that guide resource allocation and decision-making. The inclusion of third-sector institutions and a pivot from mere economic growth to comprehensive human development emerge as essential steps to nurture social well-being and justice.

The proposed interest-balanced/free system offers an alternative to the prevailing interest-based financial economy. In this system, money creation is uncoupled from debt-based lending with interest, instead aligning with profit-sharing arrangements and societal objectives that tether it to the tangible economy.

Thus, the interest-balanced/free financial economy presents a viable alternative to the interest-based paradigm, resonating with the principles of the Equitable Optimality economic model. By prioritising profit-sharing, societal objectives, and equitable resource allocation, this system strives to create a more inclusive and equitable society. Nevertheless, comprehensive research and practical implementation are imperative to fully comprehend its potential impact and address any challenges that may arise during the transition.

Hence, the Equitable Optimality economic theory offers a valuable perspective within the realm of economics. Its emphasis on ethical foundations, recognition of non-monetary values, humanisation of economic agents, and a broader policy perspective enrich our understanding of economic behaviour and the pursuit of societal welfare. While not seeking to supplant conventional economic theories, it presents an alternative framework that can inspire novel approaches to economic analysis and policymaking, all with the ultimate objective of fostering a more prosperous and harmonious society for all.

## 15.3 Internal Influences

The design and construction of the Equitable Optimality economic theory has been influenced by multi-level internal factors. As you probably have noticed I refer in this book to religious texts, and also to various economic theories that I find influential in their meaning and contextual application for a better economic theory. I take good aspects wherever I find it, and I know some may criticise this approach or argue that economics is a secular science. However, I believe this is the right approach, and as researchers we should seek the truth, knowledge, and reform whenever and wherever we find it regardless of labels. This is a call to every economist, researcher, and policymaker to leave out labels and rethink our approach to economics and reform our practices. I reiterate that I am not apologetical about this approach, however I fully respect the view of those who disagree with it.

You probably also noticed that profit and profit-share are key aspects of the Equitable Optimality economic theory in the various discussions and arguments I made throughout this book. This was not arbitrary, we need an economic culture shift and change in our current economic knowledge, theories, and implementation to reform the global economy and ensure its sustainability. This aspect is supported by various religious texts and advocated by well-known economists as argued in this book.

The Quran (Surah Ar-Rum, 9) says: "They were stronger than them in strength, and they raised the land *and built it more than they built* it (i.e., Earth), and their messengers came to them with clear evidence, so God would not wrong them …". It reminds believers to reflect on the consequences faced by those who came before them as a lesson. The verse speaks of people who inhabited the land before and how they neglected the development and progress of their societies. Instead of nurturing and building up their communities, they focused more on self-indulgence and negligence.

Despite receiving clear signs and guidance from messengers sent by God, they chose to ignore the truth and commit wrong actions, ultimately leading to their own downfall. God, in His justice, does not wrong anyone, but individuals wrong themselves by rejecting the path of righteousness and wisdom.

This verse serves as a reminder to the believers that they should learn from the mistakes of those who came before them and follow the guidance of God's messengers to avoid falling into similar pitfalls. It encourages self-reflection, seeking knowledge from history, and making wise choices to avoid repeating the errors of the past. As humans (economists, politicians, policy-makes, individuals, groups…) we seem to fail to acknowledge this fact, and even if we acknowledge it; we fail to translate it into actions or practice it.

Another verse regulates economic consumption behaviour and guides how a balanced consumption approach should be in a very nice and meaningful simile. The Quran says: 'And do not make your hand shackled to your neck, and do not spread it out to the fullest extent, lest you remain blamed, destitute' (al Isra, 17: 29).

This verse contains guidance on the importance of balanced spending and avoiding both excessive stinginess and reckless extravagance. The verse advises people not to withhold their hand from spending for the sake of good causes, such as charity and helping those in need. However, it also warns against putting undue pressure on themselves or their families by spending beyond their means. The guidance is to strike a balance in spending, avoiding both extremes.

The metaphor of "making your hand tied to your neck" refers to severe stinginess, indicating a miserly and tight-fisted attitude towards spending. On the other hand, "spreading it fully" refers to excessive spending, giving more than one can afford, leading to regret and financial difficulties. The consequence of extreme stinginess or extravagance is being "blamed" or criticised for one's actions. If someone follows either extreme, they may end up in a state of destitution or financial hardship, with no money left in their hand and no praise for their actions.

The Quran emphasises the importance of moderation and balance in all aspects of life, including spending. It encourages people to be generous and charitable while being responsible with their resources and not overspending. By striking this balance, individuals can avoid financial difficulties and ensure their actions are praiseworthy.

In the same context, the passage from Matthew (25:14–30) emphasises the concept of maximising productivity and using our creativity to create more than what previously existed. It teaches the importance of stewardship, which involves investing and utilising the resources we are given to make a profit and contribute to the common good. The notion of profit is not solely about financial gain but rather having something left over after investing time, talent, and resources. This leftover or residual assets enable us to serve others and participate in bringing about positive change and human flourishing.

Each person is uniquely crafted with different gifts and talents, and good stewardship requires us to wholeheartedly use these gifts to benefit others and society. It emphasises the importance of abundance, not for its own sake, but because it glorifies God and allows us to have more to give and share with others. Abundance enables us to have a sustainable base for service, generosity, and investment.

Without profit, it becomes challenging to have resources left over to invest in others, and the consequences of not practicing good stewardship can be detrimental to ourselves and others. Leftovers, or profits, provide us with additional opportunities to serve and advance the common good.

The passage from Jeremiah (29:7) is a message of hope and guidance from the prophet Jeremiah to the Israelites who were exiled in Babylon. In this letter, Jeremiah instructs the exiles to seek the peace and prosperity of the city where they have been taken as captives. He encourages them to contribute positively to the well-being of the society they are now a part of, even though it is not their homeland.

The essence of this message lies in the idea of mutual prosperity and inclusiveness. Jeremiah emphasises that the prosperity of the exiles is intertwined with the prosperity of the city they are living in. In other words, they should strive for the betterment of their new community, for in doing so, they will also benefit themselves.

This biblical concept of prosperity is not rooted in selfishness, exploitation, or greed. Instead, it promotes a holistic and cooperative approach to societal development. It encourages individuals to contribute positively to the welfare of their community, thus fostering a sense of unity and cooperation among its members.

Jeremiah's message is a reminder that prosperity is not solely an individual pursuit but rather a collective endeavour that benefits everyone in society. It underscores the importance of creating an environment that allows for mutual growth and well-being, where individuals work together for the common good rather than focusing solely on personal gain.

In the context of the modern world, this message remains relevant. Many nations have achieved varying degrees of prosperity, but there is a need to extend these opportunities to all members of society. By embracing principles of inclusivity, cooperation, and a focus on the common good, societies can work towards creating an environment where mutual prosperity becomes a reality for everyone. This involves addressing systemic inequalities and ensuring that all individuals have access to opportunities for growth and advancement.

The message from Jeremiah serves as a timeless reminder that true prosperity is not attained through exploitation or selfish pursuits but through collective efforts aimed at the well-being and progress of all members of society.

The pursuit of profit within Biblical parameters is seen as objectively good, as it aligns with seeking the peace and prosperity of the community. Biblical prosperity is inclusive and extends to all members of society, promoting mutual benefit and avoiding exploitative or corrupt practices. The market economy, when guided by such religious principles, encourages entrepreneurs to find innovative solutions to problems and contribute to the well-being of society.

The passage highlights the importance of stewardship, creativity, and the pursuit of profit within ethical and moral boundaries. It emphasises that when profit is pursued with a focus on the common good, it becomes a mechanism for advancing social well-being and prosperity for all members of society. By integrating spiritual values and ethical considerations into economic decision-making, a flourishing society can be achieved where mutual prosperity is the shared goal.

Reflecting on what is being discussed about the above important points profit, interest-free economy, and the role of religion, I refer to one highly regarded classical economist. Adam Smith, often considered the father of modern economics, discussed the concept of profit in his seminal work "The Wealth of Nations" (1776). Smith recognised profit as a vital component of a market economy. According to him, profit serves as the main incentive for entrepreneurs and businesses to invest their capital and engage in productive activities. In a market economy, individuals seek to maximise their own self-interest, and profit acts as a powerful motivator to achieve that goal.

Smith argued that when individuals pursue their self-interest in a competitive market, they inadvertently contribute to the overall welfare of society. Through the pursuit of profit, businesses strive to provide goods and services that meet the demands of consumers, leading to an efficient allocation of resources and an increase in the overall wealth of nations.

Smith's famous concept of the "invisible hand" captures this idea, suggesting that the pursuit of self-interest in a free market can lead to socially beneficial outcomes. In other words, when individuals and firms seek profit through voluntary exchanges in the marketplace, they inadvertently promote the well-being of society as a whole.

**Interest-Free Economy:** Adam Smith did not specifically advocate for an interest-free economy in his works. In fact, he recognised the importance of interest rates in a market economy as a mechanism for allocating capital and balancing supply and demand for funds. Interest rates play a crucial role in determining the cost of borrowing and the return on investment in an interest-based economic system. They influence decisions about saving, investment, and consumption. In a market economy, interest rates help to coordinate the actions of borrowers and lenders, facilitating the flow of funds from savers to investors.

While Smith did not argue against interest rates, he did caution against usury (excessive or exploitative interest rates) in his other work titled "Lectures on Jurisprudence." Smith was critical of usury laws that set arbitrary limits on interest rates, as he believed that such regulations could hinder productive economic activity and lead to inefficiencies. I guess Smith did not envisage an interest-free economy to exist at that time, which we argue the opposite in this book.

**Role of Religion:** Adam Smith discussed the role of religion in society in his earlier work "The Theory of Moral Sentiments" (1759). In this book, Smith explored the moral foundations of human behaviour and the role of sympathy and conscience in guiding human actions. Smith argued that religious sentiments and beliefs played a crucial role in shaping individuals' moral conduct and behaviour. He believed that religion, through its teachings and moral codes, could influence people to act with benevolence, compassion, and justice towards others. Smith saw religion as a significant force in promoting social cohesion and cooperation.

However, it is important to note that while Smith recognised the role of religion in influencing individual behaviour and social norms, he also emphasised the importance of human reason and natural moral sentiments in guiding ethical conduct. He did not advocate for religious dogma to dominate public life, and his ideas on economics and social organisation were based on reason and the observable patterns of human behaviour. Nevertheless, he acknowledged the important role of religion in consumer economic behaviour.

It is worth mentioning that Adam Smith's views on these topics were shaped by the context of his time, and his writings have been subject to various interpretations and critiques over the years. As with any historical figure, it is essential to consider the broader historical and intellectual context in which his ideas were formulated.

## 15.4 The Detrimental Impact of Human Economic Actions on the Economic Ecosystem

Human economic actions have resulted in significant negative consequences for the environment, society, Earth, and the economic ecosystem. Current economic activities contribute to environmental degradation, social inequalities, and the erosion of natural resources. We have offered analysis in this book that explores the interconnectedness of these issues and highlights the urgent need for sustainable economic practices that prioritise environmental protection, social well-being, and long-term economic stability.

**Economic Cycles:** The current trajectory of human economic actions is marked by excessive consumption, resource exploitation, and environmental degradation. Industrialisation, urbanisation, and globalisation have led to unprecedented levels of economic growth, but this has come at a significant cost to the environment and society. We explored how various economic activities, including industrial production, deforestation, and the reliance on fossil fuels, have harmed the environment, caused social disparities, and jeopardised the overall economic ecosystem. Also increasing the frequency of economic cycles. We predict that in future, in the next five (5) decades, economic cycles will become more frequent on average every eight (8) years with unconventional causes and consequences, unless we start doing something about it.

**Environmental Degradation:**

a. Climate Change: One of the most pressing consequences of human economic actions is climate change. Greenhouse gas emissions from industrial activities, transportation, and energy production have led to global warming and extreme weather events. Rising sea levels threaten coastal communities, and disruptions in weather patterns impact agriculture, water resources, and ecosystems.
b. Pollution and Resource Depletion: Economic activities, such as industrial manufacturing and intensive agriculture, release pollutants into the air, water, and soil. This leads to air pollution, water contamination, and soil degradation. Additionally, the depletion of natural resources, such as fossil fuels and minerals, is accelerating, jeopardising future economic sustainability.
c. Biodiversity Loss: Economic activities, including deforestation and habitat destruction, have caused a significant decline in global biodiversity. The loss of biodiversity disrupts ecosystems, leading to imbalances in natural processes and a reduction in ecosystem services critical for human well-being.

**Social Disparities and Inequalities:**

a) Income Inequality: Current economic systems have exacerbated income inequalities, with wealth and resources concentrated in the hands of a few, while a significant portion of the population struggles to meet basic needs. This disparity hampers social cohesion and stability, affecting overall economic productivity.

b) Exploitative Labour Practices: In pursuit of economic growth and profitability, some industries engage in exploitative labour practices, including child labour, forced labour, and poor working conditions. These practices perpetuate social injustices and undermine human dignity.
c) Displacement and Social Disruptions: Manmade disasters, such as wars and poor economic policies force people to seek a refuge in other regions and countries, looking for safety, better and dignified life. Economic development projects, such as large-scale infrastructure projects, often lead to the displacement of communities and disruptions to traditional livelihoods. Indigenous communities, in particular, are disproportionately affected, losing their land, cultural heritage, and social cohesion.

**Erosion of Natural Resources:**

a) Unsustainable Consumption: Current economic models promote a culture of excessive consumption, leading to the depletion of natural resources beyond their regenerative capacity. This overconsumption is driving ecological overshoot and increasing the strain on the planet's ecosystems.
b) Short-Term Focus: The prevailing economic mindset often prioritises short-term gains over long-term sustainability. This approach leads to the overexploitation of resources without adequate consideration of future generations' needs.

**Impact on the Economic Ecosystem:**

a) Financial Instabilities: Environmental degradation and social inequalities can contribute to financial instabilities. Climate-related events, resource scarcity, and social unrest can disrupt supply chains, increase production costs, and create uncertainties in financial markets.
b) Diminished Resilience: An economy that neglects environmental and social considerations becomes less resilient to external shocks and crises. Natural disasters, pandemics, or social unrest can have severe economic consequences.

Hence, current human economic practices have far-reaching and detrimental consequences on the environment, society, Earth, and the economic ecosystem. The interconnectedness of these issues necessitates a holistic approach to address the challenges posed by unsustainable economic practices. Transitioning towards a sustainable economic model that prioritises environmental protection, social equity, and long-term economic stability is imperative for securing a prosperous future for all. Policymakers, businesses, and individuals must collaborate to promote sustainable consumption, responsible production, and equitable distribution of resources to build a resilient and thriving global economy. The urgency of the situation demands immediate action to mitigate the harmful impacts and work towards a more sustainable and equitable world.

## 15.5 The Call for a Responsible and Equitable Economic Model: It Is Time for Reflection and Action

As I mentioned in the introduction, what motivated this book is realising and acknowledging that it is time for reflection and rethinking economics in light of new challenges and changes globally. We need to be brave and address those issues head on, even if that means we challenge the conventional status quo. I strongly believe that it is time to develop improved economic model and its theories which are compatible with the world we live in and its challenges. This is my objective and what I aim to achieve in this book.

## 15.6 What Is Proposed? The Equitable Optimality Economic Theory

The proposed Equitable Optimality economic theory aims to construct a more authentic and ethical approach to economics, grounded in socio-economic principles and values. To achieve this, economists need to re-evaluate their methodological approaches, question underlying assumptions, and embrace ethical foundations that guide decision-making and resource allocation. Incorporating third-sector institutions and shifting the focus from mere economic growth to holistic human development which are essential steps to foster social welfare and justice.

Furthermore, promoting interdisciplinary research that bridges moral economy, ethics, and economics can enrich our understanding and application of economic principles. By adopting alternative foundations, economists can pave the way for a genuine and robust economic theory that aligns with moral principles and values, leading to a more meaningful and effective approach to economic development and social welfare.

I have argued that contextual understanding is crucial in the study of economics, helping individuals internalise economic ideas and making them more applicable to real-life experiences. The proposed economic theory provides a guiding framework for a new way of economic life and behaviour, emphasising justice, fairness, and ethical conduct in economic activities, leading to a more inclusive and just society.

Overall, the proposed economic worldview governs all aspects of economic lifecycle, encouraging the pursuit of prosperity within the boundaries of justice and ethical behaviour. By adhering to this framework, individuals can achieve both material well-being and spiritual growth, leading purposeful and meaningful lives that reflect their beliefs and values.

## 15.7 The Financial Economy Proposal

The proposed interest-balanced/free banking system provides a different approach to the current financial interest-based economy. In this system, money creation is not tied to debt-based lending with interest. Instead, money is created based on profit-sharing arrangements and social objectives, which instead tie up with the real economy. For example, banks may invest in productive activities and share the profits with their depositors. This profit-sharing mechanism ensures that money creation is linked to real economic activity and shared benefits.

The interest-balanced/free banking system also eliminates the burden of interest payments on borrowers, reducing financial stress and promoting a more equitable distribution of resources. Moreover, it aligns with the principles of the Equitable Optimality economic model, which seeks to achieve social welfare, universal need fulfilment, and economic stability.

In the interest-balanced/free banking system, fiscal policy plays a significant role in achieving economic objectives. Through progressive taxation and targeted transfer payments, the government can address income and wealth inequality, promote economic development, and ensure basic needs are met for all members of society. Investment in infrastructure and strategic projects further supports economic growth and stability.

However, despite the potential benefits of the interest-balanced/free banking system, there are challenges in implementing and transitioning from the conventional interest-based system. Education and awareness are crucial to ensure a smooth transition and gain public support for the new approach. Additionally, the development of new analytical tools to study income distribution and inflation dynamics within the Equitable Optimality economic context is essential to effectively assess the system's performance and make informed policy decisions.

Therefore, the interest-balanced/free banking system offers a viable alternative to the interest-based system, aligning with the principles of the Equitable Optimality economic model. By focusing on profit-sharing, social objectives, and equitable resource allocation, this system aims to create a more inclusive and just society. However, further research and practical implementation are necessary to fully understand its potential impact and address any challenges that may arise during the transition.

Indeed, providing more specific details on the mechanics of the interest-balanced/free banking system, its implementation, regulatory framework, and potential challenges and benefits would be essential to fully understand its feasibility and impact. A comprehensive analysis of the theory would require exploring various aspects of the system to ensure its viability and effectiveness.

## 15.8 Macroeconomics and Microeconomics

Integrating insights from economic theories on the demand for money and its relationship with income-yielding assets within the context of an interest-free/balanced economy would enrich the understanding of monetary dynamics in the proposed model. Understanding how the demand for money and investment choices interplay within this economic system can shed light on the factors influencing resource allocation and economic growth.

Furthermore, conducting empirical studies and simulations to test the interest-balanced/free financial economy system's performance in different economic scenarios and conditions would be crucial. Analysing the system's stability, its ability to promote equitable wealth distribution, and its impact on economic growth and inflation would provide valuable insights for policymakers and researchers.

Moreover, examining the social and ethical implications of the proposed economic model is also essential. Understanding how profit-sharing and investment-based money creation align with the real economy and principles of justice, fairness, and social welfare can highlight the potential benefits of the system in promoting a more inclusive and just society.

Finally, exploring the transition process from a conventional interest-based system to the interest-balanced/free banking system would be crucial. Identifying the potential obstacles, challenges, and strategies for a smooth transition can provide valuable guidance for policymakers and stakeholders.

Overall, by incorporating these additional elements and conducting comprehensive research, the proposed interest-balanced/free banking system, as part of the Equitable Optimality economic model, can be further developed and refined to offer a unique and potentially more stable economic framework. This comprehensive analysis would contribute to the ongoing dialogue in economics and provide practical insights for shaping economic policies that align with the principles of justice, social welfare, and sustainable economic growth.

Hence, the Equitable Optimality economic theory perspective offers a more comprehensive and human-centred approach to economic analysis and policy-making. It recognises the inherent complexities of economic behaviour, the interplay of various motives and values, and the importance of ethical considerations in guiding economic decisions. By incorporating societal goals, ethical values, and a broader understanding of human prosperity, the theory seeks to foster a more inclusive, just, and sustainable economic system.

However, it is important to acknowledge that implementing and operationalising the Equitable Optimality economic theory would require careful consideration and research. It would entail designing appropriate policy measures, creating regulatory frameworks, and addressing potential challenges and trade-offs. Empirical studies and real-world applications would be essential to test the effectiveness and feasibility of the proposed model.

Moreover, the transition from conventional economic systems to the Equitable Optimality economic model would likely encounter resistance and barriers, given the entrenched nature of existing economic practices. Overcoming these challenges would require collaboration among policymakers, economists, businesses, and communities to build consensus and commitment towards the common goal of a more just and equitable economic system.

Thus, the Equitable Optimality economic theory perspective represents a valuable contribution to the field of economics. Its emphasis on ethical foundations, recognition of non-monetary values, humanisation of economic agents, and broader policy considerations enriches our understanding of economic behaviour and the pursuit of societal welfare. While it may not fully replace conventional economic theories, it offers an alternative framework that can inspire new approaches to economic analysis and policymaking, with the ultimate aim of creating a more prosperous and harmonious society for all.

## 15.9 A Practical Roadmap to Transition to an Equitable Optimality Economy

In the context of the Equitable Optimality economic theory, transitioning from an interest-based financial economy to an interest-free financial economy is a significant paradigm shift. This proposed roadmap outlines a practical and systematic approach to achieve this transition, considering economic, legal, and social aspects.

### *Embracing Alternative Finance Models*

One fundamental step in moving towards an interest-free financial economy is drawing inspiration from alternative finance models. These models, grounded in profit and loss-sharing arrangements and asset-backed financing, provide a promising alternative to conventional interest-based systems. To promote this transition:

- **Regulatory Framework:** Governments and central banks should create a regulatory framework that accommodates these alternative financial institutions. This framework must address taxation, accounting standards, and legal structures to ensure fair competition with conventional interest-based products.

### *Gradual Transition to an Interest-Balanced System*

Recognising the substantial challenges of an immediate shift, the roadmap proposes a gradual transition from an interest-based system to an interest-balanced economic system. The process begins with a 50/50 split between interest-based and interest-balanced systems, evolving steadily over time. Specifically, every five years, the interest-balanced portion increases by at least 7–10%. The estimate of 7-10% gradual approach is based on what is believed to be reasonable and realistic approach, similar to the approach taken currently in moving away from petrol and diesel to electric vehicles, which is considered a subestential shift. This estimate is also consistent with the Bank of England (2023) analysis regarding the debt-to-income ratio trend and its movement, as discussed earlier in this book.

## *Promoting Ethical and Socially Responsible Finance*

Transitioning to an interest-free financial economy also involves promoting ethical and socially responsible finance. This approach encourages financial institutions to consider the broader societal and environmental impacts of their investments. To facilitate this shift:

- **Incentivising Ethical Finance:** Governments can provide tax benefits or subsidies to financial institutions prioritising ethical investments. This encourages a shift towards socially responsible practices.
- **Transparency and Disclosure:** Financial institutions should be required to disclose the environmental and social impacts of their investments. Informed consumers can make conscious choices about where they deposit their funds, aligning their values with their economic behaviour.

## *Developing Innovative Financial Instruments*

Creating alternative financial instruments that offer attractive returns without relying on interest is vital for this transition. Innovative products based on profit-sharing, equity investments, and risk-sharing can help drive this change:

- **Equity-based funding:** One example is equity-based funding platforms, allowing investors to buy shares in start-ups and small businesses in exchange for a share of future profits. This offers an alternative to traditional debt financing.

## *Ensuring Financial Inclusion*

A crucial aspect of transitioning to an interest-free financial economy is ensuring universal access to financial services. Financial inclusion initiatives can bridge gaps and bring unbanked and underbanked populations into the formal financial system:

- **Digital Financial Services:** Governments and international organisations should promote digital financial services to reach underserved populations efficiently.

- **Financial Literacy Programs:** Creating educational programs that enhance financial literacy empowers individuals to make informed financial decisions.

### *Gradual Phasing Out of Interest-Based Instruments*

Transitioning away from interest-based instruments requires a gradual and phased approach:

- **Timeline for Transition:** Governments and central banks should set a clear timeline for the discontinuation of certain interest-bearing products, similar to how countries are transitioning to electric vehicles. This gradual reduction in interest-based loans minimises disruptions to the financial system.

### *International Collaboration and Standards*

Achieving a global shift to an interest-free financial economy necessitates international cooperation:

- **Global Standards:** Collaborative efforts to develop global standards for ethical and interest-free finance will create a supportive international environment and ecosystem.
- **Role of International Organisations:** International organisations like the United Nations, the World Bank, and the International Monetary Fund can facilitate this transition by advocating for ethical finance principles and providing technical assistance to countries making the shift in collaboration with other global partners.

It is vital to acknowledge that transitioning to an interest-free financial economy is a complex, long-term endeavour. Success depends on the commitment of governments, financial institutions, regulators, and society. Additionally, educating stakeholders about the benefits of this approach for the global economy and the well-being of individuals and society is crucial. Ultimately, the goal is to create a financial system that not only sustains economic soundness but also adheres to ethical and social responsibility principles, fostering prosperity for all.

## 15.10 Concluding This Journey

In this concluding chapter, I have revisited the key components of the Equitable Optimality economic theory, emphasising its ethical and moral foundations, focus on societal welfare, and emphasis on cooperation and mutual concern. The theory's core principles, such as profit-sharing, interest-balanced/free financial economy, property, and the importance of addressing income and wealth distribution, are reiterated as crucial aspects of achieving an equitable and just economic system. Some economists may argue that I am being idealistic in my approach, the proposed theory and the roadmap outlined for its implementation. However, what I have proposed and discussed can be achieved and implemented, delivering real value and benefits to all stakeholders in our global economic system. Any new innovative theory or concept has to start somewhere. It may (and will) encounter resistance from believers in the current economic order as it challenges existing assumptions and theories, but I believe this theory will evolve and will ignite scholarly discussions about its viability and importance.

Furthermore, I reflect on the journey of constructing the Equitable Optimality economic theory, highlighting the analytical tools and methodologies used to challenge conventional economic assumptions and incorporate ethical and moral economic considerations. I discussed the significance of revisiting methodological approaches, questioning underlying assumptions, and integrating social objectives in economic practices and analysis to create a more authentic and relevant economic framework. Clearly setting policy implications and steps forward for the implementation of this theory. This enables us to address current economic challenges and increased economic cycles, which are becoming more frequent and lasting longer than before. Enabling us to plan for a better economic future that is stable and resilient.

Moreover, this concluding Chapter provides insights into the key challenges and potential obstacles that may arise in the practical implementation of the Equitable Optimality economic theory. It recognises the need for further research, empirical testing, and cooperation among stakeholders to navigate the transition from the economic system to the proposed alternative.

I further argue for the above change by emphasising the transformative potential of the Equitable Optimality economic theory and its capacity to foster a more compassionate, sustainable, and inclusive economic system. It reinforces the significance of placing ethical considerations and societal welfare at the core of economic decision-making and policy formulation.

Overall, this concluding Chapter serves as a thoughtful and comprehensive closure to this book, summarising its key arguments and contributions while inspiring readers to explore the potential of the Equitable Optimality economic theory in shaping a more equitable and just economic future. With this statement I conclude this book, and I am grateful for you to accompany me on this journey and read my economic thoughts, and what I have got to say about our current economic theories.

# References


Abdul-Hakim, K. (1953). *Islam and communism*. Institute of Islamic.
ACS Z. (2000). *Regional innovation, knowledge, and global change*. Frances Pinter.
Adams, P. C. (1996). Protest and the scale politics of telecommunications. *Political Geography, 15*(5), 419–441.
Aghion P. (1998). Inequality and economic growth, in Aghion P. and Williamson J. G. Growth, inequality and globalization, pp. 5–102. Cambridge University Press, .
Agnew, J. (1993). Representing space: Space, scale and culture in social science. In J. Duncan & D. Ley (Eds.), *Place/culture/representation* (pp. 251–271). Routledge.
Agwani, M. S. (1967). Islamic fundamentalism in India (Chandigarh: TwentyFirst century India society, 1986). Ahmad, Aziz, Mawdudi and orthodox fundamentalism in Pakistan. *Middle East Journal, 21*, 369–380.
Ahmad, A. R., & Yousri. (2011). Role of finance in achieving Maqid al-Sharah. *Islamic Economic Studies, 19*(2), 1–18.
Ahmad, I. (Ed.). (1978). *Caste and stratification among Muslims in India*. Manohar.
Ahmad, K. (1957). *Islam and the west*. Jama'at-i-Islami Pakistan.
Ahmad, K. (1969). *Islam aur socialism (Islam and socialism)*. Maktabah Chiragh-e Rah.
Ahmad, K. (Ed.). (1980). *Studies in Islamic economics*. International Centre for Research in Islamic Economics, King Abdulaziz University.
Ahmad, K. (1981). Economic development in an Islamic framework. In K. Ahmad (Ed.), *Studies in Islamic economics* (pp. 171–188). Jeddah.
Ahmad, M. (1991). Islamic fundamentalism in South Asia: The Jamaati Islami and the Tablighi Jamaat of South Asia. In M. E. Marty & R. Scott Appleby (Eds.), *Fundamentalisms observed*. University of Chicago Press.
Akerlof, G. A., & Shiller, R. J. (2015). *Phishing for phools: The economics of manipulation and deception*. Princeton University Press.
Al-`Ashur, Muhammad b. al-Tahir (1366H). (n.d.). *Maqasid al-Shariah al-Islamiyah*, Tunis.
Alamad, S. (2016). Risk management methodologies: An empirical macro-prudential approach for a resilient regulatory framework for the Islamic finance industry. In M. Zulkhibri et al. (Eds.), *Macroprudential regulation and policy for the Islamic financial industry theory and applications*. Springer.
Alamad, S. (2017a). *Financial innovation and engineering in Islamic finance*. Springer.
Alamad, S. (2017b). Islamic finance ethics and perception of Western consumers. *European Journal of Islamic Finance, 6*, 2017.
Alamad, S. (2019a). *Financial and accounting principles in Islamic finance*. Springer.




S. Alamad, *Beyond Profit*, Contributions to Economics,
https://doi.org/10.1007/978-3-031-49748-3

Alamad, S. (2019b). Stress testing and reverse stress testing: An approach for a resilient Islamic financial industry. In M. Zulkhibri et al. (Eds.), *Islamic monetary economics and institutions: Theory and practice*. Springer.

Alamad, S. (2020). Case studies of Shari'ah governance in practice: United Kingdom and Europe. In N. Ali et al. (Eds.), *The Edinburgh companion to Shari'ah governance in Islamic finance*. Edinburgh University Press.

Alamad, S. (2023). Conceptualising accounting as a value-based concept in the context of alternative finance. *Journal of Accounting Literature, ahead-of-print*(ahead-of-print). https://doi.org/10.1108/JAL-03-2023-0042

Alamad, S., et al. (2021). A shared boundary object: Financial innovation and engineering in Islamic financial institutions. *The British Accounting Review, 53*(3), 100958.

al-Bukhari, Muhammad b, Isma'il. (1987). *al-Jami` al-Sahaih*. Dar al-Sha'b.

Al-Fasi, A. (1983). *Maqasid al-Shari'ah wa Makarimuha*. Ghazanfar.

Al-Ghazali, M. B. M. (1997). *Al-Mustasfa men 'Elm al-Asoul*. Beirut.

Al-Haithami, I. H. (2010). *Tuhfat al-Muhtaj Shareh al-Minhaj*. Beirut.

Ali, S. N. (2008). A roadmap for making Islamic finance sources more accessible the role of secondary Services in the Dissemination of research. In *The 7th international conference in Islamic economics* (pp. 225–233). King Abdulaziz University.

al-Jarhi, Mabid Ali. (2012). Gaps in the theory and practice of Islamic economics. In *Workshop On the future of Islamic economics*. Islamic Economics Institute, King Abdulaziz University.

Allouche, A. (1994). *Mamluk economics: A study and translation of Al-Maqrizi's Ighathah*. University of Utah Press.

Alonso, W. (1980). Five bell shapes in development. *Papers of the Regional Science Association, 45*, 5–16.

al-Sadr, M. B. (1961). *Iqtisaduna*. World Organization for Islamic Services.

al-Sadr, Muhammad Baqir. (1982-1984). *Iqtisaduna: Our economics, 4 vols. Orig. Arabic ed., 1961*. World Organization for Islamic Services.

Al-Suwaidi, A. (1993). Developments of the legal Systems of the Gulf Arab States. *Arab Law Quarterly, 8*(4), 289–301.

al-Suwailem, Sami. (2006). *Hedging in Islamic finance*. Islamic Research and Training Institute.

Aman, A. C., Jr. (1998). The globalizing state: A future-oriented perspective on the public/private distinction, federalism, and democracy. *Vanderbilt Journal of Transnational Law, 31*(4), 769, 870.

Amin, A., & Thrift, N. (1994). *Globalization, institutions and regional development in Europe*. Oxford University Press.

Amin, A., & Thrift, N. (2002). Spatialities of globalisation. *Environment and Planning A, 34*(3), 385–399. Sassen: Globalization or Denationalization?

Amsden, A. (1989). *Asia's next Giant: South Korea and late industrialization*. Oxford University Press.

Andersson, A., & Andersson, D. (Eds.). (2000). *Gateways to the global economy*. Edward Elgar.

Annheur, M. G., & Kaldor, M. (Eds.). (2002). *Global civil society yearbook* (pp. 226–227). Oxford University Press.

Ansari, S. (1991). Political legacies of Pre-1947 Sind. In D. A. Low (Ed.), *The political inheritance of Pakistan* (pp. 173–193). St. Martin's Press.

Antonelli, C. (1994). Technological districts, localized spillovers, and productivity growth: The Italian evidence of technological externalities in the core regions. *International Review of Applied Economics, 8*, 18–30.

Appadurai, A. (1996). *Modernity at large*. University of Minnesota Press.

Aquinas, St Thomas Summa Theologica in Monroe. (1948). *Early economic thought, selections from economic literature prior to Adam Smith* (pp. 51–78). Harvard University Press.

Aquinas, T. (1920). *Summa Theologica* (Fathers of the English Dominican Province, Trans.). Retrieved from http://www.newadvent.org/summa/3078.htm.

Ariely, D. (2008a). *Predictably irrational: The hidden forces that shape our decisions*. Collins.

Ariely, D. (2008b). *Predictably irrational*. Harper Collins.
Aristotle The Politics in Monroe. (1948). *Early economic thought, selections from economic literature prior to Adam Smith* (pp. 1–30). Harvard University Press.
Armstrong, K. (2000). *Islam: A short history*. Weidenfeld & Nicolson.
Arrighi, G. (1994). *The long twentieth century. Money, power, and the origins of our times*. Verso.
Asheim, B. T. (2000). Industrial districts: The contributions of Marshall and beyond. In G. L. Clark, M. P. Feldman, & M. Gertler (Eds.), *The Oxford handbook of economic geography* (pp. 413–431). Oxford University Press.
Ashraf, M., & al-Sibai, Mustafa. (1960). *al-Ishtirakiyah wa'l-Islam (the Islamic socialism)*. Damascus.
Askari, H., Iqbal, Z., Krichene, N., & Mirakhor, A. (2012). *Risk sharing in finance: The Islamic finance alternative*. John Wiley and Sons (Asia), Pte. Ltd.
Audretsch, D. B., & Feldman, M. P. (1996). R&D spillovers and the geography of innovation and production. *The American Economic Review, 86*(3), 630–640.
Autor, D. H., Levy, F., & Murnane, R. J. (2003). The skill content of recent technological change: An empirical exploration. *The Quarterly Journal of Economics, 118*(4), 1279–1333. http://www.jstor.org/stable/25053940
Aziz, K. K. (1967). *The making of Pakistan: A study in nationalism*. Chatto & Windus.
Azzoni, C. R. (1986). *Indu'stria e reversa˜o de polarizac¸a˜o no Brasil, Essays in Economics No. 58*. Institute of Economic Studies, University of Sa˜o Paulo.
Baeck, L. (1994). *The Mediterranean tradition in economic thought*. Routledge.
Bailey, M. (1971). National Income and the Price level.
Bairoch, P. (1988). *Cities and economic development*. University of Chicago Press.
Baker, J. A., & White, M. D., eds., (2016, March). *Economics and the virtues: Building a new moral foundation* (Vol. 41, No. 1, pp. 142–145). Oxford University Press.
Bakhash, S. (1989). "What Khomeini Did," New York Review of Books, July 20, 16–19.
Balassa, B. A. (1981). *The newly industrializing countries in the world economy*. Pergamon.
Balibar, E., & Wallerstein, I. (1991). *Race, nation, class: Ambiguous identities*. Verso.
Banani, A. (1961). *The modernization of Iran, 1921–1941*. Stanford University Press.
Barnes, W., & Ledebur, L. C. (1998). *The new regional economies: The US common market and the global economy*. Sage.
Bartik, T. (1991). *Who benefits from state and local economic development policies?* Upjohn Institute.
Bator, F. M. (1958). The anatomy of market failure. *The Quarterly Journal of Economics, 72*, 351–379.
Bauer, P. T., & Yamey, B. S. (1957). *The economics of under-developed countries*. University of Chicago Press.
Baumol, W. J. (1952). The transactions demand for cash: An inventory approach. *Quarterly Journal of Economics*.
Beaverstock, J., Smith, R., & Taylor, P. (2000). World city network: A new metageography? *Annals of the Association of American Geographers, 90*(1), 123–134.
Becattini, G. (1990). The Marshallian industrial district as a socio-economic notion. In F. Pyke, G. Becattini, & W. Sengenberger (Eds.), *Industrial districts and inter-firm cooperation in Italy* (pp. 37–51). International Institute for Labour Studies.
Beck, U. (1999). *World risk society*. Polity Press.
Becker, G. S. (1964). *Human capital: A theoretical and empirical analysis, with special reference to education*. University of Chicago Press.
Behdad, S. (1994). A disputed utopia: Islamic economics in revolutionary Iran. *Comparative Studies in Society and History., 36*(4), 775–813.
Behdad, S. (1989). Property rights in contemporary Islamic economic thought: A critical perspective. *Review of Social Economy, 47*, 185–211.
Belouai, A., Belabes, A., & Trullols, C. (2012). *Islamic finance in Western higher education: Developments and prospects*. Palgrave Macmillan.

Bergmann, B. (2007). Needed: A new empiricism. Economists' Voice. Available at: http://www.er.ethz.ch/inspire/Empirical_Approach_to_Economics_Bergmann.pdf
Berkes, N. (1964). *The development of secularism in Turkey*. McGill University Press.
Bernanke, B. S., Reinhart, V. R., & Sack, B. P. (2004). Monetary policy alternatives at the zero bound: An empirical assessment. *Brookings Papers on Economic Activity, 2*, 1–100.
Bianchi, P. (1992). Levels of policy and the nature of post-fordist competition. In M. Storper & A. J. Scott (Eds.), *Pathways to industrialization and regional development* (pp. 303–315). Routledge.
Biccieri, C. (2006). *The grammar of society: The nature and dynamics of social norms*. Cambridge University Press.
Binder, L. (1961). *Religion and politics in Pakistan*. University of California Press.
Black, D., & Henderson, J. V. (1998). *Urban evolution in the USA*. Department of Economics, London School of Economics (mimeo).
Blackwell, & Cox, K. R. (1997). *Spaces of globalization: Reasserting the power of the local*. Guilford.
Blackwell, & Cox, K. R. (1998). Spaces of dependence, spaces of engagement and the politics of scale, or: Looking for local politics. *Political Geography, 17*(1), 1–23.
Blanchflower, D., & Oswald, A. (2000). "Well-being over Time in Britain and USA." NBER, Working Paper No. 7487.
Blaug, M. (1985). *Economic theory in retrospect*. Cambridge University Press.
bn-al Qayyim. (n.d.). Tahdhib Sunan Abu Dawud, Vol. 5, Cairo.
Bolton, P., Roland, G., & Spolatore, E. (1996). Economic theories of the break-up and integration of nations. *European Economic Review, 40*, 700–732.
Bonilla, F., Melendez, E., Morales, R., & Torres, M. d. l. A. (1998). *Borderless Borders*. Temple University Press.
Boudeville, J.-R., & Antoine, S. (1968). *L'Espace et les Po^les de Croissance: Recherches et Textes Fondamentaux*. Presses Universitaires de France.
Boulakia, J. D. C. (1971). Ibn Khaldun: A fourteenth-century economist. *Journal of Political Economy, 79*(5), 1105–1118.
Bowles, S. (2016). *The moral economy: Why good incentives are no substitute for good citizens*. Yale University Press.
Braczyk, H., Cooke, P., & Heidenrich, M. (Eds.). (1998). *Regional innovation systems: The role of governance in a globalized world*. UCL Press.
Brennan, G., Hamlin, A., & Kliemt, H. (2010). PPE: An appraisal. *Politics, philosophy & economics, 9*(4), 363–365. https://doi.org/10.1177/1470594X10369443
Brenner, N. (1998). Global cities, glocal states: Global city formation and state territorial restructuring in contemporary Europe. *Review of International Political Economy, 5*(2), 1–37.
Brohi, A. K. (1990). Mawlana Abul A'la Mawdudi: The man, the scholar, the reformer. In K. Ahmad & Z. I. Ansari (Eds.), *Studies in honour of Mawlana sayyid Abul A'la Mawdudi*. Islamic Foundation.
Buchanan, J. M. (1975). *The Samaritan's Dilemma*. In E. S. Phelps (Ed.), *Altruism, morality and economic theory*. Russell Sage Foundation.
Buchanan, J., & Tullock, G. (1962). *The calculus of consent: Logical foundations of constitutional democracy*. University of Michigan Press.
Buchanan, & Tullock, G. (1970). The Democratic Calculus. In H. S. Kariel (Ed.), *Frontiers of democratic theory* (pp. 78–80). Random House.
Burdekin, R. C. K., & Weidenmier, M. D. (2002). Legal restrictions theory and interest-bearing money: Lessons from the southern confederacy. *Cato Journal*. in press.
Calabrese, A., & Burgelman, J.-C. (Eds.). (1999). *Communication, citizenship, and social policy. Rethinking the limits of the welfare state*. Rowman & Littlefield.
Callari, A., & Ruccio, D. F. (Eds.). (1996). *Postmodern materialism and the future of Marxist theory: Essays in the Althusserian tradition*. Wesleyan University Press.

Calmfors, L. (1995). Economic growth and unemployment: An empirical analysis. *European Economic Review, 39*(5), 837–859.

Card, D., & Krueger, A. (1997). *Myth and measurement: The economics of the minimum wage*. Princeton University Press.

Carlino, G. A. (1979). Increasing returns to scale in metropolitan manufacturing. *Journal of Regional Science, 19*, 363–373.

Carter, A. (2011). Towards a multidimensional, environmentalist ethic. *Environmental Values, 20*(3), 347–374. https://doi.org/10.3197/096327111X13077055166027

Cerny, P. G. (2000). Structuring the political arena: Public goods, states and governance in a globalizing world. In R. Palan (Ed.), *Global political economy: Contemporary theories* (pp. 21–35). Routledge.

Chamberline, E. H. (1933). *Theory of Monopolistic Competition*. Harvard University Press, Cambridge.

Chapra, M. U. (1992). *Islam and the economic challenge*. Islamic Foundation.

Chapra, M. U. (2000). *The future of economics: An Islamic perspective*. The Islamic Foundation.

Chapra, M. U. (1994). *Islam and economic development: A strategy for development with stability in the light of justice and Islamic teachings*. IIIT.

Chapra, M. U. (2008). *The Islamic vision of development in the light of Maqasid al-Shari'ah*. The International Institute of Islamic Thought.

Chehabi, H. E. (1993). Staging the Emperor's new clothes: Dress codes and nation-building under Reza Shah. *Iranian Studies, 26*, 209–223.

Chen, Y. (1996). Impact of regional factors on productivity in China. *Journal of Regional Science, 36*, 417–436.

Cheshire, P., & Gordon, I. R. (1998). Territorial competition: Some lessons for policy. *The Annals of Regional Science, 32*(3), 321–345.

Choudhury, M. A. (1974). A mathematical formulation of the principle of Mudarabah, the profit sharing in Islam. In *Proceedings of the third National Seminar*. Association of Muslim Social Scientists.

Choudhury, M. A. (1978). A social service model in the I-economy. In *Proceedings of the seventh annual conference*. Association of Muslim Social Scientists, Marion College.

Choudhury, M. A. (1980). *A specification of the social welfare function in an Islamic application to cost-benefit analysis (mimeo)*. International Centre for Research in Islamic Economics, King Abdulaziz University.

Choudhury, M. A. (1981). The rate of capitalization in valuation models in an Islamic economy. In *Proceedings of the follow up seminar on monetary and fiscal economics of Islam* (pp. 6–11).

Choudhury, M. A. (2006a). Development of Islamic economic and social thought. In M. Kabir Hassan & M. Lewis (Eds.), *Handbook of Islamic banking*. Edward Elgar Publishing Company.

Choudhury, M. A. (2006b). *Science and epistemology in the Qur'an*. The Edwin Mellen Press.

Choudhury, M. A. (2009). Islamic critique and alternative to financial engineering issues. *JKAU: Islamic Economy, 22*(2), 205–244.

Choudhury, M. A. (2010). The dynamics of the Shari'ah and the world-system. *Journal of King Abdulaziz University: Islamic Economics, 23*(2), 201–227.

Clark, G., & Feenstra, R. (2003). Technology in the great divergence. In M. D. Bordo, A. M. Taylor, & J. G. Williamson (Eds.), *Globalization in historical perspective*. University of Chicago Press.

Cleaver, H. (1998). The Zapatista effect: The internet and the rise of an alternative political fabric. *Journal of International Affairs, 51*(2), 621–640.

Cline, W. R. (1973). *Potential effects of income redistribution on economic growth*. Praeger.

Corbridge, S., Martin, R., & Thrift, N. (Eds.). (1994). *Money power and space*. Oxford University Press.

Courchene, T. (2001). Ontario as a North American region state, Toronto as a global city-region: Responding to the NAFTA challenge. In A. J. Scott (Ed.), *Global City-regions: Trends, theory, policy* (pp. 158–192). Oxford University Press.

Crafts, N., & Venables, A. J. (2003). Globalisation in history: A geographical perspective. In M. D. Bordo, A. M. Taylor, & J. G. Williamson (Eds.), *Globalisation in historical perspective*. University of Chicago Press.

Crone, P. (1987). *Meccan trade and the rise of Islam*. Princeton University Press.

Darling, M. (1947). *The Punjab peasant in prosperity and debt* (4th ed.). Manohar.

Dasgupta, P., & Stiglitz, J. (1977). Tariffs vs. quotas as revenue raising devices under uncertainty. *American Economic Review, 67*(5), 975–981.

Davezies, L. (2000). L'he'te'roge'ne'ite' locale des enjeux du de'veloppement local. *Annales de la Recherche Urbaine, spring*, 6–16.

Davis, D. E. (Ed.). (1999). *'Chaos and governance', political power and social theory. Vol. 13, part IV: Scholarly controversy*. JAI Press.

de Molinari, G. (1977). "The Production of Security," *Centre for Libertarian Studies*, Occasional Paper No. 2, New York, p. 3.

Denny, F. M. (1989). Orthopraxy in Islam and Judaism: Convictions and categories. In W. M. Brinner & S. D. Ricks (Eds.), *Studies in Islamic and Judaic traditions II*. Scholars Press.

Derrida, J. (1993). *Aporias*. Stanford University Press.

DeSmogyi, J. N. (1965). "Economic Theory in Classical Arabic Literature." *Studies in Islam*, Delhi, pp. 1–6.

Diener, E., & Oshi, S. (2000). Money and happiness: Income and subjective Well-being. In E. Diener & E. Suh (Eds.), *Culture and subjective Well-being*. MIT Press.

Dimashqi, A., & al-Fadl Ja'far ibn 'Ali. (1977). Al-Isharah ila Mahasin al-Tijarah. In Al-Bushra al-Shurbaji (Ed.). Maktabah al-Kulliyat al-Azhar.

Donahue, J. (1997a). *Disunited states*. Basic Books.

Donahue, J. (1997b). Tiebout? Or not Tiebout? The market metaphor and America's devolution. *The Journal of Economic Perspectives, 11*(4), 73–81.

Dowrick, S., & Delong, J. B. (2003). Globalisation and convergence. In M. D. Bordo, A. M. Taylor, & J. G. Williamson (Eds.), *Globalization in historical perspective*. University of Chicago Press.

Dunning, J. (1998). Regions, globalization and the knowledge economy: The issues stated. In J. Dunning (Ed.), *Regions, globalization and the knowledge-based economy* (pp. 7–41). Oxford University Press.

Duranton, G., & Monastiriotis, V. (2002). Mind the gaps: The evolution of regional inequalities in the UK, 1982–1997. *Journal of Regional Science, 42*(2), 219–256.

Duri, A. A. (1986). Baghdad. In *The Encyclopedia of Islam* (pp. 894–899). Brill.

Eade, J. (Ed.). (1996). *Living the Global City: Globalization as a local process*. Routledge.

Easterlin, R. (1974). Does economic growth improve the human lot? Some empirical evidence. In P. David & M. Reder (Eds.), *Nations and households in economic growth: Essays in honor of Moses Abramowitz*. Academic.

Easterlin, R. (1995). Will raising the income of all increase the happiness of all? *Journal of Economic Behavior and Organization, 27*(1), 35–48.

Easterlin, R. (2001). Income and happiness: Towards a unified theory. *Economic Journal, 111*, 473.

Easterlin, R. A. (1996). *Growth triumphant: The twenty-first century in historical perspective*. University of Michigan Press.

Eaton, J., & Eckstein, Z. (1997). Cities and growth: Theory and evidence from France and Japan. *Regional Science and Urban Economics, 27*, 443–474.

Eichengreen, B., & Fishlow, A. (1996). *Contending with capital flows*. The Council of Foreign Relations.

El Shaks, S. (1972). Development, primacy, and systems of cities. *Journal of Developing Areas, 7*, 11–36.

El-Gamal, M. A. (2006). *Islamic finance: Law, economics and practice*. Cambridge University Press.

Espinoza, V. (1999). Social networks among the poor: Inequality and integration in a Latin American city. In B. Wellman (Ed.), *Networks in the global village*. Westview Press.

Essid, M. Y. (1995). *A critique of the origins of Islamic economic thought*. Brill.

Fan, C. C., & Scott, A. J. (2003). Industrial agglomeration and development: A survey of spatial economic issues in East Asia and a statistical analysis of Chinese regions. *Economic Geography, 79*, 295–319.
Feenstra, R., & Hanson, G. (1996). Foreign investment, outsourcing and relative wages. In R. Feenstra, G. Grossman, & D. Irwin (Eds.), *The political economy of trade policy: Papers in honor of Jagdish Bhagwati* (pp. 89–127). MIT Press.
Feldman, M. (2000). Location and innovation: The new economic geography of innovation, spillovers, and agglomeration. In G. L. Clark, M. P. Feldman, & M. Gertler (Eds.), *The Oxford handbook of economic geography* (pp. 373–393). Oxford University Press.
Ferguson, Y. H., & Jones, R. J. B. (Eds.). (2002). *Political space. Frontiers of change and governance in a globalizing world.* SUNY Press.
Ferleger, L., & Mandle, J. R. (2000). Dimensions of globalization. In *Special millennial issue, the annals* (Vol. 570). American Academy of Political and Social Science.
Feyerabend, P. (1993). *Against method: Outline of an anarchistic theory of knowledge* (3rd ed.). Verso.
Fischel, W. J. (1992). Djahbadh. In *Encyclopedia of Islam* (Vol. 2, pp. 382–383). Brill.
Forstall, R. (1993). *Metropolitan growth and expansion in the 1980s*. US Bureau of the Census.
Frey, W. H., & Speare, A. (1988). *Regional and metropolitan growth and decline in the US*. Russell Sage Foundation.
Friedman, M. (1990). *Free to choose*. Thomson Learning.
Friedman, M. (1953). *Essays in positive economics*. University of Chicago Press.
Friedman, M. (1962). *Capitalism and freedom*. University of Chicago Press.
Friedman, M. R. (1984). *The Tyranny of the Status Quo*. New York.
Fujita, M., Krugman, P., & Venables, A. (1999). *The spatial economy: Cities, regions and international trade*. MIT Press.
Garcia, L. (2002). The architecture of global networking technologies. In S. Sassen (Ed.), *Global networks/linked cities* (pp. 39–70). Routledge.
George, H. (1955). *Progress and poverty*. Robert Schalkenback Foundation.
Gereffi, G. (1995). Global production systems and third world development. In B. Stallings (Ed.), *Global change, regional response: The new international context of development* (pp. 100–142). Cambridge University Press.
Gertler, M. S., & Digiovanna, S. (1997). In search of the new economy: Collaborative relations between users and producers of advanced manufacturing technologies. *Environment and Planning A: Economy and Space, 29*(1), 585–602.
Ghazanfar, S. M. (2003). *Medieval Islamic economic thought: Filling the great gap in European economics*. Routledge Curzon.
Gibb, H. A. R. (1947). *Modern trends in Islam*. University of Chicago Press.
Glaeser, E. (1998). Are cities dying? *Journal of Economic Perspectives, 12*(2), 139–160.
Goff, J. L. (1990). *Your money or your life – Economy and religion in the middle ages*. Zone Books.
Gordon, R. J. (2014). The Demise of U.S. Economic Growth: Restatement, Rebuttal, and Reflections. *NBER Working Paper* No. 19895.
Graafland, J. J. (2009). Calvin's Restrictions on Interest: Guidelines or the Credit Crisis, *European Banking Discussion Paper* No. 2009–22.
Grabher, G. (Ed.). (1993). *The embedded firm: On the socio-economics of industrial networks*. Routledge.
Graham, S., & Aurigi, A. (1997). Virtual cities, social polarization, and the crisis in urban public space. *Journal of Urban Technology, 4*(1), 19–52.
Granovetter, M. S. (1986). The sociological and economic approaches to labor market analysis: A social structural view. In G. Farkas & P. England (Eds.), *Industries, firms and jobs* (pp. 187–216). Plenum.
Greenwald, B. C., & Stiglitz, J. E. (1990). Asymmetric information and the new theory of the firm: Financial constraints and risk behavior. *The American Economic Review., 80*(2), 160–165.

Greenwald, B. C. N., & Stiglitz, J. E. (1991). *Information, finance, and markets: The architecture of allocative mechanisms, NBER working paper no. 3652*. National Bureau of Economic Research.

Greenwald, B., & Stiglitz, J. E. (2010). A modest proposal for international monetary reform. Time for a visible hand: Lessons from the 2008 world financial crisis. In S. GriffithJones, J. A. Ocampo, & J. E. Stiglitz (Eds.), *Initiative for policy dialogue series* (pp. 314–344). Oxford University Press.

Groenewegen, P. D. (1973). A note on the origin of the phrase, 'supply and demand.'. *Economic Journal, 83*(330), 505–509.

Grudem, W. (1994). *A systematic theology: An introduction to biblical doctrine*. Zondervan.

Gu, F. R., & Tang, Z. (2002). Shanghai: Reconnecting to the global economy. In S. Sassen (Ed.), *Global networks/Linkeed cities* (pp. 273–308). Routledge.

Haggard, S. (1990). *Pathways from the periphery*. Cornell University Press.

Hall, P. (2001). Global city-regions in the twenty-first century. In A. J. Scott (Ed.), *Global City-regions: Trends, theory, policy* (pp. 59–77). Oxford University Press.

Hall, R. B., & Biersteker, T. J. (2002). Private authority and global governance. In *Review of international political economy* (p. 20). Cambridge University Press.

Hamidullah, M. (1950). Islam and communism. *Islamic Review, 38*(3), 11–26.

Hamilton, N., & Chinchilla, N. S. (2001). *Seeking Community in a Global City: Guatemalans and Salvadorans in Los Angeles*. Temple University Press.

Haneef, M. A. (1995). Contemporary Islamic economic thought: A selected comparative analysis, (Kuala Lumpur: Ikraq, 1995). In R. Hardin (Ed.), *One for all: The logic of group conflict*. Princeton.

Haneef, M. A. (2008). Funding research in Islamic economics and finance. In *The 7th international conference in Islamic economics* (pp. 371–383). King Abdulaziz University.

Haneef, M. A. (2012). Preliminary thoughts on diagnosing some methodological issues in developing Islamic economics. In *Workshop On the future of Islamic economics*. Islamic Economics Institute, King Abdulaziz University.

Harrison, B., Glasmeier, A., & Polenske, K. (1996). *National regional and local economic development policy: New thinking about old ideas, research report*. Harvard University.

Hausman, D., & McPherson, M. (1993). Taking ethics seriously: Economics and contemporary moral philosophy. *Journal of Economic Literature, 31*(2), 671–731.

Hayek, A. (1979). *Law, legislation and liberty, the political order of a free people*. University of Chicago Press.

Hechter, M. (1987). *Principles of group solidarity*. University of California Press.

Held, D., Mcg Rew, A., Goldblatt, D., & Perraton, J. (1999). *Global transformations: Politics, economics and culture*. Stanford University Press.

Henderson, J. V. (1988). *Urban development: Theory, fact, and illusion*. Oxford University Press.

Heyworth-Dunne, J. (1939). *An introduction to the history of education in modern Egypt*. Luzac.

Hirschman, A. O. (1958). *The strategy of economic development*. Yale University Press.

Hodgson, M. G. S. (1974). *The venture of Islam: Conscience and history in a world civilization* (Vol. 1). University of Chicago Press.

Hosseini, Hamid S. (2003). "Contributions of medieval Muslim scholars to the history of economics and their impact: A refutation of the Schumpeterian," in Samuels, Warren J.; Jef E. Biddle; John B. Davis (Ed.), A companion to the history of economic thought, : Blackwell Publishing Ltd. pp. 28–45.

Hourani, A. (1983). *Arabic thought in the Liberal age, 1789–1939.*, (Reissue of 1962 ed. Cambridge University Press.

Howitt, R. (1993). A world in a grain of sand: Towards a reconceptualisation of geographical scale. *Australian Geographer, 24*(1), 33–44.

Howitt, R. (1998). Recognition, reconciliation and respect: Steps towards decolonisation? *Australian Aboriginal Studies, 1998*(1), 28–34.

Hudson, R. (1997). Restructuring region and state: The case of North East England. *Tijdschrift voor Economische en Sociale Geografie, 89*(1), 15–30.
Huntington, S. (1996). *The clash of civilizations and the remaking of world order*. Simon & Schuster.
Huntington, S. P. (1993). The clash of civilizations? *Foreign Affairs, 72*, 22–49.
Hussaini, W. A. (1971). *Principles of environmental engineering systems planning in Islamic culture: Law, politics, economics, education, and sociology of science and culture*. Stanford University. Report EEP-41.
Iannaccone, L. R. (1992). Sacrifice and stigma: Reducing free-riding in cults, communes, and other collectives. *Journal of Political Economy, 100*, 271–291.
Indiana Journal of Global Legal Studies. (2000). The state of citizenship. *Special Issue, 7*(2), 447–510.
Inman, J., & Rubinfeld, J. (1997). Rethinking federalism. *Journal of Economic Perspectives, 11*(4), 43–64.
Iqbal, M. (1964). Islam as a moral and political ideal (1909). In S. A. Vahid (Ed.), *Thoughts and reflections of Iqbal*. Sh. Muhammad Ashraf.
Isin, E. F. (Ed.). (2000). *Democracy, citizenship and the Global City*. Routledge.
Islahi, A. A. (1996). *History of economic thought in Islam*. Department of Economics, Aligharh Muslim University.
Islahi, A. A. (2015). First vs. second generation Islamic economists: Deviations and diferences in thoughts. In H. A. El-Karanshawy et al. (Eds.), *Islamic economic: Theory, policy and social justice*. Bloomsbury Qatar Foundation.
Islahi, A. A. (2008). Thirty years of research on history of Islamic economic thought: Assessment and future directions. In *The 7th international conference in Islamic economics* (pp. 347–369). King Abdulaziz University.
Islahi, A. A. (2009). *Muslim economic thinking and institutions in the 10th AH/16th AD century*. Scientiic Publishing Centre, King Abdulaziz University.
Islahi, A. A. (2010). *A study of Muslim economic thinking in the 11th AH/17th AD century*. Scientific Publishing Centre, King Abdulaziz University.
Islahi, A. A. (2011). *Islamic economic thinking in the 12th AH / 18th AD century with special reference to Shah Wali-Allah Al-Dihlawi*. Scientiic Publishing Centre, King Abdulaziz University.
Islamic Economics Research Center [IERC]. (2008). A proposed strategic vision for future research in Islamic economics. In *The 7th international conference in Islamic economics* (pp. 39–52). King Abdulaziz University.
Islamic Research and Training Institute, (IRTI). (1993). *A bibliography of Islamic economics*. IRTI.
Issawi, C. (1950). *An Arab philosophy of history: Selections from the prolegomena of Ibn Khaldun of Tunis (1332–1406)*. John Muray.
Jaffe, A. B., Trajtenberg, M., & Henderson, R. (1993). Geographic localization of knowledge spill-overs as evidenced by patent citations. *The Quarterly Journal of Economics, 108*, 577–598.
Jahiz, Amr ibn Bahr. (1983). *Kitab al-Tabassur bi al-Tijarah*. Dar al-Kitab al-Jadid.
Jalal, A. (1995). Conjuring Pakistan: History as official imagining. *International Journal of Middle East Studies, 27*, 73–89.
Jay, E., & Jay, R. (1986). *Critics of capitalism: Victorian reactions to political economy*. Cambridge University Press.
Jayet, H. (1983). Cho^mer plus souvent en re'gion urbaine, plus longtemps en re'gion rurale. *Economie et Statistique, 153*, 47–57.
Jessop, R. (1999). Reflections on globalization and its Illogics. In K. Olds et al. (Eds.), *Globalization and the Asian Pacific: Contested territories* (pp. 19–38). Routledge.
Jewish Encyclopedia. (1906). Available at: https://tbshamden.com/odds-a-ends/the-unedited-full-text-of-the-1906-jewish-encyclopedia/. [Accessed on 03/03/2024].
Joel, M. (2003). The quantitative imperative, positivism, Naïve realism and the place of qualitative methods in psychology. *Theory and Psychology., 13*(1), 5–31.

Johanssen, B., Karlsson, C., & Stough, R. (Eds.). (2001). *Theories of endogenous regional growth: Lessons for regional policies*. Springer.

Johnson, R. A. (1980). *Religious assortative marriage in the United States*. Academic.

Jonas, A. (1994). The scale politics of spatiality. *Environment and Planning D: Society and Space, 12*(3), 257–264.

Jones, K. T. (1998). Scale as epistemology. *Political Geography, 17*(1), 25–28.

Judd, D. R. (1998). The case of the missing scales: A commentary on Cox. *Political Geography, 17*(1), 29–34.

Kagel, J. H., & Roth, A. E. (Eds.). (1995). *The handbook of experimental economics. Princeton University Press.* https://doi.org/10.2307/j.ctvzsmff5

Kahf, M. (2004). *Islamic Economics: What went wrong*? Jeddah IRTI, May 26–27,2004. Available on the author's website: http://monzer.kahf.com/papers/english/ISLAMIC_ECONOMICS_what_went_wrong_ SEPT_03_IRTI.pdf

Kahf, M. (2007). *Infaq in the Islamic Economic System*. Available at: monzer.kahf.com. Accessed 30 June, 2022.

Kahneman, D., & Tversky, A. (1979). Prospect theory: An analysis of decision under risk. *Econometrica, 47*, 263–291.

Kaplan, E. A., & Sprinker, M. (Eds.). (1993). The Althusserian Legacy (Verso, 1993). (1995). *Thesis Eleven, 41*(1), 130–133. https://doi.org/10.1177/072551369504100110

Katouzian, H. (1983). Shi'ism and Islamic economics: Sadr and Bani Sadr. In R. Nikki (Ed.), *Religion and politics in Iran: Shi'ism from Quietism to revolution* (pp. 145–165). Yale University Press.

Kawashima, T. (1975). Urban agglomeration economies in manufacturing industries. *Papers of the Regional Science Association, 34*, 157–175.

Kelley, A. C., & Williamson, J. G. (1984). *What drives third World City growth?* Princeton University Press.

Kenny, C. (1999). Does growth cause happiness, or does happiness cause growth? *Kyklos, 52*(1), 3–26.

Keynes, J. M. (1936). *The general theory of employment, interest, and money*. Palgrave Macmillan.

Keynes, J. M. (1969). In J. K. Horsefield (Ed.), *1942–1943. The Keynes plan. Reproduced in the International Monetary Fund 1945–1965: Twenty years of international monetary cooperation, vol. III: Documents* (pp. 3–36). Washington.

Khaldun, I. (n.d.). *Muqaddimah*, n.p. Dar al-Fikr.

Khaldun, I. (1967). *Muqaddimah*. Cairo, Al-Maktabah al-Tijariyyah al-Kubra. See also its translation under Rosenthal, and selections from it under Issawi (1950).

Khomeini, I. [Ruhollah]. (1985). *Islam and revolution: Writings and declarations* (Hamid Algar, Trans.). London: KPI.

Kim, S. (1995). Expansion of markets and the geographic distribution of economic activities: Trends in US manufacturing structure, 1860–1987. *The Quarterly Journal of Economics, 110*, 881–908.

Kim, S. (2002). *The reconstruction of the American urban landscape in the twentieth century, NBER working paper 8857*. National Bureau of Economic Research.

Kirchgässner, G. (2005). (Why) are economists different? *European Journal of Political Economy., 21*(3), 543–562.

Kobrin, S. J. (1998). The MAI and the clash of globalizations. *Foreign Policy, 112*, 97–109.

Koehler, D. J., & Harvey, N. (2004). *Blackwell handbook of judgment and decision making*. Wiley.

Kolko, G. (1967). *The triumph of conservatism*. University Press.

Koopmans, T. C. (1969). Inter-temporal distribution and 'optimal' aggregate economic growth. In Fellner et al. (Eds.), *Ten economic studies in the tradition of Irving fisher*. John Willey and Sons.

Krasner, S. D. (1999). Globalization and sovereignty. In K. Olds et al. (Eds.), *States and sovereignty in the global economy* (pp. 34–52). Routledge.

Kratochwil, F. (1986). Of systems, boundaries and territoriality. *World Politics, 34*, 27–52.

Kris, O., Dicken, P., Kelly, P. F., Kong, L., Yeung, H. W., & Sassen: Globalization or Denationalization? 21 Chung (Eds.). (1999). *Globalizatioon and the Asian Pacific: Contested territories*. Routledge.
Krueger, A. (1993). *The political economy of policy reform in developing countries*. MIT Press.
Krugman, P. (1991). Increasing returns and economic geography. *Journal of Political Economy, 99*, 483–499.
Krugman, P., & Obstfeld, M. (1991). *International economics: Theory and policy* (2nd ed.). HarperCollins.
Krugman, P., & Venables, A. (1993). *Integration, specialization, and adjustment, NBER working paper no. 4559*. National Bureau of Economic Research.
Kung, H. (2006). *Does god exist? An answer for today*. Wipf & Stock Pub.
Kuran, T. (1997). The genesis of Islamic economics: A chapter in the politics of Muslim identity. *Social Research, 64*(2), 301–338.
Kuran, T. (1986). The economic system in contemporary Islamic thought: Interpretation and assessment. *International Journal of Middle East Studies, 18*, 135–164.
Kuran, T. (1989). On the notion of economic justice in contemporary Islamic thought. *International Journal of Middle East Studies, 21*, 171–191.
Kuran, T. (1990). Moral overload and its alleviation. In A. Ben-Ner & L. Putterman (Eds.), *Economics, values, and organization*. Cambridge University Press.
Kuran, T. (1993). The economic impact of Islamic fundamentalism. In M. E. Marty & R. S. Appleby (Eds.), *Fundamentalisms and the state: Remaking polities, economies, militance* (pp. 302–341). University of Chicago Press.
Kuran, T. (1995). Islamic economics and the Islamic subeconomy. *Journal of Economic Perspectives, 9*, 155–173.
Kuznets, S. (1955). Economic growth and income inequality. *The American Economic Review, 45*, 1–28.
Lal, D. (1983). *The poverty of development economics*. Institute of Economic Affairs.
Landau, J. (1990). *The politics of pan-Islam: Ideology and organization*. Clarendon Press.
Landes, D. (1998). *The wealth and poverty of nations*. W. W. Norton.
Leamer, E., & Storper, M. (2001). The economic geography of the internet age. *Journal of International Business Studies, 32*, 641–665.
Lee, Y. J., & Zang, H. (1998). Urbanization and regional productivity in Korean manufacturing. *Urban Studies, 35*(2), 085–099.
Lerman, E. (1981). Mawdudi's concept of Islam. *Middle Eastern Studies, 17*, 492–509.
Levine, N. (2010). *The Torah and Interest*. Retrieved from http://www.jewishencyclopedia.com/view.jsp?artid=58&letter=U&search=usury
Lewis, B. (1968). *The emergence of modern Turkey* (2d ed.). Oxford University Press.
Lewis, B. (1975). *History remembered, recovered, invented*. Princeton University Press.
Lewis, B. (1993). *Islam and the west*. Oxford University Press.
Lipton, M. (1977). *Why poor people stay poor: A study of urban bias in world development*. Temple Smith.
Little, I. M. D. (1982). *Economic development: Theory, policy, and international relations*. Basic Books.
Little, I. M. D. (2002). *Ethics, economics and politics: Principles of public policy*. Oxford University Press.
Lovink, G., & Riemens, P. (2002). Digital City Amsterdam: Local uses of global networks. In S. Sassen (Ed.), *Global networks/linked cities* (pp. 327–345). Routledge.
Lowenthal, D. (1985). *The past is a foreign country*. Cambridge University Press.
Lucas, R. (1988). On the mechanics of economic development. *Journal of Monetary Economics, 22*, 3–42.
Luckmann, T. (1967). *The invisible religion: The problem of religion in modern society*. Macmillan.
Lundvall, B. A., & Johnson, B. (1992). *The learning economy*, Paper presented to the European Association for Evolutionary Political Economy conference, November, Paris.

Macdonald, D. B. (1965). *The religious attitude and life in Islam. Orig. Ed., 1909*. Khayats.

Macdonald, D. B. (1971). *Aspects of Islam. Orig. Ed., 1911*. Books for Libraries Press.

Magnusson, W. (1996). *The search for political space*. University of Toronto Press.

Mahdi, M. (1964). *Ibn Khaldun's philosophy of history*. University of Chicago Press.

Makinen, G. E., & Woodward, T. G. (1999). Use of interest-bearing currency in the civil war: The experience below the Mason-Dixon line. *Journal of Money, Credit, and Banking, 31*(1), 121–129.

Malik, J. (1996). *Colonialization of Islam: Dissolution of traditional institutions in Pakistan*. Manohar.

Mallat, C. (1993). *The renewal of Islamic law: Muhammad Baqer as-Sadr, Najaf and the Shi'i international*. Cambridge University Press.

Mankiw, N. G., Romer, D., & Weil, D. N. (1992). A contribution to the empirics of economic growth. *Quarterly Journal of Economics, 107*, 407–437.

Mannan, M. A. (1970). *Islamic economics: Theory and practice*. Sh. Muhammad Ashraf.

Mannan, M. A. (2008). "*Comments*" on a paper by Khaled a. Hussein entitled "Islamic economics: Current state of knowledge and development of the discipline". In *The 7th international conference in Islamic economics* (pp. 61–65). King Abdulaziz University.

Maqrizi, T. a.-D. A. i. A. (1956). *Ighathah al-Ummah bi Kashf al-Ghummah*. Dar ibn al-Wahid. (See its English translation by Allouche, 1994).

Mardin, S. (1993). The Nakshibendi Order in Modern Turkey. In M. E. Marty & R. S. Appleby (Eds.), *Fundamentalisms and the state: Remaking polities, economies, militance* (pp. 204–232). University of Chicago Press.

Mark, B. (1985). *Economic theory in retrospect*. Cambridge University Press.

Marshall, A. (1890). *Principles of economics*. Macmillan.

Martimort, D. (2001). *The theory of incentives: The principal-agent model*. Princeton University Press.

Maskell, P. (Ed.). (1999). *Competition, localized learning and regional development*. Routledge.

Maslow, A. H. (1943). A theory of human motivation. *Psychological Review, 50*(4), 370–396. https://doi.org/10.1037/h0054346

Massey, D. (1993). 'Politics and Space/Time', in M. Keith and S. Pile (eds) Place and the Politics of Identity, London and New York: Routledge, pp. 141–61.

Masud, M. K. (1977). *Islamic legal philosophy, a study of Abu Ishaq al Shatibi's life and thought*. Islamic Research Institute.

Mawardi, A. a.-H. (1960). *Al-Ahkam al-Sultaniyyah wa al-Wilayat al-Diniyyah*. Mustafa al-Babi al-Halabi. (The English translation of this book by Wafa Wahba has been published under the title, *The Ordinances of Government*. Reading: Garnet, 1996.).

Mawardi, A. a.-H. '. A. (1955). *Adab al-Dunya wa al-Din. Mustafa al Saqqa, editor*. Mustafa al-Babi al Halabi.

Mawdudi, A.'l.-A.'l. (1969). *Islam aur Jadid Ma'ashi Nazariyat (Islam and modern economic theories)*. Markazi Maktabah.

Mawdudi, S. A.'l.-A.'l. (1960). *First principles of the Islamic state. Orig. Urdu ed., 1952*. Islamic Publications.

Mawdudi, S. A.'l.-A.'l. (1950). *Islamic way of life. Orig. Urdu ed., 1948*. Islamic Publications.

Mawdudi, S. A.'l.-A.'l. (1963). *Short history of the revivalist movement in Islam, tr. Al-Ash'ari. Orig. Urdu ed., 1940*. Islamic Publications.

Mawdudi, S. A.'l.-A.'l. (1976a). *Islam and ignorance. Orig. Urdu ed., 1941*. Islamic Publications.

Mawdudi, S. A.'l.-A.'l. (1976b). *Jihad in Islam. Orig. Urdu ed., 1939*. Islamic Publications.

Mawdudi, S. A.'l.-A.'l. (1978). *The economic problem of man and its Islamic solution (Orig. Urdu ed., 1941)*. Islamic Publications.

Mawdudi, S. A.'l.-A.'l. (1981). *Selected speeches and writings of Mawlana Mawdudi, vol. 1, tr. S. Zakir Aijaz*. International Islamic Publishers.

Mawdudi, S. A.'l.-A.'l. (1990). *Let us be Muslims, ed. Khurram Murad. Orig. Urdu ed., 1940*. Noordeen.

McCloskey, D. (1983). The rhetoric of economics. *The Journal of Economic Literature, 21*, 481–517.

McDowell, L. (1991). Life without Father and Ford: The new gender order of post Fordism. *Transactions of the Institute of British Geographers, New Series, 16*, 400–419.

Mehmood, S. (2011). *Eiciency wages and non-monetary motivational strategies: An experimental approach. PhD thesis*. PIDE.

Mele, C. (1999). Cyberspace and disadvantaged communities: The internet as a tool for collective action. In M. A. Smith & P. Kollock (Eds.), *Communities in cyberspace* (pp. 264–289). Routledge.

Meyer, M. S. (1989). Economic thought in the ottoman empire in the 14th – Early 19th centuries. *Archiv Orientali, 4*(57), 305–318.

Miller, D., & Slater, D. (2000). *The internet: An ethnographic approach*. Berg.

Minsky, H. P. (1982). *Can "it" happen again?: Essays on instability and finance*. M. E. Sharpe.

Mirakhor, A. (1987). Muslim scholars and the history of economics: A need for consideration. *American Journal of Islamic Social Sciences, 4*(2), 245–276.

Mirowski, P. (1991). *More heat than light*. Cambridge University Press.

Mises, L. v. (1966). *Human action*. University Press.

Mises, L. v. (1974). Profit and loss. In *Planning for freedom*. South Holland.

Mishan, E. J. (1981). *Introduction to normative economics*. Oxford University Press.

Mishkin, F. S. (2007). *The economics of money, banking, and financial markets* (8th ed.). Pearson Education.

Mishra, V. (1962). *Hinduism and economic growth*. Oxford University Press.

Misri, R. Y. (1981). *Al-Islam Wa al-Nuqud*. King Abdulaziz University.

Mitra, A. (2000). Total factor productivity growth and urbanization economies: A case of Indian industries. *Review of Urban & Regional Development Studies, 12*, 97–108.

Mokyr, J. (1985). *The economics of the industrial revolution*. Rowman & Allanheld.

Morrill, R. (1999). Inequalities of power, costs and benefits across geographic scales: The future uses of the Hanford reservation. *Political Geography, 18*, 1–23.

Mottahadeh, R. P. (1995). The clash of civilizations: An Islamicist's critique. *Harvard Middle Eastern and Islamic Review, 2*, 1–26.

Myers, M. L. (1983). *The soul of modern economic man: Ideas of self-interest, Thomas Hobbes to Adam Smith*. University of Chicago Press.

Myrdal, G. (1959). *Economic theory and under-developed regions*. Gerald Duckworth.

Nadvi, K., & Schmitz, H. (1994). *Industrial clusters in less developed countries: Review of experiences and a research agenda, discussion paper no. 339*. Institute of Development Studies, University of Sussex.

Najam, A. (2007). *Portrait of a giving community: Philanthropy by the Pakistani-American diaspora*. Harvard University Press.

Naqvi, S. N. H. (1978). Ethical foundations of Islamic economics. *Journal of Development Studies, University of Peshawar, 1*(1), 105–136.

Naqvi, S. N. H. (1994). *Islam, economic and society*. Kegan Paul International.

Nasr, S. V. R. (1996). *Mawdudi and the making of Islamic revivalism*. Oxford University Press.

Nelson, R. R. (Ed.). (1992). *National Systems of innovation*. Oxford University Press.

Nelson, J. S. (2006). *Fishes of the World* (4th ed.). John Wiley & Sons.

Newbery, D. M. G., & Stiglitz, J. E. (1984). Pareto inferior trade. *Review of Economic Studies, 51*(1), 1–12.

Nienhaus, V. (2012). Method and substance of Islamic economics: Moving where? In *Workshop on "the future of Islamic economics" during 12–13 November* (pp. 167–197). Organized by IEI.

Nietzsche, F. (1885). *Sämtliche Werke: Kritische Studienausgabe*. In G. Colli & M. Montinari (Eds.), *15 Bänden*. de Gruyter.

Nooteboom, B. (1999). Innovation, learning and industrial organization. *Cambridge Journal of Economics, 23*, 127–150.

North, D., & Thomas, R. P. (1973). *The rise of the Western world: A new economic history*. Cambridge University Press.
North, D. C. (1981). *Structure and change in economic history*. W.W. Norton.
North, D. C. (1994). Economic performance through time. *American Economic Review, 84*(2), 359–368.
Notzke, C. (1995). A new perspective in aboriginal nature resource management: Co-management. *Geoforum, 26*(2), 187–209.
Nussbaum, M. C. (2011). *Creating capabilities: The human development approach*. Harvard University Press. https://doi.org/10.2307/j.ctt2jbt31y
Obaidullah, M. (2008). *Role of Microinance in poverty alleviation*. Islamic Research and Training Institute.
Obaidullah, M., & Abdul-Latif, H. S. H. (2011). *Islamic finance for micro and medium enterprises*. Islamic Research and Training Institute.
Olson, M. (1965). *The logic of collective action*. Harvard University Press.
Olson, R. (1995). *Science Deiied and science Deied*. University of California Press.
Oran, A. F. (Ed.). (2012). *al-Azmat al-Iqtisadiyah al-Alamiyah al-Mu'asirah min Manzur Islami (The world economic crisis from Islamic perspective)*. IIIT and International Islamic University.
Organisation for Economic Cooperation and Development (OECD). (1999). *Boosting innovation: The cluster approach*. OECD.
Oswald, A. J. (1997). Happiness and economic performance. *Economic Journal, 107*(445), 1815–1831.
Palley, T. (2012). The economics of the real world: How to get started with post-Keynesianism. *Review of Political Economy, 24*(3), 391–410. https://doi.org/10.1080/09538259.2012.674390
Panitch, L. (1996). Rethinking the role of the state in an era of globalization. In Mittelman (Ed.), *Globalization: Critical reflections*. Lynne Rienner.
Parnreiter, C. (2002). The making of a Global City: Mexico City. In S. Sassen (Ed.), *Global networks/linked cities* (pp. 145–182). Routledge.
Pfeifer, K. (2001). Islamic business and business as usual: A study of firms in Egypt. *Development in Practice, Taylor & Francis Journals, 11*(1), 20–33, February.
Perroux, F. (1961). *L'Economie du XXe Sie'cle*. Presses Universitaires de France.
Petrazzini, B., & Kibati, M. (1999). The internet in developing countries. *Communications of the ACM, 42*(6), 31–36.
Phillips, K. (2002). *Wealth and democracy*. Broadway Books.
Picciotto, S., & Mayne, R. (1999). *Regulating international business: Beyond liberalization*. Macmillan, in association with OXFAM.
Pifer, J. (1978). Scholasticism. *Encyclopedia Britannica, 16*, 352–357.
Piketty, T. (2014). *Capital in the Twenty-First Century*. Harvard University Press.
Piore, M., & Sabel, C. (1984). *The second industrial divide*. Basic Books.
Pomerantz, K. (2000). *The great divergence*. Princeton University Press.
Porter, M. E. (2001). Regions and the new economics of competition. In A. J. Scott (Ed.), *Global City-regions: Trends, theory, policy* (pp. 139–157). Oxford University Press.
Poster, M. (1997). Cyberdemocracy: Internet and the public sphere. In D. Porter (Ed.), *Internet culture* (pp. 201–218). Routledge.
Prebisch, R. (1982). *La Obra de Prebisch en la CEPAL*. Fondo de Cultura Econo'mica.
Pred, A. and Watts, M. J. (1992). Reworking Modernity: Capitalisms and Symbolic Discontent. New Brunswick, N.J.: Rutgers University Press.
Puga, D., & Venables, A. (1998). The spread of industry: Spatial agglomeration and economic development. *Journal of The Japanese and International Economies, 10*, 440–464.
Puga, D., & Venables, A. (1999). Agglomeration and economic development: Import substitution versus trade liberalization. *The Econometrics Journal, 109*(455), 292–311.
Putnam, R. (2000). *Bowling alone: The collapse and revival of American community*. Simon & Schuster.
Putnam, R., Leonardi, R., & Nanetti, R. (1993). *Making democracy work*. Princeton University Press.

Quigley, C. (1979). *The evolution of civilizations: An introduction to historical analysis* (2nd ed.). Liberty Press.

Qutb, S. (1970). *Social justice in Islam, tr. John D. Hardie. Orig. Arabic ed., 1948*. American Council of Learned Societies.

Rahnema, A., & Nomani, F. (1990). *The secular miracle: Religion, politics, and economic policy in Iran*. Zed Books.

Rai'uddin, M. (1969). *The fallacy of Marxism*. Institute of Islamic Culture.

Restakis, J. (2010). *Humanizing the economy: Co-operatives in the age of capital*. New Society Publishers.

Richards, A., & Waterbury, J. (1996). *A political economy of the Middle East* (2d ed.). Westview Press.

Richardson, H. W. (1980). Polarization reversal in developing countries. *Papers of the Regional Science Association, 45*, 67–85.

Rimmer, P. J., & Morris-Suzuki, T. (1999). The Japanese internet: Visionaries and virtual democracy. *Environment and Planning A, 31*(7), 189–206.

Rivera-B Atiz, F. (1988). Increasing returns, monopolistic competition, and agglomeration economies in consumption and production. *Regional Science and Urban Economics, 34*, 380–400.

Robbins, L. (1935). *An essay on the nature and significance of economic science* (2nd ed.). Macmillan.

Rodinson, M. (1973). *Islam and capitalism, tr. Brian Pearce. Orig. French ed., 1966*. Pantheon Books.

Rodrik, D. (1999). *The new global economy and developing countries: Making openness work*. Overseas Development Council.

Romer, P. M. (1986). Increasing returns and long run growth. *Journal of Political Economy, 94*(1), 002–037.

Romer, P. M. (1990). Endogenous technological change. *Journal of Political Economy, 98*(5), S1,071–S1,102.

Ronfeldt, David, Arquilla, John, Fuller, Graham and Fuller, Melissa. (1998). The Zapatista 'social netwar' in Mexico, : RAND, MR-994-A.

Rosenberg, N. (1982). *Inside the Black box: Technology and economics*. Cambridge University Press.

Rosenfeld, S. (1996). United States: Business clusters. In *Organisation for economic cooperation and development networks of enterprises and local development*. OECD.

Rosenthal, F. (1967). *Ibn Khaldun: The Muqaddimah, an introduction to history*. Princeton University Press.

Rothbard, M. N. (1970a). *Man, economy and state*. Los Angeles.

Rothbard, M. N. (1970b). Power and market: Government and the economy, pp. xiii, 225. Institute for Humane Studies, 1970. *The ANNALS of the American Academy of Political and Social Science, 394*(1), 196–197. https://doi.org/10.1177/000271627139400193.

Rothbard, M. N. (1977). *Power and market*. Kansas City.

Roy, O. (1994). *The failure of political Islam, tr. Carol volk. Orig. French ed., 1992*. Harvard University Press.

Russo, M. (1985). Technical change and the industrial district: The role of interfirm relations in the growth and transformation of ceramic tile production in Italy. *Research Policy, 14*, 329–343.

Said, E. W. (1978). *Orientalism*. Pantheon Books.

Sala-I-M Artin, X. (2002). *The 'disturbing' rise in global income inequality, NBER working paper no. W8904*. National Bureau of Economic Research.

Samuelson, P. A., & Nordhaus, W. D. (2010). *Economics* (9th ed.). New York.

Samuelson, P. A. (1937). Some aspects of the pure theory of capital. *Quarterly Journal of Economics, 51*, 469–496.

Samuelson, P. A. (1938). Welfare economics and international trade. *American Economic Review, 28*(2), 261–266.

Samuelson, P. A. (1954). The pure theory of public expenditure. *The Review of Economics and Statistics, 36*, 387–389.

Samuelson, P. A., & Nordhaus, W. D. (1985). *Economics*. 12th edition.
Sanders, R. (1987). The pareto principle: Its use and abuse. *Journal of Services Marketing, 1*(2), 37–40. https://doi.org/10.1108/eb024706
Sarakhsi, S. a.-D. (1978). *Kitab al-Mabsut. Beirut: Dar al-ma'rifah* (Vol. 30, 3rd ed., (particularly "Kitab al-Kasb" of al-Shaybani in, pp. 245–297).
Sarton, G. (1927). *Introduction to the history of science*. Carnegie Institute. (three volumes issued between 1927 and 1948, each of the second and third volumes has two parts).
Sassen, S. (1996). *Losing control? Sovereignty in an age of globalization*. Columbia University Press.
Sassen, S. (2000a). Spatialities and temporalities of the global. *Public Culture, 12*(1) (Millenium Issue on Globalization. Re-issued by Duke University Press).
Sassen, S. (2000b). Territory and territoriality in the global economy. *International Sociology, 15*(2), 372–393.
Sassen, S. (2002). Towards a sociology of information technology. *Current Sociology*. Special Issue on the New Information Technologies.
Sassen, S. (2003). *Denationalization: Territory, authority and rights in a global digital age*. Princeton University Press.
Saxenian, A. (1994). *Regional advantage: Culture and competition in Silicon Valley and route 128*. Harvard University Press.
Schiffer Ramos, S. (2002). Sao Paulo: Articulating a cross-border regional economy. In Sassen (Ed.), *Global networks/linked cities* (pp. 209–236). Routledge.
Schmitz, H. (2001). Local governance and conflict management: Reflections on a Brazilian cluster. In A. J. Scott (Ed.), *Global City-regions: Trends, theory, policy* (pp. 401–416). Oxford University Press.
Schumpeter, J. (1968). History of economic analysis. .
Schumpeter, J. A. (1912). *Theorie der Wirtschaftlichen Entwicklung*. Duncker & Humblot. (English translation, 1934).
Schumpeter, J. A. (1954). *History of Economic Analysis*. New York: Oxford University Press.
Scott, A. J. (1998). *Regions and the world economy: The coming shape of global production, competition, and political order*. Oxford University Press.
Scott, A. J. (1999). The cultural economy: Geography and the creative field. *Media, Culture & Society, 21*, 807–817.
Scott, A. J. (2001). Industrial revitalization in the ABC municipalities, Sa˜o Paulo: Diagnostic analysis and strategic recommendations for a new economy and a new regionalism. *Regional Development Studies, 7*, 1–32.
Scott, A. J. (2002). Regional push: Towards a geography of development and growth in low- and middle-income countries. *Third World Quarterly, 23*, 137–161.
Scott, A. J., Agnew, J., Soja, E. W., & Storper, M. (2001). Global city-regions. In A. J. Scott (Ed.), *Global City-regions : Trends, theory, policy* (pp. 11–32). Oxford University Press.
Scott, A. J., & Storper, M. (1987). High technology industry and regional development: A theoretical critique and reconstruction. *International Social Science Journal, 112*, 215–232.
Sen, A. (1981). *Poverty and famines: An essay on entitlement and deprivation*. Clarendon Press.
Sen, A. (1987). *On ethics and economics*. Basil Blackwell.
Shaban, M. A. (1971). *Islamic history: A new interpretation* (Vol. 1). Cambridge University Press.
Shade, L. R. (1998). A gendered perspective on access to the information infrastructure. *The Information Society, 14*, 33–44.
Shukla, V. (1996). *Urbanization and economic growth*. Oxford University Press.
Siddiqi, M. N. (1964). "Abu Yusuf ka Ma'ashi Fikr" (economic thought of Abu Yusuf). *Fikro-Nazar, (Aligarh), 5*(1), 66–95.
Siddiqi, M. N. (1972). *Economic Enterprise in Islam*. Markazi Maktabah Islami.
Siddiqi, M. N. (1982). *Recent works on history of economic thought in Islam – A survey*. International Center for Research in Islamic Economics.
Siddiqi, M. N. (1992a). History of Islamic economic thought. In A. Ahmad & K. R. Awan (Eds.), *Lectures on Islamic economics* (pp. 69–90). IDB/IRTI.

Siddiqi, M. N. (1992b). Islamic economic thought: Foundation, evolution and needed direction. In Sadeq & Ghazali (Eds.), *Readings in Islamic economic thought* (pp. 14–32). Longman Malaysia.
Siddiqi, M. N. (2004). Riba, Bank Interest and the Rational of its Prohibition (Research Paper), Occasional Papers 205, The Islamic Research and Teaching Institute (IRTI).
Siddiqi, M. N. (2006). Islamic banking and finance in theory and practice: A survey of state of the art. *Islamic Economic Studies, 13*(2), 1–48.
Siddiqi, M. N. (2008). Obstacles of research in Islamic economics. In *The 7th international conference in Islamic economics* (pp. 3–12). King Abdulaziz University.
Siddiqi, M. N. (2009). Maqasid-e Shariat, New Delhi: Markazi Maktabah Islami. In H. A. El-Karanshawy et al. (Eds.), *21 first vs. second generation Islamic economists: Deviations and differences in thoughts*.
Siddiqi, M. N. (2012). Comments on Asad Zaman: Crisis in Islamic economics: Diagnosis and prescriptions. *JKAU: Islamic Economy, 25*(1), 173–175.
Siddiqi, M. (1975). *Marxism or Islam*. Sh.
Siddiqui, M. N. (2008). *Obstacles to Research in Islamic Economics*. In: Proceedings of The Seventh International Conference on Islamic Economics. http://islamiccenter.kaau.edu.sa/7iecon/English/English%20 Contents.htm
Silvern, S. E. (1999). Scales of justice: Law, American Indian treaty rights and political construction of scale. *Political Geography, 18*, 639–668.
Smith, A. (1776). *An inquiry into the nature and causes of the wealth of nations, complete and unabridged version (2000)*. The Modern Library.
Smith, A. (2002). *The wealth of nations*. Bibliomania.com Ltd.
Smith, A., Raphael, D. D., & Macfie, A. L. (1982). *The theory of moral sentiments* (8th ed.). Liberty Classics.
Smith, A. (1973). *An inquiry into the nature and causes of the wealth of nations*. Modern Library.
Smith, D., Solinger, D., & Topik, S. (Eds.). (1999). *States and sovereignty in the global economy*. Routledge.
Smith, M. P. (1994). Can you imagine? Transnational migration and the globalisation of grassroots politics. *Social Text, 39*, 15–34.
Smith, N. (1993). Homeless/global: Scaling places. In J. Bird, B. Curtis, T. Putnam, G. Robertson, & L. Tickner (Eds.), *Mapping the futures: Local cultures, global change* (pp. 87–119). Routledge.
Smith, R. C. (1997). Transnational migration, assimilation and political community. In M. Crahan & A. Vourvoulias-Bush (Eds.), *The City and the world*. Council of Foreign Relations.
Smith, W. C. (1957). *Islam in modern history*. Princeton University Press.
Solo, R. A. (1981). Values and judgments in the discourse of the sciences. In R. A. Solo & C. A. Anderson (Eds.), *Value judgment and income distribution* (pp. 9–40). Praeger.
Solow, R. M. (1956). A contribution to the theory of economic growth. *The Quarterly Journal of Economics, 70*(1), 65–94.
Spengler, J. (1964). Economic thought in Islam: Ibn Khaldun. *Comparative Studies in Society and History*, 268–306.
Staeheli, L. A. (1999). Globalization and the scales of citizenship. *Geography Research Forum, 19*, 60–77. Special Issue On Geography and the Nation-State, edited by Dennis Pringle and Oren Yiftachel.
Stiglitz, J. (1987). Learning to learn, localized learning, and technological progress. In P. Dasgupta & P. Stoneman (Eds.), *Economic policy and technological performance*. Cambridge University Press.
Stiglitz, J. (2002). *Globalization and its discontents*. Allen Lane/Penguin.
Stiglitz, J. E. (2011). *Of the 1%, by the 1%, for the 1%*. Vanity Fair.
Stiglitz, J. E. (2017). Macro-economic management in an electronic credit/financial system. *National Bureau of Economic Research Working Paper* No. 23032, January.

Stiglitz, J. E., Sen, A., & Fitoussi, J. P. (2009). *Report by the Commission on the Measurement of Economic Performance and Social Progress*. Retrieved from https://www.insee.fr/en/statistiques/fichier/2019951/GDPBeyond2008.pdf

Stiglitz, J. E. (2002). *Globalization and its discontents*. W.W. Norton.

Stiglitz, J. E. (2006). *Making globalization work*. W.W. Norton.

Stiglitz, J. E. (2015). *Rewriting the rules of the American economy: An agenda for growth and shared prosperity*. W.W. Norton.

Stiglitz, J. E. (2016). *The euro: How a common currency threatens the future of Europe*. W.W. Norton. 136 J. E.

Stiglitz, J. E., & Greenwald, B. (2003). *Towards a new paradigm in monetary economics*. Cambridge University Press.

Stiglitz, J. E., & Greenwald, B. (2010). Towards a new global reserve system. *Journal of Globalization and Development, 1*(2), Article 10.

Stiglitz, J. E., & Greenwald, B. (2014). *Creating a learning society: A new approach to growth, development, and social progress*. Columbia University Press.

Stiglitz, J. E., & Kaldor, M. (Eds.). (2013). *The quest for security: Protection without protectionism and the challenge of global governance*. Columbia University Press.

Stockhammer, E. (2017). Wage-led versus profit-led demand: What have we learned? A Kalecki-Minsky view. *Cambridge Journal of Economics, 41*(5), 1253–1274.

Storper, M. (1991). *Industrialization, economic development, and the regional question in the third world*. Pion.

Storper, M. (1995). The resurgence of regional economies, ten years later: The region as a nexus of untraded interdependencies. *European Urban and Regional Studies, 2*(3), 191–221. https://doi.org/10.1177/096977649500200301

Storper, M. (1997). *The regional world: Territorial development in a global economy*. Guilford Press.

Storper, M., & Venables, A. (2002). *Buzz: The economic force of the city, paper delivered to the international seminar on space and economy*. Ouro Preto.

Sueyoshi, T. (1992). Measuring the industrial performance of Chinese cities by data envelopment analysis. *Socio-economic Planning Sciences, 26*, 75–88.

Sulayman, A. H. A. A. (1968). *The theory of economics of Islam*. In *Proceedings of the Third East Coast Regional Conference*. Muslim Students Association of the United ]States and Canada.

Sum, N. L. (1999). *'Rethinking globalisation: Re-articulating the spatial scale and temporal horizons of trans-border spaces'*, Olds et al. (eds) op. cit, pp. 129–45.

Summer, A., Cheshire, P., & Senn, L. (Eds.). (1993). *Urban change in the US and Western Europe: Comparative analysis and policy*. Urban Institute Press.

Sveikauskas, L. (1975). The productivity of cities. *The Quarterly Journal of Economics, 89*, 393–413.

Svensson, L. E. O. (2011). Inflation targeting. In B. M. Friedman & M. Woodford (Eds.), *Handbook of monetary economics* (Vol. 3A, pp. 1237–1302). Elsevier.

Swyngedouw, E. (1997). Neither global nor local: "Glocalization" and the politics of scale. In K. R. Cox (Ed.), *Globalization: Reasserting the power of the review of international political economy 22 local* (pp. 137–166). New York.

Taylor, P. (1994). The state as container: Territoriality in the modern worldsystem. *Progress in Human Geography, 18*(2), 151–162.

Taylor, P. (2000). 'World cities and territorial states under conditions of contemporary globalisation', (1999 annual political geography lecture). *Political Geography, 19*(1), 5–32.

Taylor, P., Walker, D. R. F., & Beaverstock, J. V. (2002). Firms and their global service networks. In S. Sassen (Ed.), *Global networks/linked cities* (pp. 93–116). Routledge.

Taymiyyah, I. (1961). In Abd al-Rahman al-'Asimi (Ed.), *Majmu' Fatawa shaykh al-Islam Ahmad Ibn Taymiyyah*. Matabi' al-Riyad. 1961-63.

Temple, J., & Johnson, P. A. (1998). Social capability and economic growth. *The Quarterly Journal of Economics, 113*(3), 965–990.

Thaler, R. H., & Sunnstein, C. R. (2009). *Nudge: Improving decisions about health, wealth, and happiness*. Penguin Books.
Thaler, R. H. (1994). *Quasi rational economics*. Russell Sage Foundation.
Thaler, R. H., & Sunstein, C. R. (2003). Libertarian paternalism. *American Economic Review, 93*(2), 175–179.
The Holy Bible (Authorised King James Version). (n.d.). Retrieved from https://www.biblegateway.com/
The Holy Qur'an. (n.d.). *Translated by Abdullah Yusuf Ali*. Wordsworth Editions Limited.
Thrift, N. (1987). Book review: Technological change, industrial restructuring and regional development. *Progress in Human Geography, 11*(2), 307–309. https://doi.org/10.1177/030913258701100216
Thweatt, W. O. (1983). Origins of the terminology, supply and demand. *Scottish Journal of Political Economy*, 287–294.
Tobin, J. (1958). Liquidity preference and behavior towards risk. *Review of Economic Studies, 25*, 65–86.
Todaro, M. (1969). A model of labor migration and urban unemployment in less developed countries. *The American Economic Review, 59*, 138–148.
Townroe, P. M., & Keen, D. (1984). Polarization reversed in the state of Sa˜o Paulo. *Regional Studies, 18*, 45–54.
Toynbee, A. J. (1935). *A study of history* (2nd ed.). Oxford University Press.
Tullock, G. (1970). The charity of the uncharitable. *Western Economic Journal*, 9, 379–392. Reprinted in Rowley, C., (Ed). Virginia Political Economy (pp. 262–275). Liberty Fund.
Udovitch, A. L. (1970). *Partnership and profit in medieval Islam*. Princeton University Press.
US Department of Commerce. (1998). *Metropolitan area exports: An export performance report on over 250 US cities, 1993–1997, report no. 99–0064-P*. International Trade Commission, Office of Trade and Economic Analysis, United States Department of Commerce.
Uzzi, B. (1996). The sources and consequences of embeddedness for the economic performance of organizations: The network effect. *American Sociological Review, 61*(4), 674–698.
Van Greuning, H., & Iqbal, Z. (2008). *Risk analysis for Islamic banks*. The World Bank.
Wade, R. (1990). *Governing the market: Economic theory and the role of government in east Asian industrialization*. Princeton University Press.
Wagner, M. (2001a). *Decentralisation and economic performance, SIDG working paper 01(05)*. Structural Issues Development Group, HM Treasury.
Wajcman, J. (2002). Information technologies and the. *Social Sciences, Special Issue of Current Sociology (Summer), 50.*
Waliyullah, S. (1992). In M. S. Sukkar (Ed.), *Hujjatullah al-Balighah* (2nd ed.). Dar Ihya al-Ulum. two volumes.
Walker, R. B. J. (1993). *Inside/outside: International relations as political theory*. Cambridge University Press.
Warf, B., & Grimes, J. (1997). Counterhegemonic discourses and the internet. *The Geographical Review, 87*, 259–274.
Watt, W. M. (1972). *The influence of Islam on medieval Europe*. Edinburgh University Press.
Wight, J. B., & Tomer, J. F. (Eds.). (2019). *Social economics: Current and emerging avenues*. The MIT Press. http://www.jstor.org/stable/j.ctt1kk66bh
Woodford, M. (2012). Inflation Targeting and Financial Stability. *National Bureau of Economic Research (NBER) Working Paper Series*, 17967.
World Information Order. (2002). *World-information files. The politics of the info sphere*. Institute for New Culture Technologies, and Berlin: Center for Civic Education.
Yeung, Y.-M. (2000). *Globalization and networked societies*. University of Hawaii Press.
Yusof, W. S., & Wan, B. (2008). Book review introduction to microeconomics: An Islamic perspective by Zubair Hasan. *JKAU: Islamic Econ., 21*(1), 83–91.

Yusuf, A., & Ya 'qub ibn Ibrahim. (1969). *Kitab al-Kharaj*. Cairo: al-Matab'ah al-Salafiyyah, second edition, 1933/34. (This book has been translated into English by a. Ben Shemesh). In *Taxation in Islam*. E. J. Brill.
Zak, P. J., & Knack, S. (2001). Trust and growth. *The Economic Journal, 111*, 295–321. https://doi.org/10.1111/1468-0297.00609
Zaman, A. (2007). An Islamic worldview: An essential component of an Islamic education. *Lahore Journal of Policy Studies, 1*(1), 95–106.
Zaman, A. (2008). Improving social science education in Pakistan. *Lahore Journal of Policy Studies., 2*(1).
Zaman, A. (2009). Origins of Western social science. *Journal of Islamic Economics, Banking and Finance., 5*(2), 9–22.
Zaman, A. (2011). Contrast between Islamic and economic views of incentives. *Journal of Islamic Economics, Banking and Finance.*
Zaman, A. (2012a). Crisis in Islamic economics: Diagnosis and prescriptions. *JKAU: Islamic Economics, 25*(1), 147–169.
Zaman, A. (2012b). Response to comments on crisis in Islamic economics: Diagnosis and prescriptions. *JKAU: Islamic Economics, 25*(2), 227–250.
Zaman, A. (2015). Crisis in Islamic economics: Diagnosis and prescriptions. In H. A. El-Karanshawy et al. (Eds.), *Islamic economic: Theory, policy and social justice*. Doha, Qatar.
Zaman, A., & Saglam, I. (2010). *The conflict between general equilibrium and the Marshallian cross*, MPRA Paper 33256, University Library of Munich, Germany.
Zarka, M. A. (2008). Duality of sources in Islamic economics, and its methodological consequences. In *The 7th international conference in Islamic economics* (pp. 23–36). King Abdulaziz University.
Zubof, S. (2009). *The old solutions have become the new problems*. Bloomberg Business. http://www.businessweek.com/managing/content/jul2009/ca2009072_489734.htm

MIX
Papier aus verantwortungsvollen Quellen
Paper from responsible sources
FSC® C105338

If you have any concerns about our products,
you can contact us on
**ProductSafety@springernature.com**

In case Publisher is established outside the EU,
the EU authorized representative is:
**Springer Nature Customer Service Center GmbH**
**Europaplatz 3, 69115 Heidelberg, Germany**

Printed by Libri Plureos GmbH
in Hamburg, Germany